Sources

OF THE

WESTERN
TRADITION

Sources

OF THE

WESTERN

TRADITION

VOLUME II: FROM THE RENAISSANCE TO THE PRESENT

Marvin Perry
Baruch College, City University of New York

Joseph R. Peden
Baruch College, City University of New York

Theodore H. Von Laue
Clark University

George W. Bock, Editorial Associate

HOUGHTON MIFFLIN COMPANY   BOSTON

DALLAS   GENEVA, ILLINOIS   PALO ALTO   PRINCETON, NEW JERSEY

Printed in the U.S.A.
Library of Congress Catalog Card Number:
90-83043
ISBN: 0-395-47305-5

Credits

Cover: Antoine Roux, Night Festival at the Universal
Exposition of 1889. (Musée Carnavalet/Giraudon/Art
Resource)

List of Sources

Introduction
P. xv: From Marvin Perry Western Civilization: Ideas,
Politics, and Society, Third Edition, pp. 251–255.
Copyright © 1989 by Houghton Mifflin Company.
Reprinted by permission of the publisher.

Chapter 1
Section 1   P. 8: From J. H. Robinson and H. W. Rolfe,
Petrarch, the First Modern Scholar and Man of Letters (New
York: G. P. Putnam's Sons (1909), pp. 208, 210, 213.
P. 9: "Love for Greek Literature" from Henry Osborn

Credits continued on page 439.

Contents

Part Two ▼ Modern Europe   87

Chapter 4: The French Revolution   89

Chapter 5: Romanticism, Reaction, Revolution   111

Chapter 6: The Industrial Revolution   135

Ch. 26

Preface

Teachers of the Western Civilization survey have long recognized the pedagogical value of primary sources, which are the raw materials of history. The second edition of *Sources of the Western Tradition* contains a wide assortment of documents — over 300 and virtually all primary sources — that have been carefully selected and edited to fit the needs of the survey and to supplement standard texts.

We have based our choice of documents for the two volumes on several criteria. In order to introduce students to those ideas and values that characterize the Western tradition, *Sources of the Western Tradition* emphasizes primarily the works of the great thinkers. While focusing on the great ideas that have shaped the Western heritage, however, the reader also provides a balanced treatment of political, economic, and social history. We have tried to select documents that capture the characteristic outlook of an age and that provide a sense of the movement and development of Western history. The readings are of sufficient length to convey their essential meaning, and we have carefully extracted those passages that focus on the documents' main ideas.

An important feature of the reader is the grouping of several documents that illuminate a single theme; such a constellation of related readings reinforces understanding of important themes and invites comparison, analysis, and interpretation. In Volume I, Chapter 5, for example, Selection 6, "Third-Century Crisis," contains three readings: "Caracalla's Extortions" (from Dio Cassius), "Petition to Emperor Philip," and "Extortions of Maximinus" (from Herodian). In Volume II, Chapter 11, Selection 7, "The Anguish of the Intellectuals," contains readings by José Ortega y Gasset, Thomas Mann, and Arthur Koestler.

An overriding concern of the editors in preparing this compilation was to make the documents accessible — to enable students to comprehend and to interpret historical documents on their own. We have provided several pedagogical features to facilitate this aim. Introductions of three types explain the historical setting, the authors' intent, and the meaning and significance of the readings. First, introductions to each of the twenty-three chapters provide comprehensive overviews to periods. Second, introductions to each numbered section or grouping treat the historical background for the reading(s) that follow(s). Third, each reading has a brief headnote that provides specific details about that reading.

Within some readings, Interlinear Notes, clearly set off from the text of the document, serve as transitions and suggest the main themes of the passages that follow. Used primarily in longer extracts of the great thinkers, these interlinear notes help to guide students through the readings.

To aid students' comprehension, brief, bracketed editorial definitions or notes that explain unfamiliar or foreign terms are inserted into the running text. When terms or concepts in the documents require fuller explanations, these appear at the bottom of pages as editors' footnotes. Where helpful, we have retained the notes of authors, translators, or editors from whose works the documents were acquired. (The latter have asterisks, daggers, etcetera, to distinguish them from our numbered explanatory notes.) The Review Questions that appear at the end of sections enable students to check their understanding of the documents; sometimes the questions ask for comparisons with other readings, linking or contrasting key concepts.

For ancient sources, we have generally selected recent translations that are both faithful to the text and readable. For some seventeenth- and eighteenth-century English documents, the archaic spelling has been retained, when this does not preclude comprehension, in order to show students how the English language has evolved over time.

The pictures that open each chapter illustrate an important theme covered in the chapter. In addition, in each volume there is a five-page section (between Chapters 5 and 6 in Volume I and between Chapters 8 and 9 in Volume II) devoted to art. In Volume I, "Elements of Classical, Medieval, and Renaissance Art" samples sculptural and architectural styles. Volume II's "Developments in Painting from Impressionism to the Abstract" samples the varied styles of painting in the late nineteenth and early twentieth centuries.

For the second edition, we have reworked all chapters. Documents that we have retained have been re-edited; in many cases we have cut extraneous passages, inserted additional notes to clarify historical events and terms, and defined technical words. Wherever possible we have extended the constellation format; many documents used in the first edition and documents added for this edition have been grouped together to illuminate significant themes.

In virtually every chapter, readings that proved to be less useful have been replaced by new ones. The second edition of Volume I contains around twenty-five new sources. For example, in Chapter 3, "The Greeks," to illustrate the theme of humanism we have provided Pindar's ode affirming the pursuit of excellence and the famous passage from *Antigone* in which Sophocles lauds human talents. An excerpt from *Lysistrata* expands the treatment of women in ancient Greece and illustrates Aristophanes'

comic genius. Thucydides' reconstruction of a Spartan king's plea for moderation and caution raises fundamental questions about foreign policy, and the passages from *Politics* treat key themes in Aristotle's political philosophy. In Chapter 6, "Early Christianity," a new section, "Christian Worship and Organization," contains readings on church liturgy and the authority of the clergy by Saint Justin Martyr and Saint Ignatius of Antioch. Chapter 8, "The High and Late Middle Ages," includes a new section called "Medieval Universities," with excerpts from John of Salisbury, Chaucer, and medieval students.

Volume II has been more extensively revised. A major change is the new opening chapter, "The Rise of Modernity," which incorporates key readings from three chapters in Volume I: "The Renaissance," "The Reformation," and "Early Modern Society and Politics." This chapter and a new preceding introduction, "The Middle Ages and the Modern World," provide a good basis for approaching the complex issue of modernity, a natural beginning for the second half of the course.

More than fifty new readings appear in the second edition of Volume II. For example, in Chapter 7, "Politics and Society, 1850–1914," two new constellations have been inserted: "The Capitalist Ethic," which contains excerpts from Samuel Smiles's *Self-Help* and *Thrift*; and "The Lower Classes," which treats the problems of the poor in Germany and Britain at the end of the nineteenth century. Excerpts from Mary Wollstonecraft and Emmeline Pankhurst have been added to the section called "Equal Rights for Women." In that same section, the passage from John Stuart Mill has been lengthened. We have added three readings to the section on anti-Semitism: Edouard Drumont, *Jewish France,* Theodore Herzl, *The Jewish State,* and an account of the Kishinev Pogrom. In Chapter 10, "The Russian Revolution and the Soviet Union," a new section titled "The Revolution Denounced and Defended" includes the Proclamation of the Kronstadt Rebels, a socialist condemnation of the Bolshevik regime by Karl Kautsky, and a response to Kautsky by Leon Trotsky. In the last chapter, "The West in an Age of Globalism," we have introduced documents treating the ferment in the Soviet Union and Eastern Europe, women in third world development, and the environment and development (in excerpts from *Our Common Future* by the World Commission on Environment and Development).

Volume I, *From Ancient Times to the Enlightenment,* contains thirteen chapters that cover the period from the rise of civilizations in the ancient Near East to the philosphes of the eighteenth century. Volume II, *From the Renaissance to the Present,* incorporates the last two chapters of Volume I, "The Scientific Revolution" and "The Enlightenment," and has twelve chapters. Marvin Perry, senior editor of the project, researched both volumes. Joseph R. Peden contributed to Volume I and Theodore H. Von Laue to Volume II.

To accompany the second edition is a new *Instructor's Resource Manual with Test Items* by Professor Diane Moczar of Northern Virginia Community College. In addition to an introduction with suggestions on how to use *Sources of the Western Tradition* in class, there are chapter overviews, summaries of the sections, and, for each chapter, several questions for discussion or essay assignments and ten to twenty multiple-choice questions.

We wish to thank the following instructors for their critical reading of the manuscript and for their many valuable suggestions.

Donald B. Epstein, *Clackamas Community College*
Laura Gellott, *University of Wisconsin, Parkside*
Neil Heyman, *San Diego State University*
Lyle E. Linville, *Prince George's Community College*
Diane Moczar, *Northern Virginia Community College*
Walter Petry, *Fairfield University*
Jeremy D. Popkin, *University of Kentucky*
John Sommerville, *University of Florida*
Ira Spar, *Ramapo College of New Jersey*
Joshua B. Stein, *Roger Williams College*
John Turner, *C.W. Post, Long Island University*
Eric D. Weitz, *St. Olaf College*
Steven Werner, *University of Wisconsin Center–Waukesha*
Barbara Winslow, *Baruch College*
Ann Young, *Kearney State College*

We are also appreciative of the efforts of the Houghton Mifflin staff, who with their usual competent professionalism, guided the project from its inception. Joseph Peden wishes to thank his wife, Diana Peden, for her support. I wish to thank Angela Von Laue, who helped to research several chapters in Volume II and carefully read the galleys for that volume. I am especially grateful to George W. Bock, who worked closely with me in every phase of the reader's development, and to my wife, Phyllis Perry, for her encouragement.

M.P.

Introduction
The Middle Ages and the Modern World

Historians have traditionally divided Western history into three broad periods: ancient, medieval, and modern. What is meant by modernity? What has the modern world inherited from the Middle Ages? How does the modern West differ fundamentally from the Middle Ages?[1]

Medieval civilization began to decline in the fourteenth century, but no dark age comparable to the three centuries following Rome's fall descended on Europe; its economic and political institutions and technological skills had grown too strong. Instead, the waning of the Middle Ages opened up possibilities for another stage in Western civilization — the modern age.

In innumerable ways, today's world is linked to the Middle Ages. European cities, the middle class, the state system, English common law, universities — all had their origins in the Middle Ages. During that period, important advances were made in business practices. By translating and commenting on the writings of Greek and Arabic thinkers, medieval scholars preserved a priceless intellectual heritage, without which the modern mind could never have evolved. And between the thought of the scholastics and that of early modern philosophers there are numerous connecting strands.

During the Middle Ages, Europeans began to take the lead over the Muslims, the Byzantines, the Chinese, and all the other peoples in the use of technology. Medieval technology and inventiveness stemmed in part from Christianity, which taught that God had created the world specifically for human beings to subdue and exploit. Consequently, medieval people tried to employ animal power and laborsaving machinery to relieve human drudgery. Moreover, Christianity taught that God was above nature, not within it, so for the Christian there was no spiritual obstacle to exploiting nature as there was, for example, for the Hindu. Unlike classical humanism, the Christian outlook did not consider manual work degrading — even monks combined it with study.

Believing that God's law was superior to state or national decrees, medieval philosophers provided a theoretical basis for opposing tyrannical kings who violated Christian principles. The idea that both the ruler and the ruled are bound by a higher law would, in a secularized form, become a principal element of modern liberal thought.

The Christian stress on the sacred worth of the individual and on the higher law of God has never ceased to influence Western civilization. Although in modern times the various Christian churches have not often taken the lead in political and social reform, the ideals identified with the Judeo-Christian tradition have become part of the common Western heritage. As such, they have inspired social reformers who may no longer identify with their ancestral religions.

Feudal traditions lasted long after the Middle Ages. Up to the French Revolution, for instance, French aristocrats enjoyed special privileges and exercised power over local government. In England, the aristocracy controlled local government until the Industrial Revolution transformed English society in the nineteenth century. Retaining the medieval ideal of the noble warrior, aristocrats continued to dominate the officer corps of European armies through the nineteenth century and even into

---

[1]The following introduction was written by Marvin Perry for his textbook *Western Civilization: Ideas, Politics, and Society*, 3rd ed. (Boston: Houghton Mifflin, 1989), pp. 251–255.

the twentieth. Aristocratic notions of duty, honor, loyalty, and courtly love have also endured into the twentieth century.

Feudalism also contributed to the history of liberty. According to feudal theory the king, as a member of the feudal community, was duty-bound to honor agreements made by his vassals. Lords possessed personal rights that the king was obliged to respect. Resentful of a king who ran roughshod over customary feudal rights, lords also negotiated contracts with the crown, such as the famous Magna Carta, to define and guard their customary liberties. To protect themselves from the arbitrary behavior of a king, feudal lords initiated what came to be called *government by consent* and the *rule of law.*

Thus, in the Middle Ages there gradually emerged the ideas that law was not imposed on inferiors by an absolute monarch but required the collaboration of the king and his subjects; that the king, too, was bound by the law; and that lords had the right to resist a monarch who violated agreements. Related to these ideas, representative institutions also emerged with which the king was expected to consult on the realm's affairs. The most notable was the British Parliament, which, although it was subordinate to the king, became a permanent part of the state. Later, in the seventeenth century, Parliament would successfully challenge royal authority. Continuity, therefore, exists between the feudal tradition of a king bound by law and the modern practice of limiting the authority of the head of state.

Although the elements of continuity are clear, the characteristic outlook of the Middle Ages was as different from that of the modern age as it was from that of the ancient world. Religion was the integrating feature of the Middle Ages, whereas science and secularism determine the modern outlook. The period from the Italian Renaissance of the fifteenth century through the eighteenth-century Age of Enlightenment constituted a gradual breaking away from the medieval world-view — a rejection of the medieval conception of nature, so-

ciety, the individual, and the purpose of life. This transition from medieval to modern was neither sudden nor complete, for there are no sharp demarcation lines separating historical periods. While many distinctively medieval ways endured in the sixteenth, seventeenth, and even eighteenth centuries, these centuries also saw the emergence of new patterns of thought and culture and of new political and economic forms that marked the emergence of modernity.

Medieval thought began with the existence of God and the truth of his revelation as interpreted by the church, which set the standards and defined the purposes for human endeavor. Medieval thinkers regarded reason without the guidance of revelation as deficient. Thus the medieval mind rejected the fundamental principle of Greek and modern philosophy — the autonomy of reason.

Scholastics reasoned closely and carefully, drew fine distinctions, and at times demonstrated a critical attitude. They engaged in genuine philosophical speculation, but they did not allow philosophy to challenge the basic premises of their faith. Unlike either ancient or modern thinkers, medieval schoolmen believed ultimately that reason alone could not provide a unified view of nature or society. A rational soul had to be guided by a divine light. For all medieval philosophers, the natural order depended on a supernatural order for its origin and purpose. To understand the natural world properly it was necessary to know its relationship to the higher world. The discoveries of reason had to conform to Scripture as interpreted by the church.

In the modern view, both nature and the human intellect are self-sufficient. Nature is a mathematical system that operates without miracles or any other form of divine intervention. To comprehend nature and society, the mind needs no divine assistance; it accepts no authority above reason. The modern mentality finds it unacceptable to reject the conclusions of science on the basis of clerical authority and revelation, or to base politics, law, or economics on religion; it refuses to accept dogma uncritically and insists on scientific proof.

The medieval philosopher arranged both nature and society into a hierarchic order. God was the source of moral values, and the church was responsible for teaching and upholding these ethical norms. Kings acquired their right to rule from God. The entire social structure constituted a hierarchy: the clergy guided society according to Christian standards; lords defended Christian society from its enemies; serfs, lowest in the social order, toiled for the good of all. In the hierarchy of knowledge, a lower form of knowledge derived from the senses, and the highest type of knowledge, theology, dealt with God's revelation. To the medieval mind this hierarchic ordering of nature, society, and knowledge had a divine sanction.

Rejecting the medieval division of the universe into higher and lower realms and superior and inferior substances, the modern view came to regard the universe as one and nature as uniform; the modern thinker studies mathematical law and chemical composition, not grades of perfection. Spiritual meaning is not sought in an examination of the material world. Roger Bacon, for example, described seven coverings of the eye and then concluded that God had fashioned the eye in this manner in order to express the seven gifts of the Spirit. This way of thinking is alien to the modern outlook.

The modern West also broke with the rigid division of medieval society into three orders: clergy, nobles, and commoners. Opposing the feudal principle that an individual's obligations and rights are a function of his or her rank in society, the modern West stressed equality of opportunity and equal treatment under the law. It rejected the idea that society should be guided by clergymen who possess a special wisdom, by nobles who were entitled to special privileges, and by a king who received his power from God.

The modern West also rejected the personal and customary character of feudal law. As the modern state developed, law assumed an impersonal and objective character. For example,

if the lord demanded more than the customary forty days of military service, the vassal might refuse to comply, seeing the lord's request as an unpardonable violation of custom and agreement and an infringement on his liberties. In the modern state with a constitution and a representative government, if a new law increasing the length of military service is passed, it merely replaces the old law. People do not refuse to obey it because the government has broken faith or violated custom.

In the modern world, the individual's relationship to the universe has been radically transformed. Medieval people lived in a geocentric universe that was finite in space and time. The universe was small, enclosed by a sphere of stars beyond which were the heavens. The universe, it was believed, was some five thousand years old, and in the not too distant future, human history would come to an end. To medieval thinkers, human beings ranked below angels but were superior to inanimate objects, plants, and animals. People in the Middle Ages knew why they were on earth and what was expected of them; they never doubted that heaven would be their reward for living a Christian life. J. H. Randall, Jr., a historian of philosophy, eloquently sums up the medieval worldview:

> The world was governed throughout by the omnipotent will and omniscient mind of God, whose sole interests were centered in man, his trial, his fall, his suffering and his glory. Worm of the dust as he was, man was yet the central object in the whole universe. . . . And when his destiny was completed, the heavens would be rolled up as a scroll and he would dwell with the Lord forever. Only those who rejected God's freely offered grace and with hardened hearts refused repentance would be cut off from this eternal life.[2]

[2]J. H. Randall, Jr., *The Making of the Modern Mind* (Boston: Houghton Mifflin, 1940), p. 34.

This comforting medieval vision is alien to the modern outlook. Today, in a universe 15 billion years old in which the earth is a tiny speck floating in an endless cosmic ocean, where life evolved over tens of millions of years, many Westerners no longer are certain that human beings are special children of God; that heaven is their ultimate goal; that under their feet is hell; that God is an active agent in human history. To many intellectuals the universe seems unresponsive to the religious supplications of people, and life's purpose is sought within the limits of earthly existence. Science and secularism have driven Christianity and faith from their central position to the periphery of human concerns.

The modern outlook emerged gradually in the period from the Renaissance to the eighteenth-century Age of Enlightenment. Mathematics rendered the universe comprehensible. Economic and political thought broke free of the religious frame of reference. Science became the great hope of the future. The thinkers of the Enlightenment wanted to liberate humanity from superstition, ignorance, and traditions that could not pass the test of reason. Rejecting the Christian idea of a person's inherent sinfulness, they held that the individual was basically good and that evil resulted from faulty institutions, poor education, and bad leadership. Thus the concept of a rational and free society in which individuals could realize their potential slowly emerged.

Part One

Early Modern Europe

The Rise of Modernity

From the fifteenth through the seventeenth centuries, medieval attitudes and institutions broke down, and distinctly modern cultural, economic, and political forms emerged. For many historians, the Renaissance, which originated in the city-states of Italy, marks the starting point of the modern era. The Renaissance was characterized by a rebirth of interest in the humanist culture and outlook of ancient Greece and Rome. Although Renaissance individuals did not repudiate Christianity, they valued worldly activities and interests to a much greater degree than did the people of the Middle Ages, whose outlook was dominated by Christian otherworldliness. Renaissance individuals were fascinated by *this* world and by life's possibilities; they aspired to live a rich and creative life on earth and to fulfill themselves through artistic and literary activity.

Individualism was a hallmark of the Renaissance. The urban elite sought to demonstrate their unique talents, to assert their own personalities, and to gain recognition for their accomplishments. The most admired person during the Renaissance was the multitalented individual, the "universal man," who distinguished himself as a writer, artist, linguist, athlete. Disdaining Christian humility, Renaissance individuals took pride in their talents and worldly accomplishments — "I can work miracles," said the great Leonardo da Vinci.

During the High Middle Ages there had been a revival of Greek and Roman learning. Yet there were two important differences between that period called the Twelfth-Century Awakening and the Renaissance. First, many more ancient works were restored to circulation during the Renaissance than during the cultural revival of the Middle Ages. Second, medieval scholastics had tried to fit the ideas of the ancients into a Christian framework; they used Greek philosophy to explain Christian teachings. Renaissance scholars, on the other hand, valued ancient works for their own sake, believing that Greek and Roman authors could teach much about the art of living.

A distinguishing feature of the Renaissance period was the humanist movement, an educational and cultural program based on the study of ancient Greek and Latin literature. By studying the humanities — history, literature, rhetoric, moral and political philosophy — humanists aimed to

Cosimo de' Medici by Benvenuto Cellini (1500–1571). This sixteenth-century bronze bust of the duke of Florence by the famous Italian sculptor Cellini reflects the power and prestige of one of the most influential Renaissance despots. (*Alinari/Art Resource, N.Y.*)

revive the worldly spirit of the ancient Greeks and Romans, which they believed had been lost in the Middle Ages.

Humanists were thus fascinated by the writings of the ancients. From the works of Thucydides, Plato, Cicero, Seneca, and other ancient authors, humanists sought guidelines for living life well in this world and looked for stylistic models for their own literary efforts. To the humanists, the ancients had written brilliantly, in an incomparable literary style, on friendship, citizenship, love, bravery, statesmanship, beauty, excellence, and every other topic devoted to the enrichment of human life.

Like the humanist movement, Renaissance art also marked a break with medieval culture. The art of the Middle Ages had served a religious function; its purpose was to lift the mind to God. It depicted a spiritual universe in which the supernatural was the supreme reality. The Gothic cathedral, with its flying buttresses, soared toward heaven, rising in ascending tiers; it reflected the medieval conception of a hierarchical universe with God at its apex. Painting also expressed gradations of spiritual values. Traditionally, the left side of a painting portrayed the damned, the right side the saved; dark colors expressed evil, light colors good. Spatial proportion was relative to spirituality — the less spiritually valuable a thing was, the less form it had (or the more deformed it was). Medieval art perfectly expressed the Christian view of the universe and the individual. The Renaissance shattered the dominance of religion over art, shifting attention from heaven to the natural world and to the human being; Renaissance artists often dealt with religious themes but they placed their subjects in a naturalistic setting. Renaissance art also developed a new concept of visual space that was defined from the standpoint of the individual observer. It was a quantitative space in which the artist, employing reason and mathematics, portrayed the essential form of the object as it appeared in three dimensions to the human eye, that is, it depicted the object in perspective.

The Renaissance began in the middle of the fourteenth century in the northern Italian city-states, which had grown prosperous from the revival of trade in the Middle Ages. Italian merchants and bankers had the wealth to acquire libraries and fine works of art and to support art, literature, and scholarship. Surrounded by reminders of ancient Rome — amphitheaters, monuments, and sculpture — the well-to-do took an interest in classical culture and thought. In the late fifteenth and the sixteenth centuries, Renaissance ideas spread to Germany, France, Spain, and England through books available in great numbers due to the invention of the printing press.

By weakening the church and dividing Europe into Catholic and Protestant, the Reformation of the sixteenth century also contributed to the rise of modernity. The reformation of the church in the sixteenth century was rooted in demands for spiritual renewal and institutional change. These pressures began as early as the late fourteenth century and came from many sources.

The papacy and orthodox Catholic theology were challenged by English theologian John Wycliffe (c. 1320–1384) and Czech theologian John Huss (c. 1369–1415). Both attacked the bishops' involvement in temporal politics and urged a return to the simple practices of the early apostolic church; and both, claiming that the Bible alone — not the church hierarchy — was the highest authority for Christians, emphasized study of the Holy Scriptures by the laity and sermons in the common language of the people. Wycliffe, though not Huss, also undermined the clergy's authority by denying the priests' power to change the bread and wine into Christ's body and blood during the Mass. Despite severe persecution by church and state, followers of Wycliffe's and Huss's beliefs continued to exist and participated in the sixteenth-century Protestant movement.

By that time there was a widespread popular yearning for a more intense spirituality. It took many forms: the rise of new pious practices; greater interest in mystical experiences and in the study of the Bible; the development of communal ways for lay people to live and work following the apostles' example; and a heightened search for ways within secular society to imitate more perfectly the life of Christ — called the New Devotion movement.

Several secular factors contributed to this enhanced level of spiritual feeling. The many wars, famines, and plagues of the late fourteenth and the fifteenth centuries had traumatized Europe. The increasing educational level of the urban middle class and skilled laborers and the invention of the printing press allowed the rapid and relatively inexpensive spread of new ideas. Finally, there was the influence of the humanist movement, particularly in northern Europe and Spain. Many humanists dedicated themselves to promoting higher levels of religious education. They stimulated public interest in biblical study by publishing new editions of the Holy Scriptures and the writings of the church fathers, along with new devotional literature. Nearly all the religious reformers of the sixteenth century were deeply influenced by the ideals and methods of the Christian humanist movement.

In Germany economic and political considerations fused with the demand for reform of church and religious life. The middle class resented the flow of tax money from Germany to Rome; by supporting Martin Luther's break with the church, nobles saw a way of seizing church property in their territories and of resisting the centralizing efforts of Holy Roman Emperor Charles V, who sided with the papacy.

By dividing Europe into Catholic and Protestant regions, the Reformation ended medieval religious unity. It also accentuated the importance of the individual person, a distinctive feature of the modern outlook. It stressed individual conscience rather than clerical authority, called for a personal relationship between each man and woman and God, and called attention to the individual's inner religious capacities.

At the same time that the Renaissance and Reformation were transforming European cultural and religious life, the discovery of new trade routes to East Asia and of new lands across the Atlantic widened the imagination and ambitions of Europeans and precipitated a commercial revolution. Exploration and commercial expansion created the foundations of a global economy in which the European economy was tied to Asian spices, African slaves, and American silver. A wide variety of goods circulated all over the globe. From the West Indies and East Asia, sugar, rice, tea, cacao, and tobacco flowed into Europe. From the Americas, potatoes, corn, sweet potatoes, and manioc (from which tapioca is made) spread to the rest of the world. Europeans paid for Asian silks and spices with American silver.

The increasing demand for goods and a rise in prices produced more opportunities for the accumulation and investment of capital by private individuals, which is the essence of capitalism. State policies designed to increase national wealth and power also stimulated the growth of capitalism. Governments subsidized new industries, chartered joint-stock companies to engage in overseas trade, and struck at internal tariffs and guild regulations that hampered domestic economic growth. Improvements in banking, shipbuilding, mining, and manufacturing further stimulated economic growth.

In the sixteenth and seventeenth centuries the old medieval political order dissolved, and the modern state began to emerge. The modern state has a strong central government that issues laws that apply throughout the land and a permanent army of professional soldiers paid by the state.

Trained bureaucrats, responsible to the central government, collect taxes, enforce laws, and administer justice. The modern state has a secular character; promotion of religion is not the state's concern, and churches do not determine state policy. These features of the modern state were not prevalent in the Middle Ages, when the privileges of nobles, church, and towns had impeded central authority, and kings were expected to rule in accordance with Christian principles. In the sixteenth and seventeenth centuries, monarchs were exercising central authority with ever-greater effectiveness at the expense of nobles and clergy. The secularization of the state became firmly established after the Thirty Years' War (1618–1648); with their states worn out by Catholic-Protestant conflicts, kings came to act less for religious motives than for reasons of national security and power.

Historically, the modern state has been characterized by a devotion to the nation and by feelings of national pride. There is a national language that is used throughout the land, and the people have a sense of sharing a common culture and history, of being distinct from other peoples. There were some signs of growing national feeling during the sixteenth and seventeenth centuries, but this feature of the modern state did not become a major part of European political life until the nineteenth century. During the early modern period, loyalty was largely given to a town, to a province, to a noble, or to the person of the king rather than to the nation, the people as a whole.

▼▼▼

New text - p. 467 - 468
Old text - p. 431-1
          432

▼ The Humanists' Fascination with Antiquity

Humanists believed that a refined person must know the literature of Greece and Rome. They strove to imitate the style of the ancients, to speak and write as eloquently as the Greeks and Romans. Toward these ends, they sought to read, print, and restore to circulation every scrap of ancient literature that could still be found.

Petrarch
THE FATHER OF HUMANISM

During his lifetime, Francesco Petrarca, or Petrarch (1304–1374), had an astounding reputation as a poet and scholar. Often called the "father of humanism," he inspired other humanists through his love for classical learning; his criticism of medieval Latin as barbaric in contrast to the style of Cicero, Seneca, and other Romans; and his literary works based on classical models. Petrarch saw his own age as a restoration of classical brilliance after an interval of medieval darkness.

A distinctly modern element in Petrarch's thought is the subjective and individualistic character of his writing. In talking about himself and probing his own feelings, Petrarch demonstrates a self-consciousness characteristic of the modern outlook.

Like many other humanists, Petrarch remained devoted to Christianity: "When it comes to thinking or speaking of religion, that is, of the highest truth, of true happiness and eternal salvation," he declared, "I certainly am not a Ciceronian or a Platonist but a Christian." Petrarch was a forerunner of the Christian humanism best represented by Erasmus. Christian humanists combined an intense devotion to Christianity with a great love for classical literature, which they much preferred to the dull and turgid treatises written by scholastic philosophers and theologians. In the following passage, Petrarch criticizes his contemporaries for their ignorance of ancient writers and shows his commitment to classical learning.

. . . O inglorious age! that scorns antiquity, its mother, to whom it owes every noble art — that dares to declare itself not only equal but superior to the glorious past. I say nothing of the vulgar, the dregs of mankind, whose sayings and opinions may raise a laugh but hardly merit serious censure. . . .

. . . But what can be said in defense of men of education who ought not to be ignorant of antiquity and yet are plunged in this same darkness and delusion?

You see that I cannot speak of these matters without the greatest irritation and indignation. There has arisen of late a set of dialecticians [experts in logical argument],[1] who are not only ignorant but demented. Like a black army of ants from some old rotten oak, they swarm forth from their hiding places and devastate the fields of sound learning. They condemn Plato and Aristotle, and laugh at Socrates and Pytha-

goras.[2] And, good God! under what silly and incompetent leaders these opinions are put forth. . . . What shall we say of men who scorn Marcus Tullius Cicero,[3] the bright sun of eloquence? Of those who scoff at Varro and Seneca,[4] and are scandalized at what they choose to call the crude, unfinished style of Livy and Sallust [Roman historians]? . . .

Such are the times, my friend, upon which we have fallen; such is the period in which we live and are growing old. Such are the critics of today, as I so often have occasion to lament and

---

[1]Throughout the text, words in brackets have been added as glosses by the editors. Brackets around glosses from the original sources have been changed to parentheses to distinguish them.

Throughout the text, the editors' notes carry numbers, whereas notes from the original sources are indicated by asterisks, daggers, etcetera.

[2]The work of Aristotle (384–322 B.C.), a leading Greek philosopher, had an enormous influence among medieval and Renaissance scholars. A student of the philosopher Socrates, Plato (c. 427–347 B.C.) was one of the greatest philosophers of ancient Greece. His work grew to be extremely influential in the West during the Renaissance period, as new texts of his writings were discovered and translated into Latin and more Westerners could read the originals in Greek. Pythagoras (c. 582–c. 507 B.C.) was a Greek philosopher whose work influenced both Socrates and Plato.

[3]Cicero (106–43 B.C.) was a Roman statesman and rhetorician. His Latin style was especially admired and emulated during the Renaissance.

[4]Varro (116–27 B.C.) was a Roman scholar and historian. Seneca (4 B.C.–A.D. 65) was a Roman statesman, dramatist, and Stoic philosopher whose literary style was greatly admired during the Renaissance.

Why is he so angry? (What is he mad at?) (see p. 11)

Chapter 1 The Rise of Modernity   9

complain — men who are innocent of knowledge and virtue, and yet harbour the most exalted opinion of themselves. Not content with losing the words of the ancients, they must attack their genius and their ashes. They rejoice in their ignorance, as if what they did not know were not worth knowing. They give full rein to their license and conceit, and freely introduce among us new authors and outlandish teachings.

Leonardo Bruni
STUDY OF GREEK LITERATURE AND A HUMANIST EDUCATIONAL PROGRAM

CIVIC HUMANISM

Leonardo Bruni (1374–1444) was a Florentine humanist who extolled both intellectual study and active involvement in public affairs, an outlook called civic humanism. In the first reading from his *History of His Own Times in Italy*, Bruni expressed the humanist's love for ancient Greek literature and language.

In a treatise, *De Studiis et Literis* (*On Learning and Literature*), addressed to the noble lady Baptista di Montefeltro (1383–1450), daughter of the Count of Urbino, Bruni outlines the basic course of studies that the humanists recommended as the best preparation for a life of wisdom and virtue. In addition to the study of Christian literature, Bruni encourages a wide familiarity with the best minds and stylists of ancient Greek and Latin cultures.

[LOVE FOR GREEK LITERATURE]

Then first came a knowledge of Greek, which had not been in use among us for seven hundred years. Chrysoloras the Byzantine,[1] a man of noble birth and well versed in Greek letters, brought Greek learning to us. When his country was invaded by the Turks, he came by sea, first to Venice. The report of him soon spread, and he was cordially invited and besought and promised a public stipend, to come to Florence and open his store of riches to the youth. I was then studying Civil Law,[2] but . . . I burned with love of academic studies, and had spent no little pains on dialectic and rhetoric. At the coming of Chrysoloras I was torn in mind, deeming it shameful to desert the law, and yet a crime to lose such a chance of studying Greek literature; and often with youthful impulse I would say to myself: "Thou, when it is permitted thee to gaze on Homer, Plato and Demosthenes,[3] and the other [Greek] poets, philosophers, orators, of whom such glorious things are spread abroad, and speak with them and be instructed in their admirable teaching, wilt thou desert and rob thyself? Wilt thou neglect this opportunity so divinely offered? For seven hundred years, no one in Italy has possessed Greek letters; and yet we confess that all knowledge is derived from them. How great advantage to your knowledge, enhancement of your fame, increase of your pleasure, will come from an understanding of this tongue? There are doctors of civil law everywhere; and the chance of learning will not fail thee. But if this one and only doctor of Greek letters disappears, no one

[1]Chrysoloras (c. 1355–1415), a Byzantine writer and teacher, introduced the study of Greek literature to the Italians, opening a new age of Western humanistic learning.

[2]Civil Law refers to the Roman law as codified by Emperor Justinian in the early sixth century A.D. and studied in medieval law schools.

[3]Demosthenes (384–322 B.C.) was an Athenian statesman and orator whose oratorical style was much admired by Renaissance humanists.

can be found to teach thee." Overcome at length by these reasons, I gave myself to Chrysoloras, with such zeal to learn, that what through the wakeful day I gathered, I followed after in the night, even when asleep.

ON LEARNING AND LITERATURE

. . . The foundations of all true learning must be laid in the sound and thorough knowledge of Latin: which implies study marked by a broad spirit, accurate scholarship, and careful attention to details. Unless this solid basis be secured it is useless to attempt to rear an enduring edifice. Without it the great monuments of literature are unintelligible, and the art of composition impossible. To attain this essential knowledge we must never relax our careful attention to the grammar of the language, but perpetually confirm and extend our acquaintance with it until it is thoroughly our own. . . . To this end we must be supremely careful in our choice of authors, lest an inartistic and debased style infect our own writing and degrade our taste; which danger is best avoided by bringing a keen, critical sense to bear upon select works, observing the sense of each passage, the structure of the sentence, the force of every word down to the least important particle. In this way our reading reacts directly upon our style. . . .

But we must not forget that true distinction is to be gained by a wide and varied range of such studies as conduce to the profitable enjoyment of life, in which, however, we must observe due proportion in the attention and time we devote to them.

First amongst such studies I place History: a subject which must not on any account be neglected by one who aspires to true cultivation. For it is our duty to understand the origins of our own history and its development; and the achievements of Peoples and of Kings.

For the careful study of the past enlarges our foresight in contemporary affairs and affords to citizens and to monarchs lessons of incitement or warning in the ordering of public policy.

From History, also, we draw our store of examples of moral precepts.

In the monuments of ancient literature which have come down to us History holds a position of great distinction. We specially prize such [Roman] authors as Livy, Sallust and Curtius;[4] and, perhaps even above these, Julius Caesar; the style of whose Commentaries, so elegant and so limpid, entitles them to our warm admiration. . . .

The great Orators of antiquity must by all means be included. Nowhere do we find the virtues more warmly extolled, the vices so fiercely decried. From them we may learn, also, how to express consolation, encouragement, dissuasion or advice. If the principles which orators set forth are portrayed for us by philosophers, it is from the former that we learn how to employ the emotions — such as indignation, or pity — in driving home their application in individual cases. Further, from oratory we derive our store of those elegant or striking turns of expression which are used with so much effect in literary compositions. Lastly, in oratory we find that wealth of vocabulary, that clear easy-flowing style, that verve and force, which are invaluable to us both in writing and in conversation.

I come now to Poetry and the Poets. . . . For we cannot point to any great mind of the past for whom the Poets had not a powerful attraction. Aristotle, in constantly quoting Homer, Hesiod, Pindar, Euripides and other [Greek] poets, proves that he knew their works hardly less intimately than those of the philosophers. Plato, also, frequently appeals to them, and in this way covers them with his approval. If we turn to Cicero, we find him not content with quoting Ennius, Accius,[5] and others of the Lat-

---

[4]Q. Curtius Rufus, a Roman historian and rhetorician of the mid-first century A.D., composed a biography of Alexander the Great.
[5]Ennius (239–169 B.C.) wrote the first great Latin epic poem, which was based on the legends of Rome's founding and its early history. Accius (c. 170–c. 90 B.C.), also a Roman, authored a history of Greek and Latin literature.

ins, but rendering poems from the Greek and employing them habitually. . . . Hence my view that familiarity with the great poets of antiquity is essential to any claim to true education. For in their writings we find deep speculations upon Nature, and upon the Causes and Origins of things, which must carry weight with us both from their antiquity and from their authorship. Besides these, many important truths upon matters of daily life are suggested or illustrated. All this is expressed with such grace and dignity as demands our admiration. . . . To sum up what I have endeavoured to set forth. That high standard of education to which I referred at the outset is only to be reached by one who has seen many things and read much. Poet, Orator, Historian, and the rest, all must be studied, each must contribute a share. Our learning thus becomes full, ready, varied and elegant, available for action or for discourse in all subjects. But to enable us to make effectual use of what we know we must add to our knowledge the power of expression. These two sides of learning, indeed, should not be separated: they afford mutual aid and distinction. Proficiency in literary form, not accompanied by broad acquaintance with facts and truths, is a barren attainment; whilst information, however vast, which lacks all grace of expression, would seem to be put under a bushel or partly thrown away. Indeed, one may fairly ask what advantage it is to possess profound and varied learning if one cannot convey it in language worthy of the subject. Where, however, this double capacity exists — breadth of learning and grace of style — we allow the highest title to distinction and to abiding fame. If we review the great names of ancient [Greek and Roman] literature, Plato, Democritus, Aristotle, Theophrastus, Varro, Cicero, Seneca, Augustine, Jerome, Lactantius, we shall find it hard to say whether we admire more their attainments or their literary power.

REVIEW QUESTIONS

1. According to Petrarch, what was the great fault of the scholars of his own age?
2. What made Petrarch aware that a renaissance, or rebirth, of classical learning was necessary in his time?
3. Why did Leonardo Bruni abandon his earlier course of studies to pursue the study of Greek literature?
4. Why did Bruni insist on the importance of studying Latin grammar and imitating the best models of Latin style?
5. Why did Bruni consider the study of history of crucial importance?
6. Why did Bruni recommend the study of ancient classical oratory?
7. What benefit did Bruni see in the study of the ancient poets?
8. From Bruni's viewpoint, what two things were needed to acquire a good education?

2 ▼ Human Dignity

In his short lifetime, Giovanni Pico della Mirandola (1463–1494) mastered Greek, Latin, Hebrew, and Arabic and aspired to synthesize the Hebrew, Greek, and Christian traditions. His most renowned work, *Oration on the Dignity of Man,* has been called the humanist manifesto.

Pico della Mirandola
≪ *ORATION ON THE DIGNITY OF MAN* ≫

In the opening section of the *Oration,* Pico declares that unlike other creatures, human beings have not been assigned a fixed place in the universe. Our destiny is not determined by anything outside us. Rather, God has bestowed upon us a unique distinction: the liberty to determine the form and value our lives shall acquire. The notion that people have the power to shape their own lives is a key element in the emergence of the modern outlook.

I have read in the records of the Arabians, reverend Fathers, that Abdala the Saracen,[1] when questioned as to what on this stage of the world, as it were, could be seen most worthy of wonder, replied: "There is nothing to be seen more wonderful than man." In agreement with this opinion is the saying of Hermes Trismegistus: "A great miracle, Asclepius, is man."[2] But when I weighed the reason for these maxims, the many grounds for the excellence of human nature reported by many men failed to satisfy me — that man is the intermediary between creatures, the intimate of the gods, the king of the lower beings, by the acuteness of his senses, by the discernment of his reason, and by the light of his intelligence the interpreter of nature, the interval between fixed eternity and fleeting time, and (as the Persians say) the bond, nay, rather, the marriage song of the world, on David's [biblical king] testimony but little lower than the angels. Admittedly great though these reasons be, they are not the principal grounds, that is, those which may rightfully claim for themselves the privilege of the highest admiration. For why should we not admire more the angels themselves and the blessed choirs of heaven? At last it seems to me I have come to understand why man is the most fortunate of creatures and consequently worthy of all admiration and what precisely is that rank

which is his lot in the universal chain of Being — a rank to be envied not only by brutes but even by the stars and by minds beyond this world. It is a matter past faith and a wondrous one. Why should it not be? For it is on this very account that man is rightly called and judged a great miracle and a wonderful creature indeed. . . .

. . . God the Father, the supreme Architect, had already built this cosmic home we behold, the most sacred temple of His godhead, by the laws of His mysterious wisdom. The region above the heavens He had adorned with Intelligences, the heavenly spheres He had quickened with eternal souls, and the excrementary and filthy parts of the lower world He had filled with a multitude of animals of every kind. But, when the work was finished, the Craftsman kept wishing that there were someone to ponder the plan of so great a work, to love its beauty, and to wonder at its vastness. Therefore, when everything was done (as Moses and Timaeus[3] bear witness), He finally took thought concerning the creation of man. But there was not among His archetypes that from which He could fashion a new offspring, nor was there in His treasurehouses anything which He might bestow on His new son as an inheritance, nor was there in the seats of all the world a place where the latter might sit to contemplate the universe. All was now complete; all things had been assigned to the highest, the middle, and the lowest orders. But in its final

---

[1]Abdala the Saracen possibly refers to the eighth-century A.D. writer Abd-Allah Ibn al-Muqaffa.

[2]Ancient writings dealing with magic, alchemy, astrology, and occult philosophy were erroneously attributed to an assumed Egyptian priest, Hermes Trismegistus. Asclepius was a Greek god of healing.

---

[3]Timaeus, a Greek Pythagorean philosopher, was a central character in Plato's famous dialogue *Timaeus.*

creation it was not the part of the Father's power to fail as though exhausted. It was not the part of His wisdom to waver in a needful matter through poverty of counsel. It was not the part of His kindly love that he who was to praise God's divine generosity in regard to others should be compelled to condemn it in regard to himself.

At last the best of artisans [God] ordained that that creature to whom He had been able to give nothing proper to himself should have joint possession of whatever had been peculiar to each of the different kinds of being. He therefore took man as a creature of indeterminate nature and, assigning him a place in the middle of the world, addressed him thus: "Neither a fixed abode nor a form that is thine alone nor any function peculiar to thyself have we given thee, Adam, to the end that according to thy longing and according to thy judgment thou mayest have and possess what abode, what form, and what functions thou thyself shalt desire. The nature of all other beings is limited and constrained within the bounds of laws prescribed by Us. Thou, constrained by no limits, in accordance with thine own free will, in whose hand We have placed thee, shalt ordain for thyself the limits of thy nature. We have set thee at the world's center that thou mayest from thence more easily observe whatever is in the world. We have made thee neither of heaven nor of earth, neither mortal nor immortal, so that with freedom of choice and with honor, as

though the maker and molder of thyself, thou mayest fashion thyself in whatever shape thou shalt prefer. Thou shalt have the power to degenerate into the lower forms of life, which are brutish. Thou shalt have the power, out of thy soul's judgment, to be reborn into the higher forms, which are divine."

O supreme generosity of God the Father, O highest and most marvelous felicity of man! To him it is granted to have whatever he chooses, to be whatever he wills. Beasts as soon as they are born (so says Lucilius)[4] bring with them from their mother's womb all they will ever possess. Spiritual beings [angels], either from the beginning or soon thereafter, become what they are to be for ever and ever. On man when he came into life the Father conferred the seeds of all kinds and the germs of every way of life. Whatever seeds each man cultivates will grow to maturity and bear in him their own fruit. If they be vegetative, he will be like a plant. If sensitive, he will become brutish. If rational, he will grow into a heavenly being. If intellectual, he will be an angel and the son of God. And if, happy in the lot of no created thing, he withdraws into the center of his own unity, his spirit, made one with God, in the solitary darkness of God, who is set above all things, shall surpass them all.

----

[4]Lucilius, a first century A.D. Roman poet and Stoic philosopher, was a close friend of Seneca — the philosopher-dramatist.

REVIEW QUESTIONS

1. According to Giovanni Pico della Mirandola, what quality did human beings alone possess? What did its possession allow them to do?
2. How does Pico's oration on human dignity exemplify the emergence of the new psychological outlook of the Renaissance?

[handwritten: free will — shall set own limits freedom of CHOICE]

▼▼▼

3 ▼ Break with Medieval Political Theory

Turning away from the religious orientation of the Middle Ages, Renaissance thinkers discussed the human condition in secular terms and opened up possi-

bilities for thinking about moral and political problems in new ways. Thus, Niccolò Machiavelli (1469–1527), a Florentine statesman and political theorist, broke with medieval political theory. Medieval political thinkers held that the ruler derived power from God and had a religious obligation to rule in accordance with God's precepts. Machiavelli, though, ascribed no divine origin to kingship, nor did he attribute events to the mysterious will of God; and he explicitly rejected the principle that kings should adhere to Christian moral teachings. For Machiavelli, the state was a purely human creation. Successful kings or princes, he asserted, should be concerned only with preserving and strengthening the state's power and must ignore questions of good and evil, morality and immorality. Machiavelli did not assert that religion was supernatural in origin and rejected the prevailing belief that Christian morality should guide political life. For him, religion's value derived from other factors: a ruler could utilize religion to unite his subjects and to foster obedience to law.

Niccolò Machiavelli
≪ THE PRINCE ≫

In contrast to medieval thinkers, Machiavelli did not seek to construct an ideal Christian community but to discover how politics was *really* conducted. He studied politics in the cold light of reason, as the following passage from *The Prince* illustrates.

It now remains to be seen what are the methods and rules for a prince as regards his subjects and friends. And as I know that many have written of this, I fear that my writing about it may be deemed presumptuous, differing as I do, especially in this matter, from the opinions of others. But my intention being to write something of use to those who understand, it appears to me more proper to go to the real truth of the matter than to its imagination; and many have imagined republics and principalities which have never been seen or known to exist in reality; for how we live is so far removed from how we ought to live, that he who abandons what is done for what ought to be done, will rather learn to bring about his own ruin than his preservation.

▷ Machiavelli removed ethics from political thinking. A successful ruler, he contended, is indifferent to moral and religious considerations. But will not the prince be punished on the Day of Judgment for violating Christian teachings? In startling contrast to medieval theorists, Machiavelli simply ignored the question. The action of a prince, he said, should be governed solely by necessity.

A man who wishes to make a profession of goodness in everything must necessarily come to grief among so many who are not good. Therefore it is necessary for a prince, who wishes to maintain himself, to learn how not to be good, and to use this knowledge and not use it, according to the necessity of the case.

Leaving on one side, then, those things which concern only an imaginary prince, and speaking of those that are real, I state that all men, and especially princes, who are placed at a greater height, are reputed for certain qualities which bring them either praise or blame. Thus one is considered liberal, another . . . miserly; . . . one a free giver, another rapacious; one cruel, another merciful; one a breaker of his word, another trustworthy; one effeminate and pusillanimous, another fierce and high-spirited;

one humane, another haughty; one lascivious, another chaste; one frank, another astute; one hard, another easy; one serious, another frivolous; one religious, another an unbeliever, and so on. I know that every one will admit that it would be highly praiseworthy in a prince to possess all the above-named qualities that are reputed good, but as they cannot all be possessed or observed, human conditions not permitting of it, it is necessary that he should be prudent enough to avoid the scandal of those vices which would lose him the state, and guard himself if possible against those which will not lose it [for] him, but if not able to, he can indulge them with less scruple. And yet he must not mind incurring the scandal of those vices, without which it would be difficult to save the state, for if one considers well, it will be found that some things which seem virtues would, if followed, lead to one's ruin, and some others which appear vices result in one's greater security and wellbeing. . . .

. . . I say that every prince must desire to be considered merciful and not cruel. He must, however, take care not to misuse this mercifulness. Cesare Borgia was considered cruel, but his cruelty had brought order to the Romagna,[1] united it, and reduced it to peace and fealty. If this is considered well, it will be seen that he was really much more merciful than the Florentine people, who, to avoid the name of cruelty, allowed Pistoia[2] to be destroyed. A prince, therefore, must not mind incurring the charge of cruelty for the purpose of keeping his subjects united and faithful; for, with a very few

examples, he will be more merciful than those who, from excess of tenderness, allow disorders to arise, from whence spring bloodshed and rapine; for these as a rule injure the whole community, while the executions carried out by the prince injure only individuals. . . .

▷ Machiavelli's rigorous investigation of politics led him to view human nature from the standpoint of its limitations and imperfections. The astute prince, he said, recognizes that human beings are by nature selfish, cowardly, and dishonest and regulates his political strategy accordingly.

From this arises the question whether it is better to be loved more than feared, or feared more than loved. The reply is, that one ought to be both feared and loved, but as it is difficult for the two to go together, it is much safer to be feared than loved, if one of the two has to be wanting. For it may be said of men in general that they are ungrateful, voluble, dissemblers, anxious to avoid danger, and covetous of gain; as long as you benefit them, they are entirely yours; they offer you their blood, their goods, their life, and their children, as I have before said, when the necessity is remote; but when it approaches, they revolt. And the prince who has relied solely on their words, without making other preparations, is ruined; for the friendship which is gained by purchase and not through grandeur and nobility of spirit is bought but not secured, and at a pinch is not to be expended in your service. And men have less scruple in offending one who makes himself loved than one who makes himself feared; for love is held by a chain of obligation which, men being selfish, is broken whenever it serves their purpose; but fear is maintained by a dread of punishment which never fails.

Still, a prince should make himself feared in such a way that if he does not gain love, he at any rate avoids hatred; for fear and the absence of hatred may well go together, and will be always attained by one who abstains from

[handwritten margin note: Views of mankind]

---

[1]Cesare Borgia (c. 1476–1507) was the bastard son of Rodrigo Borgia, then a Spanish cardinal, and later Pope Alexander VI (1492–1503). With his father's aid he attempted to carve out for himself an independent duchy in north-central Italy, with Romagna as its heart. Through cruelty, violence, and treachery, he succeeded at first in his ambition, but ultimately his principality collapsed. Romagna was eventually incorporated into the Papal State under Pope Julius II (1503–1513). Machiavelli uses Borgia as a role model of his ideal of a modern ruler — with little justification.

[2]Pistoia, a small Italian city in Tuscany, came under the control of Florence in the fourteenth century.

interfering with the property of his citizens and subjects or with their women. And when he is obliged to take the life of any one, let him do so when there is a proper justification and manifest reason for it; but above all he must abstain from taking the property of others, for men forget more easily the death of their father than the loss of their patrimony. Then also pretexts for seizing property are never wanting, and one who begins to live by rapine will always find some reason for taking the goods of others, whereas causes for taking life are rarer and more fleeting.

But when the prince is with his army and has a large number of soldiers under his control, then it is extremely necessary that he should not mind being thought cruel; for without this reputation he could not keep an army united or disposed to any duty. Among the noteworthy actions of Hannibal[3] is numbered this, that although he had an enormous army, composed of men of all nations and fighting in foreign countries, there never arose any dissension either among them or against the prince, either in good fortune or in bad. This could not be due to anything but his inhuman cruelty, which together with his infinite other virtues, made him always venerated and terrible in the sight of his soldiers, and without it his other virtues would not have sufficed to produce that effect. Thoughtless writers admire on the one hand his actions, and on the other blame the principal cause of them. . . .

▷   Again in marked contrast to the teachings of Christian (and ancient) moralists, Machiavelli said that the successful prince will use any means to achieve and sustain political power. If the end is legitimate, all means are justified.

How laudable it is for a prince to keep good faith and live with integrity, and not with as-

---

[3]Hannibal (247–182 B.C.) was a brilliant Carthaginian general whose military victories almost destroyed Roman power. He was finally defeated at the battle of Zama in 202 B.C. by the Roman general Scipio Africanus.

tuteness, every one knows. Still the experience of our times shows those princes to have done great things who have had little regard for good faith, and have been able by astuteness to confuse men's brains, and who have ultimately overcome those who have made loyalty their foundation.

You must know, then, that there are two methods of fighting, the one by law, the other by force: the first method is that of men, the second of beasts; but as the first method is often insufficient, one must have recourse to the second. It is therefore necessary for a prince to know well how to use both the beast and the man. . . .

A prince being thus obliged to know well how to act as a beast must imitate the fox and the lion, for the lion cannot protect himself from traps, and the fox cannot defend himself from wolves. One must therefore be a fox to recognise traps, and a lion to frighten wolves. Those that wish to be only lions do not understand this. Therefore, a prudent ruler ought not to keep faith when by so doing it would be against his interest, and when the reasons which made him bind himself no longer exist. If men were all good, this precept would not be a good one; but as they are bad, and would not observe their faith with you, so you are not bound to keep faith with them. Nor have legitimate grounds ever failed a prince who wished to show [plausible] excuse for the nonfulfilment of his promise. Of this one could furnish an infinite number of modern examples, and show how many times peace has been broken, and how many promises rendered worthless, by the faithlessness of princes, and those that have been best able to imitate the fox have succeeded best. But it is necessary to be able to disguise this character well, and to be a great feigner and dissembler; and men are so simple and so ready to obey present necessities, that one who deceives will always find those who allow themselves to be deceived. . . .

. . . Thus it is well to seem merciful, faithful, humane, sincere, religious, and also to be so; but you must have the mind so disposed that when it is needful to be otherwise you may be able to change to the opposite qualities. And it must be understood that a prince, and especially a new prince, cannot observe all those things which are considered good in men, being often obliged, in order to maintain the state, to act against faith, against charity, against humanity, and against religion. And, therefore, he must have a mind disposed to adapt itself according to the wind, and as the variations of fortune dictate, and, as I said before, not deviate from what is good, if possible, but be able to do evil if constrained.

A prince must take great care that nothing goes out of his mouth which is not full of the above-named five qualities, and, to see and hear him, he should seem to be all mercy, faith, integrity, humanity, and religion. And nothing is more necessary than to seem to have this last quality, for men in general judge more by the eyes than by the hands, for every one can see,

but very few have to feel. Everybody sees what you appear to be, few feel what you are, and those few will not dare to oppose themselves to the many, who have the majesty of the state to defend them; and in the actions of men, and especially of princes, from which there is no appeal, the end justifies the means. Let a prince therefore aim at conquering and maintaining the state, and the means will always be judged honourable and praised by every one, for the vulgar is always taken by appearances and the issue of the event; and the world consists only of the vulgar, and the few who are not vulgar are isolated when the many have a rallying point in the prince. A certain prince of the present time, whom it is well not to name, never does anything but preach peace and good faith, but he is really a great enemy to both, and either of them, had he observed them, would have lost him state or reputation on many occasions.

REVIEW QUESTIONS

1. In what respect did Niccolò Machiavelli claim to be breaking new ground in his study of statecraft?
2. What was Machiavelli's view of human nature? *Selfish, cowardly, dishonest (p.15)*
3. In what ways was Machiavelli's advice to princes a break with the teachings of medieval political and moral philosophers? *Use religion to control people*
4. Compare Machiavelli's view of the political man with the picture of human beings outlined by Pico and Bruni earlier in this chapter.
5. What ethical standard did Machiavelli seem to endorse for politicians who wish to succeed? *means justify the ends*

▼▼▼

4 ▼ The Lutheran Reformation

The reformation of the Western Christian church in the sixteenth century was precipitated by Martin Luther (1483–1546). A pious German Augustinian monk and theologian, Luther had no intention of founding a new church or overthrowing the political and ecclesiastical order of late medieval Europe. He was educated in the tradition of the New Devotion, and as a theology professor at the university in Wittenberg, Germany, he opposed rationalistic, scholastic theology. Sympathetic at first to the ideas of Christian humanists like Erasmus, Luther too sought a reform of morals and an end to abusive practices within the church. But a visit to the papal court in Rome in 1510 left him profoundly shocked at its worldliness and disillusioned with the papacy's role in the church's governance.

Martin Luther
ON PAPAL POWER, JUSTIFICATION BY FAITH, AND THE INTERPRETATION OF THE BIBLE

To finance the rebuilding of St. Peter's church in Rome, the papacy in 1515 offered indulgences to those who gave alms for this pious work. An indulgence was a mitigation or remission of the austere penance imposed by a priest in absolving a penitent who confessed a sin and indicated remorse. Indulgences were granted by papal decrees for those who agreed to perform some act of charity, almsgiving, prayer, pilgrimage, or other pious work. Some preachers of this particular papal indulgence deceived people into believing that a "purchase" of this indulgence would win them, or even the dead, a secure place in heaven.

In 1517, Luther denounced the abuses connected with the preaching of papal indulgences. The quarrel led quickly to other and more profound theological issues. His opponents defended the use of indulgences on the basis of papal authority, shifting the debate to questions about the nature of papal power within the church. Luther responded with a vigorous attack on the whole system of papal governance. The principal points of his criticism were set out in his *Address to the Christian Nobility of the German Nation Concerning the Reform of the Christian Estate,* published in August 1520. In the first excerpt that follows, Luther argued that the papacy was blocking any reform of the church and appealed to the nobility of Germany to intervene by summoning a "free council" to reform the church.

A central point of contention between Luther and Catholic critics was his theological teaching on justification (salvation) by faith and on the role of good works in the scheme of salvation. Luther had suffered anguish about his unworthiness before God. Then, during a mystical experience, Luther suddenly perceived that his salvation came not because of his good works but as a free gift from God due to Luther's faith in Jesus Christ. Thus, while never denying that a Christian was obliged to perform good works, Luther argued that such pious acts were not helpful in achieving salvation. His claim that salvation or justification was attained through faith in Jesus Christ as Lord and Savior, and through that act of faith alone, became the rallying point of the Protestant reformers.

The Catholic position, not authoritatively clarified until the Council of Trent (1545–1563), argued that justification came not only through faith, but through hope and love as well, obeying God's commandments and doing good works. In *The Freedom of a Christian,* published in 1520, Luther outlined his teaching on justification by faith and on the inefficacy of good works; the second excerpt is from this work.

Another dispute between Luther and papal theologians was the question of interpretation of the Bible. In the medieval church, the final authority in any dispute over the meaning of Scriptural texts or church doctrine was ordinarily the pope alone, speaking as supreme head of the church or in concert with the bishops in an ecumenical council. The doctrine of papal infallibility (that the pope could not err in teaching matters of faith and morals) was already well known, but belief in this doctrine had not been formally required. Luther argued that the literal text of Scripture was alone the foundation of Christian truth, not the teaching of popes or councils. Moreover, Luther denied any special ordination of the clergy to power or authority in the church. He said that all believers were priests, and the clergy did not hold any power beyond that of the laity; therefore the special privileges of the clergy were unjustified. The third excerpt contains Luther's views on the interpretation of Scripture and the nature of priestly offices.

[ON PAPAL POWER]

The Romanists [traditional Catholics loyal to the papacy] have very cleverly built three walls around themselves. Hitherto they have protected themselves by these walls in such a way that no one has been able to reform them. As a result, the whole of Christendom has fallen abominably.

 In the first place, when pressed by the temporal power they have made decrees and declared that the temporal power had no jurisdiction over them, but that, on the contrary, the spiritual power is above the temporal. In the second place, when the attempt is made to reprove them with the Scriptures, they raise the objection that only the pope may interpret the Scriptures. In the third place, if threatened with a council, their story is that no one may summon a council but the pope.

In this way they have cunningly stolen our three rods from us, that they may go unpunished. They have [settled] themselves within the safe stronghold of these three walls so that they can practice all the knavery and wickedness which we see today. Even when they have been compelled to hold a council they have weakened its power in advance by putting the princes under oath to let them remain as they were. In addition, they have given the pope full authority over all decisions of a council, so that it is all the same whether there are many councils or no councils. They only deceive us with puppet shows and sham fights. They fear terribly for their skin in a really free council! They have so intimidated kings and princes with this technique that they believe it would be an offense against God not to be obedient to the Romanists in all their knavish and ghoulish deceits. . . .

The Romanists have no basis in Scripture for their claim that the pope alone has the right to call or confirm a council. This is just their own ruling, and it is only valid as long as it is not harmful to Christendom or contrary to the laws of God. Now when the pope deserves punishment, this ruling no longer obtains, for not to punish him by authority of a council is harmful to Christendom. . . .

Therefore, when necessity demands it, and the pope is an offense to Christendom, the first man who is able should, as a true member of the whole body, do what he can to bring about a truly free council. No one can do this so well as the temporal authorities, especially since they are also fellow-Christians, fellow-priests, fellow-members of the spiritual estate, fellow-lords over all things. Whenever it is necessary or profitable they ought to exercise the office and work which they have received from God over everyone.

[JUSTIFICATION BY FAITH]

You may ask, "What then is the Word of God, and how shall it be used, since there are so many words of God?" I answer: The Apostle explains this in Romans 1. The Word is the gospel of God concerning his Son, who was made flesh, suffered, rose from the dead, and was glorified through the Spirit who sanctifies. To preach Christ means to feed the soul, make it righteous, set it free, and save it, provided it believes the preaching. Faith alone is the saving and efficacious use of the Word of God, according to Rom. 10 (:9): "If you confess with your lips that Jesus is Lord and believe in your heart that God raised him from the dead, you will be saved." Furthermore, "Christ is the end of the law, that every one who has faith may be justified" (Rom. 10:4). Again, in Rom. 1 (:17), "He who through faith is righteous shall live." The Word of God cannot be received and cherished by any works whatever but only by faith. Therefore it is clear that, as the soul needs only the Word of God for its life and righteousness, so it is justified by faith alone and not any works; for if it could be justified by anything else, it would not need the Word, and consequently it would not need faith.

This faith cannot exist in connection with works — that is to say, if you at the same time claim to be justified by works, whatever their character — for that would be the same as "limping with two different opinions" (I Kings 18:21), as worshipping Baal and kissing one's own hand (Job 31:27–28), which, as Job says, is a very great iniquity. Therefore the moment you begin to have faith you learn that all things in you are altogether blameworthy, sinful, and damnable, as the Apostle says in Rom. 3 (:23), "Since all have sinned and fall short of the glory of God," and, "None is righteous, no, not one; . . . all have turned aside, together they have gone wrong" (Rom. 3:10–12). When you have learned this you will know that you need Christ, who suffered and rose again for you so that, if you believe in him, you may through this faith become a new man in so far as your sins are forgiven and you are justified by the merits of another, namely, of Christ alone.

Since, therefore, this faith can rule only in the inner man, as Rom. 10 (:10) says, "For man believes with his heart and so is justified," and since faith alone justifies, it is clear that the inner man cannot be justified, freed, or saved by any outer work or action at all, and that

these works, whatever their character, have nothing to do with this inner man. On the other hand, only ungodliness and unbelief of heart, and no outer work, make him guilty and a damnable servant of sin. Wherefore it ought to be the first concern of every Christian to lay aside all confidence in works and increasingly to strengthen faith alone and through faith to grow in the knowledge, not of works, but of Christ Jesus, who suffered and rose for him, as Peter teaches in the last chapter of his first Epistle (I Pet. 5:10). No other work makes a Christian. . . .

Our faith in Christ does not free us from works but from false opinions concerning works, that is, from the foolish presumption that justification is acquired by works. Faith redeems, corrects, and preserves our consciences so that we know that righteousness does not consist in works, although works neither can nor ought to be wanting; just as we cannot be without food and drink and all the works of this mortal body, yet our righteousness is not in them, but in faith; and yet those works of the body are not to be despised or neglected on that account. In this world we are bound by the needs of our bodily life, but we are not righteous because of them. "My kingship is not of this world" (John 18:36), says Christ. He does not, however, say, "My kingship is not here, that is, in this world." And Paul says, "Though we live in the world we are not carrying on a worldly war" (II Cor. 10:3), and in Gal. 2 (:20), "The life I now live in the flesh I live by faith in the Son of God." Thus what we do, live, and are in works and ceremonies, we do because of the necessities of this life and of the effort to rule our body. Nevertheless we are righteous, not in these, but in the faith of the Son of God.

[THE INTERPRETATION OF THE BIBLE AND THE NATURE OF THE PRIESTHOOD]

They (the Roman Catholic Popes) want to be the only masters of Scriptures. . . . They assume sole authority for themselves and would

#5

persuade us with insolent juggling of words that the Pope, whether he be bad or good, cannot err in matters of faith. . . .

. . . They cannot produce a letter to prove that the interpretation of Scripture . . . belongs to the Pope alone. They themselves have usurped this power . . . and though they allege that this power was conferred on Peter when the keys were given to him, it is plain enough that the keys were not given to Peter alone but to the entire body of Christians (Matt. 16:19; 18:18). . . .

 # 2 . . . Every baptized Christian is a priest already, not by appointment or ordination from the Pope or any other man, but because Christ Himself has begotten him as a priest . . . in baptism. . . .

The Pope has usurped the term "priest" for his anointed and tonsured hordes [clergy and monks]. By this means they have separated themselves from the ordinary Christians and have called themselves uniquely the "clergy of God," God's heritage and chosen people who must help other Christians by their sacrifice and worship. . . . Therefore the Pope argues that he alone has the right and power to ordain and do what he will. . . .

[But] the preaching office is no more than a public service which happens to be conferred on someone by the entire congregation all the members of which are priests. . . .

. . . The fact that a pope or bishop anoints, makes tonsures, ordains, consecrates (makes holy), and prescribes garb different from those of the laity . . . nevermore makes a Christian and a spiritual man. Accordingly, through baptism all of us are consecrated to the priesthood, as St. Peter says. . . . (I Peter 2:9). *# 3*

To make it still clearer, if a small group of pious Christian laymen were taken captive and settled in a wilderness and had among them no priest consecrated by a bishop, if they were to agree to choose one from their midst, married or unmarried, and were to charge him with the office of baptizing, saying Mass, absolving (forgiving of sins), and preaching, such a man would be as truly a priest as he would if all bishops and popes had consecrated him.

— it had 3 walls
① decrees for protection
② Pope interp. scripture
③ only Pope could summon council

REVIEW QUESTIONS

1. Why did Martin Luther believe it unlikely that the papacy would reform the church?
2. How did Luther hope to break papal control over summoning a church council to undertake needed reforms? *Any man could bring about a council - temporal auth.*
3. In what ways did Luther's teachings attack the hierarchical character of the church's government? *Popes & priests unnecessary - ALL are priests thru baptism*
4. How was Luther's doctrine of justification by faith alone linked to his rejection of indulgences? *You can't buy salvation - it is GIVEN to you -*
5. What was Luther's teaching on the interpretation of the Holy Scriptures? How did it conflict with the practice of the medieval church? *Not mentioned in Bible that only priests may interpret*
6. How did Luther's teaching on the common priesthood of all baptized Christians undermine the traditional view of the clerical ministry? *all are priests thru baptism*

▼▼▼

5 ▼ Justification of Absolute Monarchy by Divine Right

eliminate next year redundant

Effectively blocking royal absolutism in the Middle Ages were the dispersion of power between kings and feudal vassals, the vigorous sense of personal freedom

and urban autonomy of the townspeople, and the limitations on royal power imposed by the church. However, by the late sixteenth century, monarchs were asserting their authority over competing groups with ever-greater effectiveness. In this new balance of political forces, European kings acted out their claim to absolute power as monarchs chosen by and responsible to God alone. This theory, called the divine right of kings, became the dominant political ideology of seventeenth- and eighteenth-century Europe.

James I
≪ TRUE LAW OF FREE MONARCHIES ≫ AND A SPEECH TO PARLIAMENT

One of the most articulate defenders of the divine right of monarchy was James VI, who was king of Scotland (1567–1625) and as James I (1603–1625) also was king of England. A scholar as well as a king, James in 1598 anonymously published a widely read book called the *True Law of Free Monarchies.* He claimed that the king alone was the true legislator. James's notions of the royal prerogative and of the role of Parliament are detailed in the following passages from the *True Law* and a speech to Parliament.

TRUE LAW
Prerogative and Parliament.

According to these fundamental laws already alleged, we daily see that in the parliament (which is nothing else but the head court of the king and his vassals) the laws are but craved by his subjects, and only made by him at their [proposal] and with their advice: for albeit the king make daily statutes and ordinances, [imposing] such pains thereto as he thinks [fit], without any advice of parliament or estates, yet it lies in the power of no parliament to make any kind of law or statute, without his sceptre [that is, authority] be to it, for giving it the force of a law. . . . And as ye see it manifest that the king is over-lord of the whole land, so is he master over every person that inhabiteth the same, having power over the life and death of every one of them: for although a just prince will not take the life of any of his subjects without a clear law, yet the same laws whereby he taketh them are made by himself or his predecessors; and so the power flows always from himself. . . . Where he sees the law doubtsome or rigorous, he may interpret or mitigate the

same, lest otherwise *summum jus* be *summa injuria* [the greatest right be the greatest wrong]: and therefore general laws made publicly in parliament may upon . . . [the king's] authority be mitigated and suspended upon causes only known to him.

As likewise, although I have said a good king will frame all his actions to be according to the law, yet is he not bound thereto but of his good will, and for good example-giving to his subjects. . . . So as I have already said, a good king, though he be above the law, will subject and frame his actions thereto, for example's sake to his subjects, and of his own free will, but not as subject or bound thereto. . . .

▷ In a speech before the English Parliament in March 1610, James elaborated on his exalted theory of the monarch's absolute power.

[A SPEECH BEFORE PARLIAMENT]

. . . The state of monarchy is the supremest thing upon earth: for kings are not only God's lieutenants upon earth and sit upon God's throne, but even by God himself they are called gods. There be three principal [comparisons] that illustrate the state of monarchy: one taken out of the word of God, and the two other out of the grounds of policy and philosophy. In the Scriptures kings are called gods, and so their power after a certain relation compared to the Divine power. Kings are also compared to fathers of families: for a king is truly *parens patriae* [parent of the country], the politic father of his people. And lastly, kings are compared to the head of this microcosm of the body of man. . . .

I conclude then this point touching the power of kings with this axiom of divinity, That as to dispute what God may do is blasphemy, . . . so it is sedition in subjects to dispute what a king may do in the height of his power. But just kings will ever be willing to declare what they will do, if they will not incur the curse of God. I will not be content that my power be disputed upon; but I shall ever be willing to make the reason appear of all my doings, and rule my actions according to my laws. . . .

Now the second general ground whereof I am to speak concerns the matter of grievances. . . . First then, I am not to find fault that you inform yourselves of the particular just grievances of the people; nay I must tell you, ye can neither be just nor faithful to me or to your countries that trust and employ you, if you do it not. . . . But I would wish you to be careful to avoid [these] things in the matter of grievances.

First, that you do not meddle with the main points of government: that is my craft . . . to meddle with that, were to lesson me. I am now an old king . . . ;

I must not be taught my office.

Secondly, I would not have you meddle with such ancient rights of mine as I have received from my predecessors, possessing them *more majorum* [as ancestral customs]: such things I would be sorry should be accounted for grievances. All novelties are dangerous as well in a politic as in a natural body: and therefore I would be loath to be quarrelled in my ancient rights and possessions: for that were to judge me unworthy of that which my predecessors had and left me.

REVIEW QUESTIONS

1. According to James I, what was the role of the king within his kingdom? *master over all the land*
2. What did James concede might limit the king's exercise of power? *Example — to obey laws*
3. How did James justify his claim to mitigate or suspend the law in individual cases as he saw fit? *When law was DOUBTSOME or RIGOROUS. LAW must be flexible*
4. What did James believe was the source of kingly supreme authority? *① GOD - in BIBLE ② policy ③ philos.*
5. What did James see as the function of Parliament?
6. About what did James warn Parliament as being particularly objectionable to him? *Don't meddle*

▼▼▼

6 ▼ A Secular Defense of Absolutism

Thomas Hobbes (1588–1679), a British philosopher and political theorist, witnessed the agonies of the English civil war, including the execution of Charles I in 1649. These developments fortified Hobbes's conviction that absolutism was the most desirable and logical form of government. Only the unlimited power of a sovereign, said Hobbes, could contain human passions that disrupt the social order and threaten civilized life; only absolute rule could provide an environment secure enough for people to pursue their individual interests.

Leviathan (1651), Hobbes's principal work of political thought, broke with medieval political theory. Medieval thinkers assigned each group of people — clergy, lords, serfs, guildsmen — a place in a fixed social order; an individual's social duties were set by ancient traditions believed to have been ordained by God. During early modern times, the great expansion of commerce and capitalism spurred the new individualism already pronounced in Renaissance culture; group ties were shattered by competition and accelerating social mobility. Hobbes gave expression to a society where people confronted each other as competing individuals.

Supports ABSOLUTISM [BUT] rejects idea that monarch's

Thomas Hobbes   power came from GOD
≪ *LEVIATHAN* ≫

Hobbes was influenced by the new scientific thought that saw mathematical knowledge as the avenue to truth. Using geometry as a model, Hobbes began with what he believed were self-evident axioms regarding human nature, from which he deduced other truths. He aimed at constructing political philosophy on a scientific foundation and rejected the authority of tradition and religion as inconsistent with a science of politics. Thus, although Hobbes supported absolutism, he dismissed the idea advanced by other theorists of absolutism that the monarch's power derived from God. He also rejected the idea that the state should not be obeyed when it violated God's law. *Leviathan* is a rational and secular political statement. In this modern approach, rather than in Hobbes's justification of absolutism, lies the work's significance.

Hobbes had a pessimistic view of human nature. Believing that people are innately selfish and grasping, he maintained that competition and dissension, rather than cooperation, characterize human relations. Even when reason teaches that cooperation is more advantageous than competition, Hobbes observed that people are reluctant to alter their ways, because passion, not reason, governs their behavior. In the following passages from *Leviathan,* Hobbes described the causes of human conflicts.

Nature hath made men so equall, in the faculties of body, and mind; as that though there bee found one man sometimes manifestly stronger in body, or of quicker mind than another; yet when all is reckoned together, the difference between man, and man, is not so considerable, as that one man can thereupon claim to himselfe any benefit, to which another may not pretend, as well as he. For as to the strength of body, the weakest has strength enough to kill the strongest, either by secret machination, or by confederacy with others, that are in the same danger with himselfe. . . .

And so as to the faculties of the mind . . . men are . . . [more] equall than unequall. . . .

From this equality of ability, ariseth equality of hope in the attaining of our Ends. And therefore if any two men desire the same thing, which neverthelesse they cannot both enjoy, they become enemies; and in the way to their End, . . . endeavour to destroy, or subdue one another. . . . If one plant, sow, build, or possesse a convenient Seat, others may probably be expected to come prepared with forces united, to dispossesse, and deprive him, not only of the fruit of his labour, but also of his life, or liberty. . . .

Only a strong state will end strife

So that in the nature of man, we find three principall causes of quarrell. First, Competition; Secondly, Diffidence; Thirdly, Glory.

The first, maketh men invade for Gain; the second, for Safety; and the third, for Reputation. The first use Violence, to make themselves Masters of other men's persons, wives, children, and cattell; the second, to defend them; the third, for trifles, as a word, a smile, a different opinion, and any other signe of undervalue, either direct in their Persons, or by reflexion in their Kindred, their Friends, their Nation, their Profession, or their Name.

Hereby it is manifest, that during the time men live without a common Power to keep them all in awe, they are in that condition which is called Warre; and such a warre, as is of every man, against every man. . . .

▷ Hobbes then described a state of nature — the hypothetical condition of humanity prior to the formation of the state — as a war of all against all. For Hobbes, the state of nature is a logical abstraction, a device employed to make his point. Only a strong ruling entity — the state — will end the perpetual strife and provide security. For Hobbes, the state is merely a useful arrangement that permits individuals to exchange goods and services in a secure environment. The ruling authority in the state, the sovereign, must have supreme power, or society will collapse and the anarchy of the state of nature will return.

Whatsoever therefore is consequent to a time of Warre, where every man is Enemy to every man; the same is consequent to the time, wherein men live without other security, than what their own strength, and their own invention shall furnish them withall. In such condition, there is no place for Industry; because the fruit thereof is uncertain: and consequently no Culture of the Earth; no Navigation, nor use of the commodities that may be imported by Sea; no commodious Building; no Instruments of moving, and removing such things as require much force; no Knowledge of the face of the Earth; no account of Time; no Arts; no Letters;

no Society; and which is worst of all, continuall feare, and danger of violent death; And the life of man, solitary, poore, nasty, brutish, and short. . . .

The Passions that encline men to Peace, are Feare of Death; Desire of such things as are necessary to commodious living; and a Hope by their Industry to obtain them. And Reason suggesteth convenient Articles of Peace, upon which men may be drawn to agreement. . . .

And because the condition of Man, (as hath been declared in the precedent Chapter) is a condition of Warre of every one against every one; in which case every one is governed by his own Reason; and there is nothing he can make use of, that may not be a help unto him, in preserving his life against his enemyes; It followeth, that in such a condition, every man has a Right to every thing; even to one another's body. And therefore, as long as this naturall Right of every man to every thing endureth, there can be no security to any man, (how strong or wise soever he be,) of living out the time, which Nature ordinarily alloweth men to live. . . .

. . . If there be no Power erected, or not great enough for our security; every man will and may lawfully rely on his own strength and art, for caution against all other men. . . .

The only way to erect . . . a Common Power, as may be able to defend them from the invasion of [foreigners] and the injuries of one another, and thereby to secure them in such sort, as that by their owne industrie, and by the fruites of the Earth, they may nourish themselves and live contentedly; is, to conferre all their power and strength upon one Man, or upon one Assembly of men, that may reduce all their Wills, by plurality of voices, unto one Will . . . and therein to submit their Wills, every one to his Will, and their Judgements, to his Judgement. This is more than Consent, or Concord; it is a reall Unitie of them all, in one and the same Person, made by Covenant of every man with every man, in such manner, as if every man should say to every man, *I Authorise and give up my Right of Governing my selfe, to*

Power to ONE MAN ←

this Man, or to this Assembly of men, on this condition, that thou give up thy Right to him, and Authorise all his Actions in like manner. This done, the Multitude so united in one Person, is called a COMMON-WEALTH. . . . For by this Authoritie, given him by every particular man in the Common-wealth, he hath the use of so much Power and Strength . . . conferred on him, that by terror thereof, he is inabled to forme the wills of them all, to Peace at home, and mutuall [aid] against their enemies abroad. And in him consisteth the Essence of the Common-wealth; which (to define it), is *One Person,* of *whose Acts a great Multitude, by mutuall Covenants one with another, have made themselves every one the Author, to the end he may use the strength and means of them all, as he shall think expedient, for their Peace and Common Defence.*

And he that carryeth this Person, is called SOVERAIGNE, and said to have *Soveraigne Power;* and every one besides, his SUBJECT. . . .

. . . They that have already Instituted a Common-wealth, being thereby bound by Covenant . . . cannot lawfully make a new Covenant, amongst themselves, to be obedient to any other, in any thing whatsoever, without his permission. And therefore, they that are subjects to a Monarch, cannot without his leave

cast off Monarchy, and return to the confusion of a disunited Multitude; nor transferre their Person from him that beareth it, to another Man, or other Assembly of men: for they . . . are bound, every man to every man, to [acknowledge] . . . that he that already is their Soveraigne, shall do, and judge fit to be done; so that [those who do not obey] break their Covenant made to that man, which is injustice: and they have also every man given the Soveraignty to him that beareth their Person; and therefore if they depose him, they take from him that which is his own, and so again it is injustice. . . . And whereas some men have pretended for their disobedience to their Soveraign, a new Covenant, made, not with men, but with God; this also is unjust: for there is no Covenant with God, but by mediation of some body that representeth God's Person; which none doth but God's Lieutenant, who hath the Soveraignty under God. But this pretence of Covenant with God, is so evident a [lie], even in the pretender's own consciences, that it is not onely an act of an unjust, but also of a vile, and unmanly disposition. . . .

. . . Consequently none of [the sovereign's] Subjects, by any pretence of forfeiture, can be freed from his Subjection.

REVIEW QUESTIONS

1. What was Thomas Hobbes's view of human nature? *pessimistic*
2. What did Hobbes believe was the state of human society when man lived according to his nature? *WAR*
3. What conclusion did Hobbes draw about the best form of government? *Strong ruling state One sovereign*
4. According to Hobbes, what was the essential nature of the state or commonwealth? *State is ultimate in authority*
5. What was Hobbes's reasoning in condemning any act of rebellion against the sovereign state? *It would break the covenant by which they are bound*
6. How did Hobbes answer those who offered religious reasons for disobeying the sovereign?
7. Why is Hobbes considered a decisive thinker for the emergence of modern political thought?

There is no covenant c̄ God but only a body that represent God's person

cant change thing

▼▼▼

7 ▼ The Triumph of Constitutional Monarchy in England: The Glorious Revolution

The struggle against absolute monarchy in England during the early seventeenth century reached a climax during the reign of Charles I (1625–1649). The king's failure to support the Protestant cause during the Thirty Years' War (1618–1648) on the Continent and his fervent support of the Anglican Episcopal Church earned him many enemies. Among them were the Puritans, Presbyterians, and Independents (Congregationalists), who composed an influential minority in his early Parliaments. Faced with rising costs of government, the king tried to obtain more revenues by vote of Parliament, but the parliamentarians refused to consent to new taxes unless the king followed policies they supported. After four bitter years of controversy, the king dismissed Parliament in 1629. He ruled in an increasingly absolutist manner without calling a new Parliament for the next eleven years and levied many taxes without the consent of the people's representatives.

Charles's policies collapsed in 1640 when he was compelled to summon Parliament to raise money for an army to put down a rebellion of Scottish Presbyterians. The new Parliament set forth demands for reforms of church and state, which the king refused. He claimed monarchical power and policies to be unlimited by parliamentary controls or consent.

Parliament raised its own army as civil war broke out between its supporters and those of the king. The parties were divided not only on constitutional issues but also by religious differences. Most of the Puritans, Presbyterians, and Independents supported the parliamentary cause; Anglicans and Catholics were overwhelmingly royalist. Captured by the Scottish Presbyterian rebels in 1646 and turned over to the English parliamentary army in 1647, Charles was held prisoner for two years until the Puritan parliamentary general Oliver Cromwell (1599–1658) decided to put him on trial for treason. The king was found guilty and executed in 1649.

The revolutionary parliamentary regime evolved into a military dictatorship headed by Cromwell. After Cromwell's death, Parliament restored the monarchy in 1660 and invited the late king's heir to end his exile and take the throne. Charles II (1660–1685), by discretion and skilled statesmanship, managed to avoid a major confrontation with Parliament. When his brother James II (1685–1688), a staunch Catholic, succeeded to the throne, the hostility between Parliament and monarchy mounted. Parliament feared that James II aimed to impose Catholicism and absolutism on England.

When the king's wife gave birth to a son, making the heir to the throne another Catholic, almost all factions (except the Catholics) abandoned James II and invited the Dutch Protestant Prince William of Orange and his wife Mary, James

II's Protestant daughter, to come to England. James and his Catholic family and friends fled to France. Parliament declared the throne vacant and offered it to William and Mary as joint sovereigns. As a result of the bloodless "Glorious Revolution," the English monarchy became clearly limited by the will of Parliament.

THE ENGLISH DECLARATION OF RIGHTS

In depriving James II of the throne, Parliament had destroyed forever in Britain the theory of divine right as an operating principle of government and had firmly established a limited constitutional monarchy. The appointment of William and Mary was accompanied by a declaration of rights (later enacted as the Bill of Rights), which enumerated and declared illegal James II's arbitrary acts. The Declaration of Rights, excerpted below, compelled William and Mary and future monarchs to recognize the right of the people's representatives to dispose of the royal office and to set limits on its powers. These rights were subsequently formulated into laws passed by Parliament. Prior to the American Revolution, colonists protested that British actions in the American colonies violated certain rights guaranteed in the English Bill of Rights. Several of these rights were later included in the Constitution of the United States.

And whereas the said late king James the Second having abdicated the government and the throne being thereby vacant, His Highness the prince of Orange (whom it hath pleased Almighty God to make the glorious instrument of delivering this kingdom from popery and arbitrary power) did (by the advice of the lords spiritual and temporal and divers principal persons of the commons)[1] cause letters to be written to the lords spiritual and temporal, being Protestants; and other letters to the several counties, cities, universities, boroughs and Cinque ports[2] for the choosing of such persons to represent them, as were of right to be sent to parliament, to meet and sit at Westminster upon the two and twentieth day of January in this year one thousand six hundred eighty and eight,[3] in order to [guarantee] . . . that their religion, laws and liberties might not again be in danger of being subverted; upon which letters elections having been accordingly made,

And thereupon the said lords spiritual and temporal and commons pursuant to their respective letters and elections being now assembled in a full and free representative of this nation, taking into their most serious consideration the best means for attaining the ends aforesaid, do in the first place (as their ancestors in like case have usually done) for the vindicating and asserting their ancient rights and liberties, declare:

That the pretended power of suspending of laws or the execution of laws by regal authority without consent of parliament is illegal.

That the pretended power of dispensing with laws or the execution of laws by regal authority as it hath been assumed and exercised of late is illegal.

That the commission for erecting the late court of commissioners for ecclesiastical causes

---

[1]The lords spiritual refers to the bishops of the Church of England who sat in the House of Lords, and the lords temporal refers to the nobility entitled to sit in the House of Lords. The commons refers to the elected representatives in the House of Commons.

[2]The Cinque ports along England's southeastern coast (originally five in number) enjoyed special privileges because of their military duties in providing for coastal defense.

---

[3]The year was in fact 1689 because until 1752, the English used March 25 as the beginning of the new year.

and all other commissions and courts of like nature are illegal and pernicious.

That the levying money for or to the use of the crown by pretence of prerogative without grant of parliament for a longer time or in other manner than the same is or shall be granted is illegal.

That it is the right of the subjects to petition the king and all commitments and prosecutions for such petitioning are illegal.

That the raising or keeping a standing army within the kingdom in time of peace unless it be with consent of parliament is against law.

That the subjects which are Protestants may have arms for their defence suitable to their conditions and as allowed by law.

That election of members of parliament ought to be free.

That the freedom of speech and debates or proceedings in parliament ought not to be impeached or questioned in any court or place out of parliament.

That excessive bail ought not to be required nor excessive fines imposed nor cruel and unusual punishments inflicted.

That jurors ought to be duly impanelled and returned and jurors which pass upon men in trials for high treason ought to be freeholders.

That all grants and promises of fines and forfeitures of particular persons before conviction are illegal and void.

And that for redress of all grievances and for the amending, strengthening and preserving of the laws parliaments ought to be held frequently.

And they do claim, demand and insist upon all and singular the premises as their undoubted rights and liberties and that no declarations, judgments, doings or proceedings to the prejudice of the people in any of the said premises ought in any wise to be drawn hereafter into consequence or example.

REVIEW QUESTIONS

1. Why did Prince William of Orange summon the Parliament to meet in January 1689?
2. What ancient rights and liberties did the Parliament assert?
3. In what ways did the Declaration of Rights repudiate specific theories of monarchy held by James I?

1. He was aware of why he had been chosen to rule, he knew he had to work c̄ Parl.

2. • no laws s̄ consent of PARL • right to bear arms
• no tax s̄ " • free elections
• no standing army " • no excessive bail
• trial by jury

3. Claimed illegality of many kingly ABSOLUTIST acts

DIALOGO
di
GALILEO GALILEI LINCEO
AL SER.mo FERD. II. GRAN. DVCA DI
TOSC ANA

CHAPTER 2

SOURCES OF THE WESTERN TRADITION

The Scientific Revolution

The Scientific Revolution of the sixteenth and seventeenth centuries replaced the medieval view of the universe with a new cosmology and produced a new way of investigating nature. It overthrew the medieval conception of nature as a hierarchical order ascending toward a realm of perfection. Rejecting reliance on authority, the thinkers of the Scientific Revolution affirmed the individual's ability to know the natural world through the method of mathematical reasoning, the direct observation of nature, and carefully controlled experiments.

The medieval view of the universe had blended the theories of Aristotle and Ptolemy, two ancient Greek thinkers, with Christian teachings. In that view, a stationary earth stood in the center of the universe just above hell. Revolving around the earth were seven planets: the moon, Mercury, Venus, the sun, Mars, Jupiter, and Saturn. Because people believed that earth did not move, it was not considered a planet. Each planet was attached to a transparent sphere that turned around the earth. Encompassing the universe was a sphere of fixed stars; beyond the stars lay three heavenly spheres, the outermost of which was the abode of God. An earth-centered universe accorded with the Christian idea that God had created the universe for men and women and that salvation was the aim of life.

Also agreeable to the medieval Christian view was Aristotle's division of the universe into a lower, earthly realm and a higher realm beyond the moon. Two sets of laws operated in the universe, one on earth and the other in the celestial realm. Earthly objects were composed of four elements: earth, water, fire, and air; celestial objects were composed of the divine ether — a substance too pure, too clear, too fine, too spiritual to be found on earth. Celestial objects naturally moved in perfectly circular orbits around the earth; earthly objects, composed mainly of the heavy elements of earth and water, naturally fell downward, whereas objects made of the lighter elements of air and fire naturally flew upward toward the sky.

The destruction of the medieval world picture began with the publication in 1543 of *On the Revolutions of the Heavenly Spheres,* by Nicolaus Copernicus, a Polish mathematician, astronomer, and clergyman. In Copernicus's system, the sun was in the center of the universe, and the earth was another planet that moved around the sun. Most thinkers of the

THE FRONTISPIECE from Galileo Galilei's 1632 *Dialogue Concerning the Two Chief World Systems* depicts Aristotle, Ptolemy, and Copernicus engaged in scientific debate. (*Fotomas Index/John Freeman, London*)

31

time, committed to the Aristotelian-Ptolemaic system and to the biblical statements that seemed to support it, rejected Copernicus's conclusions.

The work of Galileo Galilei, an Italian mathematician, astronomer, and physicist, was decisive in the shattering of the medieval cosmos and the shaping of the modern scientific outlook. Galileo advanced the modern view that knowledge of nature derives from direct observation and from mathematics. For Galileo, the universe was a "grand book which . . . is written in the language of mathematics, and its characters are triangles, circles, and other geometric figures without which it is humanly impossible to understand a single word of it." Galileo also pioneered experimental physics, advanced the modern idea that nature is uniform throughout the universe, and attacked reliance on scholastic authority rather than on experimentation in resolving scientific controversies.

Johannes Kepler (1571–1630), a contemporary of Galileo, discovered three laws of planetary motion that greatly advanced astronomical knowledge. Kepler showed that the path of a planet was an ellipse, not a circle as Ptolemy (and Copernicus) had believed, and that planets do not move at uniform speed but accelerate as they near the sun. He devised formulas to calculate accurately both a planet's speed at each point in its orbit around the sun and a planet's location at a particular time. Kepler's laws provided further evidence that Copernicus had been right, for they made sense only in a sun-centered universe, but Kepler could not explain why planets stayed in their orbits rather than flying off into space or crashing into the sun. The resolution of that question was left to Sir Isaac Newton.

Newton's great achievement was integrating the findings of Copernicus, Galileo, and Kepler into a single theoretical system. Newton formulated the mechanical laws of motion and attraction that govern celestial and terrestrial objects.

The creation of a new model of the universe was one great achievement of the Scientific Revolution; another accomplishment was the formulation of the scientific method. The scientific method encompasses two approaches to knowledge, which usually complement each other: the empirical (inductive) and the rational (deductive). Although all sciences use both approaches, the inductive method is generally stressed more in such descriptive sciences as biology, anatomy, and geology, which rely on the accumulation of data. In the inductive approach, general principles are derived from analyzing external experiences — observations and the results of experiments. In the deductive approach,

(handwritten margin notes)

Galileo — knowledge from OBSERVATION & MATH

Kepler —
• ELLIPSE
• move faster as they approach sun

Newton — integrated findings of all 3 MOTION & its laws

scientific method

empirical (inductive)
rational (deductive)

Handwritten margin notes:

← accumulate DATA

Inductive used
  biology
  anatomy
  geology
  • observe
  • experiment

Deductive
  truths arrived
  at thru steps
  • self-evident
    principles in
    mind already

used in mathematics and theoretical physics, truths are derived in successive steps from indubitable axioms. Whereas the inductive method builds its concepts from an analysis of sense experience, the deductive approach constructs its ideas from self-evident principles that are conceived by the mind itself without external experience. The deductive and inductive approaches to knowledge, and their interplay, have been a constantly recurring feature in Western intellectual history since the rationalism of Plato and the empiricism of Aristotle. The success of the scientific method in modern times arose from the skillful synchronization of induction and deduction by such giants as Leonardo, Copernicus, Kepler, Galileo, and Newton.

The Scientific Revolution was instrumental in shaping the modern outlook. It destroyed the medieval conception of the universe and established the scientific method as the means for investigating nature and acquiring knowledge, even in areas having little to do with the study of the physical world. By demonstrating the powers of the human mind, the Scientific Revolution gave thinkers great confidence in reason and led eventually to a rejection of traditional beliefs in magic, astrology, and witches. In the eighteenth century, this growing skepticism led thinkers to question miracles and other Christian beliefs that seemed contrary to reason.

I ▼ The Copernican Revolution

In proclaiming that the earth was not stationary but revolved around the sun, Nicolaus Copernicus (1473–1543) revolutionized the science of astronomy. Fearing controversy and scorn, Copernicus long refused to publish his great work, *On the Revolutions of the Heavenly Spheres.* However, persuaded by friends, he finally relented and permitted publication; a copy of his book reached him on his deathbed. As Copernicus anticipated, his ideas aroused the ire of many thinkers.

Both Catholic and Protestant philosophers and theologians (including Martin Luther and John Calvin) attacked Copernicus for contradicting the Bible and Aristotle and Ptolemy, and they raised several specific objections. First, certain passages in the Bible imply a stationary earth and a sun that moves (for example, Psalm 93 says, "Yea, the world is established; it shall never be moved"; and in attacking Copernicus, Luther pointed out that "sacred Scripture tells us that Joshua commanded the sun to stand still, and not the earth"). Second, a body as heavy as the earth cannot move through space at such speed as Copernicus suggested. Third, if the earth spins on its axis, why does a stone dropped from a height land directly below instead of at a point behind where it was dropped? Fourth, if the earth moved, objects would fly off it. And finally, the moon cannot orbit both the earth and the sun at the same time.

Nicolaus Copernicus
≪ ON THE REVOLUTIONS OF THE HEAVENLY SPHERES ≫

On the Revolutions of the Heavenly Spheres **was dedicated to Pope Paul III, whom Copernicus asked to protect him from vilification. In the dedication, Copernicus explains his reason for delaying publication of** *Revolutions.*

To His Holiness, Pope Paul III,
Nicholas Copernicus' Preface
to His Books on the Revolutions

I can readily imagine, Holy Father, that as soon as some people hear that in this volume, which I have written about the revolutions of the spheres of the universe, I ascribe certain motions to the terrestrial globe, they will shout that I must be immediately repudiated together with this belief. For I am not so enamored of my own opinions that I disregard what others may think of them. I am aware that a philosopher's ideas are not subject to the judgement of ordinary persons, because it is his endeavor to seek the truth in all things, to the extent permitted to human reason by God. Yet I hold that completely erroneous views should be shunned. Those who know that the consensus of many centuries has sanctioned the conception that the earth remains at rest in the middle of the heaven as its center would, I reflected, regard it as an insane pronouncement if I made the opposite assertion that the earth moves. Therefore I debated with myself for a long time whether to publish the volume which I wrote to prove the earth's motion or rather to follow the example of the Pythagoreans[1] and certain others, who used to transmit philosophy's secrets only to kinsmen and friends, not in writing but by word of mouth. . . . And they did so, it seems to me, not, as some suppose, because they were in some way jealous about their teachings, which would be spread around; on the contrary, they wanted the very beautiful thoughts attained by great men of deep devotion not to be ridiculed by those who are reluctant to exert themselves vigorously in any literary pursuit unless it is lucrative; or if they are stimulated to the nonacquisitive study of philosophy by the exhortation and example of others, yet because of their dullness of mind they play the same part among philosophers as drones among bees. When I weighed these considerations, the scorn which I had reason to fear on account of the novelty and unconventionality of my opinion almost induced me to abandon completely the work which I had undertaken.

But while I hesitated for a long time and even resisted, my friends [encouraged me]. . . . Foremost among them was the cardinal of Capua [a city in southern Italy], Nicholas Schönberg, renowned in every field of learning. Next to him was a man who loves me dearly, Tiedemann Giese, bishop of Chelmno [a city in northern Poland], a close student of sacred letters as well as of all good literature. For he repeatedly encouraged me and, sometimes adding reproaches, urgently requested me to publish this volume and finally permit it to appear after being buried among my papers and lying concealed not merely until the ninth year but by now the fourth period of nine years. The same

[1]Pythagoreans were followers of Pythagoras, a Greek mathematician and philosopher of the sixth century B.C.; they were particularly interested in cosmology.

[Handwritten: Friends + scholars here encouraged him to publish]

conduct was recommended to me by not a few other very eminent scholars. They exhorted me no longer to refuse, on account of the fear which I felt, to make my work available for the general use of students of astronomy. The crazier my doctrine of the earth's motion now appeared to most people, the argument ran, so much the more admiration and thanks would it gain after they saw the publication of my writings dispel the fog of absurdity by most luminous proofs. Influenced therefore by these persuasive men and by this hope, in the end I allowed my friends to bring out an edition of the volume, as they had long besought me to do. . . .

But you [your Holiness] are rather waiting to hear from me how it occurred to me to venture to conceive any motion of the earth, against the traditional opinion of astronomers and almost against common sense. . . . [Copernicus then describes some of the problems connected with the Ptolemaic system.]

For a long time, then, I reflected on this confusion in the astronomical traditions concerning the derivation of the motions of the universe's spheres. I began to be annoyed that the movements of the world machine, created for our sake by the best and most systematic Artisan of all [God], were not understood with greater certainty by the philosophers, who otherwise examined so precisely the most insignificant trifles of this world. For this reason I undertook the task of rereading the works of all the philosophers which I could obtain to learn whether anyone had ever proposed other motions of the universe's spheres than those expounded by the teachers of astronomy in the schools. And in fact first I found in Cicero that Hicetas supposed the earth to move. Later I also discovered in Plutarch[2] that certain others were of this opinion. . . .

[Handwritten: all supposed the earth to move]

_____

[2]Hicetas, a Pythagorean philosopher of the fourth century B.C., taught that the earth rotated on its axis while the other heavenly bodies were at rest. Cicero was a Roman statesman of the first century B.C. Plutarch (A.D. c. 50–c. 120) was a Greek moral philosopher and biographer whose works were especially popular among Renaissance humanists.

Therefore, having obtained the opportunity from these sources, I too began to consider the mobility of the earth. . . . I thought that I too would be readily permitted to ascertain whether explanations sounder than those of my predecessors could be found for the revolution of the celestial spheres on the assumption of some motion of the earth.

Having thus assumed the motions which I ascribe to the earth later on in the volume, by long and intense study I finally found that if the motions of the other planets are correlated with the orbiting of the earth, and are computed for the revolution of each planet, not only do their phenomena follow therefrom but also the order and size of all the planets and spheres, and heaven itself is so linked together that in no portion of it can anything be shifted without disrupting the remaining parts and the universe as a whole. Accordingly in the arrangement of the volume too I have adopted the following order. In the first book I set forth the entire distribution of the spheres together with the motions which I attribute to the earth, so that this book contains, as it were, the general structure of the universe. Then in the remaining books I correlate the motions of the other planets and of all the spheres with the movement of the earth so that I may thereby determine to what extent the motions and appearances of the other planets and spheres can be saved if they are correlated with the earth's motions. I have no doubt that acute and learned astronomers will agree with me if, as this discipline especially requires, they are willing to examine and consider, not superficially but thoroughly, what I adduce in this volume in proof of these matters. However, in order that the educated and uneducated alike may see that I do not run away from the judgement of anybody at all, I have preferred dedicating my studies to Your Holiness rather than to anyone else. For even in this very remote corner of the earth where I live you are considered the highest authority by virtue of the loftiness of your office and your love for all literature and astronomy too. Hence by your prestige and

[Handwritten: OBSERVATION — earth + planets are linked]

[Handwritten: Praise for Pope]

You can defend me

judgement you can easily suppress calumnious attacks although, as the proverb has it, there is no remedy for a backbite.

Perhaps there will be babblers who claim to be judges of astronomy although completely ignorant of the subject and, badly distorting some passage of Scripture to their purpose, will dare to find fault with my undertaking and censure it. I disregard them even to the extent of despising their criticism as unfounded. For it is not unknown that Lactantius,[3] otherwise an illustrious writer but hardly an astronomer,

speaks quite childishly about the earth's shape, when he mocks those who declared that the earth has the form of a globe. Hence scholars need not be surprised if any such persons will likewise ridicule me. Astronomy is written for astronomers. To them my work too will seem, unless I am mistaken, to make some contribution.

---

[3]Renaissance humanists admired Lactantius (c. 240–c. 320), a Latin rhetorician and Christian apologist, for his classical, Ciceronian literary style.

Cardinal Bellarmine
ATTACK ON THE COPERNICAN THEORY

In 1615, Cardinal Bellarmine, who in the name of the Inquisition warned Galileo (see page 37) not to defend the Copernican theory, expressed his displeasure with heliocentrism in a letter to Paolo Antonio Foscarini. Foscarini, head of the Carmelites, an order of mendicant friars, in Calabria and professor of theology, tried to show that the earth's motion was not incompatible with biblical statements.

Cardinal Bellarmine to Foscarini (12 April 1615)

My Very Reverend Father,

I have read with interest the letter in Italian and the essay in Latin which Your [Reverence] sent me; I thank you for the one and for the other and confess that they are full of intelligence and erudition. You ask for my opinion, and so I shall give it to you, but very briefly, since now you have little time for reading and I for writing.

First, . . . to want to affirm that in reality the sun is at the center of the world and only turns on itself without moving from east to west, and the earth . . . revolves with great speed around the sun . . . is a very dangerous thing, likely not only to irritate all scholastic philosophers and theologians, but also to harm the Holy Faith by rendering Holy Scripture false. For your [Reverence] has well shown many ways of interpreting Holy Scripture, but

has not applied them to particular cases; without a doubt you would have encountered very great difficulties if you had wanted to interpret all those passages you yourself cited.

Second, I say that, as you know, the Council [of Trent] prohibits interpreting Scripture against the common consensus of the Holy Fathers; and if Your [Reverence] wants to read not only the Holy Fathers, but also the modern commentaries on Genesis, the Psalms, Ecclesiastes, and Joshua, you will find all agreeing in the literal interpretation that the sun is in heaven and turns around the earth with great speed, and that the earth is very far from heaven and sits motionless at the center of the world. Consider now, with your sense of prudence, whether the Church can tolerate giving Scripture a meaning contrary to the Holy Fathers and to all the Greek and Latin commentators. Nor can one answer that this is not a matter of faith, since if it is not a matter of faith "as re-

Makes Holy Scripture appear false

Council of Trent prohibits

gards the topic," it is a matter of faith "as regards the speaker"; and so it would be heretical to say that Abraham did not have two children and Jacob twelve, as well as to say that Christ was not born of a virgin, because both are said by the Holy Spirit through the mouth of the prophets and the apostles.

Third, I say that if there were a true demonstration that the sun is at the center of the world and the earth in the third heaven, and that the sun does not circle the earth but the earth circles the sun, then one would have to proceed with great care in explaining the Scriptures that appear contrary, and say rather that we do not understand them than that what is demonstrated is false. But I will not believe

that there is such a demonstration, until it is shown to me. . . . and in case of doubt one must not abandon the Holy Scripture as interpreted by the Holy Fathers. I add that the one who wrote, "The sun also ariseth, and the sun goeth down, and hasteth to his place where he arose," was Solomon [King of ancient Israel], who not only spoke inspired by God, but was a man above all others wise and learned in the human sciences and in the knowledge of created things; he received all this wisdom from God; therefore it is not likely that he was affirming something that was contrary to truth already demonstrated or capable of being demonstrated.

→ *how can you challenge the Scripture without stating they are false?*

REVIEW QUESTIONS

1. Why did Nicolaus Copernicus fear to publish his theory about the earth's motion? *ridiculed, shunned insane idea*
2. Why did Copernicus dedicate his work to Pope Paul III? *to suppress attacks*
3. What facts encouraged Copernicus to investigate the motions of the universe's spheres?
4. What methods did Copernicus employ in investigating the earth's motion? *— assumptions, observation, mathematical reasoning re-read all philosophers*
5. On what grounds did Cardinal Bellarmine reject the Copernican theory? *Contradicts scripture, council of Trent forbid it*

▼▼▼

2 ▼ Expanding the New Astronomy

The brilliant Italian scientist Galileo Galilei (1564–1642) rejected the medieval division of the universe into higher and lower realms and proclaimed the modern idea of nature's uniformity. Learning that a telescope had been invented in Holland, Galileo built one for himself and used it to investigate the heavens. Through his telescope, Galileo saw craters and mountains on the moon; he concluded that celestial bodies were not pure, perfect, and immutable, as had been believed. There was no difference in quality between heavenly and earthly bodies; nature was the same throughout.

built own telescope

Galileo Galilei
≪ THE STARRY MESSENGER ≫

Uniformity of Nature

In the following reading from *The Starry Messenger* (1610), Galileo reported the findings observed through his telescope, which led him to proclaim the uniformity of nature.

Planets are not Smooth or Uniform (handwritten note)

About ten months ago a report reached my ears that a certain Fleming [a native of Flanders]* had constructed a spyglass by means of which visible objects, though very distant from the eye of the observer, were distinctly seen as if nearby. Of this truly remarkable effect several experiences were related, to which some persons gave credence while others denied them. A few days later the report was confirmed to me in a letter from a noble Frenchman at Paris, Jacques Badovere,† which caused me to apply myself wholeheartedly to inquire into the means by which I might arrive at the invention of a similar instrument. This I did shortly afterwards, my basis being the theory of refraction. First I prepared a tube of lead, at the ends of which I fitted two glass lenses, both plane on one side while on the other side one was spherically convex and the other concave. Then placing my eye near the concave lens I perceived objects satisfactorily large and near, for they appeared three times closer and nine times larger than when seen with the naked eye alone. Next I constructed another one, more accurate, which represented objects as enlarged more than sixty times. Finally, sparing neither labor nor expense, I succeeded in constructing for myself so excellent an instrument that objects seen by means of it appeared nearly one thousand times larger and over thirty times closer than when regarded with our natural vision.

It would be superfluous to enumerate the number and importance of the advantages of such an instrument at sea as well as on land. But forsaking terrestrial observations, I turned to celestial ones, and first I saw the moon from as near at hand as if it were scarcely two terrestrial radii [a measure of distance, obscure today]

away. After that I observed often with wondering delight both the planets and the fixed stars, and since I saw these latter to be very crowded, I began to seek (and eventually found) a method by which I might measure their distances apart. . . .

Now let us review the observations made during the past two months, once more inviting the attention of all who are eager for true philosophy to the first steps of such important contemplations. Let us speak first of that surface of the moon which faces us. For greater clarity I distinguish two parts of this surface, a lighter and a darker; the lighter part seems to surround and to pervade the whole hemisphere, while the darker part discolors the moon's surface like a kind of cloud, and makes it appear covered with spots. Now those spots which are fairly dark and rather large are plain to everyone and have been seen throughout the ages; these I shall call the "large" or "ancient" spots, distinguishing them from others that are smaller in size but so numerous as to occur all over the lunar surface, and especially the lighter part. The latter spots had never been seen by anyone before me. From observations of these spots repeated many times I have been led to the opinion and conviction that the surface of the moon is not smooth, uniform, and precisely spherical as a great number of philosophers believe it (and the other heavenly bodies) to be, but is uneven, rough, and full of cavities and prominences, being not unlike the face of the earth, relieved by chains of mountains and deep valleys. . . .

▷ With his telescope, Galileo discovered four moons orbiting Jupiter, an observation that overcame a principal objection to the Copernican system. Galileo showed that a celestial body could indeed move around a center other than the earth; that earth was not the common center for all celestial bodies; that a celestial body (earth's moon or Jupiter's moons) could orbit a planet at the same time that the planet revolved around another body (namely, the sun).

---

*Credit for the original invention is generally assigned to Hans Lipperhey, a lens grinder in Holland who chanced upon this property of combined lenses and applied for a patent on it in 1608.
†Badovere studied in Italy toward the close of the sixteenth century and is said to have been a pupil of Galileo's about 1598. When he wrote concerning the new instrument in 1609, he was in the French diplomatic service at Paris, where he died in 1620.

On the seventh day of January in this present year 1610, at the first hour of night, when I was viewing the heavenly bodies with a telescope, Jupiter presented itself to me; and because I had prepared a very excellent instrument for myself, I perceived (as I had not before, on account of the weakness of my previous instrument) that beside the planet there were three starlets, small indeed, but very bright. Though I believed them to be among the host of fixed stars, they aroused my curiosity somewhat by appearing to lie in an exact straight line parallel to the ecliptic, and by their being more splendid than others of their size. Their arrangement with respect to Jupiter and each other was the following:

East   *   *   O   *   *West*

that is, there were two stars on the eastern side and one to the west. The most easterly star and the western one appeared larger than the other. I paid no attention to the distances between them and Jupiter, for at the outset I thought them to be fixed stars, as I have said.‡ But returning to the same investigation on January eighth — led by what, I do not know — I found a very different arrangement. The three starlets were now all to the west of Jupiter, closer together, and at equal intervals from one another as shown in the following sketch:

East   O   *   *   *   *West*

---

‡The reader should remember that the telescope was nightly revealing to Galileo hundreds of fixed stars never previously observed. His unusual gifts for astronomical observation are illustrated by his having noticed and remembered these three merely by reason of their alignment, and recalling them so well that when by chance he happened to see them the following night he was certain that they had changed their positions.

On the tenth of January, however, the stars appeared in this position with respect to Jupiter:

East   *   *   O   *West*

that is, there were but two of them, both easterly, the third (as I supposed) being hidden behind Jupiter. . . . There was no way in which such alterations could be attributed to Jupiter's motion, yet being certain that these were still the same stars I had observed . . . my perplexity was now transformed into amazement. I was sure that the apparent changes belonged not to Jupiter but to the observed stars, and I resolved to pursue this investigation with greater care and attention. . . .

I had now decided beyond all question that there existed in the heavens three stars wandering about Jupiter as do Venus and Mercury about the sun, and this became plainer than daylight from observations on similar occasions which followed. Nor were there just three such stars; four wanderers complete their revolutions about Jupiter. . . .

Here we have a fine and elegant argument for quieting the doubts of those who, while accepting with tranquil mind the revolutions of the planets about the sun in the Copernican system, are mightily disturbed to have the moon alone revolve about the earth and accompany it in an annual rotation about the sun. Some have believed that this structure of the universe should be rejected as impossible. But now we have not just one planet rotating about another while both run through a great orbit around the sun; our own eyes show us four stars which wander around Jupiter as does the moon around the earth, while all together trace out a grand revolution about the sun in the space of twelve years.

[handwritten: 4 moons orbit Jupiter]

[handwritten: all revolve around the sun]

REVIEW QUESTIONS

1. What role did technological innovation play in advancing the possibility of new scientific knowledge?

*① planets are not smooth
(as previously thought)
② they revolve around Jupiter + ALL
revolve around Sun*

2. What was the implication for modern astronomy of Galileo Galilei's observation of the surface of the moon? Of the moons of Jupiter?

3. What methods did Galileo use in his scientific investigations? *OBSERVATION DEDUCTION*

▼▼▼

3 ▼ Critique of Authority

Galileo appealed to the Roman Catholic authorities asking them to halt their actions against the theories of Copernicus, but was unsuccessful. His support of Copernicus aroused the ire of both clergy and scholastic philosophers. In 1616, the church placed Copernicus's book on the index of forbidden books, and Galileo was ordered to cease his defense of the Copernican theory. In 1632, Galileo published *Dialogue Concerning the Two Chief World Systems* in which he upheld the Copernican view. Widely distributed and acclaimed, the book antagonized Galileo's enemies, who succeeded in halting further printing. Summoned to Rome, the aging and infirm scientist was put on trial by the Inquisition and ordered to abjure the Copernican theory. Galileo bowed to the Inquisition, which condemned the *Dialogue* and sentenced him to life imprisonment — largely house arrest at his own villa near Florence, where he was treated humanely.

Galileo Galilei
LETTER TO THE GRAND DUCHESS CHRISTINA AND ≪ DIALOGUE CONCERNING THE TWO CHIEF WORLD SYSTEMS — PTOLEMAIC AND COPERNICAN ≫

The first reading illustrates Galileo's active involvement in a struggle for freedom of inquiry many years before the *Dialogue* was published. In 1615, in a letter addressed to Grand Duchess Christina of Tuscany, Galileo argued that passages from the Bible had no authority in scientific disputes.

The second reading (from the *Dialogue*) reveals Galileo's views on Aristotle. Medieval scholastics regarded Aristotle as the supreme authority on questions concerning nature, an attitude that was perpetuated by early modern scholastics. Galileo insisted that such reliance on authority was a hindrance to scientific investigation, that it is through observation, experiment, and reason that one arrives at physical truth.

[BIBLICAL AUTHORITY]

Some years ago, as Your Serene Highness well knows, I discovered in the heavens many things that had not been seen before our own age. The novelty of these things, as well as some consequences which followed from them in contradiction to the physical notions commonly held among academic philosophers, stirred up against me no small number of professors — as if I had placed these things in the sky with my own hands in order to upset nature and overturn the sciences. They seemed to forget that the increase of known truths stimulates the investigation, establishment, and growth of the arts; not their diminution or destruction.

Showing a greater fondness for their own opinions than for truth, they sought to deny and disprove the new things which, if they had cared to look for themselves, their own senses would have demonstrated to them. To this end they hurled various charges and published numerous writings filled with vain arguments, and they made the grave mistake of sprinkling these with passages taken from places in the Bible which they had failed to understand properly, and which were ill suited to their purposes. . . .

. . . Men who were well grounded in astronomical and physical science were persuaded as soon as they received my first message. There were others who denied them or remained in doubt only because of their novel and unexpected character, and because they had not yet had the opportunity to see for themselves. These men have by degrees come to be satisfied. But some, besides allegiance to their original error, possess I know not what fanciful interest in remaining hostile not so much toward the things in question as toward their discoverer. No longer being able to deny them, these men now take refuge in obstinate silence, but being more than ever exasperated by that which has pacified and quieted other men, they divert their thoughts to other fancies and seek new ways to damage me. . . .

. . . Possibly because they are disturbed by the known truth of other propositions of mine which differ from those commonly held, and therefore mistrusting their defense so long as they confine themselves to the field of philosophy, these men have resolved to fabricate a shield for their fallacies out of the mantle of pretended religion and the authority of the Bible. These they apply, with little judgment, to the refutation of arguments that they do not understand and have not even listened to.

First they have endeavored to spread the opinion that such propositions in general are contrary to the Bible and are consequently damnable and heretical. . . . Hence they have had no trouble in finding men who would preach the damnability and heresy of the new doctrine from their very pulpits with unwonted confidence, thus doing impious and inconsiderate injury not only to that doctrine and its followers but to all mathematics and mathematicians in general. . . .

. . . They go about invoking the Bible, which they would have minister to their deceitful purposes. Contrary to the sense of the Bible and the intention of the holy [Church] Fathers, if I am not mistaken, they would extend such authorities until even in purely physical matters — where faith is not involved — they would have us altogether abandon reason and the evidence of our senses in favor of some biblical passage, though under the surface meaning of its words this passage may contain a different sense.

I hope to show that I proceed with much greater piety than they do, when I argue not against condemning [Copernicus'] book, but against condemning it in the way they suggest — that is, without understanding it, weighing it, or so much as reading it. For Copernicus never discusses matters of religion or faith, nor does he use arguments that depend in any way upon the authority of sacred writings which he might have interpreted erroneously. He stands always upon physical conclusions pertaining to the celestial motions, and deals with them by astronomical and geometrical demonstrations, founded primarily upon sense experiences and very exact observations. He did not ignore the Bible, but he knew very well that if his doctrine were proved, then it could not contradict the Scriptures when they were rightly understood. . . .

The reason produced for condemning the opinion that the earth moves and the sun stands still is that in many places in the Bible one may read that the sun moves and the earth stands still. Since the Bible cannot err, it follows as a

[handwritten marginalia: ✗ Did not God give us senses, reason, intellect? for US to use]

necessary consequence that anyone takes an erroneous and heretical position who maintains that the sun is inherently motionless and the earth movable.

With regard to this argument, I think in the first place that it is very pious to say and prudent to affirm that the holy Bible can never speak untruth — whenever its true meaning is understood. But I believe nobody will deny that it is often very abstruse, and may say things which are quite different from what its bare words signify. Hence in expounding the Bible if one were always to confine oneself to the unadorned grammatical meaning, one might fall into error. . . .

[handwritten marginalia: Bible is abstruse]

. . . Now the Bible, merely to condescend to popular capacity, has not hesitated to obscure some very important pronouncements, attributing to God himself some qualities extremely remote from (and even contrary to) His essence. Who, then, would positively declare that this principle has been set aside, and the Bible has confined itself rigorously to the bare and restricted sense of its words, when speaking but casually of the earth, of water, of the sun, or of any other created thing? Especially in view of the fact that these things in no way concern the primary purpose of the sacred writings, which is the service of God and the salvation of souls — matters infinitely beyond the comprehension of the common people.

[handwritten marginalia: Bible gives God some qualities that he does not possess]

This being granted, I think that in discussions of physical problems we ought to begin not from the authority of scriptural passages, but from sense-experiences and necessary demonstrations. . . . Nothing physical which sense-experience sets before our eyes, or which necessary demonstrations prove to us, ought to be called in question (much less condemned) upon the testimony of biblical passages which may have some different meaning beneath their words. . . .

[handwritten marginalia: Nothing physical should be called in question]

. . . I do not feel obliged to believe that that same God who has endowed us with senses, reason, and intellect has intended to forgo their use and by some other means to give us knowledge which we can attain by them. He would not require us to deny sense and reason in physical matters which are set before our eyes and minds by direct experience or necessary demonstrations. . . .

It is obvious that such [anti-Copernican] authors, not having penetrated the true senses of Scripture, would impose upon others an obligation to subscribe to conclusions that are repugnant to manifest reason and sense, if they had any authority to do so. God forbid that this sort of abuse should gain countenance and authority, for then in a short time it would be necessary to proscribe all the contemplative sciences. People who are unable to understand perfectly both the Bible and the sciences far outnumber those who do understand. The former, glancing superficially through the Bible, would arrogate to themselves the authority to decree upon every question of physics on the strength of some word which they have misunderstood, and which was employed by the sacred authors for some different purpose. And the smaller number of understanding men could not dam up the furious torrent of such people, who would gain the majority of followers simply because it is much more pleasant to gain a reputation for wisdom without effort or study than to consume oneself tirelessly in the most laborious disciplines.

▷ Galileo attacked the unquestioning acceptance of Aristotle's teachings in his *Dialogue Concerning the Two Chief World Systems — Ptolemaic and Copernican.* In the *Dialogue,* Simplicio is an Aristotelian and Salviati is a spokesman for Galileo; Sagredo, a third participant, introduces the problem of relying on the authority of Aristotle.

[ARISTOTELIAN AUTHORITY]

SAGREDO One day I was at the home of a very famous doctor in Venice, where many persons came on account of their studies, and others occasionally came out of curiosity to see some anatomical dissection performed by a man who was truly no less learned than he was a careful and expert anatomist. It happened on this day that he was investigating the source and origin of the nerves, about which there exists a notorious controversy between the Galenist and Peripatetic doctors.[1] The anatomist showed that the great trunk of nerves, leaving the brain and passing through the nape, extended on down the spine and then branched out through the whole body, and that only a single strand as fine as a thread arrived at the heart. Turning to a gentleman whom we knew to be a Peripatetic philosopher, and on whose account he had been exhibiting and demonstrating everything with unusual care, he asked this man whether he was at last satisfied and convinced that the nerves originated in the brain and not in the heart. The philosopher, after considering for awhile, answered: "You have made me see this matter so plainly and palpably that if Aristotle's text were not contrary to it, stating clearly that the nerves originate in the heart, I should be forced to admit it to be true." . . .

SIMPLICIO But if Aristotle is to be abandoned, whom shall we have for a guide in philosophy? Suppose you name some author.

SALVIATI We need guides in forests and in unknown lands, but on plains and in open places only the blind need guides. It is better for such people to stay at home, but anyone with eyes in his head and his wits about him could serve as a guide for them. In saying this, I do not mean that a person should not listen to Aristotle; indeed, I applaud the reading and careful study of his works, and I reproach only those who give themselves up as slaves to him in such a way as to subscribe blindly to everything he says and take it as an inviolable decree without looking for any other reasons. This abuse carries with it another profound disorder, that other people do not try harder to comprehend the strength of his demonstrations. And what is more revolting in a public dispute, when someone is dealing with demonstrable conclusions, than to hear him interrupted by a text (often written to some quite different purpose) thrown into his teeth by an opponent? If, indeed, you wish to continue in this method of studying, then put aside the name of philosophers and call yourselves historians, or memory experts; for it is not proper that those who never philosophize should usurp the honorable title of philosopher.

---

[1]Galenist doctors followed the medical theories of Galen (A.D. 129–c. 199), a Greek anatomist and physician whose writings had great authority among medieval and early modern physicians. Peripatetic doctors followed Aristotle's teachings.

REVIEW QUESTIONS

1. What was Galileo Galilei's objection to using the Bible as a source of knowledge of physical things? According to him, how did one acquire knowledge of nature?
2. What point was Galileo making in telling the story of the anatomical dissection?
3. What was Galileo's view on the use of Aristotle's works as a basis for scientific endeavors?

▼▼▼

4 ▼ Prophet of Modern Science

Sir Francis Bacon (1561–1626), an English statesman and philosopher, vigorously supported the advancement of science and the scientific method. He believed that increased comprehension and mastery of nature would improve living conditions for people and therefore wanted science to encompass systematic research; he urged the state to fund scientific institutions. Bacon denounced universities for merely repeating Aristotelian concepts and discussing problems — Is matter formless? Are all natural substances composed of matter? — that did not increase understanding of nature or contribute to human betterment. The webs spun by these scholastics, he said, were ingenious but valueless. Bacon wanted an educational program that stressed direct contact with nature and fostered new discoveries.

Bacon was among the first to appreciate the new science's value and to explain its method clearly. Like Leonardo da Vinci, Bacon gave supreme value to the direct observation of nature; for this reason he is one of the founders of the empirical tradition in modern philosophy. Bacon upheld the inductive approach — careful investigation of nature, accumulation of data, and experimentation — as the way to truth and useful knowledge. Because he wanted science to serve a practical function, Bacon praised artisans and technicians who improved technology.

Francis Bacon
ATTACK ON AUTHORITY AND ADVOCACY OF EXPERIMENTAL SCIENCE

Bacon was not himself a scientist; he made no discoveries and had no laboratory. Nevertheless, for his advocacy of the scientific method, Bacon is deservedly regarded as a prophet of modern science. In the first passage from *Redargutio Philosophiarum (The Refutation of Philosophies),* a treatise on the "idols of the theater" — fallacious ways of thinking based on given systems of philosophy — Bacon attacks the slavish reliance on Aristotle.

But even though Aristotle were the man he is thought to be I should still warn you against receiving as oracles the thoughts and opinions of one man. What justification can there be for this self-imposed servitude [that] . . . you are content to repeat Aristotle's after two thousand [years]? . . . But if you will be guided by me you will deny, not only to this man but to any mortal now living or who shall live hereafter, the right to dictate your opinions. . . . You will never be sorry for trusting your own strength, if you but once make trial of it. You may be inferior to Aristotle on the whole, but not in everything. Finally, and this is the head and front of the whole matter, there is at least one thing in which you are far ahead of him — in precedents, in experience, in the lessons of time. Aristotle, it is said, wrote a book in which he gathered together the laws and institutions of two hundred and fifty-five cities; yet I have no doubt that the customs of Rome are worth more than all of them combined so far as military and political science are concerned. The position is the same in natural philosophy. Are you of a mind to cast aside not only your own endowments but the gifts of time? Assert yourselves before it is too late. Apply yourselves to the study of things themselves. Be not for ever the property of one man.

▷   In these scattered excerpts from *The New Organon* (1620, new system of logic), Bacon criticized contemporary methods used to inquire into nature. He expressed his ideas in the form of aphorisms — concise statements of principles or general truths.

I. Man, being the servant and interpreter of Nature, can do and understand so much and so much only as he has observed in fact or in thought of the course of nature: beyond this he neither knows anything nor can do anything.

VIII. . . . The sciences we now possess are merely systems for the nice ordering and setting forth of things already invented; not methods of invention or directions for new works.

XII. The logic now in use serves rather to fix and give stability to the errors which have their foundation in commonly received notions than to help the search after truth. So it does more harm than good.

XIX. There are and can be only two ways of searching into and discovering truth. The one flies from the senses and particulars to the most general axioms, and from these principles, the truth of which it takes for settled and immoveable, proceeds to judgment and to the discovery of middle axioms. And this way is now in fashion. The other derives axioms from the senses and particulars, rising by a gradual and unbroken ascent, so that it arrives at the most general axioms last of all. This is the true way, but as yet untried.

XXIII. There is a great difference between . . . certain empty dogmas, and the true signatures and marks set upon the works of creation as they are found in nature.

XXIV. It cannot be that axioms established by argumentation should avail for the discovery of new works; since the subtlety of nature is greater many times over than the subtlety of argument. But axioms duly and orderly formed from particulars easily discover the way to new particulars, and thus render sciences active.

XXXI. It is idle to expect any great advancement in science from the superinducing [adding] and engrafting of new things upon old. We must begin anew from the very foundations, unless we would revolve for ever in a circle with mean and contemptible progress.

CIX. There is therefore much ground for hoping that there are still laid up in the womb of nature many secrets of excellent use, having no affinity or parallelism with any thing that is now known, but lying entirely out of the beat of the imagination, which have not yet been found out. They too no doubt will some time or other, in the course and revolution of many ages, come to light of themselves, just as the others did; only by the method of which we are now treating they can be speedily and suddenly and simultaneously presented and anticipated.

▷ Bacon describes those "idols" or false notions that hamper human understanding.

XXXVIII. The idols and false notions which are now in possession of the human understanding, and have taken deep root therein, not only so beset men's minds that truth can hardly find entrance, but even after entrance obtained, they will again in the very instauration [renewal] of the sciences meet and trouble us, unless men being forewarned of the danger fortify themselves as far as may be against their assaults.

XXXIX. There are four classes of Idols which beset men's minds. To these for distinction's sake I have assigned names, — calling the first class *Idols of the Tribe*; the second, *Idols of the Cave*; the third, *Idols of the Market-place*; the fourth, *Idols of the Theatre*.

XLI. The Idols of the Tribe have their foundation in human nature itself, and in the tribe or race of men. For it is a false assertion that the sense of man is the measure of things. On the contrary, all perceptions as well of the sense as of the mind are according to the measure of the universe. And the human understanding is like a false mirror, which, receiving rays irregularly, distorts and discolours the nature of things by mingling its own nature with it.

XLII. The Idols of the Cave are the idols of the individual man. For every one (besides the errors common to human nature in general) has a cave or den of his own, which refracts and discolours the light of nature; owing either to his own proper and peculiar nature; or to his education and conversation with others; or to the reading of books, and the authority of those whom he esteems and admires; or to the differences of impressions, accordingly as they take place in a mind preoccupied and predisposed or in a mind indifferent and settled; or the like. . . .

XLIII. There are also Idols formed by the intercourse and association of men with each other, which I call Idols of the Market-place, on account of the commerce and consort of men there. For it is by discourse that men associate; and words are imposed according to the apprehension of the vulgar. And therefore the ill and unfit choice of words wonderfully obstructs the understanding. Nor do the definitions or explanations wherewith in some things learned men are wont to guard and defend themselves, by any means set the matter right. But words plainly force and overrule the understanding, and throw all into confusion, and lead men away into numberless empty controversies and idle fancies.

XLIV. Lastly, there are Idols which have immigrated into men's minds from the various dogmas of philosophies, and also from wrong laws of demonstration. These I call Idols of the Theatre; because in my judgment all the received systems are but so many stage-plays, representing worlds of their own creation after an unreal and scenic fashion. Nor is it only of the systems now in vogue, or only of the ancient sects and philosophies, that I speak; for many more plays of the same kind may yet be composed and in like artificial manner set forth; seeing that errors the most widely different have nevertheless causes for the most part alike. Neither again do I mean this only of entire systems, but also of many principles and axioms in science, which by tradition, credulity, and negligence have come to be received.

But of these several kinds of Idols I must speak more largely and exactly, that the understanding may be duly cautioned.

REVIEW QUESTIONS respect him but...
trust your own strength, apply yourself

1. What was Francis Bacon's attitude toward the wisdom of Aristotle?
2. What intellectual attitude did Bacon believe hampered new scientific discoveries in his time? Idols (4) Preconceived notions
3. What method of scientific inquiry did Bacon advocate? inductive approach AXIOMS then judgement begin anew
4. What did Bacon assume would follow from the adoption of his new method of scientific inquiry?
5. Explain how each one of Bacon's idols hamper human understanding.

▼▼▼

5 ▼ The Autonomy of the Mind

René Descartes (1596–1650), a French mathematician and philosopher, united the new currents of thought initiated during the Renaissance and the Scientific Revolution. Descartes said that the universe was a mechanical system whose inner laws could be discovered through mathematical thinking and formulated in mathematical terms. With Descartes' assertions on the power of thought, human beings became fully aware of their capacity to comprehend the world through their mental powers. For this reason he is regarded as the founder of modern philosophy.

Deductive

Innate ideas mind must intuit

The deductive approach stressed by Descartes presumes that inherent in the mind are mathematical principles, logical relationships, the principle of cause and effect, concepts of size and motion, and so on — ideas that exist independently of human experience with the external world. Descartes, for example, would say that the properties of a right-angle triangle ($a^2 + b^2 = c^2$) are implicit in human consciousness prior to any experience one might have with a triangle. These innate ideas, said Descartes, permit the mind to give order and coherence to the physical world. Descartes held that the mind arrives at truth when it "intuits" or comprehends the logical necessity of its own ideas and expresses these ideas with clarity, certainty, and precision.

René Descartes
≪ DISCOURSE ON METHOD ≫

In the *Discourse on Method* (1637), Descartes proclaimed the mind's autonomy and importance, and its ability and right to comprehend truth. In this work he offered a method whereby one could achieve certainty and thereby produce a comprehensive understanding of nature and human culture. In the following passage from the *Discourse on Method,* he explained the purpose of his inquiry. How he did so is almost as revolutionary as the ideas he wished to express. He spoke in the first person, autobiographically, as an individual employing his own reason, and he addressed himself to other individuals, inviting them to use their reason. He brought to his narrative an unprecedented confidence in the power of his own judgment and a deep disenchantment with the learning of his times.

PART ONE

From my childhood I lived in a world of books, and since I was taught that by their help I could gain a clear and assured knowledge of everything useful in life, I was eager to learn from them. But as soon as I had finished the course of studies which usually admits one to the ranks of the learned, I changed my opinion completely. For I found myself saddled with so many doubts and errors that I seemed to have gained nothing in trying to educate myself unless it was to discover more and more fully how ignorant I was.

Nevertheless I had been in one of the most celebrated schools in Europe, where I thought there should be wise men if wise men existed anywhere on earth. I had learned there everything that others learned, and, not satisfied with merely the knowledge that was taught, I had perused as many books as I could find which contained more unusual and recondite knowledge. . . . And finally, it did not seem

to me that our times were less flourishing and fertile than were any of the earlier periods. All this led me to conclude that I could judge others by myself, and to decide that there was no such wisdom in the world as I had previously hoped to find. . . .

[handwritten margin note: I could judge others by myself]

I revered our theology, and hoped as much as anyone else to get to heaven, but having learned on great authority that the road was just as open to the most ignorant as to the most learned, and that the truths of revelation which lead thereto are beyond our understanding, I would not have dared to submit them to the weakness of my reasonings. I thought that to succeed in their examination it would be necessary to have some extraordinary assistance from heaven, and to be more than a man.

I will say nothing of philosophy except that it has been studied for many centuries by the most outstanding minds without having produced anything which is not in dispute and consequently doubtful. I did not have enough presumption to hope to succeed better than the

build on new foundations

others; and when I noticed how many different opinions learned men may hold on the same subject, despite the fact that no more than one of them can ever be right, I resolved to consider almost as false any opinion which was merely plausible. . . .

This is why I gave up my studies entirely as soon as I reached the age when I was no longer under the control of my teachers. I resolved to seek no other knowledge than that which I might find within myself, or perhaps in the great book of nature. I spent a few years of my adolescence traveling, seeing courts and armies, living with people of diverse types and stations of life, acquiring varied experience, testing myself in the episodes which fortune sent me, and, above all, thinking about the things around me so that I could derive some profit from them. For it seemed to me that I might find much more of the truth in the cogitations [reflections] which each man made on things which were important to him, and where he would be the loser if he judged badly, than in the cogitations of a man of letters in his study, concerned with speculations which produce no effect, and which have no consequences to him. . . .

. . . After spending several years in thus studying the book of nature and acquiring experience, I eventually reached the decision to study my own self, and to employ all my abilities to try to choose the right path. This produced much better results in my case, I think, than would have been produced if I had never left my books and my country. . . .

PART TWO

. . . As far as the opinions which I had been receiving since my birth were concerned, I could not do better than to reject them completely for once in my lifetime, and to resume them afterwards, or perhaps accept better ones in their place, when I had determined how they fitted into a rational scheme. And I firmly believed that by this means I would succeed in conducting my life much better than if I built only upon the old foundations and gave credence to the principles which I had acquired in

reject old

my childhood without ever having examined them to see whether they were true or not. . . .

. . . Never has my intention been more than to try to reform my own ideas, and rebuild them on foundations that would be wholly mine. . . . The decision to abandon all one's preconceived notions is not an example for all to follow. . . .

As for myself, I should no doubt have . . . [never attempted it] if I had had but a single teacher or if I had not known the differences which have always existed among the most learned. I had discovered in college that one cannot imagine anything so strange and unbelievable but that it has been upheld by some philosopher; and in my travels I had found that those who held opinions contrary to ours were neither barbarians nor savages, but that many of them were at least as reasonable as ourselves. I had considered how the same man, with the same capacity for reason, becomes different as a result of being brought up among Frenchmen or Germans than he would be if he had been brought up among Chinese or cannibals; and how, in our fashions, the thing which pleased us ten years ago and perhaps will please us again ten years in the future, now seems extravagant and ridiculous; and I felt that in all these ways we are much more greatly influenced by custom and example than by any certain knowledge. Faced with this divergence of opinion, I could not accept the testimony of the majority, for I thought it worthless as a proof of anything somewhat difficult to discover, since it is much more likely that a single man will have discovered it than a whole people. Nor, on the other hand, could I select anyone whose opinions seemed to me to be preferable to those of others, and I was thus constrained to embark on the investigation for myself.

Nevertheless, like a man who walks alone in the darkness, I resolved to go so slowly and circumspectly that if I did not get ahead very rapidly I was at least safe from falling. Also, I did not want to reject all the opinions which had slipped irrationally into my consciousness since birth, until I had first spent enough time planning how to accomplish the task which I was then undertaking, and seeking the true method of obtaining knowledge of everything which my mind was capable of understanding. . . .

▷ Descartes' method consists of four principles that place the capacity to arrive at truth entirely within the province of the human mind. First one finds a self-evident principle, such as a geometric axiom. From this general principle, other truths are deduced through logical reasoning. This is accomplished by breaking a problem down into its elementary components and then, step by step, moving toward more complex knowledge.

. . . I thought that some other method [beside that of logic, algebra, and geometry] must be found to combine the advantages of these three and to escape their faults. Finally, just as the multitude of laws frequently furnishes an excuse for vice, and a state is much better governed with a few laws which are strictly adhered to, so I thought that instead of the great number of precepts of which logic is composed, I would have enough with the four following ones, provided that I made a firm and unalterable resolution not to violate them even in a single instance.

The first rule was never to accept anything as true unless I recognized it to be evidently such: that is, carefully to avoid precipitation and prejudgment, and to include nothing in my conclusions unless it presented itself so clearly and distinctly to my mind that there was no occasion to doubt it.

The second was to divide each of the difficulties which I encountered into as many parts as possible, and as might be required for an easier solution.

The third was to think in an orderly fashion, beginning with the things which were simplest and easiest to understand, and gradually and by degrees reaching toward more complex knowledge, even treating as though ordered materials which were not necessarily so.

The last was always to make enumerations so complete, and reviews so general, that I would be certain that nothing was omitted. . . .

What pleased me most about this method was that it enabled me to reason in all things, if not perfectly, at least as well as was in my power. In addition, I felt that in practicing it my mind was gradually becoming accustomed to conceive its objects more clearly and distinctly. . . .

▷ Descartes was searching for an incontrovertible truth that could serve as the first principle of philosophy. His arrival at the famous dictum "I think, therefore I am" marks the beginning of modern philosophy.

PART FOUR

. . . As I desired to devote myself wholly to the search for truth, I thought that I should . . . reject as absolutely false anything of which I could have the least doubt, in order to see whether anything would be left after this procedure which could be called wholly certain. Thus, as our senses deceive us at times, I was ready to suppose that nothing was at all the way our senses represented them to be. As there are men who make mistakes in reasoning even on the simplest topics in geometry, I judged that I was as liable to error as any other, and rejected as false all the reasoning which I had previously accepted as valid demonstration. Finally, as the same precepts which we have when awake may come to us when asleep without their being true, I decided to suppose that nothing that had ever entered my mind was more real than the illusions of my dreams. But I soon noticed that while I thus wished to think everything false, it was necessarily true that I who thought so was something. Since this truth, *I think, therefore I am,* was so firm and assured that all the most extravagant suppositions of the sceptics[1] were unable to shake it, I judged that I could safely accept it as the first principle of the philosophy I was seeking.

---

[1]The skeptics belonged to the ancient Greek philosophic school that held true knowledge to be beyond human grasp and treated all knowledge as uncertain.

REVIEW QUESTIONS

1. Why did René Descartes conclude that the teachings of his contemporaries did not conform to true reality? *they are beyond his understanding*
2. Why did Descartes exclude religious truths from his rational analysis?
3. Why was Descartes skeptical about truth being found among the philosophers? *nothing concrete had been found. opinions differed*
4. What eventually became Descartes' sole object of investigation? *HIMSELF*
5. What did Descartes discover about the basis of commonly held opinions?
6. What method for rational inquiry did Descartes finally choose? Why did he choose it? *Deduction & Logic. It allowed him to reason in all things* *4 steps*
7. What convinced Descartes that the skeptic philosophers were wrong?
8. Compare the methods of Descartes with those advocated by Bacon and Galileo.

All → rejected old. G = observation Bacon = inductive D = deductive

▼▼▼

6 ▼ The Mechanical Universe

By demonstrating that all bodies in the universe — earthly objects as well as moons, planets, and stars — obey the same laws of motion and gravitation, Sir Isaac Newton (1646–1723) completed the destruction of the medieval view of the universe. The idea that the same laws governed the movement of earthly and heavenly bodies was completely foreign to medieval thinkers, who drew a sharp division between a higher celestial world and a lower terrestrial one. In the *Principia Mathematica* (1687), Newton showed that the same forces that hold celestial bodies in their orbits around the sun make apples fall to the ground. For Newton, the universe was like a giant clock, all of whose parts obeyed strict mechanical principles and worked together in perfect precision. To Newton's contemporaries, it seemed as if mystery had been banished from the universe.

Isaac Newton
PRINCIPIA MATHEMATICA

In the first of the following passages from *Principia Mathematica*, Newton stated the principle of universal law and lauded the experimental method as the means of acquiring knowledge.

RULES OF REASONING
IN PHILOSOPHY

Rule I. We are to admit no more causes of natural things than such as are both true and sufficient to explain their appearances.

To this purpose the philosophers say that Na-ture does nothing in vain, and more is in vain when less will serve; for Nature is pleased with simplicity, and affects not the pomp of superfluous causes.

Rule II. Therefore to the same natural effects we must, as far as possible, assign the same causes.

As to respiration in a man and in a beast; the

descent of stones [meteorites] in *Europe* and in *America*; the light of our culinary fire and of the sun; the reflection of light in the earth, and in the planets.

Rule III. The qualities of bodies, which admit neither [intensification] *nor remission of degrees, and which are found to belong to all bodies within the reach of our experiments, are to be esteemed the universal qualities of all bodies whatsoever.*

For since the qualities of bodies are only known to us by experiments, we are to hold for universal all such as universally agree with experiments; and such as are not liable to diminution can never be quite taken away. We are certainly not to relinquish the evidence of experiments for the sake of dreams and vain fictions of our own devising; nor are we to recede from the analogy of Nature, which [is] . . . simple, and always consonant to itself. We no other way know the extension of bodies than by our senses, nor do these reach it in all bodies; but because we perceive extension in all that are sensible, therefore, we ascribe it universally to all others also. That abundance of bodies are hard, we learn by experience; and because the hardness of the whole arises from the hardness of the parts, we, therefore, justly infer the hardness of the undivided particles not only of the bodies we feel but of all others. That all bodies are impenetrable, we gather not from reason, but from sensation. The bodies which we handle we find impenetrable, and thence, conclude impenetrability to be an universal property of all bodies whatsoever. That all bodies are moveable, and endowed with certain powers (which we call . . . {*inertia*}) of persevering in their motion, or in their rest, we only infer from the like properties observed in the bodies which we have seen. The extension, hardness, impenetrability, mobility, . . . of the whole, result from the extension, hardness, impenetrability, mobility, . . . of the parts; and thence we conclude the least particles of all bodies to be also all extended, and hard and impenetrable, and moveable, . . . And this is the foundation of all philosophy. . . .

Lastly, if it universally appears, by experiments and astronomical observations, that all bodies about the earth gravitate towards the earth, and that in proportion to the quantity of matter which they severally contain; that the moon likewise, according to the quantity of its matter, gravitates towards the earth; that, on the other hand, our sea gravitates towards the moon; and all the planets mutually one towards another; and the comets in like manner towards the sun; we must, in consequence of this rule, universally allow that all bodies whatsoever are endowed with a principle of mutual gravitation. . . .

Rule IV. In experimental philosophy we are to look upon propositions collected by general induction from phenomena as accurately or very nearly true, notwithstanding any contrary hypotheses that may be imagined, till such time as other phenomena occur, by which they may either be made more accurate, or liable to exceptions.

This rule we must follow, that the argument of induction may not be evaded by hypotheses.

▷ Newton describes further his concepts of gravity and scientific methodology.

[GRAVITY]

Hitherto, we have explained the phenomena of the heavens and of our sea by the power of gravity, but have not yet assigned the cause of this power. This is certain, that it must proceed from a cause that penetrates to the very centres of the sun and planets, without suffering the least diminution of its force; that operates not according to the quantity of the surfaces of the particles upon which it acts (as mechanical causes used to do) but according to the quantity of the solid matter which they contain, and propagates its virtue on all sides to immense distances, decreasing always in the duplicate portion of the distances. . . .

Hitherto I have not been able to discover the

cause of those properties of gravity from the phenomena, and I frame no hypothesis; for whatever is not deduced from the phenomena is to be called an hypothesis; and hypotheses, whether metaphysical or physical, whether of occult qualities or mechanical, have no place in experimental philosophy. In this philosophy particular propositions are inferred from the phenomena, and afterward rendered general by induction. Thus it was the impenetrability, the mobility, and the impulsive forces of bodies, and the laws of motion and of gravitation were discovered. And to us it is enough that gravity does really exist, and acts according to the laws which we have explained, and abundantly serves to account for all the motions of the celestial bodies, and of our sea.

▷ A devoted Anglican, Newton believed that God had created this superbly organized universe. The following selection is also from the *Principia.*

[GOD AND THE UNIVERSE]

This most beautiful system of the sun, planets, and comets could only proceed from the counsel and dominion of an intelligent and powerful Being. And if the fixed stars are the centers of other like systems, these, being formed by the like wise counsel, must be all subject to the dominion of One, especially since the light of the fixed stars is of the same nature with the light of the sun and from every system light passes into all the other systems; and lest the systems of the fixed stars should, by their gravity, fall on each other mutually, he hath placed those systems at immense distances from one another.

This Being governs all things not as the soul of the world, but as Lord over all; and on account of his dominion he is wont to be called "Lord God" . . . or "Universal Ruler." . . . It is the dominion of a spiritual being which constitutes a God. . . . And from his true dominion it follows that the true God is a living, intelligent and powerful Being. . . . he governs all things, and knows all things that are or can be done. . . . He endures for ever, and is every where present; and by existing always and every where, he constitutes duration and space. . . . In him are all things contained and moved; yet neither affects the other: God suffers nothing from the motion of bodies; bodies find no resistance from the omnipresence of God. . . . As a blind man has no idea of colors so we have no idea of the manner by which the all-wise God preserves and understands all things. He is utterly void of all body and bodily figure, and can therefore neither be seen, nor heard, nor touched; nor ought to be worshipped under the representation of any corporeal thing. We have ideas of his attributes, but what the real substance of any thing is we know not. . . . Much less, then, have we any idea of the substance of God. We know him only by his most wise and excellent contrivances of things. . . . [W]e reverence and adore him as his servants; and a god without dominion, providence, and final causes, is nothing else but Fate and Nature. Blind metaphysical necessity, which is certainly the same always and everywhere, could produce no variety of things. All that diversity of natural things which we find suited to different times and places could arise from nothing but the ideas and will of a Being necessarily existing. . . . And thus much concerning God; to discourse of whom from the appearances of things does certainly belong to Natural Philosophy.

REVIEW QUESTIONS

1. What method did Isaac Newton use to guide his scientific investigations?
2. What would cause Newton to reject a previously held scientific truth?

3. How did Newton's method fulfill the demands set forth both by Bacon and by Descartes?
4. What kind of universe did Newton's rules of reasoning assume?
5. Summarize Newton's argument for God's existence.
6. Is Newton's idea of God compatible with his conception of the universe? What kind of God does Newton envisage?

1. drawing general conclusions by observing + using logical deductions
   * EXPERIMENTATION

3. Bacon ⟶ experimentation, Induction
   Descartes ⟶ deduction

   Newton - Senses + exp. ∈ NATURE

4. All are governed by same natural laws
   Universe is ORDERLY & PREDICTABLE

5. Such an intricate universe could only be
   Created - not arise

6. Yes - intelligent + powerful
   God - present everywhere, endures forever
   dominion over all

CHAPTER
▼▼▼
3

The Enlightenment

The Enlightenment of the eighteenth century culminated the movement toward modernity that started in the Renaissance era. The thinkers of the Enlightenment, called *philosophes,* attacked medieval otherworldliness, dethroned theology from its once-proud position as queen of the sciences, and based their understanding of nature and society on reason alone, unaided by revelation or priestly authority.

From the broad spectrum of Western history, several traditions flowed into the Enlightenment: the rational spirit born in classical Greece, the Stoic emphasis on natural law that applies to all human beings, and the Christian belief that all individuals are equal in God's eyes. A more immediate influence on the Enlightenment was Renaissance humanism, which focused on the individual and worldly human accomplishments and which criticized medieval theology-philosophy for its preoccupation with questions that seemed unrelated to the human condition. In many ways, the Enlightenment grew directly out of the Scientific Revolution. The philosophes praised both Newton's discovery of the mechanical laws that govern the universe and the scientific method that made this discovery possible. They wanted to transfer the scientific method — the reliance on experience and the critical use of the intellect — to the realm of society. They maintained that independent of clerical authority, human beings through reason — just as Newton had uncovered the laws of nature that operate in the physical world — could grasp the natural laws that govern the social world. The philosophes said that those institutions and traditions that could not meet the test of reason, because they were based on authority, ignorance, or superstition, had to be reformed or dispensed with.

For medieval philosophers, reason had been subordinate to revelation; the Christian outlook determined the medieval concept of nature, morality, government, law, and life's purpose. During the Renaissance and Scientific Revolution, reason increasingly asserted its autonomy. For example, Machiavelli rejected the principle that politics should be based on Christian teachings; he recognized no higher world as the source of a higher truth. Galileo held that on questions regarding nature, one should trust to observation, experimentation, and mathematical reasoning and should not rely on Scripture. Descartes had rejected reliance on past

MARQUISE DE POMPADOUR, mistress of the French King Louis XV, by Maurice Quentin de La Tour (1704–1788). Intellectually curious, she was interested in the philosophes' thought and encouraged the *Encyclopedia*'s writers — a volume of the work is by her side. (*Giraudon/Art Resource, N.Y.*)

authority and maintained that through thought alone one could attain knowledge that has absolute certainty. Agreeing with Descartes that the mind is self-sufficient, the philosophes rejected the guidance of revelation and its priestly interpreters. They believed that through the use of reason, individuals could comprehend and reform society.

Eighteenth-century thinkers were particularly influenced by John Locke's advocacy of religious toleration, his reliance on experience as the source of knowledge, and his concern for individual liberty. In his first *Letter Concerning Toleration,* Locke declared that Christians who persecute others in the name of their religion violate Christ's teachings. In his *Essay Concerning Human Understanding,* a work of immense significance in the history of philosophy, Locke argued that human beings are not born with innate ideas (the idea of God and principles of good and evil, for example) divinely implanted in their minds. Rather, said Locke, the human mind at birth is a blank slate upon which are imprinted sensations derived from contact with the world. These sensations, combined with the mind's reflections on them, are the source of ideas. In effect, knowledge is derived from experience. In the tradition of Francis Bacon, Locke's epistemology (theory of knowledge) implied that people should not dwell on insoluble questions, particularly sterile theological issues, but should seek practical knowledge that promotes human happiness and enlightens human beings and gives them control over their environment. Locke's empiricism, which aspired to useful knowledge and stimulated an interest in political and ethical questions that focused on human concerns, helped to mold the utilitarian and reformist spirit of the Enlightenment. If there are no innate ideas, said the philosophes, then human beings are not born with original sin, contrary to what Christians believed. All that individuals are derive from their particular experiences. If people are provided with a proper environment and education, they will become intelligent and productive citizens. This was how the reform-minded philosophes interpreted Locke. They preferred to believe that evil stemmed from faulty institutions and poor education, both of which could be remedied, rather than from a defective human nature. Locke himself favored this outlook. In his treatise on education, he wrote, "Of all the men we meet with, nine . . . of ten are what they are, good or evil, useful or not, by their education."

The Enlightenment philosophes articulated basic principles of the modern outlook: confidence in the self-sufficiency of the human mind, belief that individuals possess natural rights that governments should not violate, and the desire to reform society in accordance with rational principles. Their views influenced the reformers of the French Revolution and the Founding Fathers of the United States.

▼▼▼

I ▼ The Enlightenment Outlook

The critical use of the intellect was the central principle of the Enlightenment. The philosophes rejected beliefs and traditions that seemed to conflict with reason and attacked clerical and political authorities for interfering with the free use of the intellect.

Immanuel Kant
≪ WHAT IS ENLIGHTENMENT? ≫

The German philosopher Immanuel Kant (1724–1804) is a giant in the history of modern philosophy. Several twentieth-century philosophic movements have their origins in Kantian thought, and many issues raised by Kant still retain their importance. For example, in *Metaphysical Foundations of Morals* (1785), Kant set forth the categorical imperative that remains a crucial principle in moral philosophy. Kant asserted that when confronted with a moral choice, people should ask themselves: "Canst thou also will that thy maxim should be a universal law?" By this, Kant meant that people should ponder whether they would want the moral principle underlying their action to be elevated to a universal law that would govern others in similar circumstances. If they concluded that it should not, then the maxim should be rejected and the action avoided.

Kant valued the essential ideals of the Enlightenment and viewed the French Revolution, which put these ideals into law, as the triumph of liberty over despotism. In an essay entitled "What Is Enlightenment?" (1784), he contended that the Enlightenment marked a new way of thinking and eloquently affirmed the Enlightenment's confidence in and commitment to reason.

Enlightenment is man's leaving his self-caused immaturity. Immaturity is the incapacity to use one's intelligence without the guidance of another. Such immaturity is self-caused if it is not caused by lack of intelligence, but by lack of determination and courage to use one's intelligence without being guided by another. *Sapere Aude!* [Dare to know!] Have the courage to use your own intelligence! is therefore the motto of the enlightenment.

Through laziness and cowardice a large part of mankind, even after nature has freed them from alien guidance, gladly remain immature. It is because of laziness and cowardice that it is so easy for others to usurp the role of guardians. It is so comfortable to be a minor! If I have a book which provides meaning for me, a pastor who has conscience for me, a doctor who will judge my diet for me and so on, then I do not need to exert myself. I do not have any need to think; if I can pay, others will take over the tedious job for me. The guardians who have kindly undertaken the supervision will see to it that by far the largest part of mankind, including the entire "beautiful sex," should consider the step into maturity, not only as difficult but as very dangerous.

After having made their domestic animals dumb and having carefully prevented these quiet creatures from daring to take any step beyond the lead-strings to which they have fastened them, these guardians then show them the danger which threatens them, should they attempt to walk alone. Now this danger is not really so very great; for they would presumably learn to walk after some stumbling. However, an example of this kind intimidates and frightens people out of all further attempts.

It is difficult for the isolated individual to work himself out of the immaturity which has become almost natural for him. He has even become fond of it and for the time being is incapable of employing his own intelligence, because he has never been allowed to make the attempt. Statutes and formulas, these mechanical tools of a serviceable use, or rather misuse, of his natural faculties, are the ankle-chains of a continuous immaturity. Whoever threw it off would make an uncertain jump over the smallest trench because he is not accustomed to such free movement. Therefore there are only a few who have pursued a firm path and have succeeded in escaping from immaturity by their own cultivation of the mind.

But it is more nearly possible for a public to enlighten itself: this is even inescapable if only the public is given its freedom. For there will always be some people who think for themselves, even among the self-appointed guardians of the great mass who, after having thrown off the yoke of immaturity themselves, will spread about them the spirit of a reasonable estimate of their own value and of the need for every man to think for himself. . . . [A] public can only arrive at enlightenment slowly. Through revolution, the abandonment of personal despotism may be engendered and the end of profit-seeking and domineering oppression may occur, but never a true reform of the state of mind. Instead, new prejudices, just like the old ones, will serve as the guiding reins of the great, unthinking mass. . . .

All that is required for this enlightenment is *freedom*; and particularly the least harmful of all that may be called freedom, namely, the freedom for man to make *public use* of his reason in all matters. But I hear people clamor on all sides: Don't argue! The officer says: Don't argue, drill! The tax collector: Don't argue, pay! The pastor: Don't argue, believe! . . . Here we have restrictions on freedom everywhere. Which restriction is hampering enlightenment, and which does not, or even promotes it? I answer: The *public use* of a man's reason must be free at all times, and this alone can bring enlightenment among men. . . .

I mean by the public use of one's reason, the use which a scholar makes of it before the entire reading public. . . .

The question may now be put: Do we live at present in an enlightened age? The answer is: No, but in an age of enlightenment. Much still prevents men from being placed in a position or even being placed into position to use their own minds securely and well in matters of religion. But we do have very definite indications that this field of endeavor is being opened up for men to work freely and reduce gradually the hindrances preventing a general enlightenment and an escape from self-caused immaturity.

REVIEW QUESTIONS

1. Why did Immanuel Kant believe most persons never reached maturity?
2. What did Kant mean by the term *enlightenment*? By *freedom*?
3. What was Kant's explanation for the existence of the "guardians" in Western society?
4. What did Kant think to be the function of statutes and customs?

5. How did Kant propose to increase the maturity of individuals?
6. For Kant, what role did public liberties play in the progress of enlightenment?
7. What are the political implications of Kant's views?

---

2 ▼ Political Liberty

John Locke (1632–1704), a British statesman, philosopher, and political theorist, was a principal source of the Enlightenment. Locke's political philosophy as formulated in the *Two Treatises on Government* (1690) complements his theory of knowledge, described in the introduction to this chapter; both were rational and secular attempts to understand and improve the human condition. The Lockean spirit pervades the American Declaration of Independence, the Constitution, and the Bill of Rights and is the basis of the liberal tradition that aims to protect individual liberty from despotic state authority.

Viewing human beings as brutish and selfish, Thomas Hobbes (see Chapter 1) had prescribed a state with unlimited power; only in this way, he said, could people be protected from each other and civilized life preserved. Locke, regarding people as essentially good and humane, developed a conception of the state differing fundamentally from Hobbes's. Locke held that human beings are born with natural rights of life, liberty, and property; they establish the state to protect these rights. Consequently, neither executive nor legislature, neither king nor assembly has the authority to deprive individuals of their natural rights. Whereas Hobbes justified absolute monarchy, Locke explicitly endorsed constitutional government in which the power to govern derives from the consent of the governed and the state's authority is limited by agreement.

John Locke
≪ SECOND TREATISE ON GOVERNMENT ≫

Locke said that originally, in establishing a government, human beings had never agreed to surrender their natural rights to any state authority. The state's founders intended the new polity to preserve these natural rights and to implement the people's will. Therefore, as the following passage from Locke's *Second Treatise on Government* illustrates, the power exercised by magistrates cannot be absolute or arbitrary.

. . . *Political power* is that power, which every man having in the state of nature, has given up into the hands of the society, and therein to the governors, whom the society hath set over itself, with this express or tacit trust, that it shall be employed for their good, and the preservation of their property: now this *power*, which every man has *in the state of nature*, and which he parts with to the society in all such cases where the society can secure him, is to use such means, for the preserving of his own property, as he thinks good, and nature allows him; and to punish the breach of the law of nature in others, so as (according to the best of his reason) may most conduce to the preservation of himself, and the rest of mankind. So that the *end and measure of this power,* when in every man's hands in the state of nature, being the preservation of all of his society, that is, all mankind in general, it can have no other *end or measure,* when in the hands of the magistrate, but to preserve the members of that society in their lives, liberties, and possessions; and so cannot be an absolute, arbitrary power over their lives and fortunes, which are as much as possible to be preserved; but a *power to make laws,* and annex such *penalties* to them, as may tend to the preservation of the whole, by cutting off those parts, and those only, which are so corrupt, that they threaten the sound and healthy, without which no severity is lawful. And this *power has its original only from compact,* and agreement, and the mutual consent of those who make up the community. . . .

These are the *bounds,* which the trust, that is put in them by the society, and the law of God and nature, have *set to the legislative* power of every common-wealth, in all forms of government.

First, They are to govern by *promulgated established laws,* not to be varied in particular cases, but to have one rule for rich and poor, for the favourite at court, and the country man at plough.

Secondly, These *laws* also ought to be designed *for* no other end ultimately, but *the good of the people.*

Thirdly, They must *not raise taxes* on the *property of the people, without the consent of the people,* given by themselves, or their deputies. And this properly concerns only such governments, where the *legislative* is always in being, or at least where the people have not reserved any part of the legislative to deputies, to be from time to time chosen by themselves.

Fourthly, The *legislative* neither must *nor can transfer the power of making laws* to any body else, or place it any where, but where the people have. . . .

▷ If government fails to fulfill the end for which it was established — the preservation of the individual's right to life, liberty, and property — the people have a right to dissolve that government.

. . . The *legislative acts against the trust* reposed in them, when they endeavour to invade the property of the subject, and to make themselves, or any part of the community, masters, or arbitrary disposers of the lives, liberties, or fortunes of the people.

The reason why men enter into society, is the preservation of their property; and the end why they chuse and authorize a legislative, is, that there may be laws made, and rules set, as guards and fences to the properties of all the members of the society, to limit the power, and moderate the dominion of every part and member of the society: for since it can never be supposed to be the will of the society, that the legislative should have a power to destroy that which every one designs to secure, by entering into society, and for which the people submitted themselves to legislators of their own making; whenever the *legislators endeavour to take away, and destroy the property of the people,* or to reduce them to slavery under arbitrary power, they put themselves into a state of war with the people, who are thereupon absolved from any farther obedience, and are left to the common refuge, which God hath provided for all men, against force and violence. Whensoever therefore the *legislative* shall transgress this fundamental rule of society; and either by ambition, fear, folly or corruption, *endeavour to grasp* themselves, *or put into the hands of any other, an absolute power* over the lives, liberties, and estates of the people; by this breach of trust they *forfeit the power* the people had put into their hands for quite contrary ends, and it devolves to the people, who have a right to resume their original liberty, and, by the establishment of a new legislative, (such as they shall think fit) provide for their own safety and security, which is the end for which they are in society. What I have said here, concerning the legislative in general, holds true also concerning the supreme executor, who having a double trust put in him, both to have a part in the legislative, and the supreme execution of the law, acts against both, when he goes about to set up his own arbitrary will as the law of the society. He *acts* also *contrary to his trust,* when he either employs the force, treasure, and offices of the society, to corrupt the *representatives,* and gain them to his purposes; or openly pre-engages the *electors,* and prescribes to their choice, such, whom he has, by sollicitations, threats, promises, or otherwise, won to his designs; and employs them to bring in such, who have promised beforehand what to vote, and what to enact. . . .

▷ Locke responds to the charge that his theory will produce "frequent rebellion." Indeed, says Locke, the true rebels are the magistrates who, acting contrary to the trust granted them, violate the people's rights.

. . . Such *revolutions happen* not upon every little mismanagement in public affairs. *Great mistakes* in the ruling part, many wrong and inconvenient laws, and all the *slips* of human frailty, will be *borne by the people* without mutiny or murmur. But if a long train of abuses, prevarications and artifices, all tending the same way, make the design visible to the people, and they cannot but feel what they lie under, and see whither they are going; it is not to be wondered at, that they should then rouze themselves, and endeavour to put the rule into such

hands which may secure to them the ends for which government was at first erected. . . .

. . . I answer, that *this doctrine* of a power in the people of providing for their safety a-new, by a new legislative, when their legislators have acted contrary to their trust, by invading their property, is *the best {de}fence against rebellion,* and the probablest means to hinder it: for *rebellion* being an opposition, not to persons, but authority, which is founded only in the constitutions and laws of the government; those, whoever they be, who by force break through, and by force justify their violation of them, are truly and properly *rebels*: for when men, by entering into society and civil government, have excluded force, and introduced laws for the preservation of property, peace, and unity amongst themselves, those who set up force again in opposition to the laws, do *rebellare,* that is, bring back again the state of war, and are properly rebels: which they who are in power, (by the pretence they have to authority, the temptation of force they have in their hands, and the flattery of those about them) being likeliest to do; the properest way to prevent the evil, is to shew them the danger and injustice of it, who are under the greatest temptation to run into it.

The end of government is the good of mankind; and which is *best for mankind,* that the people should always be exposed to the boundless will of tyranny, or that the rulers should be sometimes liable to be opposed, when they grow exorbitant in the use of their power, and employ it for the destruction, and not the preservation of the properties of their people?

Thomas Jefferson
DECLARATION OF INDEPENDENCE

Written by Thomas Jefferson (1743–1826) to justify the American colonists' break with Britain, the Declaration of Independence enumerated principles that were quite familiar to English statesmen and intellectuals. The preamble to the Declaration, excerpted below, articulated clearly Locke's philosophy of natural rights. Locke had viewed life, liberty, and property as the individual's essential natural rights; Jefferson substituted the "pursuit of happiness" for property.

A DECLARATION BY THE REPRESENTATIVES OF THE UNITED STATES OF AMERICA, IN GENERAL CONGRESS ASSEMBLED.

When in the Course of human Events, it becomes necessary for one People to dissolve the Political Bands which have connected them with another, and to assume among the Powers of the Earth, the separate and equal Station to which the Laws of Nature and of Nature's God entitle them, a decent Respect to the Opinions of Mankind requires that they should declare the causes which impel them to the Separation.

We hold these Truths to be self-evident, that all Men are created equal, that they are endowed by their Creator with certain unalienable Rights, that among these are Life, Liberty, and the Pursuit of Happiness — That to secure these Rights, Governments are instituted among Men, deriving their just Powers from the Consent of the Governed, That whenever any Form of Government becomes destructive of these Ends, it is the Right of the People to alter or to abolish it, and to institute new Gov-

ernment, laying its Foundation on such Principles, and organizing its Powers in such Form, as to them shall seem most likely to effect their Safety and Happiness. Prudence, indeed, will dictate that Governments long established should not be changed for light and transient Causes; and accordingly all Experience hath shewn, that Mankind are more disposed to suffer, while Evils are sufferable, than to right themselves by abolishing the Forms to which they are accustomed. But when a long Train of Abuses and Usurpations, pursuing invariably the same Object, evinces a Design to reduce them under absolute Despotism, it is their right, it is their duty, to throw off such Government, and to provide new Guards for their future Security. Such has been the patient Sufferance of these Colonies; and such is now the Necessity which constrains them to alter their former Systems of Government. The History of the present King of Great-Britain is a History of repeated Injuries and Usurpations, all having in direct Object the Establishment of an absolute Tyranny over these States. . . .

REVIEW QUESTIONS

1. According to John Locke, what were the purposes for which governments might legitimately be formed?
2. According to Locke's theory, where did sovereignty rest in the state of nature? Where did it reside after governments were formed?
3. According to Locke, what limits bound legislators in any government?
4. What did Locke believe were the rights of the people faced with a government that failed to protect their lives, liberties, and possessions?
5. Compare the views of Locke with those of Thomas Hobbes (in Chapter 1) regarding human nature, political authority, and rebellion.
6. Compare Locke's theory of natural rights with the principles stated in the American Declaration of Independence.

▼▼▼

3 ▼ Attack on the Old Regime

François Marie Arouet (1694–1778), known to the world as Voltaire, was the recognized leader of the French Enlightenment. Few of the philosophes had a better mind, and none had a sharper wit. A relentless critic of the Old Regime (the social structure in prerevolutionary France), Voltaire attacked superstition, religious fanaticism and persecution, censorship, and other abuses of eighteenth-century French society. Spending more than two years in Great Britain, Voltaire acquired a great admiration for English liberty, toleration, commerce, and science. In *Letters Concerning the English Nation* (1733), he drew unfavorable comparisons between a progressive Britain and a reactionary France.

Voltaire's angriest words were directed against established Christianity, to which he attributed many of the ills of modern society. Voltaire regarded Christianity as "the Christ-worshiping superstition" that someday would be destroyed "by the weapons of reason." He rejected revelation and the church hierarchy and was repulsed by Christian intolerance, but he accepted Christian morality and believed in God as the prime mover who set the universe in motion.

Voltaire
A PLEA FOR TOLERANCE AND REASON

The following passages compiled from Voltaire's works — grouped according to topic — provide insight into the outlook of the philosophes. The excerpts come from sources that include his *Candide* (1759), *Treatise on Tolerance* (1763), and *The Philosophical Dictionary* (1764).

TOLERANCE

It does not require any great art or studied elocution to prove that Christians ought to tolerate one another. I will go even further and say that we ought to look upon all men as our brothers. What! call a Turk, a Jew, and a Siamese, my brother? Yes, of course; for are we not all children of the same father, and the creatures of the same God?

———

What is tolerance? . . . We are all full of weakness and errors; let us mutually pardon our follies. This is the last law of nature. . . .

It is clear that every private individual who persecutes a man, his brother, because he is not of the same opinion, is a monster. . . .

Of all religions, the Christian ought doubtless to inspire the most tolerance, although hitherto the Christians have been the most intolerant of all men.

———

. . . Tolerance has never brought civil war; intolerance has covered the earth with carnage. . . .

What! Is each citizen to be permitted to believe and to think that which his reason rightly or wrongly dictates? He should indeed, provided that he does not disturb the public order; for it is not contingent on man to believe or not to believe; but it is contingent on him to respect the usages of his country; and if you say that it is a crime not to believe in the dominant religion, you accuse then yourself the first Christians, your ancestors, and you justify those whom you accuse of having martyred them.

You reply that there is a great difference, that all religions are the work of men, and that the Apostolic Roman Catholic Church is alone the work of God. But in good faith, ought our religion because it is divine reign through hate, violence, exiles, usurpation of property, prisons, tortures, murders, and thanksgivings to God for these murders? The more the Christian religion is divine, the less it pertains to man to require it; if God made it, God will sustain it without you. You know that intolerance produces only hypocrites or rebels; what distressing alternatives! In short, do you want to sustain through executioners the religion of a God whom executioners have put to death and who taught only gentleness and patience?

———

I shall never cease, my dear sir, to preach tolerance from the housetops, despite the complaints of your priests and the outcries of ours, until persecution is no more. The progress of reason is slow, the roots of prejudice lie deep. Doubtless, I shall never see the fruits of my efforts, but they are seeds which may one day germinate.

DOGMA

. . . Is Jesus the Word? If He be the Word, did He emanate from God in time or before time? If He emanated from God, is He co-eternal and consubstantial with Him, or is He of a similar substance? Is He distinct from Him, or is He not? Is He made or begotten? Can He beget in His turn? Has He paternity? or productive virtue without paternity? Is the Holy Ghost made? or begotten? or produced? or proceeding from the Father? or proceeding from the Son? or proceeding from both? Can He beget? can He produce? is His hypostasis consubstantial with the hypostasis of the Father and the Son? and how is it that, having the same nature — the same essence as the Father and the Son, He cannot do the same things done by these persons who are Himself?

Assuredly, I understand nothing of this; no one has ever understood any of it, and that is why we have slaughtered one another.

The Christians tricked, cavilled, hated, and excommunicated one another, for some of these dogmas inaccessible to human intellect.

FANATICISM

Fanaticism is to superstition what delirium is to fever, what rage is to anger. He who has ecstasies and visions, who takes dreams for realities, and his own imaginations for prophecies is an enthusiast; he who reinforces his madness by murder is a fanatic. . . .

The most detestable example of fanaticism is that exhibited on the night of St. Bartholomew,[1] when the people of Paris rushed from house to house to stab, slaughter, throw out of the window, and tear in pieces their fellow citizens who did not go to mass.

There are some cold-blooded fanatics; such as those judges who sentence men to death for no other crime than that of thinking differently from themselves. . . .

Once fanaticism has infected a brain, the disease is almost incurable. I have seen convulsionaries who, while speaking of the miracles of Saint Paris [a fourth-century Italian bishop], gradually grew heated in spite of themselves. Their eyes became inflamed, their limbs shook, fury disfigured their face, and they would have killed anyone who contradicted them.

There is no other remedy for this epidemic malady than that philosophical spirit which, extending itself from one to another, at length softens the manners of men and prevents the access of the disease. For when the disorder has made any progress, we should, without loss of time, flee from it, and wait till the air has become purified.

PERSECUTION

What is a persecutor? He whose wounded pride and furious fanaticism arouse princes and magistrates against innocent men, whose only crime is that of being of a different opinion. "Impudent man! you have worshipped God; you have preached and practiced virtue; you have served man; you have protected the orphan, have helped the poor; you have changed deserts, in which slaves dragged on a miserable existence, into fertile lands peopled by happy families; but I have discovered that you despise me, and have

———

[1]St. Bartholomew refers to the day when the populace of Paris, instigated by King Charles IX at his mother's urging, began a week-long slaughter of Protestants that began on August 24, 1572.

never read my controversial work. You know that I am a rogue; that I have forged G[od]'s signature, that I have stolen. You might tell these things; I must anticipate you. I will, therefore, go to the confessor [spiritual counselor] of the prime minister, or the magistrate; I will show them, with outstretched neck and twisted mouth, that you hold an erroneous opinion in relation to the cells in which the Septuagint was studied; that you have even spoken disrespectfully ten years ago of Tobit's dog,[2] which you asserted to have been a spaniel, while I proved that it was a greyhound. I will denounce you as the enemy of God and man!" Such is the language of the persecutor; and if precisely these words do not issue from his lips, they are engraven on his heart with the pointed steel of fanaticism steeped in the bitterness of envy. . . .

O God of mercy! If any man can resemble that evil being who is described as ceaselessly employed in the destruction of your works, is it not the persecutor?

SUPERSTITION

In 1749 a woman was burned in the Bishopric of Würzburg [a city in central Germany], convicted of being a witch. This is an extraordinary phenomenon in the age in which we live. Is it possible that people who boast of their reformation and of trampling superstition under foot, who indeed supposed that they had reached the perfection of reason, could nevertheless believe in witchcraft, and this more than a hundred years after the so-called reformation of their reason?

In 1652 a peasant woman named Michelle Chaudron, living in the little territory of Geneva [a major city in Switzerland], met the devil going out of the city. The devil gave her

a kiss, received her homage, and imprinted on her upper lip and right breast the mark that he customarily bestows on all whom he recognizes as his favorites. This seal of the devil is a little mark which makes the skin insensitive, as all the demonographical jurists of those times affirm.

The devil ordered Michelle Chaudron to bewitch two girls. She obeyed her master punctually. The girls' parents accused her of witchcraft before the law. The girls were questioned and confronted with the accused. They declared that they felt a continual pricking in certain parts of their bodies and that they were possessed. Doctors were called, or at least, those who passed for doctors at that time. They examined the girls. They looked for the devil's seal on Michelle's body — what the statement of the case called *satanic marks*. Into them they drove a long needle, already a painful torture. Blood flowed out, and Michelle made it known, by her cries, that satanic marks certainly do not make one insensitive. The judges, seeing no definite proof that Michelle Chaudron was a witch, proceeded to torture her, a method that infallibly produces the necessary proofs: this wretched woman, yielding to the violence of torture, at last confessed everything they desired.

The doctors again looked for the satanic mark. They found a little black spot on one of her thighs. They drove in the needle. The torment of the torture had been so horrible that the poor creature hardly felt the needle; thus the crime was established. But as customs were becoming somewhat mild at that time, she was burned only after being hanged and strangled.

In those days every tribunal of Christian Europe resounded with similar arrests. The faggots were lit everywhere for witches, as for heretics. People reproached the Turks most for having neither witches nor demons among them. This absence of demons was considered an infallible proof of the falseness of a religion.

A zealous friend of public welfare, of humanity, of true religion, has stated in one of his writings on behalf of innocence, that Christian

---

[2]The Septuagint, the version of the Hebrew Scriptures used by Saint Paul and other early Christians, was a Greek translation done by Hellenized Jews in Alexandria sometime in the late third or the second century B.C. *Tobit's dog* appears in the Book of Tobit, a Hebrew book contained in the Catholic version of the Bible.

tribunals have condemned to death over a hundred thousand accused witches. If to these judicial murders are added the infinitely superior number of massacred heretics, that part of the world will seem to be nothing but a vast scaffold covered with torturers and victims, surrounded by judges, guards and spectators.

▷ The following passage is from *Candide*, Voltaire's most famous work of fiction. The king of the Bulgarians goes to war with the king of the Abares, and Candide is caught in the middle of the conflict.

WAR

Nothing could be smarter, more splendid, more brilliant, better drawn up than the two armies. Trumpets, fifes, hautboys [oboes], drums, cannons, formed a harmony such as has never been heard even in hell. The cannons first of all laid flat about six thousand men on each side; then the musketry removed from the best of worlds some nine or ten thousand blackguards who infested its surface. The bayonet also was the sufficient reason for the death of some thousands of men. The whole might amount to thirty thousand souls. Candide, who trembled like a philosopher, hid himself as well as he could during this heroic butchery. At last, while the two Kings each commanded a Te Deum[3] in his camp, Candide decided to go elsewhere to reason about effects and causes. He clambered over heaps of dead and dying men and reached a neighboring village, which was in ashes; it was an Abare village which the Bulgarians had burned in accordance with international law. Here, old men dazed with blows watched the dying agonies of their murdered wives who clutched their children to their bleeding breasts; there, disemboweled girls who had been made to satisfy the natural appetites of heroes gasped their last sighs; others, half-burned, begged to be put to death. Brains were scattered on the ground among dismembered arms and legs. Candide fled to another village as fast as he could; it belonged to the Bulgarians, and Abarian heroes had treated it in the same way. Candide, stumbling over quivering limbs or across ruins, at last escaped from the theater of war. . . .

---

[3]A Te Deum is a special liturgical hymn praising and thanking God for granting some special favor, like a military victory or the end of a war.

REVIEW QUESTIONS

1. What argument did Voltaire offer in favor of a policy of religious toleration?
2. Why was religious toleration of such central importance to enlightened philosophes like Voltaire?
3. Why did Voltaire ridicule Christian theological disputation?
4. What did Voltaire mean by the term *fanaticism*? How was it to be cured?
5. According to Voltaire, what moral evils arose from persecuting people for having differing opinions?
6. According to Voltaire, how did religion, science, and law contribute to the evil of persecuting ideological dissenters in society?
7. What did Voltaire imply about the rationality and morality of war?

▼▼▼

4 ▼ Attack on Religion

Christianity came under severe attack during the eighteenth century. The philosophes rejected Christian doctrines that seemed contrary to reason. Deism, the dominant religious outlook of the philosophes, taught that religion should accord with reason and natural law. To deists, it seemed reasonable to believe in God, for this superbly constructed universe required a creator in the same manner that a watch required a watchmaker. But, said the deists, after God had constructed the universe, he did not interfere in its operations; the universe was governed by mechanical laws. Deists denied that the Bible was God's work, rejected clerical authority, and dismissed miracles — like Jesus walking on water — as incompatible with natural law. To them, Jesus was not divine but an inspiring teacher of morality. Many deists still considered themselves Christians; the clergy, however, viewed the deists' religious views with horror.

Thomas Paine
≪ THE AGE OF REASON ≫

Exemplifying the deist outlook was Thomas Paine (1737–1809), an Englishman who moved to America in 1774. Paine's *Common Sense* (1776) was an eloquent appeal for American independence. Paine is also famous for *The Rights of Man* (1791–1792), included in the next chapter, in which he defended the French Revolution. In *The Age of Reason* (1794–1795), he denounced Christian mysteries, miracles, and prophecies as superstition and called for a natural religion that accorded with reason and science.

I believe in one God, and no more; and I hope for happiness beyond this life.

I believe in the equality of man; and I believe that religious duties consist in doing justice, loving mercy, and endeavoring to make our fellow-creatures happy.

But, lest it should be supposed that I believe many other things in addition to these, I shall, in the progress of this work, declare the things I do not believe, and my reasons for not believing them.

I do not believe in the creed professed by the Jewish church, by the Roman church, by the Greek church, by the Turkish church, by the Protestant church, nor by any church that I know of. My own mind is my own church. . . .

When Moses told the children of Israel that he received the two tables of the [Ten] commandments from the hands of God, they were not obliged to believe him, because they had no other authority for it than his telling them so; and I have no other authority for it than some historian telling me so. The commandments carry no internal evidence of divinity with them; they contain some good moral precepts, such as any man qualified to be a lawgiver, or a legislator, could produce himself, without having recourse to supernatural intervention. . . .

When also I am told that a woman called the Virgin Mary, said, or gave out, that she was with child without any cohabitation with a man, and that her betrothed husband, Joseph, said that an angel told him so, I have a right to believe them or not; such a circumstance required a much stronger evidence than their bare word for it; but we have not even this — for neither Joseph nor Mary wrote any such matter themselves; it is only reported by others that *they said so* — it is hearsay upon hearsay, and I do not choose to rest my belief upon such evidence.

It is, however, not difficult to account for the credit that was given to the story of Jesus Christ being the son of God. He was born when the heathen mythology had still some fashion and repute in the world, and that mythology had prepared the people for the belief of such a story. Almost all the extraordinary men that lived under the heathen mythology were reputed to be the sons of some of their gods. It was not a new thing, at that time, to believe a man to have been celestially begotten; the intercourse of gods with women was then a matter of familiar opinion. Their Jupiter [chief Roman god], according to their accounts, had cohabited with hundreds: the story, therefore, had nothing in it either new, wonderful, or obscene; it was conformable to the opinions that then prevailed among the people called Gentiles, or Mythologists, and it was those people only that believed it. The Jews who had kept strictly to the belief of one God, and no more, and who had always rejected the heathen mythology, never credited the story. . . .

Nothing that is here said can apply, even with the most distant disrespect, to the real character of Jesus Christ. He was a virtuous and an amiable man. The morality that he preached and practised was of the most benevolent kind; and though similar systems of morality had been preached by Confucius [Chinese philosopher], and by some of the Greek philosophers, many years before; by the Quakers [members of the Society of Friends] since; and by many good men in all ages, it has not been exceeded by any. . . .

. . . The resurrection and ascension [of Jesus Christ], supposing them to have taken place, admitted of public and ocular demonstration, like that of the ascension of a balloon, or the sun at noon-day, to all Jerusalem at least. A thing which everybody is required to believe, requires that the proof and evidence of it should be equal to all, and universal; and as the public visibility of this last related act was the only evidence that could give sanction to the former part, the whole of it falls to the ground, because that evidence never was given. Instead of this, a small number of persons, not more than eight or nine, are introduced as proxies for the whole world, to say they saw it, and all the rest of the world are called upon to believe it. But it appears that Thomas [one of Jesus' disciples] did not believe the resurrection, and, as they say, would not believe without having ocular and manual demonstration himself. *So neither will I,* and the reason is equally as good for me, and for every other person, as for Thomas.

It is in vain to attempt to palliate or disguise this matter. The story, so far as relates to the supernatural part, has every mark of fraud and imposition stamped upon the face of it. Who were the authors of it is as impossible for us now to know, as it is for us to be assured that the books in which the account is related were written by the persons whose names they bear; the best surviving evidence we now have respecting this affair is the Jews. They are regularly descended from the people who lived in the times this resurrection and ascension is said to have happened, and they say, *it is not true.*

Baron d'Holbach
≪ *GOOD SENSE* ≫

More extreme than the deists were the atheists, who denied God's existence altogether. The foremost exponent of atheism was Paul-Henri Thiry, Baron d'Holbach (1723–1789), a prominent contributor to the *Encyclopedia* (see selection 5). Holbach hosted many leading intellectuals, including Diderot, Rousseau, and Condorcet (all represented later in this chapter), at his country estate outside of Paris. He regarded the idea of God as a product of ignorance, fear, and superstition and said that terrified by natural phenomena — storms, fire, floods — humanity's primitive ancestors attributed these occurrences to unseen spirits, whom they tried to appease through rituals. In denouncing religion, Holbach was also affirming core Enlightenment ideals — reason and freedom — as the following passage from *Good Sense* reveals.

In a word, whoever will deign to consult common sense upon religious opinions, and will bestow on this inquiry the attention that is commonly given to any objects we presume interesting, will easily perceive that those opinions have no foundation; that Religion is a mere castle in the air. Theology is but the ignorance of natural causes reduced to a system; a long tissue of fallacies and contradictions. In every country, it presents us with romances void of probability. . . .

Savage and furious nations, perpetually at war, adore, under divers names, some God, conformable to their ideas, that is to say, cruel, carnivorous, selfish, bloodthirsty. We find, in all the religions of the earth, "a God of armies," a "jealous God," an "avenging God," a "destroying God," a "God," who is pleased with carnage, and whom his worshippers consider it as a duty to serve to his taste. Lambs, bulls, children, men, heretics, infidels, kings, whole nations, are sacrificed to him. Do not the zealous servants of this barbarous God think themselves obliged even to offer up themselves as a sacrifice to him? Madmen may every where be seen who, after meditating upon their terrible God, imagine that to please him they must do themselves all possible injury, and inflict on themselves, for this honour, the most exquisite torments. The gloomy ideas more usefully formed of the Deity, far from consoling them under the evils of life, have every where disquieted their minds, and produced follies destructive to their happiness.

How could the human mind make any considerable progress, while tormented with frightful phantoms, and guided by men, interested in perpetuating its ignorance and fears? Man has been forced to vegetate in his primitive stupidity: he has been taught nothing but stories about invisible powers upon whom his happiness was supposed to depend. Occupied solely by his fears, and by unintelligible reveries, he has always been at the mercy of his priests, who have reserved to themselves the right of thinking for him, and directing his actions.

Thus man has remained a child without experience, a slave without courage, fearing to reason, and unable to extricate himself from the labyrinth, in which he has so long been wandering. He believes himself forced to bend under the yoke of his gods, known to him only by the fabulous accounts given by his ministers, who, after binding each unhappy mortal in the chains of his prejudice, remain his masters, or else abandon him defenceless to the absolute power of tyrants, no less terrible than the gods, of whom they are the representatives upon earth.

Oppressed by the double yoke of spiritual and temporal power, it has been impossible for the people to know and pursue their happiness. As Religion, so Politics and Morality became sacred things, which the profane were not permitted to handle. Men have had no other Morality, than what their legislators and priests brought down from the unknown regions of heaven. The human mind, confused by its theological opinions ceased to know its own powers, mistrusted experience, feared truth and disdained reason, in order to follow authority. Man has been a mere machine in the hands of tyrants and priests, who alone have had the right of directing his actions. Always treated as a slave, he has contracted the vices of a slave.

Such are the true causes of the corruption of morals, to which Religion opposes only ideal and ineffectual barriers. Ignorance and servitude are calculated to make men wicked and unhappy. Knowledge, Reason, and Liberty, can alone reform them, and make them happier. But every thing conspires to blind them and to confirm them in their errors. Priests cheat them, tyrants corrupt, the better to enslave them. Tyranny ever was, and ever will be, the true cause of man's depravity, and also of his habitual calamities. Almost always fascinated by religious fiction, poor mortals turn not their eyes to the natural and obvious causes of their misery; but attribute their vices to the imperfection of their natures, and their unhappiness to the anger of the gods. They offer up to heaven vows, sacrifices, and presents, to obtain the end of their sufferings, which in reality, are attributable only to the negligence, ignorance, and perversity of their guides, to the folly of their customs, to the unreasonableness of their laws, and above all, to the general want of knowledge. Let men's minds be filled with true ideas; let their reason be cultivated; let justice govern them; and there will be no need of opposing to the passions, such a feeble barrier, as the fear of the gods. Men will be good, when they are well instructed, well governed, and when they are punished or despised for the evil,

and justly rewarded for the good, which they do to their fellow citizens.

To discover the true principles of Morality, men have no need of theology, of revelation, or of gods: They have need only of common sense. They have only to commune with themselves, to reflect upon their own nature, to consult their visible interests, to consider the objects of society, and of the individuals who compose it; and they will easily perceive, that virtue is advantageous, and vice disadvantageous to such beings as themselves. Let us persuade men to be just, beneficent, moderate, sociable; not because such conduct is demanded by the gods, but, because it is pleasure to men. Let us advise them to abstain from vice and crime; not because they will be punished in the other world, but because they will suffer for it in this. — *There are,* says a great man [Montesquieu], *means to prevent crimes, and these means are punishments; there are means to reform manners, and these means are good examples. . . .*

. . . Men are unhappy, only because they are ignorant; they are ignorant, only because every thing conspires to prevent their being enlightened; they are wicked, only because their reason is not sufficiently developed.

REVIEW QUESTIONS

1. What positive religious beliefs were held by a deist like Thomas Paine?
2. What Christian beliefs did Paine reject?
3. How did Paine use the new rules of scientific methodology to attack Christian beliefs?
4. What was Baron d'Holbach's view of religion?
5. Compare the views of Holbach with those of Kant (at the beginning of this chapter) on most human beings' intellectual and psychological development.
6. How did Holbach propose to change people's views on religion, politics, and morals?

▼▼▼

5 ▼ Compendium of Knowledge

A 38-volume *Encyclopedia,* whose 150 or more contributors included leading Enlightenment thinkers, was undertaken in Paris during the 1740s as a monumental effort to bring together all human knowledge and to propagate Enlightenment ideas. The *Encyclopedia*'s numerous articles on science and technology and its limited coverage of theological questions attest to the new interests of eighteenth-century intellectuals. Serving as principal editor, Denis Diderot (1713–1784) steered the project through difficult periods, including the suspension of publication by French authorities. After the first two volumes were published, the authorities denounced the work for containing "maxims that would tend to destroy royal authority, foment a spirit of independence and revolt, . . . and lay the foundations for the corruption of morals and religion." In 1759, Pope Clement XIII condemned the *Encyclopedia* for having "scandalous doctrines [and] inducing scorn for religion." It required careful diplomacy and clever ruses to finish the project and still incorporate ideas considered dangerous by religious and governmental authorities. With the project's completion in 1772, Diderot and Enlightenment opinion triumphed over clerical censors and powerful elements at the French court.

Denis Diderot
≪ ENCYCLOPEDIA ≫

The *Encyclopedia* was a monument to the Enlightenment, as Diderot himself recognized. "This work will surely produce in time a revolution in the minds of man, and I hope that tyrants, oppressors, fanatics, and the intolerant will not gain thereby. We shall have served humanity." Some articles from the *Encyclopedia* follow.

Encyclopedia . . . In truth, the aim of an *encyclopedia* is to collect all the knowledge scattered over the face of the earth, to present its general outlines and structure to the men with whom we live, and to transmit this to those who will come after us, so that the work of past centuries may be useful to the following centuries, that our children, by becoming more educated, may at the same time become more virtuous and happier, and that we may not die without having deserved well of the human race. . . .

. . . We have seen that our *Encyclopedia* could only have been the endeavor of a philosophical century. . . .

I have said that it could only belong to a philosophical age to attempt an *encyclopedia*; and I have said this because such a work constantly demands more intellectual daring than is commonly found in [less courageous periods]. All things must be examined, debated, investigated without exception and without regard for anyone's feelings. . . . We must ride roughshod over all these ancient puerilities, overturn the barriers that reason never erected, give back to the arts and sciences the liberty that is so precious to them. . . . We have for quite some time needed a reasoning age when men would no longer seek the rules in classical authors but in nature. . . .

Fanaticism . . . is blind and passionate zeal born of superstitious opinions, causing people to commit ridiculous, unjust, and cruel actions, not only without any shame or remorse, but even with a kind of joy and comfort. *Fanaticism*, therefore, is only superstition put into practice. . . .

Fanaticism has done much more harm to the world than impiety. What do impious people claim? To free themselves of a yoke, while *fanatics* want to extend their chains over all the earth. Infernal zealomania! . . .

Government . . . The good of the people must be the great purpose of the *government*. The governors are appointed to fulfill it; and the civil constitution that invests them with this power is bound therein by the laws of nature and by the law of reason, which has determined that purpose in any form of *government* as the cause of its welfare. The greatest good of the people is its liberty. Liberty is to the body of the state what health is to each individual; without health man cannot enjoy pleasure; without liberty the state of welfare is excluded from nations. A patriotic governor will therefore see that the right to defend and to maintain liberty is the most sacred of his duties. . . .

If it happens that those who hold the reins of *government* find some resistance when they use their power for the destruction and not the conservation of things that rightfully belong to the people, they must blame themselves, because the public good and the advantage of society are the purposes of establishing a *government*. Hence it necessarily follows that power cannot be arbitrary and that it must be exercised according to the established laws so that the people may know its duty and be secure within the shelter of laws, and so that governors at the same time should be held within just limits and not be tempted to employ the power they have in hand to do harmful things to the body politic. . . .

History . . . *On the usefullness of history.* The advantage consists of the comparison that a statesman or a citizen can make of foreign laws, morals, and customs with those of his country. This is what stimulates modern nations to surpass one another in the arts, in commerce, and in agriculture. The great mistakes of the past are useful in all areas. We cannot describe too often the crimes and misfortunes caused by absurd quarrels. It is certain that by refreshing our memory of these quarrels, we prevent a repetition of them. . . .

Humanity . . . is a benevolent feeling for all men, which hardly inflames anyone without a great and sensitive soul. This sublime and noble enthusiasm is troubled by the pains of other people and by the necessity to alleviate them. With these sentiments an individual would wish to cover the entire universe in order to abolish slavery, superstition, vice, and misfortune. . . .

Intolerance . . . Any method that would tend to stir up men, to arm nations, and to soak the earth with blood is impious.

It is impious to want to impose laws upon man's conscience: this is a universal rule of conduct. People must be enlightened and not constrained. . . .

What did Christ recommend to his disciples when he sent them among the Gentiles? Was it to kill or to die? Was it to persecute or to suffer? . . .

Which is the true voice of humanity, the persecutor who strikes or the persecuted who moans?

Peace . . . War is the fruit of man's depravity; it is a convulsive and violent sickness of the body politic. . . .

If reason governed men and had the influence over the heads of nations that it deserves, we would never see them inconsiderately surrender themselves to the fury of war; they would not show that ferocity that characterizes wild beasts. . . .

Political Authority   No man has received from nature the right to command others. Liberty is a gift from heaven, and each individual of the same species has the right to enjoy it as soon as he enjoys the use of reason. . . .

The prince owes to his very subjects the *authority* that he has over them; and this *authority* is limited by the laws of nature and the state. The laws of nature and the state are the conditions under which they have submitted or are supposed to have submitted to its government. . . .

Moreover the government, although hereditary in a family and placed in the hands of one person, is not private property, but public property that consequently can never be taken from the people, to whom it belongs exclusively, fundamentally, and as a freehold. Consequently it is always the people who make the lease or the agreement: they always intervene in the contract that adjudges its exercise. It is not the state that belongs to the prince, it is the prince who belongs to the state: but it does rest with the prince to govern in the state, because the state has chosen him for that purpose: he has bound himself to the people and the administration of affairs, and they in their turn are bound to obey him according to the laws. . . .

The Press   [*press* includes newspapers, magazines, books, and so forth] . . . People ask if freedom of the *press* is advantageous or prejudicial to a state. The answer is not difficult. It is of the greatest importance to conserve this practice in all states founded on liberty. I would even say that the disadvantages of this liberty are so inconsiderable compared to its advantages that this ought to be the common right of the universe, and it is certainly advisable to authorize its practice in all governments. . . .

The Slave Trade   [This trade] is the buying of unfortunate Negroes by Europeans on the coast of Africa to use as slaves in their colonies. This buying of Negroes, to reduce them to slavery, is one business that violates religion, morality, natural laws, and all the rights of human nature.

Negroes, says a modern Englishman full of enlightenment and humanity, have not become slaves by the right of war; neither do they deliver themselves voluntarily into bondage, and consequently their children are not born slaves. Nobody is unaware that they are bought from their own princes, who claim to have the right to dispose of their liberty, and that traders have them transported in the same way as their other goods, either in their colonies or in America, where they are displayed for sale.

If commerce of this kind can be justified by a moral principle, there is no crime, however atrocious it may be, that cannot be made legitimate. Kings, princes, and magistrates are not the proprietors of their subjects: they do not, therefore, have the right to dispose of their liberty and to sell them as slaves.

On the other hand, no man has the right to buy them or to make himself their master. Men and their liberty are not objects of commerce; they can be neither sold nor bought nor paid for at any price. We must conclude from this that a man whose slave has run away should only blame himself, since he had acquired for money illicit goods whose acquisition is prohibited by all the laws of humanity and equity.

There is not, therefore, a single one of these unfortunate people regarded only as slaves who does not have the right to be declared free, since he has never lost his freedom, which he could not lose and which his prince, his father, and any person whatsoever in the world had not the power to dispose of. Consequently the sale that has been completed is invalid in itself. This Negro does not divest himself and can never divest himself of his natural right; he carries it everywhere with him, and he can demand everywhere that he be allowed to enjoy it. It is, therefore, patent inhumanity on the part of judges in free countries where he is transported, not to emancipate him immediately by declaring him free, since he is their fellow man, having a soul like them.

REVIEW QUESTIONS

1. Why was the publication of the *Encyclopedia* a vital step in the philosophes' hopes for reform?

2. What was the *Encyclopedia*'s view on the nature of liberty?
3. To what extent were John Locke's political ideals reflected in the *Encyclopedia*?
4. Why did the *Encyclopedia* recommend the study of history for the "enlightened" mind?
5. What moral ideals did the authors of the *Encyclopedia* promote for "great and sensitive" souls?
6. Why was freedom of the press of such significance to the enlightened philosophes?
7. Why did the philosophes condemn slavery?

▼▼▼

6 ▼ Critique of Christian Sex Mores

Diderot reviewed Louis Antoine de Bougainville's *Voyage Around the World* (1771) and later wrote *The Supplement to the Voyage of Bougainville.* In this work, Diderot explored some ideas, particularly the sex habits of Tahitians, treated by the French explorer. Diderot also denounced European imperialism and the exploitation of non-Europeans and questioned traditional Christian sexual standards.

Denis Diderot
≪ *THE SUPPLEMENT TO THE VOYAGE OF BOUGAINVILLE* ≫

In *Supplement,* Diderot constructed a dialogue between a Tahitian (Orou), who possesses the wisdom of a French philosophe, and a chaplain, whose defense of Christian sexual mores reveals Diderot's critique of the Christian view of human nature. Diderot thus used a representative of an alien culture to attack those European customs and beliefs that the philosophes detested. In the opening passage, before Orou's dialogue, a Tahitian elder rebukes Bougainville and his companions for bringing the evils of European civilization to his island.

"We [Tahitians] are free — but see where you [Europeans] have driven into our earth the symbol of our future servitude. You are neither a god nor a devil — by what right, then, do you enslave people? Orou! You who understand the speech of these men, tell every one of us, as you have told me, what they have written on that strip of metal — 'This land belongs to us.' This land belongs to you! And why? Because you set foot in it? If some day a Tahitian should land on your shores, and if he should engrave on one of your stones or on the bark of one of your trees: 'This land belongs to the people of Tahiti,' what would you think? You are stronger than we are! And what does that signify? When one of our lads carried off some of the miserable trinkets with which your ship is loaded, what an uproar you made, and what revenge you took! And at that very moment you were plotting, in the depths of your hearts, to steal a whole country! You are not slaves; you would suffer death rather than be enslaved, yet you want to make slaves of us! Do you believe, then, that the Tahitian does not know how to die in defense of his liberty? This Tahitian, whom you want to treat as a chattel, as a dumb animal — this Tahitian is your brother. You are both children of Nature — what right do you have over him that he does not have over you?

"You came; did we attack you? Did we plunder your vessel? Did we seize you and expose you to the arrows of our enemies? Did we force you to work in the fields alongside our beasts of burden? We respected our own image in you. Leave us our own customs, which are wiser and more decent than yours. We have no wish to barter what you call our ignorance for your useless knowledge. We possess already all that is good or necessary for our existence. Do we merit your scorn because we have not been able to create superfluous wants for ourselves? When we are hungry, we have something to eat; when we are cold, we have clothing to put on. You have been in our huts — what is lacking there, in your opinion? You are welcome to drive yourselves as hard as you please in pursuit of what you call the comforts of life, but allow sensible people to stop when they see they have nothing to gain but imaginary benefits from the continuation of their painful labors. If you persuade us to go beyond the bounds of strict necessity, when shall we come to the end of our labor? When shall we have time for enjoyment? We have reduced our daily and yearly labors to the least possible amount, because to us nothing seemed more desirable than leisure. Go and bestir yourselves in your own country; there you may torment yourselves as much as you like; but leave us in peace, and do not fill our heads with a hankering after your false needs and imaginary virtues. Look at these men — see how healthy, straight and strong they are. See these women — how straight, healthy, fresh and lovely they are. Take this bow in your hands — it is my own — and call one, two, three, four of your comrades to help you try to bend it. I can bend it myself. I work the soil, I climb mountains, I make my way through the dense forest, and I can run four leagues [about 12 miles] on the plain in less than an hour.

Your young comrades have been hard put to it to keep up with me, and yet I have passed my ninetieth year. . . .

"Woe to this island! Woe to all the Tahitians now living, and to all those yet to be born, woe from the day of your arrival! We used to know but one disease — the one to which all men, all animals and all plants are subject — old age. But you have brought us a new one [venereal disease]: you have infected our blood. We shall perhaps be compelled to exterminate with our own hands some of our young girls, some of our women, some of our children, those who have lain with your women, those who have lain with your men. Our fields will be spattered with the foul blood that has passed from your veins into ours. Or else our children, condemned to die, will nourish and perpetuate the evil disease that you have given their fathers and mothers, transmitting it forever to their descendants. . . .

▷ Before the arrival of Christian Europeans, lovemaking was natural and enjoyable. Europeans introduced an alien element, guilt.

But a while ago, the young Tahitian girl blissfully abandoned herself to the embraces of a Tahitian youth and awaited impatiently the day when her mother, authorized to do so by her having reached the age of puberty, would remove her veil and uncover her breasts. She was proud of her ability to excite men's desires, to attract the amorous looks of strangers, of her own relatives, of her own brothers. In our presence, without shame, in the center of a throng of innocent Tahitians who danced and played the flute, she accepted the caresses of the young man whom her young heart and the secret promptings of her senses had marked out for her. The notion of crime and the fear of disease have come among us only with your coming. Now our enjoyments, formerly so sweet, are attended with guilt and terror. That man in black [a priest], who stands near to you and listens to me, has spoken to our young men, and I know not what he has said to our young girls, but our youths are hesitant and our girls blush. Creep away into the dark forest, if you wish, with the perverse companion of your pleasures, but allow the good, simple Tahitians to reproduce themselves without shame under the open sky and in broad daylight.

▷ In the following conversation between Orou and the chaplain, Christian sexual mores and the concept of God are questioned. Orou addresses the chaplain.

[OROU] "You are young and healthy and you have just had a good supper. He who sleeps alone, sleeps badly; at night a man needs a woman at his side. Here is my wife and here are my daughters. Choose whichever one pleases you most, but if you would like to do me a favor, you will give your preference to my youngest girl, who has not yet had any children."

The mother said: "Poor girl! I don't hold it against her. It's no fault of hers."

The chaplain replied that his religion, his holy orders, his moral standards and his sense of decency all prevented him from accepting Orou's invitation.

Orou answered: "I don't know what this thing is that you call 'religion,' but I can only have a low opinion of it because it forbids you to partake of an innocent pleasure to which Nature, the sovereign mistress of us all, invites everybody. It seems to prevent you from bringing one of your fellow creatures into the world, from doing a favor asked of you by a father, a mother and their children, from repaying the kindness of a host, and from enriching a nation by giving it an additional citizen. I don't know what it is that you call 'holy orders,' but your chief duty is to be a man and to show gratitude. . . . I hope that you will not persist in disappointing us. Look at the distress you have caused to appear on the faces of these four

women — they are afraid you have noticed some defect in them that arouses your distaste. But even if that were so, would it not be possible for you to do a good deed and have the pleasure of honoring one of my daughters in the sight of her sisters and friends? Come, be generous!"

THE CHAPLAIN You don't understand — it's not that. They are all four of them equally beautiful. But there is my religion! My holy orders! . . .

. . . [God] spoke to our ancestors and gave them laws; he prescribed to them the way in which he wishes to be honored; he ordained that certain actions are good and others he forbade them to do as being evil.

OROU I see. And one of these evil actions which he has forbidden is that of a man who goes to bed with a woman or girl. But in that case, why did he make two sexes?

THE CHAPLAIN In order that they might come together — but only when certain conditions are satisfied and only after certain initial ceremonies have been performed. By virtue of these ceremonies one man belongs to one woman and only to her; one woman belongs to one man and only to him.

OROU For their whole lives?

THE CHAPLAIN For their whole lives.

OROU So that if it should happen that a woman should go to bed with some man who was not her husband, or some man should go to bed with a woman that was not his wife . . . but that could never happen because the workman [God] would know what was going on, and since he doesn't like that sort of thing, he wouldn't let it occur.

THE CHAPLAIN No. He lets them do as they will, and they sin against the law of God (for that is the name by which we call the great workman) and against the law of the country; they commit a crime.

OROU I should be sorry to give offense by anything I might say, but if you don't mind, I'll tell you what I think.

THE CHAPLAIN Go ahead.

 OROU I find these strange precepts contrary to nature, and contrary to reason. . . . Furthermore, your laws seem to me to be contrary to the general order of things. For in truth is there anything so senseless as a precept that forbids us to heed the changing impulses that are inherent in our being, or commands that require a degree of constancy which is not possible, that violate the liberty of both male and female by chaining them perpetually to one another? Is there anything more unreasonable than this perfect fidelity that would restrict us, for the enjoyment of pleasures so capricious, to a single partner — than an oath of immutability taken by two individuals made of flesh and blood under a sky that is not the same for a moment, in a cavern that threatens to collapse upon them, at the foot of a cliff that is crumbling into dust, under a tree that is withering, on a bench of stone that is being worn away? Take my word for it, you have reduced human beings to a worse condition than that of the animals. I don't know what your great workman is, but I am very happy that he never spoke to our forefathers, and I hope that he never speaks to our children, for if he does, he may tell them the same foolishness, and they may be foolish enough to believe it. . . .

OROU Are monks faithful to their vows of sterility?

THE CHAPLAIN No.

OROU I was sure of it. Do you also have female monks?

THE CHAPLAIN Yes.

OROU As well behaved as the male monks?

THE CHAPLAIN They are kept more strictly in seclusion, they dry up from unhappiness and die of boredom.

OROU So nature is avenged for the injury done to her! Ugh! What a country! If everything is managed the way you say, you are more barbarous than we are.

REVIEW QUESTIONS

1. According to Denis Diderot, why did European imperialism violate natural law?
2. How did Europeans influence the health and sexual mores of the Tahitians?
3. How did Diderot attempt to use the Tahitians to criticize the sexual mores of Europeans?
4. How did Diderot use the concept of the law of nature to undermine Christian sexual morality?

▼▼▼

7 ▼ Rousseau: Political and Educational Reform

To the philosophes, advances in the arts were hallmarks of progress. The French philosopher Jean Jacques Rousseau (1712–1778) argued that the accumulation of knowledge improved human understanding but corrupted the morals of human beings. In *A Discourse on the Arts and Sciences* (1750) and *A Discourse on the Origin of Inequality* (1755), Rousseau diagnosed the illnesses of modern civilization. He said that human nature, which was originally good, had been corrupted by society. As a result, he stated at the beginning of *The Social Contract* (1762), "Man is born free; and everywhere he is in chains." How can humanity be made moral and free again? In *The Social Contract,* Rousseau suggested one cure: reforming the political system. He argued that in the existing civil society the rich and powerful who controlled the state oppressed the majority. Rousseau admired the small, ancient Greek city-state (polis), where citizens participated actively and directly in public affairs. A small state modeled after the ancient Greek polis, said Rousseau, would be best able to resolve the tensions between individual freedom and the requirements of the collective community. In *Émile* (1762), Rousseau sought to improve the individual through educational reforms.

Jean Jacques Rousseau
≪ *THE SOCIAL CONTRACT* ≫
AND ≪ *ÉMILE* ≫

In the opening chapters of *The Social Contract,* Rousseau rejected the principle that one person has a natural authority over others. All legitimate authority, he said, stemmed from human traditions, not from nature. Rousseau had only contempt for absolute monarchy and in *The Social Contract* sought to provide a theoretical foundation for political liberty. In *Émile,* he suggested another cure for the ills of modern society: educational reforms that would instill in children self-confidence, self-reliance, and emotional security.

THE SOCIAL CONTRACT

[To rulers who argued that they provided security for their subjects, Rousseau responded as follows:]

It will be said that the despot assures his subjects civil tranquillity. Granted; but what do they gain, if the wars his ambition brings down upon them, his insatiable avidity, and the vexatious conduct of his ministers press harder on them than their own dissensions would have done? What do they gain, if the very tranquillity they enjoy is one of their miseries? Tranquillity is found also in dungeons; but is that enough to make them desirable places to live in? The Greeks imprisoned in the cave of the Cyclops lived there very tranquilly, while they were awaiting their turn to be devoured. . . .

Even if each man could alienate himself, he could not alienate his children: they are born men and free; their liberty belongs to them, and no one but they has the right to dispose of it. Before they come to years of discretion, the father can, in their name, lay down conditions for their preservation and well-being, but he cannot give them irrevocably and without conditions: such a gift is contrary to the ends of nature, and exceeds the rights of paternity. It would therefore be necessary, in order to legitimize an arbitrary government, that in every generation the people should be in a position to accept or reject it; but, were this so, the government would be no longer arbitrary.

To renounce liberty is to renounce being a man, to surrender the rights of humanity and even its duties. For him who renounces everything no indemnity is possible. Such a renunciation is incompatible with man's nature; to remove all liberty from his will is to remove all morality from his acts.

▷ Like Hobbes and Locke, Rousseau refers to an original social contract that terminates the state of nature and establishes the civil state. The clash of particular interests in the state of nature necessitates the creation of civil authority.

I suppose men to have reached the point at which the obstacles in the way of their preservation in the state of nature show their power of resistance to be greater than the resources at the disposal of each individual for his maintenance in that state. That primitive condition can then subsist no longer; and the human race would perish unless it changed its manner of existence. . . .

This sum of forces can arise only where several persons come together: but, as the force and liberty of each man are the chief instruments of his self-preservation, how can he pledge them without harming his own interests, and neglecting the care he owes to himself? This difficulty, in its bearing on my present subject, may be stated in the following terms:

"The problem is to find a form of association which will defend and protect with the whole common force the person and goods of each associate, and in which each, while uniting himself with all, may still obey himself alone, and remain as free as before." This is the fundamental problem of which the *Social Contract* provides the solution.

▷ In entering into the social contract, the individual surrenders his rights to the community as a whole, which governs in accordance with the general will — an underlying principle that expresses what is best for the community. The general will is a plainly visible truth that is easily discerned by reason and common sense purged of self-interest and unworthy motives. For Rousseau, the general will by definition is always right and always works to the community's advantage. True freedom consists of obedience to laws that coincide with the general will. Obedience to the general will transforms an individual motivated by self-interest, appetites, and passions into a higher type of person — a citizen committed to the general good. What happens, however, if a person's private will — that is, expressions of particular, selfish interests — clashes with the general will? As private interests could ruin the body politic, says Rousseau, "whoever refuses to obey the general will shall be compelled to do so by the whole body." Thus Rousseau rejects entirely the Lockean principle that citizens possess rights independently of and against the state. Because Rousseau grants the sovereign (the people constituted as a corporate body) virtually unlimited authority over the citizenry, some critics view him as a precursor of modern dictatorship.

The clauses of this contract. . . . properly understood, may be reduced to one — the total alienation of each associate, together with all his rights, to the whole community; for, in the first place, as each gives himself absolutely, the conditions are the same for all; and, this being so, no one has any interest in making them burdensome to others.

Moreover, the alienation being without reserve, the union is as perfect as it can be, and no associate has anything more to demand: for, if the individuals retained certain rights, as there would be no common superior to decide between them and the public, each, being on one point his own judge, would ask to be so on all; the state of nature would thus continue, and the association would necessarily become inoperative or tyrannical.

Finally, each man, in giving himself to all, gives himself to nobody; and as there is no associate over which he does not acquire the same right as he yields others over himself, he gains an equivalent for everything he loses, and an increase of force for the preservation of what he has.

If then we discard from the social compact what is not of its essence, we shall find that it reduces itself to the following terms:

"Each of us puts his person and all his power in common under the supreme direction of the general will, and, in our corporate capacity, we receive each member as an indivisible part of the whole."

At once, in place of the individual personality of each contracting party, this act of association creates a moral and collective body, composed of as many members as the assembly contains voters, and receiving from this act its unity, its common identity, its life, and its will. . . .

In order then that the social compact may not be an empty formula, it tacitly includes the undertaking, which alone can give force to the rest, that whoever refuses to obey the general will shall be compelled to do so by the whole body. This means nothing less than that he will be forced to be free; for this is the condition which, by giving each citizen to his country, secures him against all personal dependence. In this lies the key to the working of the political machine; this alone legitimizes civil undertakings, which, without it, would be absurd, tyrannical, and liable to the most frightful abuses.

The passage from the state of nature to the civil state produces a very remarkable change in man, by substituting justice for instinct in his conduct, and giving his actions the morality they had formerly lacked. Then only, when the voice of duty takes the place of physical impulses and right of appetite, does man, who so far had considered only himself, find that he is forced to act on different principles, and to consult his reason before listening to his inclinations. Although, in this state, he deprives himself of some advantages which he got from nature, he gains in return others so great, his faculties are so stimulated and developed, his ideas so extended, his feelings so ennobled, and his whole soul so uplifted, that, did not the abuses of this new condition often degrade him below that which he left, he would be bound to bless continually the happy moment which took him from it for ever, and, instead of a stupid and unimaginative animal, made him an intelligent being and a man.

Let us draw up the whole account in terms easily commensurable. What man loses by the social contract is his natural liberty and an unlimited right to everything he tries to get and succeeds in getting; what he gains is civil liberty and the proprietorship of all he possesses. If we are to avoid mistake in weighing one against the other, we must clearly distinguish natural liberty, which is bounded only by the strength of the individual, from civil liberty, which is limited by the general will; and possession, which is merely the effect of force or the right of the first occupier, from property, which can be founded only on a positive title.

We might, over and above all this, add, to what man acquires in the civil state, moral liberty, which alone makes him truly master of himself; for the mere impulse of appetite is slavery, while obedience to a law which we prescribe to ourselves is liberty. . . .

The first and most important deduction from the principles we have so far laid down is that the general will alone can direct the State according to the object for which it was instituted, i.e. the common good: for if the clashing of particular interests made the establishment of societies necessary, the agreement of these very interests made it possible. The common element in these different interests is what forms the social tie; and, were there no point of agreement between them all, no society could exist. It is solely on the basis of this common interest that every society should be governed. . . .

It follows from what has gone before that the general will is always right and tends to the public advantage; but it does not follow that the deliberations of the people are always equally correct. Our will is always for our own good, but we do not always see what that is; the people is never corrupted, but it is often deceived, and on such occasions only does it seem to will what is bad.

There is often a great deal of difference between the will of all and the general will; the latter considers only the common interest, while the former takes private interest into account, and is no more than a sum of particular wills: but take away from these same wills the pluses and minuses that cancel one another, and the general will remains as the sum of the differences.

If, when the people, being furnished with

adequate information, held its deliberations, the citizens had no communication one with another, the grand total of the small differences would always give the general will, and the decision would always be good. But when factions arise, and partial associations are formed at the expense of the great association, the will of each of these associations becomes general in relation to its members, while it remains particular in relation to the State: it may then be said that there are no longer as many votes as there are men, but only as many as there are associations. The differences become less numerous and give a less general result. Lastly, when one of these associations is so great as to prevail over all the rest, the result is no longer a sum of small differences, but a single difference; in this case there is no longer a general will, and the opinion which prevails is purely particular.

It is therefore essential, if the general will is to be able to express itself, that there should be no partial society [factions] within the State, and that each citizen should think only his own thoughts. . . . But if there are partial societies, it is best to have as many as possible and to prevent them from being unequal. . . . These precautions are the only ones that can guarantee that the general will shall be always enlightened, and that the people shall in no way deceive itself.

▷ Rousseau understood that children should not be treated like little adults. He railed against chaining young children to desks and filling their heads with rote learning. Instead, he urged that children experience direct contact with the world to develop their ingenuity, resourcefulness, and imagination so that they might become productive and responsible citizens. Excerpts from Rousseau's influential treatise on education follow.

ÉMILE

When I thus get rid of children's lessons, I get rid of the chief cause of their sorrows, namely

their books. Reading is the curse of childhood, yet it is almost the only occupation you can find for children. Emile, at twelve years old, will hardly know what a book is. "But," you say, "he must, at least, know how to read." When reading is of use to him, I admit he must learn to read, but till then he will only find it a nuisance.

If children are not to be required to do anything as a matter of obedience, it follows that they will only learn what they perceive to be of real and present value, either for use or enjoyment; what other motive could they have for learning? . . .

People make a great fuss about discovering the best way to teach children to read. They invent "bureaux"* and cards, they turn the nursery into a printer's shop. Locke would have them taught to read by means of dice. What a fine idea! And the pity of it! There is a better way than any of those, and one which is generally overlooked — it consists in the desire to learn. Arouse this desire in your scholar [a student who is taught by a "learned tutor"] and have done with your "bureaux" and your dice — any method will serve.

Present interest, that is the motive power, the only motive power that takes us far and safely. Sometimes Emile receives notes of invitation from his father or mother, his relations or friends; he is invited to a dinner, a walk, a boating expedition, to see some public entertainment. These notes are short, clear, plain, and well written. Some one must read them to him, and he cannot always find anybody when wanted; no more consideration is shown to him than he himself showed to you yesterday. Time passes, the chance is lost. The note is read to him at last, but it is too late. Oh! if only he had known how to read! He receives other

---

*Translator's note — The "bureau" was a sort of case containing letters to be put together to form words. It was a favourite device for the teaching of reading and gave its name to a special method, called the bureau-method, of learning to read.

notes, so short, so interesting, he would like to try to read them. Sometimes he gets help, sometimes none. He does his best, and at last he makes out half the note; it is something about going to-morrow to drink cream — Where? With whom? He cannot tell — how hard he tries to make out the rest! I do not think Emile will need a "bureau." Shall I proceed to the teaching of writing? No, I am ashamed to toy with these trifles in a treatise on education. . . .

If, in accordance with the plan I have sketched, you follow rules which are just the opposite of the established practice, if instead of taking your scholar far afield, instead of wandering with him in distant places, in far-off lands, in remote centuries, in the ends of the earth, and in the very heavens themselves, you try to keep him to himself, to his own concerns, you will then find him able to perceive, to remember, and even to reason; this is nature's order. . . . Give his body constant exercise, make it strong and healthy, in order to make him good and wise; let him work, let him do things, let him run and shout, let him be always on the go; make a man of him in strength, and he will soon be a man in reason.

Of course by this method you will make him stupid if you are always giving him directions, always saying come here, go there, stop, do this, don't do that. If your head always guides his hands, his own mind will become useless. . . .

It is a lamentable mistake to imagine that bodily activity hinders the working of the mind, as if these two kinds of activity ought not to advance hand in hand, and as if the one were not intended to act as guide to the other. . . .

. . . Your scholar is subject to a power which is continually giving him instruction; he acts only at the word of command; he dare not eat when he is hungry, nor laugh when he is merry, nor weep when he is sad, nor offer one hand rather than the other, nor stir a foot unless he is told to do it; before long he will not venture to breathe without orders. What would you have him think about, when you do all the thinking for him? . . .

As for my pupil, or rather Nature's pupil, he has been trained from the outset to be as self-reliant as possible, he has not formed the habit of constantly seeking help from others, still less of displaying his stores of learning. On the other hand, he exercises discrimination and forethought, he reasons about everything that concerns himself. He does not chatter, he acts. Not a word does he know of what is going on in the world at large, but he knows very thoroughly what affects himself. As he is always stirring he is compelled to notice many things, to recognise many effects; he soon acquires a good deal of experience. Nature, not man, is his schoolmaster, and he learns all the quicker because he is not aware that he has any lesson to learn. So mind and body work together. He is always carrying out his own ideas, not those of other people, and thus he unites thought and action; as he grows in health and strength he grows in wisdom and discernment.

REVIEW QUESTIONS

1. What did Jean Jacques Rousseau mean by the "general will"? What function did it serve in his political theory?
2. Why do some thinkers view Rousseau as a champion of democracy, whereas others see him as a spiritual precursor of totalitarianism?
3. What was Rousseau's basic approach in educating a child?
4. What was Rousseau's view of human nature, and how did it influence his educational theory?
5. Compare and contrast the type of person produced by Rousseau's educational theory and that produced by his political theory.

8 ▼ On the Progress of Humanity

Marie Jean Antoine Nicolas Caritat, Marquis de Condorcet (1743–1794), was a French mathematician and historian of science. He contributed to the *Encyclopedia* and campaigned actively for religious toleration and the abolition of slavery. During the French Revolution, Condorcet attracted the enmity of the dominant Jacobin party and in 1793 was forced to go into hiding. Secluded in Paris, he wrote *Sketch for a Historical Picture of the Progress of the Human Mind*. Arrested in 1794, Condorcet died during his first night in prison from either exhaustion or self-inflicted poison.

Marquis de Condorcet
PROGRESS OF THE HUMAN MIND

Sharing the philosophes' confidence in human goodness and in reason, Condorcet was optimistic about humanity's future progress. Superstition, prejudice, intolerance, and tyranny — all barriers to progress in the past — would gradually be eliminated, and humanity would enter a golden age. The following excerpts are from Condorcet's *Sketch*.

. . . The aim of the work that I have undertaken, and its result will be to show by appeal to reason and fact that nature has set no term to the perfection of human faculties; that the perfectibility of man is truly indefinite; and that the progress of this perfectibility, from now onwards independent of any power that might wish to halt it, has no other limit than the duration of the globe upon which nature has cast us. This progress will doubtless vary in speed, but it will never be reversed as long as the earth occupies its present place in the system of the universe, and as long as the general laws of this system produce neither a general cataclysm nor such changes as will deprive the human race of its present faculties and its present resources. . . .

. . . It will be necessary to indicate by what stages what must appear to us today a fantastic hope ought in time to become possible, and even likely; to show why, in spite of the transitory successes of prejudice and the support that it receives from the corruption of governments or peoples, truth alone will obtain a lasting victory; we shall demonstrate how nature has joined together indissolubly the progress of knowledge and that of liberty, virtue and respect for the natural rights of man. . . .

After long periods of error, after being led astray by vague or incomplete theories, publicists have at last discovered the true rights of man and how they can all be deduced from the single truth, that *man is a sentient being, capable of reasoning and of acquiring moral ideas.* . . .

At last man could proclaim aloud his right, which for so long had been ignored, to submit all opinions to his own reason and to use in the search for truth the only instrument for its recognition that he has been given. Every man learnt with a sort of pride that nature had not forever condemned him to base his beliefs on the opinions of others; the superstitions of antiquity and the abasement of reason before the [rapture] of supernatural religion disappeared from society as from philosophy.

Thus an understanding of the natural rights of man, the belief that these rights are inalienable and [cannot be forfeited], a strongly expressed desire for liberty of thought and letters, of trade and industry, and for the alleviation of the people's suffering, for the [elimination] of all penal laws against religious dissenters and the abolition of torture and barbarous punishments, the desire for a milder system of criminal legislation and jurisprudence which should give complete security to the innocent, and for a simpler civil code, more in conformance with reason and nature, indifference in all matters of religion which now were relegated to the status of superstitions and political [deception], a hatred of hypocrisy and fanaticism, a contempt for prejudice, zeal for the propagation of enlightenment: all these principles, gradually filtering down from philosophical works to every class of society whose education went beyond the catechism and the alphabet, became the common faith . . . [of enlightened people]. In some countries these principles formed a public opinion sufficiently widespread for even the mass of the people to show a willingness to be guided by it and to obey it. . . .

Force or persuasion on the part of governments, priestly intolerance, and even national prejudices, had all lost their deadly power to smother the voice of truth, and nothing could now protect the enemies of reason or the oppressors of freedom from a sentence to which the whole of Europe would soon subscribe. . . .

Our hopes for the future condition of the human race can be subsumed under three important heads: the abolition of inequality between nations, the progress of equality within each nation, and the true perfection of mankind.

Will all nations one day attain that state of civilization which the most enlightened, the freest and the least burdened by prejudices, such as the French and the Anglo-Americans [by virtue of their revolutions], have attained already? Will the vast gulf that separates these peoples from the slavery of nations under the rule of monarchs, from the barbarism of African tribes, from the ignorance of savages, little by little disappear? . . .

Is the human race to better itself, either by discoveries in the sciences and the arts, and so in the means to individual welfare and general prosperity; or by progress in the principles of conduct or practical morality; or by a true perfection of the intellectual, moral, or physical faculties of man, an improvement which may result from a perfection either of the instruments used to heighten the intensity of these faculties and to direct their use or of the natural constitution of man?

In answering these three questions we shall find in the experience of the past, in the observation of the progress that the sciences and civilization have already made, in the analysis of the progress of the human mind and of the development of its faculties, the strongest reasons for believing that nature has set no limit to the realization of our hopes. . . .

The time will therefore come when the sun will shine only on free men who know no other master but their reason; when tyrants and slaves, priests and their stupid or hypocritical instruments will exist only in works of history and on the stage; and when we shall think of them only to pity their victims and their dupes; to maintain ourselves in a state of vigilance by thinking on their excesses; and to learn how to recognize and so to destroy, by force of reason, the first seeds of tyranny and superstition, should they ever dare to reappear amongst us.

REVIEW QUESTIONS

1. What image of human nature underlies the Marquis de Condorcet's theory of human progress?

2. According to Condorcet, what economic, political, and cultural policies were sought by enlightened philosophes?

3. According to Condorcet, what had to occur before other peoples were to achieve the goal of sharing in an enlightened civilization?

4. Was the Enlightenment philosophy an alternative moral order to that of Christianity? Or was it an internal reformation of the Christian moral order?

Part Two

▾▾

Modern Europe

The French Revolution

In 1789, many participants and observers viewed the revolutionary developments in France as the fulfillment of the Enlightenment's promise — the triumph of reason over tradition and ignorance, of liberty over despotism. It seemed that the French reformers were eliminating the abuses of an unjust system and creating a new society founded on the ideals of the philosophes.

Eighteenth-century French society, the Old Regime, was divided into three orders, or estates. The First Estate (the clergy) and the Second Estate (the nobility) enjoyed special privileges sanctioned by law and custom. The church collected tithes (taxes on the land), censored books regarded as a threat to religion and morality, and paid no taxes to the state (although the church did make a "free gift" to the royal treasury). Nobles were exempt from most taxes, collected manorial dues from peasants (even from free peasants), and held the highest positions in the church, the army, and the government. Peasants, urban workers, and members of the bourgeoisie belonged to the Third Estate, which comprised about 96 percent of the population.

The bourgeoisie — which included merchants, bankers, professionals, and government officials below the top ranks — provided the leadership and ideology for the French Revolution. In 1789 the bourgeoisie possessed wealth and talent but had no political power; it was denied equality with the aristocracy, for whom the highest positions in the land were reserved on the basis of birth. By 1789 the bourgeoisie wanted to abolish the special privileges of the nobility and to open prestigious positions to men of talent regardless of their birth; it wanted to give France a constitution that limited the monarch's power, established a parliament, and protected the rights of the individual.

The immediate cause of the French Revolution was a financial crisis. The wars of Louis XIV and subsequent foreign adventures, including French aid to the American colonists during their revolution, had emptied the royal treasury. The refusal of the clergy and the nobles to surrender their tax exemptions compelled Louis XVI to call a meeting of the Estates General — a medieval assembly that had last met in 1614 — to deal with impending bankruptcy. The nobility intended to use the Estates General to weaken the French throne and regain powers lost a century earlier under the absolute rule of Louis XIV. But the nobility's

A RAUCOUS REVOLUTIONARY COMMITTEE MEETING during the Terror in France, around 1793. Such committees tried persons accused of political crimes, thereby eliminating opposition; also, the Terror's dictatorship crushed the rights of individuals. (*Bulloz, Paris*)

plans were unrealized; their revolt against the crown paved the way for the Third Estate's eventual destruction of the Old Regime.

Between June and November 1789 the bourgeoisie, aided by uprisings of the common people of Paris and the peasants in the countryside, gained control over the state and instituted reforms. During this opening, moderate phase of the Revolution (1789–1791), the bourgeoisie abolished the special privileges of the aristocracy and clergy, formulated a declaration of human rights, subordinated the church to the state, reformed the country's administrative and judicial systems, and drew up a constitution creating a parliament and limiting the king's power.

Between 1792 and 1794 came a radical stage. Three principal factors propelled the Revolution in a radical direction: pressure from the urban poor, the *sans-culottes,* who wanted the government to do something about their poverty; a counterrevolution led by clergy and aristocrats who wanted to undo the reforms of the Revolution; and war with the European powers that sought to check French expansion and to stifle the revolutionary ideals of liberty and equality.

The dethronement of Louis XVI, the establishment of a republic in September 1792, and the king's execution in January 1793 were all signs of growing radicalism. As the new Republic tottered under the twin blows of internal insurrection and foreign invasion, the revolutionary leadership grew more extreme. In June 1793 the Jacobins took power. Tightly organized, disciplined, and fiercely devoted to the Republic, the Jacobins mobilized the nation's material and human resources to defend it against the invading foreign armies. To deal with counterrevolutionaries, the Jacobins unleashed the Reign of Terror, which took the lives of some 20,000 to 40,000 people, many of them innocent of any crime against the state. Although the Jacobins succeeded in saving the Revolution, their extreme measures aroused opposition. In the last part of 1794, power again passed into the hands of the moderate bourgeoisie, who wanted no part of Jacobin radicalism.

In 1799, Napoleon Bonaparte, a popular general with an inexhaustible yearning for power, overthrew the government and pushed the Revolution in still another direction, toward military dictatorship. Although Napoleon subverted the revolutionary ideal of liberty, he preserved the social gains of the Revolution — the abolition of the special privileges of the nobility and the clergy.

The era of French Revolution was a decisive period in the shaping of the modern West. By destroying aristocratic privileges and opening careers to talent, it advanced the cause of equality under the law. By weakening the power of the clergy, it promoted the secularization of society. By abolishing the divine right of monarchy, drafting a constitution, and establishing a parliament, it accelerated the growth of the liberal-democratic state. By eliminating serfdom and the sale of government offices and by reforming the tax system, it fostered a rational approach to administration. In the nineteenth century, the ideals and reforms of the French Revolution spread in shock waves across Europe; in country after country, the old order was challenged by the ideals of liberty and equality.

▼▼▼

I ▼ Abuses of the Old Regime

The roots of the French Revolution lay in the aristocratic structure of French society. The Third Estate resented the special privileges of the aristocracy, a legacy of the Middle Ages, and the inefficient and corrupt methods of government. To many French people influenced by the ideas of the philosophes, French society seemed an affront to reason. By 1789, reformers sought a new social order based on rationality and equality.

Arthur Young
PLIGHT OF THE FRENCH PEASANTS

French peasants in the late eighteenth century were better off than the peasants of eastern and central Europe, where serfdom predominated. The great majority of France's 21 million peasants were free; many owned their own land, and some were prosperous. Yet the countryside was burdened with severe problems, which sparked a spontaneous revolution in 1789.

A rising birthrate led to the continual subdivision of French farms among peasant sons; on the resulting small holdings, peasants struggled to squeeze out a living. Many landless peasants, who were forced to work as day laborers, were also hurt by the soaring population. An oversupply of rural day laborers reduced many of the landless to beggary. An unjust and corrupt tax system also contributed to the peasants' poverty. Peasants paid excessive taxes to the state, church, and lords; taxes and obligations due the lords were particularly onerous medieval vestiges, as most peasants were no longer serfs. Inflation and a poor harvest in 1788–1789 worsened conditions.

Arthur Young (1741–1820), an English agricultural expert with a keen eye for detail, traveled through France just prior to the Revolution. In *Travels During the Years 1787, 1788, and 1789,* he reported on conditions in the countryside.

. . . The abuses attending the levy of taxes were heavy and universal. The kingdom was parceled into generalities [administrative units], with an intendant at the head of each, into whose hands the whole power of the crown was delegated for everything except the military authority; but particularly for all affairs of finance. The generalities were subdivided into elections, at the head of which was a *sub-delegue* appointed by the intendant. The rolls of the *taille*, capitation, *vingtièmes*,[1] and other taxes, were distributed among districts, parishes, and individuals, at the pleasure of the intendant, who could exempt, change, add, or diminish at pleasure. Such an enormous power, constantly acting, and from which no man was free, must, in the nature of things, degenerate in many cases into absolute tyranny. It must be obvious that the friends, acquaintances, and dependents of the intendant, and of all his *sub-delegues,* and the friends of these friends, to a long chain of dependence, might be favoured in taxation at the expense of their miserable neighbours; and that noblemen in favour at court, to whose protection the intendant himself would naturally look up, could find little difficulty in throwing much of the weight of their taxes on others, without a similar support. Instances, and even gross ones, have been reported to me in many parts of the kingdom, that made me shudder at the oppression to which [people have been subjected] by the undue favours granted to such crooked influence. But, without recurring to such cases, what must have been the state of the poor people paying heavy taxes, from which the nobility and clergy were exempted? A cruel aggravation of their misery, to see those who could best afford to pay, exempted because able! . . . The *corvées* [taxes paid in labor, often road building], or police of the roads, were annually the ruin of many hundreds of farmers; more than 300 were reduced to beggary in filling up

one vale in Lorraine: all these oppressions fell on the *tiers etat* [Third Estate] only; the nobility and clergy having been equally exempted from *tailles,* militia and *corvées.* The penal code of finance makes one shudder at the horrors of punishment inadequate to the crime. . . .

1. Smugglers of salt, armed and assembled to the number of five, in Provence, a fine of 500 liv. [*livres*, French coins] and nine years galleys [sentenced to backbreaking labor — rowing sea vessels], in all the rest of the kingdom, death.
2. Smugglers, armed, assembled, but in number under five, a fine of 300 liv. and three years galleys. Second offense, death. . . .
10. Buying smuggled salt, to resell it, the same punishments as for smuggling. . . .

The *Capitaineries* [lords' exclusive hunting rights] were a dreadful scourge on all the occupiers of land. By this term is to be understood the paramountship of certain districts, granted by the king to princes of the blood, by which they were put in possession of the property of all game, even on lands not belonging to them. . . . In speaking of the preservation of the game in these *capitaineries,* it must be observed that by game must be understood whole droves of wild boars, and herds of deer not confined by any wall or pale, but wandering at pleasure over the whole country, to the destruction of crops; and to the peopling of the galleys by the wretched peasants, who presumed to kill them in order to save that food which was to support their helpless children. . . . Now an English reader will scarcely understand it without being told, that there were numerous edicts for preserving the game which prohibited weeding and hoeing, lest the young partridges should be disturbed; . . . manuring with night soil, lest the flavour of the partridges should be injured by feeding on the corn so produced; . . . and taking away the stubble, which would deprive the birds of shelter. The tyranny exercised in these *capitaineries,* which

---

[1]A *taille* was a tax levied on the value of a peasant's land or wealth. A capitation was a head or poll tax paid for each person. A *vingtième* was a tax on income and was paid chiefly by peasants.

extended over 400 leagues[2] of country, was so great that many *cahiers* [lists of the Third Estate's grievances] demanded the utter suppression of them. Such were the exertions of arbitrary power which the lower orders felt directly from the royal authority; but, heavy as they were, it is a question whether the [abuses], suffered [indirectly] through the nobility and the clergy, were not yet more oppressive. Nothing can exceed the complaints made in the *cahiers* under this head. They speak of the dispensation of justice in the manorial courts, as comprising every species of despotism; the districts indeterminate — appeals endless — irreconcilable to liberty and prosperity — and irrevocably [condemned] in the opinion of the

public — augmenting litigations — favouring every [form of trickery] — ruining the parties — not only by enormous expenses on the most petty objects, but by a dreadful loss of time. The judges, commonly ignorant pretenders, who hold their courts in *cabarets* [taverns] . . . are absolutely dependent on the seigneurs [lords]. Nothing can exceed the force of expression used in painting the oppressions of the seigneurs, in consequence of their feudal powers. . . . The countryman is tyrannically enslaved by it. . . . In passing through many of the French provinces, I was struck with the various and heavy complaints of the farmers and little proprietors of the feudal grievances, with the weight of which their industry was [burdened]; but I could not then conceive the multiplicity of the shackles which kept them poor and depressed. I understood it better afterwards.

[2]Various units of distance were called leagues, and their length was from about 2.4 to 4.6 miles.

GRIEVANCES OF THE THIRD ESTATE

At the same time that elections were held for the Estates General, the three estates drafted *cahiers de doléances,* the lists of grievances that deputies would take with them when the Estates General convened. The cahiers from all three estates expressed loyalty to the monarchy and the church and called for a written constitution and an elected assembly. The cahiers of the clergy and the nobility insisted on the preservation of traditional rights and privileges. The Cahier of the Third Estate of Dourdan, in the *généralité* of Orléans (one of the thirty-four administrative units into which prerevolutionary France was divided), expressed the reformist hopes of the Third Estate. Some of the grievances in the cahier follow.

29 March, 1789

The order of the third estate of the City, *Bailliage* [judicial district], and County of Dourdan, imbued with gratitude prompted by the paternal kindness of the King, who deigns to restore its former rights and its former constitution, forgets at this moment its misfortunes and impotence, to harken only to its foremost sentiment and its foremost duty, that of

sacrificing everything to the glory of the *Patrie* [nation] and the service of His Majesty. It supplicates him to accept the grievances, complaints, and remonstrances which it is permitted to bring to the foot of the throne, and to see therein only the expression of its zeal and the homage of its obedience.

It wishes:

1. That his subjects of the third estate, equal by such status to all other citizens, pre-

sent themselves before the common father without other distinction which might degrade them.

2. That all the orders [the three estates], already united by duty and a common desire to contribute equally to the needs of the State, also deliberate in common concerning its needs.

3. That no citizen lose his liberty except according to law; that, consequently, no one be arrested by virtue of special orders, or, if imperative circumstances necessitate such orders, that the prisoner be handed over to the regular courts of justice within forty-eight hours at the latest.

4. That no letters or writings intercepted in the post [mails] be the cause of the detention of any citizen, or be produced in court against him, except in case of conspiracy or undertaking against the State.

5. That the property of all citizens be inviolable, and that no one be required to make sacrifice thereof for the public welfare, except upon assurance of indemnification based upon the statement of freely selected appraisers. . . .

15. That every personal tax be abolished; that thus the *capitation* and the *taille* and its accessories be merged with the *vingtièmes*[1] in a tax on land and real or nominal property.

16. That such tax be borne equally, without distinction, by all classes of citizens and by all kinds of property, even feudal and contingent rights.

17. That the tax substituted for the *corvée* [taxes paid in labor] be borne by all classes of citizens equally and without distinction. That said tax, at present beyond the capacity of those who pay it and the needs to which it is destined, be reduced by at least one-half. . . .

JUSTICE

1. That the administration of justice be reformed, either by restoring strict execution of ordinances, or by reforming the sections thereof that are contrary to the dispatch and welfare of justice. . . .

7. That venality [sale] of offices be suppressed. . . .

8. That the excessive number of offices in the necessary courts be reduced in just measure, and that no one be given an office of magistracy if he is not at least twenty-five years of age, and until after a substantial public examination has verified his morality, integrity, and ability. . . .

10. That the study of law be reformed; that it be directed in a manner analogous to our legislation, and that candidates for degrees be subjected to rigorous tests which may not be evaded; that no dispensation of age or time be granted.

11. That a body of general customary law be drafted of all articles common to all the customs of the several provinces and *bailliages*. . . .

12. That deliberations of courts . . . which tend to prevent entry of the third estate thereto be rescinded and annulled as injurious to the citizens of that order, in contempt of the authority of the King, whose choice they limit, and contrary to the welfare of justice, the administration of which would become the patrimony of those of noble birth instead of being entrusted to merit, enlightenment, and virtue.

13. That military ordinances which restrict entrance to the service to those possessing nobility be reformed.

That naval ordinances establishing a degrading distinction between officers born into the order of nobility and those born into that of the third estate be revoked, as thoroughly injurious to an order of citizens and destructive of the competition so necessary to the glory and prosperity of the State.

FINANCES

1. That if the Estates General considers it necessary to preserve the fees of *aides* [tax on commodities], such fees be made uniform throughout the entire kingdom and reduced to a single denomination. . . .

---

[1]For an explanation of taxes, see footnote 1 on page 92.

2. That the tax of the *gabelle* [tax on salt] be eliminated if possible, or that it be regulated among the several provinces of the kingdom. . . .

3. That the taxes on hides, which have totally destroyed that branch of commerce and caused it to go abroad, be suppressed forever.

4. That . . . all useless offices, either in police or in the administration of justice, be abolished and suppressed.

AGRICULTURE

4. That the right to hunt may never affect the property of the citizen; that, accordingly, he may at all times travel over his lands, have injurious herbs uprooted, and cut *luzernes* [alfalfa], *sainfoins* [fodder], and other produce whenever it suits him; and that stubble may be freely raked immediately after the harvest. . . .[2]

11. . . .That individuals as well as communities be permitted to free themselves from the rights of *banalité* [peasants were required to use the lord's mill, winepress, and oven], and *corvée,* by payments in money or in kind, at a rate likewise established by His Majesty on the basis of the deliberations of the Estates General. . . .

15. That the militia, which devastates the country, takes workers away from husbandry, produces premature and ill-matched marriages, and imposes secret and arbitrary taxes upon those who are subject thereto, be suppressed and replaced by voluntary enlistment at the expense of the provinces.

---

[2]See the discussion of nobles' hunting rights and the peasants' hatred of this practice in the preceding reading by Arthur Young.

Emmanuel Sieyès
BOURGEOIS DISDAIN FOR SPECIAL PRIVILEGES OF THE ARISTOCRACY

In a series of pamphlets, including *The Essay on Privileges* (1788) and *What Is the Third Estate?* (1789), Abbé Emmanuel Sieyès (1748–1836) expressed the bourgeoisie's disdain for the nobility. Although educated at Jesuit schools to become a priest, Sieyès had come under the influence of Enlightenment ideas. In *What Is the Third Estate?* he denounced the special privileges of the nobility, asserted that the people are the source of political authority, and maintained that national unity stands above estate or local interests. The ideals of the Revolution — liberty, equality, and fraternity — are found in Sieyès's pamphlet, excerpts of which follow.

The plan of this book is fairly simple. We must ask ourselves three questions.

1. What is the Third State? *Everything.*
2. What has it been until now in the political order? *Nothing.*
3. What does it want to be? *Something. . . .*

. . . Only the well-paid and honorific posts are filled by members of the privileged order [nobles]. Are we to give them credit for this? We could do so only if the Third Estate was unable or unwilling to fill these posts. We know the answer. Nevertheless, the privileged have dared to preclude the Third Estate. "No matter how useful you are," they said, "no matter how able you are, you can go so far and no further. Honors are not for the like of you.". . .

. . . Has nobody observed that as soon as the government becomes the property of a separate class, it starts to grow out of all proportion and that posts are created not to meet the needs of the governed but of those who govern them? . . .

It suffices to have made the point that the so-called usefulness of a privileged order to the public service is a fallacy; that, without help from this order, all the arduous tasks in the service are performed by the Third Estate; that without this order the higher posts could be infinitely better filled; that they ought to be the natural prize and reward of recognised ability and service; and that if the privileged have succeeded in usurping all well-paid and honorific posts, this is both a hateful iniquity towards the generality of citizens and an act of treason to the commonwealth.

Who is bold enough to maintain that the Third Estate does not contain within itself everything needful to constitute a complete nation? It is like a strong and robust man with one arm still in chains. If the privileged order were removed, the nation would not be something less but something more. What then is the Third Estate? All; but an "all" that is fettered and oppressed. What would it be without the privileged order? It would be all; but free and flourishing. Nothing will go well without the Third Estate; everything would go considerably better without the two others. . . .

. . . The privileged, far from being useful to the nation, can only weaken and injure it; . . . the nobility may be a *burden* for the nation. . . .

The nobility, however, is . . . a foreigner in our midst because of its *civil and political* prerogatives.

What is a nation? A body of associates living under *common* laws and represented by the same *legislative assembly*, etc.

Is it not obvious that the nobility possesses privileges and exemptions which it brazenly calls its rights and which stand distinct from the rights of the great body of citizens? Because of these special rights, the nobility does not belong to the common order, nor is it subjected to the common laws. Thus its private rights make it a people apart in the great nation.

REVIEW QUESTIONS

1. What abuses did Arthur Young see in the French systems of taxation and justice?
2. Why did Young consider the *capitaineries* (nobles' hunting rights) to be a particularly "dreadful scourge" on the peasants?
3. The principle of equality pervaded the cahiers of the Third Estate. Discuss this statement.
4. How did the Cahier of the Third Estate of Dourdan try to correct some of the abuses discussed by Arthur Young?
5. How important did Emmanuel Sieyès say the nobility (the privileged order) was to the life of the nation?
6. What importance did Sieyès attach to the contribution of the Third Estate (the bourgeoisie) to the life of the nation?
7. How did Sieyès define the nation? Why did he believe that the privileged order was a barrier to national unity?

▼▼▼

2 ▼ Liberty, Equality, Fraternity

In August 1789 the French National Assembly adopted the Declaration of the Rights of Man and of Citizens, which expressed the liberal and universal ideals of the Enlightenment. The Declaration proclaimed that sovereignty derives from the people, that is, that the people are the source of political power; that men are born free and equal in rights; and that it is the purpose of government to protect the natural rights of the individual. Because these ideals contrasted markedly with the outlook of an absolute monarchy, a privileged aristocracy, and an intolerant clergy, some historians view the Declaration of Rights as the death knell of the Old Regime. Its affirmation of liberty, reason, and natural rights inspired liberal reformers in other lands.

DECLARATION OF THE RIGHTS OF MAN AND OF CITIZENS

Together with John Locke's *Second Treatise on Government,* the American Declaration of Independence, and the Constitution of the United States, the Declaration of the Rights of Man and of Citizens, which follows, is a pivotal document in the development of modern liberalism.

The Representatives of the people of FRANCE, formed into a NATIONAL ASSEMBLY, considering that ignorance, neglect, or contempt of human rights, are the sole causes of public misfortunes and corruptions of Government, have resolved to set forth in a solemn declaration, these natural, imprescriptible, and unalienable rights: that this declaration, being constantly present to the minds of the members of the body social, they may be ever kept attentive to their rights and their duties: that the acts of the legislative and executive powers of Government, being capable of being every moment compared with the end of political institutions, may be more respected: and also, that the future claims of the citizens, being directed by simple and incontestible principles, may always tend to the maintenance of the Constitution, and the general happiness.

For these reasons the NATIONAL ASSEMBLY doth recognize and declare, in the presence of the Supreme Being, and with the hope of his blessing and favor, the following *sacred* rights of men and of citizens:

I. *Men are born, and always continue, free, and equal in respect of their rights. Civil distinctions, therefore, can be founded only on public utility.*

II. *The end of all political associations, is, the preservation of the natural and imprescriptible rights of man; and these rights are liberty, property, security, and resistance of oppression.*

III. *The nation is essentially the source of all sovereignty; nor can any* INDIVIDUAL *or* ANY BODY OF MEN, *be entitled to any authority which is not expressly derived from it.*

IV. Political Liberty consists in the power of doing whatever does not injure another. The exercise of the natural rights of every man, has no other limits than those which are necessary to secure to every *other* man the free exercise of the same rights; and these limits are determinable only by the law.

V. The law ought to prohibit only actions hurtful to society. What is not prohibited by the law, should not be hindered; nor should any one be compelled to that which the law does not require.

VI. The law is an expression of the will of the community. All citizens have a right to concur, either personally, or by their representatives, in its formation. It should be the same to all, whether it protects or punishes; and *all being equal in its sight, are equally eligible to all honors, places, and employments, according to their different abilities, without any other distinction than that created by their virtues and talents.*

VII. No man should be accused, arrested, or held in confinement, except in cases determined by the law, and according to the forms which it has prescribed. All who promote, solicit, execute, or cause to be executed, arbitrary orders, ought to be punished; and every citizen called upon or apprehended by virtue of the law, ought immediately to obey, and renders himself culpable by resistance.

VIII. The law ought to impose no other penalties but such as are absolutely and evidently necessary; and no one ought to be punished, but in virtue of a law promulgated before the offence, and legally applied.

IX. Every man being presumed innocent till he has been convicted, whenever his detention becomes indispensible, all rigor [harshness] to him, more than is necessary to secure his person, ought to be provided against by the law.

X. No man ought to be molested on account of his opinions, not even on account of his *religious* opinions, provided his avowal of them does not disturb the public order established by the law.

XI. The unrestrained communication of thoughts and opinions being one of the most precious rights of man, every citizen may speak, write, and publish freely, provided he is responsible for the abuse of this liberty in cases determined by the law.

XII. A public force being necessary to give security to the rights of men and of citizens, that force is instituted for the benefit of the community, and not for the particular benefit of the persons with whom it is entrusted.

XIII. A common contribution being necessary for the support of the public force, and for defraying the other expenses of government, it ought to be divided equally among the members of the community, according to their abilities.

XIV. Every citizen has a right, either by himself or his representative, to a free voice in determining the necessity of public contributions, the appropriation of them, and their amount, mode of assessment and duration.

XV. Every community has a right to demand of all its agents, an account of their conduct.

XVI. Every community in which a separation of powers and a security of rights is not provided for, wants a constitution.

XVII. The rights to property being inviolable and sacred, no one ought to be deprived of it, except in cases of evident public necessity, legally ascertained, and on condition of a previous just indemnity.

REVIEW QUESTIONS

1. What purpose did the writers of the Declaration of Rights intend the document to have? Was it supposed to describe reality as it was? Was it a law to be obeyed? Was it a standard against which to measure reality?
2. According to the Declaration, what do all men share by birth and what makes it possible for them to differ from one another in public life?
3. What does the Declaration say about the nature of political liberty? What are its limits, and how are they determined?
4. How does the Declaration show the influence of John Locke (see Chapter 3 in this volume)?

5. The ideals of the Declaration have become deeply embedded in the Western outlook. Discuss this statement.

▼▼▼

3 ▼ The Revolution Debated

There were mixed reactions to the French Revolution among thinkers and statesmen in Europe and the United States. In *Reflections on the Revolution in France* (1790), Edmund Burke (1729–1797), a leading British statesman and political thinker, attacked the violence and fundamental principles of the Revolution. Thomas Paine (1737–1809), a prominent figure in the American Revolution — his *Common Sense* (1776) was a stirring appeal for independence — responded to Burke's attack on the French Revolution in his *Rights of Man* (1791–1792).

Edmund Burke
≪ REFLECTIONS ON THE REVOLUTION IN FRANCE ≫

Burke regarded the revolutionaries as wild-eyed fanatics who had uprooted all established authority, tradition, and institutions, thereby plunging France into anarchy. Not sharing the faith of the philosophes in human goodness, Burke held that without the restraints of established authority, people revert to savagery. For Burke, monarchy, aristocracy, and Christianity represented civilizing forces that tamed the beast in human nature. By undermining venerable institutions, he said, the French revolutionaries had opened the door to anarchy and terror. Burke's *Reflections,* excerpts of which follow, was instrumental in the shaping of conservative thought.

. . . You [revolutionaries] chose to act as if you had never been moulded into civil society, and had every thing to begin anew. You began ill, because you began by despising every thing that belonged to you. . . . If the last generations of your country appeared without much lustre in your eyes, you might have passed them by, and derived your claims from a more early race of ancestors. Under a pious predilection for those ancestors, your imaginations would have realized in them a standard of virtue and wisdom, beyond the vulgar practice of the hour: and you would have risen with the example to whose imitation you aspired. Respecting your forefathers, you would have been taught to re-spect yourselves. You would not have chosen to consider the French as a people of yesterday, as a nation of low-born servile wretches, until the emancipating year of 1789. . . . By following wise examples you would have given new examples of wisdom to the world. You would have rendered the cause of liberty venerable in the eyes of every worthy mind in every nation. . . . You would have had a free constitution; a potent monarchy; a disciplined army; a reformed and venerated clergy; a mitigated but spirited nobility, to lead your virtue. . . .

Compute your gains: see what is got by those extravagant and presumptuous speculations which have taught your leaders to despise all their predecessors, and all their contemporaries, and even to despise themselves, until the moment in which they became truly despicable. By following those false lights, France has bought undisguised calamities at a higher price than any nation has purchased the most unequivocal blessings! . . . France, when she let loose the reins of regal authority, doubled the licence, of a ferocious dissoluteness in manners, and of an insolent irreligion in opinions and practices; and has extended through all ranks of life. . . . all the unhappy corruptions that usually were the disease of wealth and power. This is one of the new principles of equality in France. . . .

. . . The science of government being therefore so practical in itself, and intended for such practical purposes, a matter which requires experience, and even more experience than any person can gain in his whole life, however sagacious and observing he may be, it is with infinite caution that any man ought to venture upon pulling down an edifice which has answered in any tolerable degree for ages the common purposes of society, or on building it up again, without having models and patterns of approved utility before his eyes. . . .

. . . The nature of man is intricate; the objects of society are of the greatest possible complexity; and therefore no simple disposition or direction of power can be suitable either to man's nature, or to the quality of his affairs.

When ancient opinions of life are taken away, the loss cannot possibly be estimated. From that moment we have no compass to govern us; nor can we know distinctly to what port we steer. . . .

. . . Nothing is more certain than that our manners, our civilization, and all the good things which are connected with manners and with civilization have, in this European world of ours, depended for ages upon two principles and were, indeed, the result of both combined: I mean the spirit of a gentleman and the spirit of religion. . . .

▷ Burke next compares the English people with the French revolutionaries.

. . . Thanks to our sullen resistance to innovation, thanks to the cold sluggishness of our national character, we still bear the stamp of our forefathers. . . . We are not the converts of Rousseau; we are not the disciples of Voltaire; Helvetius has made no progress amongst us.[1] Atheists are not our preachers; madmen are not our lawgivers. We know that *we* have made no discoveries, and we think that no discoveries are to be made, in morality nor many in the great principles of government. . . . We fear God; we look up with awe to kings, with affection to parliaments, with duty to magistrates, with reverence to priests, and with respect to nobility. . . .

. . . We are afraid to put men to live and trade each on his own private stock of reason, because we suspect that this stock in each man is small, and that the individuals would do better to avail themselves of the general bank and capital of nations and of ages.

---

[1]Rousseau, Voltaire, and Helvetius were French philosophes of the eighteenth century noted, respectively, for advocating democracy, attacking the abuses of the Old Regime, and applying scientific reason to moral principles.

Thomas Paine
≪ RIGHTS OF MAN ≫

In his *Rights of Man,* excerpted below, Thomas Paine argued that reason, not tradition, was the proper foundation of government. He defended the principle of natural rights and insisted that as a form of government, a republic was superior to hereditary monarchy or aristocracy.

Among the incivilities by which nations or individuals provoke and irritate each other, Mr. Burke's pamphlet on the French Revolution is an extraordinary instance. . . . There is scarcely an epithet of abuse to be found in the English language with which Mr. Burke has not loaded the French nation and the National Assembly. Everything which rancor, prejudice, ignorance, or knowledge could suggest are poured forth in the copious fury of near four hundred pages. . . .

The two modes of government which prevail in the world are, first, government by election and representation; secondly, government by hereditary succession. The former is generally known by the name of republic; the latter by that of monarchy and aristocracy.

Those two distinct and opposite forms erect themselves on the two distinct and opposite bases of reason and ignorance. As the exercise of government requires talents and abilities, and as talents and abilities cannot have hereditary descent, it is evident that hereditary succession requires a belief from man to which his reason cannot subscribe and which can only be established upon his ignorance; and the more ignorant any country is, the better it is fitted for this species of government.

On the contrary, government in a well-constituted republic requires no belief from man beyond what his reason can give. He sees the rationale of the whole system, its origin and its operation; and as it is best supported when best understood, the human faculties act with boldness and acquire, under this form of government, a gigantic manliness.

. . . Each of those forms acts on a different base — the one moving freely by the aid of reason, the other by ignorance. . . .

All hereditary government is in its nature tyranny. A heritable crown or a heritable throne, or by what other fanciful name such things may be called, have no other significant explanation than that mankind are heritable property. To inherit a government is to inherit the people, as if they were flocks and herds. . . .

We have heard the rights of man called a *leveling* system,[1] but the only system to which the word "leveling" is truly applicable is the hereditary monarchical system. It is a system of *mental leveling*. It indiscriminately admits every species of character to the same authority. Vice and virtue, ignorance and wisdom, in short, every quality, good or bad, is put on the same level. Kings succeed each other, not as [rational men], but as animals. It signifies not what their mental or moral characters are.

Passing over, for the present, all the evils and mischiefs which monarchy has occasioned in the world, nothing can more effectually prove its uselessness in a state of *civil government* than making it hereditary. Would we make any office hereditary that required wisdom and abilities to fill it? . . .

It requires some talents to be a common mechanic, but to be a king requires only the animal figure of a man — a sort of breathing automaton. This sort of superstition may last a few years more, but it cannot long resist the awakened reason and interest of man. . . .

As this is the order of nature, the order of government must necessarily follow it, or government will, as we see it does, degenerate into ignorance. The hereditary system, therefore, is as repugnant to human wisdom as to human rights and is as absurd as it is unjust.

As the republic of letters brings forward the best literary productions by giving to genius a fair and universal chance, so the representative system of government is calculated to produce the wisest laws by collecting wisdom where it can be found. I smile to myself when I contem-

[1]To aristocratic critics, the principle of the rights of man reduced those who were naturally better to the level of their inferiors.

plate the ridiculous insignificance into which literature and all the sciences would sink were they made hereditary, and I carry the same idea into governments. A hereditary governor is as inconsistent as a hereditary author. I know not whether Homer or Euclid[2] had sons, but I will venture an opinion that if they had, and had left their works unfinished, those sons could not have completed them.

Do we need a stronger evidence of the ab-

surdity of hereditary government than is seen in the descendants of those men, in any line of life, who once were famous? Is there scarcely an instance in which there is not a total reverse of character? It appears as if the tide of mental faculties flowed as far as it could in certain channels, and then forsook its course and arose in others. How irrational then is the hereditary system which establishes channels of power, in company with which wisdom refuses to flow! By continuing this absurdity, man is perpetually in contradiction with himself; he accepts for a king or a chief magistrate or a legislator a person whom he would not elect for a constable.

---

[2]Homer, ancient Greek epic poet, composed the *Odyssey* and the *Iliad*. Euclid was a Greek mathematician of the third century B.C. who systematized the principles of geometry.

REVIEW QUESTIONS

1. Why was Edmund Burke opposed to the French Revolution?
2. Why did Burke regard "resistance to innovation" and the "cold sluggishness of our national character" as virtues?
3. On what grounds did Thomas Paine defend the French Revolution?
4. According to Paine, how did the two modes of government that prevailed in the world — monarchy and republic — differ from one another?
5. Compare and contrast the attitudes of Burke and Paine toward (1) the historical past, (2) liberty and natural rights, (3) reason, and (4) the philosophes.

▼▼▼

4 ▼ Robespierre and the Reign of Terror

In the summer of 1793 the French Republic was threatened with internal insurrection and foreign invasion. During this period of acute crisis, the Jacobins provided strong leadership. They organized a large national army of citizen soldiers who, imbued with love for the nation, routed the invaders on the northern frontier. To deal with internal enemies, the Jacobins instituted the Reign of Terror, in which Maximilien Robespierre (1758–1794) played a pivotal role.

Most Jacobins, including Robespierre, supported terror not because they were bloodthirsty or power mad. Rather, they were idealists who believed that terror was necessary to rescue the Republic and the Revolution from destruction. Deeply committed to republican democracy, Robespierre saw himself as the bearer of a higher faith, molding a new society founded on reason, good citizenship, patriotism, and virtue. Robespierre viewed those who prevented the implementation of this new society as traitors and sinners who had to be killed for the good of humanity.

Maximilien Robespierre
REPUBLIC OF VIRTUE

In his speech of February 5, 1794, Robespierre provided a comprehensive statement of his political theory in which he equated democracy with virtue and justified the use of terror in defending democracy.

What is the objective toward which we are reaching? The peaceful enjoyment of liberty and equality; the reign of that eternal justice whose laws are engraved not on marble or stone but in the hearts of all men, even in the heart of the slave who has forgotten them or of the tyrant who disowns them.

We wish an order of things where all the low and cruel passions will be curbed, all the beneficent and generous passions awakened by the laws, where ambition will be a desire to deserve glory and serve the *patrie* [nation]; where distinctions grow only out of the very system of equality; where the citizen will be subject to the authority of the magistrate, the magistrate to that of the people, and the people to that of justice; where the *patrie* assures the well-being of each individual, and where each individual shares with pride the prosperity and glory of the *patrie*; where every soul expands by the continual communication of republican sentiments, and by the need to merit the esteem of a great people; where the arts will embellish the liberty that ennobles them, and commerce will be the source of public wealth and not merely of the monstrous riches of a few families.

We wish to substitute in our country . . . all the virtues and miracles of the republic for all the vices and absurdities of the monarchy.

We wish, in a word, to fulfill the intentions of nature and the destiny of humanity, realize the promises of philosophy, and acquit providence of the long reign of crime and tyranny. We wish that France, once illustrious among enslaved nations, may, while eclipsing the glory of all the free peoples that ever existed, become a model to nations, a terror to oppressors, a consolation to the oppressed, an ornament of the universe; and that, by sealing our work with our blood, we may witness at least the dawn of universal happiness — this is our ambition, this is our aim.

What kind of government can realize these prodigies [great deeds]? A democratic or republican government only. . . .

A democracy is a state where the sovereign people, guided by laws of their own making, do for themselves everything that they can do well, and by means of delegates everything that they cannot do for themselves.

It is therefore in the principles of democratic government that you must seek the rules of your political conduct.

But in order to found democracy and consolidate it among us, in order to attain the peaceful reign of constitutional laws, we must complete the war of liberty against tyranny; . . . [S]uch is the aim of the revolutionary government that you have organized. . . .

But the French are the first people in the world who have established true democracy by calling all men to equality and to full enjoyment of the rights of citizenship; and that is, in my opinion, the true reason why all the tyrants leagued against the republic will be vanquished.

There are from this moment great conclusions to be drawn from the principles that we have just laid down.

Since virtue [good citizenship] and equality are the soul of the republic, and your aim is to found and to consolidate the republic, it follows that the first rule of your political conduct must be to relate all of your measures to the maintenance of equality and to the development of virtue; for the first care of the legislator must be to strengthen the principles on which the government rests. Hence all that tends to excite a love of country, to purify moral standards, to exalt souls, to direct the passions of the human heart toward the public good must be adopted or established by you. All that tends to concentrate and debase them into selfish egotism, to awaken an infatuation for trivial things, and scorn for great ones, must be rejected or repressed by you. In the system of the French revolution, that which is immoral is impolitic, and that which tends to corrupt is counterrevolutionary. Weakness, vices, and prejudices are the road to monarchy. . . .

. . . Externally all the despots surround you; internally all the friends of tyranny conspire. . . . It is necessary to annihilate both the internal and external enemies of the republic or perish with its fall. Now, in this situation your first political maxim should be that one guides the people by reason, and the enemies of the people by terror.

If the driving force of popular government in peacetime is virtue, that of popular government during a revolution is both *virtue and terror*: virtue, without which terror is destructive; terror, without which virtue is impotent. Terror is only justice that is prompt, severe, and inflexible; it is thus an emanation of virtue; it is less a distinct principle than a consequence of the general principle of democracy applied to the most pressing needs of the *patrie*.

▷   In a series of notes written in the summer of 1793, Robespierre expressed his policy toward counterrevolutionaries.

[DESPOTISM IN DEFENSE OF LIBERTY]

What is our goal? The enforcement of the constitution for the benefit of the people.

Who will our enemies be? The vicious and the rich.

What means will they employ? Slander and hypocrisy.

What things may be favorable for the employment of these? The ignorance of the *sans-culottes*.[1]

The people must therefore be enlightened. But what are the obstacles to the enlightenment of the people? Mercenary writers who daily mislead them with impudent falsehoods.

What conclusions may be drawn from this? 1. These writers must be proscribed as the most dangerous enemies of the people. 2. Right-minded literature must be scattered about in profusion.

What are the other obstacles to the establishment of liberty? Foreign war and civil war.

How can foreign war be ended? By putting republican generals in command of our armies and punishing those who have betrayed us.

How can civil war be ended? By punishing traitors and conspirators, particularly if they are deputies or administrators; by sending loyal troops under patriotic leaders to subdue the aristocrats of Lyon, Marseille, Toulon, the Vendée, the Jura, and all other regions in which the standards of rebellion and royalism have been raised; and by making frightful examples of all scoundrels who have outraged liberty and spilled the blood of patriots.

1. Proscription [condemnation] of perfidious and counter-revolutionary writers and propagation of proper literature.
2. Punishment of traitors and conspirators, particularly deputies and administrators.
3. Appointment of patriotic generals; dismissal and punishment of others.
4. Sustenance and laws for the people.

---

[1]*Sans-culottes* literally means without the fancy breeches worn by the aristocracy. The term refers generally to a poor city dweller (who wore simple trousers). Champions of equality, the sans-culottes hated the aristocracy and the powerful bourgeoisie.

REVIEW QUESTIONS

1. Compare and contrast Maximilien Robespierre's vision of the Republic of Virtue with the ideals of the Declaration of the Rights of Man and of Citizens in Section 2. What did Robespierre mean by virtue?
2. What distinction did Robespierre draw between constitutional and revolutionary government?
3. On what grounds did Robespierre justify terror?
4. Like medieval inquisitors, Robespierre regarded people with different views not as opponents but as sinners. Discuss this statement.

▼▼▼

5 ▼ Napoleon: Destroyer and Preserver of the Revolution

In 1799, a group of conspirators that included Napoleon Bonaparte (1769–1821), an ambitious and popular general, staged a successful coup d'état. Within a short time, Napoleon became a one-man ruler, and in 1804 he crowned himself emperor of the French. Under Napoleon's military dictatorship, political freedom (a principal goal of the French Revolution) was suppressed. Nevertheless, Napoleon preserved, strengthened, and spread to other lands many of the Revolution's reforms. He supported religious tolerance, secular education, and access to positions according to ability; he would not restore the privileges of the aristocracy and church.

Napoleon Bonaparte LEADER, GENERAL, TYRANT, REFORMER

Napoleon was a brilliant military commander who carefully planned each campaign and resorted to speed, deception, and surprise to confuse and demoralize his opponents. By rapid marches, Napoleon would concentrate a superior force against a segment of the enemy's strung-out forces. Recognizing the importance of good morale, he sought to inspire his troops by appealing to their honor, their vanity, and their love of France.

In 1796, Napoleon, then a young officer, was given command of the French army in Italy. In the Italian campaign, he demonstrated a genius for propaganda and psychological warfare, as the following proclamations to his troops indicate.

[LEADER AND GENERAL]

[March 27, 1796]

Soldiers, you are naked, ill fed! The Government owes you much; it can give you nothing.

Your patience, the courage you display in the midst of these rocks, are admirable; but they procure you no glory, no fame is reflected upon you. I seek to lead you into the most fertile plains in the world. Rich provinces, great cities will be in your power. There you will find honor, glory, and riches. Soldiers of Italy, would you be lacking in courage or constancy?

[*April 26, 1796*]

Soldiers:

In a fortnight you have won six victories, taken twenty-one standards, fifty-five pieces of artillery, several strong positions, and conquered the richest part of Piedmont [a region in northern Italy]; you have captured 15,000 prisoners and killed or wounded more than 10,000 men. . . .

. . . You have won battles without cannon, crossed rivers without bridges, made forced marches without shoes, camped without brandy and often without bread. Soldiers of liberty, only republican phalanxes [infantry troops] could have endured what you have endured. Soldiers, you have our thanks! The grateful *Patrie* [nation] will owe its prosperity to you. . . .

The two armies which but recently attacked you with audacity are fleeing before you in terror; the wicked men who laughed at your misery and rejoiced at the thought of the triumphs of your enemies are confounded and trembling.

But, soldiers, as yet you have done nothing compared with what remains to be done. . . .

. . . Undoubtedly the greatest obstacles have been overcome; but you still have battles to fight, cities to capture, rivers to cross. Is there one among you whose courage is abating? . . . No. . . . All of you are consumed with a desire to extend the glory of the French people; all of you long to humiliate those arrogant kings who dare to contemplate placing us in fetters; all of you desire to dictate a glorious peace, one which will indemnify the *Patrie* for the immense sacrifices it has made; all of you wish to be able to say with pride as you return to your villages, "I was with the victorious army of Italy!"

Friends, I promise you this conquest; but there is one condition you must swear to fulfill — to respect the people whom you liberate,

to repress the horrible pillaging committed by scoundrels incited by our enemies. Otherwise you would not be the liberators of the people; you would be their scourge. . . . Plunderers will be shot without mercy; already, several have been. . . .

Peoples of Italy, the French army comes to break your chains; the French people is the friend of all peoples; approach it with confidence; your property, your religion, and your customs will be respected.

We are waging war as generous enemies, and we wish only to crush the tyrants who enslave you.

▷   The following passages from Napoleon's diary shed light on his generalship, ambition, and leadership qualities.

[*1800*]

What a thing is imagination! Here are men who don't know me, who have never seen me, but who only knew of me, and they are moved by my presence, they would do anything for me! And this same incident arises in all centuries and in all countries! Such is fanaticism! Yes, imagination rules the world. The defect of our modern institutions is that they do not speak to the imagination. By that alone can man be governed; without it he is but a brute.

[*1800*]

The impact of an army, like the total of mechanical coefficients, is equal to the mass multiplied by the velocity.

A battle is a dramatic action which has its beginning, its middle, and its conclusion. The result of a battle depends on the instantaneous flash of an idea. When you are about to give battle concentrate all your strength, neglect nothing; a battalion often decides the day.

In warfare every opportunity must be seized; for fortune is a woman: if you miss her to-day, you need not expect to find her to-morrow.

There is nothing in the military profession I cannot do for myself. If there is no one to make gunpowder, I know how to make it; gun carriages, I know how to construct them; if it is founding a cannon, I know that; or if the details of tactics must be taught, I can teach them.

The presence of a general is necessary: he is the head, he is the all in all of an army. It was not the Roman army conquered Gaul, but Cæsar; it was not the Carthaginians made the armies of the Republic tremble at the very gates of Rome, but Hannibal; it was not the Macedonian army marched to the Indus [River], but Alexander; . . . it was not the Prussian army that defended Prussia during seven years against the three strongest Powers of Europe, but Frederick the Great.

Concentration of forces, activity, activity with the firm resolve to die gloriously: these are the three great principles of the military art that have always made fortune favourable in all my operations. Death is nothing; but to live defeated and ingloriously, is to die every day.

I am a soldier, because that is the special faculty I was born with; that is my life, my habit. I have commanded wherever I have been. I commanded, when twenty-three years old, at the siege of Toulon; . . . I carried the soldiers of the army of Italy with me as soon as I appeared among them; I was born that way. . . .

It was by becoming a Catholic that I pacified the Vendée [region in western France], and a [Muslim] that I established myself in Egypt; it was by becoming ultramontane[1] that I won over public opinion in Italy. If I ruled a people of Jews, I would rebuild the temple of Solomon! Paradise is a central spot whither the souls of men proceed along different roads; every sect has a road of its own. . . .

[*1802*]

My power proceeds from my reputation, and my reputation from the victories I have won.

My power would fall if I were not to support it with more glory and more victories. Conquest has made me what I am; only conquest can maintain me. . . .

[*1804*]

My mistress is power; I have done too much to conquer her to let her be snatched away from me. Although it may be said that power came to me of its own accord, yet I know what labour, what sleepless nights, what scheming, it has involved. . . .

[*1809*]

Again I repeat that in war morale and opinion are half the battle. The art of the great captain has always been to make his troops appear very numerous to the enemy, and the enemy's very few to his own. So that to-day, in spite of the long time we have spent in Germany, the enemy do not know my real strength. We are constantly striving to magnify our numbers. Far from confessing that I had only 100,000 men at Wagram [French victory over Austria in 1809] I am constantly suggesting that I had 220,000. In my Italian campaigns, in which I had only a handful of troops, I always exaggerated my numbers. It served my purpose, and has not lessened my glory. My generals and practised soldiers could always perceive, after the event, all the skilfulness of my operations, even that of having exaggerated the numbers of my troops.

▷ In several ways, Napoleon anticipated the strategies of twentieth-century dictators. He concentrated power in his own hands, suppressed opposition, and sought to mold public opinion by controlling the press and education. The following Imperial Catechism of 1806, which schoolchildren were required to memorize and recite, is a pointed example of Napoleonic indoctrination.

---

[1]Favoring the pope over competing authorities.

[TYRANT]

Lesson VII. Continuation of the Fourth Commandment.

Q. What are the duties of Christians with respect to the princes who govern them, and what in particular are our duties towards Napoleon I, our Emperor?

A. Christians owe to the princes who govern them, and we owe in particular to Napoleon I, our Emperor, *love, respect, obedience, fidelity, military service* and the tributes laid for the preservation and defence of the Empire and of his throne; we also owe to him fervent prayers for his safety and the spiritual and temporal prosperity of the state.

Q. Why are we bound to all these duties towards our Emperor?

A. First of all, because God, who creates empires and distributes them according to His will, in loading our Emperor with gifts, both in peace and in war, has established him as our sovereign and has made him the minister of His power and His image upon the earth. *To honor and to serve our Emperor is then to honor and to serve God himself.* Secondly, because our Lord Jesus Christ by His doctrine as well as by His example, has Himself taught us what we owe to our sovereign: He was born the subject of Caesar Augustus;[1] He paid the prescribed impost; and just as He ordered to render to God that which belongs to God, so He ordered to render to Caesar that which belongs to Caesar.

Q. Are there not particular reasons which ought to attach us more strongly to Napoleon I, our Emperor?

A. Yes; for it is he whom God has raised up under difficult circumstances to re-establish the public worship of the holy religion of our fathers and to be the protector of it. He has restored and preserved public order by his profound and active wisdom; he defends the state by his powerful arm; he has become the anointed of the Lord through the consecration

which he received from the sovereign pontiff, head of the universal church.

Q. What ought to be thought of those who may be lacking in their duty towards our Emperor?

A. According to the apostle Saint Paul, they would be resisting the order established by God himself and would render themselves *worthy of eternal damnation.*

Q. Will the duties which are required of us towards our Emperor be equally binding with respect to his lawful successors in the order established by the constitutions of the Empire?

A. Yes, without doubt; for we read in the holy scriptures, that God, Lord of heaven and earth, by an order of His supreme will and through His providence, gives empires not only to one person in particular, but also to his family.

▷ In the following letter (April 22, 1805) to Joseph Fouché, minister of police, Napoleon reveals his intention to regulate public opinion.

Repress the journals a little; make them produce wholesome articles. I want you to write to the editors of the . . . newspapers that are most widely read in order to let them know that the time is not far away when, seeing that they are no longer of service to me, I shall suppress them along with all the others. . . . Tell them that the . . . Revolution is over, and that there is now only one party in France; that I shall never allow the newspapers to say anything contrary to my interests; that they may publish a few little articles with just a bit of poison in them, but that one fine day somebody will shut their mouths.

▷ With varying degrees of success, Napoleon's administrations in conquered lands provided positions based on talent, equalized taxes, and abolished serfdom and the courts of the nobility. They promoted freedom of religion, fought clerical interference with secular authority, and promoted secular education. By undermining the power of European clergy and aristocrats,

---

[1]Caesar Augustus (27 B.C.–A.D. 14) was the Roman emperor at the time that Jesus was born.

Napoleon weakened the Old Regime irreparably in much of Europe. A letter from Napoleon to his brother Jérôme, King of Westphalia, illustrates Napoleon's desire for enlightened rule.

[REFORMER]

To Jérôme Napoléon, King of Westphalia
Fontainebleau, November 15, 1807.

I enclose the Constitution for your Kingdom. It embodies the conditions on which I renounce all my rights of conquest, and all the claims I have acquired over your state. You must faithfully observe it. I am concerned for the happiness of your subjects, not only as it affects your reputation, and my own, but also for its influence on the whole European situation. Don't listen to those who say that your subjects are so accustomed to slavery that they will feel no gratitude for the benefits you give them. There is more intelligence in the Kingdom of Westphalia than they would have you believe; and your throne will never be firmly established except upon the trust and affection of the common people. What German opinion impatiently demands is that men of no rank, but of marked ability, shall have an equal claim upon your favour and your employment, and that every trace of serfdom, or of a feudal hierarchy between the sovereign and the lowest class of his subjects, shall be done away. The benefits of the Code Napoléon, public trial, and the introduction of juries, will be the leading features of your government. And to tell you the truth, I count more upon their effects, for the extension and consolidation of your rule, than upon the most resounding victories. I want your subjects to enjoy a degree of liberty, equality, and prosperity hitherto unknown to the German people. I want this liberal regime to produce, one way or another, changes which will be of the utmost benefit to the system of the Confederation, and to the strength of your monarchy. Such a method of government will be a stronger barrier between you and Prussia than the Elbe [River], the fortresses, and the protection of France. What people will want to return under the arbitrary Prussian rule, once it has tasted the benefits of a wise and liberal administration? In Germany, as in France, Italy, and Spain, people long for equality and liberalism. I have been managing the affairs of Europe long enough now to know that the burden of the privileged classes was resented everywhere. Rule constitutionally. Even if reason, and the enlightenment of the age, were not sufficient cause, it would be good policy for one in your position; and you will find that the backing of public opinion gives you a great natural advantage over the absolute Kings who are your neighbours.

REVIEW QUESTIONS

how does he describe fortune?

1. In his proclamations how did Napoleon Bonaparte try to raise the morale of his troops? *promises of greater things, extend glory of Fr.*
2. How did Napoleon try to appeal to the Italians? — *we come to break your chains*
3. What did Napoleon mean by imagination? Why did he value it? *Rules the world - how easily men are led*
4. What was the role of the general in Napoleon's view of military strategy? *- necessary, leader*
5. How did Napoleon use propaganda to achieve his goals?
6. What was the purpose of Napoleon's Imperial Catechism of 1806? *to bind people to emp.'s will*
7. How did the appeal to religion help to fulfill the underlying purpose of the catechism? What would Machiavelli have thought of this device?
8. Do you see any similarities of method between Napoleon's proclamations to his troops and the Imperial Catechism? Any differences?
9. How seriously did Napoleon adhere to the ideals of the Enlightenment and French Revolution?
10. Show how Napoleon spread the reforms of the Enlightenment.

CHAPTER

▼▼▼

5

Romanticism, Reaction, Revolution

In 1815 the European scene had changed. Napoleon was exiled to the island of St. Helena, and a Bourbon king, in the person of Louis XVIII, again reigned in France. The Great Powers of Europe, meeting at Vienna, had drawn up a peace settlement that awarded territory to the states that had fought Napoleon and restored to power some rulers dethroned by the French emperor. The Congress of Vienna also organized the Concert of Europe to guard against a resurgence of the revolutionary spirit that had kept Europe in turmoil for some twenty-five years. The conservative leaders of Europe wanted no more Robespierres who resorted to terror and no more Napoleons who sought to dominate the continent.

However, reactionary rulers' efforts to turn the clock back to the Old Regime could not contain the forces unleashed by the French Revolution. Between 1820 and 1848 a series of revolts rocked Europe. The principal causes were liberalism (which demanded constitutional government and the protection of the freedom and rights of the individual citizen) and nationalism (which called for the reawakening and unification of the nation and its liberation from foreign domination).

In the 1820s, the Concert of Europe crushed a quasi-liberal revolution in Spain and liberal uprisings in Italy, and Tsar Nicholas I subdued liberal aristocrats who challenged tsarist autocracy. The Greeks, however, successfully fought for independence from the Ottoman Turks.

Between 1830 and 1832, another wave of revolutions swept over Europe. Italian liberals and nationalists failed to free Italy from foreign rule or to wrest reforms from autocratic princes, and the tsar's troops crushed a Polish bid for independence from Russian rule. But in France, rebels overthrew the reactionary Bourbon Charles X in 1830 and replaced him with a more moderate ruler, Louis Philippe; a little later Belgium gained its independence from Holland.

The year 1848 was decisive in the struggle for liberty and nationhood. In France, democrats overthrew Louis Philippe and established a republic that gave all men the right to vote. However, in Italy and Germany, revolutions attempting to unify each land failed, as did a bid in Hungary for

LIBERTY LEADING THE PEOPLE, 1830, by Eugene Delacroix (1798–1863). Combining Romantic style with political beliefs in this painting, Delacroix commemorates the French Revolution of 1830, when the reactionary Charles X was replaced by Louis Philippe. (*Giraudon/Art Resource, N.Y.*)

111

independence from the Hapsburg Empire. After enjoying initial successes, the revolutionaries were crushed by superior might, and their liberal and nationalist objectives remained largely unfulfilled. By 1870, however, many nationalist aspirations had been realized. The Hapsburg Empire granted Hungary autonomy in 1867, and during 1870–1871, the period of the Franco-Prussian War, Germany and Italy became unified states. That authoritarian and militaristic Prussia unified Germany, rather than liberals like those who had fought in the revolutions of 1848, affected the future of Europe.

In the early nineteenth century a new cultural orientation, romanticism, emphasized the liberation of human emotions and the free expression of personality in artistic creations. The romantics' attack on the rationalism of the Enlightenment and their veneration of the past influenced conservative thought, and their concern for a people's history and traditions contributed to the development of nationalism. By encouraging innovation in art, music, and literature, the romantics greatly enriched European cultural life.

▼▼▼

I ▼ Romanticism

Romantics attacked the outlook of the Enlightenment, protesting that the philosophes' excessive intellectualizing and their mechanistic view of the physical world and human nature distorted and fettered the human spirit and thwarted cultural creativity. The rationalism of the philosophes, said the romantics, had reduced human beings into soulless thinking machines, and vibrant nature into lifeless wheels, cogs, and pulleys. In contrast to the philosophes' scientific and analytic approach, the romantics asserted the intrinsic value of emotions and imagination and extolled the spontaneity, richness, and uniqueness of the human spirit. To the philosophes, the emotions obstructed clear thinking.

For romantics, feelings and imagination were the human essence, the source of cultural creativity, and the avenue to true understanding. Their beliefs led the romantics to rebel against strict standards of esthetics that governed artistic creations. They held that artists, musicians, and writers must trust their own sensibilities and inventiveness and must not be bound by textbook rules; the romantics focused on the creative capacities inherent in the emotions and urged individuality and freedom of expression in the arts. In the Age of Romanticism, the artist and poet succeeded the scientist as the arbiters of Western civilization.

William Wordsworth
≪ LYRICAL BALLADS ≫
AND ≪ TABLES TURNED ≫

The works of the great English poet William Wordsworth (1770–1850) exemplify many tendencies of the Romantic Movement. In the interval during which he tried to come to grips with his disenchantment with the French Revolution, Wordsworth's creativity reached its height. In the preface to *Lyrical Ballads* (1798), excerpted below, Wordsworth produced what has become known as the manifesto of romanticism. He wanted poetry to express powerful feelings and also contended that because it is a vehicle for the imagination, poetry is the source of truth. Wordsworth thus represented a shift in perspective comparable to the shift begun by Descartes in philosophy, but for Wordsworth imagination and feeling, not mathematics and logic, yielded highest truth.

The philosophes had regarded nature as a giant machine, all of whose parts worked in perfect precision and whose laws could be uncovered through the scientific method. The romantics rejected this mechanical model. To them, nature was a living organism filled with beautiful forms whose inner meaning was grasped through the human imagination; they sought from nature a higher truth than mechanical law. In "Tables Turned," Wordsworth exalts nature as humanity's teacher.

PREFACE TO LYRICAL BALLADS

. . . Aristotle, I have been told, hath said, that Poetry is the most philosophic of all writing: it is so: its object is truth, not individual and local, but general, and operative; not standing upon external testimony, but carried alive into the heart by passion; truth which is its own testimony, which gives strength and divinity to the tribunal to which it appeals, and receives them from the same tribunal. Poetry is the image of man and nature. . . .

To this knowledge which all men carry about with them, and to these sympathies in which without any other discipline than that of our daily life we are fitted to take delight, the Poet principally directs his attention. He considers man and nature as essentially adapted to each other, and the mind of man as naturally the mirror of the fairest and most interesting qualities of nature. . . . The Man of Science seeks truth as a remote and unknown benefactor; he cherishes and loves it in his solitude: the Poet,

singing a song in which all human beings join with him, rejoices in the presence of truth as our visible friend and hourly companion. Poetry is the breath and finer spirit of all knowledge: it is the impassioned expression which is in the countenance of all Science. Emphatically may it be said of the Poet, as Shakespeare hath said of man, "that he looks before and after." He is the rock of defence of human nature; an upholder and preserver, carrying every where with him relationship and love. In spite of difference of soil and climate, of language and manners, of laws and customs, in spite of things silently gone out of mind and things violently destroyed, the Poet binds together by passion and knowledge the vast empire of human society, as it is spread over the whole earth, and over all time. The objects of the Poet's thoughts are every where; though the eyes and senses of men are, it is true, his favourite guides, yet he will follow wheresoever he can find an atmosphere of sensation in which to move his wings. Poetry is the first and last of all knowledge — it is as immortal as the heart of man.

TABLES TURNED

Up! up! my Friend, and quit your books;
Or surely you'll grow double:
Up! up! my Friend, and clear your looks;
Why all this toil and trouble?

The sun, above the mountain's head,
A freshening lustre mellow
Through all the long green fields has spread,
His first sweet evening yellow.

Books! 'tis a dull and endless strife:
Come, hear the woodland linnet [Old World
   finch],
How sweet his music! on my life,
There's more of wisdom in it.

And hark! how blithe the throstle [thrush] sings!
He, too, is no mean preacher:
Come forth into the light of things,
Let Nature be your Teacher.

She has a world of ready wealth,
Our minds and hearts to bless —
Spontaneous wisdom breathed by health,
Truth breathed by cheerfulness.

One impulse from a vernal wood
May teach you more of man,
Of moral evil and of good,
Than all the sages can.

Sweet is the lore which Nature brings;
Our meddling intellect
Mis-shapes the beauteous forms of things: —
We murder to dissect.

Enough of Science and of Art;
Close up those barren leaves [book pages];
Come forth, and bring with you a heart
That watches and receives.

William Blake
≪ MILTON ≫

William Blake (1757–1827) was a British engraver, poet, and religious mystic. He also affirmed the creative potential of the imagination and expressed distaste for the rationalist-scientific outlook of the Enlightenment, as is clear from these lines in his poem "Milton."

. . . the Reasoning Power in Man:
This is a false Body; an Incrustation [scab] over
   my Immortal
Spirit; a Selfhood, which must be put off &
   annihilated alway[s]
To cleanse the Face of my Spirit by Self-
   examination,

41 . . .

To bathe in the Waters of Life, to wash off the
   Not Human,
I come in Self-annihilation & the grandeur of
   Inspiration,

To cast off Rational Demonstration by Faith in
   the Saviour,
To cast off the rotten rags of Memory by
   Inspiration,
To cast off Bacon, Locke & Newton from
   Albion's covering,[1]
To take off his filthy garments & clothe him
   with Imagination,
To cast aside from Poetry all that is not
   Inspiration,

---

[1]Bacon, Locke, and Newton were British thinkers who valued reason and science, and Albion is an ancient name for England.

That it no longer shall dare to mock with the aspersion of Madness

. . .

To cast off the idiot Questioner who is always questioning
But never capable of answering, who sits with a sly grin
Silent plotting when to question, like a thief in a cave,
Who publishes doubt & calls it knowledge, whose Science is Despair,
Whose pretence to knowledge is Envy, whose whole Science is

To destroy the wisdom of ages to gratify ravenous Envy
That rages round him like a Wolf day & night without rest:
He smiles with condescension, he talks of Benevolence & Virtue,
And those who act with Benevolence & Virtue they murder time on time.
These are the destroyers of Jerusalem, these are the murderers
Of Jesus, who deny the Faith & mock at Eternal Life. . . .

Johann Wolfgang von Goethe
≪ *FAUST* ≫

In *Faust,* Johann Wolfgang von Goethe (1749–1832), Germany's greatest poet, gave expression to the romantic's anguish and yearnings. The play begins in the study of the learned Dr. Faustus. He is a master of all knowledge but is spiritually anguished. He yearns for the innocence and life-affirming wisdom of youth, the inspiration of nature, and the joy and excitement of life's experiences. Science, philosophy, and theology no longer stimulate the troubled professor.

THE FIRST PART OF THE TRAGEDY
Night

(FAUST *in a narrow, high-vaulted Gothic chamber, sitting uneasily at the desk in his armchair.*)

FAUST Ah me! I've now studied thoroughly and with ardent effort philosophy, law, medicine, and even, alas! theology. And here I stand, poor fool, and am no wiser than before. I've the title of Master, even Doctor, and for ten years now I've been leading my pupils by the nose, up and down and back and forth — and realize that we can't know anything! And that is eating my heart out. True, I'm smarter than all these fops of Doctors, Masters, clerks, and preachers; nor am I tormented by scruple or doubt, or any fear of hell or devil. In return, I'm deprived of all joy. For I don't pretend to know anything worth knowing, or to be able to teach anything that might improve men or convert them. Then too, I've neither goods nor gold, nor is any worldly honor or glory mine. No dog would lead such a life as this! And so I've devoted myself to magic, hoping that through the power and speech of the spirit many a secret might become known to me; so that no longer, in a bitter sweat, I'll need to say things that I don't know to be true; and so that I may discern what holds the universe together in its deepest center, view all the working and germinal forces, and be done with this traffic in words.

O light of the full moon, would that you were gazing for the last time upon my pain, you whom I have seen, as I sat awake at this desk, rise through so many a midnight hour. Then, as now, it was over books and papers, mournful friend, that you appeared to me. Ah! could I but walk on mountain heights in your beloved radiance, hover with spirits about mountain caverns, rove over meadows in your dimness, and, unburdened of all this fog of learning, find health by bathing in your dew!

Woe! still stuck in this dungeon here? Accursed, musty hole-in-the-wall, where even the blessed light of heaven breaks but dimly through the painted panes! Hemmed in by this pile of books, which is gnawed by worms and covered with dust, and into which smoke-blackened papers are thrust all the way up to the vaulted ceiling; cluttered everywhere with flasks and jars, the place stuffed full of old instruments, and the junk of generations on top of that — that's your world! Men call that a world!

And still you ask why your heart is cramped with fear? Why an inexplicable pain inhibits every stir of life within you? Instead of living Nature, into which God put man at his creation, what surrounds you in smoke and mold is nothing but animal bones and human skeletons.

Up! flee! out into the open country! And this mysterious book, from the hand of Nostradamus* himself, is not guide enough for you? Then you will come to know the course of the stars, and with Nature instructing you the spirit power will dawn on you that tells you how spirit speaks with spirit. In vain does arid speculation try to explain the sacred symbols to you: Spirits, you are hovering near me: answer me, if you hear me! (*He opens the volume, and his glance falls on the sign of the Macrocosm.*†) Ha! what rapture, at this sight, floods all my senses at once! I feel a youthful, holy joy of life coursing like a new fire through my nerves and veins. Was it a god that wrote these symbols which still the turmoil within me, fill my poor heart with joy, and with a mysterious force unveil the powers of Nature round about me? Am I a god? Such brightness grows in me! In these pure lines I see before me creative Nature at work. Only now do I grasp the meaning of the Sage's word, "The spirit world is not barred; it is your mind that is closed, your heart that is dead! Up, neophyte, and bathe your earthly breast tirelessly in the glow of morning!" (*He studies the sign.*) How all things interweave to form the whole, each one working and living in the other, as if the heavenly forces were ascending and descending, passing the golden buckets from hand to hand, and pressing forward from heaven through the earth, their wings fragrant with blessings, until the entire universe resounds in one great harmony!

What a spectacle! But alas, no more than a spectacle. Where can I grasp you, infinite Nature? You breasts, where? Fountains of all life, to which both earth and heaven cling, toward which my languishing breast is straining — you swell, you give suck, and must I pine for you in vain?

---

*Nostradamus is the Latinized name of a French astrologer, Michel de Notredame (1503–66), who published a collection of prophecies which are still occasionally quoted; he wrote no such book as is attributed to him here.

†Medieval astrologers contrasted the "Macrocosm," their conception of the universe, with the "Microcosm" . . . man as a world-in-little.

REVIEW QUESTIONS

1. How did William Wordsworth feel that the human mind could arrive at truth? In what way did science and poetry diverge in the way they attained truth?
2. According to Wordsworth, how could the human being achieve goodness?
3. What did Wordsworth believe the role of the poet was?
4. In "Tables Turned," what connection did Wordsworth see between nature and the human mind? How did his idea of nature differ from that of the scientist's? According to Wordsworth, what effect did nature have on the imagination?
5. Why did William Blake attack reason?
6. How does the passage from *Faust* illustrate the romantic temperament?

7. The Romantic Movement was a reaction against the dominant ideas of the Enlightenment. Discuss this statement.

▼▼▼

2 ▼ Conservatism

In the period after 1815, conservatism was the principal ideology of those who repudiated the Enlightenment and the French Revolution. Conservatives valued tradition over reason, aristocratic and clerical authority over equality, and the community over the individual. Edmund Burke's *Reflections on the Revolution in France* (see page 99) was instrumental in shaping the conservative outlook. Another leading conservative was Joseph de Maistre (1753–1821), who fled his native Sardinia in 1792 (and again in 1793) after it was invaded by the armies of the new French Republic. De Maistre denounced the Enlightenment for spawning the French Revolution, defended the church as a civilizing agent that made individuals aware of their social obligations, and affirmed tradition as a model more valuable than instant reforms embodied in "paper constitutions."

The symbol of conservatism in the first half of the nineteenth century was Prince Klemens von Metternich (1773–1859) of Austria. A bitter opponent of Jacobinism and Napoleon, he became the pivotal figure at the Congress of Vienna (1814–1815), where European powers met to redraw the map of Europe after their victory over France. Metternich said that the Jacobins had subverted the pillars of civilization and that Napoleon, by harnessing the forces of the Revolution, had destroyed the traditional European state system. No peace was possible with Napoleon, who championed revolutionary doctrines and dethroned kings, and whose rule rested not on legitimacy but on conquest and charisma. No balance of power could endure such an adventurer who obliterated states and sought European domination.

Klemens von Metternich
CONFESSION OF POLITICAL FAITH

Two decades of revolutionary warfare had shaped Metternich's political thinking. After the fall of Napoleon, Metternich worked to restore the European balance and to suppress revolutionary movements. The following excerpt from his *Memoirs,* a memorandum to Tsar Alexander I, dated December 15, 1820, reveals Metternich's conservative outlook.

"L'Europe," a celebrated writer has recently said, *"fait aujourd'hui pitié à l'homme d'esprit et horreur à l'homme vertueux."*[1]

It would be difficult to comprise in a few words a more exact picture of the situation at the time we are writing these lines!

Kings have to calculate the chances of their very existence in the immediate future; passions are let loose, and league together to overthrow

---

[1]Europe today arouses pity in an intelligent man and horror in a man of virtue.

everything which society respects as the basis of its existence; religion, public morality, laws, customs, rights, and duties, all are attacked, confounded, overthrown, or called in question. . . .

What is the cause of all these evils? By what methods has this evil established itself, and how is it that it penetrates into every vein of the social body?

Do remedies still exist to arrest the progress of this evil, and what are they? . . .

Let us examine the matter!

▷ Metternich denounces the French philosophes for their "false systems" and "fatal errors" that weakened the social fabric and gave rise to the French Revolution. In their presumption, the philosophes forsook the experience and wisdom of the past, trusting only their own thoughts and inclinations.

The progress of the human mind has been extremely rapid in the course of the last three centuries. This progress having been accelerated more rapidly than the growth of wisdom (the only counterpoise to passions and to error); a revolution prepared by the false systems . . . has at last broken out. . . .

. . . There were . . . some men [the philosophes], unhappily endowed with great talents, who felt their own strength, and . . . who had the art to prepare and conduct men's minds to the triumph of their detestable enterprise — an enterprise all the more odious as it was pursued without regard to results, simply abandoning themselves to the one feeling of hatred of God and of His immutable moral laws.

France had the misfortune to produce the greatest number of these men. It is in her midst that religion and all that she holds sacred, that morality and authority, and all connected with them, have been attacked with a steady and systematic animosity, and it is there that the weapon of ridicule has been used with the most ease and success.

Drag through the mud the name of God and

the powers instituted by His divine decrees, and the revolution will be prepared! Speak of a social contract,[2] and the revolution is accomplished! The revolution was already completed in the palaces of Kings, in the drawing-rooms and boudoirs of certain cities, while among the great mass of the people it was still only in a state of preparation. . . .

. . . The French Revolution broke out, and has gone through a complete revolutionary cycle in a very short period, which could only have appeared long to its victims and to its contemporaries. . . .

. . . The revolutionary seed had penetrated into every country. . . . It was greatly developed under the *régime* of the military despotism of Bonaparte. His conquests displaced a number of laws, institutions, and customs; broke through bonds sacred among all nations, strong enough to resist time itself; which is more than can be said of certain benefits conferred by these innovators. . . .

▷ Metternich attacks the middle class for adopting and spreading these dangerous ideas.

It is principally the middle classes of society which this moral gangrene has affected, and it is only among them that the real heads of the party are found. . . .

In all four countries [France, Germany, Italy, and Spain] the agitated classes are principally composed of wealthy men — real cosmopolitans, securing their personal advantage at the expense of any order of things whatever — paid State officials, men of letters, lawyers, and the individuals charged with public education. . . .

---

[2]The social contract theory consisted essentially of the following principles: (1) people voluntarily enter into an agreement to establish a political community; (2) government rests on the consent of the governed; (3) people possess natural freedom and equality, which they do not surrender to the state. These principles were used to challenge the divine right of kings and absolute monarchy.

We see this intermediary class abandon itself with a blind fury and animosity which proves much more its own fears than any confidence in the success of its enterprises, to all the means which seem proper to assuage its thirst for power, applying itself to the task of persuading Kings that their rights are confined to sitting upon a throne, while those of the people are to govern, and to attack all that centuries have bequeathed as holy and worthy of man's respect — denying, in fact, the value of the past, and declaring themselves the masters of the future. We see this class take all sorts of disguises, uniting and subdividing as occasion offers, helping each other in the hour of danger, and the next day depriving each other of all their conquests. It takes possession of the press, and employs it to promote impiety, disobedience to the laws of religion and the State, and goes so far as to preach murder as a duty for those who desire what is good. . . .

▷ Metternich wants governments to band together to suppress dangerous ideas, the free press, and secret societies and to preserve religious principles.

We are convinced that society can no longer be saved without strong and vigorous resolutions on the part of the Governments still free in their opinions and actions.

We are also convinced that this may be, if the Governments face the truth, if they free themselves from all illusion, if they join their ranks and take their stand on a line of correct, unambiguous, and frankly announced principles.

By this course the monarchs will fulfill the duties imposed upon them by [God] who, by entrusting them with power, has charged them to watch over the maintenance of justice, and the rights of all, to avoid the paths of error, and tread firmly in the way of truth. . . .

There is a rule of conduct common to individuals and to States, established by the experience of centuries as by that of everyday life.

This rule declares "that one must not dream of reformation while agitated by passion; wisdom directs that at such moments we should limit ourselves to maintaining."

Let the monarchs vigorously adopt this principle; let all their resolutions bear the impression of it. Let their actions, their measures, and even their words announce and prove to the world this determination — they will find allies everywhere. The Governments, in establishing the principle of *stability,* will in no wise exclude the development of what is good, for stability is not immobility. . . .

If the same elements of destruction which are now throwing society into convulsions have existed in all ages — for every age has seen immoral and ambitious men, hypocrites, men of heated imaginations, wrong motives, and wild projects — yet ours, by the single fact of the liberty of the press, possesses more than any preceding age the means of contact, seduction, and attraction whereby to act on these different classes of men.

We are certainly not alone in questioning if society can exist with the liberty of the press, a scourge unknown to the world before the latter half of the seventeenth century, and restrained until the end of the eighteenth, with scarcely any exceptions but England — a part of Europe separated from the continent by the sea, as well as by her language and by her peculiar manners.

The first principle to be followed by the monarchs, united as they are by the coincidence of their desires and opinions, should be that of maintaining the stability of political institutions against the disorganised excitement which has taken possession of men's minds; the immutability of principles against the madness of their interpretation; and respect for laws actually in force against a desire for their destruction. . . .

. . . The first and greatest concern for the immense majority of every nation is the stability of the laws, and their uninterrupted action — never their change. Therefore let the Governments govern, let them maintain the groundwork of their institutions, both ancient and modern; for if it is at all times dangerous to touch them, it certainly would not now, in the general confusion, be wise to do so. . . .

Let them maintain religious principles in all their purity, and not allow the faith to be attacked and morality interpreted according to the *social contract* or the visions of foolish sectarians.

Let them suppress Secret Societies, that gangrene of society. . . .

To every great State determined to survive the storm there still remain many chances of salvation, and a strong union between the States on the principles we have announced will overcome the storm itself.

Joseph de Maistre
≪ ESSAY ON THE GENERATIVE PRINCIPLE OF POLITICAL CONSTITUTIONS ≫

The following critique of the philosophes, the French Revolution, and manufactured constitutions is taken from Joseph de Maistre's *Essay on the Generative Principle of Political Constitutions* (1808–1809).

One of the greatest errors of a century which professed them all was to believe that a political constitution could be created and written *a priori,* whereas reason and experience unite in proving that a constitution is a divine work and that precisely the most fundamental and essentially constitutional of a nation's laws could not possibly be written. . . .

. . . Was it not a common belief everywhere that a constitution was the work of the intellect, like an ode or a tragedy? Had not Thomas Paine declared, with a profundity that charmed the universities, that a constitution does not exist as long as one cannot put it in his pocket? The unsuspecting, overweening self-confidence of the eighteenth century balked at nothing, and I do not believe that it produced a single stripling of any talent who did not make three things when he left school: an educational system, a constitution, and a world. . . .

. . . I do not believe that the slightest doubt remains as to the unquestionable truth of the following propositions:

The fundamental principles of political constitutions exist prior to all written law.

Constitutional law (*loi*) is and can only be the development or sanction of a pre-existing and unwritten law (*droit*). . . .

. . . [H]e who believes himself able by writing alone to establish a clear and lasting doctrine IS A GREAT FOOL. If he really possessed the seeds of truth, he could never believe that a little black liquid and a pen could germinate them in the world, protect them from harsh weather, and make them sufficiently effective. As for whoever undertakes writing *laws or civil constitutions* in the belief that he can give them adequate conviction and stability because he has written them, he disgraces himself, whether or no other people say so. He shows an equal ignorance of the nature of inspiration and delirium, right and wrong, good and evil. This ignorance is shameful, even when approved by the whole body of the common people.

. . . [N]o real and great institution can be based on written law, since men themselves, instruments, in turn, of the established institution, do not know what it is to become and since imperceptible growth is the true promise of durability in all things. . . .

Everything brings us back to the general rule. *Man cannot create a constitution, and no le-*

gitimate constitution can be written. The collection of fundamental laws which necessarily constitute a civil or religious society never has been or will be written *a priori.*

▷ De Maistre assails the philosophes for attacking religion. Without Christianity, he says, people become brutalized, and civilization degenerates into anarchy.

Religion alone civilizes nations. No other known force can influence the savage. . . . [W]hat shall we think of a generation which has thrown everything to the winds, including the very foundations of the structure of society, by making education exclusively scientific? It was impossible to err more frightfully. For every educational system which does not have religion as its basis will collapse in an instant, or else diffuse only poisons throughout the State . . . if the guidance of education is not returned to the priests, and if science is not uniformly relegated to a subordinate rank, incalculable evils await us. We shall become brutalized by science, and that is the worst sort of brutality. . . .

Not until the first half of the eighteenth century did impiety really become a force. We see it at first spreading in every direction with amazing energy. From palaces to hovels, it insinuates itself everywhere, infesting everything. . . .

REVIEW QUESTIONS

1. What was Klemens von Metternich's opinion of "the progress of the human mind . . . in the . . . last three centuries" and its effect upon the society of his times?
2. What did Metternich mean by "Drag through the mud the name of God and the powers instituted by His divine decrees, and the revolution will be prepared!"?
3. How did Metternich regard the middle classes?
4. What strategy did Metternich propose to bring stability back to political life?
5. Why did Joseph de Maistre believe that man cannot create a constitution and no legitimate constitution can be written?
6. What faults did de Maistre find with the education of his day?

▼▼▼

3 ▼ Liberalism

Conservatism was the ideology of the old order that was hostile to the Enlightenment and the French Revolution; in contrast, liberalism aspired to carry out the promise of the philosophes and the Revolution. Liberals called for a constitution that protected individual liberty and denounced censorship, arbitrary arrest, and other forms of repression. They believed that through reason and education, social evils could be remedied. Liberals rejected an essential feature of the Old Regime — the special privileges of the aristocracy and the clergy — and held that the individual should be judged on the basis of achievement, not of birth. At the core of the liberal outlook lay the conviction that the individual would develop into a good and productive human being and citizen if not coerced by governments and churches.

John Stuart Mill
ON LIBERTY

Freedom of thought and expression were principal concerns of nineteenth-century liberals. The classic defense of intellectual freedom is *On Liberty* (1859), written by John Stuart Mill (1806–1873), a prominent British philosopher. Mill argued that no individual or government has a monopoly on truth, for all human beings are fallible. Therefore, the government and the majority have no legitimate authority to suppress views, however unpopular; they have no right to interfere with a person's liberty so long as that person's actions do no injury to others. Nothing is more absolute, contended Mill, than the inviolable right of all adults to think and live as they please so long as they respect the rights of others. For Mill, toleration of opposing and unpopular viewpoints is a necessary trait in order for a person to become rational, moral, and civilized.

The object of this essay is to assert one very simple principle, as entitled to govern absolutely the dealings of society with the individual. . . . That principle is that the sole end for which mankind are warranted, individually or collectively, in interfering with the liberty of action of any of their number is self-protection. That the only purpose for which power can be rightfully exercised over any member of a civilized community, against his will, is to prevent harm to others. His own good, either physical or moral, is not a sufficient warrant. He cannot rightfully be compelled to do or forbear because it will be better for him to do so, because it will make him happier, because, in the opinions of others, to do so would be wise or even right. These are good reasons for remonstrating with him, or reasoning with him, or persuading him, or entreating him, but not for compelling him or visiting him with any evil in case he do otherwise. To justify that, the conduct from which it is desired to deter him must be calculated to produce evil to someone else. The only part of the conduct of anyone for which he is amenable to society is that which concerns others. In the part which merely concerns himself, his independence is, of right, absolute. Over himself, over his own body and mind, the individual is sovereign. . . .

. . . This, then, is the appropriate region of human liberty. It comprises, first, the inward domain of consciousness, demanding liberty of conscience in the most comprehensive sense, liberty of thought and feeling, absolute freedom of opinion and sentiment on all subjects, practical or speculative, scientific, moral, or theological. The liberty of expressing and publishing opinions may seem to fall under a different principle, since it belongs to that part of the conduct of an individual which concerns other people, but, being almost of as much importance as the liberty of thought itself and resting in great part on the same reasons, is practically inseparable from it. Secondly, the principle requires liberty of tastes and pursuits, of framing the plan of our life to suit our own character, of doing as we like, subject to such consequences as may follow, without impediment from our fellow creatures, so long as what we do does not harm them, even though they should think our conduct foolish, perverse, or wrong. Thirdly, from this liberty of each individual follows the liberty, within the same limits, of combination among individuals; freedom to unite for any purpose not involving harm to others: the persons combining being supposed to be of full age and not forced or deceived.

No society in which these liberties are not, on the whole, respected is free, whatever may be its form of government; and none is completely free in which they do not exist absolute and unqualified. The only freedom which deserves the name is that of pursuing our own good in our own way, so long as we do not attempt to deprive others of theirs or impede their efforts to obtain it. Each is the proper guardian of his own health, whether bodily *or* mental and spiritual. Mankind are greater gainers by suffering each other to live as seems good to themselves than by compelling each to live as seems good to the rest. . . .

. . . Let us suppose, therefore, that the government is entirely at one with the people, and never thinks of exerting any power of coercion unless in agreement with what it conceives to be their voice. But I deny the right of the people to exercise such coercion, either by themselves or by their government. The power itself is illegitimate. The best government has no more title to it than the worst. It is as noxious, or more noxious, when exerted in accordance with public opinion than when in opposition to it. If all mankind minus one were of one opinion, mankind would be no more justified in silencing that one person than he, if he had the power, would be justified in silencing mankind. Were an opinion a personal possession of no value except to the owner, if to be obstructed in the enjoyment of it were simply a private injury, it would make some difference whether the injury was inflicted only on a few persons or on many. But the peculiar evil of silencing the expression of an opinion is that it is robbing the human race, posterity as well as the existing generation — those who dissent from the opinion, still more than those who hold it. If the opinion is right, they are deprived of the opportunity of exchanging error for truth; if wrong, they lose, what is almost as great a benefit, the clearer perception and livelier impression of truth produced by its collision with error.

REVIEW QUESTIONS

1. What was the purpose of John Stuart Mill's essay?
2. For Mill, what is the "peculiar evil of silencing the expression of an opinion," however unpopular?
3. On what grounds would Mill permit society to restrict individual liberty?

▼▼▼

4 ▼ Nationalism and Repression in Germany

Nationalism espoused the individual's allegiance to the national community and sought to unify divided nations and to liberate subject peoples. In the early nineteenth century, most nationalists were liberals who viewed the struggle for unification and freedom from foreign oppression as an extension of the struggle for individual rights. Few liberals recognized that nationalism was a potentially dangerous force that could threaten liberal ideals of freedom and equality.

By glorifying a nation's language and ancient traditions and folkways, romanticism contributed to the evolution of modern nationalism, particularly in Germany. German romantics longed to create a true folk community in which the individual's soul would be immersed in the nation's soul. Through the national community, individuals could find the meaning in life for which they yearned. The romantic veneration of the past produced a mythical way of thinking about politics and history, one that subordinated reason to powerful emotions. In particular, some German romantics attacked the liberal-rational tradition of the Enlightenment and the French Revolution as hostile to the true German spirit.

Ernst Moritz Arndt
THE WAR OF LIBERATION

The Napoleonic wars kindled nationalist sentiments in the German states. Hatred of the French occupier evoked a feeling of outrage and a desire for national unity among some Germans, who before the occupation had thought not of a German fatherland but of their own states and princes. These Germans called for a war of liberation against Napoleon. Attracting mostly intellectuals, the idea of political unification had limited impact on the rest of the people, who remained loyal to local princes and local territories. Nevertheless, the embryo of nationalism was conceived in the German uprising against Napoleon in 1813. The writings of Ernst Moritz Arndt (1769–1860) vividly express the emerging nationalism. The following excerpts describe Arndt's view of the War of Liberation and present his appeal for German unity.

Fired with enthusiasm, the people rose, "with God for King and Fatherland." Among the Prussians there was only one voice, one feeling, one anger and one love, to save the Fatherland and to free Germany. The Prussians wanted war; war and death they wanted; peace they feared because they could hope for no honorable peace from Napoleon. War, war, sounded the cry from the Carpathians [mountains] to the Baltic [Sea], from the Niemen to the Elbe [rivers]. War! cried the nobleman and landed proprietor who had become impoverished. War! the peasant who was driving his last horse to death. . . . War! the citizen who was growing exhausted from quartering soldiers and paying taxes. War! the widow who was sending her only son to the front. War! the young girl who, with tears of pride and pain, was leaving her betrothed. Youths who were hardly able to bear arms, men with gray hair, officers who on account of wounds and mutilations had long ago been honorably discharged, rich landed proprietors and officials, fathers of large families and managers of extensive businesses — all were unwilling to remain behind. Even young women, under all sorts of disguises, rushed to arms; all wanted to drill, arm themselves and fight and die for the Fatherland. . . .

The most beautiful thing about all this holy zeal and happy confusion was that all differences of position, class, and age were forgotten . . . that the one great feeling for the Fatherland, its freedom and honor, swallowed all other feelings, caused all other considerations and relationships to be forgotten.

▷   In another passage, Arndt appealed for German unity.

German man, feel again God, hear and fear the eternal, and you hear and fear also your *Volk* [folk, people, nation]; you feel again in God the honor and dignity of your fathers, their glorious history rejuvenates itself again in you, their firm and gallant virtue reblossoms in you, the whole German Fatherland stands again before you in the august halo of past centuries! Then, when you feel and fear and honor all this, then you cry, then you lament, then you wrathfully reproach yourself that you have become so miserable and evil: then starts your new life and your new history. . . . From the North Sea to the Carpathians, from the Baltic to the Alps, from the Vistula to the Schelde [rivers], one faith, one love, one courage, and one enthusiasm must gather again the whole German folk in brotherly community; they must learn to feel how great, mighty, and happy their fathers were in obedience to one German emperor and one Reich, at a time when the many discords had not yet turned one against the other, when the many cowards and knaves had not yet betrayed them; . . . above the ruins and ashes of their destroyed Fatherland they must weepingly join hands and pray and swear all to stand like one man and to fight until the sacred land will be free. . . . Feel the infinite and sublime which slumbers hidden in the lap of the days, those light and mighty spirits which now glimmer in isolated meteors but which soon will shine in all suns and stars; feel the new birth of times, the higher, cleaner breath of spiritual life and do not longer be fooled and confused by the insignificant and small. No longer Catholics and Protestants, no longer Prussians and Austrians, Saxons and Bavarians, Silesians and Hanoverians, no longer of different faith, different mentality, and different will — be Germans, be one, will to be one by love and loyalty, and no devil will vanquish you.

Heinrich von Gagern
THE CALL FOR GERMAN UNITY

Heinrich von Gagern (1799–1880) was a liberal who helped to organize the *Burschenschaften*, German student fraternities dedicated to national unity. In the passage that follows, von Gagern explained the nationalist purpose of the German student movement.

It is very hard to explain the spirit of the student movement to you, but I shall try, even though I can only give you a few characteristics. . . .

. . . Those who share in this spirit have [a] . . . tendency in their student life, Love of Fatherland is their guiding principle. Their purpose is to make a better future for the Fatherland, each as best he can, to spread national consciousness, or to use the much ridiculed and maligned Germanic expression, more folkishness, and to work for better constitutions. . . .

. . . We want more sense of community among the several states of Germany, greater unity in their policies and in their principles of government; no separate policy for each state, but the nearest possible relations with one another; above all, we want Germany to be considered *one* land and the German people *one* people. In the forms of our student comradeship we show how we want to approach this as nearly as possible in the real world. Regional fraternities are forbidden, and we live in a German comradeship, one people in spirit, as we want it for all Germany in reality. We give our selves the freest of constitutions, just as we should like Germany to have the freest possible one, insofar as that is suitable for the German people. We want a constitution for the people that fits in with the spirit of the times and with the people's own level of enlightenment, rather than what each prince gives his people according to what he likes and what serves his private interest. Above all, we want the princes to understand and to follow the principle that they exist for the country and not the country for them. In fact, the prevailing view is that the constitution should not come from the individual states at all. The main principles of the German constitution should apply to all states in common, and should be expressed by the German federal assembly. This constitution should deal not only with the absolute necessities, like fiscal administration and justice, general administration and church and military affairs and so on; this constitution ought to be extended to the education of the young, at least at the upper age levels, and to many other such things.

KARLSBAD DECREES

In 1819, Metternich and representatives from other German states meeting at Karlsbad drew up several decrees designed to stifle liberalism and nationalism. The Karlsbad Decrees called for the dissolution of the *Burschenschaften*, the censoring of books and newspapers, and the dismissal of professors who spread liberal doctrines.

Provisional Decree relative to the Measures to be taken concerning the Universities.

Sect. 1. The Sovereign shall make choice for each university of an extraordinary commissioner, furnished with suitable instructions and powers, residing in the place where the university is established. . . .

The duty of this commissioner shall be to . . . observe carefully the spirit with which the professors and tutors are guided in their public and private lectures; . . . and to devote a constant attention to every thing which may tend to the maintenance of morality, good order and decency among the youths.

Sect. 2. The governments of the states, members of the confederation, reciprocally engage to remove from their universities and other establishments of instruction, the professors and other public teachers, against whom it may be proved, that in departing from their duty, in overstepping the bounds of their duty, in abusing their legitimate influence over the minds of youth, by the propagation of pernicious dogmas, hostile to order and public tranquility, or in sapping the foundation of existing establishments, they have shown themselves incapable of executing the important functions entrusted to them. . . .

A professor or tutor thus excluded, cannot be admitted in any other state of the confederation to any other establishment of public instruction.

Sect. 3. The laws long since made against secret or unauthorized associations at the universities, shall be maintained in all their force and rigour, and shall be particularly extended with so much the more severity against the well-known society formed some years ago under the name of the General Burgenschaft, as it has for its basis an idea, absolutely inadmissible, of community and continued correspondence between the different universities.

The governments shall mutually engage to admit to no public employment any individuals who may continue or enter into any of those associations after the publication of the present decree.

Decree relative to the Measures for preventing the Abuses of the Press.

Sect. 1. . . . No writing appearing in the form of a daily paper or periodical pamphlet . . . shall be issued from the press without the previous consent of the public authority. . . .

Sect. 7. The editor of a journal, or other periodical publication, that may be suppressed by command of the Diet, shall not be allowed, during the space of five years, to conduct any similar publication in any states of the confederation. . . .

Decree relative to the formation of a Central Commission, for the purpose of Ulterior Inquiry respecting Revolutionary Plots, discovered in some of the States of the Confederation.

Art. 1. In 15 days from the date of this decree, an extraordinary commission of inquiry, appointed by the Diet and composed of 7 members, including the President, shall assemble in the city of Mentz, a fortress of the confederation.

2. The object of this commission is, to make careful and detailed inquiries respecting the facts, the origin and the multiplied ramifications of the secret revolutionary and demagogic

associations, directed against the political constitution and internal repose, as well of the confederation in general, as of the individual members thereof.

REVIEW QUESTIONS

1. According to Ernst Arndt, what was the effect upon German people of different classes and ages of the rising feeling of nationalism?
2. Arndt's writings show the interconnection between Romanticism and nationalism. Discuss this statement.
3. What was the guiding principle behind Heinrich von Gagern's characterization of the German student movement? What were its political implications?
4. By what methods did the Karlsbad Decrees propose to preserve political stability, and on what grounds was this proposal made?
5. The Karlsbad Decrees seem to have assumed that unregulated ideas were powerful factors in disrupting civilization. If this is so, do you feel that the methods proposed to restrain ideas indicated a genuine understanding of their force and were equal to the task of repressing them? Discuss.

▼▼▼

5 ▼ The Call for Italian Unity

In 1815, Italy was a fragmented nation. Hapsburg Austria ruled Lombardy and Venetia in the north and a Bourbon king sat on the throne of the Kingdom of the Two Sicilies in the south. The duchies of Tuscany, Parma, and Modena were ruled by Hapsburg princes subservient to Austria. The papal states in central Italy were ruled by the pope. The House of Savoy, an Italian dynasty, ruled the Kingdom of Piedmont, which became the cornerstone of Italian unification. Inspired by past Italian glories — the Roman Empire and the Renaissance — Italian nationalists demanded an end to foreign occupation and the unification of the Italian peninsula. As in other lands, national revival and unification appealed principally to intellectuals and the middle class.

Giuseppe Mazzini
YOUNG ITALY

A leading figure in the *Risorgimento* — the struggle for Italian nationhood — was Giuseppe Mazzini (1805–1872). Often called the "soul of the Risorgimento," Mazzini devoted his life to the creation of a unified and republican Italy; he believed that a free and democratic Italy would serve as a model to the other nations of Europe. In 1831, he founded Young Italy, a society dedicated to the cause of Italian unity. The following reading includes the oath taken by members of Young Italy.

Young Italy is a brotherhood of Italians who believe in a law of Progress and Duty, and are convinced that Italy is destined to become one nation, — convinced also that she possesses sufficient strength within herself to become one, and that the ill success of her former efforts is to be attributed not to the weakness, but to the misdirection of the revolutionary elements within her, — that the secret of force lies in constancy and unity of effort. They join this association in the firm intent of consecrating both thought and action to the great aim of reconstituting Italy as one independent sovereign nation of free men and equals. . . .

Young Italy is Republican. . . . Republican, — Because theoretically every nation is destined, by the law of God and humanity, to form a free and equal community of brothers; and the republican is the only form of government that insures this future. . . .

The means by which Young Italy proposes to reach its aim are — education and insurrection, to be adopted simultaneously, and made to harmonize with each other. Education must ever be directed to teach by example, word, and pen the necessity of insurrection. Insurrection, whenever it can be realized, must be so conducted as to render it a means of national education. . . .

Insurrection — by means of guerrilla bands — is the true method of warfare for all nations desirous of emancipating themselves from a foreign yoke. This method of warfare supplies the want — inevitable at the commencement of the insurrection — of a regular army; it calls the greatest number of elements into the field, and yet may be sustained by the smallest number. It forms the military education of the people, and consecrates every foot of the native soil by the memory of some warlike deed. . . .

Each member will, upon his initiation into the association of Young Italy, pronounce the following form of oath, in the presence of the initiator:

In the name of God and of Italy;

In the name of all the martyrs of the holy Italian cause who have fallen beneath foreign and domestic tyranny;

By the duties which bind me to the land wherein God has placed me, and to the brothers whom God has given me;

By the love — innate in all men — I bear to the country that gave my mother birth, and will be the home of my children;

By the hatred — innate in all men — I bear to evil, injustice, usurpation and arbitrary rule;

By the blush that rises to my brow when I stand before the citizens of other lands, to know that I have no rights of citizenship, no country, and no national flag;

By the aspiration that thrills my soul towards that liberty for which it was created, and is impotent to exert; towards the good it was created to strive after, and is impotent to achieve in the silence and isolation of slavery;

By the memory of our former greatness, and the sense of our present degradation;

By the tears of Italian mothers for their sons dead on the scaffold, in prison, or in exile;

By the sufferings of the millions, —

I, . . . believing in the mission intrusted by God to Italy, and the duty of every Italian to strive to attempt its fulfillment; convinced that where God has ordained that a nation shall be, He has given the requisite power to create it; that the people are the depositaries of that power, and that in its right direction for the people, and by the people, lies the secret of victory; convinced that virtue consists in action and sacrifice, and strength in union and constancy of purpose: I give my name to Young Italy, an association of men holding the same faith, and swear:

To dedicate myself wholly and forever to the endeavor with them to constitute Italy one free, independent, republican nation; to promote by every means in my power — whether by written or spoken word, or by action — the education of my Italian brothers towards the aim of Young Italy; towards association, the sole means of its accomplishment, and to virtue, which alone can render the conquest lasting; to abstain from enrolling myself in any other association from this time forth; to obey all the instructions, in conformity with the spirit of Young Italy, given me by those who represent with me the union of my Italian brothers; and to keep the secret of these instructions, even at the cost of my life; to assist my brothers of the association both by action and counsel —

NOW AND FOREVER.

This do I swear, invoking upon my head the wrath of God, the abhorrence of man, and the infamy of the perjurer, if I ever betray the whole or a part of this my oath.

REVIEW QUESTIONS

1. What bonds united members of Giuseppe Mazzini's Young Italy?
2. Why do you suppose many students were attracted to Young Italy?
3. Mazzini was a democrat, a nationalist, and a romantic. Discuss this statement.

▼▼▼

6 ▼ 1848: The Year of Revolutions

In 1848, revolutions for political liberty and nationhood broke out in many parts of Europe. An uprising in Paris set this revolutionary tidal wave in motion. In February 1848, democrats seeking to create a French republic and to institute universal manhood suffrage precipitated a crisis; the following uprising in Paris forced King Louis Philippe to abdicate. The leaders of the new French Republic championed political democracy but, with some notable exceptions like Louis Blanc (1811–1882), had little concern for the plight of the laboring poor.

The publication of the *Organization of Labor* (1839) had established Blanc as a leading French social reformer. Blanc urged the government to finance national workshops — industrial corporations, in which the directors would be elected by the workers — to provide employment for the urban poor. The government responded to Blanc's insistence that all workers have the "right to work" by indeed establishing national workshops, but these provided jobs for only a fraction of the unemployed, and many workers were given wages for doing nothing. Property owners regarded the workshops as a waste of government funds and as nests of working-class radicalism. When the government closed the workshops in June 1848, Parisian workers revolted.

Alexis de Tocqueville
THE JUNE DAYS

To the French workers the June 1848 revolt was against poverty and for a fairer distribution of property. Viewing this uprising as a threat to property and indeed to civilization, the rest of France rallied against the workers, who were crushed after several days of bitter street fighting. In his *Recollections,* Alexis de Tocqueville (1805–1859), a leading statesman and political theorist, included a speech he made on January 29, 1848, before the French Chamber of Deputies, in which he warned the officials about the mood of the laboring poor.

. . . I am told that there is no danger because there are no riots; I am told that, because there is no visible disorder on the surface of society, there is no revolution at hand.

Gentlemen, permit me to say that I believe you are deceived. True, there is no actual disorder; but it has entered deeply into men's minds. See what is passing in the breasts of the working classes, who, I grant, are at present quiet. No doubt they are not disturbed by political passion, properly so-called, to the same extent that they have been; but can you not see that their passions, instead of political, have become social? Do you not see that there are gradually forming in their breasts opinions and ideas which are destined not only to upset this or that law, ministry, or even form of government, but society itself, until it totters upon the foundations on which it rests today? Do you not listen to what they say to themselves each day? Do you not hear them repeating unceasingly that all that is above them is incapable and unworthy of governing them; that the present distribution of goods throughout the world is unjust; that property rests on a foundation which is not an equitable foundation? And do you not realize that when such opinions take root, when they spread in an almost universal manner, when they sink deeply into the masses, they are bound to bring with them sooner or later, I know not when nor how, a most formidable revolution?

This, gentlemen, is my profound conviction: I believe that we are at this moment sleeping on a volcano. I am profoundly convinced of it. . . .

▷ Later in his *Recollections,* de Tocqueville describes the second uprising in 1848, called the June Days.

I come at last to the insurrection of June, the most extensive and the most singular that has occurred in our history, and perhaps in any other: the most extensive, because, during four days, more than a hundred thousand men were engaged in it; the most singular, because the insurgents fought without a war-cry, without leaders, without flags, and yet with a marvellous harmony and an amount of military experience that astonished the oldest officers.

What distinguished it also, among all the events of this kind which have succeeded one another in France for sixty years, is that it did not aim at changing the form of government, but at altering the order of society. It was not, strictly speaking, a political struggle, in the

sense which until then we had given to the word, but a combat of class against class, a sort of Servile War [slave uprising in ancient Rome]. It represented the facts of the Revolution of February in the same manner as the theories of Socialism represented its ideas; or rather it issued naturally from these ideas, as a son does from his mother. We behold in it nothing more than a blind and rude, but powerful, effort on the part of the workmen to escape from the necessities of their condition, which had been depicted to them as one of unlawful oppression, and to open up by main force a road towards that imaginary comfort with which they had been deluded. It was this mixture of greed and false theory which first gave birth to the insurrection and then made it so formidable. These poor people had been told that the wealth of the rich was in some way the produce of a theft practised upon themselves. They had been assured that the inequality of fortunes was as opposed to morality and the welfare of society as it was to nature. Prompted by their needs and their passions, many had believed this obscure and erroneous notion of right, which, mingled with brute force, imparted to the latter an energy, a tenacity and a power which it would never have possessed unaided.

It must also be observed that this formidable insurrection was not the enterprise of a certain number of conspirators, but the revolt of one whole section of the population against another. Women took part in it as well as men. While the latter fought, the former prepared and carried ammunition; and when at last the time had come to surrender, the women were the last to yield. These women went to battle with, as it were, a housewifely ardour: they looked to victory for the comfort of their husbands and the education of their children. . . .

As we know, it was the closing of the national workshops that occasioned the rising. Dreading to disband this formidable soldiery at one stroke, the Government had tried to disperse it by sending part of the workmen into the country. They refused to leave. On the 22nd of June, they marched through Paris in troops, singing in cadence, in a monotonous chant, "We won't be sent away, we won't be sent away. . . ."

. . . The spirit of insurrection circulated from one to the other of this immense class, and in each of its parts, as the blood does in the body; it filled the quarters where there was no fighting, as well as those which served as the scene of battle; it had penetrated into our houses, around, above, below us. The very places in which we thought ourselves the masters swarmed with domestic enemies; one might say that an atmosphere of civil war enveloped the whole of Paris, amid which, to whatever part we withdrew, we had to live. . . .

. . . It was easy to perceive through the multitude of contradictory reports that we had to do with the most universal, the best armed, and the most furious insurrection ever known in Paris. The national workshops and various revolutionary bands that had just been disbanded supplied it with trained and disciplined soldiers and with leaders. It was extending every moment, and it was difficult to believe that it would not end by being victorious, . . . all the great insurrections of the last sixty years had triumphed. . . .

Nevertheless, we succeeded in triumphing over this so formidable insurrection; nay more, it was just that which rendered it so terrible which saved us. . . . Had the revolt borne a less radical character and a less ferocious aspect, it is probable that the greater part of the middle class would have stayed at home; France would not have come to our aid; the National Assembly itself would perhaps have yielded, or at least a minority of its members would have advised it; and the energy of the whole body would have been greatly unnerved. But the insurrection was of such a nature that any understanding with it became at once impossible, and from the first it left us no alternative but to defeat it or to be destroyed ourselves.

Carl Schurz
REVOLUTION SPREADS TO THE GERMAN STATES

The February Revolution in Paris was eagerly received by German liberals and nationalists who yearned for a Germany governed by national parliament and a constitution that guaranteed basic liberties. In the following excerpt from his *Reminiscences*, Carl Schurz (1829–1906), then a student at the University of Bonn, recalled the expectations of German liberal-nationalists. After the revolution failed, Schurz fled to Switzerland and eventually went to the United States, where he had a distinguished career as a senator, cabinet member, and journalist.

One morning, toward the end of February, 1848, I sat quietly in my attic-chamber, working hard at my tragedy of "Ulrich von Hutten," when suddenly a friend rushed breathlessly into the room, exclaiming: "What, you sitting here! Do you not know what has happened?"

"No; what?"

"The French have driven away Louis Philippe and proclaimed the republic."

I threw down my pen — and that was the end of "Ulrich von Hutten." I never touched the manuscript again. We tore down the stairs, into the street, to the market-square, the accustomed meeting-place for all the student societies after their midday dinner. Although it was still forenoon, the market was already crowded with young men talking excitedly. There was no shouting, no noise, only agitated conversation. What did we want there? This probably no one knew. But since the French had driven away Louis Philippe and proclaimed the republic, something of course must happen here, too. Some of the students had brought their rapiers along, as if it were necessary at once to make an attack or to defend ourselves. We were dominated by a vague feeling as if a great outbreak of elemental forces had begun, as if an earthquake was impending of which we had felt the first shock, and we instinctively crowded together. Thus we wandered about in numerous bands . . . [and] fell into conversation with all manner of strangers, to find in them the same confused, astonished and expectant state of mind; then back to the market-square, to see what might be going on there; then again somewhere else, and so on, without aim and end, until finally late in the night fatigue compelled us to find the way home.

The next morning there were the usual lectures to be attended. But how profitless! The voice of the professor sounded like a monotonous drone coming from far away. What he had to say did not seem to concern us. The pen that should have taken notes remained idle. At last we closed with a sigh the notebook and went away, impelled by a feeling that now we had something more important to do — to devote ourselves to the affairs of the fatherland. And this we did by seeking as quickly as possible again the company of our friends, in order to discuss what had happened and what was to come. In these conversations, excited as they were, certain ideas and catchwords worked themselves to the surface, which expressed more or less the feelings of the people. Now had arrived in Germany the day for the establishment of "German Unity," and the founding of a great, powerful national German Empire. In the first line the convocation of a national parliament. Then the demands for civil rights and liberties, free speech, free press, the right of free assembly, equality before the law, a freely elected representation of the people with legislative power, responsibility of ministers, self-government of the communes, the right of the people to carry arms, the formation of a civic guard with elective officers, and so on — in short, that which was called a "constitutional form of government on a broad democratic basis." Republican ideas were at first only spar-

ingly expressed. But the word democracy was soon on all tongues, and many, too, thought it a matter of course that if the princes should try to withhold from the people the rights and liberties demanded, force would take the place of mere petition. Of course the regeneration of the fatherland must, if possible, be accomplished by peaceable means. A few days after the outbreak of this commotion I reached my nineteenth birthday. I remember to have been so entirely absorbed by what was happening that I could hardly turn my thoughts to anything else. Like many of my friends, I was dominated by the feeling that at last the great opportunity had arrived for giving to the German people the liberty which was their birthright and to the German fatherland its unity and greatness, and that it was now the first duty of every German to do and to sacrifice everything for this sacred object. We were profoundly, solemnly in earnest. . . .

Exciting news came from all sides. In Cologne a threatening ferment prevailed. In the taverns and on the streets resounded the "Marseillaise" [French national anthem, symbol of the Revolution], which at that time still passed in all Europe as the "hymn of liberty." On the public places great meetings were held to consult about the demands to be made by the people. A large deputation, headed by the late lieutenant of artillery, August von Willich, forced its way into the hall of the city council, vehemently insisting that the municipality present as its own the demands of the people of Cologne to the king. The streets resounded with the military drumbeat; the soldiery marched upon the popular gatherings, and Willich, as well as another ex-artillery officer, Fritz Anneke, were arrested; whereupon increasing excitement. . . .

. . . In Coblenz, Düsseldorf, Aachen, Crefeld, Cleves and other cities on the Rhine similar demonstrations took place. In South Germany — in Baden, Hessen-on-the-Rhine, Nassau, Würtemberg, Bavaria — the same revolutionary spirit burst forth like a prairie-fire. In Baden the Grand Duke acceded almost at once to what was asked of him, and so did the rulers of Würtemberg, Nassau, and Hessen-Darmstadt. . . .

Great news came from Vienna. There the students of the university were the first to assail the Emperor of Austria with the cry for liberty and citizens' rights. Blood flowed in the streets, and the downfall of Prince Metternich was the result. The students organized themselves as the armed guard of liberty. In the great cities of Prussia there was a mighty commotion. Not only Cologne, Coblenz and Trier, but also Breslau, Königsberg and Frankfurt-on-the-Oder, sent deputations to Berlin to entreat the king. In the Prussian capital the masses surged upon the streets, and everybody looked for events of great import.

While such tidings rushed in upon us from all sides like a roaring hurricane, we in the little university town of Bonn were also busy preparing addresses to the sovereign, to circulate them for signature and to send them to Berlin. On the 18th of March we too had our mass demonstration. A great multitude gathered for a solemn procession through the streets of the town. The most respectable citizens, not a few professors and a great number of students and people of all grades marched in close ranks. At the head of the procession Professor Kinkel bore the tricolor, black, red and gold, which so long had been prohibited as the revolutionary flag. Arrived on the market-square he mounted the steps of the city hall and spoke to the assembled throng. He spoke with wonderful eloquence, his voice ringing out in its most powerful tones as he depicted a resurrection of German unity and greatness and of the liberties and rights of the German people, which now must be conceded by the princes or won by force by the people. And when at last he waved the black, red and gold banner, and predicted to a free German nation a magnificent future, enthusiasm without bounds broke forth. People clapped their hands, they shouted, they embraced one another, they shed tears. In a moment the city was covered with black, red and gold flags, and not only the Burschenschaft, but almost everybody wore a black-red-gold cockade on his hat. While on that 18th of March we were parading through the streets suddenly sinister rumors flew from mouth to mouth. It had been reported that the king of Prussia, after long hesitation, had finally concluded, like the other German princes, to concede the demands that were pouring upon him from all sides. But now a whispered report flew around that the soldiery had suddenly fired upon the people and that a bloody struggle was raging in the streets of Berlin.

REVIEW QUESTIONS

1. According to Alexis de Tocqueville, why did Parisian workers revolt in 1848?
2. How did the goals of Parisian workers who revolted in 1848 differ from those of members of Giuseppe Mazzini's Young Italy?
3. In de Tocqueville's view, the most dangerous revolutions are invisible. Explain.
4. Why did the leaders of France resolve to crush the revolt and what enabled them to succeed?
5. De Tocqueville observed that what distinguished this revolt was that it aimed to change the order of society, not the form of government. What kind of revolt did this produce, and how did it differ from nationalist uprisings?
6. What effect did the news of Louis Philippe's overthrow and the founding of the French Republic have on Carl Schurz and the young students of his day? How did they behave?
7. What were the goals of Schurz and many of his colleagues? How did they seek to reconcile nationalism and liberalism?
8. Compare the goals of the German revolutionaries of 1848 with those of Young Italy's members.
9. Why have university students often been attracted to revolutions? Provide examples from the twentieth century.

The Industrial Revolution

In the last part of the eighteenth century, as a revolution for liberty and equality swept across France and sent shock waves across Europe, a different kind of revolution, a revolution in industry, was transforming life in Great Britain. In the nineteenth century the Industrial Revolution spread to the United States and to the European continent. Today, it encompasses virtually the entire world; everywhere the drive to substitute machines for human labor continues at a rapid pace.

After 1760, dramatic changes occurred in Britain in the way goods were produced and labor organized. New forms of power, particularly steam, replaced animal strength and human muscle. Better ways of obtaining and using raw materials were discovered, and a new form of organizing production and workers — the factory — came into common use. In the nineteenth century, technology moved from triumph to triumph with a momentum unprecedented in human history. The resulting explosion in economic production and productivity transformed society with breathtaking speed.

Rapid industrialization caused hardships for the new class of industrial workers, many of them recent arrivals from the countryside. Arduous and monotonous, factory labor was geared to the strict discipline of the clock, the machine, and the production schedule. Employment was never secure. Sick workers received no pay and were often fired; aged workers suffered pay cuts or lost their jobs. During business slumps, employers lowered wages with impunity, and laid-off workers had nowhere to turn for assistance. Because factory owners did not consider safety an important concern, accidents were frequent. Yet the Industrial Revolution was also a great force for human betterment. Ultimately it raised the standard of living, even for the lowest classes, lengthened life expectancy, and provided more leisure time and more possibilities for people to fulfill their potential.

The Industrial Revolution dramatically altered political and social life at all levels, but especially for the middle class, whose engagement in capitalist ventures brought greater political power and social recognition. During the course of the nineteenth century, the bourgeoisie came to hold many of the highest offices in western European states, completing a trend that had begun with the French Revolution.

LUDGATE HILL by Gustave Doré (1833–1883). This French artist depicted London slums in many of his engravings. This London street scene captures the crowds, filthy streets, and chaotic traffic that pervaded cities in the new industrial age and diminished the quality of urban life. (*Historical Pictures Service, Chicago*)

Cities grew in size, number, and importance. Municipal authorities were unable to cope with the rapid pace of urbanization, and without adequate housing, sanitation, or recreational facilities, the exploding urban centers were another source of working-class misery. In preindustrial Britain, most people had lived in small villages. They knew where their roots were; relatives, friends, and the village church gave them a sense of belonging. The industrial centers separated people from nature and from their places of origin, shattering traditional ways of life that had given men and women a sense of security.

The plight of the working class created a demand for reform, but the British government, committed to laissez-faire economic principles that militated against state involvement, was slow to act. In the last part of the nineteenth century, however, the development of labor unions, the rising political voice of the working class, and the growing recognition that the problems created by industrialization required government intervention speeded up the pace of reform. Rejecting the road of reform, **Karl Marx** called for a working-class revolution that would destroy the capitalist system.

▼▼▼

I ▼ Early Industrialization

Several factors help to explain why the Industrial Revolution began in Great Britain. That country had an abundant labor supply, large deposits of coal and iron ore, and capital available for investing in new industries. A large domestic middle class and overseas colonies provided markets for manufactured goods. Colonies were also a source for raw materials, particularly cotton for the textile industry. The Scientific Revolution and an enthusiasm for engineering fostered a spirit of curiosity and inventiveness. Britain had enterprising and daring entrepreneurs who organized new businesses and discovered new methods of production.

Edward Baines
BRITAIN'S INDUSTRIAL ADVANTAGES AND THE FACTORY SYSTEM

In 1835, Edward Baines (1800–1890), an early student of industrialization, wrote *The History of the Cotton Manufacture in Great Britain* — about one of the leading industries in the early days of the Industrial Revolution. In the passages that follow, Baines discusses the reasons for Britain's industrial transformation and the advantages of the factory system.

Three things may be regarded as of primary importance for the successful prosecution of manufactures, namely, water-power, fuel, and iron. Wherever these exist in combination, and where they are abundant and cheap, machinery may be manufactured and put in motion at small cost; and most of the processes of making and finishing cloth, whether chemical or mechanical, depending, as they do, mainly on the two great agents of water and heat, may likewise be performed with advantage.

. . . A great number of streams . . . furnish water-power adequate to turn many hundred mills: they afford the element of water, indispensable for scouring, bleaching, printing, dyeing, and other processes of manufacture: and when collected in their larger channels, or employed to feed canals, they supply a superior inland navigation, so important for the transit of raw materials and merchandise.

Not less important for manufactures than the copious supply of good water, is the great abundance of coal. . . . This mineral fuel animates the thousand arms of the steam-engine, and furnishes the most powerful agent in all chemical and mechanical operations.

In mentioning the advantages which Lancashire [the major cotton manufacturing area] possesses as a seat of manufactures, we must not omit its ready communication with the sea by means of its well-situated port, Liverpool, through the medium of which it receives, from Ireland, a large proportion of the food that supports its population, and whose commerce brings from distant shores the raw materials of its manufactures, and again distributes them, converted into useful and elegant clothing, amongst all the nations of the earth. Through the same means a plentiful supply of timber is obtained, so needful for building purposes.

To the above natural advantages, we must add, the acquired advantage of a canal communication, which ramifies itself through all the populous parts of this country, and connects it with the inland counties, the seats of other flourishing manufactures, and the sources whence iron, lime, salt, stone, and other articles in which Lancashire is deficient, are obtained. By this means Lancashire, being already possessed of the primary requisites for manufactures, is enabled, at a very small expense, to command things of secondary importance, and to appropriate to its use the natural advantages of the whole kingdom. The canals, having been accomplished by individual enterprise, not by national funds, were constructed to supply a want already existing: they were not, therefore, original sources of the manufactures, but have extended together with them, and are to be considered as having essentially aided and accelerated that prosperity from whose beginnings they themselves arose. The recent introduction of railways will have a great effect in making the operations of trade more intensely active, and perfecting the division of labour, already carried to so high a point. By the railway and the locomotive engine, the extremities of the land will, for every beneficial purpose, be united.

In comparing the advantages of England for manufactures with those of other countries, we can by no means overlook the excellent commercial position of the country — intermediate between the north and south of Europe; and its insular situation, which, combined with the command of the seas, secures our territory from invasion or annoyance. The German ocean, the Baltic, and the Mediterranean are the regular highways for our ships; and our western ports command an unobstructed passage to the Atlantic, and to every quarter of the world.

A temperate climate, and a hardy race of men, have also greatly contributed to promote the manufacturing industry of England.

The political and moral advantages of this country, as a seat of manufactures, are not less remarkable than its physical advantages. The arts are the daughters of peace and liberty. In no country have these blessings been enjoyed in so high a degree, or for so long a continuance, as in England. Under the reign of just laws, personal liberty and property have been secure; mercantile enterprise has been allowed to reap its reward; capital has accumulated in safety; the workman has "gone forth to his work and to his labour until the evening;" and, thus protected and favoured, the manufacturing prosperity of the country has struck its roots deep, and spread forth its branches to the ends of the earth.

England has also gained by the calamities of other countries, and the intolerance of other governments. At different periods, the Flemish and French protestants, expelled from their native lands, have taken refuge in England, and have repaid the protection given them by practising and teaching branches of industry, in which the English were then less expert than their neighbours. The wars which have at different times desolated the rest of Europe, and especially those which followed the French revolution, (when mechanical invention was producing the most wonderful effects in England,) checked the progress of manufacturing improvement on the continent, and left England for many years without a competitor. At the same time, the English navy held the sovereignty of the ocean, and under its protection the commerce of this country extended beyond all former bounds, and established a firm connexion between the manufacturers of Lancashire and their customers in the most distant lands.

When the natural, political, and adventitious causes, thus enumerated, are viewed together, it cannnot be [a] matter of surprise that England has obtained a preeminence over the rest of the world in manufactures.

▷ A crucial feature of the Industrial Revolution was a new production system — the making of goods in factories. By bringing all the operations of manufacturing under one roof, industrialists made the process of production more efficient. Baines describes the factory system's advantages over former methods.

. . . Hitherto the cotton manufacture had been carried on almost entirely in the houses of the workmen: the hand or stock cards,[1] the spinning wheel, and the loom, required no larger apartment than that of a cottage. A spinning jenny[2] of small size might also be used in a cottage, and in many instances was so used: when the number of spindles was considerably increased, adjacent work-shops were used. But the water-frame, the carding engine, and the other machines which [Richard] Arkwright brought out in a finished state, required both more space than could be found in a cottage, and more power than could be applied by the human arm. Their weight also rendered it necessary to place them in strongly-built mills, and they could not be advantageously turned by any power then known but that of water.

The use of machinery was accompanied by a greater division of labour than existed in the primitive state of the manufacture; the material went through many more processes; and of course the loss of time and the risk of waste would have been much increased, if its removal from house to house at every stage of the manufacture had been necessary. It became obvious that there were several important advantages in carrying on the numerous operations of an extensive manufacture in the same building. Where water power was required, it was economy to build one mill, and put up one waterwheel, rather than several. This arrangement also enabled the master spinner himself to superintend every stage of the manufacture: it gave him a greater security against the wasteful or fraudulent consumption of the material: it saved time in the transference of the work from hand to hand: and it prevented the extreme inconvenience which would have resulted from the failure of one class of workmen to perform their part, when several other classes of work-

---

[1]Prior to spinning, raw fibers had to be carded with a brushlike tool that cleaned and separated them.
[2]The spinning jenny, which was hand-powered, was the first machine that spun fiber onto multiple spindles at the same time; that is, it produced more thread or yarn in less time than the single-thread spinning wheel.

men were dependent upon them. Another circumstance which made it advantageous to have a large number of machines in one manufactory was, that mechanics must be employed on the spot, to construct and repair the machinery, and that their time could not be fully occupied with only a few machines.

All these considerations drove the cotton spinners to that important change in the economy of English manufactures, the introduction of the factory system; and when that system had once been adopted, such were its pecuniary advantages, that mercantile competition would have rendered it impossible, even had it been desirable, to abandon it.

Adam Smith
THE DIVISION OF LABOR

Baines's emphasis on the division of labor in the expanding use of machinery can be traced to Adam Smith, who in the eighteenth century pioneered the study of economics. Adam Smith (1723–1790) was a bright and thoughtful academic who had attended Glasgow University in his native Scotland and then Oxford University in England before being appointed professor of logic at Glasgow at age twenty-eight and professor of moral philosophy at twenty-nine. After some years of travel on the Continent, Smith wrote over a span of years his masterpiece; *An Inquiry into the Nature and Causes of the Wealth of Nations* (see also page 152), published in 1776, made him instantly famous. He began *The Wealth of Nations* by analyzing the benefits of the division of labor — the system in which each worker performs a single set task or a single step in the manufacturing process.

The greatest improvement in the productive powers of Labour, and the greater skill, dexterity, and judgment with which it is anywhere directed, or applied, seem to have been the effects of the division of labour. . . .

This great increase of the quantity of work, which, in consequence of the division of labour, the same number of people are capable of performing, is owing to three different circumstances; first, to the increase of dexterity in every particular workman; secondly, to the saving of the time which is commonly lost in passing from one species of work to another; and lastly, to the invention of a great number of machines which facilitate and abridge labour, and enable one man to do the work of many. . . .

To take an example, therefore, from a very trifling manufacture; but one in which the division of labour has been very often taken notice of, the trade of the pin-maker; a workman not educated to this business (which the division of labour has rendered a distinct trade), nor acquainted with the use of the machinery employed in it (to the invention of which the same division of labour has probably given occasion), could scarce, perhaps, with his utmost industry, make one pin in a day, and certainly could not make twenty. But in the way in which this business is now carried on, not only the whole work is a peculiar trade, but it is divided into a number of branches, of which the greater part are likewise peculiar trades. One man draws out the wire, another straightens it, a third cuts it, a fourth points it, a fifth grinds it at the top for receiving the head: to make the head requires two or three distinct operations; to put it on is a peculiar business; to whiten the pins is another; it is even a trade by itself to put them into the paper; and the important business of making a pin is, in this manner, divided into about eighteen distinct operations, which, in some manufactories, are all performed by distinct hands, though in others the same man will sometimes perform two or three of them. I have seen a small manufactory of this kind where ten men only were employed, and where some of them consequently performed two or three distinct operations. But though they were very poor [craftsmen], and therefore but indifferently accommodated with the necessary machinery, they could, when they exerted themselves, make among them about twelve pounds of pins in a day. There are in a pound upwards of four thousand pins of a middling size. Those ten persons, therefore, could make among them upwards of forty-eight thousand pins in a day. Each person, therefore, making a tenth part of forty-eight thousand pins, might be considered as making four thousand eight hundred pins in a day. But if they had all wrought separately and independently, and without any of them having been educated to this peculiar business, they certainly could not each of them have made twenty, perhaps not one pin in a day; that is, certainly, not the two hundred and fortieth, perhaps not the four thousand eight hundredth part of what they are at present capable of performing, in consequence of a proper division and combination of their different operations. . . .

REVIEW QUESTIONS

1. What natural assets for industrial development did England possess?
2. How did England's location in Europe and the world affect its industrial development?
3. What characteristics of English society and government contributed to the rise of the Industrial Revolution?
4. What was the role of British sea power in the Industrial Revolution?
5. What were the factory system's advantages over the domestic system of production?
6. How, according to Adam Smith, did the division of labor lead to increased productivity?

▼▼▼

2 ▼ Industrialism and the Spirit of Private Enterprise

A vigorous spirit of enterprise and the opportunity for men of ability to rise from common origins to riches and fame help explain the growth of industrialism in England. These industrial capitalists adopted the attitude of medieval monks that "idleness is the enemy of the soul," to which they added "time is money."

Edward Baines
THE CAREER OF RICHARD ARKWRIGHT

The spirit of enterprise is illustrated in the career of Richard Arkwright (1732–1792), one of the leading pioneers in the cotton industry. Arkwright began as an inventor of spinning machines and a promoter of factories and soon progressed to full-blown entrepreneurship. He was eventually knighted for his accomplishments. In the following excerpt from *The History of the Cotton Manufacture in Great Britain,* Edward Baines (see page 136) describes Arkwright's extraordinary rise to success and prominence.

Richard Arkwright rose by the force of his natural talents from a very humble condition in society. He was born at Preston on the 23d of December, 1732, of poor parents: being the youngest of thirteen children, his parents could only afford to give him an education of the humblest kind, and he was scarcely able to write. He was brought up to the trade of a barber at Kirkham and Preston, and established himself in that business at Bolton in the year 1760. Having become possessed of a chemical process for dyeing human hair, which in that day (when wigs were universal) was of considerable value, he travelled about collecting hair, and again disposing of it when dyed. In 1761, he married a wife from Leigh, and the connexions he thus formed in that town are supposed to have afterwards brought him acquainted with Highs's experiments in making spinning machines. He himself manifested a strong bent for experiments in mechanics, which he is stated to have followed with so much devotedness as to have neglected his business and injured his circumstances. His natural disposition was ardent, enterprising, and stubbornly persevering: his mind was as coarse as it was bold and active, and his manners were rough and unpleasing.

▷ This uncouth mechanic produced a series of power-driven machines for all phases of textile manufacture — from carding to spinning — that revolutionized the industry and made him rich.

When this admirable series of machines was made known, and by their means yarns were produced far superior in quality to any before spun in England, as well as lower in price, a mighty impulse was communicated to the cotton manufacture. Weavers could now obtain an unlimited quantity of yarn, at a reasonable price; manufacturers could use warps [crossthreads in woven fabric] of cotton, which were much cheaper than the linen warps formerly used. Cotton fabrics could be sold lower than had ever before been known. The demand for them consequently increased. The shuttle [tool that carries thread in a loom] flew with fresh energy, and the weavers earned immoderately high wages. Spinning mills were erected to supply the requisite quantity of yarn. The fame of Arkwright resounded through the land; and capitalists flocked to him to buy his patent machines, or permission to use them. . . .

The most marked traits in the character of Arkwright were his wonderful ardour, energy, and perseverance. He commonly laboured in his multifarious concerns from five o'clock in the morning till nine at night; and when considerably more than fifty years of age, — feeling that the defects of his education placed him under great difficulty and inconvenience in conducting his correspondence, and in the general management of his business, — he encroached upon his sleep, in order to gain an hour each day to learn English grammar, and another hour to improve his writing and orthography [spelling]! He was impatient of whatever interfered with his favourite pursuits; and the fact is too strikingly characteristic not to be mentioned, that he separated from his wife not many years after their marriage, because she, convinced that he would starve his family . . . [because of the impracticality of some of his schemes], broke some of his experimental models of machinery. Arkwright was a severe economist of time; and, that he might not waste a moment, he generally travelled with four horses, and at a very rapid speed. His concerns in Derbyshire, Lancashire, and Scotland were so extensive and numerous, as to [show] at once his astonishing power of transacting business and his all-grasping spirit. In many of these he had partners, but he generally managed in such a way, that, whoever lost, he himself was a gainer. . . . His speculative schemes were vast and daring; he contemplated entering into the most extensive mercantile transactions, and buying up all the cotton in the world, in order to make an enormous profit by the monopoly: and from the extravagance of some of these designs, his judicious friends were of opinion, that if he had lived to put them in practice, he might have [impoverished himself].

REVIEW QUESTIONS

1. What character traits enabled Richard Arkwright, a poor barber, to rise to knighthood, fortune, and fame?
2. What social, economic, and political conditions do you think made Arkwright's remarkable success possible?
3. What qualities made Arkwright a capitalist?

"rags to riches" story could move up. *"spirit of Rev".*

Indust. Rev. cheap labor avail. cons... *Support of Parl. to protect textile industry*

3 ▼ Factory Discipline

For the new industries to succeed, workers needed to adopt the rigorous discipline exercised by the new industrial capitalists themselves. But adapting to labor with machines in factories proved traumatic for the poor, uneducated, and often unruly folk, who previously had toiled on farms and in village workshops and were used to a less demanding pace.

FACTORY RULES

The problem of adapting a preindustrial labor force to the discipline needed for coordinating large numbers of workers in the factory was common to all industrializing countries. The Foundry and Engineering Works of the Royal Overseas Trading Company, in the Moabit section of Berlin, issued the following rules in 1844. The rules aimed at instilling obedience and honesty as well as "good order and harmony" among the factory's workers. The rules not only stressed time-keeping (with appropriate fines for latecomers), but also proper conduct in all aspects of life and work in the factory.

In every large works, and in the co-ordination of any large number of workmen, good order and harmony must be looked upon as the fundamentals of success, and therefore the following rules shall be strictly observed.

Every man employed in the concern . . . shall receive a copy of these rules, so that no one can plead ignorance. Its acceptance shall be deemed to mean consent to submit to its regulations.

(1) The normal working day begins at all seasons at 6 A.M. precisely and ends, after the usual break of half an hour for breakfast, an hour for dinner and half an hour for tea, at 7 P.M., and it shall be strictly observed.

Five minutes before the beginning of the

stated hours of work until their actual commencement, a bell shall ring and indicate that every worker employed in the concern has to proceed to his place of work, in order to start as soon as the bell stops.

The doorkeeper shall lock the door punctually at 6 A.M., 8:30 A.M., 1 P.M. and 4:30 P.M.

Workers arriving 2 minutes late shall lose half an hour's wages; whoever is more than 2 minutes late may not start work until after the next break, or at least shall lose his wages until then. Any disputes about the correct time shall be settled by the clock mounted above the gatekeeper's lodge.

These rules are valid both for time- and for piece-workers, and in cases of breaches of these rules, workmen shall be fined in proportion to their earnings. The deductions from the wage shall be entered in the wage-book of the gatekeeper whose duty they are; they shall be unconditionally accepted as it will not be possible to enter into any discussions about them.

(2) When the bell is rung to denote the end of the working day, every workman, both on piece- and on day-wage, shall leave his workshop and the yard, but is not allowed to make preparations for his departure before the bell rings. Every breach of this rule shall lead to a fine of five silver groschen [pennies] to the sick fund. Only those who have obtained special permission by the overseer may stay on in the workshop in order to work. — If a workman has worked beyond the closing bell, he must give his name to the gatekeeper on leaving, on pain of losing his payment for the overtime.

(3) No workman, whether employed by time or piece, may leave before the end of the working day, without having first received permission from the overseer and having given his name to the gatekeeper. Omission of these two actions shall lead to a fine of ten silver groschen payable to the sick fund.

(4) Repeated irregular arrival at work shall lead to dismissal. This shall also apply to those who are found idling by an official or overseer, and refuse to obey their order to resume work.

(5) Entry to the firm's property by any but the designated gateway, and exit by any prohibited route, e.g. by climbing fences or walls, or by crossing the Spree [River], shall be punished by a fine of fifteen silver groschen to the sick fund for the first offences, and dismissal for the second.

(6) No worker may leave his place of work otherwise than for reasons connected with his work.

(7) All conversation with fellow-workers is prohibited; if any worker requires information about his work, he must turn to the overseer, or to the particular fellow-worker designated for the purpose.

(8) Smoking in the workshops or in the yard is prohibited during working hours; anyone caught smoking shall be fined five silver groschen for the sick fund for every such offence.

(9) Every worker is responsible for cleaning up his space in the workshop, and if in doubt, he is to turn to his overseer. — All tools must always be kept in good condition, and must be cleaned after use. This applies particularly to the turner, regarding his lathe.

(10) Natural functions must be performed at the appropriate places, and whoever is found soiling walls, fences, squares, etc., and similarly, whoever is found washing his face and hands in the workshop and not in the places assigned for the purpose, shall be fined five silver groschen for the sick fund.

(11) On completion of his piece of work, every workman must hand it over at once to his foreman or superior, in order to receive a fresh piece of work. Pattern makers must on no account hand over their patterns to the foundry without express order of their supervisors. No workman may take over work from his fellow-workman without instruction to that effect by the foreman.

(12) It goes without saying that all overseers and officials of the firm shall be obeyed without question, and shall be treated with due deference. Disobedience will be punished by dismissal.

(13) Immediate dismissal shall also be the fate of anyone found drunk in any of the workshops.

(14) Untrue allegations against superiors or officials of the concern shall lead to stern reprimand, and may lead to dismissal. The same punishment shall be meted out to those who knowingly allow errors to slip through when supervising or stocktaking.

(15) Every workman is obliged to report to his superiors any acts of dishonesty or embezzlement on the part of his fellow workmen. If he omits to do so, and it is shown after subsequent discovery of a misdemeanour that he knew about it at the time, he shall be liable to be taken to court as an accessory after the fact and the wage due to him shall be retained as punishment. Conversely, anyone denouncing a theft in such a way as to allow conviction of the thief shall receive a reward of two Thaler [dollar equivalent], and, if necessary, his name shall be kept confidential. — Further, the gatekeeper and the watchman, as well as every official, are entitled to search the baskets, parcels, aprons etc. of the women and children who are taking the dinners into the works, on their departure, as well as search any worker suspected of stealing any article whatever. . . .

(18) Advances shall be granted only to the older workers, and even to them only in exceptional circumstances. As long as he is working by the piece, the workman is entitled merely to his fixed weekly wage as subsistence pay; the extra earnings shall be paid out only on completion of the whole piece contract. If a workman leaves before his piece contract is completed, either of his own free will, or on being dismissed as punishment, or because of illness, the partly completed work shall be valued by the general manager with the help of two overseers, and he will be paid accordingly. There is no appeal against the decision of these experts.

(19) A free copy of these rules is handed to every workman, but whoever loses it and requires a new one, or cannot produce it on leaving, shall be fined 2½ silver groschen, payable to the sick fund.

REVIEW QUESTIONS

1. How long was the working day in the Berlin factory? How much time off were the workers allowed?
2. Besides punctuality, what other aspects of factory work required official regulation?
3. Judging by the Berlin factory rules, what were the differences between preindustrial and industrial work routines?
4. How might these rules have affected the lives of families?

▼▼▼

4 ▼ The Dark Side of Industrialization

Among the numerous problems caused by rapid industrialization, none aroused greater concern among humanitarians than child labor in factories and mines. In preindustrial times, children had always been part of the labor force, indoors and out, a practice that was continued during the early days of the Industrial Revolution. In the cotton industry, for instance, the proportion of children and adolescents under eighteen was around 40–45 percent of the labor force; in some large firms the proportion was even greater. Employers discovered early that youngsters adapted more easily to machines and factory discipline than did adults, who were used to traditional handicraft routines. Child labor took children away from their parents, undermined family life, and deprived children of schooling. Factory routines dulled their minds, and the long hours spent in often unsanitary environments endangered their health.

Sadler Commission
REPORT ON CHILD LABOR

Due to concern about child labor, in 1832 a parliamentary committee chaired by Michael Thomas Sadler investigated the situation of children employed in British factories. The following testimonies are drawn from the records of the Sadler Commission.

COMMITTEE ON FACTORIES BILL: MINUTES OF EVIDENCE.

[April 12,] 1832.
Michael Thomas Sadler, Esquire, in the Chair.
William Cooper, called in: and Examined.

What is your business? — I follow the cloth-dressing at present.[1]

What is your age? — I was eight-and-twenty last February.

When did you first begin to work in mills or factories? — When I was about ten years of age.

With whom did you first work? — At Mr. Benyon's flax mills, in Meadowlane, Leeds.

What were your usual hours of working? — We began at five, and gave over at nine; at five o'clock in the morning.

And you gave over at nine o'clock? — At nine at night.

At what distance might you have lived from the mill? — About a mile and a half.

At what time had you to get up in the morning to attend to your labour? — I had to be up soon after four o'clock.

Every morning? — Every morning.

What intermissions had you for meals? — When we began at five in the morning, we went on until noon, and then we had 40 minutes for dinner.

Had you no time for breakfast? — No, we got it as we could, while we were working.

Had you any time for an afternoon refreshment, or what is called in Yorkshire your "drinking?" — No; when we began at noon, we went on till night; there was only one stoppage, the 40 minutes for dinner.

Then as you had to get your breakfast, and what is called "drinking" in that manner, you had to put it on one side? — Yes, we had to put it on one side; and when we got our frames doffed,[2] we ate two or three mouthfuls, and then put it by again.

Is there not considerable dust in a flax mill? — A flax mill is very dusty indeed.

Was not your food therefore frequently spoiled? — Yes, at times with the dust; sometimes we could not eat it, when it had got a lot of dust on.

What were you when you were ten years old? — What is called a bobbin-doffer;[3] when the frames are quite full, we have to doff them.

Then as you lived so far from home, you took your dinner to the mill? — We took all our meals with us, living so far off.

During the 40 minutes which you were al-

---

[1]In the original source, each paragraph was numbered; paragraphs 1–18 and 21–35 are in this section.

[2]*Frames* refers to the spinning machines, which were built on a bulky framework; *doff* means to lift off the spindles full of yarn.

[3]A bobbin-doffer was usually a child, whose job was to remove the spindles (bobbins) when filled with thread or yarn.

lowed for dinner, had you ever to employ that time in your turn in cleaning the machinery? — At times we had to stop to clean the machinery, and then we got our dinner as well as we could; they paid us for that. . . .

Did you ever work even later than the time you have mentioned? — I cannot say that I worked later there. I had a sister who worked up stairs, and she worked till 11 at night, in what they call the card-room.[4]

At what time in the morning did she begin work? — At the same time as myself.

And they kept her there till 11 at night? — Till 11 at night.

You say that your sister was in the card-room? — Yes.

Is not that a very dusty department? — Yes, very dusty indeed.

She had to be at the mill at five, and was kept at work till eleven at night? — Yes.

During the whole time she was there? — During the whole time; there was only 40 minutes allowed at dinner out of that.

To keep you at your work for such a length of time, and especially towards the termination of such a day's labour as that, what means were taken to keep you awake and attentive? — They strapped [beat] us at times, when we were not quite ready to be doffing the frame when it was full.

Were you frequently strapped? — At times we were frequently strapped.

What sort of strap was it? — About this length (describing it).

What was it made of? — Of leather.

Were you occasionally very considerably hurt with the strap? — Sometimes it hurt us very much, and sometimes they did not lay on so hard as they did at others.

Were the girls strapped in that sort of way? — They did not strap what they called the grown-up women.

Were any of the female children strapped? —

Yes; they were strapped in the same way as the lesser boys.

What were your wages at 10 years old at Mr. Benyon's? — I think it was 4 *s*. [shillings][5] a week.

[*May 18,*] *1832.*
Michael Thomas Sadler, Esquire, in the chair.
Mr. Matthew Crabtree, called in; and Examined.

What age are you? — Twenty-two.[6]

What is your occupation? — A blanket manufacturer.

Have you ever been employed in a factory? — Yes.

At what age did you first go to work in one? — Eight.

How long did you continue in that occupation? — Four years.

Will you state the hours of labour at the period when you first went to the factory, in ordinary times? — From 6 in the morning to 8 at night.

Fourteen hours? — Yes.

With what intervals for refreshment and rest? — An hour at noon.

Then you had no resting time allowed in which to take your breakfast, or what is in Yorkshire called your "drinking"? — No.

When trade was brisk what were your hours? — From 5 in the morning to 9 in the evening.

Sixteen hours? — Yes.

With what intervals at dinner? — An hour.

How far did you live from the mill? — About two miles.

Was there any time allowed for you to get your breakfast in the mill? — No.

Did you take it before you left home? — Generally.

During those long hours of labour could you be punctual, how did you awake? — I seldom

---

[4]In the card-room was a machine for separating fibers from one another, prior to being spun into yarn.

[5]A shilling equals 12 pence or 1/20 of a British pound.
[6]Like the preceding section, each paragraph in this section is numbered in the original source: 2481–2519 and 2597–2604.

did awake spontaneously. I was most generally awoke or lifted out of bed, sometimes asleep, by my parents.

Were you always in time? — No.

What was the consequence if you had been too late? — I was most commonly beaten.

Severely? — Very severely, I thought.

In whose factory was this? — Messrs. Hague & Cook's, of Dewsbury.

Will you state the effect that those long hours had upon the state of your health and feelings? — I was, when working those long hours, commonly very much fatigued at night, when I left my work, so much so that I sometimes should have slept as I walked if I had not stumbled and started awake again, and so sick often that I could not eat, and what I did eat I vomited.

Did this labour destroy your appetite? — It did.

In what situation were you in that mill? — I was a piecener [see below].

Will you state to the Committee whether piecening is a very laborious employment for children, or not? — It is a very laborious employment. Pieceners are continually running to and fro, and on their feet the whole day.

The duty of the piecener is to take the cardings from one part of the machinery, and to place them on another? — Yes.

So that the labour is not only continual, but it is unabated to the last? — It is unabated to the last.

Do you not think, from your own experience, that the speed of the machinery is so calculated as to demand the utmost exertions of a child, supposing the hours were moderate? — It is as much as they could do at the best; they are always upon the stretch, and it is commonly very difficult to keep up with their work.

State the condition of the children towards the latter part of the day, who have thus to keep up with the machinery? — It is as much as they can do when they are not very much fatigued to keep up with their work, and towards the close of the day, when they come to be more fatigued, they cannot keep up with it very well,

and the consequence is that they are beaten to spur them on.

Were you beaten under those circumstances? — Yes.

Frequently? — Very frequently.

And principally at the latter end of the day? — Yes.

And is it your belief that if you had not been so beaten, you should not have got through the work? — I should not if I had not been kept up to it by some means.

Does beating then principally occur at the latter end of the day, when the children are exceedingly fatigued? — It does at the latter end of the day, and in the morning sometimes, when they are very drowsy, and have not got rid of the fatigue of the day before.

What were you beaten with principally? — A strap.

Any thing else? — Yes, a stick sometimes; and there is a kind of roller which runs on the top of the machine called a billy, perhaps two or three yards in length, and perhaps an inch and a half, or more, in diameter; the circumference would be four or five inches, I cannot speak exactly.

Were you beaten with that instrument? — Yes.

Have you yourself been beaten, and have you seen other children struck severely with that roller? — I have been struck very severely with it myself, so much so as to knock me down, and I have seen other children have their heads broken with it.

You think that it is a general practice to beat the children with the roller? — It is.

You do not think then that you were worse treated than other children in the mill? — No, I was not, perhaps not so bad as some were. . . .

Can you speak as to the effect of this labour in the mills and factories on the morals of the children, as far as you have observed? — As far as I have observed with regard to morals in the mills, there is every thing about them that is disgusting to every one conscious of correct morality.

Do you find that the children, the females especially, are very early demoralized in them? — They are.

Is their language indecent? — Very indecent; and both sexes take great familiarities with each other in the mills, without at all being ashamed of their conduct.

Do you connect their immorality of language and conduct with their excessive labour? — It may be somewhat connected with it, for it is to be observed that most of that goes on towards night, when they begin to be drowsy; it is a kind of stimulus which they use to keep them awake; they say some pert thing or other to keep themselves from drowsiness, and it generally happens to be some obscene language.

Have not a considerable number of the females employed in mills illegitimate children very early in life? — I believe there are; I have known some of them have illegitimate children when they were between 16 and 17 years of age.

How many grown up females had you in the mill? — I cannot speak to the exact number that were grown up; perhaps there might be thirty-four or so that worked in the mill at that time.

How many of those had illegitimate children? — A great many of them, eighteen or nineteen of them, I think.

Did they generally marry the men by whom they had the children? — No, it sometimes happens that young women have children by married men, and I have known an instance, a few weeks since, where one of the young women had a child by a married man.

Friedrich Engels
≪ THE CONDITION OF THE WORKING CLASS IN ENGLAND ≫

Rapid industrialization produced a drastic change of environment for workers, who moved from the casual, slow-paced English villages and small towns to large, congested, and impersonal industrial cities. The familiar social patterns and cherished values by which preindustrial people had oriented themselves grew weak or disappeared, for these patterns and values clashed with the requirements of the new industrial age. Many people in England, from the highest to the lowest classes, still felt wedded to the old ways and hated the congested industrial centers. The miseries of the industrial towns distressed Friedrich Engels (1820–1895), a well-to-do German intellectual and son of a prosperous German manufacturer. In the early 1840s, Engels moved to Manchester, a great English industrial center, where he eventually established himself in business. In that decade, he also entered into a lifelong collaboration with Karl Marx, the founder of modern socialism (see page 156). Engels yearned for the fellowship and the pleasures of nature that he had experienced in preindustrial Germany. In the new urban centers, even in cosmopolitan London, he found only alienation and human degradation, which he described in his *Condition of the Working Class in England* (1844).

. . . It is only when [a person] has visited the slums of this great city that it dawns upon him that the inhabitants of modern London have had to sacrifice so much that is best in human nature in order to create those wonders of civilisation with which their city teems. The vast majority of Londoners have had to let so many of their potential creative faculties lie dormant, stunted and unused in order that a small, closely-knit group of their fellow citizens could develop to the full the qualities with which nature has endowed them. The restless and noisy activity of the crowded streets is highly distasteful, and it is surely abhorrent to human nature itself. Hundreds of thousands of men and women drawn from all classes and ranks of society pack the streets of London. Are they not all human beings with the same innate characteristics and potentialities? Are they not all equally interested in the pursuit of happiness? And do they not all aim at happiness by following similar methods? Yet they rush past each other as if they had nothing in common. They are tacitly agreed on one thing only — that everyone should keep to the right of the pavement so as not to collide with the stream of people moving in the opposite direction. No one even thinks of sparing a glance for his neighbour in the streets. The more that Londoners are packed into a tiny space, the more repulsive and disgraceful becomes the brutal indifference with which they ignore their neighbours and selfishly concentrate upon their private affairs. We know well enough that this isolation of the individual — this narrowminded egotism — is everywhere the fundamental principle of modern society. But nowhere is this selfish egotism so blatantly evident as in the frantic bustle of the great city. The disintegration of society into individuals, each guided by his private principles and each pursuing his own aims, has been pushed to its furthest limits in London. Here indeed human society has been split into its component atoms.

From this it follows that the social conflict — the war of all against all — is fought in the open. . . . Here men regard their fellows not as human beings, but as pawns in the struggle for existence. Everyone exploits his neighbour with the result that the stronger tramples the weaker under foot. The strongest of all, a tiny group of capitalists, monopolise everything, while the weakest, who are in the vast majority, succumb to the most abject poverty.

What is true of London, is true also of all the great towns, such as Manchester, Birmingham and Leeds. Everywhere one finds on the one hand the most barbarous indifference and selfish egotism and on the other the most distressing scenes of misery and poverty. . . .

Every great town has one or more slum areas into which the working classes are packed. Sometimes, of course, poverty is to be found hidden away in alleys close to the stately homes of the wealthy. Generally, however, the workers are segregated in separate districts where they struggle through life as best they can out of sight of the more fortunate classes of society. The slums of the English towns have much in common — the worst houses in a town being found in the worst districts. They are generally unplanned wildernesses of one- or two-storied terrace houses built of brick. Wherever possible these have cellars which are also used as dwellings. These little houses of three or four rooms and a kitchen are called cottages, and throughout England, except for some parts of London, are where the working classes normally live. The streets themselves are usually unpaved and full of holes. They are filthy and strewn with animal and vegetable refuse. Since they have neither gutters nor drains the refuse accumulates in stagnant, stinking puddles. Ventilation in the slums is inadequate owing to the hopelessly unplanned nature of these areas. A great many people live huddled together in a very small area, and so it is easy to imagine the nature of the air in these workers' quarters.

REVIEW QUESTIONS

1. According to the testimonies given the Sadler Commission, how young were the children employed in the factories? How many hours and at what times of day did they work?

2. What do you think were the reasons for the employment of children from the employers' point of view? From the parents' point of view?
3. What measures were employed in the factories to keep children alert at their tasks?
4. According to Friedrich Engels, how had the industrial city caused deterioration in the quality of human relationships? What did he mean by the statement that "human society has been split into its component atoms"?

▼▼▼

5 ▼ The Brighter Side of Industrialization

While rapid industrialization produced numerous instances of working-class distress, historians largely agree that the workers' standard of living generally increased over the short term and increased substantially over the long term. The new mechanical methods of production made it possible to feed and clothe an expanding population and ultimately reduced the burdens of heavy labor. Moreover, there were numerous examples of factory owners who treated their employees well.

Andrew Ure
DECENT WORKING AND LIVING CONDITIONS

Andrew Ure (1778–1857), a scientist and an early observer of industrialization, challenged the pessimists of his day. In the following passages from his *Philosophy of Manufactures* (1835), Ure disagreed with the testimony given to the Sadler Commission and stressed the benefits to workers accruing from the factory system.

Of all the common prejudices that exist with regard to factory labour, there is none more unfounded than that which ascribes to it excessive tedium and irksomeness above other occupations, owing to its being carried on in conjunction with the "unceasing motion of the steam-engine." In an establishment for spinning or weaving cotton, all the hard work is performed by the steam-engine which leaves for the attendant no hard labour at all, and literally nothing to do in general; but at intervals to perform some delicate operation, such as joining the threads that break, taking the cops off the spindles, &c. And it is so far from being true that the work in a factory is incessant, because the motion of the steam-engine is incessant, that the fact is, that the labour is not incessant on that very account, because it is performed in conjunction with the steam-engine. Of all manufacturing employments, those are by far the most irksome and incessant in which steam-engines are not employed, as in lace-running and stocking-weaving; and the way to prevent an employment from being incessant, is to introduce a steam-engine into it. These remarks certainly apply more especially to the labour of children in factories. Three-fourths of the children so employed are engaged in piecing at the mules.[1] "When the carriages of these have re-

---

[1]Mules are machines that draw and twist fiber into thread and wind this into cops (pyramids of threads wound on tubes). A piecener moves the wool from one part of the machinery to another.

ceded a foot and a half or two feet from the rollers," says Mr. Tufnell, "nothing is to be done, not even attention is required from either spinner or piecer." Both of them stand idle for a time, and in fine spinning particularly, for three-quarters of a minute, or more. Consequently, if a child remains at this business twelve hours daily, he has nine hours of inaction. And though he attends two mules, he has still six hours of non-exertion. Spinners sometimes dedicate these intervals to the perusal of books. The scavengers,[2] who in Mr. Sadler's report have been described as being "constantly in a state of grief, always in terror, and every moment they have to spare stretched all their length upon the floor in a state of perspiration," may be observed in cotton-factories idle for *four* minutes at a time, or moving about in a sportive mood, utterly unconscious of the tragical scenes in which they were dramatized.

Occupations which are assisted by steam-engines require for the most part a higher, or at least a steadier species of labour, than those which are not; the exercise of the mind being then partially substituted for that of the muscles, constituting skilled labour, which is always paid more highly than unskilled. On this principle we can readily account for the comparatively high wages which the inmates of a factory, whether children or adults, obtain. . . .

What I have myself witnessed at several times, both on Sundays and working-days, has convinced me that the population of Belper is, in reference to health, domestic comfort, and religious culture, in a truly enviable state, compared with the average of our agricultural villages. The factory rooms are well aired, and as clean as any gentleman's parlour. The children are well-complexioned, and work with cheerful dexterity at their respective occupations.

At Quarry Bank, near Wilmslow, in Cheshire, is situated the oldest of the five establishments belonging to the great firm of Messrs.

Greg and Sons, of Manchester, who work up the one-hundredth part of all the cotton consumed in Great Britain. It is driven by an elegant water-wheel, 32 feet in diameter, and 24 feet broad, equivalent in power to 120 horses. The country road is beautiful, and presents a succession of picturesque wooded dells interspersed with richly cultivated fields. At a little distance from the factory, on a sunny slope, stands a handsome house, two stories high, built for the accommodation of the female apprentices. Here are well fed, clothed, educated, and lodged, under kind superintendence, sixty young girls, who by their deportment at the mill, as well as in Wilmslow Church on Sunday, where I saw them assembled, evince a degree of comfort most creditable to the humane and intelligent proprietors. . . .

Sufficient evidence has been adduced to convince the candid mind, that factories, more especially cotton-mills, are so organized as to afford as easy and comfortable occupation as anywhere can fall to the lot of the labouring classes.

What a pity it is that the party who lately declaimed so loudly about the inmates of factories being universally victims of oppression, misery, and vice, did not, from their rural or civic retreats, examine first of all into the relative condition of their own rustic operatives, and dispassionately see how the balance stood betwixt them! . . . It is, in fact, in the factory districts alone that the demoralizing agency of pauperism has been effectually resisted, and a noble spirit of industry, enterprise, and intelligence, called forth. What a contrast is there at this day, between the torpor and brutality which pervade very many of the farming parishes, as delineated in the official reports, and the beneficent activity which animates all the cotton factory towns, villages, and hamlets!

The regularity required in mills is such as to render persons who are in the habit of getting intoxicated unfit to be employed there, and all respectable manufacturers object to employ persons guilty of that vice; and thus mill-work tends to check drunkenness. Mr. Marshall,

---

[2]Scavengers were children who collected the loose cotton lying on the floor and around the machinery.

M.P. [Member of Parliament] of Leeds, thinks that the health of persons employed in mills is better from the regularity of their habits, than of those employed at home in weaving.

REVIEW QUESTIONS

1. How did Andrew Ure respond to the argument that factory work entailed incessant hard labor?
2. What was his opinion of the working and living conditions in the districts that he had visited? What comparison did he draw between factory districts and farming parishes?

▼▼▼

6 ▼ The New Science of Political Economy

The new spirit of scientific inquiry manifest in the seventeenth and eighteenth centuries extended also into the economic field, creating the new science of political economy. Its pioneer was Adam Smith, author of the classic book *The Wealth of Nations* (1776; see also page 139). Smith was an optimist, in favor of leaving individuals' economic activities to their own devices. For that reason he condemned government interference in the economy — so common in his day under the protectionist government's mercantilism policy, which sought to increase the nation's wealth by expanding exports while minimizing imports. The "invisible hand," which according to Smith turned individual gain into social advantage, also favored free trade among nations based on an international division of labor.

Adam Smith's optimistic assumptions were soon called into question by Thomas Robert Malthus (1766–1834). A Church of England clergyman and professor of history and political economy at a small college run by the East India Company, Malthus gave the study of political economy not only a moral but also a pessimistic twist; he was more concerned with the poverty of nations. He contributed two books to the science of political economy. The first, *An Essay on the Principle of Population, as It Affects the Future Improvement of Society,* was published in 1798. It was followed in 1803 by a second and enlarged edition entitled *An Essay on the Principle of Population, or, a View of Its Past and Present Effects on Human Happiness.* In these works Malthus argued that population growth was the true reason for the poverty of the poor.

Adam Smith
≪ THE WEALTH OF NATIONS ≫

The Wealth of Nations carries the important message of *laissez-faire,* which means that the government should intervene as little as possible in economic affairs and leave the market to its own devices. It advocates the liberation of economic production from all limiting regulation in order to benefit "the people and the sovereign," not only in Great Britain but in the community of countries. Admittedly, in his advocacy of free trade Smith made allowance for the national interest, justifying "certain public works and certain public institutions," including the government and the state. He defended, for instance, the Navigation Acts, which stipulated that goods brought from its overseas colonies into England be carried in British ships. Neither did he want to ruin established industries by introducing free trade too suddenly. His preference was clearly for economic cooperation among nations as a source of peace. Adam Smith was an eighteenth-century cosmopolitan who viewed political economy as an international system. In the passage that follows, Smith argues that economic activity unrestricted by government best serves the individual and society.

Every individual is continually exerting himself to find out the most advantageous employment for whatever capital he can command. It is his own advantage, indeed, and not that of the society, which he has in view. But the study of his own advantage, naturally, or rather necessarily, leads him to prefer that employment which is most advantageous to the society. . . .

. . . As every individual, therefore, endeavours as much as he can both to employ his capital in the support of domestic industry, and so to direct that industry that its produce may be of the greatest value, every individual necessarily labours to render the annual revenue of the society as great as he can. He generally, indeed, neither intends to promote the public interest, nor knows how much he is promoting it. By preferring the support of domestic to that of foreign industry, he intends only his own security; and by directing that industry in such a manner as its produce may be of the greatest value, he intends only his own gain, and he is in this, as in many other cases, led by an invisible hand to promote an end which was no part of his intention. Nor is it always the worse for the society that it was no part of it. By pursuing his own interest he frequently promotes that of the society more effectually than when he really intends to promote it. I have never known much good done by those who affected to trade for the public good. . . .

. . . The statesman who should attempt to direct private people in what manner they ought to employ their capitals, would not only load himself with a most unnecessary attention, but assume an authority which could safely be trusted, not only to no single person, but to no council or senate whatever, and which would nowhere be so dangerous as in the hands of a man who had folly and presumption enough to fancy himself fit to exercise it. . . .

It is thus that every system which endeavours, either by extraordinary encouragements to draw towards a particular species of industry a greater share of the capital of the society than would naturally go to it, or, by extraordinary restraints, force from a particular species of industry some share of the capital which would otherwise be employed in it, is in reality subversive to the great purpose which it means to promote. It retards, instead of accelerating, the progress of the society towards real wealth and greatness; and diminishes, instead of increasing, the real value of the annual produce of its land and labour.

All systems either of preference or of restraint, therefore, being thus completely taken away, the obvious and simple system of natural liberty establishes itself of its own accord. Every man, as long as he does not violate the laws of justice, is left perfectly free to pursue his own interest his own way, and to bring both his industry and capital into competition with those of any other man, or order of men. The sovereign is completely discharged from a duty, in the attempting to perform which he must always be exposed to innumerable delusions, and for the proper performance of which no human wisdom or knowledge could ever be sufficient; the duty of superintending the industry of private people, and of directing it towards the employments most suitable to the interest of the society. According to the system of natural liberty, the sovereign has only three duties to attend to; three duties of great importance, indeed, but plain and intelligible to common understandings: first, the duty of protecting the society from the violence and invasion of other independent societies: secondly, the duty of protecting, as far as possible, every member of the society from the injustice or oppression of every other member of it, or the duty of establishing an exact administration of justice; and, thirdly, the duty of erecting and maintaining certain public works and certain public institutions which it can never be for the interest of any individual, or small number of individuals, to erect and maintain; because the profit could never repay the expense to any individual or small number of individuals, though it may frequently do much more than repay it to a great society.

Thomas R. Malthus
≪ ON THE PRINCIPLE OF POPULATION ≫

Malthus assumed that population tended forever to outgrow the resources needed to sustain it. The balance between population and its life-sustaining resources was elementally maintained, he gloomily argued, by famine, war, and other fatal calamities. As a clergyman, he believed in sexual abstinence as the means of limiting population growth. He also saw little need to better the condition of the poor, whom he considered the most licentious part of the population, because he believed that they would then breed faster and, by upsetting the population/resource balance, bring misery to all. This view that poverty was an iron law of nature buttressed supporters of strict laissez-faire who opposed government action to aid the poor.

[POPULATION'S EFFECTS ON SOCIETY]

I have read some of the speculations on the perfectibility of man and of society with great pleasure. I have been warmed and delighted with the enchanting picture which they hold forth. I ardently wish for such happy improvements. But I see great and, to my understanding, unconquerable difficulties in the way to them. These difficulties it is my present purpose to state, declaring, at the same time, that so far from exulting in them, as a cause of triumphing over the friends of innovation, nothing would give me greater pleasure than to see them completely removed. . . .

[These difficulties are]

First, That food is necessary to the existence of man.

Secondly, That the passion between the sexes is necessary and will remain nearly in its present state.

These two laws, ever since we have had any knowledge of mankind, appear to have been fixed laws of our nature; and as we have not hitherto seen any alteration in them, we have no right to conclude that they will ever cease to be what they are now, without an immediate act of power in that Being who first arranged the system of the universe, and for the advantage of His creatures, still executes, according to fixed laws, all its various operations. . . .

Assuming, then, my postulata as granted, I say that the power of population is indefinitely greater than the power in the earth to produce subsistence for man.

Population, when unchecked, increases in a geometrical ratio. Subsistence only increases in an arithmetical ratio. A slight acquaintance with numbers will show the immensity of the first power in comparison of the second.

By that law of our nature which makes food necessary to the life of man, the effects of these two unequal powers must be kept equal.

This implies a strong and constantly operating check on population from the difficulty of subsistence. This difficulty must fall somewhere and must necessarily be severely felt by a large portion of mankind. . . .

This natural inequality of the two powers of population and of production in the earth, and that great law of our nature which must constantly keep their efforts equal, form the great difficulty that to me appears insurmountable in the way to perfectibility of society. . . .

Consequently, if the premises are just, the argument is conclusive against the perfectibility of the mass of mankind.

[POPULATION'S EFFECTS ON HUMAN HAPPINESS]

The ultimate check to population appears then to be a want of food, arising necessarily from the different ratios according to which population and food increase. But this ultimate check is never the immediate check, except in cases of actual famine.

The immediate check may be stated to consist in all those customs, and all those diseases, which seem to be generated by a scarcity of the means of subsistence; and all those causes, independent of this scarcity, which tend prematurely to weaken and destroy the human frame.

These checks to population, which are constantly operating with more or less force in every society, and keep down the number to the level of the means of subsistence, may be classed under two general heads — the preventive and the positive checks.

The preventive check, as far as it is voluntary, is peculiar to man, and arises from that distinctive superiority in his reasoning faculties which enables him to calculate distant consequences. Man cannot look around him and see the distress which frequently presses upon those who have large families; he cannot contemplate his present possessions or earnings which he now nearly consumes himself, and calculate the amount of each share, when with a little addition they must be divided, perhaps, among seven or eight, without feeling a doubt whether, if he follow the bent of his inclinations, he may be able to support the offspring which he will probably bring into the world. . . .

The conditions are calculated to prevent, and certainly do prevent, a great number of persons in all civilized nations from pursuing the dictate of nature in an early attachment to one woman. . . .

The positive checks to population are extremely various, and include every cause, whether arising from vice or misery, which in any degree contributes to shorten the natural duration of human life. Under this head, therefore, may be enumerated all unwholesome occupations, severe labor and exposure to the seasons, extreme poverty, bad nursing of children, great towns, excesses of all kinds, the whole train of common diseases and epidemics, wars, plague, and famine. . . .

[POPULATION AND POVERTY]

Almost everything that has been hitherto done for the poor, has tended, as if with solicitous care, to throw a veil of obscurity over this subject and to hide from them the true cause of their poverty. When the wages of labour are hardly sufficient to maintain two children, a man marries and has five or six. He of course finds himself miserably distressed. . . . He accuses his parish. . . . He accuses the avarice of the rich. . . . He accuses the partial and unjust institutions of society. . . . In searching for objects of accusation, he never [alludes] to the quarter from which all his misfortunes originate. The last person that he would think of accusing is himself. . . .

We cannot justly accuse them (the common people) of improvidence [thriftlessness] and want of industry, till . . . after it has been brought home to their comprehensions, that they are themselves the cause of their own poverty; that the means of redress are in their own hands, and in the hands of no other persons whatever; that the society in which they live and the government which presides over it, are totally without power in this respect; and however ardently they [government] may desire to relieve them, and whatever attempts they may make to do so, they are really and truly unable to execute what they benevolently wish, but unjustly promise.

[handwritten: Food is necessary for existence]
[handwritten: Passion is " + will remain]
[handwritten: POP. WILL ALWAYS OUTGROW FOOD PRODUCTION]

REVIEW QUESTIONS

1. What were Adam Smith's objections to the policy of mercantilism?
2. What did Smith say were the results of a laissez-faire policy?
3. What are the "fixed laws" of human nature according to Thomas Malthus? For Malthus, how did the power of population growth compare with that of the means to increase food?
4. What distinction did Malthus draw between preventive and positive checks to population growth?
5. Why is Malthus considered to have been a pessimist? *[handwritten: Man will have more children than he can support – they are the cause of their own distress]*

7 ▾ The Socialist Revolution

After completing a doctorate at the University of Jena in 1841, Karl Marx (1818–1883) edited a newspaper that was suppressed by the Prussian authorities for its radicalism and atheism. He left his native Rhineland for Paris, where he became friendly with Friedrich Engels. Expelled from France at the request of Prussia, Marx went to Brussels. In 1848, Marx and Engels produced for the Communist League the *Communist Manifesto*, advocating the violent overthrow of capitalism and the creation of a socialist society. Marx returned to Prussia and participated in a minor way in the Revolutions of 1848 in Germany. Expelled from Prussia in 1849, he went to England. He spent the rest of his life there, writing and agitating for the cause of socialism.

The *Communist Manifesto* presented a philosophy of history and a theory of society that Marx expanded upon in his later works, particularly *Capital* (1867). In the tradition of the Enlightenment, he maintained that history, like the operations of nature, was governed by scientific law. To understand the past and the present and to predict the essential outlines of the future, said Marx, one must concentrate on economic forces, on how goods are produced and how wealth is distributed. Marx's call for a working-class revolution against capitalism and for the establishment of a classless society established the ideology of twentieth-century communist revolutionaries.

Karl Marx and Friedrich Engels
≪ *COMMUNIST MANIFESTO* ≫

In the opening section of the *Manifesto*, a basic premise of the Marxian philosophy of history is advanced: class conflict — the idea that the social order is divided into classes based on conflicting economic interests.

BOURGEOIS AND PROLETARIANS

The history of all hitherto existing society is the history of class struggles.

Freeman and slave, patrician and plebian [aristocrat and commoner, in the ancient world], lord and serf, guild-master [master craftsman] and journeyman [who worked for a guild-master], in a word, oppressor and oppressed, stood in constant opposition to one another, carried on an uninterrupted, now hidden, now open fight, that each time ended, either in a revolutionary reconstitution of society at large, or in the common ruin of the contending classes.

In the earlier epochs of history we find almost everywhere a complicated arrangement of society into various orders, a manifold gradation of social rank. In ancient Rome we have patricians, knights, plebeians, slaves; in the Middle Ages, feudal lords, vassals [landowners pledged to lords], guild-masters, journeymen, apprentices, serfs; in almost all of these classes, again, subordinate gradations.

The modern bourgeois society that has sprouted from the ruins of feudal society, has not done away with class antagonisms. It has but established new forms of struggle in place of the old ones.

Our epoch, the epoch of the bourgeoisie [capitalist class], possesses, however, this distinctive feature; it has simplified the class antagonisms. Society as a whole is more and more splitting up into two great hostile camps, into two great classes directly facing each other: Bourgeoisie and Proletariat [industrial workers].

From the serfs of the middle ages sprang the chartered burghers of the earliest towns. From these burgesses the first elements of the bourgeoisie were developed.

The discovery of America, the rounding of the Cape, opened up fresh ground for the rising bourgeoisie. The East-Indian and Chinese markets, the colonization of America, trade with the colonies, the increase in the means of exchange and in commodities generally, gave to commerce, to navigation, to industry, an impulse never before known, and thereby, to the revolutionary element in the tottering feudal society, a rapid development.

The feudal system of industry, under which industrial production was monopolized by closed guilds, now no longer sufficed for the growing wants of the new market. The manufacturing system took its place. The guild-masters were pushed on one side by the manufacturing middle class; division of labor between the different corporate guilds vanished in the face of division of labor in each single workshop.

Meantime the markets kept ever growing, the demand ever rising. . . . Thereupon steam and machinery revolutionized industrial production. The place of manufacture was taken by the giant, Modern Industry, the place of the industrial middle class, by industrial millionaires, the leaders of whole industrial armies, the modern bourgeois.

Modern Industry has established the world's market, for which the discovery of America paved the way. This market has given an immense development to commerce, to navigation, to communication by land. This development has, in its turn, reacted on the extension of industry; and in proportion, as in-

replaced agrarian

dustry, commerce, navigation, railways extended, in the same proportion, the bourgeoisie developed, increased its capital, and pushed into the background every class handed down from the Middle Ages.

We see, therefore, how the modern bourgeoisie is itself the product of a long course of development, of a series of revolutions in the modes of production and of exchange.

Each step in the development of the bourgeoisie was accompanied by a corresponding political advance of that class. An oppressed class under the sway of the feudal nobility, an armed and self-governing association in the mediaeval commune [town], . . . the bourgeoisie has at last, since the establishment of Modern Industry and of the world's market, conquered for itself, in the modern representative State, exclusive political sway. The executive of the modern State is but a committee for managing the common affairs of the whole bourgeoisie.

The bourgeoisie, historically, has played a most revolutionary part.

The bourgeoisie, wherever it has got the upper hand, has put an end to all feudal, patriarchal, idyllic relations. It has pitilessly torn asunder the motley feudal ties that bound man to his "natural superiors," and has left remaining no other nexus [link] between man and man than naked self-interest, than callous "cash payment." It has drowned the most heavenly ecstasies of religious fervor, of chivalrous enthusiasm, . . . in the icy water of egotistical calculation. It has resolved personal worth into exchange value, and in place of the numberless indefeasible chartered freedoms, has set up that single, unconscionable freedom — Free Trade. In one word, for exploitation, veiled by religious and political illusions, it has substituted naked, shameless, direct, brutal exploitation. . . .

▷   The bourgeoisie, states the *Manifesto,* has subjected nature's forces to human control to an unprecedented degree and has replaced feudal organization of agriculture (serfdom) and man-

ufacturing (guild system) with capitalist free competition. But the capitalists cannot control these "gigantic means of production and exchange." Periodically, capitalist society is burdened by severe economic crises; capitalism is afflicted with overproduction — more goods are produced than the market will absorb. In all earlier epochs, which were afflicted with scarcity, the *Manifesto* declares, such a condition "would have seemed an absurdity." To deal with the crisis, the capitalists curtail production, thereby intensifying the poverty of the proletariat. In capitalist society, the exploited worker suffers from physical poverty — a result of low wages — and spiritual poverty — a result of the monotony, regimentation, and impersonal character of the capitalist factory system. For the proletariat, work is not the satisfaction of a need but a repulsive means for survival. The products they help make bring them no satisfaction; they are alienated from their labor.

In proportion as the bourgeoisie, *i.e.,* capital, is developed, in the same proportion is the proletariat, the modern working class, developed — a class of laborers, who live only so long as they find work, and who find work only so long as their labor increases capital. These laborers, who must sell themselves piecemeal, are a commodity, like every other article of commerce, and are consequently exposed to all the vicissitudes of competition, to all the fluctuations of the market.

Owing to the extensive use of machinery and to division of labor, the work of the proletarians has lost all individual character, and, consequently, all charm for the workman. He becomes an appendage of the machine, and it is only the most simple, most monotonous, and most easily acquired knack, that is required of him. Hence, the cost of production of a workman is restricted, almost entirely, to the means of subsistence that he requires for his maintenance, and for the propagation of his race. But the price of a commodity, and therefore also of labor, is equal to its cost of production. In proportion, therefore, as the repulsiveness of the work increases, the wage decreases. Nay more, in proportion as the use of machinery and division of labor increases, in the same proportion the burden of toil also increases, whether by prolongation of the working hours, by increase of the work exacted in a given time, or by increased speed of the machinery, etc.

Modern industry has converted the little workshop of the patriarchal master into the great factory of the industrial capitalist. Masses of laborers, crowded into the factory, are organized like soldiers. As privates of the industrial army they are placed under the command of a perfect hierarchy of officers and sergeants. Not only are they slaves of the bourgeois class, and of the bourgeois state; they are daily and hourly enslaved by the machine, by the overlooker, and, above all, by the individual bourgeois manufacturer himself. The more openly this despotism proclaims gain to be its end and aim, the more petty, the more hateful and the more embittering it is.

The less the skill and exertion of strength implied in manual labor, in other words, the more modern industry develops, the more is the labor of men superseded by that of women. Differences of age and sex have no longer any distinctive social validity for the working class. All are instruments of labor, more or less expensive to use, according to their age and sex.

No sooner has the laborer received his wages in cash, for the moment escaping exploitation by the manufacturer, than he is set upon by the other portions of the bourgeoisie, the landlord, the shop-keeper, the pawnbroker, etc. . . .

▷ The exploited workers organize to defend their interests against the capitalist oppressors.

But with the development of industry the proletariat not only increases in number; it becomes concentrated in greater masses, its strength grows, and it feels that strength more. The various interests and conditions of life within the ranks of the proletariat are more and more equalized, in proportion as machinery obliterates all distinctions of labor and nearly everywhere reduces wages to the same low level. The growing competition among the bourgeois, and the resulting commercial crises, make the wages of the workers ever more fluctuating. The unceasing improvement of machinery, ever more rapidly developing, makes their livelihood more and more precarious: the collisions between individual workmen and individual bourgeois take more and more the character of collisions between two classes. Thereupon the workers begin to form combinations (trade unions) against the bourgeoisie; they club together in order to keep up the rate of wages; they found permanent associations in order to make provision beforehand for these occasional revolts. Here and there the contest breaks out into riots.

Now and then the workers are victorious, but only for a time. The real fruit of their battles lies, not in the immediate results, but in [their ever-expanding unity]. . . .

This organization of the proletarians into a class, and consequently into a political party, is continually being upset again by the competition between the workers themselves. But it ever rises up again, stronger, firmer, mightier. It compels legislative recognition of particular interests of the workers, by taking advantage of the divisions among the bourgeoisie itself. Thus the ten-hour bill[1] in England was carried. . . .

▷ Increasingly, the proletariat, no longer feeling part of the old society, seeks to destroy it.

In the conditions of the proletariat, those of the old society at large are already virtually swamped. The proletarian is without property;

[1]The Ten Hours Act (1847) provided a ten and a half hour day from 6 A.M. to 6 P.M., with an hour and a half for meals for women and children.

his relation to his wife and children has no longer anything in common with the bourgeois family relations; modern industrial labor, modern subjection to capital, the same in England as in France, in America as in Germany, has stripped him of every trace of national character. Law, morality, religion, are to him so many bourgeois prejudices, behind which lurk in ambush just as many bourgeois interests.

All the preceding classes that got the upper hand sought to fortify their already acquired status by subjecting society at large to their conditions of appropriation. The proletarians cannot become masters of the productive forces of society, except by abolishing their own previous mode of appropriation, and thereby also every other previous mode of appropriation. They have nothing of their own to secure and to fortify; their mission is to destroy all previous securities for, and insurances of, individual property.

All previous historical movements were movements of minorities, or in the interest of minorities. The proletarian movement is the self-conscious, independent movement of the immense majority, in the interest of the immense majority. The proletariat, the lowest stratum of our present society, cannot stir, cannot raise itself up, without the whole super-incumbent [overlying] strata of official society being sprung into the air.

Though not in substance, yet in form, the struggle of the proletariat with the bourgeoisie is at first a national struggle. The proletariat of each country must, of course, first of all settle matters with its own bourgeoisie.

In depicting the most general phases of the development of the proletariat, we traced the more or less veiled civil war, raging within existing society, up to the point where that war breaks out into open revolution, and where the violent overthrow of the bourgeoisie lays the foundation for the sway of the proletariat. . . .

The modern laborer . . . instead of rising with the progress of industry, sinks deeper and deeper below the conditions of existence of his own class. He becomes a pauper, and pauperism develops more rapidly than population and wealth. And here it becomes evident that the bourgeoisie is unfit any longer to be the ruling class in society and to impose its conditions of existence upon society as an overriding law. It is unfit to rule because it is incompetent to assure an existence to its slave within his slavery, because it cannot help letting him sink into such a state that it has to feed him instead of being fed by him. Society can no longer live under this bourgeoisie, in other words its existence is no longer compatible with society.

The essential condition for the existence and for the sway of the bourgeois class, is the formation and augmentation of capital; the condition for capital is wage-labor. Wage-labor rests exclusively on competition between the laborers. The advance of industry, whose involuntary promoter is the bourgeoisie, replaces the isolation of the laborers, due to competition, by their revolutionary combination, due to association. The development of modern industry, therefore, cuts from under its feet the very foundation on which the bourgeoisie produces and appropriates products. What the bourgeoisie therefore produces above all, are its own gravediggers. Its fall and the victory of the proletariat are equally inevitable. . . .

▷ Communists, says the *Manifesto,* are the most advanced and determined members of working-class parties. Among the aims of the communists are organizations of the working class into a revolutionary party; overthrow of bourgeois power and the assumption of political power by the proletariat; and an end to exploitation of one individual by another and the creation of a classless society. These aims will be achieved by the abolition of bourgeois private property (private ownership of the means of production) and the abolition of the bourgeoisie as a class.

The Communists, therefore, are on the one hand, practically, the most advanced and resolute section of the working class parties of every country, that section which pushes forward all others; on the other hand, theoretically, they have over the great mass of the proletariat the advantage of clearly understanding the line of march, the conditions, and the ultimate general results of the proletarian movement.

The immediate aim of the Communists is the same as that of all the other proletarian parties: formation of the proletariat into a class, overthrow of the bourgeois supremacy, conquest of political power by the proletariat. . . .

The distinguishing feature of Communism is not the abolition of property generally, but the abolition of bourgeois property. But modern bourgeois private property is the final and most complete expression of the system of producing and appropriating products, that is based on class antagonisms, on the exploitation of the many by the few.

In this sense the theory of the Communists may be summed up in the single sentence: Abolition of private property. . . .

▷ One argument leveled against communists by bourgeois critics, says the *Manifesto*, is that the destruction of the bourgeoisie would lead to the disappearance of bourgeois culture, which is "identical with the disappearance of all culture," and the loss of all moral and religious truths. Marx insists that these ethical and religious ideals lauded by the bourgeoisie are not universal truths at all but are common expressions of the ruling class at a particular stage in history.

That culture, the loss of which he [the bourgeois] laments, is for the enormous majority, a mere training to act as a machine.

But don't wangle with us so long as you [the bourgeoisie] apply to our [the communists'] intended abolition of bourgeois property, the standard of your bourgeois notions of freedom, culture, law, etc. Your very ideas are but the outgrowth of the conditions of your bourgeois

production and bourgeois property, just as your jurisprudence is but the will of your class made into a law for all, a will, whose essential character and direction are determined by the economical conditions of existence of your class.

The selfish misconception that induces you to transform into eternal laws of nature and of reason, the social forms springing from your present mode of production and form of property — historical relations that rise and disappear in the progress of production — this misconception you share with every ruling class that has preceded you. What you see clearly in the case of ancient property, what you admit in the case of feudal property, you are of course forbidden to admit in the case of your own bourgeois form of property. . . .

The charges against Communism made from a religious, a philosophical, and, generally, from an ideological standpoint, are not deserving of serious examination.

Does it require deep intuition to comprehend that man's ideas, views, and conceptions, in one word, man's consciousness changes with every change in the conditions of his material existence, in his social relations and in his social life?

What else does the history of ideas prove than that intellectual production changes its character in proportion as material production is changed? The ruling ideas of each age have ever been the ideas of its ruling class. . . .

. . . The ideas of religious liberty and freedom of conscience merely gave expression to the sway of free competition within the domain of knowledge.

"Undoubtedly," it will be said, "religious, moral, philosophical, and juridical ideas have been modified in the course of historic development. But religion, morality, philosophy, political science, and law, constantly survived this change.

"There are besides, eternal truths, such as Freedom, Justice, etc., that are common to all states of society. But Communism abolishes eternal truths, it abolishes all religion and all morality, instead of constituting them on a new basis; it therefore acts as a contradiction to all past historical experience."

What does this accusation reduce itself to? The history of all past society has consisted in the development of class antagonisms, antagonisms that assumed different forms at different epochs.

But whatever form they may have taken, one fact is common to all past ages, *viz.*, the exploitation of one part of society by the other. No wonder, then, that the social consciousness of past ages, despite all the multiplicity and variety it displays, moves within certain common forms, or general ideas, which cannot completely vanish except with the total disappearance of class antagonisms.

The Communist revolution is the most radical rupture with traditional property relations; no wonder that its development involves the most radical rupture with traditional ideas.

▷   Aroused and united by communist intellectuals, says the *Manifesto*, the proletariat will wrest power from the bourgeoisie and overthrow the capitalist system that has oppressed them. In the new society, people will be fully free.

But let us have done with the bourgeois objections to Communism.

We have seen above that the first step in the revolution by the working class is to raise the proletariat to the position of the ruling class, to win the battle of democracy.

The proletariat will use its political suprem-

acy to wrest, by degrees, all capital from the bourgeoisie; to centralize all instruments of production in the hands of the State, *i.e.*, of the proletariat organized as the ruling class; and to increase the total of productive forces as rapidly as possible. . . .

When, in the course of development, class distinctions have disappeared and all production has been concentrated in the hands of a vast association of the whole nation, the public power will lose its political character. Political power, properly so called, is merely the organized power of one class for oppressing another. If the proletariat during its contest with the bourgeoisie is compelled, by the force of circumstances, to organize itself as a class, if, by means of a revolution, it makes itself the ruling class, and, as such, sweeps away by force the old conditions of production, then it will, along with these conditions, have swept away the conditions for the existence of class antagonism, and of classes generally, and will thereby have abolished its own supremacy as a class.

In place of the old bourgeois society with its classes and class antagonisms we shall have an association in which the free development of each is the condition for the free development of all. . . .

The Communist disdain to conceal their views and aims. They openly declare that their ends can be attained only by the forcible overthrow of all existing social conditions. Let the ruling classes tremble at a communistic revolution. The proletarians have nothing to lose but their chains. They have a world to win.

Working men of all countries, unite!

REVIEW QUESTIONS

1. What do Karl Marx and Friedrich Engels mean by the term *class conflict*? What historical examples of class conflict are provided?
2. According to the *Manifesto*, what role has the state played in the class conflict?
3. How does the *Manifesto* describe the condition of the working class under capitalism?

4. According to the *Manifesto,* why is capitalism doomed? What conditions will bring about the end of capitalism?
5. "The ruling ideas of each age have ever been the ideas of its ruling class." What is meant by this statement? Do you agree or disagree? Explain.
6. What does the culture of an age owe to its mode of material production, according to the *Manifesto?*

+ opinion

②. State → tool of ruling class
    used by bourgeas to control prol.

③ Workers under capitalism
        exploited by bourgeois
        subject to fluctuations of market

④ proletariat will bond together, become larger
    - will overthrow the bourgeois
    - will destroy capitalism by abolishing private property

⑥ Intellectual production changes in character in proportion
        to its material production   (p. 161, 162)
    The ruling class determines the ideas
    Communism raises social conscience

SOURCES OF THE WESTERN TRADITION

CHAPTER
▼▼▼
7

Politics and Society, 1850–1914

In the years just prior to World War I, Europe reached the climax of its power and influence in the world. These were peaceful and unprecedentedly prosperous years and only vaguely disturbed by battles at the periphery — the Russo-Japanese War (1904–1905), wars in the Balkans stemming from the decline of the Ottoman Empire, and conflicts in European overseas empires. Europe had not experienced a major war since the Franco-Prussian War (1870–1871) and no general European war since the time of Napoleon. More numerous than ever and concentrated in ever-growing cities, the peoples of Europe interacted with each other in a busy exchange of goods, ideas, and services, which led to remarkable creativity in industry, science, and the arts. The physical sciences flourished; medical science advanced; the psychoanalytic method developed under Sigmund Freud. New technologies speeded communication and transportation, which intensified human contact and competition. Industrialization, promoted by capitalist enterprise, spread throughout Europe and the United States, raising the standard of living and advancing expectations among the poor for a better life. The new mobility and social interdependence provided greater opportunity for individual gain, but they also increased social tensions.

One source of tension was the agitation for women's rights to be equal with those of men in education and politics. Although women faced strenuous resistance with regard to suffrage, they fought toward that goal, gaining some concessions. Conflict also arose over social justice for workers — for their material security and their right to vote and organize. In England, improvement for the working class resulted from joint efforts by the workers, members of the privileged classes, and the government. In Germany, the state, afraid of revolution, took a more active role, organizing the first social security program for workers. Meanwhile, among workers able to improve their lot by voting and organizing, desire for revolution receded. Higher living standards and devotion to the nation made workers loyal to the capitalist order; even workers aspired to bourgeois respectability. And rather than falling prey to all-consuming monopolies, as Marx had predicted, the middle classes

HOMELESS CHILDREN, 1875, new arrivals at the London orphanage of Dr. Barnardo. This orphanage represents the nineteenth-century spirit of reform that tried to address the evils and injustices of the industrial age that often affected children of the poor. (*Barnardo's Photographic Archive, London*)

thrived, at least in the countries of western and central Europe.

In eastern Europe, social and political tensions were greater. In the Austro-Hungarian Empire, reaching east from the Alps into the Balkans, nationalist agitation was on the rise. The Slavic peoples, resenting their domination by Germans and Magyars, threatened the very survival of that multinational monarchy, one of the major states of Europe. A sociopolitical crisis also threatened the Russian Empire. Contact with western Europe convinced the tsarist government of the need to modernize the country's backward economy and catch up with "the West," as Russians called the richer lands of Europe. In the absence of capable capitalists, the government assumed direct responsibility for industrialization. At the same time, the workers, prompted by westernized intellectuals, compared their lot with that of their counterparts in western Europe and saw themselves as exploited. Like privileged Russians familiar with western Europe, they blamed their country's backwardness on the tsars; disaffected, they called for a constitutional government with universal suffrage. When Japan defeated Russia in 1905, revolution broke out, spearheaded by the workers of St. Petersburg. The revolution failed but weakened the tsarist regime and strengthened the resolve of the revolutionaries. Russia's woeful conditions encouraged an especially militant brand of revolutionary Marxism.

Meanwhile the traditional rivalry of the major European states spread from Europe to the world at large. The Spanish and Portuguese empires had faded, but the British had long gloried in their overseas expansion. They used extravagant — even racist — language to justify their ambition, claiming to be the fittest in the struggle for survival. But in the newly united Germany, intellectuals and politicians enviously asked why their country should not be equal to Great Britain. They too wanted a world-spanning empire. Against the militant promoters of imperialism in Britain, Germany, and other aspiring powers, anti-imperialists speaking on behalf of the conquered peoples and peaceful relations among nations made little headway. The power competition between the major states of Europe grew to global dimensions.

In 1884, virtually all of Africa not yet under colonial rule was divided among England, France, and Germany. Africans trying to resist lacked the resources of the Europeans, who quickly overpowered them. In the Far East, too, along the Chinese coast, ports and spheres of influence were carved out of the tottering Chinese Empire.

By the early 1900s, European civilization had produced impressive achievements in all spheres of human activity, and European states dominated the globe. Yet the great advances also increasingly divided Europe; competition for wealth and power heightened international rivalries. Nationalist ambitions, backed in most countries by popular support, and an arms race further worsened international relations. Although few people at the time recognized it, Europe's period of peace and security was ending. World War I, which broke out in 1914, was on the horizon.

▼▼▼

I ▼ The Capitalist Ethic

The remarkable advance in industry and material prosperity in the nineteenth century has been hailed as the triumph of the middle class, or bourgeoisie, which included bankers, merchants, factory owners, professionals, and government officials. Unlike the upper classes, which lived on inherited wealth, middle-class people supported themselves by diligent, assiduous activity — what has been called "the capitalist (or bourgeois) ethic."

The ideal of dedicated and responsible hard work directed by an internal rather than an external discipline remained the ultimate source of human merit and inspired men like Richard Arkwright (see page 140), who had risen from rags to riches. This ideal was widely publicized in the nineteenth century, encouraging upward mobility among the lower classes and sustaining the morale of ambitious middle-class people immersed in the keen competition of private enterprise. By shaping highly motivated private citizens, the capitalist ethic also provided a vital source of national strength.

Samuel Smiles
≪ SELF-HELP ≫ AND ≪ THRIFT ≫

Samuel Smiles (1812–1904) was the most famous messenger of the capitalist ethic at its best. His father, a Scottish papermaker and general merchant, died early, leaving his eleven children to fend for themselves. Samuel was apprenticed to a medical office, in due time becoming a physician in general practice. Turned journalist, he edited the local newspaper in the English city of Leeds, hoping to cure the ills of society by promoting the social and intellectual development of the working classes. Leaving his editorial office, he stepped into railroad management as a friend of George Stephenson, the inventor of the locomotive and promoter of railroads, whose biography Smiles wrote in 1857. Two years later he published *Self-Help,* which had grown out of a lecture to a small mutual-improvement society in which people sought each other's help in bettering their condition. The book was an instant success and was translated into many languages, including Japanese. Having retired, after twenty-one years as a railway administrator and prolific author, Smiles suffered a stroke caused by overwork. Recovered, he traveled widely, writing more books about deserving but often unknown achievers. All along, he practiced in his personal life the virtues that he preached. The following selections set forth the essence not only of Samuel Smiles's philosophy of life but also of the values inspiring the achievements of capitalism.

SELF-HELP

"Heaven helps those who help themselves" is a well-tried maxim, embodying in a small compass the results of vast human experience. The spirit of self-help is the root of all genuine growth in the individual; and, exhibited in the lives of many, it constitutes the true source of national vigour and strength. Help from without is often enfeebling in its effects, but help from within invariably invigorates. Whatever is done *for* men or classes, to a certain extent takes away the stimulus and necessity of doing for themselves; and where men are subjected to over-guidance and over-government, the inevitable tendency is to render them comparatively helpless.

Even the best institutions can give a man no active help. Perhaps the most they can do is, to leave him free to develop himself and improve his individual condition. But in all times men have been prone to believe that their happiness and well-being were to be secured by means of institutions rather than by their own conduct. Hence the value of legislation as an agent in human advancement has usually been much over-estimated. . . . [N]o laws, however stringent, can make the idle industrious, the thriftless provident, or the drunken sober. Such reforms can only be effected by means of individual action, economy, and self-denial; by better habits, rather than by greater rights. . . .

National progress is the sum of individual industry, energy, and uprightness, as national decay is of individual idleness, selfishness, and vice. What we are accustomed to decry as great social evils, will, for the most part, be found to be but the outgrowth of man's own perverted life; and though we may endeavour to cut them down and extirpate them by means of Law, they will only spring up again with fresh luxuriance in some other form, unless the conditions of personal life and character are radically improved. If this view be correct, then it follows that the highest patriotism and philanthropy consist, not so much in altering laws and modifying institutions, as in helping and stimulating men to elevate and improve themselves by their own free and independent individual action.

It may be of comparatively little consequence how a man is governed from without, whilst everything depends upon how he governs himself from within. The greatest slave is not he who is ruled by a despot, great though that evil be, but he who is the thrall of his own moral ignorance, selfishness, and vice. . . .

▷ Smiles's book *Thrift*, published in 1875, restates and expands on the themes stressed in *Self-Help*.

THRIFT

Every man is bound to do what he can to elevate his social state, and to secure his independence. For this purpose he must spare from his means in order to be independent in his condition. Industry enables men to earn their living; it should also enable them to learn to live. Independence can only be established by the exercise of forethought, prudence, frugality, and self-denial. To be just as well as generous, men must deny themselves. The essence of generosity is self-sacrifice.

The object of this book is to induce men to

employ their means for worthy purposes, and not to waste them upon selfish indulgences. Many enemies have to be encountered in accomplishing this object. There are idleness, thoughtlessness, vanity, vice, intemperance. The last is the worst enemy of all. Numerous cases are cited in the course of the following book, which show that one of the best methods of abating the curse of Drink is to induce old and young to practice the virtue of Thrift. . . .

It is the savings of individuals which compose the wealth — in other words, the well-being — of every nation. On the other hand, it is the wastefulness of individuals which occasions the impoverishment of states. So that every thrifty person may be regarded as a public benefactor, and every thriftless person as a public enemy. . . .

. . . All that is great in man comes of labor — greatness in art, in literature, in science. Knowledge — "the wing wherewith we fly to heaven" — is only acquired through labor. Genius is but a capability of laboring intensely: it is the power of making great and sustained efforts. Labor may be a chastisement, but it is indeed a glorious one. It is worship, duty, praise, and immortality — for those who labor with the highest aims and for the purest purposes. . . .

. . . Of all wretched men, surely the idle are the most so — those whose life is barren of utility, who have nothing to do except to gratify their senses. Are not such men the most querulous, miserable, and dissatisfied of all, constantly in a state of *ennui* [boredom], alike useless to themselves and to others — mere cumberers [troublesome occupiers] of the earth, who, when removed, are missed by none, and whom none regret? Most wretched and ignoble lot, indeed, is the lot of the idlers.

Who have helped the world onward so much as the workers; men who have had to work from necessity or from choice? All that we call progress — civilization, well-being, and prosperity — depends upon industry, diligently applied — from the culture of a barley-stalk to the construction of a steamship; from the stitching of a collar to the sculpturing of "the statue that enchants the world."

All useful and beautiful thoughts, in like manner, are the issue of labor, of study, of observation, of research, of diligent elaboration. . . .

By the working-man we do not mean merely the man who labors with his muscles and sinews. A horse can do this. But *he* is pre-eminently the working-man who works with his brain also, and whose whole physical system is under the influence of his higher faculties. The man who paints a picture, who writes a book, who makes a law, who creates a poem, is a working-man of the highest order; not so necessary to the physical sustainment of the community as the plowman or the shepherd, but not less important as providing for society its highest intellectual nourishment. . . .

But a large proportion of men do not provide for the future. They do not remember the past. They think only of the present. They preserve nothing. They spend all that they earn. They do not provide for themselves; they do not provide for their families. They may make high wages, but eat and drink the whole of what they earn. Such people are constantly poor, and hanging on the verge of destitution. . . .

REVIEW QUESTIONS

1. What, according to Samuel Smiles, were the key values that should guide the individual?
2. How did Smiles define success in life?
3. What, in his opinion, were the enemies of individual and national achievement?
4. Do Smiles's writings offer good advice to the poor in the United States today? Explain why or why not.

▼▼▼

2 ▾ The Lower Classes

The members of the upper and middle classes in society looked down on "the lower classes" — industrial workers, domestic help, and peasants; and still further down, the street people, the mentally disturbed, the homeless, the unemployed, and vagrants; and at the bottom, the criminal underworld. These "lower classes" were most vulnerable to the vicissitudes of the business cycle and dependent on small and uncertain incomes; commonly they worked long hours under dehumanizing strain and were housed most likely in urban slums under unsanitary conditions; they were hungry, illiterate, often reduced to outright destitution, and desperate to earn some money. In the slums of London's East End, one could see ragged men collect dog excrement for use in tanning leather; prostitution thrived.

In the economic progress of the nineteenth century, the overall material conditions of society improved remarkably, sharpening the social contrasts. Concerned people spoke of "two nations," the rich and the poor. The poor, however, were not entirely passive; workers began to rally, trying to improve their condition by political action, thereby scaring the upper classes into social awareness. At the same time, humanitarian concerns, often rising from religious inspiration, stirred some of the well-to-do. Toward the end of the nineteenth century, the misery of the poor caused lively public debate and heated political agitation.

Nikolaus Osterroth
THE YEARNING FOR SOCIAL JUSTICE

Nikolaus Osterroth (1875–1933), the son of a butcher, was a clay miner from the Palatinate, a region in western Germany. His and his fellow miners' resentment at the deterioration of their working conditions undermined their traditional loyalty to their Catholic faith and prepared them for the appeal of the Social Democratic party, which, under the guidance of Marxist intellectuals, represented the interests of the German working class. Osterroth became a union and party organizer before World War I; after the war he played a part in the politics of the Weimar Republic.

This selection, taken from his autobiography published in 1920, describes in telling detail his transition from a docile clay miner to a Social Democratic agitator and organizer.

The hardest work is the rough cutting with the ax and cutting away the clumps from the seam. You can't take it for more than three hours because your hands get completely exhausted. So the shift is divided into four two-hour sections separated by breakfast, lunch, and the afternoon break. In his youth a miner's arms twitch from exhaustion even when he sleeps. . . .

. . . When there are a great number of people employed in a mine, then two tunnels on opposite sides of the shaft are worked, and one man works steadily at piling up the clumps. He also has to load the clumps onto wagons at the top of the shaft. The poor devil has to transport 800–1,000 wet, slippery clumps, each of which weighs 100 pounds. After years of this, his back gets all crooked and his arms get long like an ape's, so that he can scratch his knees without bending over.

For several hours every day the clumps are lifted up the shaft with a winch. In earlier days this work was usually done by women or girls. It was a really murderous job and frequently resulted in premature births or great damage to the child-bearing organs of the women workers. After protracted pressure from the miners, the Bavarian Mining Law finally put an end to this disgraceful women's work. . . .

▷ The clay-mining industry in Bavaria suffered hard times in the 1890s. The mine owners sought to reduce production costs at the expense of the workers, causing great friction.

MY FIRST ACQUAINTANCE WITH THE SOCIAL DEMOCRATS

. . . The attempt to introduce these work rules created bad blood among the miners and stirred them to resistance, which at first found an outlet only in tavern debates.

When the mine owners stood by their plan . . . the miners turned to the priest, so that he might help them fight against this obvious injustice. But instead of standing by them, the priest preached that the employer was an authority appointed by God whom one had to obey. Humble obedience was the greatest virtue of subordinates. There had always been master and servant, and God had given the master the right to command his servant.

The workers could see what the priest was driving at, and they streamed from the church over to the tavern. There they reviled the priest in most unchristian language as one who, in exchange for the gift of a new church window

from a mine owner, would preach patience to the workers instead of instilling humanity and righteousness in the mine owners. . . .

. . .[W]hen I heard with my own ears how the priest unambiguously sided against the workers instead of speaking to the conscience of the mine owners, I was angry and saw the priest above all as a Center party[1] man . . . groveling to the upper classes and ready for any betrayal of the people; leading the people by the nose with religion; and always representing the "heretics" as the only danger. . . .

. . . And how did the priest use his influence? Instead of defending the rights of the oppressed, whose leadership he regarded as his monopoly, he preached submission and patience to the workers. He sat at the table of the rich and accepted the gifts that they had wrung from the poor, instead of reminding them that their actions were hardhearted and unchristian. Instead of saying to the mine owners, "Thou shalt love thy neighbor as thyself," he said to the exploited and raped workers, "You are servants, and servants you must remain; God wills it for your salvation."

A terrible storm raged through me. I doubted everything that up until then I had held as noble and good. . . .

On the last Sunday in April a leaflet was thrown through the open window while we were eating lunch. For a while it went unnoticed. After lunch I picked up the sheet of paper and glanced at the front and back sides, without reading the text. It was labeled, "To the Voters for the Reichstag!" and on the bottom of the back side it said, "The Social Democratic Reichstag Members." Now some life came into me. That was what I was looking for: a program, an authentic pronouncement of Social Democracy!

I began to read. Sentence by sentence there was an indictment against the government and the bourgeois parties, against armaments

---

[1]The Center party, representing the interests of the Catholic Church in Germany, generally followed a socially conservative course.

expenditures that had been driven to unbearable heights, against the insanely increasing debt burden of the Empire, against the excess of the new naval appropriations that oppressed the people, and against the plundering of the masses by tariffs and indirect taxes. And there was more: The stagnation of social welfare; the misery and lack of rights of the working class; the prison terms that the Emperor threatened, which would destroy the workers' right to organize! All that made an enormous, totally new impression on me.

Suddenly I saw the world from the other side, from a side that up to now had been dark for me. . . . I was seized by a feeling of wild fury about the obvious injustice of a tax system that spared the ones who could best pay and plundered those who already despaired of life in their bitter misery.

But then I found something new that really gripped me: The Social Democratic leaflet not only criticized, it not only put its finger on the festering wounds and showed that the class character of society was the cause of the wrongs — no, it also produced a series of highly illuminating suggestions for the abolition of these wrongs. Numerous demands for the betterment of the condition of the people were made to the state. And then the leaflet turned to the voters, with a flaming appeal to them to make use of the universal suffrage, the greatest right of a citizen, in order to retaliate in the name of the people against a hostile government and treacherous parties.

▷ He searches for the people who had distributed the leaflet.

The leaflet affected me like a revelation. . . .

. . . [T]hey sat down again and for a whole hour they told me about the aspirations of Social Democracy and the growth of the young union movement. How heartily they laughed at the hopes I'd placed in the priest, and how convincingly and plainly they described how above all we workers lacked union organization. A union would bring together the weak uninfluential workers in order to counter the employers with the power of united action.

God, how clear and simple it all was! This new world of thought that gave the worker the weapons of self-awareness and self-consciousness was very different from the old world of priestly and economic authority where the worker was merely an object of domination and exploitation!

Once I'd gotten hold of these bringers of enlightenment I wouldn't let them go; I didn't have to be invited twice to help distribute leaflets in the remaining two villages of the county. With the winged zeal of the newly converted, I leaped from house to house, taking three steps at a time and feeling lighter and happier than ever before in my life. My new friends liked my zeal. When we parted late in the evening, they gave me an "Erfurt Program"[2] and some newspapers, and promised that they would soon send me a package of pamphlets and newspapers. I spent almost the whole night studying the program, and I had the feeling that all these thoughts were etched into my brain with flamed writing.

The next day was the first of May. After a short, feverish sleep I awoke — for the first time as a Social Democrat. This was the day that the new work rules were to go into effect. . . .

▷ On May Day — a holiday recently proclaimed by socialists to demonstrate workers' solidarity and their defiance of capitalism — Osterroth, inciting the workers to skip work, gives a speech.

At first I stammered and got confused when I saw the many curious people hanging on my every word. But soon the joyous shouts of

---

[2]Adopted in 1891, this was the official, Marxist-oriented program of the Social Democratic party.

agreement made me overcome all obstacles. I was amazed at myself, at how fast the new ideas from the article and the leaflet popped, one after another, into my mouth. And they were as new to my audience as to me. I discussed the purpose of our festival; I spoke of how our helplessness and powerlessness had emboldened our enemies, the mine owners, to impose the oppressive measures, the wage cuts, and the work rules, and to curtail our rights. I showed my comrades how impressive our unity was, and how it would help us further if we recognized the misery of our situation and got to know and value the means of improvement. I described how the workers were politically and economically exploited, deprived of their rights, duped, and deceived, and how deliverance from economic and political misery had to come from the working class itself. I described how the workers had to be unified and could not be allowed to fight among themselves for religious or political reasons. There were only two opposing sides that affected the workers very deeply and they were not "here the Catholics, there the non-Catholics"; rather, they were "here capital, there labor" — "here masters, there slaves"! If we wanted to prevent the deterioration of our working conditions and fight for improvements, then we needed an organization that included all of us; and if we wanted to protest against political injustice and strive for healthier political conditions, then we had to vote for the Social Democratic candidate in the upcoming Reichstag election. Only the Social Democratic party dealt fairly with the workers, for it was the only workers' party that the upper classes fought against.

William Booth
≪ *IN DARKEST ENGLAND* ≫

The poor were not without compassionate friends. One of them was William Booth, the founder of the Salvation Army. Growing up poor himself, he was apprenticed to a pawnbroker while still a boy. At fifteen, under Methodist influence, he experienced a religious conversion, which eventually turned him into a Methodist minister; his wife and helpmate was one of the first Methodist woman preachers. Settled in London, he combined work at a pawnshop with ministering to the poor in the slums of London's East End. Booth and his wife devoted themselves to rescuing and rehabilitating the homeless, the unemployed, and the sinners of the urban underworld. In 1879 the organization that they had evolved officially became the Salvation Army. William Booth was its general; ordained ministers were its officers; the soldiers were men and women dedicated to save others from the misery from which they themselves had escaped. All wore the Salvation Army's special uniform. The Salvation Army grew rapidly, spreading over the world. It now serves in seventy-seven countries, with over 300,000 soldiers in the United States.

In 1890 General Booth published *In Darkest England and the Way Out,* describing the misery of the poor and outlining his methods of achieving spiritual salvation through social service. In the opening two chapters, Booth outlined the extent of poverty in England at the height of its imperial glory. He begins by comparing England with journalist-explorer Henry Stanley's description of the brutality, slavery, and disease that he witnessed in "Darkest Africa."

WHY "DARKEST ENGLAND"?

This summer the attention of the civilised world has been arrested by the story which Mr. Stanley has told of "Darkest Africa" and his journeyings across the heart of the Lost Continent. . . .

It is a terrible picture, and one that has engraved itself deep on the heart of civilisation. But while brooding over the awful presentation of life as it exists in the vast African forest, it seemed to me only too vivid a picture of many parts of our own land. As there is a darkest Africa is there not also a darkest England? Civilisation, which can breed its own barbarians, does it not also breed its own pygmies? May we not find a parallel at our own doors, and discover within a stone's throw of our cathedrals and palaces similar horrors to those which Stanley has found existing in the great Equatorial forest?

The more the mind dwells upon the subject, the closer the analogy appears. The [Arab] ivory raiders who brutally traffic in the unfortunate denizens of the forest glades, what are they but the [exploiters] who flourish on the weakness of our poor? . . . As in Africa, it is all trees, trees, trees with no other world conceivable; so is it here — it is all vice and poverty and crime. To many the world is all slum, with the Workhouse as an intermediate purgatory before the grave. . . . Who can battle against the ten thousand million trees? Who can hope to make headway against the innumerable adverse conditions which doom the dweller in Darkest England to eternal and immutable misery?

. . . Talk about Dante's Hell, and all the horrors and cruelties of the torture-chamber of the lost! The man who walks with open eyes and with bleeding heart through the shambles of our civilisation needs no such fantastic images of the poet to teach him horror. Often and often, when I have seen the young and the poor and the helpless go down before my eyes into the morass, trampled underfoot by beasts of prey in human shape that haunt these regions, it seemed as if God were no longer in His world, but that in His stead reigned a fiend, merciless as Hell, ruthless as the grave. Hard it is, no doubt, to read in Stanley's pages of the slave-traders coldly arranging for the surprise of a village, the capture of the inhabitants, the massacre of those who resist, and the violation of all the women; but the stony streets of London, if they could but speak, would tell of tragedies as awful, of ruin as complete, of ravishments as horrible, as if we were in Central Africa; only the ghastly devastation is covered, corpse-like, with the artificialities and hypocrisies of modern civilisation.

The lot of a negress in the Equatorial Forest is not, perhaps, a very happy one, but is it so very much worse than that of many a pretty orphan girl in our Christian capital? . . . A young penniless girl, if she be pretty, is often hunted from pillar to post by her employers, confronted always by the alternative — Starve or Sin. And when once the poor girl has consented to buy the right to earn her living by the sacrifice of her virtue, then she is treated as a slave and an outcast by the very men who have ruined her. . . . [A]nd she is swept downward. . . .

The blood boils with impotent rage at the sight of these enormities, callously inflicted, and silently borne by these miserable victims. Nor is it only women who are the victims, although their fate is the most tragic. Those firms which reduce sweating [hard labor at low wages] to a fine art, who systematically and deliberately defraud the workman of his pay, who grind the faces of the poor, and who rob the widow and the orphan, and who for a pretence make great professions of public-spirit and philanthropy, those men nowadays are sent to Parliament to make laws for the people. The old prophets sent them to Hell — but we have changed all that. They send their victims to Hell, and are rewarded by all that wealth can do to make their lives comfortable. Read the House of Lords' Report on the Sweating System, and ask if any African slave system, making due allowance for the superior civilisation, and therefore sensitiveness, of the victims, reveals more misery.

Darkest England, like Darkest Africa, reeks with malaria. The foul and fetid breath of our slums is almost as poisonous as that of the African swamp. Fever is almost as chronic there as on the Equator. Every year thousands of children are killed off by what is called defects of our sanitary system. They are in reality starved and poisoned, and all that can be said is that, in many cases, it is better for them that they were taken away from the trouble to come.

Just as in Darkest Africa it is only a part of the evil and misery that comes from the superior race who invade the forest to enslave and massacre its miserable inhabitants, so with us, much of the misery of those whose lot we are considering arises from their own habits. Drunkenness and all manner of uncleanness, moral and physical, abound. Have you ever watched by the bedside of a man in delirium tremens [trembling and delusions brought on by alcohol abuse]? Multiply the sufferings of that one drunkard by the hundred thousand, and you have some idea of what scenes are being witnessed in all our great cities at this moment. . . . A population sodden with drink, steeped in vice, eaten up by every social and physical malady, these are the denizens of Darkest England amidst whom my life has been spent, and to whose rescue I would now summon all that is best in the manhood and womanhood of our land. . . .

. . . [T]he grimmest social problems of our time should be sternly faced, not with a view to the generation of profitless emotion, but with a view to its solution. . . .

▷ Relying on the statistics of Charles Booth (no relation), William Booth concluded that three million people, one-tenth of the population, were pauperized and degraded.

THE SUBMERGED TENTH

What, then, is Darkest England? For whom do we claim that "urgency" which gives their case priority over that of all other sections of their countrymen and countrywomen? . . .

. . . The [people] in Darkest England, for whom I appeal, are (1) those who, having no capital or income of their own, would in a month be dead from sheer starvation were they exclusively dependent upon the money earned by their own work; and (2) those who by their utmost exertions are unable to attain the regulation allowance of food which the law prescribes as indispensable even for the worst criminals in our gaols.

I sorrowfully admit that it would be Utopian in our present social arrangements to dream of attaining for every honest Englishman a gaol standard of all the necessaries of life. Some time, perhaps, we may venture to hope that every honest worker on English soil will always be as warmly clad, as healthily housed, and as regularly fed as our criminal convicts — but that is not yet.

Neither is it possible to hope for many years to come that human beings generally will be as well cared for as horses. Mr. Carlyle long ago remarked that the four-footed worker has already got all that this two-handed one is clamouring for. . . .

What, then, is the standard towards which we may venture to aim with some prospect of réalisation in our time? It is a very humble one, but if realised it would solve the worst problems of modern Society.

It is the standard of the London Cab Horse. . . .

The first question, then, which confronts us is, what are the dimensions of the Evil? How many of our fellow-men dwell in this Darkest England? How can we take the census of those who have fallen below the Cab Horse standard to which it is our aim to elevate the most wretched of our countrymen? . . .

REVIEW QUESTIONS

1. Describe the role of the Catholic priest in the discontent of Nikolaus Osterroth and the miners.
2. Describe how the ideas expressed in the Social Democrat pamphlet were seized by Osterroth and transformed his life.
3. What, according to William Booth, were the essential aspects of life in "Darkest England"? Why did he draw the comparison to darkest Africa?
4. What view of human nature underlies Booth's critique of society?
5. Do any of Booth's scathing criticisms apply to contemporary America?

▼▼▼

3 ▼ The Evolution of Liberalism

The principal concern of early-nineteenth-century liberalism was protecting the rights of the individual against the demands of the state. For this reason, liberals advocated a constitution that limited the state's authority and a bill of rights that stipulated the citizen's basic freedoms. Believing that state interference in the economy endangered individual liberty and private property, liberals were strong advocates of laissez-faire — leaving the market to its own devices. And convinced that the unpropertied and uneducated masses were not deeply committed to individual freedom, liberals approved property requirements for voting and office holding.

In the last part of the nineteenth century, however, liberalism changed substantially as many liberals came to support government reforms to deal with the problems created by unregulated industrialization. By the early twentieth century, liberalism — not without reservation and opposition on the part of some liberals — had evolved into social democracy, which maintains that government has an obligation to assist the needy.

Thomas Hill Green
≪ LIBERAL LEGISLATION AND FREEDOM OF CONTRACT ≫

Arguing that laissez-faire enabled the powerful to exploit the weak, Thomas Hill Green (1836–1882), a British political theorist, urged legislation to promote better conditions of labor, education, and health. In a truly liberal society, said Green, individuals have the opportunity to develop their moral and intellectual abilities. But poor education, inadequate housing, and unhealthy living and working environments deprive people of the opportunity for self-enhancement. For these people, freedom is an empty word. Green insisted that the liberal state must concern itself not just with individual rights but with the common good. The following reading is excerpted from his lecture "Liberal Legislation and Freedom of Contract," delivered in 1881.

We shall probably all agree that freedom, rightly understood, is the greatest of blessings; that its attainment is the true end of all our effort as citizens. But when we thus speak of freedom, we should consider carefully what we mean by it. . . . When we measure the progress of a society by its growth in freedom, we measure it by . . . the greater power on the part of the citizens as a body to make the most and best of themselves. . . . If the ideal of true freedom is the maximum of power for all members of human society alike to make the best of themselves, we are right in refusing to ascribe the glory of freedom to a state in which the apparent elevation of the few is founded on the degradation of the many. . . .

If I have given a true account of that freedom which forms the goal of social effort, we shall see that freedom of contract, freedom in all the forms of doing what one will with one's own, is valuable only as a means to an end. That end is . . . the liberation of the powers of all men equally for contributions to a common good. No one has a right to do what he will with his own [property] in such a way as to contravene this end [the common good]. . . . Every one has an interest in securing to every one else the free use and enjoyment and disposal of his possessions, so long as that freedom on the part of one does not interfere with a like freedom on the part of others, because such freedom contributes to that equal development of the faculties of all which is the highest good for all. This is the true and the only justification of rights of property. Rights of property, however, have been and are claimed which cannot be thus justified. We are all now agreed that men cannot rightly be the property of men. The institution of property being only justifiable as a means to the free exercise of the social capabilities of all, there can be no true right to property of a kind which debars one class of men from such free exercise altogether. We condemn slavery no less when it arises out of a voluntary agreement on the part of the enslaved person. A contract by which any one agreed for a certain consideration to become the slave of another we should reckon a void contract. Here, then, is a limitation upon freedom of contract which we all recognise as rightful. No contract is valid in which human persons, willingly or unwillingly, are dealt with as commodities, because such contracts of necessity defeat the end for which alone society enforces contracts at all.

▷ Green argued that the state must correct abuses in society for people to develop their capacities and reap the harvest of freedom. For all members of society to make the best of themselves, it is necessary to place some limits on individual freedom. For instance, Green denied the freedom to contract for labor in a way that is detrimental to health. When people injure themselves, they also damage the community at large.

Are there no other contracts which, less obviously perhaps but really, are open to the same objection? In the first place, let us consider contracts affecting labour. Labour, the economist tells us, is a commodity exchangeable like other commodities. This is in a certain sense true, but it is a commodity which attaches in a peculiar manner to the person of man. Hence restrictions may need to be placed on the sale of this commodity which would be unnecessary in other cases, in order to prevent labour from being sold under conditions which make it impossible for the person selling it ever to become a free contributor to social good in any form. This is most plainly the case when a man bargains to work under conditions fatal to health, *e.g.,* in an unventilated factory. Every injury to the health of the individual is, so far as it goes, a public injury. It is an impediment to the general freedom; so much deduction from our power, as members of society, to make the best of ourselves. Society is, therefore, plainly within its right when it limits freedom of contract for the sale of labour, so far as is done by our laws for the sanitary regulations of factories, workshops, and mines. It is equally within its right in prohibiting the labour of women and young persons beyond certain hours. If they work beyond those hours, the result is demonstrably physical deterioration; which, as demonstrably, carries with it a lowering of the moral forces of society. For the sake of that general freedom of its members to make the best of themselves, which it is the object of civil society to secure, a prohibition should be put by law, which is the deliberate voice of society, on all such contracts of service as in a general way yield such a result. The purchase or hire of unwholesome dwellings is properly forbidden on the same principle. Its application to compulsory education may not be quite so obvious, but it will appear on a little reflection. Without a command of certain elementary arts and knowledge, the individual in modern society is as effectually crippled as by the loss of a limb or a broken constitution. He is not free to develop his faculties. With a view to securing such freedom among its members it is as certainly within the province of the state to prevent children from growing up in that kind of ignorance which practically excludes them from a free career in life, as it is within its province to require the sort of building and drainage necessary for public health.

Our modern legislation then with reference to labour, and education, and health, involving as it does manifold interference with freedom of contract, is justified on the ground that it is the business of the state, not indeed directly to promote moral goodness, for that, from the very nature of moral goodness, it cannot do, but to maintain the conditions without which a free exercise of the human faculties is impossible. . . . But there are some political speculators . . . [who] think that the individual ought to be left much more to himself than has of late been the case. Might not our people, they ask, have been trusted to learn in time for themselves to eschew unhealthy dwellings, to refuse dangerous and degrading employment, to get their children the schooling necessary for making their way in the world? Would they not for their own comfort, if not from more chivalrous

feeling, keep their wives and daughters from overwork? Or, failing this, ought not women, like men, to learn to protect themselves? Might not all the rules, in short, which legislation of the kind we have been discussing is intended to attain, have been attained without it; not so quickly, perhaps, but without tampering so dangerously with the independence and self-reliance of the people?

Now, we shall probably all agree that a society in which the public health was duly protected, and necessary education duly provided for, by the spontaneous action of individuals, was in a higher condition than one in which the compulsion of law was needed to secure these ends. But we must take men as we find them. Until such a condition of society is reached, it is the business of the state to take the best security it can for the young citizens growing up in such health and with so much knowledge as is necessary for their real freedom. . . . It was the overworked women, the ill-housed and untaught families, for whose benefit they [laws] were intended. And the question is whether without these laws the suffering classes could have been delivered quickly or slowly from the condition they were in. Could the enlightened self-interest or benevolence of individuals, working under a system of unlimited freedom of contract, have ever brought them into a state compatible with the free development of the human faculties? No one considering the facts can have any doubt as to the answer to this question. Left to itself, or to the operation of casual benevolence, a degraded population perpetuates and increases itself. Read any of the authorised accounts, given before royal or parliamentary commissions, of the state of the labourers, especially of the women and children, as they were in our great industries before the law was first brought to bear on them, and before freedom of contract was first interfered with in them. Ask yourself what chance there was of a generation, born and bred under such conditions, ever contracting itself out of them. . . . If labour is to be had under conditions incompatible with the health or decent housing or education of the labourer, there will always be plenty of people [employers] to buy it under those conditions. . . . Either the standard of well-being on the part of the sellers of labour [workers] must prevent them from selling their labour under those conditions, or the law must prevent it. With a population such as ours was forty years ago, and still largely is, the law must prevent it and continue the prevention for some generations, before the sellers will be in a state to prevent it for themselves.

Herbert Spencer
≪ *THE MAN VERSUS THE STATE* ≫

Committed to a traditional laissez-faire policy, however, some liberals attacked state intervention as a threat to personal freedom and a betrayal of central liberal principles. In *The Man versus the State* (1884), British philosopher Herbert Spencer (1820–1903) warned that increased government regulation would lead to socialism and slavery.

The extension of this policy . . . [of government legislation] fosters everywhere the tacit assumption that Government should step in whenever anything is not going right. "Surely you would not have this misery continue!" exclaims some one, if you hint . . . [an objection] to much that is now being said and done. Observe what is implied by this exclamation. It takes for granted. . . . that every evil can be removed: the truth being that with the existing defects of human nature, many evils can only be thrust out of one place or form into another place or form — often being increased by the change. The exclamation also implies the unhesitating belief, here especially concerning us, that evils of all kinds should be dealt with by the State. . . . Obviously, the more numerous governmental interventions become, the more confirmed does this habit of thought grow, and the more loud and perpetual the demands for intervention.

Every extension of the regulative policy involves an addition to the regulative agents — a further growth of officialism and an increasing power of the organization formed of officials. . . .

. . . Moreover, every additional State-interference strengthens the tacit assumption that it is the duty of the State to deal with all evils and secure all benefits. Increasing power of a growing administrative organization is accompanied by decreasing power of the rest of the society to resist its further growth and control. . . .

"But why is this change described as 'the coming-slavery'?" is a question which many will still ask. The reply is simple. All socialism involves slavery. . . .

Evidently then, the changes made, the changes in progress, and the changes urged, will carry us not only towards State-ownership of land and dwellings and means of communication, all to be administered and worked by State-agents, but towards State-usurpation of all industries: the private forms of which, disadvantaged more and more in competition with the State, which can arrange everything for its own convenience, will more and more die away, just as many voluntary schools have, in presence of Board-schools. And so will be brought about the desired ideal of the socialists. . . .

. . . It is a matter of common remark, often made when a marriage is impending, that those possessed by strong hopes habitually dwell on the promised pleasures and think nothing of the accompanying pains. A further exemplification of this truth is supplied by these political enthusiasts and fanatical revolutionists. Impressed with the miseries existing under our present social arrangements, and not regarding these miseries as caused by the ill-working of a human nature but partially adapted to the social state, they imagine them to be forthwith curable by this or that rearrangement. Yet, even did their plans succeed it could only be by substituting one kind of evil for another. A little deliberate thought would show that under their proposed arrangements, their liberties must be surrendered in proportion as their material welfares were cared for.

For no form of co-operation, small or great, can be carried on without regulation, and an implied submission to the regulating agencies. . . .

. . . So that each [individual] would stand toward the governing agency in the relation of slave to master.

"But the governing agency would be a master which he and others made and kept constantly in check; and one which therefore would not control him or others more than was needful for the benefit of each and all."

To which reply the first rejoinder is that,

even if so, each member of the community as an individual would be a slave to the community as a whole. Such a relation has habitually existed in militant communities, even under quasi-popular forms of government. In ancient Greece the accepted principle was that the citizen belonged neither to himself nor to his family, but belonged to his city — the city being with the Greek equivalent to the community. And this doctrine, proper to a state of constant warfare, is a doctrine which socialism unawares re-introduces into a state intended to be purely industrial. The services of each will belong to the aggregate of all; and for these services, such returns will be given as the authorities think proper. So that even if the administration is of the beneficent kind intended to be secured, slavery, however mild, must be the outcome of the arrangement. . . .

The function of Liberalism in the past was that of putting a limit to the powers of kings. The function of true Liberalism in the future will be that of putting a limit to the powers of Parliaments.

REVIEW QUESTIONS

1. How did Green define freedom? Do you agree or disagree with his definition? Explain.
2. On what basis would Green restrict property rights?
3. On what basis does he justify state intervention in social and economic life?
4. What was Herbert Spencer's answer to the argument that government legislation is necessary to relieve human misery?
5. What did Spencer mean by the dictum "All socialism involves slavery"?
6. According to Spencer, what was true liberalism? Compare his conception of liberalism with that of Thomas Hill Green.

4 ▼ Equal Rights for Women

Inspired by the ideals of equality voiced in the Enlightenment and the French Revolution, women in nineteenth-century Europe and the United States began to demand equal rights. In the United States, the Women's Suffrage Movement held its first convention in 1848 in Seneca Falls, New York. The women passed a Declaration of Principles that said in part: "We hold these truths to be self-evident: that all men and women are created equal." The struggle for equal rights and voting privileges continued, and by the end of the century, women were voting in a few state elections. Finally, in 1920, the Nineteenth Amendment gave women voting privileges throughout the United States.

In England, having failed to persuade Parliament in the mid-1860s to give them the vote, women organized reform societies, drew up petitions, and protested unfair treatment. The Women's Social and Political Union (WSPU), organized by Emmeline Pankhurst, employed militant tactics.

During World War I, women worked in offices, factories, and service industries at jobs formerly held by men. Their wartime service made it clear that women played an essential role in the economic life of nations, and many political leaders argued for the extension of the vote to them. In 1918, British women over the age of thirty gained the vote, and in 1928, Parliament lowered the voting age for British women to twenty-one, the same as for men.

The first countries to permit women to vote were New Zealand in 1893 and Australia in 1902. In Europe, women were granted voting rights by stages, first for municipal elections, later for national ones. Finland extended voting rights to women in 1906; the other Scandinavian countries followed suit, but the majority of European countries did not allow women to vote until after World War I.

Mary Wollstonecraft
VINDICATION OF THE RIGHTS OF WOMAN

When in 1789 the French revolutionaries issued their "Declaration of the Rights of Man," it was only a matter of time before a woman published a declaration of the rights of woman. That feat was accomplished in the same year in France by Olympe de Gouges. In England, Mary Wollstonecraft, strongly influenced by her, published her own statement *Vindication of the Rights of Woman* in 1792. Her protest against the prevailing submissiveness of women was reinforced by the philosophy of the Enlightenment and the ideals of the French Revolution, which she observed firsthand from 1792 to 1794. A career woman, she made her living as a prolific writer closely associated with the radicals of her time, one of whom, William Godwin, she married shortly before her death. Wollstonecraft became famous for her vigorous protests against the subjection of women. Children, husbands, and society generally, she pleaded in *Vindication of the Rights of Woman,* were best served by well-educated, self-reliant, and strong women capable of holding their own in the world.

. . . I have turned over various books written on the subject of education, and patiently observed the conduct of parents and the management of schools; but what has been the result? — a profound conviction that the neglected education of my fellow creatures is the grand source of the misery I deplore, and that women, in particular, are rendered weak and wretched. . . . The conduct and manners of women, in fact, evidently prove that their minds are not in a healthy state. . . . One cause of this . . . I attribute to a false system of education, gathered from the books written on this subject by men who, considering females rather as women than human creatures, have been more anxious to make them alluring mistresses than affectionate wives and rational mothers. . . .

. . . A degree of physical superiority of men cannot . . . be denied, and it is a noble prerogative! But not content with this natural pre-eminence, men endeavour to sink us still lower, merely to render us alluring objects for a moment. . . .

My own sex, I hope, will excuse me, if I treat them like rational creatures, instead of flattering their *fascinating* graces, and viewing them as if they were in a state of perpetual childhood, unable to stand alone. I earnestly wish to point out in what true dignity and human happiness consists. I wish to persuade women to endeavour to acquire strength, both of mind and body. . . .

Dismissing, then, those pretty feminine phrases, which the men condescendingly use to soften our slavish dependence, and despising that weak elegancy of mind, exquisite sensibility, and sweet docility of manners, supposed to be the sexual characteristics of the weaker vessel, I wish to show that elegance is inferior to virtue, that the first object of laudable ambition is to obtain a character as a human being, regardless of the distinction of sex. . . .

The education of women has of late been more attended to than formerly; yet they are still reckoned a frivolous sex, and ridiculed or pitied by the writers who endeavour by satire or instruction to improve them. It is acknowledged that they spend many of the first years of their lives in acquiring a smattering of accomplishments; meanwhile strength of body and mind are sacrificed to libertine notions of beauty, to the desire of establishing themselves — the only way women can rise in the world — by marriage. And this desire making mere animals of them, when they marry they act as such children may be expected to act, — they dress, they paint, and nickname God's creatures. Surely these weak beings are only fit for a seraglio [harem]! Can they be expected to govern a family with judgment, or take care of the poor babes whom they bring into the world? . . .

Contending for the rights of woman, my main argument is built on this simple principle, that if she be not prepared by education to become the companion of man, she will stop the progress of knowledge and virtue; for truth must be common to all, or it will be inefficacious with respect to its influence on general practice. And how can woman be expected to co-operate unless she knows why she ought to be virtuous? unless freedom strengthens her reason till she comprehends her duty, and see in what manner it is connected with her real good. If children are to be educated to understand the true principle of patriotism, their mother must be a patriot; and the love of mankind, from which an orderly train of virtues spring, can only be produced by considering the moral and civil interest of mankind; but the education and situation of woman at present shuts her out from such investigations. . . .

Consider — I address you as a legislator — whether, when men contend for their freedom, and to be allowed to judge for themselves respecting their own happiness, it be not inconsistent and unjust to subjugate women, even though you firmly believe that you are acting in the manner best calculated to promote their happiness? Who made man the exclusive judge, if woman partake with him of the gift of reason?

In this style argue tyrants of every denomination, from the weak king to the weak father of a family; they are all eager to crush reason, yet always assert that they usurp its throne only to be useful. Do you not act a similar part when you *force* all women, by denying them civil and political rights, to remain immured [imprisoned] in their families groping in the dark? for surely, sir, you will not assert that a duty can be binding which is not founded on reason? If, indeed, this be their destination, arguments may be drawn from reason; and thus augustly supported, the more understanding women acquire, the more they will be attached to their duty — comprehending it — for unless they comprehend it, unless their morals be fixed on the same immutable principle as those of man, no authority can make them discharge it in a virtuous manner. They may be convenient slaves, but slavery will have its constant effect, degrading the master and the abject dependent.

But if women are to be excluded, without having a voice, from a participation of the natural rights of mankind, prove first, to ward off the charge of injustice and inconsistency, that they [lack] reason, else this flaw in your NEW CONSTITUTION will ever show that man must, in some shape, act like a tyrant, and tyranny, in whatever part of society it rears its brazen front, will ever undermine morality. . . .

In what does man's pre-eminence over the brute creation consist? The answer is as clear as that a half is less than the whole, in Reason. . . . Yet . . . deeply rooted processes have clouded reason. . . . Men, in general, seem to employ their reason to justify prejudices, which they have imbibed, they can scarcely trace how, rather than to root them out.

The power of generalising ideas, of drawing comprehensive conclusions from individual observations . . . has not only been denied to women; but writers have insisted that it is inconsistent, with a few exceptions, with their sexual character. Let men prove this, and I shall grant that woman only exists for man. I must, however, previously remark, that the power of generalising ideas, to any great extent, is not very common amongst men or women. But this exercise is the true cultivation of the understanding; and everything conspires to render the cultivation of the understanding more difficult in the female than male world. . . .

I shall not go back to the remote annals of antiquity to trace the history of woman; it is sufficient to allow that she has always been either a slave or a despot, and to remark that each of these situations equally retards the progress of reason. The grand source of female folly and vice has ever appeared to me to arise from narrowness of mind; and the very constitution of civil governments has put almost insuperable obstacles in the way to prevent the cultivation of the female understanding; yet virtue can be built on no other foundation. . . .

When do we hear of women who, starting out of obscurity, boldly claim respect on account of their great abilities or daring virtues? Where are they to be found? . . .

With respect to women, when they receive a careful education, they are either made fine ladies, brimful of sensibility, and teeming with capricious fancies, or mere notable women. The latter are often friendly, honest creatures, and have a shrewd kind of good sense, joined with worldly prudence, that often render them more useful members of society than the fine sentimental lady, though they possess neither greatness of mind nor taste. The intellectual world is shut against them. Take them out of their family or neighbourhood, and they stand still; the mind finding no employment, for literature affords a fund of amusement which they have never sought to relish, but frequently to despise. The sentiments and taste of more cultivated minds appear ridiculous, even in those whom chance and family connections have led them to love; but in mere acquaintance they think it all affectation.

A man of sense can only love such a woman on account of her sex, and respect her because she is a trusty servant. He lets her, to preserve his own peace, scold the servants, and go to church in clothes made of the very best materials. . . . [W]omen, whose minds are not enlarged by cultivation, or . . . by reflection, are very unfit to manage a family, for, by an undue stretch of power, they are always tyrannising to support a superiority that only rests on the arbitrary distinction of fortune.

Women have seldom sufficient serious employment to silence their feelings; a round of little cares, or vain pursuits frittering away all strength of mind and organs, they become naturally only objects of sense. In short, the whole tenor of female education (the education of society) tends to render the best disposed romantic and inconstant; and the remainder vain and [contemptible]. In the present state of society this evil can scarcely be remedied, I am afraid, in the slightest degree; should a more laudable ambition ever gain ground they may be brought nearer to nature and reason, and become more virtuous and useful as they grow more respectable. . . .

Women . . . all want to be ladies. Which is simply to have nothing to do, but listlessly to go they scarcely care where, for they cannot tell what.

But what have women to do in society? I may be asked, but to loiter with easy grace. . . . Women might certainly study the art of healing, and be physicians as well as nurses. . . . They might also study politics . . . for the reading of history will scarcely be more useful than the study of romances. . . . Business of various kinds, they might likewise pursue, if they were educated in a more orderly manner, which might save many from common and legal prostitution. . . . The few employments open to a woman, so far from being liberal, are menial. . . .

Some of these women might be restrained from marrying by a proper spirit of delicacy, and others may not have had it in their power to escape in this pitiful way from servitude; is not that Government then very defective, and very unmindful of the happiness of one-half of its members, that does not provide for honest, independent women, by encouraging them to fill respectable stations? . . .

It is a melancholy truth; yet such is the blessed effect of civilisation! the most respectable women are the most oppressed; and, unless they have understandings far superior to the common run of understandings, taking in both sexes, they must, from being treated like contemptible beings, become contemptible. How many women thus waste life away the prey of discontent, who might have practised as physicians, regulated a farm, managed a shop, and stood erect, supported by their own industry, instead of hanging their heads. . . .

Would men but generously snap our chains, and be content with rational fellowship instead of slavish obedience, they would find us more observant daughters, more affectionate sisters, more faithful wives, more reasonable mothers — in a word, better citizens. We should then love them with true affection, because we should learn to respect ourselves; and the peace of mind of a worthy man would not be interrupted by the idle vanity of his wife, nor the babes sent to nestle in a strange bosom, having never found a home in their mother's. . . .

. . . The sexual distinction which men have so warmly insisted upon, is arbitrary. . . . Asserting the rights which women in common with men ought to contend for, I have not attempted to [make light of] their faults; but to prove them to be the natural consequence of their education and station in society. If so, it is reasonable to suppose that they will change their character, and correct their vices and follies, when they are allowed to be free in a physical, moral, and civil sense.

Let woman share the rights, and she will emulate the virtues of man; for she must grow more perfect when emancipated. . . .

John Stuart Mill
≪ THE SUBJECTION OF WOMEN ≫

John Stuart Mill (see page 122), a British philosopher and a liberal, championed women's rights. In 1867, Mill, as a member of Parliament, proposed that the suffrage be extended to women (the proposal was rejected by a vote of 194 to 74). In *The Subjection of Women* (1869), written in collaboration with his stepdaughter Helen Taylor, Mill argued that male dominance of women constituted a flagrant abuse of power. He maintained that female inequality, "a single relic of an old world of thought and practice exploded in everything else," violated the principle of individual rights and hindered the progress of humanity. Excerpts from Mill's classic in the history of femininism follow.

The object of this Essay is to explain, as clearly as I am able, the grounds of an opinion which I have held from the very earliest period when I had formed any opinions at all on social or political matters, and which, instead of being weakened or modified, has been constantly growing stronger by the progress of reflection and the experience of life: That the principle which regulates the existing social relations between the two sexes — the legal subordination of one sex to the other — is wrong in itself, and now one of the chief hindrances to human improvement; and that it ought to be replaced by a principle of perfect equality, admitting no power or privilege on the one side, nor disability on the other. . . .

. . . The adoption of this system of inequality never was the result of deliberation, or forethought, or any social ideas, or any notion whatever of what conduced to the benefit of humanity or the good order of society. It arose simply from the fact that from the very earliest twilight of human society, every woman (owing to the value attached to her by men, combined with her inferiority in muscular strength) was found in a state of bondage to some man. . . .

But, it will be said, the rule of men over women differs from all these others in not being a rule of force: it is accepted voluntarily; women make no complaint, and are consenting parties to it. In the first place, a great number of women do not accept it. Ever since there have been women able to make their sentiments known by their writings (the only mode of publicity which society permits to them), an increasing number of them have recorded protests against their present social condition: and recently many thousands of them, headed by the most eminent women known to the public, have petitioned Parliament for their admission to the parliamentary suffrage. The claim of women to be educated as solidly, and in the same branches of knowledge, as men, is urged with growing intensity, and with a great pros-

pect of success; while the demand for their admission into professions and occupations hitherto closed against them becomes every year more urgent. Though there are not in this country, as there are in the United States, periodical Conventions and an organized party to agitate for the Rights of Women, there is a numerous and active Society organized and managed by women, for the more limited object of obtaining the political franchise. Nor is it only in our own country and in America that women are beginning to protest, more or less collectively, against the disabilities under which they labour. France, and Italy, and Switzerland, and Russia now afford examples of the same thing. How many more women there are who silently cherish similar aspirations, no one can possibly know; but there are abundant tokens how many *would* cherish them, were they not so strenuously taught to repress them as contrary to the proprieties of their sex. . . .

Men do not want solely the obedience of women, they want their sentiments. All men, except the most brutish, desire to have, in the woman most nearly connected with them, not a forced slave but a willing one; not a slave merely, but a favourite. They have therefore put everything in practice to enslave their minds. The masters of all other slaves rely, for maintaining obedience, on fear; either fear of themselves, or religious fears. The masters of women wanted more than simple obedience, and they turned the whole force of education to effect their purpose. All women are brought up from the very earliest years in the belief that their ideal of character is the very opposite to that of men; not self-will, and government by self-control, but submission, and yielding to the control of others. All the moralities tell them that it is the duty of women, and all the current sentimentalities that it is their nature, to live for others; to make complete abnegation of themselves, and to have no life but in their affections. And by their affections are meant the only ones they are allowed to have — those to the men with whom they are connected, or to the children who constitute an additional and indefeasible tie between them and a man. When we put together three things — first, the natural attraction between opposite sexes; secondly, the wife's entire dependence on the husband, every privilege or pleasure she has being either his gift, or depending entirely on his will; and lastly, that the principal object of human pursuit, consideration, and all objects of social ambition, can in general be sought or obtained by her only through him — it would be a miracle if the object of being attractive to men had not become the polar star of feminine education and formation of character. And, this great means of influence over the minds of women having been acquired, an instinct of selfishness made men avail themselves of it to the utmost as a means of holding women in subjection, by representing to them meekness, submissiveness, and resignation of all individual will into the hands of a man, as an essential part of sexual attractiveness. Can it be doubted that any of the other yokes which mankind have succeeded in breaking would have subsisted till now if the same means had existed, and had been as sedulously [diligently] used to bow down their minds to it?

▷   Mill argues that women should be able to participate in political life and should not be barred from entering the professions.

On the other point which is involved in the just equality of women, their admissibility to all the functions and occupations hitherto retained as the monopoly of the stronger sex. . . . I believe that their disabilities [in occupation and civil life] elsewhere are only clung to in order to maintain their subordination in domestic life; because the generality of the male sex cannot yet tolerate the idea of living with an equal. Were it not for that, I think that almost every one, in the existing state of opinion in politics and political economy, would admit

the injustice of excluding half the human race from the greater number of lucrative occupations, and from almost all high social functions; ordaining from their birth either that they are not, and cannot by any possibility become, fit for employments which are legally open to the stupidest and basest of the other sex, or else that however fit they may be, those employments shall be interdicted to them, in order to be preserved for the exclusive benefit of males. . . .

It will perhaps be sufficient if I confine myself, in the details of my argument, to functions of a public nature: since, if I am successful as to those, it probably will be readily granted that women should be admissible to all other occupations. . . . And here let me begin . . . [with] the suffrage, both parliamentary and municipal. . . .

. . . To have a voice in choosing those by whom one is to be governed, is a means of self-protection due to every one, though he were to remain for ever excluded from the function of governing. . . . Under whatever conditions, and within whatever limits, men are admitted to the suffrage, there is not a shadow of justification for not admitting women under the same. The majority of the women of any class are not likely to differ in political opinion from the majority of the men of the same class, unless the question be one in which the interests of women, as such, are in some way involved; and if they are so, women require the suffrage, as their guarantee of just and equal consideration. . . .

With regard to the fitness of women, not only to participate in elections, but themselves to hold offices or practise professions involving important public responsibilities; I have already observed that this consideration is not essential to the practical question in dispute: since any woman, who succeeds in an open profession, proves by that very fact that she is qualified for it. And in the case of public offices, if the political system of the country is such as to exclude unfit men, it will equally exclude unfit women: while if it is not, there is no additional evil in the fact that the unfit persons whom it admits may be either women or men. . . .

. . . There is no country of Europe in which the ablest men have not frequently experienced, and keenly appreciated, the value of the advice and help of clever and experienced women of the world, in the attainment both of private and of public objects; and there are important matters of public administration to which few men are equally competent with such women; among others, the detailed control of expenditure. But what we are now discussing is not the need which society has of the services of women in public business, but the dull and hopeless life to which it so often condemns them, by forbidding them to exercise the practical abilities which many of them are conscious of, in any wider field than one which to some of them never was, and to others is no longer, open. If there is anything vitally important to the happiness of human beings, it is that they should relish their habitual pursuit [that is, they should be happy in their work]. This requisite of an enjoyable life is very imperfectly granted, or altogether denied, to a large part of mankind; and by its absence many a life is a failure, which is provided, in appearance, with every requisite of success.

Emmeline Pankhurst
≪ WHY WE ARE MILITANT ≫

Agitation in Great Britain for woman suffrage reached a peak during the turbulent years of parliamentary reform, 1909–1911. Under the leadership of Emmeline Pankhurst and her daughter Christabel, women engaged in demonstrations, disrupted political meetings, and when dragged off to jail, resorted to passive resistance and hunger strikes. Some hunger strikers were subjected to the cruelty of force feeding. In 1913 Emmeline Pankhurst carried her appeal to the United States, where she delivered the speech printed below.

I know that in your minds there are questions like these; you are saying, "Woman Suffrage is sure to come; the emancipation of humanity is an evolutionary process, and how is it that some women, instead of trusting to that evolution, instead of educating the masses of people of their country, instead of educating their own sex to prepare them for citizenship, how is it that these militant women are using violence and upsetting the business arrangements of the country in their undue impatience to attain their end?"

Let me try to explain to you the situation. . . .

The extensions of the franchise to the men of my country have been preceded by very great violence, by something like a revolution, by something like civil war. In 1832, you know we were on the edge of a civil war and on the edge of revolution, and it was at the point of the sword — no, not at the point of the sword — it was after the practice of arson on so large a scale that half the city of Bristol was burned down in a single night, it was because more and greater violence and arson were feared that the Reform Bill of 1832 [which gave the vote to the middle class] was allowed to pass into law. In 1867, . . . [r]ioting went on all over the country, and as the result of that rioting, as the result of that unrest, . . . as a result of the fear of more rioting and violence the Reform Act of 1867 [which gave workers the vote] was put upon the statute books.

In 1884 . . . [r]ioting was threatened and feared, and so the agricultural labourers got the vote.

Meanwhile, during the '80's, women, like men, were asking for the franchise. Appeals, larger and more numerous than for any other reform, were presented in support of Woman's Suffrage, Meetings of the great corporations [group of principal officials in a town or city government], great town councils, and city councils, passed resolutions asking that women should have the vote. More meetings were held, and larger, for Woman Suffrage than were held for votes for men, and yet the women did not get it. Men got the vote because they were and would be violent. The women did not get it because they were constitutional and law-abiding. . . .

I believed, as many women still in England believe, that women could get their way in some mysterious manner, by purely peaceful methods. We have been so accustomed, we women, to accept one standard for men and another standard for women, that we have even applied that variation of standard to the injury of our political welfare.

Having had better opportunities of education, and having had some training in politics, having in political life come so near to the "superior" being as to see that he was not altogether such a fount of wisdom as they had supposed, that he had his human weaknesses as we had, the twentieth century women began to say to themselves, "Is it not time, since our methods have failed and the men's have succeeded, that we should take a leaf out of their political book?" . . .

Well, we in Great Britain, on the eve of the General Election of 1905, a mere handful of us — why, you could almost count us on the fingers of both hands — set out on the wonderful adventure of forcing the strongest Government of modern times to give the women the vote. . . .

The Suffrage movement was almost dead. The women had lost heart. You could not get a Suffrage meeting that was attended by members of the general public. . . .

Two women changed that in a twinkling of an eye at a great Liberal demonstration in Manchester, where a Liberal leader, Sir Edward Grey, was explaining the programme to be carried out during the Liberals' next turn of office. The two women put the fateful question, "When are you going to give votes to women?" and refused to sit down until they had been answered. These two women were sent to gaol, and from that day to this the women's movement, both militant and constitutional, has never looked back. We had little more than one moribund society for Woman Suffrage in those days. Now we have nearly 50 societies for Woman Suffrage, and they are large in membership, they are rich in money, and their ranks are swelling every day that passes. That is how militancy has put back the clock of Woman Suffrage in Great Britain. . . .

I want to say here and now that the only justification for violence, the only justification for damage to property, the only justification for risk to the comfort of other human beings is the fact that you have tried all other available means and have failed to secure justice, and as a law-abiding person — and I am by nature a law-abiding person, as one hating violence, hating disorder — I want to say that from the moment we began our militant agitation to this day I have felt absolutely guiltless in this matter.

I tell you that in Great Britain there is no other way. . . .

Well, I say the time is long past when it became necessary for women to revolt in order to maintain their self respect in Great Britain. The women who are waging this war are women who would fight, if it were only for the idea of liberty — if it were only that they might be free citizens of a free country — I myself would fight for that idea alone. But we have, in addition to this love of freedom, intolerable grievances to redress. . . .

Those grievances are so pressing that, so far from it being a duty to be patient and to wait for evolution, in thinking of those grievances the idea of patience is intolerable. We feel that patience is something akin to crime when our patience involves continued suffering on the part of the oppressed.

We are fighting to get the power to alter bad laws; but some people say to us, "Go to the representatives in the House of Commons, point out to them that these laws are bad, and you will find them quite ready to alter them."

Ladies and gentlemen, there are women in my country who have spent long and useful lives trying to get reforms, and because of their voteless condition, they are unable even to get the ear of Members of Parliament, much less are they able to secure those reforms.

Our marriage and divorce laws are a disgrace to civilisation. I sometimes wonder, looking back from the serenity of past middle age, at the courage of women. I wonder that women have the courage to take upon themselves the responsibilities of marriage and motherhood when I see how little protection the law of my country affords them. I wonder that a woman will face the ordeal of childbirth with the knowledge that after she has risked her life to bring a child into the world she has absolutely no parental rights over the future of that child. Think what trust women have in men when a woman will marry a man, knowing, if she has knowledge of the law, that if that man is not all she in her love for him thinks him, he may even bring a strange woman into the house, bring his mistress into the house to live with her, and she cannot get legal relief from such a marriage as that. . . .

. . . [W]e realise how political power, how political influence, which would enable us to get better laws, would make it possible for thousands upon thousands of unhappy women to live happier lives. . . .

Take the industrial side of the question: have men's wages for a hard day's work ever been so low and inadequate as are women's wages today? Have men ever had to suffer from the laws, more injustice than women suffer? Is there a single reason which men have had for demanding liberty that does not also apply to women?

Why, if you were talking to the *men* of any other nation you would not hesitate to reply in the affirmative. There is not a man in this meeting who has not felt sympathy with the uprising of the men of other lands when suffering from intolerable tyranny, when deprived of all representative rights. You are full of sympathy with men in Russia. You are full of sympathy with nations that rise against the domination of the Turk. You are full of sympathy with all struggling people striving for independence. How is it, then, that some of you have nothing but ridicule and contempt and [condemnation] for women who are fighting for exactly the same thing?

All my life I have tried to understand why it is that men who value their citizenship as their dearest possession seem to think citizenship ridiculous when it is to be applied to the women of their race. And I find an explanation, and it is the only one I can think of. It came to me when I was in a prison cell, remembering how I had seen men laugh at the idea of women going to prison. Why they would confess they could not bear a cell door to be shut upon themselves for a single hour without asking to be let out. A thought came to me in my prison cell, and it was this: that to men women are not human beings like themselves. Some men think we are superhuman; they put us on pedestals; they revere us; they think we are too fine and too delicate to come down into the hurly-burly of life. Other men think us sub-human; they think we are a strange species unfortunately having to exist for the perpetuation of the race. They think that we are fit for drudgery, but that in some strange way our minds are not like theirs, our love for great things is not like theirs, and so we are a sort of sub-human species.

We are neither superhuman nor are we sub-human. We are just human beings like yourselves.

Our hearts burn within us when we read the great mottoes which celebrate the liberty of your country; when we go to France and we read the words, liberty, fraternity and equality, don't you think that we appreciate the meaning of those words? And then when we wake to the knowledge that these things are not for us, they are only for our brothers, then there comes a sense of bitterness into the hearts of some women, and they say to themselves, "Will men never understand?" But so far as we in England are concerned, we have come to the conclusion that we are not going to leave men any illusions upon the question.

When we were patient, when we believed in argument and persuasion, they said, "You don't really want it because, if you did, you would do something unmistakable to show you were determined to have it." And then when we did something unmistakable they said, "You are behaving so badly that you show you are not fit for it."

Now, gentlemen, in your heart of hearts you do not believe that. You know perfectly well that there never was a thing worth having that was not worth fighting for. You know perfectly well that if the situation were reversed, if you had no constitutional rights and we had all of them, if you had the duty of paying and obeying and trying to look as pleasant, and we were the proud citizens who could decide our fate and yours, because we knew what was good for you better than you knew yourselves, you know perfectly well that you wouldn't stand it for a single day, and you would be perfectly justified in rebelling against such intolerable conditions.

Hubertine Auclert
≪ *LA CITOYENNE* ≫

The leading voice for women's rights in late-nineteenth-century France was the newspaper *La Citoyenne (The Female Citizen),* started in 1881 by Hubertine Auclert (1848–1914). But in socially conservative France, progress was slow — women did not receive the vote until 1944. In the following passage, Auclert stated the case for female equality.

It is the humiliating law that, for purposes of giving verbal or written testimony, lumps women together with male idiots and men deprived by law of their civil rights. Women are not allowed to act as witness to the registration of a birth or a marriage, or the execution of an act of sale. What am I saying? A woman is not even allowed to attest to the identity of another woman for the notarization of a signature.

By the civil emancipation of woman, I mean, in a word, the abrogation of every one of these laws of exception that release men from responsibilities and weigh down women with the heaviest burdens. . . .

Now, what do we mean by the political emancipation of woman? We mean women's receiving the right that confers the power to make laws: by itself, if one is elected deputy; by delegation, if one is a voter.

Thus, it is evident that political rights are for woman the keystone that will give her all other rights.

When women are able to intervene in public affairs, their first concern will be to reform unjust legislation; their first act will be to use the right given them to change their situation.

But since woman does not have the power to weaken the laws that oppress her, whom can she count on to do it? On man? But it is man who has established the existing laws and these laws do not trouble him. On the contrary, they give him all the facilities to trouble us; thus, instead of suppressing these laws that enslave woman, man busies himself with creating laws that will further enlarge his horizons. In this country where there are seventeen million sovereigns — men — and more than seventeen million slaves — women — the reforms that men perceive as essential are the reforms that will grant them still more privileges.

This means that it is beyond any doubt that as long as woman does not possess this weapon — the vote — she will suffer the rule of masculine law. All her efforts to conquer her civil and economic liberties will be in vain.

What women need to free themselves from masculine tyranny — made law — is the possession of their share of sovereignty; they need the title of *citoyenne française;* they need the ballot.

The French citizeness: this means that woman invested with the highest social rights will, by freedom, have her dignity restored; by the sense of responsibility, her character enlarged.

The French citizeness will promptly rise out of her distressing economic situation; the State and the laws will no longer render her inferior; the schooling of woman being, like that of man, essentially useful, every career, every profession will be open to her; and whatever her work, woman will no longer see it deprecated under the ridiculous pretext that it was done by a woman.

The French citizeness will quintuple the effectiveness of her maternal influence; she will raise the child not for herself alone, or for itself, but for society. She will inculcate those private and public virtues that will contribute to the child's happiness and that of his fellow-creatures.

The woman invested with the highest social rights, the French citizeness, will have the power to endow generations with such a sweeping moral vision, that fraternity will replace egoism in human relationships, and harmony — the goal to which all aspire — will supplant the present conflict in society.

In as much as we believe that from the emancipation of woman will flow a source of good for all humanity, we can do no better than to consecrate all our efforts to this cause.

REVIEW QUESTIONS

1. According to Mary Wollstonecraft, what benefits would society derive from giving equal rights to women?
2. Why did Wollstonecraft object to the traditional attitudes of men toward women?
3. How, in Wollstonecraft's opinion, should women change?
4. In John Stuart Mill's view, what was the ultimate origin of the subjection of women?
5. According to Mill, what character qualities did men seek to instill in women?
6. Why, according to Mill's argument, should women have the right to participate in politics and public affairs on equal terms with men?
7. Why did Emmeline Pankhurst think that violence was justified in fighting for women's rights?
8. What conditions in the lives of women drew Emmeline Pankhurst to advocate violence?
9. Why, according to her, did men, who valued their citizenship as their dearest possession, feel it was ridiculous to grant it to women?
10. What were the "laws that enslave women" in France, according to Hubertine Auclert?
11. What did Auclert mean by "the political emancipation of women"? What did she expect would result from this emancipation?

▼▼▼

5 ▼ Social Reform

Prince Otto von Bismarck (1815–1898), first chancellor of the German Empire, was the architect of a united Germany under Prussian auspices. A conservative Prussian aristocrat, he nevertheless adopted the liberal goal of national unity, giving the German Empire a broad political base. He was concerned with the need to tie the emerging industrial working class to his state by supporting "state socialism." To establish itself in the world, the New Germany could not afford domestic discord or class struggle.

The workers in the fast-expanding German industries, however, were attracted to the Social Democratic party inspired by Marx and Engels, which favored a democratic republic and even talked of a socialist revolution. After an attempt on the emperor's life in 1878 was blamed on the Social Democrats, Bismarck stepped forward with his Anti-Socialist Law — he called it the "exceptional law" — designed to suppress Social Democratic agitation. Aware that repression alone would not yield tranquility, he introduced positive measures during the 1880s in the form of state-organized social insurance for industrial workers. The program guaranteed workers a minimum income in case of sickness, accident, disability, and old age. By giving workers a stake in the social order, Bismarck effectively undercut revolutionary fervor.

Bismarck's pioneer program in state socialism set a model for other countries as well. As part of Liberal party reforms in 1910–1911, Britain adopted a state-sponsored social insurance scheme, the beginning of the British welfare state.

Otto von Bismarck
PROMOTION OF THE WORKERS' WELFARE

Bismarck's motives for state socialism — as well as aspects of his political philosophy, with its religious overtones — are evident in the following selection from a speech he gave to the Reichstag, the German national assembly, on March 10, 1884.

The positive efforts began really only in the year . . . 1881 . . . with the imperial message . . . in which His Majesty William I said: "Already in February of this year, we have expressed our conviction that the healing of social ills is not to be sought exclusively by means of repression of Social Democratic excesses, but equally in the positive promotion of the workers' welfare. . . ."

In consequence of this, first of all, the insurance law against accidents was submitted. . . .

And . . . it reads . . . "But those who have, through age or disability, become incapable of working have a confirmed claim on all for a higher degree of state care than could have been their share heretofore. . . ."

The plan of reform which we adhere to according to the will of the Emperor and of the allied governments cannot be implemented in a short time; it needs a period of years for its accomplishment. We have bestirred ourselves to improve the laborers' position in three directions. One, at a time when opportunity for work is slight and wages have become low, we have taken the necessary steps to protect work in our native land against competition; in other words, we have introduced protective tariffs to protect domestic labor. As a result of these measures, a real improvement of wages and a diminution of unemployment has taken place. Since then, work has reappeared more and more, and you trouble yourself in vain in seeking other grounds for that. On the contrary, I believe this event must have a considerable effect in the quietening down of socialist efforts. The person who still remembers the period from 1877 and 1878 and the conditions at the time will not deny that even in foreign writings the hope of connecting their revolutionary plans to the workers' dissatisfaction has declined to some degree. Therefore, this protective tariff system has usefulness for the goal.

A second plan, which is in the government's mind, is the improvement of tax conditions, in that a fit division of them is sought, by which particularly oppressive [sales taxes] on account of small amounts are, if not eliminated, then, at least, decreased, which perhaps will lead to a further decrease. [Sales taxes] have earlier destroyed and broken down many small individuals in the working class and the few groschen [pennies] which they brought in taxes at the stipulated time also often were the reason why a family, which did not stand right on the lowest rung of affluence, was thrown back into want. . . .

The third branch of reforms, which we strive for, lies in direct provision for the workers. The question of labor time and wage increases is extraordinarily difficult to solve through state intervention, through legislation at all; for in any settlement that one makes, one runs the danger of interfering very considerably and unnecessarily in the personal freedom of getting value for one's services. . . . Then the worker suffers from that as well as the entrepreneur. That therefore is the governing borderline, and every legislative intervention must stop before that. . . . The workers' real sore point is the insecur-

ity of his existence. He is not always sure he will always have work. He is not sure he will always be healthy, and he foresees some day he will be old and incapable of work. But also if he falls into poverty as a result of long illness, he is completely helpless with his own powers, and society hitherto does not recognize a real obligation to him beyond ordinary poor relief, even when he has worked ever so faithfully and diligently before. But ordinary poor relief leaves much to be desired, especially in the great cities where it is extraordinarily much worse than in the country. . . . We read in Berlin newspapers of suicide because of difficulty in making both ends meet, of people who died from direct hunger and have hanged themselves because they have nothing to eat, of people who announce in the paper they were tossed out homeless and have no income. . . .

. . . For the worker it is always a fact that falling into poverty and onto poor relief in a great city is synonymous with misery, and this insecurity makes him hostile and mistrustful of society. That is humanly not unnatural, and as long as the state does not meet him halfway, just as long will this trust in the state's honesty be taken from him by accusations against the government, which he will find where he wills; always running back again to the socialist quacks . . . and, without great reflection, letting himself be promised things, which will not be fulfilled. On this account, I believe that accident insurance, with which we show the way, especially as soon as it covers agriculture completely, the construction industry above all, and all trades, will still work amelioratingly on the anxieties and ill-feeling of the working class. The sickness is not entirely curable, but through suppression of its external symptoms by coercive legislation we only arrest it and drive it inward. I cannot have anything to do with that alone. . . .

. . . I have, of course, said: We derive our right to let the exceptional law continue from duty and from the fulfillment of the duty of Christian legislation. On the Progressive side, you call it "socialist legislation"; I prefer the term "Christian." At the time of the Apostles, socialism went very much further still. If perhaps you will read the Bible once, you will find out various things about it in the Acts of the Apostles. I don't go as far in our own times. But I get the courage for repressive measures only from my good intention of working to the end that, so far as a Christian-minded state society may do it, the real grievances, the real hardships of fate, about which the workers have to complain, will be alleviated and will be redressed. How far? That, indeed, is a matter of implementation, but the duty of doing what one recognizes to be a duty is not annulled by the difficulty of implementation, and . . . our action is completely independent of success.

REVIEW QUESTIONS

1. What were the political motives behind Otto von Bismarck's social reforms?
2. What, according to Bismarck, were the causes of revolution?
3. What economic program did Bismarck propose for improving the conditions of the working class?
4. Describe the Christian strains in Bismarck's arguments.
5. Did Bismarck believe that the state has a moral obligation to care for the welfare of the working class? Explain your answer.

▼▼▼

6 ▼ Russia: Autocracy and Modernization

To the east of Germany stretched the vastness of Imperial Russia, which extended from the Russian heartland deep into Central Asia and to Siberia and the shores of the Pacific. By any comparison with western Europe — and all of Europe west of Russia was called the West — Russia was backward. Although liberal democracy advanced in western Europe, the Russian tsars embodied repressive monarchism. By the end of the nineteenth century, Russia was a police state; this was the only form in which the tsarist regime could hold its government together in this strikingly poor country, inhabited mostly by peasants barely emancipated from serfdom. Western travelers found Russia lacking in sanitation and other "essentials" of civilization, a situation that worsened the further east they ventured. Even though Russian intellectuals familiar with western Europe cherished their homeland, they deplored their country's inferiority in government and material culture. In spite of its backwardness, though, Russia played an important role in European politics.

Sergei Witte
A REPORT FOR TSAR NICHOLAS II

In 1899, Sergei Witte (1849–1915), Russia's minister of finance, prepared a report for Tsar Nicholas II (1894–1917) on the necessity of industrialization. This report offers unusual insights into the tsarist empire's economic weakness and the problems of trying to overcome that weakness. Witte's emphasis on the need for economic mobilization with the help of a carefully planned system foreshadows the subsequent industrialization drive under the Communist regime.

The Witte system, as it came to be called, justified the high tariff on imports originally imposed in 1891. The tariff raised the prices of imported manufactured goods (as well as of luxuries), which upset the landed nobility — Russia's chief agricultural producers and exporters and the tsar's major support group. The nobility not only preferred Western manufactured goods and resented having to pay more for them but also feared that European nations would impose a retaliatory tariff on Russian agricultural exports. The spokesmen for Russian agriculture demanded free trade and opposed Witte who, in promoting industrial development with the help of foreign capital and know-how, also had to combat widespread nationalist hostility toward foreigners.

In his report, Witte left no doubt that rapid economic development would bring much hardship for the Russian people, and he therefore pressed the emperor to be bold in his support for these policies. His "firm and strict economic system" was absolutely necessary if the Russian Empire, virtually a colony of western Europe, were to become as strong economically as the United States, already in 1900 serving as a yardstick for Russia's progress. Witte believed that only through industrialization could Russia maintain itself as a great power. Excerpts from Witte's report follow.

Russia remains even at the present essentially an agricultural country. It pays for all its obligations to foreigners by exporting raw materials, chiefly of an agricultural nature, principally grain. It meets its demand for finished goods by imports from abroad. The economic relations of Russia with western Europe are fully comparable to the relations of colonial countries with their [ruling states]. The latter consider their colonies as advantageous markets in which they can freely sell the products of their labor and of their industry and from which they can draw with a powerful hand the raw materials necessary for them. This is the basis of the economic power of the governments of western Europe, and chiefly for that end do they guard their existing colonies or acquire new ones. Russia was, and to a considerable extent still is, such a hospitable colony for all industrially developed states, generously providing them with the cheap products of her soil and buying dearly the products of their labor. But there is a radical difference between Russia and a colony: Russia is an independent and strong power. She has the right and the strength not to want to be the eternal handmaiden of states which are more developed economically. She should know the price of her raw materials and of the natural riches hidden in the womb of her abundant territories, and she is conscious of the great, not yet fully displayed, capacity for work among her people. She is proud of her great might, by which she jealously guards not only the political but also the economic independence of her empire. She wants to be a metropolis herself. On the basis of the people's labor, liberated from the bonds of serfdom, there began to grow our own national economy, which bids fair to become a reliable counterweight to the domination of foreign industry.

The creation of our own national industry — that is the profound task, both economic and political, from which our protectionist system [that is, tariffs to protect emerging Russian industries from foreign competition] arises. . . . The task of our present commercial and industrial policy is thus still a very difficult one. It is necessary not only to create industries but to force them to work cheaply; it is necessary to develop in our growing industrial community an energetic and active life — in a word, to raise our industries qualitatively and quantitatively to such a high level that they cease to be a drain and become a source of prosperity in our national economy.

What do we need to accomplish that? We need capital, knowledge, and the spirit of enterprise. Only these three factors can speed up the creation of a fully independent national industry. But, unfortunately, not all these forces can be artificially implanted. They are mutually interconnected; their own proper development depends upon the very growth of industry. . . .

We have . . . neither capital, nor knowledge, nor the spirit of enterprise. The extension of popular education through general, technical, and commercial schools can have, of course, a beneficial influence; and Your Majesty's government is working on that. But no matter how significant the promotion of enlightenment, that road is too slow; by itself it cannot realize our goal. The natural school of industry is first of all a lively industry. Institutions of learning serve only as one aid toward that end. The first investment of savings awakens in man the restlessness of enterprise, and with the first investment in industry the powerful stimulus of personal interest calls forth such curiosity and love of learning as to make an illiterate peasant into a railway builder, a bold and progressive organizer of industry, and a versatile financier.

Industry gives birth to capital; capital gives rise to enterprise and love of learning; and knowledge, enterprise, and capital combined create new industries. Such is the eternal cycle of economic life, and by the succession of such turns our national economy moves ahead in the process of its natural growth. In Russia this growth is yet too slow, because there is yet too little industry, capital, and spirit of enterprise. But we cannot be content with the continuation of such slow growth. . . .

We must give the country such industrial perfection as has been reached by the United States of America, which firmly bases its prosperity on two pillars — agriculture and industry. . . . I have now analysed the chief bases of the economic system which has been followed in Russia since the reign of Alexander III. . . .

To obtain cheaper goods, of which the population stands in such urgent need, by a substantial tariff reduction would be too expensive. It would forever deprive the country of the positive results of the protective system, for which a whole generation has made sacrifices; it would upset the industries which we have created with so much effort just when they were ready to repay the nation for its sacrifices.

It would be very dangerous to rely on the competition of foreign goods for the lowering of our prices. But we can attain the same results with the help of the competition of foreign capital, which, by coming into Russia, will help Russian enterprise to promote native industry and speed up the accumulation of native capital. Any obstructions to the influx of foreign capital will only delay the establishment of a mature and all-powerful industry. The country cannot afford to defer that goal for long. . . .

Your Imperial Highness may see from the foregoing that the economic policy which the Russian government has followed for the last eight years is a carefully planned system, in which all parts are inseparably interconnected.

George Gapon and Ivan Vasimov
THE REVOLUTION OF 1905

Revolution had long been brewing in the Russian Empire. The peasants had always been restless, ready for an uprising whenever conditions seemed favor-

able. The government regarded industrial workers, numerous in towns and cities, as troublemakers. The leaders of business and finance cautiously favored a constitution, and liberal intellectuals had been agitating for one for decades. Meanwhile, the revolutionary underground waited in the wings. Then war broke out with Japan in 1904 as a result of Russian expansion into Manchuria after the completion of the Trans-Siberian railway. When the Russian forces were defeated, the disastrous loss of prestige encouraged the revolutionaries.

The opening shots in the revolution of 1905, however, came not from revolutionaries but from soldiers who fired at a peaceful procession of workers led by Father George Gapon (1870–1906), an orthodox priest known for his loyalty to the throne. The workers intended to petition the tsar to relieve their plight; instead they were fired on by order of officials afraid of mob violence in front of the imperial palace. Several hundred people were killed or injured. The mishandling of this incident, called "Bloody Sunday," further revealed the government's incompetence; it became the signal for revolutionary action throughout the country. Violence spread among peasants, followed by uprisings in the industrial centers that culminated in a general strike in October. At its height, a workers' council (or *soviet*) was formed in St. Petersburg to run the city. Nicholas II, his army still in the Far East, feared losing his throne unless he quickly granted a constitution. In late October he issued the October Manifesto allowing limited popular participation in the government.

These extracts from the workers' petition to the tsar have a peaceful tone, although the workers called for a freely elected constituent assembly that would limit the tsar's powers. The petition's content provides insight into the conditions experienced by Russian workers that turned them into a revolutionary force.

Sovereign!

We, the workers and the inhabitants of various social strata of the city of St. Petersburg, our wives, children, and helpless old parents, have come to you, Sovereign, to seek justice and protection. We are impoverished; our employers oppress us, overburden us with work, insult us, consider us inhuman, and treat us as slaves who must suffer a bitter fate in silence. Though we have suffered, they push us deeper and deeper into a gulf of misery, disfranchisement, and ignorance. Despotism and arbitrariness strangle us and we are gasping for breath. Sovereign, we have no strength left. We have reached the limit of endurance. We have reached that terrible moment when death is preferable to the continuance of unbearable sufferings.

And so we left our work and informed our employers that we shall not resume work until they meet our demands. We do not demand much; we only want what is indispensable to life and without which life is nothing but hard labor and eternal suffering. Our first request was that our employers discuss our needs jointly with us. But they refused to do this; they even denied us the right to speak about our needs, saying that the law does not give us such a right. Also unlawful were our requests to reduce the working day to eight hours, to set wages jointly with us; to examine our disputes with lower echelons of factory administration; to increase the wages of unskilled workers and women to one ruble [about $1.00] per day; to abolish overtime work; to provide medical care without insult. . . .

Sovereign, there are thousands of us here; outwardly we resemble human beings, but in reality neither we nor the Russian people as a whole enjoy any human right, have any right to speak, to think, to assemble, to discuss our needs, or to take measures to improve our conditions. They have enslaved us and they did it under the protection of your officials, with their aid and with their cooperation. They imprison and [even] send into exile any one of us who has the courage to speak on behalf of the interests of the working class and of the people. They punish us for our good heartedness and sympathy as if for a crime. To pity a downtrodden, disfranchised, and oppressed man is to commit a major crime. All the workers and the peasants are at the mercy of bureaucratic administrators consisting of embezzlers of public funds and thieves who not only disregard the interests of the people but also scorn these interests. The bureaucratic administration has brought the country to complete ruin, has brought upon it a disgraceful war [Russo-Japanese war, 1904–1905], and continues to lead it further and further into destruction. We, the workers and the people, have absolutely nothing to say in the matter of expenditure of huge taxes that are collected from us. In fact, we do not know where or for what the money collected from the impoverished people goes. The people are deprived of the opportunity to express their wishes and their demands and to participate in determining taxes and expenditures. The workers are deprived of the opportunity to organize themselves in unions to protect their interests.

Sovereign! Is all this compatible with God's laws, by the grace of which you reign? And is it possible to live under such laws? Wouldn't it be better for all of us if we, the toiling people of all Russia, died? Let the capitalist-exploiters of the working class, the bureaucratic embezzlers of public funds, and the pillagers of the Russian people live and enjoy themselves. Sovereign, these are the problems that we face and these are the reasons that we have gathered before the walls of your palace. Here we seek our last salvation. Do not refuse to come to the aid of your people; lead them out of the grave of disfranchisement [inability to participate in the political process], poverty, and ignorance; grant them an opportunity to determine their own destiny, and remove from them the unbearable yoke of bureaucrats. Tear down the wall that separates you from your people and let them rule the country with you. . . . Russia is too great, her needs too diverse and numerous to be administered by bureaucrats only. It is essential to have a popular representation; it is essential that the people help themselves and that they govern themselves. Only they know their real needs. Do not spurn their help; accept it; decree immediately to summon at once representatives of the Russian land from all classes, from all strata, including workers' representatives. Let there be present a capitalist, a worker, a bureaucrat, a priest, a doctor, and a teacher — let everyone regardless of who they are elect their own representatives. Let everyone be equal and free to elect or be elected, and toward that end decree that the elections to the Constituent Assembly be carried out on the basis of universal, secret, and equal suffrage. . . .

Here, Sovereign, are our principal needs with which we came to you. Only if and when they are fulfilled will it be possible to free our country from Slavery and poverty; will it be possible for it to flourish; will it be possible for the workers to organize themselves to protect their interests against the insolent exploitation of the capitalists and the thievish government of bureaucrats who strangle the people. Decree and swear that you will realize these [requests] and you will make Russia happy, famous and will imprint forever your name in our hearts and in the hearts of our descendants. And if you will not decree it, if you will not respond to our plea, we shall die here, in this square, before your palace. We have nowhere else to go and it is useless to go. We have only two roads open to us: one leading to freedom and happiness, the other to the grave. Let our life be a sacrifice for suffering Russia. We do not regret this sacrifice. We offer it willingly.

George Gapon, Priest   *Ivan Vasimov, Worker*

M. I. Pokzovskaya
WORKING CONDITIONS FOR WOMEN IN THE FACTORIES

If the misery of the workers as described in Father Gapon's petition was deplorable, the lot of women workers was even more harrowing. Their helplessness in the face of ruthless exploitation and sexual abuse highlighted the widespread absence in Russia of those social traditions and working conditions that had promoted Western standards of humaneness and civility. This report describing how women were treated in Russian factories was written by a Russian woman doctor and published in an English suffragist magazine in 1914.

The matter of fines which are exacted from factory workers by their employers is a very serious one. Fines are imposed for: late arrival, work which is not found to be up to standard, for laughter, even for indisposition. At a certain well-known calendar factory in St. Petersburg the women workers receive 0.45 rbls. [rubles] a day, and the fines have been known to amount to 0.50 rbls. a day. At a weaving factory, also in St. Petersburg, women operatives may earn as much as 1.25 rbls. a day, but owing to deductions for various fines the earnings often sink to as low as 0.25 rbls. a day. If a worker is feeling unwell and sits down, a fine is incurred. . . . If an article is dropped, the fine is [levied and] . . . if the worker fails to "stand to attention" at the entrance of employer or foreman and until he leaves the room, she is fined. . . . At a well-known chocolate factory in Moscow the fine for laughing is 0.75 rbls. and if a worker is 15 minutes late she is dismissed for one week. At another old established and famous chocolate factory in case of sudden illness a woman employee is instantly discharged. In a certain cartridge factory the workers are searched before leaving, and those who persist in having pockets are fined. . . .

In the majority of factories where women are employed the working day is from 10 to 11½ hours, after deducting the dinner and breakfast intervals. On Saturday, in many factories . . .

the work sometimes lasts 16 and 18 hours per day. The workers are forced to work overtime on pain of instant dismissal or of transference to inferior employment, and in the case of children actual physical force is used to make them continue in their places. Dining and lunch rooms are rarely provided, and in many places no definite time is allowed for meals. In one well-known factory one hour is allowed for meals, but there is no place where the workers can eat their food except in the work-rooms or in the lavatories.

The position of women workers on the tobacco plantations is the worst. According to a report published by the Sevastopol branch of the Women's Protective Union, young girls are sometimes kept at work during 22 hours in the day. Owing to the difficulties of carrying on the process of breaking the tobacco leaves in the daytime, the girl-workers are driven into the plantations at 4 A.M. where they work until 9 A.M. After that they are engaged in the processes of weighing and tying the packets of tobacco, which work is continued through practically the whole day, with the exception of short intervals for meals. At the same time the women workers are continually exposed to brutal and degrading treatment and assault. Not infrequently their earnings are not paid to them. . . .

It happens sometimes, as on April 25th,

1913, at a cotton spinning factory in St. Petersburg, that the workers strike as a protest against the dismissal of old workers and their replacement by girls between 14 and 16 years of age. The result of the strike was a wholesale dismissal of all the women, whose places were filled by young girls. Not infrequently the women strike on account of the rude treatment which they receive from the foreman, actual bodily ill-treatment not being unknown. Such strikes rarely accomplish anything.

The worst aspect of woman's factory labour is, however, the moral danger to which women are exposed from those in power over them.

Immoral proposals from foremen and from their assistants are of general occurrence, and women who resist are persecuted in every possible way, and sometimes actually violated.

In a large tobacco factory in St. Petersburg the women workers who were asking for raised pay were cynically informed that they could augment their income by prostitution.

All these hard conditions in connection with factory life have the result of driving a certain number of women workers into tolerated houses of prostitution or into the streets. This is directly encouraged by the management of some factories.

REVIEW QUESTIONS

1. What assessment did Sergei Witte make of the economic position of Russia in relation to the major states of western Europe and to the United States?
2. What, according to Witte, did Russia lack in comparison with the economically developed countries?
3. What measures did Witte propose in order to create a Russian "national industry"?
4. What, according to Father George Gapon's petition, were the conditions of life and work for Russian workers?
5. What were the workers' demands as outlined in the petition?
6. Do the demands in Father Gapon's petition indicate that these workers were revolutionaries? Explain your answer.
7. What were the working conditions for women as described in M. I. Pokzovskaya's report?
8. What did the working conditions and the treatment of women workers indicate about the position of women in Russian working-class society?

▼▼▼

7 ▼ Anti-Semitism: Regression to the Irrational

Anti-Semitism, a European phenomenon of long standing, rose to new prominence in the late nineteenth century. Formerly segregated by law into ghettoes, Jews, under the aegis of the Enlightenment and the French Revolution, had gained legal equality in most European lands. In the nineteenth century, Jews participated in the economic and cultural progress of the times and often achieved distinction in business, the professions, and the arts and sciences. However, driven by irrational fears and mythical conceptions that had survived

from the Middle Ages, many people regarded Jews as a dangerous race of international conspirators and foreign intruders who threatened their nations.

Throughout the nineteenth century, anti-Semitic outrages occurred in many European lands. Russian anti-Semitism assumed a particularly violent form in the infamous pogroms — murderous mob attacks on Jews — occasionally fomented by government officials. Even in highly civilized France, anti-Semitism proved a powerful force. At the time of the Dreyfus affair, Catholic and nationalist zealots demanded that Jews be deprived of their civil rights. In Germany, anti-Semitism became associated with the ideological defense of a distinctive German culture, the volkish thought popular in the last part of the nineteenth century. After the foundation of the German Empire in 1871, the pace of economic and cultural change quickened, and with it the cultural disorientation that fanned anti-Semitism. Volkish thinkers, who valued traditional Germany — the landscape, the peasant, and the village — associated Jews with the changes brought about by rapid industrialization and modernization. Compounding the problem was the influx into Germany of Jewish immigrants from the Russian Empire, who were searching for a better life and brought with them their own distinctive culture and religion. Nationalists and conservatives used anti-Semitism in an effort to gain a mass following.

Racial-nationalist considerations were the decisive force behind modern anti-Semitism. Racists said that the Jews were a wicked race of Asiatics, condemned by their genes; they differed physically, intellectually, and spiritually from Europeans who were descendants of ancient Aryans. (The Aryans emerged some 4,000 years ago, probably between the Caspian Sea and the Hindu Kush Mountains. Intermingling with others, the Aryans lost whatever identity as a people they might have had.) After discovering similarities between core European languages (Greek, Latin, German) and ancient Persian and ancient Sanskrit (the language of the conquerors of India), nineteenth-century scholars believed that these languages all stemmed from a common tongue spoken by the Aryans. From there, some leaped to the conclusion that the Aryans constituted a distinct race endowed with superior racial qualities.

German racists in particular embraced the ideas of Stewart Houston Chamberlain (1855–1927), an Englishman whose boundless admiration for Germandom, led him to adopt German citizenship. In *Foundations of the Nineteenth Century* (1899), Chamberlain argued that the Germans, blond, blue-eyed, long-skulled, and distinguished by an inner spiritual depth, possessed the strongest strain of Aryan blood; they were the true shapers and guardians of high civilization.

Chamberlain pitted Aryans and Jews against each other in a struggle of world historical importance. As agents of a spiritually empty capitalism and divisive liberalism, the Jews, said Chamberlain, were the opposite of the idealistic, heroic, and faithful Germans. Chamberlain denied that Jesus was a Jew, hinting that he was of Aryan stock, and held that the goal of the Jew was "to put his foot upon the neck of all the nations of the world and be lord and possessor of the whole earth." Racial anti-Semitism became a powerful force in European intellectual life, especially in Germany. It was the seedbed of Hitler's movement.

Hermann Ahlwardt
THE SEMITIC VERSUS THE TEUTONIC RACE

In the following reading, Hermann Ahlwardt, an anti-Semitic member of the Reichstag and author of *The Desperate Struggle Between Aryan and Jew,* addresses the chamber on March 6, 1895, with a plea to close Germany's borders to Jewish immigrants. His speech reflects the anti-Semitic rhetoric popular among German conservatives before World War I. The material in parentheses is by Paul W. Massing, translator and editor.

It is certainly true that there are Jews in our country of whom nothing adverse can be said. Nevertheless, the Jews as a whole must be considered harmful, for the racial traits of this people are of a kind that in the long run do not agree with the racial traits of the Teutons.[1] Every Jew who at this very moment has not as yet transgressed is likely to do so at some future time under given circumstances because his racial characteristics drive him on in that direction. . . .

My political friends do not hold the view that we fight the Jews because of their religion. . . . We would not dream of waging a political struggle against anyone because of his religion. . . . We hold the view that the Jews are a different race, a different people with entirely different character traits.

Experience in all fields of nature shows that innate racial characteristics which have been acquired by the race in the course of many thousands of years are the strongest and most enduring factors that exist, and that therefore we can rid ourselves of the characteristics of our race no more than can the Jews. One need not fight the Jew individually, and we are not doing that, by the way. But, when countless specimens prove the existence of certain racial characteristics and when these characteristics are such as to make impossible a common life, well, then I believe that we who are natives here, who have tilled the soil and defended it against all enemies — that we have a duty to

take a stand against the Jews who are of a quite different nature.

We Teutons are rooted in the cultural soil of labor. . . . The Jews do not believe in the culture of labor, they do not want to create values themselves, but want to appropriate, without working, the values which others have created; that is the cardinal difference that guides us in all our considerations. . . .

Herr Deputy Rickert[2] here has just expounded how few Jews we have altogether and that their number is steadily declining. Well, gentlemen, why don't you go to the main business centers and see for yourselves whether the percentages indicated by Herr Rickert prevail there too. Why don't you walk along the Leipzigerstrasse (in Berlin) or the Zeil in Frankfurt and have a look at the shops? Wherever there are opportunities to make money, the Jews have established themselves, but not in order to work — no, they let others work for them and take what the others have produced by their labor.

Deputy Hasse . . . has committed the grave mistake of putting the Jews and other peoples on the same level, and that is the worst mistake that we could possibly make.

The Jews have an attitude toward us which differs totally from that of other peoples. It is one thing when a Pole, a Russian, a French-

---

[1] Teutons refers to the quintessential Germans. The name comes from a German tribe that once defeated a Roman army.

[2] Heinrich Rickert, a leader of the Progressives and an outspoken opponent of anti-Semitism, had pointed out that the Jews constituted only 1.29 percent of the population of Prussia. What enraged the German Right was that the Jews accounted for 9.58 percent of the university students in Prussia.

man, a Dane immigrates to our country, and quite another thing when a Jew settles here. . . . Once our (Polish, etc.) guests have lived here for ten, twenty years, they come to resemble us. For they have stood with us on the same cultural soil of labor. . . . After thirty, forty years they have become Germans and their grandchildren would be indistinguishable from us except for the strange-sounding names they still bear. The Jews have lived here for 700, 800 years, but have they become Germans? Have they placed themselves on the cultural soil of labor? They never even dreamed of such a thing; as soon as they arrived, they started to cheat and they have been doing that ever since they have been in Germany. . . .

The Jews should not be admitted, whether or not there is overpopulation, for they do not belong to a productive race, they are exploiters, parasites. . . .

(Answering Rickert's arguments that . . . it would be a shame if fifty million Germans were afraid of a few Jews, Ahlwardt continued:) . . .

Herr Rickert, who is just as tall as I am, is afraid of one single cholera bacillus — well, gentlemen, the Jews are just that, cholera bacilli!

Gentlemen, the crux of the matter is Jewry's capacity for contagion and exploitation. . . . How many thousands of Germans have perished as a result of this Jewish exploitation, how many may have hanged themselves, shot themselves, drowned themselves, how many may have ended by the wayside as tramps in America or drawn their last breath in the gutter, all of them people who had worked industriously on the soil their fathers had acquired, perhaps in hundreds of years of hard work. . . . Don't you feel any pity for those countless Germans? Are they to perish unsung? Ah, why were they foolish enough to let themselves be cheated? But the Germans are by no means so foolish, they are far more intelligent than the Jews. All inventions, all great ideas come from the Germans and not from the Jews. No, I shall tell you the national difference: The German is fundamentally trusting, his heart is full of loyalty

and confidence. The Jew gains this confidence, only to betray it at the proper moment, ruining and pauperizing the German. This abuse of confidence on the part of the Jews is their main weapon. And these Jewish scoundrels are to be defended here! Is there no one to think of all those hundreds of thousands, nor of those millions of workers whose wages grow smaller and smaller because Jewish competition brings the prices down? One always hears: you must be humane toward the Jews. The humanitarianism of our century . . . is our curse. Why aren't you for once humane toward the oppressed? You'd better exterminate those beasts of prey and you'd better start by not letting any more of them into our country. . . .

(Taking issue with the liberals' argument of Jewish achievements in the arts, Ahlwardt declared:)

Art in my opinion is the capacity for expressing one's innermost feelings in such a way as to arouse the same feelings in the other person. Now the Jewish world of emotions (*Gefühlswelt*) and the Teutonic world of emotions are two quite different things. German art can express only German feelings; Jewish art only Jewish feelings. Because Jewry has been thrusting itself forward everywhere, it has also thrust itself forward in the field of art and therefore the art that is now in the foreground is Jewish art. Nowadays the head of a family must be very careful when he decides to take his family to the theater lest his Teutonic feelings be outraged by the infamous Jewish art that has spread everywhere.

The Jew is no German. If you say, the Jew was born in Germany, he was nursed by a German wetnurse, he abides by German laws, he has to serve as a soldier — and what kind of a soldier at that! let's not talk about it — he fulfills all his obligations, he pays his taxes — then I say that all this is not the crucial factor with regard to his nationality; the crucial factor is the race from which he stems. Permit me to make a rather trite comparison which I have already used elsewhere in my speeches: a horse that is born in a cowshed is far from being a cow.

A Jew who was born in Germany does not thereby become a German; he is still a Jew. Therefore it is imperative that we realize that Jewish racial characteristics differ so greatly from ours that a common life of Jews and Germans under the same laws is quite impossible because the Germans will perish. . . .

. . . I beg you from the bottom of my heart not to take this matter* lightly but as a very serious thing. It is a question of life and death for our people. . . .

_____

*Prohibition of Jewish immigration.

We wouldn't think of going as far as have the Austrian anti-Semites in the Federal Council (*Reichsrat*) and to move that a bounty be paid for every Jew shot or to decree that he who kills a Jew shall inherit his property. We have no such intention. We shall not go as far as that. What we want is a clear and reasonable separation of the Jews from the Germans. An immediate prerequisite is that we slam the door and see to it that no more of them get in.†

_____

†At the end of the debate a vote was taken, with 218 representatives present. Of these, 51 voted for, 167 against the motion.

Édouard Drumont
≪ JEWISH FRANCE ≫

Édouard Drumont (1842–1917), a journalist and rabid conservative, became in the 1880s the mouthpiece of French anti-Semitism. Drumont glorified attachment to the soil, obedience to authority, and the moral discipline of an authoritarian Catholic church, addressing himself to peasants and petty bourgeois folk — to those layers of the population that preferred the simplicity of the past to the fast-moving, urban complexity of the late nineteenth century. He especially deplored the new materialism with its self-indulgence and moral laxity.

To him the chief source of the contemporary degeneracy was the Jews. In 1886 he published the book that made him famous, called *La France Juive (Jewish France)*. Advertised as an essay on contemporary history, it ascribed to Jews repulsive moral attributes, repeated the medieval myth that Jews murdered Christian children for ritual purposes, and propagated the bizarre theory that Jews were in a conspiracy to dominate France and the rest of Europe. The Jews, said Drumont, caused the ruin of Europe. Reprinted many times — his book sold over a million copies — it shaped public opinion for the conviction in 1894 of Captain Alfred Dreyfus, the first Jewish officer to be appointed to the General Staff of the French army, on faked evidence of high treason. In the following passage from *La France Juive,* Drumont contrasts the Semitic Jews with the Aryan French.

Let us examine now the essential traits which differentiate Jews from other people, beginning with ethnographic, physiological, and psychological comparisons of the Semite with the Aryan. These are two distinct races irremediably hostile to each other, whose antagonism has troubled the past and will cause still more trouble in the future.

The generic name Aryan derives from a Sanskrit word signifying "noble," "illustrious," "generous," standing for the superior family of the Indo-European family. . . . All the nations of Europe are descended by a straight line from the Aryan race, from which all great civilizations have sprung. . . . The Aryan or Indo-European race alone possesses the notion of justice, the sentiment of freedom, and the concept of the Beautiful. . . .

From the earliest moment of history we find the Aryan at war with the Semite. The dream of the Semite, indeed its obsession, has always been to reduce the Aryan into servants, to throw them into subjection. . . . Today Semitism feels sure of victory. It has replaced violence by wily tricks. The noisy invasion has been replaced by silent, progressive, slow penetration. Armed hordes no longer announce their arrival by shouts, but separate individuals, gathering in small groups, opportunistically infiltrate the state, taking possession of all important positions, all the functions in the country from the lowest to the highest. Spreading out from the area of Vilna [in Russia] they have occupied Germany, leaped over the Vosges mountains, and conquered France.

There was nothing brutal in this advance; it was a soft takeover accomplished in an insinuating manner of chasing the indigenous people from their homes, their source of income, in a velvety way depriving them of their goods, their tradition, their morals, and eventually their religion. . . . By their qualities as well as their faults, the two races [Jews and Aryans] are condemned to hurt each other.

The Semite is mercantile, greedy, scheming, subtle, crafty. The Aryan is enthusiastic, heroic, chivalrous, disinterested, straight-forward, trusting to the point of naiveté. The Semite is earthbound, seeing nothing beyond the present life. The Aryan is the child of heaven, relentlessly preoccupied with superior aspirations. One lives among realities, the other among ideals.

The Semite operates by instinct; he has the vocation of a trader, a genius for exchange, for every occasion to take advantage of his fellow man. The Aryan is devoted to life on the land, a poet, a monk and above all a soldier. War is his true element; he exposes himself joyfully to danger; he braves death. The Semite lacks any creative faculty. By contrast the Aryan is an inventor. The Jew has not made the least invention. He rather exploits, organizes, and utilizes the inventions of creative Aryans, guarding them as though they were his own. . . . The Aryan organizes voyages of adventure and discovers America. The Semite. . . . attends to all that has been explored and developed in order to enrich himself at the expense of others.

THE KISHINEV POGROM, 1903

Between 1881 and 1921 there were three large-scale waves of pogroms (mob attacks against Jews) in Russia. The civil and military authorities generally made no attempt to stop the murderous rampages and, at times, provided support. The worst of the pogroms occurred during the Civil War that followed the Bolshevik Revolution of 1917; some 60,000 Jews were slaughtered, particularly in the Ukraine, long a hotbed of anti-Semitism.

None of the numerous anti-Semitic outbreaks against Russian Jews in the years before World War I had a greater impact than that of the Kishinev pogrom, in southwestern Russia, in 1903. Its exceptional brutalities left a deep mark on Jewish consciousness. In 1903 almost half of Kishinev's population was Jewish; having achieved success in commerce and petty industry, Jews were the mainstay of the city's prosperity. This condition aroused the anti-Semitic feelings of their neighbors, already predisposed to hatred of Jews by a deeply embedded Christian bias.

After the assassination of Tsar Alexander II in 1881, the anti-Semitism of the Russian government gained ground. With influential support, a journalist named Pavolski Krushevan founded a newspaper in 1897 called *The Bessara-*

bian, which stirred up anti-Semitic sentiment. He accused the Jews of exploiting the Christian population, and worse, of ritual murder. In the course of five years, Krushevan stepped up his agitation, printing lurid stories designed to incite popular violence against Jews. He and his like-minded associates brought public indignation to the boiling point in the spring of 1903. Calling for "a bloody reckoning with the Jews," he prepared the attack for April 6. It was Easter Sunday for the Christians and part of the Passover week for the Jews. The details of what happened in Kishinev on April 6 and 7 are taken from a report entitled *Die Judenpogrome in Russland (The Jewish Pogroms in Russia),* prepared by a Zionist organization in London and published in Germany in 1910.

Sunday morning the weather cleared. The Jews were celebrating the last two days of Passover. Not anticipating trouble, they put on their holiday clothes and went to the synagogue. . . .

. . . Suddenly at about 3 P.M. a crowd of men appeared on the square Novyi Bazar, all dressed in red shirts. The men howled like madmen, incessantly shouting: "Death to the Jews. Beat the Jews." In front of the Moscow Tavern the crowd of some hundred split into 24 groups of 10–15 men each. There and then the systematic destruction, pillaging, and robbing of Jewish houses and shops began. At first they threw stones in great quantity and force, breaking windows and shutters. Then they tore open doors and windows, breaking into the Jewish houses and living quarters, smashing whatever furniture and equipment they found. The Jews had to hand over to the robbers their jewelry, money, and whatever other valuables they possessed. If they offered the slightest resistance, they were beaten over the head with pieces of their broken furniture. The storerooms were ransacked with special fury. The goods were either carried away or thrown on the street and destroyed. A large crowd of Christians followed the rioters, members of the intelligentsia, officials, students in the theological school, and others. . . .

At 5 P.M. the first Jew was murdered. The robbers stormed a trolley car with a Jewish passenger on board, shouting "Throw out the Jew." The Jew was pushed out and from all sides beaten on his head until his skull cracked and his brains spilled out. At first the sight of

a dead Jew seemed to momentarily scare the bandits, but when they saw that the police did not care, they dispersed in all directions, shouting "Kill the Jews!"

On those streets where the pillaging took place Jews had to give up all attempts at self-defense. . . . But on the square Novyi Bazar the Jewish butchers gathered to defend themselves and their families. They bravely fought back and chased away the attackers, who were as cowardly as they were wild. Then the police came and arrested the Jews.

That was the final signal for the organizers of the mob. Until 10 P.M. the unleashed passions were vented in plunder, robbery, and destruction. Seven other murders took place. . . .

The Jews spent the night from Sunday to Monday in indescribable fear, yet hoping that the terror might be over.

During that night the leaders of the *pogrom* prepared further attacks, as in war. First the gangs which during the previous evening had arrived from the countryside were equipped with weapons. All weapons were of the same kind: axes, iron bars, and clubs, all strong enough to break doors and shutters, and even metal cabinets and safes. All men wore the same outfit: the red workshirts were worn by all members of the rabble, by peasants, workers, petty bourgeois, even seminary students and police. The second systematic action was the marking of all Jewish houses by the committee organizing the pogrom. During the night all Jewish houses and shops were painted with white chalk. Next came the organization of a permanent information and communication network among the various gangs. Several bicyclists were engaged, who subsequently played an important role. The bicyclists were high school students, theological students, and officials. The organization covered more than the city of Kishinev. Messengers were sent out to the nearest villages inviting the peasants: "Come to the city and help plunder the Jews. Bring big bags." Around 3 A.M. the preparations were finished. The signal for the attack was given.

The terror that now followed can hardly be described — orgies of loathsome savagery, blood-thirsty brutishness, and devilish lechery claimed their victims. Forty-nine Jews were murdered in Kishinev. When one hears about the excess of horror, one recognizes that only a few victims were lucky enough to die a simple death. Most of them had to suffer a variety of unbelievable abuse and repulsive torture unusual even among barbarians.

From 3 A.M. to 8 P.M. on Monday the gangs raged through the ruins and rubble which they themselves had piled up. They plundered, robbed, destroyed Jewish property, stole it, burned it, devastated it. They chased, slew, raped, and martyred the Jews. Representatives of all layers of the population took part in this witches' sabbath: soldiers, policemen, officials, and priests; children and women; peasants, workers, and vagabonds.

Major streets resounded with the terrifying roar of murdering gangs and the heartrending cries of the unfortunate victims. . . . The storerooms and shops were robbed, as on the previous day, down to the last item. . . . In the Jewish houses, the gangs burst into the living quarters with murderous howls, demanding all money and valuables. . . . If, however, the Jews could offer nothing or did not respond quickly enough, or if the gangsters were in a murderous mood, the men were knocked down, badly wounded, or killed. The women were raped one after the other in front of their men and children. They tore the arms and legs off the children, or broke them; some children

were carried to the top floor and thrown out of the window. . . .

Early Monday morning a Jewish deputation hurried to the Governor of the province to plead for protection. He answered that he could do nothing, since he had no orders from St. Petersburg [the capital]. At the same time he refused to accept private telegrams from St. Petersburg.

The vain appeal of the Jews to the governor was followed by a catastrophic worsening of their fate. The gangs henceforth could count on the patronage of the highest authority. . . .

In ever-rising fury the robbery, murder, and desecration continued. Jews had their heads hacked off. Towels were soaked in their blood and then waved like red flags. The murderers wrote with Jewish blood on white flags in large letters: "Death to the Jews!" They slit open the bodies of men and women, ripped out their guts and filled the hollows with feathers. They jumped on the corpses and danced, roaring, and drunk with vodka — men and women of "the best society." Officials and policemen laughed at the spectacle and joined in the fun. They beat pregnant women on their stomachs until they bled to death. . . .

They cut off the breasts of women after raping them. . . . Nails were driven into Chaja Sarah Phonarji's nostrils until they penetrated her skull. They hacked off the upper jaw of David Chariton, with all his teeth and his upper lip. Another man, Jechiel Selzer, had his ears pulled off before being beaten on the head until he became insane. . . .

These are some of the inhumanities committed during the pogrom. They are certified as true by eyewitnesses and the testimony of Christian physicians and Russian newspapers, which had passed through the most anti-Semitic and despotic censorship.

The synagogues were stormed and plundered with special spite. In one synagogue the *gabai* [sexton] braved death in front of the holy ark holding the Torah. Dressed in the *tales* [prayer shawl] and with the *tephalin* [phylacteries] on his forehead, he prepared for the onslaught of the murderers in order to protect the sacred scroll. He was cut down in the foulest manner. Then they tore, here and elsewhere, the Torah from the holy ark and cut the parchment into small scraps (Christian children later sold them on the streets for a few kopeks as mementos of Kishinev). After that the mobsters demolished, here as elsewhere, the synagogue's interior.

The barbarism of these scenes was so shatter-ing that no less than 13 Jews went out of their minds. . . .

It would be unjust and ungrateful not to mention those Christians who in those days of mad brutality proved themselves true human beings and illustrious exceptions. They deserve to be remembered with special esteem because they were so few. . . .

Theodor Herzl
≪ THE JEWISH STATE ≫

Theodor Herzl (1860–1904) was raised in a comfortable, Jewish, middle-class home. Moving from Budapest, where he was born, to Vienna, the capital of the Austro-Hungarian Empire, he started to practice law, but soon turned to jour-nalism, writing from Paris for the leading Vienna newspaper. A keen observer of the contemporary scene, he vigorously agitated for the ideal of an indepen-dent Jewish state. It was not a new idea but one whose time had come. Nation-alist ferment was rising everywhere, often combined with virulent anti-Semi-tism. Under the circumstances, Herzl argued, security for Jews could be guaranteed only by a separate national state for Jews, preferably in Palestine.

In 1896 he published his program in a book, *Der Judenstaat (The Jewish State),* in which he envisaged a glorious future for an independent Jewish state harmoniously cooperating with the local population. In the following year he presided over the first Congress of Zionist Organizations held in Basel (Switzer-land), attended mostly by Jews from central and eastern Europe. In its program the congress called for "a publicly guaranteed homeland for the Jewish people in the land of Israel." Subsequently, Herzl negotiated with the German emperor, the British government, and the sultan of the Ottoman Empire (of which Pal-estine was a part) for diplomatic support. In 1901 the Jewish National Fund was created to help settlers purchase land in Palestine. At his death, Herzl firmly expected a Jewish state to arise sometime in the future. The following excerpts from his book express the main points in his plea for a Jewish state.

We are a people — one people.

We have honestly endeavored everywhere to merge ourselves in the social life of surrounding communities and to preserve the faith of our fathers. We are not permitted to do so. In vain are we loyal patriots, our loyalty in some places running to extremes; in vain do we make the same sacrifices of life and property as our fel-low-citizens; in vain do we strive to increase the fame of our native land in science and art, or her wealth by trade and commerce. In countries where we have lived for centuries we are still cried down as strangers, and often by those whose ancestors were not yet domiciled in the land where Jews had already had experience of suffering. . . .

But I think we shall not be left in peace.

Oppression and persecution cannot exterminate us. No nation on earth has survived such struggles and sufferings as we have gone through. Jew-baiting has merely stripped off our weaklings; the strong among us were invariably true to their race when persecution broke out against them. . . .

. . . [O]ld prejudices against us still lie deep in the hearts of the people. He who would have proofs of this need only listen to the people where they speak with frankness and simplicity: proverb and fairy-tale are both Anti-Semitic. . . .

No one can deny the gravity of the situation of the Jews. Wherever they live in perceptible numbers, they are more or less persecuted. Their equality before the law, granted by statute, has become practically a dead letter. They are debarred from filling even moderately high positions, either in the army, or in any public or private capacity. And attempts are made to thrust them out of business also: "Don't buy from Jews!"

Attacks in Parliaments, in assemblies, in the press, in the pulpit, in the street, on journeys — for example, their exclusion from certain hotels — even in places of recreation, become daily more numerous. The forms of persecutions varying according to the countries and social circles in which they occur. In Russia, imposts are levied on Jewish villages; in Rumania, a few persons are put to death; in Germany, they get a good beating occasionally; in Austria, Anti-Semites exercise terrorism over all public life; in Algeria, there are travelling agitators; in Paris, the Jews are shut out of the so-called best social circles and excluded from clubs. Shades of anti-Jewish feeling are innumerable. But this is not to be an attempt to make out a doleful category of Jewish hardships.

I do not intend to arouse sympathetic emotions on our behalf. That would be foolish, futile, and undignified proceeding. I shall content myself with putting the following questions to the Jews: Is it not true that, in countries where we live in perceptible numbers, the position of Jewish lawyers, doctors, technicians, teachers, and employees of all descriptions becomes daily more intolerable? Is it not true, that the Jewish middle classes are seriously threatened? Is it not true, that the passions of the mob are incited against our wealthy people? Is it not true, that our poor endure greater sufferings than any other proletariat? I think that this external pressure makes itself felt everywhere. In our economically upper classes it causes discomfort, in our middle classes continual and grave anxieties, in our lower classes absolute despair.

Everything tends, in fact, to one and the same conclusion, which is clearly enunciated in that classic Berlin phrase: *"Juden Raus!"* (Out with the Jews!)

I shall now put the Question in the briefest possible form: Are we to "get out" now and where to?

Or, may we yet remain? And, how long?

Let us first settle the point of staying where we are. Can we hope for better days, can we possess our souls in patience, can we wait in pious resignation till the princes and peoples of this earth are more mercifully disposed towards us? I say that we cannot hope for a change in the current of feeling. . . . The nations in whose midst Jews live are all either covertly or openly Anti-Semitic. . . .

. . . We might perhaps be able to merge ourselves entirely into surrounding races, if these were to leave us in peace for a period of two generations. But they will not leave us in peace. For a little period they manage to tolerate us, and then their hostility breaks out again and again. . . .

Thus, whether we like it or not, we are now, and shall henceforth remain, a historic group with unmistakable characteristics common to us all.

We are one people — our enemies have made us one without our consent, as repeatedly happens in history. Distress binds us together, and, thus united, we suddenly discover our strength. Yes, we are strong enough to form a State, and, indeed, a model State. We possess all human and material resources necessary for the purpose. . . .

Let the sovereignty be granted us over a portion of the globe large enough to satisfy the rightful requirements of a nation; the rest we shall manage for ourselves.

The creation of a new State is neither ridiculous nor impossible. We have in our day witnessed the process in connection with nations which were not largely members of the middle class, but poorer, less educated, and consequently weaker than ourselves. . . .

Palestine is our ever-memorable historic home. The very name of Palestine would attract our people with a force of marvellous potency. If His Majesty the Sultan were to give us Pal-

estine, we could in return undertake to regulate the whole finances of Turkey. We should there form a portion of a rampart of Europe against Asia, an outpost of civilization as opposed to barbarism. We should as a neutral State remain in contact with all Europe, which would have to guarantee our existence. The sanctuaries of Christendom would be safeguarded by assigning to them an extra-territorial status such as is well-known to the law of nations. We should form a guard of honor about these sanctuaries, answering for the fulfillment of this duty with our existence. This guard of honor would be the great symbol of the solution of the Jewish Question after eighteen centuries of Jewish suffering.

REVIEW QUESTIONS

1. What, according to Hermann Ahlwardt, were the racial characteristics of Jews? What, in contrast, were the racial characteristics of Germans?
2. What, said Ahlwardt, would be the ultimate result if Jewish immigration into Germany was not stopped?
3. Judging by Ahlwardt's specific arguments and their emotional tone, to what kind of people and to what class in society do you think he was appealing? How did Ahlwardt's anti-Semitism differ from traditional Christian anti-Semitism?
4. What kind of human needs did anti-Semitism seem to satisfy? What type of people is often attracted to anti-Semitic thinking? How may anti-Semitism be regarded as a regression to mythical modes of thinking?
5. What qualities, according to Édouard Drumont, separate Jews from the Aryans?
6. What social groups in Kishinev took part in the attack upon the Jews? What does the pogrom reveal about human nature? What role did government officials play?
7. Why did Theodor Herzl believe that the creation of a Jewish state was the only solution to the Jewish question?

▼▼▼

8 ▼ The Spirit of British Imperialism

In 1872, British statesman Benjamin Disraeli (1804–1881) delivered a speech at the Crystal Palace in London that expressed the ambitions driving the British to imperialist expansion. Disraeli posed a choice for his country: comfortable insignificance in world affairs or imperial power with prosperity and global prestige. Disraeli's espousal of the second alternative met with support from many Englishmen, including Cecil Rhodes.

Cecil Rhodes
≪ CONFESSION OF FAITH ≫

One ardent supporter of British expansion was Cecil Rhodes (1853–1902). Raised in a parsonage north of London, Rhodes went to southern Africa at the age of seventeen for his health and to join his brother. Within two years he had established himself in the diamond industry. In the 1870s, he divided his time between Africa and studying at Oxford University. While at Oxford, Rhodes heard John Ruskin (1819–1900), social reformer and Slade Professor of Art, deliver an address echoing Disraeli's Crystal Palace speech. Ruskin expressed great pride in the British race and great enthusiasm for imperial ventures. He urged England "to found colonies as fast and as far as she is able, formed of the most energetic and worthiest of men." To the impressionable Rhodes, Ruskin was a prophet outlining England's future. Ruskin inspired Rhodes to write a "Confession of Faith," which represented an extravagant dream of a world empire ruled by "the most honorable race the world possesses."

The "Confession of Faith" guided Rhodes's life to the end. His company, De Beers Consolidated Mines, Ltd., controlled 90 percent of the world's diamond production and had a large stake in South Africa's gold fields. Never regarding wealth as an end in itself, Rhodes sought to extend British influence and institutions into the interior of Africa and to bring lands settled and dominated by Dutch-descended Boers under the British flag. Through his efforts, Rhodesia (now Zimbabwe) was added to the British Empire.

Excerpts follow from "Confession of Faith" of 1877. The "Confession" is included in the appendix of John E. Flint's biography of Cecil Rhodes. Flint reproduced the document "in its original form without any editing of spelling or punctuation."

It often strikes a man to inquire what is the chief good in life; to one the thought comes that it is a happy marriage, to another great wealth, and as each seizes on his idea, for that he more or less works for the rest of his existence. To myself thinking over the same question the wish came to render myself useful to my country. I then asked myself how could I and after reviewing the various methods I have felt that at the present day we are actually limiting our children and perhaps bringing into the world half the human beings we might owing to the lack of country for them to inhabit that if we had retained America there would at this moment be millions more of English living. I contend that we are the finest race in the world and that the more of the world we in-habit the better it is for the human race. Just fancy those parts that are at present inhabited by the most despicable specimens of human beings what an alteration there would be if they were brought under Anglo-Saxon influence, look again at the extra employment a new country added to our dominions gives. I contend that every acre added to our territory means in the future birth to some more of the English race who otherwise would not be brought into existence. Added to this the absorption of the greater portion of the world under our rule simply means the end of all wars. . . .

The idea gleaming and dancing before ones eyes like a will-of-the-wisp at last frames itself into a plan. Why should we not form a secret society with but one object the furtherance of the British Empire and the bringing of the whole uncivilised world under British rule for the recovery of the United States for the making the Anglo-Saxon race but one Empire. What a dream, but yet it is probable, it is possible. I once heard it argued by a fellow in my own college, I am sorry to own it by an Englishman, that it was a good thing for us that we have lost the United States. There are some subjects on which there can be no arguments, and to an Englishman this is one of them, but even from an American's point of view just picture what they have lost, look at their government, are not the frauds that yearly come before the public view a disgrace to any country and especially their's which is the finest in the world. Would they have occurred had they remained under English rule great as they have become how infinitely greater they would have been with the softening and elevating influences of English rule, think of those countless 000's [thousands] of Englishmen that during the last 100 years would have crossed the Atlantic and settled and populated the United States. Would they have not made without any prejudice a finer country of it than the low class Irish and German emigrants? All this we have lost and that country loses owing to whom? Owing to two or three ignorant pig-headed statesmen of the last century, at their door lies the blame. Do you ever feel mad? do you ever feel murderous. I think I do with those men. I bring facts to prove my assertion. Does an English father when his sons wish to emigrate ever think of suggesting emigration to a country under another flag, never — it would seem a disgrace to suggest such a thing I think that we all think that poverty is better under our own flag than wealth under a foreign one.

Put your mind into another train of thought. Fancy Australia discovered and colonised under the French flag. . . . We learn from having lost to cling to what we possess. We know the size of the world we know the total extent. Africa is still lying ready for us it is our duty to take

it. It is our duty to seize every opportunity of acquiring more territory and we should keep this one idea steadily before our eyes that more territory simply means more of the Anglo-Saxon race more of the best the most human, most honourable race the world possesses.

To forward such a scheme what a splendid help a secret society would be a society not openly acknowledgèd but who would work in secret for such an object.

I contend that there are at the present moment numbers of the ablest men in the world who would devote their whole lives to it. . . . What has been the main cause of the success of the Romish Church? The fact that every enthusiast, call it if you like every madman finds employment in it. Let us form the same kind of society a Church for the extension of the British Empire. A society which should have its members in every part of the British Empire working with one object and one idea. . . .

(In every Colonial legislature the Society should attempt to have its members prepared at all times to vote or speak and advocate the closer union of England and the colonies, to crush all disloyalty and every movement for the severance of our Empire. The Society should inspire and even own portions of the press for the press rules the mind of the people. The Society should always be searching for members who might by their position in the world by their energies or character forward the object but the ballot and test for admittance should be severe). . . .[1]

For fear that death might cut me off before the time for attempting its development I leave all my worldly goods in trust to S. G. Shippard and the Secretary for the Colonies at the time of my death to try to form such a Society with such an object.

---

[1] It is not clear why Rhodes placed this paragraph in parentheses.

Joseph Chamberlain
THE BRITISH EMPIRE: COLONIAL COMMERCE AND THE WHITE MAN'S BURDEN

British imperialists like Joseph Chamberlain (1836–1914) argued that the welfare of Britain depended upon the preservation and extension of the empire, for colonies fostered trade and served as a source of raw materials. In addition, Chamberlain asserted that the British Empire had a sacred duty to carry civilization, Christianity, and British law to the "backward" peoples of Africa and Asia. As a leading statesman, Chamberlain made many speeches, both in Parliament and before local political groups, that endorsed imperialist ventures. Excerpts from these speeches, later collected and published under the title *Foreign and Colonial Speeches,* follow.

{June 10, 1896}

. . . The Empire, to parody a celebrated expression, is commerce. It was created by commerce, it is founded on commerce, and it could not exist a day without commerce. (Cheers). . . . The fact is history teaches us that no nation has ever achieved real greatness without the aid of commerce, and the greatness of no nation has survived the decay of its trade. Well, then, gentlemen, we have reason to be proud of our commerce and to be resolved to guard it from attack. (Cheers.). . . .

{March 31, 1897}

. . . We have suffered much in this country from depression of trade. We know how many of our fellow-subjects are at this moment unemployed. Is there any man in his senses who believes that the crowded population of these islands could exist for a single day if we were to cut adrift from us the great dependencies which now look to us for protection and assistance, and which are the natural markets for our trade? (Cheers.) The area of the United Kingdom is only 120,000 miles; the area of the British Empire is over 9,000,000 square miles, of which nearly 500,000 are to be found in the portion of Africa with which we have been dealing. If tomorrow it were possible, as some people apparently desire, to reduce by a stroke of the pen the British Empire to the dimensions of the United Kingdom, half at least of our population would be starved (cheers). . . .

{January 22, 1894}

We must look this matter in the face, and must recognise that in order that we may have more employment to give we must create more demand. (Hear, hear.) Give me the demand for more goods and then I will undertake to give plenty of employment in making the goods; and the only thing, in my opinion, that the Government can do in order to meet this great difficulty that we are considering, is so to arrange its policy that every inducement shall be given to the demand; that new markets shall be created, and that old markets shall be effectually developed. (Cheers.) . . . I am convinced that it is a necessity as well as a duty for us to uphold the dominion and empire which we now possess. (Loud cheers.) . . . I would never lose the hold which we now have over our great Indian dependency — (hear, hear) — by far the greatest and most valuable of all the customers we have or ever shall have in this country. For the same reasons I approve of the continued occupation of Egypt; and for the same reasons I have urged upon this Government, and upon previous Governments, the necessity for using every legitimate opportunity to extend our influence and control in that great African continent which is now being opened up to civilisation and to commerce; and, lastly, it is for the same reasons that I hold that our navy should be strengthened — (loud cheers) — until its supremacy is so assured that we cannot be shaken in any of the possessions which we hold or may hold hereafter.

Believe me, if in any one of the places to which I have referred any change took place which deprived us of that control and influence of which I have been speaking, the first to suffer would be the working-men of this country. Then, indeed, we should see a distress which would not be temporary, but which would be chronic, and we should find that England was entirely unable to support the enormous population which is now maintained by the aid of her foreign trade. If the working-men of this country understand, as I believe they do — I am one of those who have had good reason through my life to rely upon their intelligence and shrewdness — if they understand their own interests, they will never lend any countenance to the doctrines of those politicians who never lose an opportunity of pouring contempt and abuse upon the brave Englishmen, who, even at this moment, in all parts of the world are carving out new dominions for Britain, and are opening up fresh markets for British commerce, and laying out fresh fields for British labour. (Applause.) . . .

March 31, 1897

. . . We feel now that our rule over these territories can only be justified if we can show that it adds to the happiness and prosperity of the people — (cheers) — and I maintain that our rule does, and has, brought security and peace and comparative prosperity to countries that never knew these blessings before. (Cheers.)

In carrying out this work of civilisation we are fulfilling what I believe to be our national mission, and we are finding scope for the exercise of those faculties and qualities which have made of us a great governing race. (Cheers.) I do not say that our success has been perfect in every case, I do not say that all our methods have been beyond reproach; but I do say that in almost every instance in which the rule of the Queen has been established and the great *Pax Britannica*[1] has been enforced, there has come with it greater security to life and property, and a material improvement in the condition of the bulk of the population. (Cheers.) No doubt, in the first instance, when these conquests have been made, there has been bloodshed, there has been loss of life among the native populations, loss of still more precious lives among those who have been sent out to bring these countries into some kind of disciplined order, but it must be remembered that this is the condition of the mission we have to fulfil. . . .

. . . You cannot have omelettes without breaking eggs; you cannot destroy the practices of barbarism, of slavery, of superstition, which for centuries have desolated the interior of Africa, without the use of force; but if you will fairly contrast the gain to humanity with the price which we are bound to pay for it, I think you may well rejoice in the result of such expeditions as those which have recently been conducted with such signal success — (cheers) — in Nyassaland, Ashanti, Benin, and Nupé [regions in Africa] — expeditions which may have, and indeed have, cost valuable lives, but as to which we may rest assured that for one life lost a hundred will be gained, and the cause of civilisation and the prosperity of the people will in the long run be eminently advanced. (Cheers.) But no doubt such a state of things, such a mission as I have described, involve heavy responsibility. . . . and it is a gigantic task that we have undertaken when we have de-

---

[1]*Pax Britannica* means "British Peace" in the tradition of the *Pax Romana* — the peace, stability, and prosperity that characterized the Roman Empire at its height in the first two centuries A.D.

termined to wield the sceptre of empire. Great is the task, great is the responsibility, but great is the honour — (cheers); and I am convinced that the conscience and the spirit of the country will rise to the height of its obligations, and that we shall have the strength to fulfil the mission which our history and our national character have imposed upon us. (Cheers.)

Karl Pearson
SOCIAL DARWINISM: IMPERIALISM JUSTIFIED BY NATURE

In the last part of the nineteenth century, the spirit of expansionism was buttressed by application of Darwin's theory of evolution to human society. Theorists called Social Darwinists argued that nations and races, like the species of animals, were locked in a struggle for existence in which only the fittest survived and deserved to survive. British and American imperialists employed the language of Social Darwinism to promote and justify Anglo-Saxon expansion and domination of other peoples. Social Darwinist ideas spread to Germany, which was inspired by the examples of British and American expansion. In a lecture given in 1900 and titled "National Life from the Standpoint of Science," Karl Pearson (1857–1936), a British professor of mathematics, expressed the beliefs of Social Darwinists.

What I have said about bad stock seems to me to hold for the lower races of man. How many centuries, how many thousands of years, have the Kaffir [a tribe in southern Africa] or the negro held large districts in Africa undisturbed by the white man? Yet their intertribal struggles have not yet produced a civilization in the least comparable with the Aryan[1] [western European]. Educate and nurture them as you will, I do not believe that you will succeed in modifying the stock. History shows me one way, and one way only, in which a high state of civilization has been produced, namely, the struggle of race with race, and the survival of the physically and mentally fitter race. . . .

. . . Let us suppose we could prevent the white man, if we liked, from going to lands of which the agricultural and mineral resources are not worked to the full; then I should say a thousand times better for him that he should not go than that he should settle down and live alongside the inferior race. The only healthy alternative is that he should go and completely drive out the inferior race. That is practically what the white man has done in North America. . . . But I venture to say that no man calmly judging will wish either that the whites had never gone to America, or would desire that whites and Red Indians were to-day living alongside each other as negro and white in the Southern States, as Kaffir and European in South Africa, still less that they had mixed their blood as Spaniard and Indian in South America. . . . I venture to assert, then, that the struggle for existence between white and red man, painful and even terrible as it was in its details, has given us a good far outbalancing its immediate evil. In place of the red man, contributing practically nothing to the work and thought of the world, we have a great nation, mistress of many arts, and able, with its

[1]Most European languages derive from the Aryan language spoken by people who lived thousands of years ago in the region from the Caspian Sea to the Hindu Kush Mountains. Around 2000 B.C., some Aryan-speaking people migrated to Europe and India. Nineteenth-century racialist thinkers held that Europeans, descendants of the ancient Aryans, were racially superior to other peoples.

youthful imagination and fresh, untrammelled impulses, to contribute much to the common stock of civilized man. . . .

But America is but one case in which we have to mark a masterful human progress following an inter-racial struggle. The Australian nation is another case of great civilization supplanting a lower race unable to work to the full the land and its resources. . . . The struggle means suffering, intense suffering, while it is in progress; but that struggle and that suffering have been the stages by which the white man has reached his present stage of development, and they account for the fact that he no longer lives in caves and feeds on roots and nuts. This dependence of progress on the survival of the fitter race, terribly black as it may seem to some of you, gives the struggle for existence its redeeming features; it is the fiery crucible out of which comes the finer metal. You may hope for a time when the sword shall be turned into the ploughshare, when American and German and English traders shall no longer compete in the markets of the world for their raw material and for their food supply, when the white man and the dark shall share the soil between them, and each till it as he lists [pleases]. But, believe me, when that day comes mankind will no longer progress; there will be nothing to check the fertility of inferior stock; the relentless law of heredity will not be controlled and guided by natural selection. Man will stagnate. . . .

The . . . great function of science in national life . . . is to show us what national life means, and how the nation is a vast organism subject . . . to the great forces of evolution. . . . There is a struggle of race against race and of nation against nation. In the early days of that struggle it was a blind, unconscious struggle of barbaric tribes. At the present day, in the case of the civilized white man, it has become more and more the conscious, carefully directed attempt of the nation to fit itself to a continuously changing environment. The nation has to foresee how and where the struggle will be carried on; the maintenance of national position is becoming more and more a conscious preparation for changing conditions, an insight into the needs of coming environments. . . .

. . . If a nation is to maintain its position in this struggle, it must be fully provided with trained brains in every department of national activity, from the government to the factory, and have, if possible, a *reserve of brain and physique* to fall back upon in times of national crisis. . . .

You will see that my view — and I think it may be called the scientific view of a nation — is that of an organized whole, kept up to a high pitch of internal efficiency by insuring that its numbers are substantially recruited from the better stocks, and kept up to a high pitch of external efficiency by contest, chiefly by way of war with inferior races, and with equal races by the struggle for trade-routes and for the sources of raw material and of food supply. This is the natural history view of mankind, and I do not think you can in its main features subvert it. . . .

. . . Is it not a fact that the daily bread of our millions of workers depends on their having somebody to work for? that if we give up the contest for trade-routes and for free markets and for waste lands, we indirectly give up our food-supply? Is it not a fact that our strength depends on these and upon our colonies, and that our colonies have been won by the ejection of inferior races, and are maintained against equal races only by respect for the present power of our empire? . . .

. . . We find that the law of the survival of the fitter is true of mankind, but that the struggle is that of the gregarious animal. A community not knit together by strong social instincts, by sympathy between man and man, and class and class, cannot face the external contest, the competition with other nations, by peace or by war, for the raw material of production and for its food supply. This struggle of tribe with tribe, and nation with nation, may have its mournful side; but we see as a result of it the gradual progress of mankind to higher intellectual and physical efficiency. It is idle to condemn it; we can only see that it exists and recognise what we have gained by it — civilization and social sympathy. But while the statesman has to watch this external struggle, . . . he must be very cautious that the nation is not silently rotting at its core. He must insure that the fertility of the inferior stocks is checked, and that of the superior stocks encouraged; he must regard with suspicion anything that tempts the physically and mentally fitter men and women to remain childless. . . .

. . . The path of progress is strewn with the wrecks of nations; traces are everywhere to be seen of the hecatombs [slaughtered remains] of inferior races, and of victims who found not the narrow way to perfection. Yet these dead people are, in very truth, the stepping stones on which mankind has arisen to the higher intellectual and deeper emotional life of today.

REVIEW QUESTIONS

1. What nationalistic views were expressed in Cecil Rhodes's "Confession of Faith"?
2. What role did the concept of race — the English or Anglo-Saxon race — play in the arguments of Rhodes? Compare his views with those advanced by Hermann Ahlwardt in the preceding selection.
3. How do Joseph Chamberlain's arguments in favor of British expansion compare with those of Rhodes?
4. What, according to Chamberlain, were the economic benefits of British expansion?
5. How did Chamberlain define the national mission of the "great governing race," the English?
6. What does the phrase, "you cannot make omelettes without breaking eggs," have to do with British imperialism?
7. What, according to Karl Pearson, was the "natural history view of mankind"?
8. How did Pearson define the difference between inferior and superior races?
9. What measures did Pearson advocate for keeping the race fit?
10. How did Pearson portray the effects of the survival of the fittest on international relations?

▼▼▼

9 ▼ Anti-imperialism

The early protests of non-European victims of colonialism were reinforced by anti-imperialist agitation within Europe itself. Although the statesmen in power, with the support of parliamentary majorities, backed colonial expansion, the spokesmen of the opposition, labor leaders and socialist intellectuals, spoke out on behalf of the colonized peoples.

John Atkinson Hobson
AN EARLY CRITIQUE OF IMPERIALISM

One of the early English critics of imperialism was the social reformer and economist John Atkinson Hobson (1858–1940). Hobson's primary interest was social reform, and he turned to economics to try to solve the problem of poverty. Like Rhodes, he was influenced by Ruskin's ideas, but his interpretation of them led him to a diametrically opposed view of colonialism. As an economist, he argued that the unequal distribution of income made capitalism unproductive and unstable. It could not maintain itself except through investing in less-developed countries on an increasing scale, thus fostering colonial expansion. Lenin, leader of the Russian Revolution, later adopted this thesis. Hobson's stress upon the economic causes of imperialism has been disputed by some historians who see the desire for national power and glory as a far more important cause. Hobson attacked imperialism in the following passages from his book *Imperialism* (1902).

. . . The decades of Imperialism have been prolific in wars; most of these wars have been directly motivated by aggression of white races upon "lower races," and have issued in the forcible seizure of territory. Every one of the steps of expansion in Africa, Asia, and the Pacific has been accompanied by bloodshed; each imperialist Power keeps an increasing army available for foreign service; rectification of frontiers, punitive expeditions, and other euphemisms for war are in incessant progress. The *pax Britannica,* always an impudent falsehood, has become of recent years a grotesque monster of hypocrisy; along our Indian frontiers, in West Africa, in the Soudan, in Uganda, in Rhodesia fighting has been well-nigh incessant. Although the great imperialist Powers have kept their hands off one another, save where the rising empire of the United States has found its opportunity in the falling empire of Spain, the self-restraint has been costly and precarious. Peace as a national policy is antagonised not merely by war, but by militarism, an even graver injury. Apart from the enmity of France and Germany, the main cause of the vast armaments which are draining the resources of most European countries is their conflicting interests in territorial and commercial expansion. Where thirty years ago there existed one sensitive spot in our relations with France, or Germany, or Russia, there are a dozen now; diplomatic strains are of almost monthly occurrence between Powers with African or Chinese interests, and the chiefly business nature of the national antagonisms renders them more dangerous, inasmuch as the policy of Governments passes more under the influence of distinctively financial juntos [cliques]. . . .

Our economic analysis has disclosed the fact that it is only the interests of competing cliques of business men — investors, contractors, export manufacturers, and certain professional classes — that are antagonistic; that these cliques, usurping the authority and voice of the people, use the public resources to push their private businesses, and spend the blood and money of the people in this vast and disastrous military game, feigning national antagonisms which have no basis in reality. It is not to the interest of the British people, either as producers of wealth or as tax-payers, to risk a war with Russia and France in order to join Japan in preventing Russia from seizing [K]orea; but it may serve the interests of a group of commercial politicians to promote this dangerous policy. The South African war [the Boer War, 1899–1902], openly fomented by gold speculators for their private purposes, will rank in history as a leading case of this usurpation of nationalism. . . .

. . . So long as this competitive expansion for territory and foreign markets is permitted to misrepresent itself as "national policy" the antagonism of interests seems real, and the peoples must sweat and bleed and toil to keep up an ever more expensive machinery of war. . . .

. . . The industrial and financial forces of Imperialism, operating through the party, the press, the church, the school, mould public opinion and public policy by the false idealisation of those primitive lusts of struggle, domination, and acquisitiveness which have survived throughout the eras of peaceful industrial order and whose stimulation is needed once again for the work of imperial aggression, expansion, and the forceful exploitation of lower races. For these business politicians biology and sociology weave thin convenient theories of a race struggle for the subjugation of the inferior peoples, in order that we, the Anglo-Saxon, may take their lands and live upon their labours; while economics buttresses the argument by representing our work in conquering and ruling them as our share in the division of labour among nations, and history devises reasons why the lessons of past empire do not apply to ours, while social ethics paints the motive of "Imperialism" as the desire to bear the "burden" of educating and elevating races of "children." Thus are the "cultured" or semi-cultured classes indoctrinated with the intellectual and moral grandeur of Imperialism. For the masses there is a cruder appeal to hero-worship and sensational glory, adventure and the sporting spirit: current history falsified in coarse flaring colours, for the direct stimulation of the combative instincts. But while various methods are employed, some delicate and indirect, others coarse and flamboyant, the operation everywhere resolves itself into an incitation and direction of the brute lusts of human domination which are everywhere latent in civilised humanity, for the pursuance of a policy fraught with material gain to a minority of co-operative vested interests which usurp the title of the commonwealth. . . .

. . . The presence of a scattering of white officials, missionaries, traders, mining or plantation overseers, a dominant male caste with little knowledge of or sympathy for the institutions of the people, is ill-calculated to give to these lower races even such gains as Western civilisation might be capable of giving.

The condition of the white rulers of these lower races is distinctively parasitic; they live upon these natives, their chief work being that of organising native labour for their support. The normal state of such a country is one in which the most fertile lands and the mineral resources are owned by white aliens and worked by natives under their direction, primarily for their gain: they do not identify themselves with the interests of the nation or its people, but remain an alien body of sojourners, a "parasite" upon the carcass of its "host," destined to extract wealth from the country and retire to consume it at home. All the hard manual or other severe routine work is done by natives. . . .

Nowhere under such conditions is the theory of white government as a trust for civilisation made valid; nowhere is there any provision to secure the predominance of the interests, either of the world at large or of the governed people, over those of the encroaching nation, or more commonly a section of that nation. The relations subsisting between the superior and the inferior nations, commonly established by pure force, and resting on that basis, are such as preclude the genuine sympathy essential to the operation of the best civilising influences, and usually resolve themselves into the maintenance of external good order so as to forward the profitable development of certain natural resources of the land, under "forced" native labour, primarily for the benefit of white traders and investors, and secondarily for the benefit of the world of white Western consumers.

This failure to justify by results the forcible rule over alien peoples is attributable to no special defect of the British or other modern European nations. It is inherent in the nature of such domination. . . .

REVIEW QUESTIONS

1. Why, in J. A. Hobson's opinion, was the *pax Britannica* an "impudent falsehood"?
2. According to Hobson, what were the driving forces behind imperialism? And how did the special interests behind imperialism dominate public opinion?
3. How was imperialism endangering international relations among western European nations, according to Hobson?
4. One ideal of imperialism was to spread civilizing influences among native populations. How did Hobson interpret this sense of mission?
5. If, as Hobson asserted, "the brute lusts of human domination . . . are everywhere latent in civilised humanity," why did he especially blame "the competing cliques of business men" for the inhumanities and violence of imperialism?

Changing Patterns of Thought and Culture

Romanticism dominated European art, literature, and music in the early nineteenth century. Stressing the feelings and the free expression of personality, the Romantic Movement was a reaction against the rationalism of the Enlightenment. In the middle decades of the century, realism and its close auxiliary naturalism supplanted romanticism as the chief norm of cultural expression. Rejecting religious, metaphysical, and romantic interpretations of reality, realists aspired to an exact and accurate portrayal of the external world and daily life. Realist and naturalist writers like Émile Zola used the empirical approach: the careful collection, ordering, and interpretation of facts employed in science, which was advancing steadily in the nineteenth century. Among the most important scientific theories formulated was Charles Darwin's theory on evolution, which revolutionized conceptions of time and the origins of the human species.

The closing decades of the nineteenth century and the opening of the twentieth witnessed a crisis in Western thought. Rejecting the Enlightenment belief in the essential rationality of human beings, some thinkers — such as Fyodor Dostoyevsky, Friedrich Nietzsche, and Sigmund Freud — stressed the immense power of the nonrational in individual and social life. They held that subconscious drives, impulses, and instincts lay at the core of human nature, that people were moved more by religious-mythic images and symbols than by logical thought, that feelings determine human conduct more than reason does. This new image of the individual led to unsettling conclusions. If human beings are not fundamentally rational, then what are the prospects of resolving the immense problems of an industrial civilization? Although most thinkers shared the Enlightenment's vision of humanity's future progress, doubters were also heard.

The crisis of thought also found expression in art and literature. Artists like Pablo Picasso and writers like James Joyce and Franz Kafka exhibited a growing fascination with the nonrational — with dreams, fantasies, sexual conflicts, and guilt, with tortured, fragmented, and dislocated inner lives. In the process, they rejected traditional esthetic standards established during the Renaissance and the

SIGMUND FREUD, the eminent and influential twentieth-century German psychiatrist, photographed in 1914 in Vienna by one of his sons. Beside Freud is a reproduction of Michelangelo's *Dying Slave.* (*Mary Evans/Sigmund Freud Copyrights*)

221

Enlightenment and experimented with new forms of artistic and literary representation.

These developments in thought and culture produced insights into human nature and society and opened up new possibilities in art and literature. But such changes also contributed to the disorientation and insecurity that characterizes the twentieth century.

▼▼▼

I ▼ Realism and Naturalism

The middle decades of the nineteenth century were characterized by the growing importance of science and industrialization in European life. A movement known as positivism sought to apply the scientific method to the study of society. Rejecting theological and metaphysical theories as unscientific, positivists sought to arrive at the general laws that underlie society by carefully assembling and classifying data.

This stress on a rigorous observation of reality also characterized realism and naturalism, the dominant movements in art and literature. In several ways, realism differed from romanticism, the dominant cultural movement in the first half of the century. Romantics were concerned with the inner life — with feelings, intuition, and imagination. They sought escape from the city into natural beauty, and they venerated the past, particularly the Middle Ages, which they viewed as noble, idyllic, and good in contrast to the spiritually impoverished present. Realists, on the other hand, shifted attention away from individual human feelings to the external world, which they investigated with the meticulous care of the scientist. Preoccupied with reality as it actually is, realist writers and artists depicted ordinary people, including the poor and humble, in ordinary circumstances. With a careful eye for detail and in a matter-of-fact way devoid of romantic exuberance and exaggeration, realists described peasants, factory workers, laundresses, beggars, criminals, and prostitutes.

Realism quickly evolved into naturalism. Naturalist writers held that human behavior was determined by the social environment, that certain social and economic conditions produced predictable traits in men and women, that cause and effect operated in society as well as in physical nature.

Émile Zola
≪ THE EXPERIMENTAL NOVEL ≫

Émile Zola (1840–1902) was one of France's great novelists. Coming from the provinces to Paris, the young Zola, after failing to get a law degree, worked as an ill-paid clerk. Then unemployed for two years, he learned firsthand how the poor suffered. His life improved when he got a job in the sales department of a publishing house. He became a columnist and art critic, intensely studying life among all classes of the population but with special concern for the poor. His description of the Paris slums made him famous as both a social critic and a literary innovator. In his writing style, he combined realistic attention to detail, almost in the manner of a social scientist, with a compassionate symbolism and a poetic imagination. Living up to his ideals of hard work and social justice, he published many works and spoke out on public issues. In 1898, he wrote a famous letter in defense of Captain Alfred Dreyfus, a victim of anti-Semitism; threatened with arrest, he fled to England where he lived in exile for a time. In the following reading from *The Experimental Novel,* Zola asserted that literature too can be a science.

. . . Some day the physiologist[1] will explain to us the mechanism of the thoughts and the passions; we shall know how the individual machinery of each man works; how he thinks, how he loves, how he goes from reason to passion and folly; but these phenomena, resulting as they do from the mechanism of the organs, acting under the influence of an interior condition, are not produced in isolation or in the bare void. Man is not alone; he lives in society, in a social condition; and consequently, for us novelists, this social condition unceasingly modifies the phenomena. Indeed our great study is just there, in the reciprocal effect of society on the individual and the individual on society. For the physiologist, the exterior and interior conditions are purely chemical and physical, and this aids him in finding the laws which govern them easily. We are not yet able to prove that the social condition is also physical and chemical. It is that certainly, or rather it is the variable product of a group of living beings, who themselves are absolutely submissive to the physical and chemical laws which govern alike living beings and inanimate. From this we shall see that we can act upon the social conditions, in acting upon the phenomena of which we have made ourselves master in man. And this is what constitutes the experimental novel: to possess a knowledge of the mechanism of the phenomena inherent in man, to show the ma-

chinery of his intellectual and sensory manifestations, under the influences of heredity and environment, such as physiology shall give them to us, and then finally to exhibit man living in social conditions produced by himself, which he modifies daily, and in the heart of which he himself experiences a continual transformation. Thus, then, we lean on physiology; we take man from the hands of the physiologist solely, in order to continue the solution of the problem, and to solve scientifically the question of how men behave when they are in society. . . .

I have reached this point: the experimental novel is a consequence of the scientific evolution of the century; it continues and completes physiology, which itself leans for support on chemistry and medicine; it substitutes for the study of the abstract and the metaphysical[2] man the study of the natural man, governed by physical and chemical laws, and modified by the influences of his surroundings; it is in one word the literature of our scientific age. . . .

. . . The metaphysical man is dead; our whole territory is transformed by the advent of the physiological man. No doubt "Achilles' Anger," "Dido's Love,"[3] will last forever on

---

[1] Physiology is the study of the functions of living organisms.

[2] Metaphysics is a branch of philosophy concerned with the first principle of things, with the ultimate reality beyond the physical appearance of things.

[3] "Achilles' anger" is a reference to Homer's *Iliad*; Achilles, the great Greek warrior, is infuriated when King Agamemnon deprives him of his prize, the captive girl Briseis. "Dido's love" is a reference to Virgil's *Aeneid*; Dido, the queen of Carthage, has a great love for Aeneas, the Trojan prince.

account of their beauty; but today we feel the necessity of analyzing anger and love, of discovering exactly how such passions work in the human being. This view of the matter is a new one; we have become experimentalists instead of philosophers. In short, everything is summed up in this great fact: the experimental method in letters, as in the sciences, is on the way to explain the natural phenomena, both individual and social, of which metaphysics, until now, has given only irrational and supernatural explanations.

REVIEW QUESTIONS

1. How did Émile Zola define the experimental novel?
2. What relationship did Zola draw between the experimental novel and the scientific age?
3. What view of the individual and society did Zola's conception of the experimental novel present? To what extent, in his view, could individuals control social conditions and how?

▼▼▼

2 ▼ Theory of Evolution

In a century of outstanding scientific discoveries, none was more significant than the theory of evolution formulated by the English naturalist Charles Darwin (1809–1882). From December 1831 to 1836, Darwin had served as naturalist at sea on the *H.M.S. Beagle,* which surveyed parts of South America and some Pacific islands. He collected and classified many specimens of animal and plant life and from his investigations eventually drew several conclusions that startled the scientific community and enraged many clergy.

Before Darwin's theory of evolution, most people adhered to the biblical account of creation found in Genesis, which said that God had created the universe, the various species of animal and plant life, and human beings, all in six days. The creation account also said that God had given each species of animal and plant a form that distinguished it from every other species. It was commonly held that the creation of the universe and of the first human beings had occurred some six thousand years earlier.

Based on his study, Darwin maintained that all life on earth had descended from earlier living forms; that human beings had evolved from lower, nonhuman species; and that the process had taken millions of years. Adopting the Malthusian idea that population reproduces faster than the food supply increases, Darwin held that within nature there is a continual struggle for existence. He said that the advantage lies with those living things that are stronger, faster, better camouflaged from their enemies, or better fitted in some way for survival than are other members of their species; those more fit to survive pass along the advantageous trait to offspring. This principle of *natural selection* explains why some members of a species survive and reproduce and why those less fit perish.

Charles Darwin
NATURAL SELECTION

According to Darwin, members of a species inherit variations that distinguish them from others in the species, and over many generations these variations become more pronounced. In time, a new variety of life evolves that can no longer breed with the species from which it descended. In this way, new species emerge and older ones die out. Human beings were also a product of natural selection, evolving from earlier, lower, nonhuman forms of life. In this first passage, from his autobiography, Darwin described his empirical method and his discovery of a general theory that coordinated and illuminated the data he found. Succeeding excerpts are from his *Origin of Species* (1859) and *The Descent of Man* (1871).

[DARWIN'S DESCRIPTION OF HIS METHOD AND DISCOVERY]

From September 1854 I devoted my whole time to arranging my huge pile of notes, to observing, and to experimenting in relation to the transmutation of species. During the voyage of the *Beagle* I had been deeply impressed by discovering in the Pampean formation[1] great fossil animals covered with armour like that on the existing armadillos; secondly, by the manner in which closely allied animals replace one another in proceeding southwards over the Continent; and thirdly, by the South American character of most of the productions of the Galapagos archipelago,[2] and more especially by the manner in which they differ slightly on each island of the group; none of the islands appearing to be very ancient in a geological sense.

It was evident that such facts as these, as well as many others, could only be explained on the supposition that species gradually become modified; and the subject haunted me. But it was equally evident that neither the action of the surrounding conditions, nor the will of the or-

ganisms (especially in the case of plants) could account for the innumerable cases in which organisms of every kind are beautifully adapted to their habits of life — for instance, a woodpecker or a tree-frog to climb trees, or a seed for dispersal by hooks or plumes. I had always been much struck by such adaptations, and until these could be explained it seemed to me almost useless to endeavour to prove by indirect evidence that species have been modified.

After my return to England it appeared to me that by following the example of Lyell[3] in Geology, and by collecting all facts which bore in any way on the variation of animals and plants under domestication and nature, some light might perhaps be thrown on the whole subject. My first note-book was opened in July 1837. I worked on true Baconian principles,[4] and without any theory collected facts on a wholesale scale, more especially with respect to domesticated productions, by printed enquiries, by conversation with skilful breeders and gardeners, and by extensive reading. When I

---

[1]The Pampean formation refers to the vast plain that stretches across Argentina, from the Atlantic Ocean to the foothills of the Andes Mountains.
[2]The Galapagos Islands, a Pacific archipelago 650 miles west of Ecuador, are noted for their unusual wildlife, which Darwin observed.

[3]Sir Charles Lyell (1797–1875) was a Scottish geologist whose work showed that the planet had evolved slowly over many ages. Like Lyell, Darwin sought to interpret natural history by observing processes still going on.
[4]"Baconian principles" refers to Sir Francis Bacon (1561–1626), one of the first to insist that new knowledge should be acquired through experimentation and the accumulation of data.

see the list of books of all kinds which I read and abstracted, including whole series of Journals and Transactions, I am surprised at my industry. I soon perceived that selection was the keystone of man's success in making useful races of animals and plants. But how selection could be applied to organisms living in a state of nature remained for some time a mystery to me.

In October 1838, that is, fifteen months after I had begun my systematic enquiry, I happened to read for amusement Malthus[5] on *Population,* and being well prepared to appreciate the struggle for existence which everywhere goes on from long-continued observation of the habits of animals and plants, it at once struck me that under these circumstances favourable variations would tend to be preserved and unfavourable ones to be destroyed. The result of this would be the formation of new species. Here, then, I had at last got a theory by which to work. . . .

It has sometimes been said that the success of the *Origin {of Species}* proved "that the subject was in the air," or "that men's minds were prepared for it." I do not think that this is strictly true, for I occasionally sounded not a few naturalists, and never happened to come across a single one who seemed to doubt about the permanence of species. Even Lyell and Hooker,[6] though they would listen with interest to me, never seemed to agree. I tried once or twice to explain to able men what I meant by Natural Selection, but signally failed. What I believe was strictly true is that innumerable well-observed facts were stored in the minds of naturalists ready to take their proper places as soon as any theory which would receive them was sufficiently explained. . . .

My *Descent of Man* was published in February 1871. As soon as I had become, in the year of 1837 or 1838, convinced that species were mutable productions, I could not avoid the belief that man must come under the same law.

▷   In the following excerpt from *The Origin of Species* (1859), Darwin explained the struggle for existence and the principle of natural selection.

ON THE ORIGIN OF SPECIES

. . . Owing to this struggle [for existence], variations, however slight . . . , if they be in any degree profitable to the individuals of a species, in their infinitely complex relations to other organic beings and to their physical conditions of life, will tend to the preservation of such individuals, and will generally be inherited by the offspring. The offspring, also, will thus have a better chance of surviving, for, of the many individuals of any species which are periodically born, but a small number can survive. I have called this principle, by which each slight variation, if useful, is preserved, by the term Natural Selection, in order to mark its relation to man's power of selection. But the expression often used by Mr. Herbert Spencer[7] of the Survival of the Fittest is more accurate, and is sometimes equally convenient. . . .

A struggle for existence inevitably follows from the high rate at which all organic beings tend to increase. Every being, which during its natural lifetime produces several eggs or seeds, must suffer destruction during some period of its life, and during some season or occasional year, otherwise, on the principle of geometrical increase, its numbers would quickly become so inordinately great that no country could support the product. Hence, as more individuals are produced than can possibly survive, there must in every case be a struggle for existence,

---

[5]Thomas Malthus (1766–1834) was an English economist who maintained that population increases geometrically (2, 4, 8, 16, and so on) but the food supply increases arithmetically (1, 2, 3, 4, and so on). (See page 155.)

[6]Sir Joseph Dalton Hooker (1817–1911) was an English botanist who supported Darwin's ideas.

[7]The British philosopher Herbert Spencer (1820–1903) coined the term *survival of the fittest.* (See page 179.)

either one individual with another of the same species, or with the individuals of distinct species, or with the physical conditions of life. It is the doctrine of Malthus applied with manifold force to the whole animal and vegetable kingdoms; for in this case there can be no artificial increase of food, and no prudential restraint from marriage. Although some species may be now increasing, more or less rapidly, in numbers, all cannot do so, for the world would not hold them.

There is no exception to the rule that every organic being naturally increases at so high a rate, that, if not destroyed, the earth would soon be covered by the progeny of a single pair. Even slow-breeding man has doubled in twenty-five years, and at this rate, in less than a thousand years, there would literally not be standing-room for his progeny. . . . The elephant is reckoned the slowest breeder of all known animals, and I have taken some pains to estimate its probable minimum rate of natural increase; it will be safest to assume that it begins breeding when thirty years old, and goes on breeding till ninety years old, bringing forth six young in the interval, and surviving till one hundred years old; if this be so, after a period of from 740 to 750 years there would be nearly nineteen million elephants alive, descended from the first pair. . . .

. . . Can we doubt (remembering that many more individuals are born than can possibly survive) that individuals having any advantage, however slight, over others, would have the best chance of surviving and of procreating their kind? On the other hand, we may feel sure that any variation in the least degree injurious would be rigidly destroyed. This preservation of favourable individual differences and variations, and the destruction of those which are injurious, I have called Natural Selection, or the Survival of the Fittest. . . .

. . . Natural Selection acts solely through the preservation of variations in some way advantageous, which consequently endure. Owing to the high geometrical rate of increase of all organic beings, each area is already fully stocked with inhabitants; and it follows from this, that as the favoured forms increase in number, so, generally, will the less favoured decrease and become rare. . . .

From these several considerations I think it inevitably follows, that as new species in the course of time are formed through natural selection, others will become rarer and rarer, and finally extinct. The forms which stand in closest competition with those undergoing modification and improvement will naturally suffer most. And we have seen in the chapter on the Struggle for Existence that it is the most closely-allied forms — varieties of the same species, and species of the same genus or of related genera — which, from having nearly the same structure, constitution, and habits, generally come into the severest competition with each other; consequently, each new variety or species, during the progress of its formation, will generally press hardest on its nearest kindred, and tend to exterminate them. We see the same process of extermination amongst our domesticated productions, through the selection of improved forms by man.

▷ In *The Descent of Man* (1871), Darwin argued that human beings have evolved from lower forms of life.

THE DESCENT OF MAN

The main conclusion here arrived at, and now held by many naturalists who are well competent to form a sound judgment, is that man is descended from some less highly organised form. The grounds upon which this conclusion rests will never be shaken, for the close similarity between man and the lower animals in embryonic development, as well as in innumerable points of structure and constitution, both of high and of the most trifling importance, — the rudiments which he retains, and the abnormal reversions to which he is occasionally liable, — are facts which cannot be disputed. They have long been known, but until recently they told us nothing with respect to the origin of man. Now when viewed by the light of our knowledge of the whole organic world, their meaning is unmistakable. The great principle of evolution stands up clear and firm, when these groups of facts are considered in connection with others, such as the mutual affinities of the members of the same group, their geographical distribution in past and present times, and their geological succession. It is incredible that all these facts should speak falsely. He who is not content to look, like a savage, at the phenomena of nature as disconnected, cannot any longer believe that man is the work of a separate act of creation. He will be forced to admit that the close resemblance of the embryo of man to that, for instance, of a dog — the construction of his skull, limbs and whole frame on the same plan with that of other mammals, independently of the uses to which the parts may be put — the occasional reappearance of various structures, for instance of several muscles, which man does not normally possess, but which are common to the Quadrumana[8] — and a crowd of analogous facts — all point in the plainest manner to the conclusion that man is the co-descendant with other mammals of a common progenitor.

We have seen that man incessantly presents

---

[8]An order of mammals, Quadrumana includes all primates (monkeys, apes, and baboons) except human beings; the primates' hind and forefeet can be used as hands as they have opposable first digits.

individual differences in all parts of his body and in his mental faculties. These differences or variations seem to be induced by the same general causes, and to obey the same laws as with the lower animals. In both cases similar laws of inheritance prevail. Man tends to increase at a greater rate than his means of subsistence; consequently he is occasionally subjected to a severe struggle for existence, and natural selection will have effected whatever lies within its scope. A succession of strongly-marked variations of a similar nature is by no means requisite; slight fluctuating differences in the individual suffice for the work of natural selection. . . .

Man may be excused for feeling some pride at having risen, though not through his own exertions, to the very summit of the organic scale; and the fact of his having thus risen, instead of having been aboriginally placed there, may give him hope for a still higher destiny in the distant future. But we are not here concerned with hopes or fears, only with the truth as far as our reason permits us to discover it; and I have given the evidence to the best of my ability. We must, however, acknowledge, as it seems to me, that man with all his noble qualities, with sympathy which feels for the most debased, with benevolence which extends not only to other men but to the humblest living creature, with his god-like intellect which has penetrated into the movements and constitution of the solar system — with all these exalted powers — Man still bears in his bodily frame the indelible stamp of his lowly origin.

REVIEW QUESTIONS

1. How did Charles Darwin make use of Thomas Malthus's theory of population growth?
2. To what did Darwin attribute the struggle for existence?
3. How did Darwin account for the extinction of old species and the emergence of new ones?
4. What did Darwin mean when he said that man "with his god-like intellect . . . still bears in his bodily frame the indelible stamp of his lowly origins"?

▼▼▼

3 ▼ Darwinism and Religion

Many clergymen regarded the theory of evolution as a threat to the infallibility of the Bible. Darwinism attacked the traditional belief that some six thousand years ago God had created all animal and plant species and had given each one a permanent form; evolution seemed to relegate Adam and Eve to the realm of myth. The conflict between fundamentalists — those who believed in a literal interpretation of the Bible — and advocates of the new biology was marked by great bitterness. In time, however, many Christians reconciled the theory of evolution and the biblical account of creation. They maintained that God directed the evolutionary process and that the timespan of six days for creation given in Genesis is not meant to be taken literally.

In the early seventeenth century, Galileo (see Chapter 2) had insisted that on questions concerning nature, scientists should not turn to the Bible as an authority but should rely on the evidence of observation and experiments. The controversy over evolution reaffirmed this conviction for the scientific community, which more than ever saw the scientific method as the incontestable authority for interpreting nature. The theory of evolution also contributed to a growing secularism. The central doctrine of Christianity — that human beings were created by God and that salvation was the ultimate aim of life — rested more than ever on faith rather than on reason.

Andrew D. White
≪ A HISTORY OF THE WARFARE OF SCIENCE WITH THEOLOGY ≫

In the following passage, Andrew D. White (1832–1918), scholar, diplomat, and president of Cornell University in Ithaca, New York, described the controversy that raged over the publication of *The Origin of Species* and *The Descent of Man*. A founder of Cornell, White himself came under attack by clergy who feared that the new institution of higher learning would teach "atheism" and "infidelity." The passage is taken from *A History of the Warfare of Science with Theology in Christendom* (1894).

Darwin's *Origin of Species* had come into the theological world like a plough into an ant-hill. Everywhere those thus rudely awakened from their old comfort and repose had swarmed forth angry and confused. Reviews, sermons, books light and heavy, came flying at the new thinker from all sides.

The keynote was struck at once in the *Quar-terly Review* by Wilberforce, Bishop of Oxford. He declared that Darwin was guilty of "a tendency to limit God's glory in creation"; that "the principle of natural selection is absolutely incompatible with the word of God"; that it "contradicts the revealed relations of creation to its Creator"; that it is "inconsistent with the fullness of his glory"; that it is "a dishonouring view of Nature"; and that there is "a simpler explanation of the presence of these strange forms among the works of God": that explanation being — "the fall of Adam." Nor did the bishop's efforts end here; at the meeting of the British Association for the Advancement of Science he again disported himself in the tide of popular applause. Referring to the ideas of Darwin, who was absent on account of illness, he congratulated himself in a public speech that he was not descended from a monkey. The reply came from Huxley,[1] who said in substance: "If I had to choose, I would prefer to be a descendant of a humble monkey rather than of a man who employs his knowledge and eloquence in misrepresenting those who are wearing out their lives in the search for truth."

This shot reverberated through England, and indeed through other countries.

The utterances of this the most brilliant prelate of the Anglican Church received a sort of antiphonal response from the leaders of the English Catholics. . . . Cardinal Manning declared his abhorrence of the new view of Nature, and described it as "a brutal philosophy — to wit, there is no God, and the ape is our Adam."

These attacks from such eminent sources set the clerical fashion for several years. . . . Another distinguished clergyman, vice-president of a Protestant institute to combat "dangerous" science, declared Darwinism "an attempt to dethrone God." . . . Another spoke of Darwin's views as suggesting that "God is dead," and declared that Darwin's work "does open violence to everything which the Creator himself has told us in the Scriptures of the methods and results of his work." Still another theological authority asserted: "If the Darwinian theory is true, Genesis is a lie, the whole framework of the book of life falls to pieces, and the revelation of God to man, as we Christians know it, is a delusion and a snare." Another, who had shown excellent qualities as an observing natu-

ralist, declared the Darwinian view "a huge imposture from the beginning."

Echoes came from America. One review . . . denounced Darwin's views as "infidelity"; another, representing the American branch of the Anglican Church. . . . plunged into an exceedingly dangerous line of argument in the following words: "If this hypothesis be true, then is the Bible an unbearable fiction; . . . then have Christians for nearly two thousand years been duped by a monstrous lie. . . . Darwin requires us to disbelieve the authoritative word of the Creator." . . .

Nor was the older branch of the Church to be left behind in this chorus. Bayma, in the *Catholic World,* declared, "Mr. Darwin is, we have reason to believe, the mouthpiece or chief trumpeter of that infidel clique whose well-known object is to do away with all idea of a God."

Worthy of especial note as showing the determination of the theological side at that period was the foundation of sacro-scientific organizations to combat the new ideas. First to be noted is the "Academia," planned by Cardinal Wiseman. In a circular letter the cardinal, usually so moderate and just, sounded an alarm and summed up by saying, "Now it is for the Church, which alone possesses divine certainty and divine discernment, to place itself at once in the front of a movement which threatens even the fragmentary remains of Christian belief in England." The necessary permission was obtained from Rome, the Academia was founded. . . . A similar effort was seen in Protestant quarters; the "Victoria Institute" was created, and perhaps the most noted utterance which ever came from it was the declaration of its vice-president, the Rev. Walter Mitchell, that "Darwinism endeavours to dethrone God."

In France the attack was even more violent. Fabre d'Envieu brought out the heavy artillery of theology, and in a long series of elaborate propositions demonstrated that any other doctrine than that of the fixity and persistence of species is absolutely contrary to Scripture. . . .

In Germany . . . Catholic theologians vied

---

[1]Thomas Henry Huxley (1825–1895) was an English biologist and a staunch defender of Darwin.

with Protestants in bitterness. Prof. Michelis declared Darwin's theory "a caricature of creation." Dr. Hagermann asserted that it "turned the Creator out of doors." Dr. Schund insisted that "every idea of the Holy Scriptures, from the first to the last page, stands in diametrical opposition to the Darwinian theory"; and, "if Darwin be right in his view of the development of man out of a brutal condition, then the Bible teaching in regard to man is utterly annihilated." Rougemont in Switzerland called for a crusade against the obnoxious doctrine. Luthardt, Professor of Theology at Leipsic, declared: "The idea of creation belongs to religion and not to natural science; the whole superstructure of personal religion is built upon the doctrine of creation"; and he showed the evolution theory to be in direct contradiction to Holy Writ. . . .

In 1871 was published Darwin's *Descent of Man.* Its doctrine had been anticipated by critics of his previous books, but it made, none the less, a great stir; again the opposing army trooped forth, though evidently with much less heart than before. A few were very violent. The *Dublin University Magazine,* . . . charged Mr. Darwin with . . . being "resolved to hunt God out of the world."

From America there came new echoes. . . . The Rev. Dr. Hodge, of Princeton . . . denounced it as thoroughly "atheistic"; he insisted that Christians "have a right to protest against the arraying of probabilities against the clear evidence of the Scriptures"; . . . and declared that the Darwinian theory of natural selection is "utterly inconsistent with the Scriptures," and that "an absent God, who does nothing, is to us no God"; that "to ignore design as manifested in God's creation is to dethrone God"; that "a denial of design in Nature is virtually a denial of God." . . .

Fortunately, at about the time when Dar-

win's *Descent of Man* was published, there had come into Princeton University a Dr. James McCosh. Called to the presidency, he at once took his stand against teachings so dangerous to Christianity as those of Drs. Hodge, Duffield, and their associates. . . . He saw that the most dangerous thing which could be done to Christianity at Princeton was to reiterate in the university pulpit, week after week, solemn declarations that if evolution by natural selection, or indeed evolution at all, be true, the Scriptures are false. He tells us that he saw that this was the certain way to make the students unbelievers; he therefore not only checked this dangerous preaching but preached an opposite doctrine. With him began the inevitable compromise, and, in spite of mutterings against him as a Darwinian, he carried the day. Whatever may be thought of his general system of philosophy, no one can deny his great service in neutralizing the teachings of his predecessors and colleagues — so dangerous to all that is essential in Christianity.

Other divines of strong sense in other parts of the country began to take similar ground — namely, that men could be Christians and at the same time Darwinians. . . .

In view of the proofs accumulating in favour of the new evolutionary hypothesis, the change in the tone of controlling theologians was now rapid. From all sides came evidences of desire to compromise with the theory. . . .

Whatever additional factors may be added to natural selection — and Darwin himself fully admitted that there might be others — the theory of an evolution process in the formation of the universe and of animated nature is established, and the old theory of direct creation is gone forever. In place of it science has given us conceptions far more noble, and opened the way to an argument for design infinitely more beautiful than any ever developed by theology.

REVIEW QUESTIONS

1. For what reasons did the clergy denounce Charles Darwin's theories?
2. Darwin and the clergy who attacked his theories perceived truth differently. Discuss this statement.

▼▼▼

4 ▼ The Futility of Reason and the Power of the Will

The outlook of the Enlightenment, which stressed science, political freedom, the rational reform of society, and the certainty of progress, was the dominant intellectual current in the late nineteenth century. However, in the closing decades of the century, several thinkers challenged and rejected the Enlightenment outlook. In particular, they maintained that people are not fundamentally rational, that below surface rationality lie impulses, instincts, and drives that constitute a deeper reality.

A powerful attack on the rational-scientific tradition of the Enlightenment came from Fyodor Dostoyevsky (1821–1881), a Russian novelist and essayist whose masterpieces include *Crime and Punishment* (1866), *The Idiot* (1868), and *The Brothers Karamazov* (1879–1880).

Fyodor Dostoyevsky
≪ NOTES FROM THE UNDERGROUND ≫

In *Notes from the Underground* (1864), Dostoyevsky attacked thinkers who enshrined reason and science and believed that scientific laws govern human behavior. He rejected the notion that once these laws were understood, people could create (as socialists in fact tried to do) utopian communities in which society would be rationally planned and organized to promote human betterment. The narrator in the novel, called the Underground Man, rebels against the efforts of rationalists, positivists, liberals, and socialists to define human nature according to universal principles and to reform society so as to promote greater happiness and security. For the Underground Man, there are no objective truths; there are only individuals with subjective desires and unpredictable, irrepressible wills.

Dostoyevsky maintained that human beings cannot be defined by reason alone — human nature is too dynamic, too diversified, too volcanic to be schematized and programmed by the theoretical mind. He urged a new definition of human beings, one that would affirm each person's individuality and subjectivity and encompass the total personality — feelings and will as well as reason.

In the first part of *Notes from the Underground*, the Underground Man addresses an imaginary audience. In a long monologue, he expresses a revulsion for the liberal-rationalist assertion that with increased enlightenment, people would "become good and noble," that they would realize it was to their advantage to pursue "prosperity, wealth, [political] freedom, peace." The Underground Man retorts that the individual's principal concern is not happiness or security but a free and unfettered will.

. . . Oh, tell me, who first declared, who first proclaimed, that man only does nasty things because he does not know his own real interests; and that if he were enlightened, if his eyes were opened to his real normal interests, man would at once cease to do nasty things, would at once become good and noble because, being enlightened and understanding his real advantage, he would see his own advantage in the good and nothing else, and we all know that not a single man can knowingly act to his own disadvantage. Consequently, so to say, he would begin doing good through necessity. Oh, the babe! Oh, the pure, innocent child! Why, in the first place, when in all these thousands of years has there ever been a time when man has acted only for his own advantage? What is to be done with the millions of facts that bear witness that men, *knowingly,* that is, fully understanding their real advantages, have left them in the background and have rushed headlong on another path, to risk, to chance, compelled to this course by nobody and by nothing, but, as it were, precisely because they did not want the beaten track, and stubbornly, wilfully, went off on another difficult, absurd way seeking it almost in the darkness. After all, it means that this stubbornness and willfulness were more pleasant to them than any advantage. Advantage! What is advantage? And will you take it upon yourself to define with perfect accuracy in exactly what the advantage of man consists of? And what if it so happens that a man's advantage *sometimes* not only may, but even must, consist exactly in his desiring under certain conditions what is harmful to himself and not what is advantageous. . . . After all, you, [imaginary] gentlemen, so far as I know, have taken your whole register of human advantages from the average of statistical figures and scientific-economic formulas. After all, your advantages are prosperity, wealth, freedom, peace — and so on, and so on. So that a man who, for instance, would openly and knowingly oppose that whole list would, to your thinking, and indeed to mine too, of course, be an ob-

scurantist [one who prevents enlightenment] or an absolute madman, would he not? But, after all, here is something amazing: why does it happen that all these statisticians, sages and lovers of humanity, when they calculate human advantages invariably leave one out? . . .

. . . The fact is, gentlemen, it seems that something that is dearer to almost every man than his greatest advantages must really exist, or (not to be illogical) there is one most advantageous advantage (the very one omitted of which we spoke just now) which is more important and more advantageous than all other advantages, for which, if necessary, a man is ready to act in opposition to all laws, that is, in opposition to reason, honor, peace, prosperity — in short, in opposition to all those wonderful and useful things if only he can attain that fundamental, most advantageous advantage which is dearer to him than all. . . .

. . . Why, one may choose what is contrary to one's own interests, and sometimes one *positively ought* (that is my idea). One's own free unfettered choice, one's own fancy, however wild it may be, one's own fancy worked up at times to frenzy — why that is that very "most advantageous advantage" which we have overlooked, which comes under no classification and through which all systems and theories are continually being sent to the devil. And how do these sages know that man must necessarily need a rationally advantageous choice? What man needs is simply *independent* choice, whatever that independence may cost and wherever it may lead. Well, choice, after all, the devil only knows. . . .

▷ Life is more than reasoning, more than "simply extracting square roots," declares the Underground Man. The will, which is "a manifestation of all life," is more precious than reason. Simply to have their own way, human beings will do something stupid, self-destructive, irrational. Reason constitutes only a small part of the human personality.

. . . You see, gentlemen, reason, gentlemen, is an excellent thing, there is no disputing that, but reason is only reason and can only satisfy man's rational faculty, while will is a manifestation of all life, that is, of all human life including reason as well as all impulses. And although our life, in this manifestation of it, is often worthless, yet it is life nevertheless and not simply extracting square roots. After all, here I, for instance, quite naturally want to live, in order to satisfy all my faculties for life, and not simply my rational faculty, that is, not simply one-twentieth of all my faculties for life. What does reason know? Reason only knows what it has succeeded in learning (some things it will perhaps never learn; while this is nevertheless no comfort, why not say so frankly?) and human nature acts as a whole, with everything that is in it, consciously or unconsciously, and, even if it goes wrong, it lives. I suspect, gentlemen, that you are looking at me with compassion; you repeat to me that an enlightened and developed man, such, in short, as the future man will be, cannot knowingly desire anything disadvantageous to himself, that this can be proved mathematically. I thoroughly agree, it really can — by mathematics. But I repeat for the hundredth time, there is one case, one only, when man may purposely, consciously, desire what is injurious to himself, what is stupid, very stupid — simply in order *to have the right* to desire for himself even what is very stupid and not to be bound by an obligation to desire only what is rational. After all, this very stupid thing, after all, this caprice of ours, may really be more advantageous for us, gentlemen, than anything else on earth, especially in some cases. And in particular it may be more advantageous than any advantages even when it does us obvious harm, and contradicts the soundest conclusions of our reason about our advantage — because in any case it preserves for us what is most precious and most important — that is, our personality, our individuality. Some, you see, maintain that this really is the most precious thing for man; desire can, of course, if it desires, be in agreement with reason; particu-

larly if it does not abuse this practice but does so in moderation, it is both useful and sometimes even praiseworthy. But very often, and even most often, desire completely and stubbornly opposes reason, and . . . and . . . and do you know that that, too, is useful and sometimes even praiseworthy?

▷ To intellectuals who want to "cure men of their old habits and reform their will in accordance with science and common sense," the Underground Man asks: Is it possible or even desirable to reform men? Perhaps they prefer uncertainty and caprice, chaos and destruction, or just living in their own way. How else do they preserve their uniqueness?

. . . In short, one may say anything about the history of the world — anything that might enter the most disordered imagination. The only thing one cannot say is that it is rational. The very word sticks in one's throat. And, indeed, this is even the kind of thing that continually happens. After all, there are continually turning up in life moral and rational people, sages, and lovers of humanity, who make it their goal for life to live as morally and rationally as possible, to be, so to speak, a light to their neighbors, simply in order to show them that it is really possible to live morally and rationally in this world. And so what? We all know that those very people sooner or later toward the end of their lives have been false to themselves, playing some trick, often a most indecent one. Now I ask you: What can one expect from man since he is a creature endowed with such strange qualities? Shower upon him every earthly blessing, drown him in bliss so that nothing but bubbles would dance on the surface of his bliss, as on a sea; give him such economic prosperity that he would have nothing else to do but sleep, eat cakes and busy himself with ensuring the continuation of world history and even then man, out of sheer ingratitude, sheer libel, would play you some loathsome trick. He would even risk his cakes and would deliberately desire the most fatal rubbish, the most uneconomical absurdity, simply to introduce into all this positive rationality his fatal fantastic element. It is just his fantastic dreams, his vulgar folly, that he will desire to retain, simply in order to prove to himself (as though that were so necessary) that men still are men and not piano keys, which even if played by the laws of nature themselves threaten to be controlled so completely that soon one will be able to desire nothing but by the calendar. And, after all, that is not all: even if man really were nothing but a piano key, even if this were proved to him by natural science and mathematics, even then he would not become reasonable, but would purposely do something perverse out of sheer ingratitude, simply to have his own way. And if he does not find any means he will devise destruction and chaos, will devise sufferings of all sorts, and will thereby have his own way. He will launch a curse upon the world . . . [to] convince himself that he is a man and not a piano key! If you say that all this, too, can be calculated and tabulated, chaos and darkness and curses, so that the mere possibility of calculating it all beforehand would stop it all, and reason would reassert itself — then man would purposely go mad in order to be rid of reason and have his own way! I believe in that, I vouch for it, because, after all, the whole work of man seems really to consist in nothing but proving to himself continually that he is a man and not an organ stop. It may be at the cost of his skin! But he has proved it; he may become a caveman, but he will have proved it. And after that can one help sinning, rejoicing that it has not yet come, and that desire still depends on the devil knows what! . . .

. . . Gentlemen, I am tormented by questions; answer them for me. Now you, for instance, want to cure men of their old habits and reform their will in accordance with science and common sense. But how do you know, not only that it is possible, but also that it is *desirable,* to reform man in that way? And what leads you to the conclusion that it is so *necessary* to reform man's desires? In short, how do you know that such a reformation will really be advantageous to man? And go to the heart of the matter, why are you *so sure* of your conviction that not to act against his real normal advantages guaranteed by the conclusions of reason and arithmetic is always advantageous for man and must be a law for all mankind? . . .

And why are you so firmly, so triumphantly convinced that only the normal and the positive — in short, only prosperity — is to the advantage of man? Is not reason mistaken about advantage? After all, perhaps man likes something besides prosperity? Perhaps he likes suffering just as much? Perhaps suffering is just as great an advantage to him as prosperity? Man is sometimes fearfully, passionately in love with suffering and that is a fact. There is no need to appeal to universal history to prove that; only ask yourself, if only you are a man and have lived at all. As far as my own personal opinion is concerned, to care only for prosperity seems to me somehow even ill-bred. Whether it's good or bad, it is sometimes very pleasant to smash things, too. After all, I do not really insist on suffering or on prosperity either. I insist on my caprice, and its being guaranteed to me when necessary. Suffering would be out of place in vaudevilles, for instance; I know that. In the crystal palace [utopia] it is even unthinkable; suffering means doubt, means negation, and what would be the good of a crystal palace if there could be any doubt about it? And yet I am sure man will never renounce real suffering, that is, destruction and chaos.

REVIEW QUESTIONS

1. Why did Fyodor Dostoyevsky believe that people will act in opposition to their own interest?

2. How did Dostoyevsky regard intellectuals who sought to "cure men of their old habits and reform their will in accordance with science and common sense"?
3. What did Dostoyevsky mean when he said that "the whole work of man seems really to consist in nothing but proving to himself continually that he is a man and not an organ stop"?
4. What role did reason play in Dostoyevsky's view of human nature and society?

5 ▼ The Overman and the Will to Power

Few modern thinkers have aroused more controversy than the German philosopher Friedrich Nietzsche (1844–1900). Although scholars pay tribute to Nietzsche's originality and genius, they are often in sharp disagreement over the meaning and influence of his work. Nietzsche was a relentless critic of modern society. He attacked democracy, universal suffrage, equality, and socialism for suppressing a higher type of human existence. Nietzsche was also critical of the Western rational tradition. The theoretical outlook, the excessive intellectualizing of philosophers, he said, smothers the will, thereby stifling creativity and nobility; reason also falsifies life through the claim that it allows apprehension of universal truth. Nietzsche was not opposed to the critical use of the intellect, but like the romantics, he focused on the immense vitality of the emotions. He also held that life is a senseless flux devoid of any overarching purpose. There are no moral values revealed by God. Indeed, Nietzsche proclaimed that God is dead. Nor are values and certainties woven into the fabric of nature that can be apprehended by reason — the "natural rights of man," for example. All the values taught by Christian and bourgeois thinkers are without foundation, said Nietzsche. There is only naked man living in a godless and absurd world.

Nietzsche called for the emergence of the *overman* or *superman,* a higher type of man who asserts his will, gives order to chaotic passions, makes great demands on himself, and lives life with a fierce joy. The overman aspires to self-perfection. Without fear or guilt, he creates his own values and defines his own life. In this way, he overcomes nihilism — the belief that there is nothing of ultimate value. It is such rare individuals, the highest specimens of humanity, that concern Nietzsche, not the herdlike masses.

The superman grasps the central reality of human existence — that people instinctively, uncompromisingly, ceaselessly, strive for power. The will to exert power is the determining factor in domestic politics and international affairs. Life is a contest in which the enhancement of power is the ultimate purpose of our actions; it brings supreme enjoyment: "the love of power is the demon of men. Let them have everything — health, food, a place to live, entertainment — they are and remain unhappy and low-spirited: for the demon waits and waits and will be satisfied. Take everything from them and satisfy this and they are almost happy — as happy as men and demons can be."

Friedrich Nietzsche
≪ THE BIRTH OF TRAGEDY ≫
≪ THE WILL TO POWER ≫
AND ≪ THE ANTICHRIST ≫

Three of Nietzsche's works — *The Birth of Tragedy, The Will to Power,* and *The Antichrist* — are represented in the following readings. In *The Birth of Tragedy* (1872), his first major work, Nietzsche offered an unconventional interpretation of ancient Greek culture. Traditionally, scholars and philosophers had lauded the Greeks for their rationality — for originating scientific and philosophic thought and for aspiring to balance, harmony, and moderation both in the arts and in ethics. Nietzsche chose to emphasize the emotional roots of Greek culture — the Dionysian spirit that springs from the soil of myth and ritual, passion and frenzy, instinct and intuition, heroism and suffering. He maintained that this Dionysian spirit, rooted in the nonrational, was the source of Greek creativity in art and drama.

In the following excerpt from *The Birth of Tragedy,* Nietzsche attributed to Socrates the rise of scientific thought, which aspires to separate truth from myth, illusion, and error. He said that this scientific outlook, which began essentially with Socrates and achieved its height in the ancient world in Alexandria, has become the basis of modern culture. Modern westerners admire the theoretical man and not the man of instinct and action. But he said that in modern times doubts have arisen about science's claim to the attainment of certainty. Westerners are beginning to recognize the limitations of reason and to appreciate the creative potential inherent in the nonrational side of human nature.

THE BIRTH OF TRAGEDY

Once we have fully realized how, after Socrates, the mystagogue [a teacher who initiates followers into the mysteries of his discipline] of science, one school of philosophers after another came upon the scene and departed; how generation after generation of inquirers, spurred by an insatiable thirst for knowledge, explored every aspect of the universe; and how by that ecumenical concern a common net of knowledge was spread over the whole globe, affording glimpses into the workings of an entire solar system — once we have realized all this, and the monumental pyramid of present-day knowledge, we cannot help viewing Socrates as the vortex and turning point of Western civilization. . . .

. . . Socrates represents the archetype of the theoretical optimist, who, strong in the belief that nature can be fathomed, considers knowledge to be the true panacea and error to be radical evil. To Socratic man the one noble and truly human occupation was that of laying bare the workings of nature, of separating true knowledge from illusion and error. So it happened that ever since Socrates the mechanism of concepts, judgments, and syllogisms [logical arguments] has come to be regarded as the highest exercise of man's powers, nature's most admirable gift. Socrates and his successors, down to our own day, have considered all moral and sentimental accomplishments — noble deeds, compassion, self-sacrifice, heroism, even that spiritual calm, so difficult of attainment, which the Apollonian[1] Greek called *sophrosyne* — to be ultimately derived from the dialectic of knowledge, and therefore teachable. Whoever has tasted the delight of a Socratic perception, experienced how it moves to encompass the whole world of phenomena in ever widening circles, knows no sharper incentive to life than his desire to complete the conquest, to weave the net absolutely tight. . . .

Our whole modern world is caught in the net of Alexandrian culture and recognizes as its ideal the man of theory, equipped with the highest cognitive powers, working in the service of science, and whose archetype and progenitor is Socrates. All our pedagogic devices are oriented toward this ideal. Any type of existence that deviates from this model has a hard struggle and lives, at best, on sufferance. It is a rather frightening thought that for centuries the only form of educated man to be found was the scholar. Even our literary arts have been forced to develop out of learned imitations, and the important role rhyme plays in our poetry still betokens the derivation of our poetic forms from artificial experiments with a language not vernacular but properly learned. To any true Greek, that product of modern culture, *Faust,*[2] would have seemed quite unintelligible, though we ourselves understand it well enough. We have only to place Faust, who storms unsatisfied through all the provinces of knowledge and is driven to make a bargain with the powers of darkness, beside Socrates in order to realize that modern man has begun to be aware of the limits of Socratic curiosity and to long, in the wide, waste ocean of knowledge, for a shore. Goethe once said to Eckermann, referring to Napoleon: "Yes indeed, my friend,

there is also a productivity of actions." This *aperçu* [insight] suggests that for us moderns the man of action is something amazing and incredible, so that the wisdom of a Goethe was needed to find such a strange mode of existence comprehensible, even excusable.

We should acknowledge, then, that Socratic culture is rooted in an optimism which believes itself omnipotent. . . .

The blight which threatens theoretical culture has only begun to frighten modern man, and he is groping uneasily for remedies out of the storehouse of his experience, without having any real conviction that these remedies will prevail against disaster. In the meantime, there have arisen certain men of genius who, with admirable circumspection and consequence, have used the arsenal of science to demonstrate the limitations of science and of the cognitive faculty itself. They have authoritatively rejected science's claim to universal validity and to the attainment of universal goals and exploded for the first time the belief that man may plumb the universe by means of the law of causation. The extraordinary courage and wisdom of Kant and Schopenhauer[3] have won the most difficult victory, that over the optimistic foundations of logic, which form the underpinnings of our culture. Whereas the current optimism had treated the universe as knowable, in the presumption of eternal truths, and space, time, and causality as absolute and universally valid laws, Kant showed how these supposed laws serve only to raise appearance . . . to the status of true reality, thereby rendering impossible a genuine understanding of that reality: in the words of Schopenhauer, binding the dreamer even faster in sleep. . . .

. . . Socratic culture has been shaken and has begun to doubt its own infallibility. . . . The

---

[1] *Apollonian* derives from Apollo — the Greek god of sunlight, prophecy, music, and poetry — and refers to calm, measured, balanced form. Nietzsche opposes the term to *Dionysian.*

[2] *Faust* is a play written by Johann Goethe (1749–1832), often considered Germany's greatest writer. In the play, Dr. Faustus, a man of learning, determines that reason cannot solve the mysteries of the universe. Seeking to experience life fully, Faust enters into a pact with the devil. See *Faust* in Chapter 5, Section 1.

[3] Immanuel Kant (1724–1804), a German philosopher, held that scientific knowledge is based on appearances (phenomena) and that absolute knowledge of reality is unattainable. Arthur Schopenhauer (1788–1860), another German philosopher, declared that beneath the conscious intellect is the will, a striving, demanding force that is the real basis of human behavior.

man of theory, having begun to dread the consequences of his views, no longer dares commit himself freely to the icy flood of existence but runs nervously up and down the bank.

▷ First published in 1901, one year after Nietzsche's death, *The Will to Power* consists of the author's notes written in the years 1883 to 1888. The following passages from this work show Nietzsche's contempt for democracy and socialism and proclaim the will to power.

THE WILL TO POWER

720 (1886–1887)

The most fearful and fundamental desire in man, his drive for power — this drive is called "freedom" — must be held in check the longest. This is why ethics . . . has hitherto aimed at holding the desire for power in check: it disparages the tyrannical individual and with its glorification of social welfare and patriotism emphasizes the power-instinct of the herd.

728 (March–June 1888)

. . . A society that definitely and *instinctively* gives up war and conquest is in decline: it is ripe for democracy and the rule of shopkeepers — In most cases, to be sure, assurances of peace are merely narcotics.

751 (March–June 1888)

"The will to power" is so hated in democratic ages that their entire psychology seems directed toward belittling and defaming it. . . .

752 (1884)

. . . Democracy represents the disbelief in great human beings and an elite society: "Everyone is equal to everyone else." "At bottom we are one and all self-seeking cattle and mob."

753 (1885)

I am opposed to 1. socialism, because it dreams quite naively of "the good, true, and beautiful" and of "equal rights" (— anarchism also desires the same ideal, but in a more brutal fashion); 2. parliamentary government and the press, because these are the means by which the herd animal becomes master.

762 (1885)

European democracy represents a release of forces only to a very small degree. It is above all a release of laziness, of weariness, of *weakness*.

765 (Jan.–Fall 1888)

. . . Another Christian concept, no less crazy, has passed even more deeply into the tissue of modernity: the concept of the "equality of souls before God." This concept furnishes the prototype of all theories of equal rights: mankind was first taught to stammer the proposition of equality in a religious context, and only later was it made into morality: no wonder that man ended by taking it seriously, taking it practically! — that is to say, politically, democratically, socialistically, in the spirit of the pessimism of indignation.

854 (1884)

In the age of *suffrage universel*, i.e., when everyone may sit in judgment on everyone and everything, I feel impelled to reestablish *order of rank*.

855 (Spring–Fall 1887)

What determines rank, sets off rank, is only quanta of power, and nothing else.

857 (Jan.–Fall 1888)

I distinguish between a type of ascending life and another type of decay, disintegration, weakness. Is it credible that the question of the relative rank of these two types still needs to be posed?

858 (Nov. 1887–March 1888)

What determines your rank is the quantum of power you are: the rest is cowardice.

861 (1884)

A declaration of war on the masses by *higher men* is needed! Everywhere the mediocre are combining in order to make themselves master! Everything that makes soft and effeminate, that serves the ends of the "people" or the "feminine," works in favor of *suffrage universel,* i.e., the dominion of *inferior* men. But we should take reprisal and bring this whole affair (which in Europe commenced with Christianity) to light and to the bar of judgment.

862 (1884)

A doctrine is needed powerful enough to work as a breeding agent: strengthening the strong, paralyzing and destructive for the world-weary.

The annihilation of the decaying races. Decay of Europe. — The annihilation of slavish evaluations. — Dominion over the earth as a means of producing a higher type. — The annihilation of the tartuffery [hypocrisy] called "morality." . . . The annihilation of *suffrage universel*; i.e., the system through which the lowest natures prescribe themselves as laws for the higher. — The annihilation of mediocrity and its acceptance. (The onesided, individuals — peoples; to strive for fullness of nature through the pairing of opposites: race mixture to this end). — The new courage — no *a priori* [innate and universal] truths (such truths were sought by those accustomed to faith!), but a *free* subordination to a ruling idea that has its time: e.g., time as a property of space, etc.

870 (1884)

The root of all evil: that the slavish morality of meekness, chastity, selflessness, absolute obedience, has triumphed — ruling natures were thus condemned (1) to hypocrisy, (2) to torments of conscience — creative natures felt like rebels against God, uncertain and inhibited by eternal values. . . .

In summa: the best things have been slandered because the weak or the immoderate swine have cast a bad light on them — and the best men have remained hidden — and have often misunderstood themselves.

874 (1884)

The degeneration of the rulers and the ruling classes has been the cause of the greatest mischief in history! Without the Roman Caesars and Roman society, the insanity of Christianity would never have come to power.

When lesser men begin to doubt whether higher men exist, then the danger is great! And one ends by discovering that there is *virtue* also among the lowly and subjugated, the poor in spirit, and that *before God* men are equal — which has so far been the . . . [height] of nonsense on earth! For ultimately, the higher men measured themselves according to the standard of virtue of slaves — found they were "proud," etc., found all their higher qualities reprehensible.

997 (1884)

I teach: that there are higher and lower men, and that a single individual can under certain circumstances justify the existence of whole millennia — that is, a full, rich, great, whole human being in relation to countless incomplete fragmentary men.

998 (1884)

The highest men live beyond the rulers, freed from all bonds; and in the rulers they have their instruments.

999 (1884)

Order of rank: He who *determines* values and directs the will of millennia by giving direction to the highest natures is the *highest* man.

1001 (1884)

Not "mankind" but *overman* is the goal!

1067 (1885)

. . . This world is the will to power — and nothing besides! And you yourselves are also this will to power — and nothing besides!

▷ Nietzsche regarded Christianity as a life-denying religion that appeals to the masses. Fearful and resentful of their betters, he said, the masses espouse a faith that preaches equality and compassion. He maintained that Christianity has "waged a war to the death against (the) higher type of man." The following passages are from *The Antichrist,* written in 1888.

THE ANTICHRIST

2. What is good? — All that heightens the feeling of power, the will to power, power itself in man.

What is bad? — All that proceeds from weakness.

What is happiness? — The feeling that power *increases* — that a resistance is overcome.

Not contentment, but more power; *not* peace at all, but war; *not* virtue, but proficiency (virtue in the Renaissance style, *virtù,* virtue free of moralic acid).

The weak and ill-constituted shall perish: first principle of *our* philanthropy. And one shall help them to do so.

What is more harmful than any vice? — Active sympathy for the ill-constituted and weak — Christianity. . . .

3. The problem I raise here is not what ought to succeed mankind in the sequence of species (— the human being is an *end* —): but what type of human being one ought to *breed,* ought to *will,* as more valuable, more worthy of life, more certain of the future.

This more valuable type has existed often enough already: but as a lucky accident, as an exception, never as *willed. He* has rather been the most feared, he has hitherto been virtually *the* thing to be feared — and out of fear the reverse type has been willed, bred, *achieved:* the domestic animal, the herd animal, the sick animal man — the Christian. . . .

5. One should not embellish or dress up Christianity: it has waged *a war to the death* against this *higher* type of man, it has excom-municated all the fundamental instincts of this type, it has distilled evil, the *Evil One,* out of these instincts — the strong human being as the type of reprehensibility, as the "outcast." Christianity has taken the side of everything weak, base, ill-constituted, it has made an ideal out of *opposition* to the preservative instincts of strong life; it has depraved the reason even of the intellectually strongest natures by teaching men to feel the supreme values of intellectuality as sinful, as misleading, as *temptations.* The most deplorable example: the depraving of Pascal,[1] who believed his reason had been depraved by original sin while it had only been depraved by his Christianity!

6. . . . Christianity is a revolt of everything that crawls along the ground directed against that which is elevated. . . .

7. Christianity is called the religion of *pity.* — Pity stands in antithesis to the tonic emotions which enhance the energy of the feeling of life: it has a depressive effect. One loses force when one pities. . . .

15. In Christianity neither morality nor religion come into contact with reality at any point. Nothing but imaginary *causes* ("God," "soul," "ego," "spirit," "free will" — or "unfree will"): nothing but imaginary *effects* ("sin," "redemption," "grace," "punishment," "forgiveness of sins"). . . .

18. The Christian conception of God — God as God of the sick, God as spider, God as spirit — is one of the most corrupt conceptions of God arrived at on earth: perhaps it even represents the low-water mark in the descending development of the God type. God degenerated to the *contradiction of life,* instead of being its transfiguration and eternal *Yes!* In God a declaration of hostility towards life, nature, the will to life! God the formula for every calumny of "this world," for every lie about 'the next

---

[1]Blaise Pascal (1623–1662) was a French mathematician, philosopher, and eloquent defender of the Christian faith.

world'! In God, nothingness deified, the will to nothingness sanctified! . . .

21. In Christianity the instincts of the subjugated and oppressed come into the foreground: it is the lowest classes which seek their salvation in it. . . .

43. The poison of the doctrine "*equal* rights for all" — this has been more thoroughly sowed by Christianity than by anything else; from the most secret recesses of base instincts, Christianity has waged a war to the death against every feeling of reverence and distance between man and man, against, that is, the *precondition* of every elevation, every increase in culture — it has forged out of the [resentment] of the masses its *chief weapon* against *us,* against everything noble, joyful, high-spirited on earth, against our happiness on earth. . . . "Immortality" granted to every Peter and Paul has been the greatest and most malicious outrage on *noble*

mankind ever committed. — *And* let us not underestimate the fatality that has crept out of Christianity even into politics! No one any longer possesses today the courage to claim special privileges or the right to rule, the courage to feel a sense of reverence towards himself and towards his equals — the courage for a *pathos of distance.* . . . Our politics is *morbid* from this lack of courage! — The aristocratic outlook has been undermined most deeply by the lie of equality of souls; and if the belief in the "prerogative of the majority" makes revolutions and *will continue to make them* — it is Christianity, let there be no doubt about it, *Christian* value judgement which translates every revolution into mere blood and crime! Christianity is a revolt of everything that crawls along the ground directed against that which is *elevated*: the Gospel of the "lowly" *makes* low. . . .

REVIEW QUESTIONS

1. Why did Friedrich Nietzsche criticize Socrates?
2. According to Nietzsche, how was "Socratic culture" undermined in the nineteenth century?
3. What did Nietzsche consider to be a human being's most elemental desire?
4. Why did Nietzsche attack democracy and socialism? How do you respond to his attack?
5. What were Nietzsche's criticisms of Christianity? How do you respond to this attack?
6. How does Nietzsche's philosophy stand in relation to the Enlightenment?
7. What did Nietzsche affirm and extol?

▼▼▼

6 ▼ The Unconscious

After graduating from medical school in Vienna, Sigmund Freud (1856–1939), the founder of psychoanalysis, specialized in the treatment of nervous disorders. By encouraging his patients to speak to him about their troubles, Freud was able to probe deeper into their minds. These investigations led him to conclude that childhood fears and experiences, often sexual in nature, accounted for neuroses — hysteria, anxiety, depression, obsessions, and so on. So threatening and painful were these childhood emotions and experiences that his patients banished them from conscious memory to the realm of the unconscious. To understand and treat neurotic behavior, Freud said it is necessary to look behind overt symptoms and bring to the surface emotionally charged experiences and fears — childhood traumas — that lie buried in the unconscious. Freud probed the unconscious by urging his patients to say whatever came to their minds. This procedure, called free association, rests on the premise that spontaneous and uninhibited talk reveals a person's underlying preoccupations, his or her inner world. A second avenue to the unconscious is the analysis of dreams; an individual's dreams, said Freud, reveal his or her secret wishes.

Sigmund Freud
THE UNCONSCIOUS, PSYCHOANALYSIS, AND ≪ CIVILIZATION AND ITS DISCONTENTS ≫

Readings from these three works of Freud are included: *A Note on the Unconscious in Psychoanalysis, Five Lectures on Psychoanalysis,* and *Civilization and Its Discontents.* Freud's scientific investigation of psychic development led him to conclude that powerful mental processes hidden from consciousness govern human behavior more than reason does. His exploration of the unconscious produced a new image of the human being that has had a profound impact on twentieth-century thought. In the following excerpt from *A Note on the Unconscious in Psychoanalysis* (1912), Freud defined the term *unconscious.*

A NOTE ON THE UNCONSCIOUS IN PSYCHOANALYSIS

I wish to expound in a few words and as plainly as possible what the term 'unconscious' has come to mean in psychoanalysis and in psychoanalysis alone. . . .

. . . The well-known experiment, . . . of the 'post-hypnotic suggestion' teaches us to insist upon the importance of the distinction between *conscious* and *unconscious* and seems to increase its value.

In this experiment, as performed by Bernheim,[1] a person is put into a hypnotic state and is subsequently aroused. While he was in the hypnotic state, under the influence of the physician, he was ordered to execute a certain action at a certain fixed moment after his awakening, say half an hour later. He awakes, and seems fully conscious and in his ordinary condition; he has no recollection of his hypnotic

state, and yet at the prearranged moment there rushes into his mind the impulse to do such and such a thing, and he does it consciously, though not knowing why. It seems impossible to give any other description of the phenomenon than to say that the order has been present in the mind of the person in a condition of latency, or had been present unconsciously, until the given moment came, and then had become conscious. But not the whole of it emerged into consciousness: only the conception of the act to be executed. All the other ideas associated with this conception — the order, the influence of the physician, the recollection of the hypnotic state, remained unconscious even then. . . .

The mind of the hysterical patient is full of active yet unconscious ideas; all her symptoms proceed from such ideas. It is in fact the most striking character of the hysterical mind to be ruled by them. If the hysterical woman vomits, she may do so from the idea of being pregnant. She has, however, no knowledge of this idea, although it can easily be detected in her mind, and made conscious to her, by one of the technical procedures of psychoanalysis. If she is

---

[1]Hippolyte Bernheim (1840–1919), a French physician, used hypnosis in the treatment of his patients and published a successful book on the subject.

executing the jerks and movements constituting her 'fit,' she does not even consciously represent to herself the intended actions, and she may perceive those actions with the detached feelings of an onlooker. Nevertheless analysis will show that she was acting her part in the dramatic reproduction of some incident in her life, the memory of which was unconsciously active during the attack. The same preponderance of active unconscious ideas is revealed by analysis as the essential fact in the psychology of all other forms of neurosis. . . .

. . . The term *unconscious* . . . designates . . . ideas with a certain dynamic character, ideas keeping apart from consciousness in spite of their intensity and activity.

▷ This passage from a lecture given in 1909 describes Freud's attempt to penetrate the world of the unconscious.

FIVE LECTURES ON PSYCHOANALYSIS

. . . At first, I must confess, this seemed a senseless and hopeless undertaking. I was set the task of learning from the patient something that I did not know and that he did not know himself. How could one hope to elicit it? But there came to my help a recollection of a most remarkable and instructive experiment which I had witnessed when I was with Bernheim at Nancy [in 1889]. Bernheim showed us that people whom he had put into a state of hypnotic somnambulism [a hypnotically induced condition of sleep in which acts are performed], and who had had all kinds of experiences while they were in that state, only *appeared* to have lost the memory of what they had experienced during somnambulism; it was possible to revive these memories in their normal state. It is true that, when he questioned them about their somnambulistic experiences, they began by maintaining that they knew nothing about them; but if he refused to give way, and in-

sisted, and assured them that they *did* know about them, the forgotten experiences always reappeared.

So I did the same thing with my patients. When I reached a point with them at which they maintained that they knew nothing more, I assured them that they *did* know it all the same, and that they had only to say it; and I ventured to declare that the right memory would occur to them at the moment at which I laid my hand on their forehead. In that way I succeeded, without using hypnosis, in obtaining from the patients whatever was required for establishing the connection between the pathogenic [capable of causing disease] scenes they had forgotten and the symptoms left over from those scenes. But it was a laborious procedure, and in the long run an exhausting one; and it was unsuited to serve as a permanent technique.

I did not abandon it, however, before the observations I made during my use of it afforded me decisive evidence. I found confirmation of the fact that the forgotten memories were not lost. They were in the patient's possession and were ready to emerge in association to what was still known by him; but there was some force that prevented them from becoming conscious and compelled them to remain unconscious. The existence of this force could be assumed with certainty, since one became aware of an effort corresponding to it if, in opposition to it, one tried to introduce the unconscious memories into the patient's consciousness. The force which was maintaining the pathological condition became apparent in the form of *resistance* on the part of the patient.

It was on this idea of resistance, then, that I based my view of the course of psychical events in hysteria. In order to effect a recovery, it had proved necessary to remove these resistances. Starting out from the mechanism of cure, it now became possible to construct quite definite ideas of the origin of the illness. The same forces which, in the form of resistance, were now offering opposition to the forgotten material's being made conscious, must formerly have brought about the forgetting and must have pushed the pathogenic experiences in question out of consciousness. I gave the name of *"repression"* to this hypothetical process, and I considered that it was proved by the undeniable existence of resistance.

The further question could then be raised as to what these forces were and what the determinants were of the repression in which we now recognized the pathogenic mechanism of hysteria. A comparative study of the pathogenic situations which we had come to know through the cathartic procedure made it possible to answer this question. All these experiences had involved the emergence of a wishful impulse which was in sharp contrast to the subject's other wishes and which proved incompatible with the ethical and aesthetic standards of his personality. There had been a short conflict, and the end of this internal struggle was that the idea which had appeared before consciousness as the vehicle of this irreconcilable wish fell a victim to repression, was pushed out of consciousness with all its attached memories, and was forgotten. Thus the incompatibility of the wish in question with the patient's ego was the motive for the repression; the subject's ethical and other standards were the repressing forces. An acceptance of the incompatible wishful impulse or a prolongation of the conflict would have produced a high degree of unpleasure; this unpleasure was avoided by means of repression, which was thus revealed as one of the devices serving to protect the mental personality.

To take the place of a number of instances, I will relate a single one of my cases, in which the determinants and advantages of repression are sufficiently evident. For my present purpose I shall have once again to abridge the case history and omit some important underlying material. The patient was a girl, who had lost her beloved father after she had taken a share in nursing him — a situation analogous to that of Breuer's[2] patient. Soon afterwards her elder

[2]Joseph Breuer (1842–1925) was an Austrian physician and Freud's early collaborator.

sister married, and her new brother-in-law aroused in her a peculiar feeling of sympathy which was easily masked under a disguise of family affection. Not long afterwards her sister fell ill and died, in the absence of the patient and her mother. They were summoned in all haste without being given any definite information of the tragic event. When the girl reached the bedside of her dead sister, there came to her for a brief moment an idea that might be expressed in these words: "Now he is free and can marry me." We may assume with certainty that this idea, which betrayed to her consciousness the intense love for her brother-in-law of which she had not herself been conscious, was surrendered to repression a moment later, owing to the revolt of her feelings. The girl fell ill with severe hysterical symptoms; and while she was under my treatment it turned out that she had completely forgotten the scene by her sister's bedside and the odious egoistic impulse that had emerged in her. She remembered it during the treatment and reproduced the pathogenic moment with signs of the most violent emotion, and, as a result of the treatment, she became healthy once more.

▷ In the tradition of the Enlightenment philosophes, Freud valued reason and science, but he did not share the philosophes' confidence in human goodness and humanity's capacity for future progress. In *Civilization and Its Discontents* (1930), Freud posited the frightening theory that human beings are driven by an inherent aggressiveness that threatens civilized life — that civilization is fighting a losing battle with our aggressive instincts. Although Freud's pessimism was no doubt influenced by the tragedy of World War I, many ideas expressed in *Civilization and Its Discontents* derived from views that he had formulated decades earlier.

CIVILIZATION AND ITS DISCONTENTS

The element of truth behind all this, which people are so ready to disavow, is that men are not gentle creatures who want to be loved, and who at most can defend themselves if they are attacked; they are, on the contrary, creatures among whose instinctual endowments is to be reckoned a powerful share of aggressiveness. As a result, their neighbour is for them not only a potential helper or sexual object, but also someone who tempts them to satisfy their aggressiveness on him, to exploit his capacity for work without compensation, to use him sexually without his consent, to seize his possessions, to humiliate him, to cause him pain, to torture and to kill him. *Homo homini lupus.* [Man is wolf to man.] Who, in the face of all his experience of life and of history, will have the courage to dispute this assertion? As a rule this cruel aggressiveness waits for some provocation or puts itself at the service of some other purpose, whose goal might also have been reached by milder measures. In circumstances that are favourable to it, when the mental counter-forces which ordinarily inhibit it are out of action, it also manifests itself spontaneously and reveals man as a savage beast to whom consideration towards his own kind is something alien. Anyone who calls to mind the atrocities committed during the racial migrations or the invasions of the Huns, or by the people known as Mongols under Jenghiz Khan and Tamerlane, or at the capture of Jerusalem by the pious Crusaders, or even, indeed, the horrors of the recent World War — anyone who calls these things to mind will have to bow humbly before the truth of this view.

The existence of this inclination to aggression, which we can detect in ourselves and justly assume to be present in others, is the factor which disturbs our relations with our neighbour and which forces civilization into such a high expenditure [of energy]. In consequence of this primary mutual hostility of human beings, civilized society is perpetually threatened with disintegration. The interest of work in common would not hold it together; instinctual passions are stronger than reasonable interests. Civilization has to use its utmost efforts in order to set limits to man's aggressive instincts and to hold

the manifestations of them in check by psychical reaction-formations. Hence, therefore, the use of methods intended to incite people into identifications and aim-inhibited relationships of love, hence the restriction upon sexual life, and hence too the ideal's commandment to love one's neighbour as oneself — a commandment which is really justified by the fact that nothing else runs so strongly counter to the original nature of man. In spite of every effort, these endeavours of civilization have not so far achieved very much. It hopes to prevent the crudest excesses of brutal violence by itself assuming the right to use violence against criminals, but the law is not able to lay hold of the more cautious and refined manifestations of human aggressiveness. The time comes when each one of us has to give up as illusions the expectations which, in his youth, he pinned upon his fellowmen, and when he may learn how much difficulty and pain has been added to his life by their ill-will. At the same time, it would be unfair to reproach civilization with trying to eliminate strife and competition from human activity. These things are undoubtedly indispensable. But opposition is not necessarily enmity; it is merely misused and made an *occasion* for enmity.

The communists believe that they have found the path to deliverance from our evils. According to them, man is wholly good and is well-disposed to his neighbour; but the institution of private property has corrupted his nature. The ownership of private wealth gives the individual power, and with it the temptation to ill-treat his neighbour; while the man who is excluded from possession is bound to rebel in hostility against his oppressor. If private property were abolished, all wealth held in common, and everyone allowed to share in the enjoyment of it, ill-will and hostility would disappear among men. Since everyone's needs would be satisfied, no one would have any reason to regard another as his enemy; all would willingly undertake the work that was necessary. I have no concern with any economic criticisms of the communist system. . . . But I am able to recognize that the psychological premises on which the system is based are an untenable illusion. In abolishing private property we deprive the human love of aggression of one of its instruments, certainly a strong one, though certainly not the strongest; but we have in no way altered the differences in power and influence which are misused by aggressiveness, nor have we altered anything in its nature. Aggressiveness was not created by property. It reigned almost without limit in primitive times, when property was still very scanty, and it already shows itself in the nursery almost before property has given up its primal, anal form; it forms the basis of every relation of affection and love among people (with the single exception, perhaps, of the mother's relation to her male child). If we do away with personal rights over material wealth, there still remains prerogative in the field of sexual relationships, which is bound to become the source of the strongest dislike and the most violent hostility among men who in other respects are on an equal footing. If we were to remove this factor, too, by allowing complete freedom of sexual life and thus abolishing the family, the germ-cell of civilization, we cannot, it is true, easily foresee what new paths the development of civilization could take; but one thing we can expect, and that is that this indestructible feature of human nature will follow it there.

It is clearly not easy for men to give up the satisfaction of this inclination to aggression. They do not feel comfortable without it. . . .

If civilization imposes such great sacrifices not only on man's sexuality but on his aggressivity, we can understand better why it is hard for him to be happy in that civilization. . . .

In all that follows I adopt the standpoint, therefore, that the inclination to aggression is an original, self-subsisting instinctual disposition in man, and I return to my view that it constitutes the greatest impediment to civilization.

REVIEW QUESTIONS

1. What was Sigmund Freud's definition of the *unconscious*? What examples of the power of the unconscious did he provide?
2. What did Freud mean by *repression*? What examples of repression did he provide?
3. Compare and contrast the approaches of Freud and Nietzsche to the nonrational.
4. What did Freud consider the "greatest impediment to civilization"? Why?
5. How did Freud react to the Marxist view that private property is the source of evil?
6. Compare Freud's view of human nature and reason to that of Enlightenment philosophes.

DEVELOPMENTS IN PAINTING FROM IMPRESSIONISM TO THE ABSTRACT

Claude Monet (1840–1926): *On the Seine at Bennecourt*, 1868, oil on canvas, 32″ (height) × 39 1/2″. The French impressionist painters provided the nineteenth century art world with a fresh perspective on painting, one that focused on scenes of nature and upper-class leisure that were imbued with a new sense of color and light. Impressionist painters, such as Monet, painted their sun- and color-drenched landscapes outdoors, which gave them a sense of immediacy and reality. This early painting shows Monet's lifelong concern with the changing play of light on water. (© *1990 The Art Institute of Chicago. All Rights Reserved.*)

Georges Seurat (1859–1891): *A Sunday Afternoon on the Island of La Grande Jatte,* 1884–1886, oil on canvas, 81″ × 121″. Seurat, a pointillist rather than a true impressionist, aimed at making impressionist paintings more solid and durable. While this French artist's colors and light have an impressionistic quality, his firm shapes and immobile figures have quite the opposite effect. Seurat's brushstrokes are staccato points of color and light, rather than the loose brushstrokes of the impressionists, giving his paintings a greater sense of order and permanence. (© 1990 *The Art Institute of Chicago. All Rights Reserved.*)

Paul Gauguin (1848–1903): *Two Tahitian Women with Mangoes,* 1899, oil on canvas, 37″ × 28½″. Gauguin left France for Tahiti because of his disaffection for Western civilization, and this move had a profound impact upon his artistic style. Like other artists of his day, Gauguin saw the power of non-Western art and was drawn to the art of "primitive" people, uncorrupted by industrial society and close to nature. The brilliant colorization, casual composition, and sun-drenched South Seas women reveal this strong, tropical influence. (*The Metropolitan Museum of Art. Gift of William Church Osborn, 1949. [49.58.1]*)

Vincent van Gogh (1853–1890): *The Starry Night*, 1889, oil on canvas, 29″ × 36 1/4″. A Dutch postimpressionist painter, Van Gogh abandoned impressionism because he felt that the style did not allow him the freedom to express his emotions. He adopted a more dramatic color palette and dynamic brush technique that enabled him to create powerful paintings that also reflected his own inner turmoil. He incorporated a much greater sense of movement and strength in his works than the impressionists — here the exploding and whirling stars, the intrusive large cypress trees, and the diminutive human buildings. (*Collection, The Museum of Modern Art, New York. Acquired by the Lillie P. Bliss Bequest*)

Henri Rousseau (1844–1910): *The Dream,* 1910, oil on canvas, 6′ 8 1/2″
× 9′ 9 1/2″. Rousseau was a folk artist whose paintings conveyed magical
and enchanted worlds. A retired French customs collector with no training
in art, Rousseau began to paint in his middle age. Painted in the last year of
his life, *The Dream* is extremely vibrant, filled with an intense, but controlled
energy, characteristic of most of his work. While the figures are simplistic,
the dramatic colors and the composition are highly complex and structured,
creating an effect of childlike innocence and directness. (*Collection, The Museum of Modern Art, New York. Gift of Nelson A. Rockefeller*)

Vasili Kandinski (1866–1944): *Abstraction,* 1923, oil on canvas, 16″ × 15 1/8″. One of the first artists to successfully abandon representational images in his art, Kandinski declared his independence from observed reality and entered the world of artistic abstraction. While his art is nonrepresentational, there is still a strong, pervading sense of unity and vitality within each painting. Because his use of abstract symbols and images lends itself to a variety of different interpretations, people find this Russian's work intriguing. (*Art Resource, N.Y.*)

Pablo Picasso (1881–1973): *Guernica,* 1937, oil on canvas, 11′ 6″ × 25′ 8 1/4″. Perhaps the most famous artist of this century, this Spanish painter worked in several styles and media. While living in France, he developed the Cubist style with Georges Braque. This compelling painting was inspired by the German terror bombing that leveled the town of Guernica during the Spanish Civil War. His cubist style in this painting creates a powerful collage of images that symbolize the agony of all war. (*Giraudon/Art Resource, N.Y.*)

Part Three

▼▼▼

Western Civilization

in Crisis

CHAPTER

▼▼▼

9

World War I

To many Europeans, the opening years of the twentieth century seemed full of promise. Advances in science and technology, the rising standard of living, the expansion of education, and the absence of wars between the Great Powers since the Franco-Prussian War (1870–1871) all contributed to a general feeling of optimism. Yet these accomplishments hid disruptive forces that were propelling Europe toward a cataclysm. On June 28, 1914, Archduke Francis Ferdinand, heir to the throne of Austria-Hungary, was assassinated by Gavrilo Princip, a young Serbian nationalist (and Austrian subject), at Sarajevo in the Austrian province of Bosnia, inhabited largely by South Slavs. The assassination triggered those explosive forces that lay below the surface of European life, and six weeks later, Europe was engulfed in a general war that altered the course of Western civilization.

Belligerent, irrational, and extreme nationalism was a principal cause of World War I. Placing their country above everything, nationalists in various countries fomented hatred of other nationalities and called for the expansion of their nation's borders — attitudes that fostered belligerence in foreign relations. Wedded to nationalism was a militaristic view that regarded war as heroic and as the highest expression of individual and national life.

Yet Europe might have avoided the world war had the nations not been divided into hostile alliance systems. By 1907, the Triple Alliance of Germany, Austria-Hungary, and Italy confronted the loosely organized Triple Entente of France, Russia, and Great Britain. What German chancellor Otto von Bismarck said in 1879 was just as true in 1914: "The great powers of our time are like travellers, unknown to one another, whom chance has brought together in a carriage. They watch each other, and when one of them puts his hand into his pocket, his neighbor gets ready his own revolver in order to be able to fire the first shot."

A danger inherent in an alliance is that a country, knowing that it has the support of allies, may pursue an aggressive foreign policy and may be less likely to compromise during a crisis; also, a war between two states may well draw in the other allied powers. These dangers materialized in 1914.

In the diplomatic furor of July and early August 1914, following the assassination of Francis Ferdinand, several patterns emerged. Austria-Hungary, a multinational empire

WOUNDED BELGIAN SOLDIERS, assisting one another in their flight from Ostend into France, show the pain and despair experienced by troops on both sides of the conflict. (*The Bettmann Archive*)

dominated by Germans and Hungarians, feared the nationalist aspirations of its Slavic minorities. The nationalist
yearnings of neighboring Serbia aggravated Austria-Hungary's problems, for the Serbs, a South Slav people, wanted
to create a Greater Serbia by uniting with South Slavs of
Austria-Hungary. If Slavic nationalism gained in intensity,
the Austro-Hungarian (or Hapsburg) Empire would be broken into states based on nationality. Austria-Hungary decided to use the assassination as justification for crushing
Serbia.

The system of alliances escalated the tensions between
Austria-Hungary and Serbia into a general European war.
Germany saw itself threatened by the Triple Entente (a conviction based more on paranoia than on objective fact) and
regarded Austria-Hungary as its only reliable ally. Holding
that at all costs its ally must be kept strong, German officials
supported Austria-Hungary's decision to crush Serbia. Fearing that Germany and Austria-Hungary aimed to extend
their power into southeastern Europe, Russia would not
permit the destruction of Serbia. With the support of
France, Russia began to mobilize, and when it moved to full
mobilization, Germany declared war. As German battle
plans, drawn up years before, called for a war with both
France and Russia, France was drawn into the conflict; Germany's invasion of neutral Belgium brought Great Britain
into the war.

Most European statesmen and military men believed the
war would be over in a few months. Virtually no one anticipated that it would last more than four years and that the
casualties would number in the millions.

World War I was a turning point in Western history. In
Russia, it led to the downfall of the tsarist autocracy and the
rise of the Soviet state. The war created unsettling conditions that led to the emergence of fascist movements in Italy
and Germany, and it shattered, perhaps forever, the Enlightenment belief in the inevitable and perpetual progress
of Western civilization.

▼▼▼

I ▼ Militarism

Historians regard a surging militarism as an underlying cause of World War I.
One sign of militarism was the rapid increase in expenditures for armaments in
the years prior to 1914. Between 1910 and 1914, both Austria-Hungary and

Germany, for example, doubled their military budgets. The arms race intensified suspicion among the Great Powers. A second danger was the increased power of the military in policy making, particularly in Austria-Hungary and Germany, and in the crisis following the assassination, generals tended to press for a military solution.

Heinrich von Treitschke
THE GREATNESS OF WAR

Coupled with the military's influence on state decisions was a romantic glorification of the nation and war, an attitude shared by both the elite and the masses. Although militarism generally pervaded Europe, it was particularly strong in Germany. In the following reading from *Politics* (1907), German historian Heinrich von Treitschke (1834–1896) glorified warfare.

. . . One must say with the greatest determination: War is for an afflicted people the only remedy. When the State exclaims: My very existence is at stake! then social self-seeking must disappear and all party hatred be silent. The individual must forget his own *ego* and feel himself a member of the whole, he must recognize how negligible is his life compared with the good of the whole. Therein lies the greatness of war that the little man completely vanishes before the great thought of the State. The sacrifice of nationalities for one another is nowhere invested with such beauty as in war. At such a time the corn is separated from the chaff. All who lived through 1870 will understand the saying of Niebuhr[1] with regard to the year 1813, that he then experienced the "bliss of sharing with all his fellow citizens, with the scholar and the ignorant, the one common feeling — no man who enjoyed this experience will to his dying day forget how loving, friendly and strong he felt."

It is indeed political idealism which fosters war, whereas materialism rejects it. What a perversion of morality to want to banish heroism from human life. The heroes of a people are the personalities who fill the youthful souls with delight and enthusiasm, and amongst authors we as boys and youths admire most those whose words sound like a flourish of trumpets. He who cannot take pleasure therein, is too cowardly to take up arms himself for his fatherland. All appeal to Christianity in this matter is perverted. The Bible states expressly that the man in authority shall wield the sword; it states likewise that: "Greater love hath no man than this that he giveth his life for his friend." Those who preach the nonsense about everlasting peace do not understand the life of the Aryan race, the Aryans are before all brave. They have always been men enough to protect by the sword what they had won by the intellect. . . .

To the historian who lives in the realms of the Will, it is quite clear that the furtherance of an everlasting peace is fundamentally reactionary. He sees that to banish war from history would be to banish all progress and becoming. It is only the periods of exhaustion, weariness and mental stagnation that have dallied with the dream of everlasting peace. . . . The living God will see to it that war returns again and again as a terrible medicine for humanity.

---

[1]Barthold G. Niebuhr (1776–1831) was a Prussian historian. The passage refers to the German War of Liberation against Napoleon, which German patriots regarded as a glorious episode in their national history.

REVIEW QUESTIONS

1. Why did Heinrich von Treitschke regard war as a far more desirable condition than peace?
2. According to Treitschke, what is the individual's highest responsibility?
3. According to Treitschke, what function does the hero serve in national life?

▼▼▼

2 ▼ Pan-Serbism: Nationalism and Terrorism

The conspiracy to assassinate Archduke Francis Ferdinand was organized by a secret Serbian society called Union or Death, more popularly known as the Black Hand. Founded in 1911, the Black Hand aspired to create a Greater Serbia by uniting with their kinsmen, the South Slavs dwelling in Austria-Hungary. Thus, Austrian officials regarded the aspirations of Pan-Serbs as a significant threat to the Hapsburg Empire.

THE BLACK HAND

In 1914, the Black Hand had some 2,500 members, most of them army officers. The society indoctrinated members with a fanatic nationalism and trained them in terrorist methods. The initiation ceremony, designed to strengthen a new member's commitment to the cause and to foster obedience to the society's leaders, had the appearance of a sacred rite. The candidate entered a dark room in which a table stood covered with a black cloth; resting on the table were a dagger, a revolver, and a crucifix. When the candidate declared his readiness to take the oath of allegiance, a masked member of the society's elite entered the room and stood in silence. After the initiate pronounced the oath, the masked man shook his hand and departed without uttering a word. Excerpts of the Black Hand's by-laws, including the oath of allegiance, follow.

BY-LAWS OF THE ORGANIZATION UNION OR DEATH

Article 1. This organization is created for the purpose of realizing the national ideal: the union of all Serbs. Membership is open to every Serb, without distinction of sex, religion, or place of birth, and to all those who are sincerely devoted to this cause.

Article 2. This organization prefers terrorist action to intellectual propaganda, and for this reason it must remain absolutely secret.

Article 3. The organization bears the name *Ujedinjenje ili Smirt* (Union or Death).

Article 4. To fulfill its purpose, the organization will do the following:

1. Exercise influence on government circles, on the various social classes, and on the entire social life of the kingdom of Serbia, which is considered the Piedmont[1] of the Serbian nation;

---

[1]The Piedmont was the Italian state that served as the nucleus for the unification of Italy.

2. Organize revolutionary action in all territories inhabited by Serbs;

3. Beyond the frontiers of Serbia, fight with all means the enemies of the Serbian national idea;

4. Maintain amicable relations with all states, peoples, organizations, and individuals who support Serbia and the Serbian element;

5. Assist those nations and organizations that are fighting for their own national liberation and unification. . . .

Article 24. Every member has a duty to recruit new members, but the member shall guarantee with his life those whom he introduces into the organization.

Article 25. Members of the organization are forbidden to know each other personally. Only members of the central committee are known to each other.

Article 26. In the organization itself, the members are designated by numbers. Only the central committee in Belgrade knows their names.

Article 27. Members of the organization must obey absolutely the commands given to them by their superiors.

Article 28. Each member has a duty to communicate to the central committee at Belgrade all information that may be of interest to the organization.

Article 29. The interests of the organization stand above all other interests.

Article 30. On entering the organization, each member must know that he loses his own personality, that he can expect neither personal glory nor personal profit, material or moral. Consequently, any member who endeavors to exploit the organization for personal, social, or party motives, will be punished. If by his acts he harms the organization itself, his punishment will be death.

Article 31. Those who enter the organization may never leave it, and no one has the authority to accept a member's resignation.

Article 32. Each member must aid the organization, with weekly contributions. If need be, the organization may procure funds through coercion. . . .

Article 33. When the central committee of Belgrade pronounces a death sentence the only thing that matters is that the execution is carried out unfailingly. The method of execution is of little importance.

Article 34. The organization's seal is composed as follows. On the center of the seal a powerful arm holds in its hand an unfurled flag. On the flag, as a coat of arms, are a skull and crossed bones; by the side of the flag are a knife, a bomb and poison. Around, in a circle, are inscribed the following words reading from left to right: "Unification or Death," and at the base "The Supreme Central Directorate."

Article 35. On joining the organization, the recruit takes the following oath:

"I (name), in becoming a member of the organization, 'Unification or Death,' do swear by the sun that shines on me, by the earth that nourishes me, by God, by the blood of my ancestors, on my honor and my life that from this moment until my death, I shall be faithful to the regulations of the organization and that I will be prepared to make any sacrifice for it. I swear before God, on my honor and on my life, that I shall carry with me to the grave the organization's secrets. May God condemn me and my comrades judge me if I violate or do not respect, consciously or not, my oath."

Article 36. These regulations come into force immediately.

Article 37. These regulations must not be changed.

Belgrade, 9 May 1911.

REVIEW QUESTIONS

1. How did Union or Death seek to accomplish its goal of uniting all Serbs?
2. What type of people do you think were attracted to the objectives and methods of the Black Hand?

▼▼▼

3 ▼ British Fear of German Power

The completion of German unification under Prussian leadership in 1870–1871 upset the European balance of power. A militarily powerful, rapidly industrializing, and increasingly nationalist Germany aroused fear among other European states, particularly after Chancellor Otto von Bismarck (1815–1898) was forced out of office in 1890. The new German leadership became increasingly more aggressive and more susceptible to nationalist demands. German nationalists argued that the unification of Germany was more than the culmination of a deeply felt German goal; it was the starting point for German world power.

Eyre Crowe
GERMANY'S YEARNING FOR EXPANSION AND POWER

Fearful of Germany's growing industrial might, acquisition of colonies, and military preparations, particularly in naval armament, Britain ended its "splendid isolation" and entered into what was in effect a loose alliance with France in 1904 and with Russia in 1907. In 1907, Sir Eyre Crowe, an official in the British Foreign Office, assessed Germany's *Weltpolitik* — its desire to play a greater role on the world stage. Some historians regard that desire as a primary cause of World War I. Excerpts from Crowe's memorandum follow.

For purposes of foreign policy the modern German Empire may be regarded as the heir, or descendant of Prussia. . . .

. . . With "blood and iron" Prussia had forged her position in the councils of the Great Powers of Europe. In due course it came to pass that, with the impetus given to every branch of national activity by the newly-won unity, and more especially by the growing development of oversea trade flowing in ever-increasing volume . . . , the young empire found opened to its energy a whole world outside Europe, of which it had previously hardly had the opportunity to become more than dimly conscious. Sailing across the ocean in German ships, German merchants began for the first time to divine the true position of countries such as England, the United States, France, and even the Netherlands, whose political influence extends to distant seas and continents. The colonies and foreign possessions of England more especially were seen to give to that country a recognized and enviable status in a world where the name of Germany, if mentioned at all, excited no particular interest. . . . Here was distinct inequality, with a heavy bias in favour of the maritime and colonizing Powers.

Such a state of things was not welcome to German patriotic pride. Germany had won her place as one of the leading, if not, in fact, the foremost Power on the European continent. But over and beyond the European Great Powers there seemed to stand the "World Powers." It was at once clear that Germany must become a "World Power." The evolution of this idea and its translation into practical politics followed with singular consistency the line of thought that had inspired the Prussian Kings in their efforts to make Prussia great. "If Prussia," said Frederick the Great, "is to count for something in the councils of Europe, she must be made a Great Power." And the echo: "If Germany wants to have a voice in the affairs of the larger oceanic world she must be made a 'World Power.'" "I want more territory," said Prussia. "Germany must have Colonies," says the new world-policy. And Colonies were accordingly established, in such spots as were found to be still unappropriated, or out of which others could be pushed by the vigorous assertion of a German demand for "a place in the sun." . . .

Meanwhile the dream of a Colonial Empire had taken deep hold on the German imagination. Emperor, statesmen, journalists, geographers, economists, commercial and shipping houses, and the whole mass of educated and uneducated public opinion continue with one voice to declare: We *must* have real Colonies, where German emigrants can settle and spread the national ideals of the Fatherland, and we *must* have a fleet and coaling stations to keep together the Colonies which we are bound to acquire. To the question, "Why *must?*" the ready answer is: "A healthy and powerful State like Germany, with its 60,000,000 inhabitants, must expand, it cannot stand still, it must have territories to which its overflowing population can emigrate without giving up its nationality." When it is objected that the world is now actually parcelled out among independent States, and that territory for colonization cannot be had except by taking it from the rightful possessor, the reply again is: "We cannot enter into such considerations. Necessity has no law. The world belongs to the strong. A vigorous nation cannot allow its growth to be hampered by blind adherence to the *status quo.* We have no designs on other people's possessions, but where States are too feeble to put their territory to the best possible use, it is the manifest destiny of those who can and will do so to take their places." . . .

The significance of these individual utterances may easily be exaggerated. Taken together, their cumulative effect is to confirm the impression that Germany distinctly aims at playing on the world's political stage a much larger and much more dominant part than she finds allotted to herself under the present distribution of material power. . . .

. . . No modern German would plead guilty to a mere lust of conquest for the sake of conquest. But the vague and undefined schemes of Teutonic expansion . . . are but the expression of the deeply rooted feeling that Germany has by the strength and purity of her national purpose, the fervour of her patriotism, the depth of her religious feeling, the high standard of competency, and the perspicuous honesty of her administration, the successful pursuit of every branch of public and scientific activity, and the elevated character of her philosophy, art, and ethics, established for herself the right to assert the primacy of German national ideals. And as it is an axiom of her political faith that right, in order that it may prevail, must be backed by force, the transition is easy to the belief that the "good German sword," which plays so large a part in patriotic speech, is there to solve any difficulties that may be in the way of establishing the reign of those ideals in a Germanized world. . . .

So long . . . as Germany competes for an intellectual and moral leadership of the world in reliance on her own national advantages and energies England can but admire, applaud, and join in the race. If, on the other hand, Germany believes that greater relative preponderance of material power, wider extent of territory, inviolable frontiers, and supremacy at sea are the necessary and preliminary possessions without which any aspirations to such leadership must end in failure, then England must expect that Germany will surely seek to diminish the power of any rivals, to enhance her own by extending her dominion, to hinder the co-operation of other States, and ultimately to break up and supplant the British empire. . . .

England seeks no quarrels, and will never give Germany cause for legitimate offence.

But this is not a matter in which England can safely run any risks. . . .

. . . A German maritime supremacy must be acknowledged to be incompatible with the existence of the British Empire, and even if that Empire disappeared, the union of the greatest military with the greatest naval Power in one State would compel the world to combine for the riddance of such an incubus [nightmare].

REVIEW QUESTIONS

1. How did Sir Eyre Crowe interpret the principle of the balance of power as it applied to Britain? How was Britain's foreign policy related to its geographic position?
2. According to Crowe, what did Germany's foreign policy owe to its Prussian background?
3. How did Crowe regard German demands for colonies?

▼▼▼

4 ▼ War as Celebration: The Mood in European Capitals

An outpouring of patriotism greeted the proclamation of war. Huge crowds thronged the avenues and squares of capital cities to express their devotion to their nations and their willingness to bear arms. Many Europeans regarded war as a sacred moment that held the promise of adventure and an escape from a humdrum and purposeless daily existence. Going to war seemed to satisfy a yearning to surrender oneself to a noble cause: the greatness of the nation. The image of the nation united in a spirit of fraternity and self-sacrifice was immensely appealing.

Roland Doregelès
PARIS: "THAT FABULOUS DAY"

In "After Fifty Years," Roland Doregelès (1886–1973), a distinguished French writer, recalled the mood in Paris at the outbreak of the war.

"It's come!* It's posted at the district mayor's office," a passserby shouted to me as he ran.

I reached the Rue Drouot in one leap and shouldered through the mob that already filled the courtyard to approach the fascinating white sheet pasted to the door. I read the message at a glance, then reread it slowly, word for word, to convince myself that it was true:

THE FIRST DAY OF
MOBILIZATION WILL BE
SUNDAY, AUGUST 2

Only three lines, written hastily by a hand that trembled. It was an announcement to a million and a half Frenchmen.

The people who had read it moved away, stunned, while others crowded in, but this silent numbness did not last. Suddenly a heroic

---

*Translated from the French by Sally Abeles.

wind lifted their heads. What? War, was it? Well, then, let's go! Without any signal, the "Marseillaise" poured from thousands of throats, sheafs of flags appeared at windows, and howling processions rolled out on the boulevards. Each column brandished a placard: AL-SACE VOLUNTEERS, JEWISH VOLUNTEERS, POL-ISH VOLUNTEERS. They hailed one another above the bravos of the crowd, and this human torrent, swelling at every corner, moved on to circle around the Place de la Concorde, before the statue of Strasbourg banked with flowers, then flowed toward the Place de la République, where mobs from Belleville and the Faubourg St. Antoine yelled themselves hoarse on the refrain from the great days, *"Aux armes, citoyens!"* (To arms, citizens!) But this time it was better than a song.

To gather the news for my paper, I ran around the city in every direction. At the Cours la Reine I saw the fabled cuirassiers [cavalry] in their horsetail plumes march by, and at the Rue La Fayette footsoldiers in battle garb with women throwing flowers and kisses to them. In a marshaling yard I saw guns being loaded, their long, thin barrels twined around with branches and laurel leaves, while troops in red breeches piled gaily into delivery vans they were scrawling with challenges and caricatures. Young and old, civilians and military men burned with the same excitement. It was like a Brotherhood Day.

Dead tired but still exhilarated, I got back to *L'Homme libre* and burst into the office of Georges Clemenceau, our chief.†

"What is Paris saying?" he asked me.

"It's singing, sir!"

"Then everything will be all right. . . ."

His old patriot's heart was not wrong; no cloud marred that fabulous day. . . .

---

†*L'Homme libre* (The Free Man) was but one of several periodicals Clemenceau founded and directed during his long political career. — Tr.

Less than twenty-four hours later, seeing their old dreams of peace crumble [socialist workers] would stream out into the boulevards . . . [but] they would break into the "Marseillaise," not the "Internationale"; they would cry, "To Berlin!," not 'Down with war!"

What did they have to defend, these black-nailed patriots? Not even a shack, an acre to till, indeed hardly a patch of ground reserved at the Pantin Cemetery; yet they would depart, like their rivals of yesterday, a heroic song on their lips and a flower in their guns. No more poor or rich, proletarians or bourgeois, right-wingers or militant leftists; there were only Frenchmen.

Beginning the next day, thousands of men eager to fight would jostle one another outside recruiting offices, waiting to join up. Men who could have stayed home, with their wives and children or an imploring mama. But no. The word "duty" had a meaning for them, and the word "country" had regained its splendor.

I close my eyes, and they appear to me, those volunteers on the great day; then I see them again in the old kepi [military cap] or blue helmet, shouting, "Here!" when somebody called for men for a raid, or hurling themselves into an attack with fixed bayonets, and I wonder, and I question their bloody [ghosts].

Tell me, comrades in eternal silence, would you have besieged the enlistment offices with the same enthusiasm, would you have fought such a courageous fight had you known that fifty years later those men in gray knit caps or steel helmets you were ordered to kill would no longer be enemies and that we would have to open our arms to them? Wouldn't the heroic "Let's go!" you shouted as you cleared the parapets have stuck in your throats? Deep in the grave where you dwell, don't you regret your sacrifice? "Why did we fight? Why did we let ourselves get killed?" This is the murmur of a million and a half voices rising from the bowels of the earth, and we, the survivors, do not know what to answer.

Stefan Zweig
VIENNA: "THE RUSHING FEELING OF FRATERNITY"

Some intellectuals viewed the war as a way of regenerating Europe; nobility and glory would triumph over life's petty concerns. In the following reading, Stefan Zweig (1881–1942), a prominent Austrian literary figure, recalled the scene in Vienna, the capital of the Austro-Hungarian Empire, at the outbreak of World War I. This passage comes from Zweig's autobiography written in 1941.

The next morning I was in Austria. In every station placards had been put up announcing general mobilization. The trains were filled with fresh recruits, banners were flying, music sounded, and in Vienna I found the entire city in a tumult. The first shock at the news of war — the war that no one, people or government, had wanted — the war which had slipped, much against their will, out of the clumsy hands of the diplomats who had been bluffing and toying with it, had suddenly been transformed into enthusiasm. There were parades in the street, flags, ribbons, and music burst forth everywhere, young recruits were marching triumphantly, their faces lighting up at the cheering — they, the John Does and Richard Roes who usually go unnoticed and uncelebrated.

And to be truthful, I must acknowledge that there was a majestic, rapturous, and even seductive something in this first outbreak of the people from which one could escape only with difficulty. And in spite of all my hatred and aversion for war, I should not like to have missed the memory of those first days. As never before, thousands and hundreds of thousands felt what they should have felt in peace time, that they belonged together. A city of two million, a country of nearly fifty million, in that hour felt that they were participating in world history, in a moment which would never recur, and that each one was called upon to cast his infinitesimal self into the glowing mass, there to be purified of all selfishness. All differences of class, rank, and language were flooded over at that moment by the rushing feeling of fraternity. Strangers spoke to one another in the streets, people who had avoided each other for years shook hands, everywhere one saw excited faces. Each individual experienced an exaltation of his ego, he was no longer the isolated person of former times, he had been incorporated into the mass, he was part of the people, and his person, his hitherto unnoticed person, had been given meaning. The petty mail clerk, who ordinarily sorted letters early and late, who sorted constantly, who sorted from Monday until Saturday without interruption; the clerk, the cobbler, had suddenly achieved a romantic possibility in life: he could become a hero, and everyone who wore a uniform was already being cheered by the women, and greeted beforehand with this romantic appellation by those who had to remain behind. They acknowledged the unknown power which had lifted them out of their everyday existence. Even mothers with their grief, and women with their fears, were ashamed to manifest their quite natural emotions in the face of this first transformation. But it is quite possible that a deeper, more secret power was at work in this frenzy. So deeply, so quickly did the tide break over humanity that, foaming over the surface, it churned up the depths, the subconscious primitive instincts of the human animal — that which Freud so meaningfully calls "the revulsion from culture," the desire to break out of the conventional bourgeois world of codes and statutes, and to permit the primitive instincts of the blood to rage at will. It is also possible that these powers of darkness had their share in the wild frenzy into which everything was thrown — self-sacrifice and alcohol, the spirit of adventure and the spirit of pure faith, the old magic of flags and patriotic slogans, that mysterious frenzy of the millions which can hardly be described in words, but which, for the moment, gave a wild and almost rapturous impetus to the greatest crime of our time. . . .

. . . What did the great mass know of war in 1914, after nearly half a century of peace? They did not know war, they had hardly given it a thought. It had become legendary, and distance had made it seem romantic and heroic. They still saw it in the perspective of their school readers and of paintings in museums; brilliant cavalry attacks in glittering uniforms, the fatal shot always straight through the heart, the entire campaign a resounding march of vic-

tory — "We'll be home at Christmas," the recruits shouted laughingly to their mothers in August of 1914. Who in the villages and the cities of Austria remembered "real" war? A few ancients at best, who in 1866 had fought against Prussia, which was now their ally. But what a quick, bloodless far-off war that had been, a campaign that had ended in three weeks with few victims and before it had well started! A rapid excursion into the romantic, a wild, manly adventure — that is how the war of 1914 was painted in the imagination of the simple man, and the young people were honestly afraid that they might miss this most wonderful and exciting experience of their lives; that is why they hurried and thronged to the colors, and that is why they shouted and sang in the trains that carried them to the slaughter; wildly and feverishly the red wave of blood coursed through the veins of the entire nation.

Philipp Scheidemann
BERLIN: "THE HOUR WE YEARNED FOR"

Philipp Scheidemann (1865–1939), one of the founding fathers of the Weimar Republic, described Berlin's martial mood in his memoirs, published in 1929.

At express speed I had returned to Berlin. Everywhere a word could be heard the conversation was of war and rumours of war. There was only one topic of conversation — war. The supporters of war seemed to be in a great majority. Were these pugnacious fellows, young and old, bereft of their senses? Were they so ignorant of the horrors of war? . . . Vast crowds of demonstrators paraded. . . . Schoolboys and students were there in their thousands; their bearded seniors, with their Iron Crosses of 1870–71 on their breasts, were there too in huge numbers.

Treitschke and Bernhardi[1] (to say nothing

of the National Liberal beer-swilling heroes) seemed to have multiplied a thousandfold. Patriotic demonstrations had an intoxicating effect and excited the war-mongers to excess. "A call like the voice of thunder." Cheers! "In triumph we will smite France to the ground." "All hail to thee in victor's crown." Cheers! Hurrah!

The counter-demonstrations immediately organized by the Berlin Social Democrats were imposing, and certainly more disciplined than the Jingo [extremely nationalistic] processions, but could not outdo the shouts of the fire-eaters. "Good luck to him who cares for truth and right. Stand firmly round the flag." "Long live peace!" "Socialists, close up your ranks." The Socialist International cheer. The patriots were sometimes silenced by the Proletarians; then

[1]Both Heinrich von Treitschke (see page 259) and General von Bernhardi glorified war.

they came out on top again. This choral contest . . . went on for days.

"It is the hour we yearned for — our friends know that," so the Pan-German[2] papers shouted, that had for years been shouting for war. The *Post,* conducted by von Stumm, the Independent Conservative leader and big Industrial, had thus moaned in all its columns in 1900, at the fortieth celebration of the Franco-German War: "Another forty years of peace would be a national misfortune for Germany."

[2]The Pan-German Association, whose membership included professors, schoolteachers, journalists, lawyers, and aristocrats, spread nationalist and racial theories and glorified war as an expression of national vitality.

Now these firebrands saw the seeds they had planted ripening. Perhaps in the heads of many who had been called upon to make every effort to keep the peace Bernhardi's words, that "the preservation of peace can and never shall be the aim of politics," had done mischief. These words are infernally like the secret instructions given by Baron von Holstein to the German delegates to the first Peace Conference at The Hague:

"For the State there is no higher aim than the preservation of its own interests; among the Great Powers these will not necessarily coincide with the maintenance of peace, but rather with the hostile policy of enemies and rivals."

REVIEW QUESTIONS

1. Why did the mood in Paris at the outbreak of war seem like a Brotherhood Day to Roland Doregelès?
2. Why, according to Stefan Zweig, did the prospects of war appeal so seductively to the emotions?
3. According to Philipp Scheidemann, why did many Germans welcome the war?
4. Why was war welcomed as a positive event by so many different peoples?
5. Do you think human beings are aggressive by nature? Explain your answer.

▼▼▼

5 ▼ Trench Warfare

In 1914 the young men of European nations marched off to war believing that they were embarking on a glorious and chivalrous adventure. They were eager to serve their countries, to demonstrate personal valor, and to experience life at its most intense moments. But in the trenches, where unseen enemies fired machine guns and artillery that killed indiscriminately and relentlessly, this romantic illusion about combat disintegrated.

Erich Maria Remarque
≪ ALL QUIET ON THE WESTERN FRONT ≫

The following reading is taken from Erich Maria Remarque's novel *All Quiet on the Western Front* (1929), the most famous literary work to emerge from World War I. A veteran of the trenches himself, Remarque graphically described the slaughter that robbed Europe of its young men. His narrator is a young German soldier.

We wake up in the middle of the night. The earth booms. Heavy fire is falling on us. We crouch into corners. We distinguish shells of every calibre.

Each man lays hold of his things and looks again every minute to reassure himself that they are still there. The dug-out heaves, the night roars and flashes. We look at each other in the momentary flashes of light, and with pale faces and pressed lips shake our heads.

Every man is aware of the heavy shells tearing down the parapet, rooting up the embankment and demolishing the upper layers of concrete. When a shell lands in the trench we note how the hollow, furious blast is like a blow from the paw of a raging beast of prey. Already by morning a few of the recruits are green and vomiting. They are too inexperienced. . . .

The bombardment does not diminish. It is falling in the rear too. As far as one can see spout fountains of mud and iron. A wide belt is being raked.

The attack does not come, but the bombardment continues. We are gradually benumbed. Hardly a man speaks. We cannot make ourselves understood.

Our trench is almost gone. At many places it is only eighteen inches high, it is broken by holes, and craters, and mountains of earth. A shell lands square in front of our post. At once it is dark. We are buried and must dig ourselves out. . . .

Towards morning, while it is still dark, there is some excitement. Through the entrance rushes in a swarm of fleeing rats that try to storm the walls. Torches light up the confusion. Everyone yells and curses and slaughters. The madness and despair of many hours unloads itself in this outburst. Faces are distorted, arms strike out, the beasts scream; we just stop in time to avoid attacking one another. . . .

Suddenly it howls and flashes terrifically, the dug-out cracks in all its joints under a direct hit, fortunately only a light one that the concrete blocks are able to withstand. It rings metallically, the walls reel, rifles, helmets, earth, mud, and dust fly everywhere. Sulphur fumes pour in.

If we were in one of those light dug-outs that they have been building lately instead of this deeper one, none of us would be alive.

But the effect is bad enough even so. The recruit starts to rave again and two others follow suit. One jumps up and rushes out, we have trouble with the other two. I start after the one who escapes and wonder whether to shoot him in the leg — then it shrieks again, I fling myself down and when I stand up the wall of the trench is plastered with smoking splinters, lumps of flesh, and bits of uniform. I scramble back.

The first recruit seems actually to have gone insane. He butts his head against the wall like a goat. We must try to-night to take him to the rear. Meanwhile we bind him, but in such a way that in case of attack he can be released at once. . . .

Suddenly the nearer explosions cease. The shelling continues but it has lifted and falls behind us, our trench is free. We seize the hand-grenades, pitch them out in front of the dug-out and jump after them. The bombardment has stopped and a heavy barrage now falls behind us. The attack has come.

No one would believe that in this howling waste there could still be men; but steel helmets now appear on all sides out of the trench, and fifty yards from us a machine-gun is already in position and barking.

The wire entanglements are torn to pieces. Yet they offer some obstacle. We see the storm-troops coming. Our artillery opens fire. Machine-guns rattle, rifles crack. The charge works its way across. Haie and Kropp begin with the hand-grenades. They throw as fast as they can, others pass them, the handles with the strings already pulled. Haie throws seventy-five yards, Kropp sixty, it has been measured, the distance is important. The enemy as they run cannot do much before they are within forty yards.

We recognize the smooth distorted faces, the helmets: they are French. They have already suffered heavily when they reach the remnants of the barbed wire entanglements. A whole line has gone down before our machine-guns; then we have a lot of stoppages and they come nearer.

I see one of them, his face upturned, fall into a wire cradle. His body collapses, his hands remain suspended as though he were praying. Then his body drops clean away and only his hands with the stumps of his arms, shot off, now hang in the wire.

The moment we are about to retreat three faces rise up from the ground in front of us. Under one of the helmets a dark pointed beard and two eyes that are fastened on me. I raise my hand, but I cannot throw into those strange eyes; for one mad moment the whole slaughter whirls like a circus round me, and these two eyes alone are motionless; then the head rises up, a hand, a movement, and my hand-grenade flies through the air and into him.

We make for the rear, pull wire cradles into the trench and leave bombs behind us with the strings pulled, which ensures us a fiery retreat. The machine-guns are already firing from the next position.

We have become wild beasts. We do not fight, we defend ourselves against annihilation. It is not against men that we fling our bombs, what do we know of men in this moment when Death is hunting us down — now, for the first time in three days we can see his face, now for the first time in three days we can oppose him; we feel a mad anger. No longer do we lie helpless, waiting on the scaffold, we can destroy and kill, to save ourselves, to save ourselves and to be revenged.

We crouch behind every corner, behind every barrier of barbed wire, and hurl heaps of explosives at the feet of the advancing enemy before we run. The blast of the hand-grenades impinges powerfully on our arms and legs; crouching like cats we run on, overwhelmed by this wave that bears us along, that fills us with ferocity, turns us into thugs, into murderers, into God only knows what devils; this wave that multiplies our strength with fear and madness and greed of life, seeking and fighting for noth-

ing but our deliverance. If your own father came over with them you would not hesitate to fling a bomb at him.

The forward trenches have been abandoned. Are they still trenches? They are blown to pieces, annihilated — there are only broken bits of trenches, holes linked by cracks, nests of craters, that is all. But the enemy's casualties increase. They did not count on so much resistance.

———

It is nearly noon. The sun blazes hotly, the sweat stings in our eyes, we wipe it off on our sleeves and often blood with it. At last we reach a trench that is in a somewhat better condition. It is manned and ready for the counter-attack, it receives us. Our guns open in full blast and cut off the enemy attack.

The lines behind us stop. They can advance no farther. The attack is crushed by our artillery. We watch. The fire lifts a hundred yards and we break forward. Beside me a lance-corporal has his head torn off. He runs a few steps more while the blood spouts from his neck like a fountain.

It does not come quite to hand-to-hand fighting; they are driven back. We arrive once again at our shattered trench and pass on beyond it. . . .

We have lost all feeling for one another. We can hardly control ourselves when our glance lights on the form of some other man. We are insensible, dead men, who through some trick, some dreadful magic, are still able to run and to kill.

A young Frenchman lags behind, he is overtaken, he puts up his hands, in one he still holds his revolver — does he mean to shoot or to give himself! — a blow from a spade cleaves through his face. A second sees it and tries to run farther; a bayonet jabs into his back. He leaps in the air, his arms thrown wide, his mouth wide open, yelling; he staggers, in his back the bayonet quivers. A third throws away his rifle, cowers down with his hands before his eyes. He is left behind with a few other prisoners to carry off the wounded.

Suddenly in the pursuit we reach the enemy line.

We are so close on the heels of our retreating enemies that we reach it almost at the same time as they. In this way we suffer few casualties. A machine-gun barks, but is silenced with a bomb. Nevertheless, the couple of seconds has sufficed to give us five stomach wounds. With the butt of his rifle Kat smashes to pulp the face of one of the unwounded machine-gunners. We bayonet the others before they have time to get out their bombs. Then thirstily we drink the water they have for cooling the gun.

Everywhere wire-cutters are snapping, planks are thrown across the entanglements, we jump through the narrow entrances into the trenches. Haie strikes his spade into the neck of a gigantic Frenchman and throws the first hand-grenade; we duck behind a breastwork for a few seconds, then the straight bit of trench ahead of us is empty. The next throw whizzes obliquely over the corner and clears a passage; as we run past we toss handfuls down into the dug-outs, the earth shudders, it crashes, smokes and groans, we stumble over slippery lumps of flesh, over yielding bodies; I fall into an open belly on which lies a clean, new officer's cap.

The fight ceases. We lose touch with the enemy. We cannot stay here long but must retire under cover of our artillery to our own position. No sooner do we know this than we dive into the nearest dug-outs, and with the utmost haste seize on whatever provisions we can see, especially the tins of corned beef and butter, before we clear out.

We get back pretty well. There is no further attack by the enemy. We lie for an hour panting and resting before anyone speaks. We are so completely played out that in spite of our great hunger we do not think of the provisions. Then gradually we become something like men again.

REVIEW QUESTIONS

1. How did the soldiers in the trenches react to artillery bombardment?
2. What ordeal did the attacking soldiers encounter as they neared the enemy trenches?
3. What were the feelings of the soldiers as they engaged the attackers?

▼▼▼

6 ▼ The War and British Women

At the outbreak of war, British suffragists set aside their political activism and responded to their country's wartime needs. To release men for military service, many women took jobs in offices, factories, and service industries. They drove ambulances, mail trucks, and buses; worked in munitions factories; read gas meters; and collected railway tickets. They worked as laboratory assistants, plumbers' helpers, and bank clerks. By performing effectively in jobs formerly reserved for men, women demonstrated that they had an essential role to play in Britain's economic life. By the end of the war, little opposition remained to granting women political rights, and in 1918 women over the age of thirty gained the vote. In 1928, Parliament lowered the voting age to twenty-one, the same as for men.

Naomi Loughnan
GENTEEL WOMEN IN THE FACTORIES

Naomi Loughnan was one of millions of women who replaced men in all branches of civilian life, in allied and enemy countries alike, during World War I. She was a young, upper-middle-class woman who lived with her family in London and had never had to work for her living. In her job in a munitions plant, she had to adjust to close association with women from the London slums, to hostel life, and to twelve-hour shifts doing heavy and sometimes dangerous work. The chief motivation for British women of her class was their desire to aid the war effort, not the opportunity to earn substantial wages.

We little thought when we first put on our overalls and caps and enlisted in the Munition Army how much more inspiring our life was to be than we had dared to hope. Though we munition workers sacrifice our ease we gain a life worth living. Our long days are filled with interest, and with the zest of doing work for our country in the grand cause of Freedom. As we handle the weapons of war we are learning great lessons of life. In the busy, noisy workshops we come face to face with every kind of class, and each one of these classes has something to learn from the others. Our muscles may be aching, and the brightness fading a little from our eyes, but our minds are expanding, our very souls are growing stronger. And excellent, too, is the discipline for our bodies, though we do not always recognize this. . . .

The day is long, the atmosphere is breathed and rebreathed, and the oil smells. Our hands are black with warm, thick oozings from the machines, which coat the work and, incidentally, the workers. We regard our horrible, begrimed members [limbs] with disgust and secret pride. . . .

. . . The genteel among us wear gloves. We vie with each other in finding the most up-to-date grease-removers, just as we used to vie about hats. Our hands are not alone in suffering from dirt. . . . [D]ust-clouds, filled with unwelcome life, find a resting-place in our lungs and noses.

The work is hard. It may be, perhaps, from sheer lifting and carrying and weighing, or merely because of those long dragging hours that keep us sitting on little stools in front of whirring, clattering machines that are all too easy to work. We wish sometimes they were not quite so "fool-proof," for monotony is painful. Or life may appear hard to us by reason of those same creeping hours spent on our feet, up and down, to and fro, and up and down again, hour after hour, until something altogether queer takes place in the muscles of our legs. But we go on. . . . It is amazing what we can do when there is no way of escape but desertion. . . .

. . . The first thing that strikes the newcomer, as the shop door opens, is the great wall of noise that seems to rise and confront one like a tangible substance. The crashing, tearing, rattling whirr of machinery is deafening. And yet, though this may seem almost impossible, the workers get so accustomed to it after a little time that they do not notice it until it stops. . . .

The twelve-hour shift at night, though taking greater toll of nerve and energy, has distinct charms of its own. . . . The first hours seem to go more quickly than the corresponding ones on day work, until at last two o'clock is reached. Then begins a hand-to-hand struggle with Morpheus [Greek god of dreams]. . . . A stern sense of duty, growing feebler as the moments pass, is our only weapon of defence, whereas the crafty god has a veritable armoury of leaden eyelids, weakening pulses, sleep-weighted heads, and slackening wills. He even leads the foremen away to their offices and softens the hearts of languid overlookers. Some of us succumb, but there are those among us who will not give in. An unbecoming greyness alters our faces, however young and fresh by day, a strange wilting process that steals all youth and beauty from us — until the morning. . . .

Engineering mankind is possessed of the unshakable opinion that no woman can have the mechanical sense. If one of us asks humbly why such and such an alteration is not made to prevent this or that drawback to a machine, she is told, with a superior smile, that a man has worked her machine before her for years, and that therefore if there were any improvement possible it would have been made. As long as we do exactly what we are told and do not attempt to use our brains, we give entire satisfaction, and are treated as nice, good children. Any swerving from the easy path prepared for us by our males arouses the most scathing contempt in their manly bosoms. The exceptions are as delightful to meet as they are rare. Women have, however, proved that their entry into the munition world has increased the output. Employers who forget things personal in their patriotic desire for large results are enthusiastic over the success of women in the shops. But their workmen have to be handled with the utmost tenderness and caution lest they should actually imagine it was being suggested that women could do their work equally well, given equal conditions of training — at least where muscle is not the driving force. This undercurrent of jealousy rises to the surface rather often, but as a general rule the men behave with much kindness, and are ready to help with muscle and advice whenever called upon. If eyes are very bright and hair inclined to curl, the muscle and advice do not even wait for a call.

The coming of the mixed classes of women into the factory is slowly but surely having an educative effect upon the men. "Language" is almost unconsciously becoming subdued. There are fiery exceptions who make our hair stand up on end under our close-fitting caps, but a sharp rebuke or a look of horror will often

[straighten out] the most truculent. He will at the moment, perhaps, sneer at the "blooming milksop fools of women," but he will be more careful next time. It is grievous to hear the girls also swearing and using disgusting language. Shoulder to shoulder with the children of the slums, the upper classes are having their eyes prised open at last to the awful conditions among which their sisters have dwelt. Foul language, immorality, and many other evils are but the natural outcome of overcrowding and bitter poverty. If some of us, still blind and ignorant of our responsibilities, shrink horrified and repelled from the rougher set, the compliment is returned with open derision and ribald laughter. There is something, too, about the prim prudery of the "genteel" that tickles the East-Ender's [a lower-class person] sharp wit. On the other hand, attempts at friendliness from the more understanding are treated with the utmost suspicion, though once that suspicion is overcome and friendship is established, it is unshakable. Our working hours are highly flavoured by our neighbours' treatment of ourselves and of each other. Laughter, anger, acute confusion, and laughter again, are constantly changing our immediate outlook on life. Sometimes disgust will overcome us, but we are learning with painful clarity that the fault is not theirs whose actions disgust us, but must be placed to the discredit of those other classes who have allowed the continued existence of conditions which generate the things from which we shrink appalled. . . .

Whatever sacrifice we make of wearied bodies, brains dulled by interminable night-shifts, of roughened hands, and faces robbed of their soft curves, it is, after all, so small a thing. We live in safety, we have shelter, and food whenever necessary, and we are even earning quite a lot of money. What is ours beside the great sacrifice? Men in their prime, on the verge of ambition realized, surrounded by the benefits won by their earlier struggles, are offering up their very lives. And those boys with Life, all glorious and untried, spread before them at their feet, are turning a smiling face to Death.

REVIEW QUESTIONS

1. How was Naomi Loughnan's life transformed by her job as a munitions worker?
2. What insights into gender and class distinctions at the time of World War I does she provide?

▼▼▼

7 ▼ The Paris Peace Conference

The most terrible war the world had experienced ended in November 1918; in January 1919, representatives of the victorious powers assembled in Paris to draw up a peace settlement. The principal figures at the Paris Peace Conference were Woodrow Wilson (1856–1924), president of the United States; David Lloyd George (1863–1945), prime minister of Great Britain; Georges Clemenceau (1841–1929), premier of France; and Vittorio Orlando (1860–1952), premier of Italy. Disillusioned intellectuals and the war-weary masses turned to Wilson as the prince of peace who would fashion a new and better world.

Woodrow Wilson
THE IDEALISTIC VIEW

Wilson sought a peace of justice and reconciliation, one based on democratic and Christian ideals, as the following excerpts from his speeches illustrate.

(May 26, 1917)

We are fighting for the liberty, the self-government, and the undictated development of all peoples, and every feature of the settlement that concludes this war must be conceived and executed for that purpose. Wrongs must first be righted and then adequate safeguards must be created to prevent their being committed again. . . .

. . . No people must be forced under sovereignty under which it does not wish to live. No territory must change hands except for the purpose of securing those who inhabit it a fair chance of life and liberty. No indemnities must be insisted on except those that constitute payment for manifest wrongs done. No readjustments of power must be made except such as will tend to secure the future peace of the world and the future welfare and happiness of its peoples.

And then the free peoples of the world must draw together in some common covenant, some genuine and practical co-öperation that will in effect combine their force to secure peace and justice in the dealings of nations with one another.

▷ The following are excerpts from Wilson's Fourteen Points of January 18, 1918.

IV. Adequate guarantees given and taken that national armaments will be reduced to the lowest point consistent with domestic safety.

V. A free, open-minded, and absolutely impartial adjustment of all colonial claims, based upon a strict observance of the principle that in determining all such questions of sovereignty the interests of the populations concerned must have equal weight with the equitable claims of the government whose title is to be determined. . . .

VIII. All French territory should be freed and the invaded portions restored, and the wrong done to France by Prussia in 1871 in the matter of Alsace-Lorraine, which has unsettled the peace of the world for nearly fifty years, should be righted, in order that peace may once more be made secure in the interest of all.

IX. A readjustment of the frontiers of Italy should be effected along clearly recognizable lines of nationality.

X. The peoples of Austria-Hungary, whose place among the nations we wish to see safeguarded and assured, should be accorded the freest opportunity of autonomous development. . . .

XII. The Turkish portions of the present Ottoman Empire should be assured a secure sovereignty, but the other nationalities which are now under Turkish rule should be assured an undoubted security of life and an absolutely unmolested opportunity of autonomous development, and the Dardanelles should be permanently opened as a free passage to the ships and commerce of all nations under international guarantees.

XIII. An independent Polish state should be erected which should include the territories inhabited by indisputably Polish populations, which should be assured a free and secure access to the sea, and whose political and economic independence and territorial integrity should be guaranteed by international covenant.

XIV. A general association of nations must be formed under specific covenants for the purpose of affording mutual guarantees of political independence and territorial integrity to great and small states alike.

(February 11, 1918)

. . . The principles to be applied [in the peace settlement] are these:

First, that each part of the final settlement must be based upon the essential justice of that particular case and upon such adjustments as are most likely to bring a peace that will be permanent;

Second, that peoples and provinces are not to be bartered about from sovereignty to sovereignty as if they were mere chattels and pawns in a game, even the great game, now forever discredited, of the balance of power; but that

Third, every territorial settlement involved in this war must be made in the interest and for the benefit of the populations concerned, and not as a part of any mere adjustment or compromise of claims amongst rival states; and

Fourth, that all well-defined national aspiration shall be accorded the utmost satisfaction that can be accorded them without introducing new or perpetuating old elements of discord and antagonism that would be likely in time to break the peace of Europe and consequently of the world.

(April 6, 1918)

. . . We are ready, whenever the final reckoning is made, to be just to the German people, deal fairly with the German power, as with all others. There can be no difference between peoples in the final judgment, if it is indeed to be a righteous judgment. To propose anything but justice, even-handed and dispassionate justice, to Germany at any time, whatever the outcome of the war, would be to renounce and dishonor our own cause. For we ask nothing that we are not willing to accord.

(December 16, 1918)

. . . The war through which we have just passed has illustrated in a way which never can be forgotten the extraordinary wrongs which can be perpetrated by arbitrary and irresponsible power.

It is not possible to secure the happiness and prosperity of the world, to establish an enduring peace, unless the repetition of such wrongs is rendered impossible. This has indeed been a people's war. It has been waged against absolutism and militarism, and these enemies of liberty must from this time forth be shut out from the possibility of working their cruel will upon mankind.

(January 3, 1919)

. . . Our task at Paris is to organize the friendship of the world, to see to it that all the moral forces that make for right and justice and liberty are united and are given a vital organization to which the peoples of the world will readily and gladly respond. In other words, our task is no less colossal than this, to set up a new international psychology, to have a new atmosphere.

(January 25, 1919)

. . . We are . . . here to see that every people in the world shall choose its own masters and govern its own destinies, not as we wish, but as it wishes. We are here to see, in short, that the very foundations of this war are swept away. Those foundations were the private choice of small coteries of civil rulers and military staffs. Those foundations were the aggression of great powers upon the small. Those foundations were the holding together of empires of unwilling subjects by the duress of arms. Those foundations were the power of small bodies of men to work their will upon mankind and use them as pawns in a game. And nothing less than the emancipation of the world from these things will accomplish peace.

Georges Clemenceau
FRENCH DEMANDS FOR SECURITY AND REVENGE

Wilson's promised new world clashed with French demands for security and revenge. Almost all the fighting on the war's western front had taken place in France; its industries and farmlands lay in ruins, and many of its young men had perished. France had been invaded by Germany in 1870 as well as in 1914, so the French believed that only by crippling Germany could they gain security. Premier Clemenceau, who was called "the Tiger," dismisssed Wilson's vision of a new world as mere noble sentiment divorced from reality, and he fought tenaciously to gain security for France. Clemenceau's profound hatred and mistrust of Germany are revealed in his book *Grandeur and Misery of Victory* (1930), written a decade after the Paris Peace Conference.

For the catastrophe of 1914 the Germans are responsible. Only a professional liar would deny this. . . .

What after all is this war, prepared, undertaken, and waged by the German people, who flung aside every scruple of conscience to let it loose, hoping for a peace of enslavement under the yoke of a militarism destructive of all human dignity? It is simply the continuance, the recrudescence, of those never-ending acts of violence by which the first savage tribes carried

out their depredations with all the resources of barbarism. The means improve with the ages. The ends remain the same. . . .

Germany, in this matter, was unfortunate enough to allow herself (in spite of her skill at dissimulation) to be betrayed into an excess of candour by her characteristic tendency to go to extremes. *Deutschland über alles. Germany above everything!* That, and nothing less, is what she asks, and when once her demand is satisfied she will let you enjoy a peace under the yoke. Not only does she make no secret of her aim, but the intolerable arrogance of the German aristocracy, the servile good nature of the intellectual and the scholar, the gross vanity of the most competent leaders in industry, and the widespread influence of a violent popular poetry conspire to shatter throughout the world all the time-honoured traditions of individual, as well as international, dignity. . . .

On November 11, 1918, the fighting ceased.

It is not I who will dispute the German soldier's qualities of endurance. But he had been promised a *fresh and frolicsome war,* and for four years he had been pinned down between the anvil and the hammer. . . . Our defeat would have resulted in a relapse of human civilization into violence and bloodshed. . . .

Outrages against human civilization are in the long run defeated by their own excess, and thus I discern in the peculiar mentality of the German soldier, with his *"Deutschland über alles,"* the cause of the premature exhaustion that brought him to beg for an armistice before the French soldier, who was fighting for his independence. . . .

And what is this "Germanic civilization," this monstrous explosion of the will to power, which threatens openly to do away entirely with the diversities established by many evolutions, to set in their place the implacable mastery of a race whose lordly part would be to substitute itself, by force of arms, for all national developments? We need only read [General Friedrich von] Bernhardi's famous pamphlet *Our Future,* in which it is alleged that Germany sums up within herself, as the historian Treitschke asserts, the greatest manifestation of human supremacy, and finds herself condemned, by her very greatness, either to absorb all nations in herself or to return to nothingness. . . . Ought we not all to feel menaced in our very vitals by this mad doctrine of universal Germanic supremacy over England, France, America, and every other country? . . .

What document more suitable to reveal the direction of "German culture" than the famous manifesto of the ninety-three super-intellectuals of Germany,[1] issued to justify the bloodiest and the least excusable of military aggressions against the great centres of civilization? At the moment . . . violated Belgium lay beneath the heel of the malefactor (October 1914) . . . [and German troops were] razing . . . great historical buildings to the ground [and] burning down . . . libraries. It would need a whole book to tell of the infamous treatment inflicted upon noncombatants, to reckon up those who were shot down, or put to death, or deported, or condemned to forced labour. . . .

Well, this was the hour chosen by German intellectuals to make themselves heard. Let all the nations give ear! . . .

. . . Their learning made of them merely Germans better than all others qualified to formulate, on their own account, the extravagances of Germanic arrogance. The only difference is that they speak louder than the common people, those docile automatons. The fact is that they really believe themselves to be the representatives of a privileged *"culture"* that sets them above the errors of the human race, and confers on them the prerogative of a superior power. . . .

The whole document is nothing but denials without the support of a single proof. *"It is not true* that Germany wanted the War." [Kaiser] William II had for years been *"mocked at by his adversaries of today on account of his unshakable love of peace."* They neglect to tell us whence they got this lie. They forget that from 1871 till 1914 we received from Germany a series of war threats in the course of which Queen Victoria and also the Czar had to intervene with the *Kaiser* direct for the maintenance of peace.

I have already recalled how our German intellectuals account for the violation of the Belgian frontier:

---

[1]Shortly after the outbreak of war, ninety-three leading German scholars and scientists addressed a letter to the world, defending Germany's actions.

It is not true that we criminally violated Belgian neutrality. It can be proved that France and England had made up their minds to violate it. It can be proved that Belgium was willing. It would have been suicide not to forestall them. . . .

. . . And when a great chemist such as Ostwald tells us, with his colleagues, that our struggle *"against the so-called German militarism"* is really directed *"against German culture,"* we must remember that *this same savant published a history of chemistry* IN WHICH THE NAME OF [eighteenth-century French chemist Antoine] LAVOISIER WAS NOT MENTIONED.

The "intellectuals" take their place in public opinion as the most ardent propagandists of the thesis which makes Germany the very model of the *"chosen people."* The same Professor Ostwald had already written, *"Germany has reached a higher stage of civilization than the other peoples, and the result of the War will be an organization of Europe under German leadership."* Professor Haeckel had demanded *the conquest of London, the division of Belgium between Germany and Holland, the annexation of North-east France, of Poland, the Baltic Provinces, the Congo, and a great part of the English colonies.* Professor Lasson went further still:

We are morally and intellectually superior to all men. We are peerless. So too are our organizations and our institutions. *Germany is the most perfect creation known in history,* and the Imperial Chancellor, Herr von Bethmann-Hollweg, is *the most eminent of living men.*

Ordinary laymen who talked in this strain would be taken off to some safe asylum. Coming from duly hallmarked professors, such statements explain all German warfare by alleging that Germany's destiny is universal domination, and that for this very reason she is bound either to disappear altogether or to exercise violence on all nations with a view to their own betterment. . . .

May I further recall, since we have to emphasize the point, that on September 17, 1914, Erzberger, the well-known German statesman, an eminent member of the Catholic Party, wrote to the Minister of War, General von Falkenhayn, *"We must not worry about committing an offence against the rights of nations nor about violating the laws of humanity. Such feelings today are of secondary importance"*? A month later, on October 21, 1914, he wrote in *Der Tag, "If a way was found of entirely wiping out the whole of London it would be more humane to employ it* than to allow the blood of A SINGLE GERMAN SOLDIER to be shed on the battlefield!" . . .

. . . General von Bernhardi himself, the best pupil, as I have already said, of the historian Treitschke, whose ideas are law in Germany, has just preached the doctrine of "World power or Downfall" at us. So there is nothing left for other nations, as a way of salvation, but to be conquered by Germany. . . .

I have sometimes penetrated into the sacred cave of the Germanic cult, which is, as every one knows, the *Bierhaus* [beer hall]. A great aisle of massive humanity where there accumulate, amid the fumes of tobacco and beer, the popular rumblings of a nationalism upheld by the sonorous brasses blaring to the heavens the supreme voice of Germany, *"Deutschland über alles!"* Men, women, and children, all petrified in reverence before the divine stoneware pot, brows furrowed with irrepressible power, eyes lost in a dream of infinity, mouths twisted by the intensity of will-power, drink in long draughts the celestial hope of vague expectations. These only remain to be realized presently when the chief marked out by Destiny shall have given the word. There you have the ultimate framework of an old but childish race.

REVIEW QUESTIONS

1. What principles did Woodrow Wilson want to serve as the basis of the peace settlement?

2. What were Wilson's objectives for the peoples of Austria-Hungary? The Poles? Alsace and Lorraine?
3. According to Wilson, what were the principal reasons for the outbreak of war in 1914?
4. What accusations did Georges Clemenceau make against the German national character? What contrasts did he draw between the Germans and the French?
5. How did Clemenceau respond to the manifesto of the German intellectuals?
6. Why, more than a decade after the war, did Clemenceau believe that Germany should still be feared?

▼▼▼

8 ▼ German Denunciation of the Versailles Treaty

A debate raged over the Versailles Treaty, the peace settlement imposed on Germany by the Paris Peace Conference. The treaty's defenders argued that if Germany had won the war, it would have forced far more ruthless terms on France and other losing countries. These defenders pointed to the Treaty of Brest-Litovsk, which Germany compelled the new and weak revolutionary Russian government to sign in 1918, as an example of German peacemaking. Through this treaty, Germany seized 34 percent of Russia's population, 32 percent of its farmland, 54 percent of its industrial enterprise, and 89 percent of its coal mines.

The Germans denounced the Versailles Treaty, which they regarded both as a violation of Wilson's principles as enunciated in the Fourteen Points and other statements and as an Anglo-French plot to keep Germany economically and militarily weak. Leaders of the new German Weimar Republic, formed after a revolution had forced the emperor to abdicate, protested that in punishing and humiliating the new republic for the sins of the monarchy and the military, the peacemakers weakened the foundations of democracy in Germany, kept alive old hatreds, and planted the seeds of future conflicts. Enraged nationalists swore to erase this blot on German honor.

German Delegation to the Paris Peace Conference
A PEACE OF MIGHT

In the excerpts that follow, the German delegation to the Paris Peace Conference voiced its criticism of the Versailles Treaty.

The peace to be concluded with Germany was to be a peace of right, not a peace of might.

In his address to the Mexican journalists on the 9th of June, 1918, President Wilson promised to maintain the principle that the interests of the weakest and of the strongest should be equally sacred. . . . And in his speech before Congress on the 11th of February 1918, the President described the aim of peace as follows: "What we are striving for is a new international order based upon broad and universal principles of right and justice — no mere peace of shreds and patches." . . .

To begin with the territorial questions:

In the West, a purely German territory on the Saar with a population of at least 650,000 inhabitants is to be separated from the German Empire for at least fifteen years merely for the reason that claims are asserted to the coal abounding there.

The other cessions in the West, German-Austria and German-Bohemia will be mentioned in connection with the right of self-determination.

In Schleswig, the line of demarcation for voting has been traced through purely German districts and goes farther than Denmark herself wishes.

In the East, Upper Silesia is to be separated from Germany and given to Poland, although it has had no political connexion with Poland for the last 750 years. Contrary to this, the provinces of Posen and almost the whole of West Prussia are to be separated from the German Empire in consideration of the former extent of the old Polish state, although millions of Germans are living there. Again, the district of Memel is separated from Germany quite regardless of its historical past, in the obvious attempt to separate Germany from Russia for economic reasons. For the purpose of securing to Poland free access to the sea, East Prussia is to be completely cut off from the rest of the Empire and thereby condemned to economic and national decay. The purely German city of Danzig is to become a Free State under the suzerainty of Poland. Such terms are not founded on any principle of justice. Quite arbitrarily, here the idea of an imprescribable historical right, there the idea of ethnographical possession, there the standpoint of economic interest shall prevail, in every case the decision being unfavourable to Germany.

The settlement of the colonial question is equally contradictory to a peace of justice. For the essence of activity in colonial work does not consist in capitalistic exploitation of a less developed human race, but in raising backward peoples to a higher civilization. This gives the Powers which are advanced in culture a natural claim to take part in colonial work. Germany, whose colonial accomplishments cannot be denied, has also this natural claim, which is not recognized by a treaty of peace that deprives Germany of all of her colonies.

Not only the settlement of the territorial questions but each and every provision of the treaty of peace is governed by the ill-renowned phrase: "Might above Right!" — Here are a few illustrations: . . .

Although President Wilson . . . has acknowledged that "no single fact caused the war, but that in the last analysis the whole European system is in a deeper sense responsible for the war, with its combination of alliances and understandings, a complicated texture of intrigues and espionage that unfailingly caught the whole family of nations in its meshes," . . . Germany is to acknowledge that Germany and her allies are responsible for all damages which the enemy Governments or their subjects have incurred by her and her allies' aggression. . . . Apart from the consideration that there is no incontestable legal foundation for the obligation for reparation imposed upon Germany, the amount of such compensation is to be determined by a commission nominated solely by Germany's enemies, Germany taking no part in the findings of the commission. The commission is plainly to have power to administer Germany like the estate of a bankrupt. . . .

. . . Germany must promise to pay an indemnity, the amount of which at present is not even stated. . . .

These few instances show that that is not the just peace we were promised, not the peace "the very principle of which," according to a word of President Wilson, "is equality and the common participation in a common benefit. The equality of nations upon which peace must be founded if it is to last must be an equality of rights." . . .

In this war, a new fundamental law has arisen which the statesmen of all belligerent peoples have again and again acknowledged to be their aim: the right of self-determination. To make it possible for all nations to put this privilege into practice was intended to be one achievement of the war. . . . On February 11, 1918, President Wilson said in Congress: "Peoples and provinces are not to be bartered about from sovereignty to sovereignty as if they were mere chattels and pawns in a game." . . .

Neither the treatment described above of the inhabitants of the Saar region . . . of consulting the population in the districts of Eupen, Malmédy, and Prussian Moresnet — which, moreover, shall not take place before they have been put under Belgian sovereignty — comply in the least with such a solemn recognition of the right of self-determination.

The same is also true with regard to Alsace-Lorraine. If Germany has pledged herself "to right the wrong of 1871," this does not mean any renunciation of the right of self-determination of the inhabitants of Alsace-Lorraine. A cession of the country without consulting the population would be a new wrong, if for no other reason, because it would be inconsistent with a recognized principle of peace.

On the other hand, it is incompatible with the idea of national self-determination for two and one-half million Germans to be torn away from their native land against their own will. By the proposed demarcation of the boundary, unmistakably German territories are disposed of in favor of their Polish neighbours. Thus, from the Central Silesian districts of Guhrau and Militsch certain portions are to be wrenched away, in which, besides 44,900 Germans, reside at the utmost 3,700 Poles. The same may be said with reference to the towns of Schneidemühl and Bromberg of which the latter has, at the utmost, eighteen per cent. Polish inhabitants, whereas in the rural district of Bromberg the Poles do not form even forty per cent of the population. . . . This disrespect of the right of self-determination is shown most grossly in the fact that Danzig is to be separated from the German Empire and made a free state. Neither historical rights nor the present ethnographical conditions of ownership of the Polish people can have any weight as compared with the German past and the German character of that city. Free access to the sea, satisfying the economic wants of Poland, can be secured by guarantees founded on international law, by the creating of free ports. Likewise the cession of the commercial town of Memel, which is to be exacted from Germany, is in no way consistent with the right of self-determination. The same may be said with reference to the fact that millions of Germans in German-Austria are to be denied the union with Germany which they desire and that, further, millions of Germans dwelling along our frontiers are to be forced to remain part of the newly created Czecho-Slovakian State.

Philipp Scheidemann
THE DEBATE WITHIN GERMANY

The following reading is taken from the memoirs of Philipp Scheidemann (see page 267), prime minister of the Weimar Republic during the time of the debate over signing the Versailles Treaty.

On the afternoon of 12th May a meeting of the National Assembly took place in the new Aula [assembly hall] of the University. As Prime Minister, I spoke on behalf of the Government on the Versailles Treaty. A few extracts from the speech may be given here:

On strange premises in emergency quarters, the representatives of the nation have met together, like a last remnant of loyal men, at a time when the Fatherland is in the gravest danger. All are present except the Alsace-Lorrainers, from whom the right of being here represented has been taken away, as well as the right of exercising their privilege of self-determination as free men.

When I see lined up here the representatives of German stock and nationality, men chosen from the Rhineland, the Saar Basin, West and East Prussia, Posen, Silesia and Memel, side by side with Parliamentarians from [regions] that are not threatened and men from [regions] that are, who, if the will of our enemies becomes law, will now for the last time meet Germans as Germans, I am conscious of being one with you in spirit at this sad and solemn hour when we have only one command to obey: We must hold together. We must stick together. We are one flesh and one blood, and he who tries to separate us cuts with a murderous knife into the live flesh of the German people. To preserve the life of our people is our highest duty.

We are chasing no nationalistic phantoms; no question of prestige and no thirst of power have any part or lot in our deliberations. For country and people we must save life — a bare, poor life now, when everyone feels the throttling hand on his throat. Let me speak without mincing my words; what lies at the root of our deliberations is this thick book (pointing to the Peace Terms), in which hundreds of paragraphs begin with "Germany renounces — renounces — renounces" — this *malleus maleficarum* [hammer of evil-doing countries] by which the confession of our own unworthiness, the consent to our own merciless dismemberment, the agreement to our enslavement and bondage, are to be wrung and extorted from a great people — this book shall not be our law manual for the future!

Then followed comparisons of the dictated Peace with Wilson's fourteen points, and a description of the devastating effect of the Treaty for Germany in home and foreign policy. Then I continued:

I ask you: who can, as an honest man, I will not say as a German, but only as an honest, straightforward man, accept such terms? What hand would not wither that binds itself and us in these fetters? (Great applause.) And now I've said enough, more than enough. We have made counter proposals; we shall make others. We see, with your approval, that our sacred duty lies in negotiation. This Treaty, in the opinion of the Government, cannot be accepted. (Tumultuous cheering, lasting for minutes in the Hall and galleries. The meeting rises.)

PRESIDENT: I ask you to allow the speaker to continue his speech.

SCHEIDEMANN, THE PRIME MINISTER: This Treaty is so impossible that I cannot yet realize the world containing such a book without millions and trillions of throats in all lands and of all parties yelling out: "Away with this organized murder."

My speech ended with these words:

We have done with fighting; we want peace. We behold in horror from the example of our enemies what convulsions a policy of force and brutal militarism have caused. With a shudder we turn our heads away from these long years of murder.

Yes, we do. Woe to them who have conjured up the War. But threefold woe to them who postpone a real peace for a single day.

Vociferous cheers and clapping of hands followed. . . .

The Peace delegates returned from Versailles to Weimar on 17th June. . . . Count Brockdorff-Rantzau [head of the Foreign Office] reported to the Government on behalf of the delegates on 18th June. He asked for the rejection of the Treaty as being intolerable and impracticable. "There is no one in Germany who considers the Peace proposed to us can be carried out. In our eyes honesty is the best policy. This precept does not admit of our accepting impossible obligations." In the last sentence it says: "If our enemies intend using force against us, we can be sure that the peaceable course of the world will soon set up for us an impartial tribunal, before which we shall plead for our rights."

The pros and cons were debated from late at night till three o'clock in the morning. It was out of the question that one side would persuade the other. . . . Why continue this quibbling that could lead to nothing? I cried off this cruel game by . . . tendering my resignation. . . .

The new Cabinet, now consisting of members of the Centre [Catholic Center party] and the S.P.D. [Social Democratic party] made frantic efforts to get concessions here and there and also tried to amend certain reservations. Clemenceau brutally put a stop to this by saying: "You have only twenty-four hours to decide. The time allowed for discussion is past. Either — yes or no."

. . . The People's Representatives were flocking to the National Assembly. There they decided by 237 votes to 138 to sign the peace proposals. Five members abstained from voting. . . .

. . . Generals von Hindenburg and Groener frankly admitted, when asked by the Government, that no serious resistance could be offered. If such were not the case why had they asked for an armistice and peace? Hindenburg supplemented his opinion with the words that he, as a soldier, would prefer utter ruin to a disgraceful peace. This was the soldier's point of view, who was ready to give his own life, not the politician's point of view, who was responsible for the life of the entire people and had to try to keep them together. . . .

On the top of all these unheard-of difficulties came many others. The people were without clothing, underlinen, boots and shoes and — bread. The people must go on starving. "Sign! Then there'll be bread" — that was the hope of millions. Many hundreds of thousands racked with worry had their kith and kin in foreign prison camps. We were required to return our prisoners of war at once, but when would our fathers, brothers and sons who had been captured be released from bondage? No one knew, but all knew that they were badly treated, especially in France, and were badly fed.

REVIEW QUESTIONS

1. According to the German delegation, how did the Treaty of Versailles violate the principle of self-determination championed by Woodrow Wilson?
2. In addition to the loss of territory, what other features of the Treaty of Versailles angered the Germans?
3. Why, despite its hatred of the treaty, did the German government ratify it?

▼▼▼

9 ▼ The War and European Consciousness

World War I caused many intellectuals to have grave doubts about the Enlightenment tradition and the future of Western civilization. More than ever the belief in human goodness, reason, and the progress of humanity seemed an illusion. Despite its many accomplishments, intellectuals contended that Western civilization was flawed and might die.

Paul Valéry
DISILLUSIONMENT

Shortly after World War I, Paul Valéry (1871–1945), a prominent French writer, expressed the mood of disillusionment that gripped many intellectuals. The following reading was written in 1919; the second reading is from a 1922 speech. Both were published in *Variety*, a collection of some of Valéry's works.

We modern civilizations have learned to recognize that we are mortal like the others.

We had heard tell of whole worlds vanished, of empires foundered with all their men and all their engines, sunk to the inexplorable depths of the centuries with their gods and laws, their academies and their pure and applied sciences, their grammars, dictionaries, classics, romantics, symbolists, their critics and the critics of their critics. We knew that all the apparent earth is made of ashes, and that ashes have a meaning. We perceived, through the misty bulk of history, the phantoms of huge vessels once laden with riches and learning. We could not count them. But these wrecks, after all, were no concern of ours.

Elam, Nineveh, Babylon were vague and splendid names; the total ruin of these worlds, for us, meant as little as did their existence. But *France, England, Russia* . . . these names, too, are splendid. . . . And now we see that the abyss of history is deep enough to bury all the world. We feel that a civilization is fragile as a life. The circumstances which will send the works of [John] Keats [English poet] and the works of [Charles] Baudelaire [French poet] to join those of Menander[1] are not at all inconceivable; they are found in the daily papers.

▷   The following passage is from an address that Valéry delivered at the University of Zurich on November 15, 1922

The storm has died away, and still we are restless, uneasy, as if the storm were about to break. Almost all the affairs of men remain in a terrible uncertainty. We think of what has disappeared, we are almost destroyed by what has been destroyed; we do not know what will be born, and we fear the future, not without reason. We hope vaguely, we dread precisely; our fears are infinitely more precise than our hopes; we confess that the charm of life is behind us, abundance is behind us, but doubt and disorder are in us and with us. There is no thinking man, however shrewd or learned he may be, who can hope to dominate this anxiety, to escape from this impression of darkness, to measure the probable duration of this period when the vital relations of humanity are disturbed profoundly.

We are a very unfortunate generation, whose lot has been to see the moment of our passage through life coincide with the arrival of great and terrifying events, the echo of which will resound through all our lives.

One can say that all the fundamentals of the world have been affected by the war, or more exactly, by the circumstances of the war; something deeper has been worn away than the renewable parts of the machine. You know how greatly the general economic situation has been disturbed, and the polity of states, and the very life of the individual; you are familiar with the universal discomfort, hesitation, apprehension. *But among all these injured things is the Mind.* The Mind has indeed been cruelly wounded; its complaint is heard in the hearts of intellectual man; it passes a mournful judgment on itself. It doubts itself profoundly.

---

[1]Menander was an ancient Greek poet whose works were lost until fragments were found in Egypt at the end of the nineteenth century.

Erich Maria Remarque
THE LOST GENERATION

In Erich Maria Remarque's *All Quiet on the Western Front,* a wounded German soldier reflects on the war and his future. He sees himself as part of a lost generation. (See also page 268.)

Gradually a few of us are allowed to get up. And I am given crutches to hobble around on. But I do not make much use of them; I cannot bear Albert's gaze as I move about the room. His eyes always follow me with such a strange look. So I sometimes escape to the corridor; — there I can move about more freely.

On the next floor below are the abdominal and spine cases, head wounds and double amputations. On the right side of the wing are the jaw wounds, gas cases, nose, ear, and neck wounds. On the left the blind and the lung wounds, pelvis wounds, wounds in the joints, wounds in the kidneys, wounds in the testicles, wounds in the intestines. Here a man realizes for the first time in how many places a man can get hit.

Two fellows die of tetanus. Their skin turns pale, their limbs stiffen, at last only their eyes live — stubbornly. Many of the wounded have their shattered limbs hanging free in the air from a gallows; underneath the wound a basin is placed into which drips the pus. Every two or three hours the vessel is emptied. Other men lie in stretching bandages with heavy weights hanging from the end of the bed. I see intestine wounds that are constantly full of excreta. The surgeon's clerk shows me X-ray photographs of completely smashed hip-bones, knees, and shoulders.

A man cannot realize that above such shattered bodies there are still human faces in which life goes its daily round. And this is only one hospital, one single station; there are hundreds of thousands in Germany, hundreds of thousands in France, hundreds of thousands in Russia. How senseless is everything that can ever be written, done, or thought, when such things are possible. It must be all lies and of no account when the culture of a thousand years could not prevent this stream of blood being poured out, these torture-chambers in their hundreds of thousands. A hospital alone shows what war is.

I am young, I am twenty years old; yet I know nothing of life but despair, death, fear, and fatuous superficiality cast over an abyss of sorrow. I see how peoples are set against one another, and in silence, unknowingly, foolishly, obediently, innocently slay one another. I see that the keenest brains of the world invent weapons and words to make it yet more refined and enduring. And all men of my age, here and over there, throughout the whole world see these things; all my generation is experiencing these things with me. What would our fathers do if we suddenly stood up and came before them and proffered our account? What do they expect of us if a time ever comes when the war is over? Through the years our business has been killing; — it was our first calling in life. Our knowledge of life is limited to death. What will happen afterwards? And what shall come out of us?

Ernst von Salomon
BRUTALIZATION OF THE INDIVIDUAL

The war also produced a fascination for violence that persisted after peace had been declared. Many returned veterans, their whole being enveloped by the war, continued to yearn for the excitement of battle and the fellowship of the trenches. Brutalized by the war, these men became ideal recruits for fascist parties that relished violence and sought the destruction of the liberal state.

Immediately after the war ended, thousands of soldiers and adventurers joined the Free Corps — volunteer brigades that defended Germany's eastern borders against encroachments by the new states of Poland, Latvia, and Estonia, and fought communist revolutionaries. Many of these freebooters later became members of Hitler's movement. Ernst von Salomon, a leading spokesman of the Free Corps movement, was a sixteen-year-old student in Berlin when the defeated German army marched home. In the passage that follows, he described the soldiers who "will always carry the trenches in their blood."

The soldiers walked quickly, pressed closely to each other. Suddenly the first four came into sight, looking lifeless. They had stony, rigid faces. . . .

Then came the others. Their eyes lay deep in dark, gray, sharp-edged hollows under the shadow of their helmets. They looked neither right nor left, but straight ahead, as if under the power of a terrifying target in front of them; as if they peered from a mud hole or a trench over torn-up earth. In front of them lay emptiness. They spoke not a word. . . .

O God, how these men looked, as they came nearer — those utterly exhausted, immobile faces under their steel helmets, those bony limbs, those ragged dusty uniforms! And around them an infinite void. It was as if they had drawn a magic circle around themselves, in which dangerous forces, invisible to outsiders, worked their secret spell. Did they still carry in their minds the madness of a thousand battles compressed into whirling visions, as they carried in their uniforms the dirt and the dust of shell-torn fields? The sight was unbearable. They marched like envoys of death, of dread, of the most deadly and solitary coldness. And here was their homeland, warmth, and happiness.

Why were they so silent? Whey did they not smile?

. . . When I saw these deadly determined faces, these faces as hard as if hacked out of wood, these eyes that glanced past the onlookers, unresponsive, hostile — yes, hostile indeed — then I knew — it suddenly came over me in a fright — that everything had been utterly different from what we had thought, all of us who stood here watching. . . . What did we know about these men? About the war in the trenches? About our soldiers? Oh God, it was terrible: What we had been told was all untrue. We had been told lies. These were not our beloved heroes, the protectors of our homes — these were men who did not belong to us, gathered here to meet them. They did not want to belong to us; they came from other worlds with other laws and other friendships. And all of a sudden everything that I had hoped and wished for, that had inspired me, turned shallow and empty. . . . What an abysmal error it had been to believe for four years that these men belonged to us. Now that misunderstanding vanished. . . .

Then I suddenly understood. These were not workers, peasants, students; no, these were not mechanics, white-collar employees, business-men, officials — these were soldiers. . . . These were men who had responded to the secret call of blood, of spirit, volunteers one way or the other, men who had experienced exacting comradeship and the things behind things — who had found a home in war, a fatherland, a community, and a nation. . . .

The homeland belonged to them; the nation belonged to them. What we had blabbered like marketwomen, they had actually lived. . . . The trenches were their home, their fatherland, their nation. And they had never used these words; they never believed in them; they believed in themselves. The war held them in its grip and dominated them; the war will never discharge them; they will never return home; they will always carry the trenches in their blood, the closeness of death, the dread, the intoxication, the iron. And suddenly they were to become peaceful citizens, set again in solid every-day routines? Never! That would mean a counterfeit that was bound to fail. The war is over; the warriors are still marching, . . . dissatisfied when they are demobilized, explosive when they stay together. The war had not given them answers; it had achieved no decision. The soldiers continue to march. . . .

Appeals were posted on the street corners for volunteer units to defend Germany's eastern borders. The day after the troops marched into our town, I volunteered. I was accepted and outfitted. Now I too was a soldier.

Sigmund Freud
A LEGACY OF EMBITTERMENT

In his 1915 essay, "Thoughts for the Times on War and Death," Sigmund Freud (see page 243) said that World War I's fury would shatter the bonds of a common European civilization and engulf Europeans in hatred for years to come.

We cannot but feel that no event [World War I] has ever destroyed so much that is precious in the common possessions of humanity, confused so many of the clearest intelligences, or so thoroughly debased what is highest. Science herself has lost her passionless impartiality; her deeply embittered servants seek for weapons from her with which to contribute towards the struggle with the enemy. Anthropologists feel driven to declare him [the enemy] inferior and degenerate, psychiatrists issue a diagnosis of his disease of mind or spirit. . . .

We had expected the great world-dominating nations of white race upon whom the leadership of the human species has fallen, who were known to have world-wide interests as their concern, to whose creative powers were due not only our technical advances towards the control of nature but the artistic and scientific standards of civilization — we had expected these peoples to succeed in discovering another way of settling misunderstandings and conflicts of interest. Within each of these nations high norms of moral conduct were laid down for the individual, to which his manner of life was bound to conform if he desired to take part in a civilized community. . . .

Relying on this unity among the civilized peoples, countless men and women have exchanged their native home for a foreign one, and made their existence dependent on the intercommunications between friendly nations. Moreover anyone who was not by stress of circumstance confined to one spot could create for himself out of all the advantages and attractions of these civilized countries a new and wider fatherland, in which he could move about without hindrance or suspicion. In this way he enjoyed the blue sea and the grey; the beauty of snow-covered mountains and of green meadow lands; the magic of northern forests and the splendour of southern vegetation; the mood evoked by landscapes that recall great historical events, and the silence of untouched nature. This new fatherland was a museum for him, too, filled with all the treasures which the artists of civilized humanity had in the successive centuries created and left behind. As he wandered from one gallery to another in this museum, he could recognize with impartial appreciation what varied types of perfection a mixture of blood, the course of history, and the special quality of their mother-earth had produced among his compatriots in this wider sense. Here he would find cool, inflexible energy developed to the highest point; there, the graceful art of beautifying existence; elsewhere the feeling for orderliness and law, or others among the qualities which have made mankind the lords of the earth.

Nor must we forget that each of these citizens of the civilized world had created for himself a "Parnassus" and a "School of Athens" [that is, a center of high culture and learning] of his own. From among the great thinkers, writers and artists of all nations he had chosen those to whom he considered he owed the best of what he had been able to achieve in enjoyment and understanding of life, and he had venerated them along with the immortal ancients as well as with the familiar masters of his own tongue. None of these great men had seemed to him foreign because they spoke another language — neither the incomparable explorer of human passions, nor the intoxicated worshipper of beauty, nor the powerful and menacing prophet, nor the subtle satirist; and he never reproached himself on that account for being a renegade towards his own nation and his beloved mother-tongue.

The enjoyment of this common civilization was disturbed from time to time by warning voices, which declared that old traditional differences made wars inevitable, even among the members of a community such as this. We re-fused to believe it; but if such a war were to happen, how did we picture it? . . . [W]e pictured it as a chivalrous passage of arms, which would limit itself to establishing the superiority of one side in the struggle, while as far as possible avoiding acute suffering that could contribute nothing to the decision, and granting complete immunity for the wounded who had to withdraw from the contest, as well as for the doctors and nurses who devoted themselves to their recovery. There would, of course, be the utmost consideration for the non-combatant classes of the population — for women who take no part in war-work, and for the children who, when they are grown up, should become on both sides one another's friends and helpers. And again, all the international undertakings and institutions in which the common civilization of peace-time had been embodied would be maintained.

Even a war like this would have produced enough horror and suffering; but it would not have interrupted the development of ethical relations between the collective individuals of mankind — the peoples and states.

Then the war in which we had refused to believe broke out, and it brought — disillusionment. Not only is it more bloody and more destructive than any war of other days, because of the enormously increased perfection of weapons of attack and defence; it is at least as cruel, as embittered, as implacable as any that has preceded it. It disregards all the restrictions known as International Law, which in peace-time the states had bound themselves to observe; it ignores the prerogatives of the wounded and the medical service, the distinction between civil and military sections of the population, the claims of private property. It tramples in blind fury on all that comes in its way, as though there were to be no future and no peace among men after it is over. It cuts all the common bonds between the contending peoples, and threatens to leave a legacy of embitterment that will make any renewal of those bonds impossible for a long time to come.

REVIEW QUESTIONS

1. What did Paul Valéry mean in saying that the mind of Europe doubted itself profoundly?
2. Why do you think many veterans felt that they were part of a lost generation?
3. What reasons can you think of why many Germans were attracted to paramilitary organizations immediately after the war?
4. How did Sigmund Freud describe the prevailing mood in Europe just prior to the war? How did the war alter this mood and create a "legacy of embitterment"?

The Russian Revolution and the Soviet Union

On the eve of World War I the Russian Empire faced a profound crisis. Ever-closer contact with the West, industrialization, and socioeconomic mobility resulting from a new railroad network were undermining the traditional foundations of state and society. Peasant unrest was mounting; the new factories had spawned a rebellious working class. The tsar had never trusted the country's intellectuals — too many of them had turned into revolutionaries. Defeat in the war with Japan had led to the revolution of 1905, nearly toppling the tsarist regime. Less than a decade later, as worldwide war approached, conservatives recognized and dreaded the prospect of military collapse followed by revolutionary anarchy. Liberals, less realistically, hoped for a constitutional regime that would let backward Russia catch up to the West. Radicals of utopian vision, like V. I. Lenin, expected the Russian workers to become the vanguard of a revolutionary advance that would bring freedom and justice to oppressed peoples all over the world.

Toward the end of World War I, the conservatives' fears came true. Nicholas II was overthrown in the March revolution of 1917; in the ensuing civic disorganization, the Russian state faced dissolution. The Germans were ready to partition the country. The liberal coalition that had formed a provisional government after the abdication of Nicholas II broke apart in early November. At that point, Lenin's Bolsheviks seized power, supported by the workers and soldiers in the country's capital of Petrograd (formerly St. Petersburg and after 1924 called Leningrad). In the civil war that followed, the Bolsheviks proved to be the only force capable of holding together a country faced with defeat, revolution, civil war, foreign intervention, and economic ruin. The government became a socialist dictatorship with Lenin at its head. Soviet Russia was guided by Marxist ideology adapted by Lenin to Russian conditions, and it was run by the professional revolutionaries of the Communist party in the name of elected councils (called Soviets) of workers and peasants. To counter the prevailing anarchy, Lenin preached discipline, the discipline of responsible social cooperation, which in Western countries had become, to a large extent, part of civic routine. Lenin believed that among the raw and

VLADIMIR LENIN in Theater Square, Leningrad, addresses troops during the Russian Revolution. Leon Trotsky can be seen to the right of the platform. (© Archive/Photo Researchers, Inc.)

violence-prone peoples of Russia discipline had to be enforced by compulsion and even terror. The counterrevolution that threatened the very existence of the Communist regime was for Lenin a pressing reason for employing terror. By the end of the civil war, even the workers and soldiers of Petrograd protested against the Communist dictatorship, and the garrison at the nearby Kronstadt naval base rose in revolt in 1921.

The years after the Kronstadt uprising were relatively calm. Russia regained its prewar standards of productivity, but it did not overcome the weaknesses that had led to catastrophe in World War I. To guard Soviet Russia against a similar fate was the burning ambition of Joseph Stalin, who in 1929, after a prolonged struggle, took over the leadership role left vacant when Lenin died in 1924. The product of violence and revolutionary agitation since youth, Stalin started a second revolution far more brutal than Lenin's.

Rapid industrialization under successive Five-Year Plans led to appalling confusion, waste, and hardship, yet also to an impressive increase in production. The forcible collectivization of agriculture, designed to crush the spirit of ever-rebellious peasants and to bring agricultural production under the planned economy, proved a savage process. All along, Stalin's revolution was accompanied by well-orchestrated methods of disciplining the country's heterogeneous, stubborn, and willful peoples into docile citizens ready for the sacrifices of overly rapid industrialization and driven by patriotic dedication. The second revolution created a sense of citizenship among the peoples of Russia that was unique in the country's history.

Stalin burned to achieve the age-old Russian dream of overcoming the country's backwardness and matching the advanced Western countries in world power and prestige. His program was a desperate effort to create deliberately by compulsion and in the shortest time possible a modern Russian state that would hold its own in a ruthlessly competitive, modern world. With harsh and cruel methods, so repulsive to Western values, Stalin transformed the Soviet Union into an industrial and world power, respected and feared for the next half century.

▼▼▼

I ▾ Theory and Practice of Bolshevism

As events in 1917 proved, Russian liberals were not capable of ruling the country in times of supreme crisis. The question then became what political system and ideology could overcome anarchy. Could the rebellious peasants and work-ers — the working class — mount a successful revolution and build a Russian government more effective than that of the tsars? That question had long agi-tated Russian revolutionary leaders, and the answer would determine not only the fate of the revolution but also the survival of Russia as an independent state.

V. I. Lenin
≪ WHAT IS TO BE DONE? ≫

Lenin (Vladimir Ilyich Ulyanov, 1870–1924) believed that on its own, the work-ing class could never achieve a successful revolution; workers without leader-ship could not rise above petty trade unionism. Throughout his career, Lenin contrasted ignorant working-class "spontaneity" with revolutionary "conscious-ness," meaning deliberate action guided by the proper comprehension of the conditions under which revolutionaries must work. Under his leadership, the guiding ideology of the Soviet Union became Marxism-Leninism, that is, Marxist theory as applied by Lenin to the special conditions of Russia.

A seminal document of Marxism-Leninism was Lenin's pamphlet *What Is to Be Done?* published in 1902, fifteen years before the tsar's overthrow. In this tract Lenin addressed the big questions facing Russian Marxists (who called themselves Social Democrats after the German Social Democratic party that served as their model). How could they effectively channel the mounting dis-content in Russian society and especially in the new industrial working class? How could they prevail against the secret police in the tsarist police state (re-ferred to by Lenin as autocracy)? How could they find Russia's way among the complexities of the modern world and master them? The answers Lenin offered to these difficult questions — found in the following passages — helped shape the Soviet regime.

Without revolutionary theory there can be no revolutionary movement. This idea cannot be insisted upon too strongly. . . . Yet, for Rus-sian Social-Democrats the importance of theory is enhanced by three other circumstances, which are often forgotten: first, by the fact that our Party is only in process of formation, its features are only just becoming defined, and it has as yet far from settled accounts with the other trends of revolutionary thought that threaten to divert the movement from the cor-rect path. . . .

Secondly, the Social-Democratic movement is in its very essence an international move-ment. This means, not only that we must com-bat national chauvinism, but that an incipient movement in a young country can be successful only if it makes use of the experiences of other countries. In order to make use of these expe-riences it is not enough merely to be acquainted with them, or simply to copy out the latest res-olutions. What is required is the ability to treat these experiences critically and to test them in-dependently. He who realises how enormously the modern working-class movement has grown and branched out will understand what a re-serve of theoretical forces and political (as well as revolutionary) experience is required to carry out this task.

[T]he national tasks of Russian Social-Democracy are such as have never confronted any other socialist party in the world. We shall have occasion further on to deal with the polit-ical and organisational duties which the task of emancipating the whole people from the yoke of autocracy imposes upon us. At this point, we wish to state only that the *role of vanguard fighter can be fulfilled only by a party that is guided by the most advanced theory.* . . .

We have said that there *could not have been* Social-Democratic consciousness among the workers. It would have to be brought to them from without. The history of all countries shows that the working class, exclusively by its own effort, is able to develop only trade-union consciousness, i.e. the conviction that it is necessary to combine in unions, fight the employers, and strive to compel the government to pass necessary labour legislation, etc. The theory of socialism, however, grew out of the philosophic, historical, and economic theories elaborated by educated representatives of the propertied classes, by intellectuals. By their social status, the founders of modern scientific socialism, Marx and Engels, themselves belonged to the bourgeois intelligentsia. In the very same way, in Russia, the theoretical doctrine of Social-Democracy arose altogether independently of the spontaneous growth of the working-class movement; it arose as a natural and inevitable outcome of the development of thought among the revolutionary socialist intelligentsia. . . .

▷ Given the ignorance of the working class, said Lenin, revolutionary leadership had to come from a close-knit vanguard of dedicated and disciplined professional revolutionaries as well trained as the tsarist police and always in close touch with the masses. The revolutionary leaders had to raise working-class awareness to a comprehensive understanding of the coming crisis in Russia and the capitalist world generally.

. . . I assert: (1) that no revolutionary movement can endure without a stable organisation of leaders maintaining continuity; (2) that the broader the popular mass drawn spontaneously into the struggle, which forms the basis of the movement and participates in it, the more urgent the need for such an organisation, and the

more solid this organisation must be (for it is much easier for all sorts of demagogues to sidetrack the more backward sections of the masses); (3) that such an organisation must consist chiefly of people professionally engaged in revolutionary activity; (4) that in an autocratic state, the more we *confine* the membership of such an organisation to people who are professionally engaged in revolutionary activity and who have been professionally trained in the art of combating the political police, the more difficult will it be to unearth the organisation; and (5) the *greater* will be the number of people from the working class and from the other social classes who will be able to join the movement and perform active work in it. . . .

. . . Social-Democracy leads the struggle of the working class, not only for better terms for the sale of labour-power, but for the abolition of the social system that compels the propertyless to sell themselves to the rich. Social-Democracy represents the working class, not in its relation to a given group of employers alone, but in its relation to all classes of modern society and to the state as an organised political force. Hence, it follows that not only must Social-Democrats not confine themselves exclusively to the economic struggle, but that they must not allow [investigating mismanagement of the economy] to become the predominant part of their activities. We must take up actively the political education of the working class and the development of its political consciousness.

▷ Lenin did not think there was a danger that the secret, tightly centralized revolutionary organization would establish a dictatorship over the proletariat. He trusted that close comradeship and a sense of responsibility would lead to a superior revolutionary "democratism." He looked to the Russian revolutionaries as the vanguard of the international revolutionary movement.

. . . We can never give a mass organisation that degree of secrecy without which there can be no question of persistent and continuous struggle against the government. To concentrate all secret functions in the hands of as small a number of professional revolutionaries as possible does not mean that the latter will "do the thinking for all" and that the rank and file will not take an active part in the *movement*. On the contrary, the membership will promote increasing numbers of the professional revolutionaries from its ranks; for it will know that it is not enough for a few students and for a few working men waging the economic struggle to gather in order to form a "committee," but that it takes years to train oneself to be a professional revolutionary. . . . Centralisation of the most secret functions in an organisation of revolutionaries will not diminish, but rather increase the extent and enhance the quality of the activity of a large number of other organisations, that are intended for a broad public and are therefore as loose and as non-secret as possible, such as workers' trade unions; workers' self-education circles and circles for reading illegal literature; and socialist, as well as democratic, circles among *all* other sections of the population; etc., etc. We must have such circles, trade unions, and organisations everywhere in *as large a number as possible* and with the widest variety of functions. . . .

. . . The only serious organisational principle for the active workers of our movement should be the strictest secrecy, the strictest selection of members, and the training of professional revolutionaries. Given these qualities, something even more than "democratism" would be guaranteed to us, namely, complete, comradely, mutual confidence among revolutionaries. . . . They have a lively sense of their *responsibility,* knowing as they do from experience that an organisation of real revolutionaries will stop at nothing to rid itself of an unworthy member. . . .

. . . Our worst sin with regard to organisation consists in the fact that *by our primitiveness we have lowered the prestige of revolutionaries in Russia.* A person who is flabby and shaky on questions of theory, who has a narrow outlook, who pleads the spontaneity of the masses as an excuse for his own sluggishness, who resembles a trade-union secretary more than a spokesman of the people, who is unable to conceive of a broad and bold plan that would command the respect even of opponents, and who is inexperienced and clumsy in his own professional art — the art of combating the political police — such a man is not a revolutionary, but a wretched amateur!

REVIEW QUESTIONS

1. How did V. I. Lenin think revolutionary theory that originated outside the working class could be in the interest of the working class?
2. According to Lenin, why did the revolutionary movement in Russia call for an elite of professional revolutionaries?
3. What did Lenin say were the qualities of the revolutionary elite?
4. How democratic was the organization of the revolutionary elite as described by Lenin?
5. Do you see an element of Russian nationalism in the special role Lenin assigned to the Russian workers?

2 ▾ The Bolshevik Revolution

In March 1917, in the middle of World War I, Russians were demoralized. The army, poorly trained, inadequately equipped, and incompetently led, had suffered staggering losses; everywhere soldiers were deserting. Food shortages and low wages drove workers to desperation; the loss of fathers and sons at the front embittered peasants. Discontent was keenest in Petrograd, where on March 9, 200,000 striking workers shouting "Down with autocracy!" packed the streets. After some bloodshed, government troops refused to fire on the workers. Faced with a broad and debilitating crisis — violence and anarchy in the capital, breakdown of transport, uncertain food and fuel supplies, and general disorder — Tsar Nicholas II was forced to turn over authority to a provisional government, thereby ending three centuries of tsarist rule under the Romanov dynasty.

The Provisional Government, after July 1917 guided by Aleksandr Kerensky (1881–1970), sought to transform Russia into a Western-style liberal state, but the government failed to comprehend the urgency with which the Russian peasants wanted the landlords' land, and soldiers and the masses wanted peace. Resentment spiraled. Kerensky's increasing unpopularity and the magnitude of popular unrest seemed to Lenin, then in hiding, to offer the long-expected opportunity for the Bolsheviks to seize power.

N. N. Sukhanov
TROTSKY AROUSES THE PEOPLE

Playing a crucial role in the Bolshevik seizure of power on November 7, 1917, was Leon Trotsky (1879–1940). Born Lev Davidovich Bronstein, the son of a prosperous Jewish farmer in the Ukraine, Trotsky was attracted early into the ranks of the revolutionaries, and he shared their fate. Exiled to Siberia in 1902, he escaped to Switzerland with a faked passport in the name of Leon Trotsky. Back in Russia for the Revolution of 1905, he was again exiled and again escaped. After a period abroad, he returned to Russia after the overthrow of the tsar in March 1917 and soon assumed a leading role among the Bolsheviks. In September 1917, as the moderate regime of Kerensky began to totter, Trotsky was elected chairman of the Petrograd soviet; soon afterward he masterminded the Military-Revolutionary Committee, the Bolshevik strike force.

On the evening of November 4, Trotsky delivered a rousing speech at the Peoples' House, a popular theater much used for working-class meetings. His speech is described by an eyewitness, the Menshevik (a Social Democratic moderate) leader N. N. Sukhanov, in his 1917 book, *The Russian Revolution*.

The mood of the people, more than 3,000, who filled the hall was definitely tense; they were all silently waiting for something. The audience was of course primarily workers and soldiers, but more than a few typically lower-middle-class men's and women's figures were visible.

Trotsky's ovation seemed to be cut short prematurely, out of curiosity and impatience: what was he going to say? Trotsky at once began to heat up the atmosphere, with his skill and brilliance. I remember that at length and with

extraordinary power he drew a picture of the suffering of the trenches. Thoughts flashed through my mind of the inevitable incongruity of the parts in this oratorical whole. But Trotsky knew what he was doing. The whole point lay in the mood. The political conclusions had long been familiar. They could be condensed, as long as there were enough highlights.

Trotsky did this — with enough highlights. The Soviet regime was not only called upon to put an end to the suffering of the trenches. It would give land and heal the internal disorder. Once again the recipes against hunger were repeated: a soldier, a sailor, and a working girl, who would requisition bread from those who had it and distribute it gratis to the cities and front. But Trotsky went even further on this decisive "Day of the Petersburg Soviet."

"The Soviet Government will give everything the country contains to the poor and the men in the trenches. You, bourgeois, have got two fur caps! — give one of them to the soldier, who's freezing in the trenches. Have you got warm boots? Stay at home. The worker needs your boots. . . ."

These were very good and just ideas. They could not but excite the enthusiasm of a crowd who had been reared on the Tsarist whip. In any case, I certify as a direct witness that this was what was said on this last day.

All round me was a mood bordering on ecstasy. It seemed as though the crowd, spontaneously and of its own accord, would break into some religious hymn. Trotsky formulated a brief and general resolution, or pronounced some general formula like "we will defend the worker-peasant cause to the last drop of our blood."

Who was — for? The crowd of thousands, as one man, raised their hands. I saw the raised hands and burning eyes of men, women, youths, soldiers, peasants, and typically lower-middle-class faces. Were they in spiritual transport? Did they see, through the raised curtain, a corner of the "righteous land" of their longing? Or were they penetrated by a consciousness of the *political occasion,* under the influence of the political agitation of a *Socialist?* Ask no questions! Accept it as it was. . . .

Trotsky went on speaking. The innumerable crowd went on holding their hands up. Trotsky rapped out the words: "Let this vote of yours be your vow — with all your strength and at any sacrifice to support the Soviet that has taken on itself the glorious burden of bringing to a conclusion the victory of the revolution and of giving land, bread, and peace!"

The vast crowd was holding up its hands. It agreed. It vowed. Once again, accept this as it was. With an unusual feeling of oppression I looked on at this really magnificent scene.

Trotsky finished. Someone else went out on to the stage. But there was no point in waiting and looking any more.

Throughout Petersburg more or less the same thing was going on. Everywhere there were final reviews and final vows. Thousands, tens of thousands and hundreds of thousands of people . . . This, actually, was already an insurrection. Things had started. . . .

V. I. Lenin
THE CALL TO POWER

On November 6 (October 24 by the old-style calendar then in use in Russia), Lenin urged immediate action, as the following document reveals.

. . . The situation is critical in the extreme. In fact it is now absolutely clear that to delay the uprising would be fatal.

With all my might I urge comrades to realise that everything now hangs by a thread; that we are confronted by problems which are not to be solved by conferences or congresses (even congresses of Soviets), but exclusively by peoples, by the masses, by the struggle of the armed people.

The bourgeois onslaught of the Kornilovites [followers of General Kornilov, who tried to establish a military dictatorship] show that we must not wait. We must at all costs, this very evening, this very night, arrest the government, having first disarmed the officer cadets (defeating them, if they resist), and so on.

We must not wait! We may lose everything! Who must take power?

That is not important at present. Let the Revolutionary Military Committee [Bolshevik organization working within the army and navy] do it, or "some other institution" which will declare that it will relinquish power only to the true representatives of the interests of the people, the interests of the army (the immediate proposal of peace), the interests of the peasants (the land to be taken immediately and private property abolished), the interests of the starving.

All districts, all regiments, all forces must be mobilised at once and must immediately send their delegations to the Revolutionary Military Committee and to the Central Committee of the Bolsheviks [governing organization of the Bolshevik party] with the insistent demand that under no circumstances should power be left in the hands of Kerensky and Co. . . . not under any circumstances; the matter must be decided without fail this very evening, or this very night.

History will not forgive revolutionaries for procrastinating when they could be victorious today (and they certainly will be victorious today), while they risk losing much tomorrow, in fact, they risk losing everything.

If we seize power today, we seize it not in opposition to the Soviets but on their behalf.

The seizure of power is the business of the uprising; its political purpose will become clear after the seizure. . . .

. . . It would be an infinite crime on the part of the revolutionaries were they to let the chance slip, knowing that the *salvation of the revolution,* the offer of peace, the salvation of Petrograd, salvation from famine, the transfer of the land to the peasants depend upon them.

The government is tottering. It must be *given the death-blow* at all costs.

To delay action is fatal.

REVIEW QUESTIONS

1. With what issues and what promises did Leon Trotsky arouse the masses in support of the Bolshevik seizure of power?
2. Why was his speech so effective?
3. What promises did V. I. Lenin hold out to his supporters should the revolution succeed?
4. How would you characterize Lenin's mood on the eve of the Bolshevik seizure of power?

▼▼▼

3 ▼ The Revolution Denounced and Defended

The Bolshevik Revolution's call for a new society free of exploitation made a profound impression around the world. Yet its reliance on force and compulsion, entailing gross disregard for human life and dignity, also aroused strong protest within the socialist camp.

PROCLAMATION OF THE KRONSTADT REBELS

In March 1921 the sailors at the Kronstadt naval base, in league with the workers of nearby Petrograd — all ardent allies of the Bolsheviks in 1917–1918 — revolted against the repressive Communist government. The high expectations created by the revolution clashed brutally with Lenin's ruthless determination to restore order to a country utterly defeated in World War I and threatened with anarchy and dissolution. In their disillusionment the Kronstadt sailors and their working-class allies reaffirmed their revolutionary ideals by taking up arms against "the dictatorship of the proletariat."

Their rebellion, a profound embarrassment to the communist regime, was quickly crushed by Red troops. But it also persuaded Lenin, now that the White Army had been defeated in the civil war, to relax the grip of the Communist party and to restore a measure of private enterprise under the New Economic Policy (NEP), lasting until the Stalin revolution of 1929. Under Gorbachev the idealism of the Kronstadt sailors is being recognized and revived at last.

With the October Revolution the working class had hoped to achieve its emancipation. But there resulted an even greater enslavement of human personality.

The power of the police and gendarme monarchy fell into the hands of usurpers — the Communists — who, instead of giving the people liberty, have instilled in them only the constant fear of the Tcheka [secret police], which by its horrors surpasses even the gendarme regime of Tsarism. . . . Worst and most criminal of all is the spiritual cabal of the Communists: they have laid their hand also on the internal world of the laboring masses, compelling everyone to think according to Communist prescription.

. . . Russia of the toilers, the first to raise the red banner of labor's emancipation, is drenched with the blood of those martyred for the greater glory of Communist dominion. In that sea of blood the Communists are drowning all the bright promises and possibilities of the workers' revolution. It has now become clear that the Russian Communist Party is not the defender of the laboring masses, as it pretends to be. The interests of the working people are foreign to it. Having gained power it is now fearful only of losing it, and therefore it considers all means permissible: defamation, deceit,

violence, murder, and vengeance upon the families of the rebels.

There is an end to long-suffering patience. Here and there the land is lit up by the fires of rebellion in a struggle against oppression and violence. Strikes of workers have multiplied, but the Bolshevik police regime has taken every precaution against the outbreak of the inevitable Third Revolution.

But in spite of it all it has come, and it is made by the hands of the laboring masses. The Generals of Communism see clearly that it is the people who have risen, the people who have become convinced that the Communists have betrayed the ideas of Socialism. Fearing for their safety and knowing that there is no place they can hide in from the wrath of the workers, the Communists still try to terrorise the rebels with prison, shooting, and other barbarities. But life under the Communist dictatorship is more terrible than death. . . .

There is no middle road. To conquer or to die! The example is being set by Kronstadt, the terror of counter-revolution from the right and from the left. Here has taken place the great revolutionary deed. Here is raised the banner of rebellion against the three-year-old tyranny and oppression of Communist autocracy, which has put in the shade the three-hundred-year-old despotism of monarchism. Here, in Kronstadt, has been laid the cornerstone of the Third Revolution which is to break the last chains of the worker and open the new, broad road to Socialist creativeness.

This new Revolution will rouse the masses of the East and the West, and it will serve as an example of new Socialist constructiveness, in contradistinction to the governmental, cut-and-dried Communist "construction." The laboring masses will learn that what has been done till now in the name of the workers and peasants was not Socialism.

Without firing a single shot, without shedding a drop of blood, the first step has been taken. Those who labor need no blood. They will shed it only in self-defense. . . . The workers and peasants march on: they are leaving behind them the *utchredilka* (Constituent Assembly) with its bourgeois regime and the Communist Party dictatorship with its Tcheka and State capitalism, which have put the noose around the neck of the workers and threaten to strangle them to death.

The present change offers the laboring masses the opportunity of securing, at last, freely elected Soviets which will function without fear of the Party whip; they can now reorganise the governmentalised labor unions into voluntary associations of workers, peasants, and the working intelligentsia. At last is broken the police club of Communist autocracy.

Karl Kautsky
SOCIALIST CONDEMNATION OF THE BOLSHEVIK REGIME

Karl Kautsky (1854–1938), a leading German Marxist, denounced the Bolshevik regime for its terrorism, repression, and authoritarianism. Kautsky viewed the course of the Russian Revolution from the humanitarian perspectives of German socialists. Eager to safeguard the moral purity of the Marxist creed, he deplored the Bolsheviks' brutality. The following reflections, written in 1919, spell out his reactions to the course of the revolution in Russia.

The world-war made the working class take a backward step both morally and intellectually. It brutalised almost every strata of the population; it set the most undeveloped elements of the proletariat in the forefront of the movement, and finally increased the [impoverished] state of the proletariat to such an extent, that it brought despair in the place of quiet thought and reflection. The war also encouraged primitive ideas in the working-classes, by developing the military way of thinking, that form of thinking which, as it is, lies very near the surface in the thoughts of the average unintelligent man, who imagines that mere power is the determining factor in the world history — as if one needed only the necessary force and recklessness to accomplish everything that one undertakes. Marx and Engels have always attacked and opposed this conception. . . .

The Bolsheviks . . . have . . . kept themselves going by discarding one after another some part of their programme, so that finally they have achieved the very contrary to that which they set out to obtain. For instance, in order to come into power they threw overboard all their democratic principles. In order to keep themselves in power they have had to let their Socialist principles go the way of the democratic. They have . . . sacrificed their principles, and have proved themselves to be thoroughgoing opportunists.

Bolshevism has, up to the present, triumphed in Russia, but Socialism has already suffered a defeat. We have only to look at the form of society which has developed under the Bolshevik regime, and which was bound so to develop, as soon as the Bolshevik method was applied. . . .

Among the phenomena for which Bolshevism has been responsible, Terrorism, which begins with the abolition of every form of freedom of the Press, and ends in a system of wholesale execution, is certainly the most striking and the most repellant of all. It is that which gave rise to the greatest hatred against the Bolsheviks. . . .

The instruments of terrorism were the revolutionary tribunals and the extraordinary commissions. . . . Both have carried on fearful work, quite apart from the so-called military punitive expeditions, the victims of which are incalculable. The number of victims of the extraordinary commissions will never be easy to ascertain. In any case they number their thousands. The lowest estimate puts the number at 6,000; others give the total as double that number, others treble; and over and above these are numberless cases of people who have been immured alive or ill-treated and tortured to death.

Those who defend Bolshevism do so by pointing out that their opponents, the White Guards of the Finns, the Baltic barons, the counter-revolutionary Tsarist generals and admirals have not done any better. But is it a justification of theft to show that others steal? In any case, these others do not go against their own principles, if they deliberately sacrifice human life in order to maintain their power; whereas the Bolsheviks most certainly do. For they thus become unfaithful to the principles of the sanctity of human life, which they themselves openly proclaimed, and by means of which they have themselves become raised to power and justified in their actions. . . .

But not even the aim of the Bolsheviks is free from objection. Its immediate endeavour is to preserve the militarist bureaucratic apparatus of power, which it has created. . . .

Shooting — that is the Alpha and Omega [the beginning and the end] of Communist government wisdom. . . .

. . . The Extraordinary Commissions of the Soviet Republic deliberate in secret, without any sort of guarantee that the accused shall have their due rights. For it is not absolutely imperative that the accused himself should be heard, let alone his witnesses. A mere denunciation, a mere suspicion suffices to remove him. . . .

Originally [the Bolsheviks] were wholehearted protagonists of a National Assembly, elected on the strength of a universal and equal vote. But they set this aside, as soon as it stood in their way. They were thorough-going opponents of the death penalty, yet they established a bloody rule. . . . [They were] fiery upholders of democracy within the proletariat, but they are repressing this democracy more and more by means of their personal dictatorship. . . . At the beginning of their regime they declared it to be their object to smash the bureaucratic apparatus, which represented the means of power of the old State; but they have introduced in its place a new form of bureaucratic rule. . . . [They] strove to reduce all classes to the same level, instead of which they have called into being a new class distinction. They have created a class which stands on a lower level than the proletariat, which latter they have raised to a privileged class; and over and above this they have caused still another class to appear, which is in receipt of large incomes and enjoys high privileges. . . .

. . . The hereditary sin of Bolshevism has been its suppression of democracy through a form of government, namely, the dictatorship, which has no meaning unless it represents the unlimited and despotic power, either of one single person or of a small organisation intimately bound together. . . .

. . . The opposition against the Bolsheviks has been increasing from day to day. The growing nervousness betrayed by its disciples over every kind of Press which is not official, as well as the exclusion of Socialist critics from the Soviets, shows the transition to the Regiment of Terror. In such a situation, to demolish the dictatorship in order gradually to return to democracy is scarcely possible. All such attempts hitherto have quickly come to an end. The Bolsheviks are prepared, in order to maintain their position, to make all sorts of possible concessions to bureaucracy, to militarism, and to capitalism, whereas any concession to democracy seems to them to be sheer suicide.

Leon Trotsky
RESPONDING TO KAUTSKY

Would a spirited Bolshevik allow Kautsky's accusation to go unanswered? Speaking from his intimate knowledge of Russian conditions, the radical Russian Marxist Leon Trotsky was bound to resent the presumption of outsiders from the West, like Kautsky, who imposed their values upon the alien realities of Russia. Trotsky was a seasoned insider. He had stood at the center of the revolution of November 1917 (see page 296). Thereafter he assumed charge of Soviet foreign relations before creating the Red Army, which prevailed over the Whites in the civil war (and also suppressed the Kronstadt rebellion). He knew firsthand "what war is in general, and the civil war in particular." As he protested in 1920, Kautsky's "liberalism" did not apply to the extreme conditions of the Bolshevik Revolution.

Kautsky, in spite of all the happenings in the world to-day, completely fails to realize what war is in general, and the civil war in particular. . . . The enemy must be made harmless, and in wartime this means that he must be destroyed.

The problem of revolution, as of war, consists in breaking the will of the foe, forcing him to capitulate and to accept the conditions of the conqueror. . . . The bourgeoisie itself conquered power by means of revolts, and consolidated it by the civil war. In the peaceful period, it retains power by means of a system of repression. As long as class society, founded on the most deep-rooted antagonisms, continues to exist, repression remains a necessary means of breaking the will of the opposing side.

Even if, in one country or another, the dictatorship of the proletariat grew up within the external framework of democracy, this would by no means avert the civil war. The question as to who is to rule the country, *i.e.,* of the life or death of the bourgeoisie, will be decided on either side, not by references to the paragraphs of the constitution, but by the employment of all forms of violence. . . .

In history [there is] no other way of breaking the class will of the enemy except the systematic and energetic use of violence.

The degree of ferocity of the struggle depends on a series of internal and international circumstances. The more ferocious and dangerous is the resistance of the class enemy who have been overthrown, the more inevitably does the system of repression take the form of a system of terror.

But here Kautsky unexpectedly takes up a new position in his struggle with Soviet terrorism. He simply waves aside all reference to the ferocity of the counter-revolutionary opposition of the Russian bourgeoisie. . . .

The working class, which seized power in battle, had as its object and its duty to establish that power unshakeably, to guarantee its own supremacy beyond question, to destroy its enemies' hankering for a new revolution, and thereby to make sure of carrying out Socialist reforms. Otherwise there would be no point in seizing power.

The revolution "logically" does not demand terrorism, just as "logically" it does not demand an armed insurrection. What a profound commonplace! But the revolution does require of the revolutionary class that it should attain its end by all methods at its disposal — if necessary, by an armed rising: if required, by terrorism. A revolutionary class which has conquered power with arms in its hands is bound to, and will, suppress, rifle in hand, all attempts to tear the power out of its hands. Where it has against it a hostile army, it will oppose to it its own army. Where it is confronted with armed conspiracy, attempt at murder, or rising, it will hurl at the heads of its enemies an unsparing penalty. Perhaps Kautsky has invented other methods? Or does he reduce the whole question to the *degree* of repression, and recommend in all circumstances imprisonment instead of execution?

. . . [T]error can be very efficient against a reactionary class which does not want to leave the scene of operations. *Intimidation* is a powerful weapon of policy, both internationally and internally. War, like revolution, is founded upon intimidation. A victorious war, generally speaking, destroys only an insignificant part of the conquered army, intimidating the remainder and breaking their will. The revolution works in the same way: it kills individuals, and intimidates thousands. In this sense, the Red Terror is not distinguishable from the armed insurrection, the direct continuation of which it represents. The State terror of a revolutionary class can be condemned "morally" only by a man who, as a principle, rejects (in words) every form of violence whatsoever — consequently, every war and every rising. For this one has to be merely and simply a hypocritical Quaker.

"But, in that case, in what do your tactics differ from the tactics of Tsarism?" we are asked, by the high priests of Liberalism and Kautskianism.

You do not understand this, holy men? We shall explain to you. The terror of Tsarism was directed against the proletariat. The gendarmerie of Tsarism throttled the workers who were fighting for the Socialist order. Our Extraordinary Commissions shoot landlords, capitalists, and generals who are striving to restore the capitalist order. Do you grasp this . . . distinction? Yes? For us Communists it is quite sufficient.

One point particularly worries Kautsky, the author of a great many books and articles — the freedom of the Press. Is it permissible to suppress newspapers?

During war all institutions and organs of the State and of public opinion become, directly or indirectly, weapons of warfare. This is particularly true of the Press. No government carrying on a serious war will allow publications to exist on its territory which, openly or indirectly, support the enemy. Still more so in a civil war. The nature of the latter is such that each of the struggling sides has in the rear of its armies considerable circles of the population on the side of the enemy. In war, where both success and failure are repaid by death, hostile agents who penetrate into the rear are subject to execution. This is inhuman, but no one ever considered war a school of humanity — still less civil war. Can it be seriously demanded that, during a civil war with the White Guards of Denikin,[1] the publications of parties supporting Denikin should come out unhindered in Moscow and Petrograd? To propose this in the name of the "freedom" of the Press is just the same as, in the name of open dealing, to demand the publication of military secrets. . . .

We are fighting. We are fighting a life-and-death struggle. The Press is a weapon not of an abstract society, but of two irreconcilable, armed and contending sides. We are destroying the Press of the counter-revolution, just as we destroyed its fortified positions, its stores, its communications, and its intelligence systems. . . . [W]e were never concerned with the Kantian-priestly [moralistic] and vegetarian-Quaker prattle about the "sacredness of human life." We were revolutionaries in opposition, and have remained revolutionaries in power. To make the individual sacred we must destroy the

---

[1]General Denikin was the leader of the strongest White armies.

social order which crucifies him. And this problem can only be solved by blood and iron. . . .

. . . The bourgeoisie to-day is a falling class. It not only no longer plays an essential part in production, but by its imperialist methods of appropriation is destroying the economic structure of the world and human culture generally. Nevertheless, the historical persistence of the bourgeoisie is colossal. It holds to power, and does not wish to abandon it. Thereby it threatens to drag after it into the abyss the whole of society. We are forced to tear it off, to chop it away. The Red Terror is a weapon utilized against a class, doomed to destruction, which

does not wish to perish. If the White Terror[2] can only retard the historical rise of the proletariat, the Red Terror hastens the destruction of the bourgeoisie. This hastening — a pure question of acceleration — is at certain periods of decisive importance. Without the Red Terror, the Russian bourgeoisie, together with the world bourgeoisie, would throttle us long before the coming of the revolution in Europe. One must be blind not to see this, or a swindler to deny it.

_____
[2]Terror and counterterror were common during the civil war in both White and Red armies.

REVIEW QUESTIONS

1. How, according to the Kronstadt rebels, had the communists betrayed the ideas of socialism?
2. Where, according to Karl Kautsky, had the Bolsheviks strayed from the true spirit of socialism?
3. How did Leon Trotsky answer Kautsky's critique of terror?
4. Who had the better arguments, Kautsky or Trotsky?

4 ▾ Modernize or Perish

Joseph Stalin (1879–1953) was the communist leader who made the Soviet Union into a superpower. He was born Iosif Vissarionovich Dzhugashvili in Trans-Caucasus Georgia. A rebel from childhood, he was one of Lenin's favored professional revolutionaries, trained in the tough schools of underground agitation, tsarist prisons, and Siberian exile. Unscrupulous, energetic, and endowed with a keen nose for the realities of power within the party and the country as a whole, Stalin surpassed his political rivals in strength of will and organizational astuteness. After he was appointed secretary-general of the Communist party (then considered a minor post) in 1922, he concentrated on building, amid the disorganization caused by war, revolution, and civil war, an effective party organization adapted to the temper of the Russian people. With this structure's help, he established himself as Lenin's successor. Stalin, more powerful and more ruthless than Lenin, was determined to force his country to overcome the economic and political weakness that had led to defeat and ruin in 1917. After Lenin's death, Stalin preached the "Leninist style of work," which combined "Russian revolutionary sweep" with "American efficiency."

Joseph Stalin
THE HARD LINE

Firmly entrenched in power by 1929, Stalin started a second revolution (called the Stalin revolution), mobilizing at top speed the potential of the country, however limited the human and material resources available, whatever the obstacles, and whatever the human price. The alternative, he was sure, was foreign domination that would totally destroy his country's independence. In this spirit, he addressed a gathering of industrial managers in 1931, talking to them not in Marxist-Leninist jargon, but in terms of hard-line Russian nationalism.

It is sometimes asked whether it is not possible to slow down the tempo a bit, to put a check on the movement. No, comrades, it is not possible! The tempo must not be reduced! On the contrary, we must increase it as much as is within our powers and possibilities. This is dictated to us by our obligations to the workers and peasants of the U.S.S.R. This is dictated to us by our obligations to the working class of the whole world.

To slacken the tempo would mean falling behind. And those who fall behind get beaten. But we do not want to be beaten. No, we refuse to be beaten! One feature of the history of old Russia was the continual beatings she suffered for falling behind, for her backwardness. She was beaten by the Mongol Khans. She was beaten by the Turkish beys. She was beaten by the Swedish feudal lords. She was beaten by the Polish and Lithuanian gentry. She was beaten by the British and French capitalists. She was beaten by the Japanese barons. All beat her — for her backwardness: for military backwardness, for cultural backwardness, for political backwardness, for industrial backwardness, for agricultural backwardness. She was beaten because to do so was profitable and could be done with impunity. Do you remember the words of the pre-revolutionary poet [Nikolai Nekrassov]: "You are poor and abundant, mighty and impotent, Mother Russia." These words of the old poet were well learned by those gentlemen.

They beat her, saying: "You are abundant," so one can enrich oneself at your expense. They beat her, saying: "You are poor and impotent," so you can be beaten and plundered with impunity. Such is the law of the exploiters — to beat the backward and the weak. It is the jungle law of capitalism. You are backward, you are weak — therefore you are wrong; hence, you can be beaten and enslaved. You are mighty — therefore you are right; hence, we must be wary of you.

That is why we must no longer lag behind.

In the past we had no fatherland, nor could we have one. But now that we have overthrown capitalism and power is in the hands of the working class, we have a fatherland, and we will defend its independence. Do you want our socialist fatherland to be beaten and to lose its independence? If you do not want this you must put an end to its backwardness in the shortest possible time and develop genuine Bolshevik tempo in building up its socialist system of economy. There is no other way. That is why Lenin said during the October Revolution: "Either perish, or overtake and outstrip the advanced capitalist countries."

We are fifty or a hundred years behind the advanced countries. We must make good this distance in ten years. Either we do it, or they crush us.

This is what our obligations to the workers and peasants of the U.S.S.R. dictate to us.

REVIEW QUESTIONS

1. Why did Joseph Stalin argue that the tempo of industrialization could not be slowed down?
2. Which sentences in Stalin's statement seem to you the most quotable or the most important?
3. How important is the idea of "fatherland" to Stalin?

▼▼▼

5 ▼ Forced Collectivization

The forced collectivization of agriculture from 1929 to 1933 was an integral part of the Stalin revolution. His argument in favor of it was simple: an economy divided against itself cannot stand — planned industrial mobilization was incompatible with small-scale private agriculture in the traditional manner. Collectivization meant combining many small peasant holdings into a single large unit run in theory by the peasants (now called collective farmers), but in practice by the collective farm chairman guided by the government's Five-Year Plan.

Joseph Stalin
LIQUIDATION OF THE KULAKS

Collectivization, not surprisingly, met with fierce resistance, especially from the more efficient peasants called kulaks, who were averse to surrendering their private plots and their freedom in running their households. Their resistance therefore had to be broken, and the Communist party fomented a rural class-struggle, seeking help in this effort from the poorer peasants. Sometimes even the poorest peasants sided with the local kulaks. Under these conditions, Stalin did not shrink from unleashing violence in the countryside aimed at the "liquidation of the kulaks as a class." For Stalin the collectivization drive meant an all-out war on what was for him the citadel of backwardness: the peasant tradition and rebelliousness so prominent under the tsars. The following reading — Stalin's address to the Conference of Marxist Students of the Agrarian Question, December 1929 — conveys his intentions.

The characteristic feature of our work during the past year is: (a) that we, the party and the Soviet government, have developed an offensive on the whole front against the capitalist elements in the countryside; and (b) that this offensive, as you know, has brought about and is bringing about very palpable, *positive* results.

What does this mean? It means that we have passed from the policy of *restricting* the exploit-ing proclivities of the kulaks to the policy of *eliminating* the kulaks as a class. This means that we have made, and are still making, one of the most decisive turns in our whole policy.

. . . Could we have undertaken such an offensive against the kulaks five years or three years ago? Could we then have counted on success in such an offensive? No, we could not. That would have been the most dangerous adventurism! That would have been playing a very dangerous game at offensive. We would certainly have come to grief and, once we had come to grief, we would have strengthened the position of the kulaks. Why? Because we did not yet have strongholds in the rural districts in the shape of a wide network of state farms and collective farms upon which to rely in a determined offensive against the kulaks. Because at that time we were not yet able to *substitute* for the capitalist production of the kulaks socialist production in the shape of the collective farms and state farms. . . .

But today? What is the position? Today, we have an adequate material base which enables us to strike at the kulaks, to break their resistance, to eliminate them as a class, and to *substitute* for their output the output of the collective farms and state farms. . . .

Now, as you see, we have the material base which enables us to *substitute* for kulak output the output of the collective farms and state farms. That is why our offensive against the kulaks is now meeting with undeniable success.

That is how the offensive against the kulaks must be carried on, if we mean a real offensive and not futile declamations against the kulaks.

That is why we have recently passed from the policy of *restricting* the exploiting *proclivities* of the kulaks to the policy of *eliminating the kulaks as a class*. . . . Now we are able to carry on a determined offensive against the kulaks, to break their resistance, to eliminate them as a class and substitute for their output the output of the collective farms and state farms. Now, the kulaks are being expropriated by the masses of poor and middle peasants themselves, by the masses who are putting solid collectivization into practice. Now the expropriation of the kulaks in the regions of solid collectivization is no longer just an administrative measure. Now, the expropriation of the kulaks is an integral part of the formation and development of the collective farms. . . .

. . . [Should] the kulak . . . be permitted to join the collective farms[?] Of course not, for he is a sworn enemy of the collective farm movement. Clear, one would think.

Lev Kopelev
TERROR IN THE COUNTRYSIDE

The liquidation of the kulaks began in late 1929, extending through the length and breadth of the country during the winter. The killing rose to a brutal climax in the following spring and continued for another two years, by which time the bulk of the private farms had been eliminated. By some estimates, almost five million people were liquidated. Some were driven from their huts, deprived of all possessions, and left destitute in the dead of winter; the men were sent to forced labor and their families left abandoned. Others killed themselves or were killed outright, sometimes in pitched battles involving a whole village — men, women, and children.

The upheaval destroyed agricultural production in these years; farm animals died or were killed in huge numbers; fields lay barren. In 1932 and 1933, famine stalked the south and southeast, killing additional millions; it was especially severe in the Ukraine. The vast tragedy caused by collectivization did not deter Stalin from pursuing his goals: the establishment of state farms run like factories and the subordination of the rebellious and willful peasantry to state authority.

Here a militant participant in the collectivization drive, Lev Kopelev, recalls some of his experiences. Kopelev, born in 1912 and raised in a Ukrainian, middle-class Jewish family, evolved from a youthful Stalinist into a tolerant, gentle person in later years; he was chastened after World War II by a term in a labor camp reserved for scientists. Subsequently out of favor because of his literary protests against the inhumanities of the Soviet system, he was exiled from the Soviet Union to West Germany in 1980.

The grain front! Stalin said the struggle for grain was the struggle for socialism. I was convinced that we were warriors on an invisible front, fighting against kulak sabotage for the grain which was needed by the country, by the five-year plan. Above all, for the grain, but also for the souls of these peasants who were mired in unconscientiousness, in ignorance, who succumbed to enemy agitation, who did not understand the great truth of communism. . . .

The highest measure of coercion on the hard-core holdouts was "undisputed confiscation."

A team consisting of several young kolkhozniks [collective farmers] and members of the village soviet . . . would search the hut, barn, yard, and take away all the stores of seed, lead away the cow, the horse, the pigs.

In some cases they would be merciful and leave some potatoes, peas, corn for feeding the family. But the stricter ones would make a clean sweep. They would take not only the food and livestock, but also "all valuables and surpluses of clothing," including icons in their frames, samovars, painted carpets and even metal kitchen utensils which might be silver. And any money they found stashed away. Special instructions ordered the removal of gold, silver and currency. . . .

Several times Volodya and I were present at such plundering raids. We even took part: we were entrusted to draw up inventories of the confiscated goods. . . . The women howled hysterically, clinging to the bags.

"Oy, that's the last thing we have! That was for the children's kasha! Honest to God, the children will starve!"

They wailed, falling on their trunks:

"Oy, that's a keepsake from my dead mama! People, come to my aid, this is my trousseau, never e'en put on!"

I heard the children echoing them with screams, choking, coughing with screams. And I saw the looks of the men: frightened, pleading, hateful, dully impassive, extinguished with despair or flaring up with half-mad, daring ferocity.

"Take it. Take it away. Take everything away. There's still a pot of borscht on the stove. It's plain, got no meat. But still it's got beets, taters 'n' cabbage. And it's salted! Better take it, comrade citizens! Here, hang on, I'll take off my shoes. They're patched and re-patched, but maybe they'll have some use for the proletariat, for our dear Soviet power."

It was excruciating to see and hear all this. And even worse to take part in it. . . . And I persuaded myself, explained to myself. I mustn't give in to debilitating pity. We were realizing historical necessity. We were performing our revolutionary duty. We were obtaining grain for the socialist fatherland. For the five-year plan. . . .

I have always remembered the winter of the last grain collections, the weeks of the great famine. And I have always told about it. But I did not begin to write it down until many years later. . . .

How could all this have happened?

Who was guilty of the famine which destroyed millions of lives?

How could I have participated in it? . . .

We were raised as the fanatical [believers] of a new creed, the only true *religion* of scientific socialism. The party became our church militant, bequeathing to all mankind eternal salvation, eternal peace and the bliss of an earthly paradise. It victoriously surmounted all other churches, schisms and heresies. The works of Marx, Engels and Lenin were accepted as holy writ, and Stalin was the infallible high priest.

. . . Stalin was the most perspicacious, the most wise (at that time they hadn't yet started calling him "great" and "brilliant"). He said: "The struggle for grain is the struggle for socialism." And we believed him unconditionally. And later we believed that unconditional collectivization was unavoidable if we were to overcome the capriciousness and uncertainty of the market and the backwardness of individual farming, to guarantee a steady supply of grain, milk and meat to the cities. And also if we were to reeducate millions of peasants, those petty landowners and hence potential bourgeoisie, potential kulaks, to transform them into laborers with a social conscience, to liberate them from "the idiocy of country life," from ignorance and prejudice, and to accustom them to culture, to all the boons of socialism. . . .

▷ In the following passage Kopelev reflects, even more searchingly, on his own motivation and state of mind as a participant in Stalin's collectivization drive.

With the rest of my generation I firmly believed that the ends justified the means. Our great goal was the universal triumph of Communism, and for the sake of that goal everything was permissible — to lie, to steal, to destroy hundreds of thousands and even millions of people, all those who were hindering our work or could hinder it, everyone who stood in the way. And to hesitate or doubt about all this was to give in to "intellectual squeamishness" and "stupid liberalism," the attributes of people who "could not see the forest for the trees."

That was how I had reasoned, and everyone like me, even when I did have my doubts, when I saw what "total collectivization" meant — how . . . mercilessly they stripped the peasants in the winter of 1932–33. I took part in this myself, scouring the countryside, searching for hidden grain, testing the earth with an iron rod for loose spots that might lead to buried grain. With the others, I emptied out the old folks'

storage chests, stopping my ears to the children's crying and the women's wails. For I was convinced that I was accomplishing the great and necessary transformation of the countryside; that in the days to come the people who lived there would be better off for it; that their distress and suffering were a result of their own ignorance or the machinations of the class enemy; that those who sent me — and I myself — knew better than the peasants how they should live, what they should sow and when they should plow.

In the terrible spring of 1933 I saw people dying from hunger. I saw women and children with distended bellies, turning blue, still breathing but with vacant, lifeless eyes. And corpses — corpses in ragged sheepskin coats and cheap felt boots; corpses in peasant huts, in the melting snow of old Vologda, under the bridges of Kharkov. . . . I saw all this and did not go out of my mind or commit suicide. Nor did I curse those who had sent me to take away the peasants' grain in the winter, and in the spring to persuade the barely walking, skeleton-thin or sickly-swollen people to go into the fields in order to "fulfill the Bolshevik sowing plan in shock-worker style."

Nor did I lose my faith. As before, I believed because I wanted to believe. Thus from time immemorial men have believed when possessed by a desire to serve powers and values above and beyond humanity: gods, emperors, states; ideals of virtue, freedom, nation, race, class, party. . . .

Any single-minded attempt to realize these ideals exacts its toll of human sacrifice. In the name of the noblest visions promising eternal happiness to their descendants, such men bring merciless ruin on their contemporaries. Bestowing paradise on the dead, they maim and destroy the living. They become unprincipled liars and unrelenting executioners, all the while seeing themselves as virtuous and honorable militants — convinced that if they are forced into villainy, it is for the sake of future good, and that if they have to lie, it is in the name of eternal truths.

. . . That was how we thought and acted — we, the fanatical disciples of the all-saving ideals of Communism. When we saw the base and cruel acts that were committed in the name of our exalted notions of good, and when we ourselves took part in those actions, what we feared most was to lose our heads, fall into doubt or heresy and forfeit our unbounded faith. . . . The concepts of conscience, honor, humaneness we dismissed as idealistic prejudices, "intellectual" or "bourgeois," and hence, perverse.

REVIEW QUESTIONS

1. How, in Joseph Stalin's view, did socialist farming differ from capitalist farming?
2. Why were the kulaks selected as special targets in the drive for collectivization?
3. How would you characterize the motivation of the young Lev Kopelev and his associates in carrying out the collectivization of agriculture?
4. How, in retrospect, did Kopelev explain his role in the collectivization drive?
5. Looking at both Stalin's and Kopelev's accounts, what was at stake in the conflict between ends and means in the collectivization of agriculture?

▼▼▼

6 ▼ Soviet Indoctrination

Pressed by the necessity to transform their country into a modern state, the communist leaders used every opportunity to force the population to adopt the attitudes and motivation necessary to effect such a transformation. Education, from nursery school to university, provided special opportunities to mold attitudes. The Soviet regime made impressive gains in promoting education among its diverse people; it also used education to foster dedication to hard work, discipline in social cooperation, and pride in the nation. For a backward country that, as Lenin had said, must "either perish or overtake and outstrip the advanced capitalist countries," such changes were considered essential.

During the Stalin era, artists and writers were compelled to promote the ideals of the Stalin revolution. In the style of "socialist realism," their heroes were factory workers and farmers who labored tirelessly and enthusiastically to build a new society. Even romance served a political purpose. Novelists wrote love stories following limited, prosaic themes. For example, a young girl might lose her heart to a co-worker who is a leader in the communist youth organization and who outproduces his comrades at his job; as the newly married couple is needed at the factory, they choose to forgo a honeymoon.

A. O. Avdienko
THE CULT OF STALIN

Among a people so deeply divided by ethnicity and petty localism and limited by a pervasive narrowness of perspective, building countrywide unity and consensus was a crucial challenge for the government. In the Russian past the worship of saints and the veneration of the tsar had served that purpose. The political mobilization of the masses during the revolution required an intensification of that tradition. It led to the "cult of personality," the deliberate fixation of individual dedication and loyalty on the all-powerful leader, whose personality exemplified the challenge of extraordinary times. The following selection illustrates by what emotional bonds the individual was tied to Stalin, and through Stalin to the prodigious transformation of Russian state and society that he was attempting.

Thank you, Stalin. Thank you because I am joyful. Thank you because I am well. No matter how old I become, I shall never forget how we received Stalin two days ago. Centuries will pass, and the generations still to come will regard us as the happiest of mortals, as the most fortunate of men, because we lived in the century of centuries, because we were privileged to see Stalin, our inspired leader. Yes, and we regard ourselves as the happiest of mortals because we are the contemporaries of a man who never had an equal in world history.

The men of all ages will call on thy name, which is strong, beautiful, wise and marvellous. Thy name is engraven on every factory, every machine, every place on the earth, and in the hearts of all men.

Every time I have found myself in his presence I have been subjugated by his strength, his charm, his grandeur. I have experienced a great desire to sing, to cry out, to shout with joy and happiness. And now see me — me! — on the same platform where the Great Stalin stood a year ago. In what country, in what part of the world could such a thing happen.

I write books. I am an author. All thanks to thee, O great educator, Stalin. I love a young woman with a renewed love and shall perpetuate myself in my children — all thanks to thee, great educator, Stalin. I shall be eternally happy and joyous, all thanks to thee, great educator, Stalin. Everything belongs to thee, chief of our great country. And when the woman I love presents me with a child the first word it shall utter will be: Stalin.

O great Stalin, O leader of the peoples,
Thou who broughtest man to birth.
Thou who fructifiest the earth,
Thou who restorest the centuries,
Thou who makest bloom the spring,
Thou who makest vibrate the musical
    chords . . .
Thou, splendour of my spring, O Thou,
Sun reflected by millions of hearts . . .

Yevgeny Yevtushenko
LITERATURE AS PROPAGANDA

After Stalin's death in 1953, Soviet intellectuals breathed more freely, and they protested against the rigid Stalinist controls. In the following extract from his *Precocious Autobiography,* Russian poet Yevgeny Yevtushenko (b. 1933) looks back to the raw days of intellectual repression under Stalin.

Blankly smiling workers and collective farmers looked out from the covers of books. Almost every novel and short story had a happy ending. Painters more and more often took as their subject state banquets, weddings, solemn public meetings, and parades.

The apotheosis of this trend was a movie which in its grand finale showed thousands of collective farmers having a gargantuan feast against the background of a new power station.

Recently I had a talk with its producer, a gifted and intelligent man.

"How could you produce such a film?" I asked. "It is true that I also once wrote verses in that vein, but I was still wet behind the ears, whereas you were adult and mature."

The producer smiled a sad smile. "You know, the strangest thing to me is that I was absolutely sincere. I thought all this was a necessary part of building communism. And then I believed Stalin."

So when we talk about "the cult of personality," we should not be too hasty in accusing all those who, one way or another, were involved in it, debasing themselves with their flattery. There were of course sycophants [servile flatterers] who used the situation for their own ends. But that many people connected with the arts sang Stalin's praises was often not vice but tragedy.

How was it possible for even gifted and intelligent people to be deceived?

To begin with, Stalin was a strong and vivid personality. When he wanted to, Stalin knew how to charm people. He charmed Gorky and Barbusse. In 1937, the cruelest year of the purges, he managed to charm that tough and experienced observer, Lion Feuchtwanger.[1]

In the second place, in the minds of the Soviet people, Stalin's name was indissolubly linked with Lenin's. Stalin knew how popular Lenin was and saw to it that history was rewritten in such a way as to make his own relations with Lenin seem much more friendly than they had been in fact. The rewriting was so thorough that perhaps Stalin himself believed his own version in the end.

There can be no doubt of Stalin's love for

---

[1]Gorky was a prominent Russian writer; Barbusse and Feuchtwanger were well-known Western European writers.

Lenin. His speech on Lenin's death, beginning with the words, "In leaving us, Comrade Lenin has bequeathed . . ." reads like a poem in prose. He wanted to stand as Lenin's heir not only in other people's eyes, but in his own eyes too. He deceived himself as well as the others. Even [Boris] Pasternak put the two names side by side:

> Laughter in the village,
> Voice behind the plow,
> Lenin and Stalin,
> And these verses now . . .

In reality, however, Stalin distorted Lenin's ideas, because to Lenin — and this was the whole meaning of his work — communism was to serve man, whereas under Stalin it appeared that man served communism.

Stalin's theory that people were the little cogwheels of communism was put into practice and with horrifying results. . . . Russian poets, who had produced some fine works during the war, turned dull again. If a good poem did appear now and then, it was likely to be about the war — this was simpler to write about.

Poets visited factories and construction sites but wrote more about machines than about the men who made them work. If machines could read, they might have found such poems interesting. Human beings did not.

The size of a printing was not determined by demand but by the poet's official standing. As a result bookstores were cluttered up with books of poetry which no one wanted. . . . A simple, touching poem by the young poet Vanshenkin, about a boy's first love, caused almost a sensation against this background of industrial-agricultural verse. Vinokurov's first poems, handsomely disheveled among the general sleekness, were avidly seized upon — they had human warmth. But the general situation was unchanged. Poetry remained unpopular. The older poets were silent, and when they did break their silence, it was even worse. The generation of poets that had been spawned by the war and that had raised so many hopes had petered out. Life in peacetime turned out to be more complicated than life at the front. Two of the greatest Russian poets, Zabolotsky and Smelyakov, were in concentration camps. The young poet Mandel (Korzhavin) had been deported. I don't know if Mandel's name will be remembered in the history of Russian poets but it will certainly be remembered in the history of Russian social thought.

He was the only poet who openly wrote and recited verses against Stalin while Stalin was alive. That he recited them seems to be what saved his life, for the authorities evidently thought him insane. In one poem he wrote of Stalin:

There in Moscow, in whirling darkness,
Wrapped in his military coat,
Not understanding Pasternak,
A hard and cruel man stared at the snow.

. . . Now that ten years have gone by, I realize that Stalin's greatest crime was not the arrests and the shootings he ordered. His greatest crime was the corruption of the human spirit.

Vladimir Polyakov
AN ATTACK ON CENSORSHIP
≪ THE STORY OF FIREMAN PROKHORCHUK ≫

The following reading by Soviet writer Vladimir Polyakov was published in Moscow the year Stalin died. This "story of a story" is a humorous attack on censorship.

(The action takes place in the editorial offices of a Soviet magazine. A woman writer — a beginner — shyly enters the editors' office.)

SHE Pardon me. . . . please excuse me. . . . You're the editor of the magazine, aren't you?

HE That's right.

SHE My name is Krapivina. I've written a little story for your magazine.

HE All right, leave it here.

SHE I was wondering whether I couldn't get your opinion of it right away. If you'll permit me, I'll read it to you. It won't take more than three or four minutes. May I?

HE All right, read it.

SHE It is entitled "A Noble Deed." (She begins to read.)

It was the dead of night — three o'clock. Everybody in the town was asleep. Not a single electric light was burning. It was dark and quiet. But suddenly a gory tongue of flame shot out of the fourth-floor window of a large gray house. "Help!" someone shouted. "We're on fire!" This was the voice of a careless tenant who, when he went to bed, had forgotten to switch off the electric hot plate, the cause of the fire. Both the fire and the tenant were darting around the room. The siren of a fire engine wailed. Firemen jumped down from the engine and dashed into the house. The room where the tenant was darting around was a sea of flames. Fireman Prokhorchuk, a middle-age Ukrainian with large black mustachios, stood in front of the door. The fireman stood and thought. Suddenly he rushed into the room, pulled the smoldering tenant out, and aimed his extinguisher at the flames. The fire was put out, thanks to the daring of Prokhorchuk. Fire Chief Gorbushin approached him. "Good boy, Prokhorchuk," he said, "you've acted according to the regulations!" Whereupon the fire chief smiled and added: "You haven't noticed it, but your right mustachio is aflame." Prokhorchuk smiled and aimed a jet at his mustachio. It was dawning.

HE The story isn't bad. The title's suitable too: "A Noble Deed." But there are some passages in it that must be revised. You see, it's a shame when a story is good and you come across things that are different from what you'd wish. Let's see, how does it start, your story?

SHE It was the dead of night — three o'clock. Everybody in the town was asleep. . . .

HE No good at all. It implies that the police are asleep, and those on watch are asleep, and. . . . No, won't do at all. It indicates a lack of vigilance. That passage must be changed. Better write it like this: It was dead of night — three o'clock. No one in the town was asleep.

SHE But that's impossible, it's nighttime and people do sleep.

HE Yes, I suppose you're right. Then let's have it this way: Everybody in the town was asleep but was at his post.

SHE Asleep at their posts?

HE No, that's complete nonsense. Better write: Some people slept while others kept a sharp lookout. What comes next?

SHE Not a single electric light was burning.

HE What's this? Sounds as if, in our country, we make bulbs that don't work?

SHE But it's night. They were turned off.

HE It could reflect on our bulbs. Delete it! If they aren't lit, what need is there to mention them?

SHE (reading on) But suddenly a gory tongue of flame shot out of the fourth-floor window of a large gray house. "Help!" someone shouted, "we're on fire!"

HE What's that, panic?

SHE Yes.

HE And it is your opinion that panic ought to be publicized in the columns of our periodicals?

SHE No, of course not. But this is fiction, . . . a creative work. I'm describing a fire.

HE And you portray a man who spreads panic instead of a civic-minded citizen? If I were you, I'd replace that cry of "help" by some more rallying cry.

SHE For instance?

HE For instance, say . . . ". . . We shall put it out!" someone shouted. "Nothing to worry about, there's no fire."

SHE What do you mean, "there's no fire," when there *is* a fire?

HE No, "there's no fire" in the sense of "we shall put it out, nothing to worry about."

SHE It's impossible.

HE It's possible. And then, you could do away with the cry.

SHE (reads on) This was the voice of the careless tenant who, when he went to bed, had forgotten to switch off the electric hot plate.

HE The what tenant?

SHE Careless.

HE Do you think that carelessness should be popularized in the columns of our periodicals? I shouldn't think so. And then why did you write that he forgot to switch off the electric hot plate? Is that an appropriate example to set for the education of the readers?

SHE I didn't intend to use it educationally, but without the hot plate there'd have been no fire.

HE And would we be much worse off?

SHE No, better, of course.

HE Well then, that's how you should have written it. Away with the hot plate and then you won't have to mention the fire. Go on, read, how does it go after that? Come straight to the portrayal of the fireman.

SHE Fireman Prokhorchuk, a middle-aged Ukrainian . . .

HE That's nicely caught.

SHE . . . with large black mustachios, stopped in front of the door. The fireman stood there and thought.

HE Bad. A fireman mustn't think. He must put the fire out without thinking.

SHE But it is a fine point in the story.

HE In a story it may be a fine point but not in a fireman. Then also, since we have no fire, there's no need to drag the fireman into the house.

SHE But then, what about his dialogue with the fire chief?

HE Let them talk in the fire house. How does the dialogue go?

SHE (reads) Fire Chief Gorbushin approached him. "Good boy, Prokhorchuk," he said, "you've acted according to regulations!" Whereupon the fire chief smiled and added: "You haven't noticed it, but your right mustachio is aflame." Prokhorchuk smiled and aimed a jet at his mustachio. It was dawning.

HE Why must you have that?

SHE What?

HE The burning mustachio.

SHE I put it in for the humor of the thing. The man was so absorbed in his work that he didn't notice that his mustache was ablaze.

HE Believe me, you should delete it. Since there's no fire, the house isn't burning and there's no need to burn any mustachios.

SHE And what about the element of laughter?

HE There'll be laughter all right. When do people laugh? When things are good for them. And isn't it good that there's no fire? It's very good. And so everybody will laugh. Read what you have now.

SHE (reading) "A Noble Deed." It was the dead of night — three o'clock. Some people slept while others kept a sharp lookout. From the fourth-floor window of a large gray house somebody shouted: "We are not on fire!" "Good boy, Prokhorchuk!" said Fire Chief Gorbushin to Fireman Prokhorchuk, a middle-aged Ukrainian with large black mustachios, "you're following the regulations." Prokhorchuk smiled and aimed a jet of water at his mustachio. It was dawning.

HE There we have a good piece of writing! Now it can be published!

REVIEW QUESTIONS

1. From the A. O. Avdienko reading, how were communists supposed to feel about Stalin?
2. What were Yevgeny Yevtushenko's reasons for denouncing Stalin?
3. Describe the contrasting attitudes toward art in Yevtushenko's reading, first before Stalin's death and then afterward.
4. What do you think Yevtushenko meant by "the corruption of the human spirit" under Stalin?
5. What values did the censor strive to uphold in Vladimir Polyakov's story?
6. What does the story suggest about the impact of censorship on creativity?

▼▼▼

7 ▼ Stalin's Terror

The victims of Stalin's terror number in the many millions. Stalin had no qualms about sacrificing multitudes of people to build up the Soviet Union's strength and to make it a powerful factor in world politics. In addition, he felt entitled to settle his own private scores as well as national ones against secessionist Ukrainians. The Soviet government's first acknowledgment of Stalin's terror were made by Khrushchev. The full scope of it has begun to emerge only under Gorbachev.

Nikita Khrushchev
KHRUSHCHEV'S SECRET SPEECH

Nikita Khrushchev (1894–1971), first secretary of the Communist party (1953–1964) and premier of the Soviet Union (1958–1964), delivered a famous speech to an unofficial, closed session of the twentieth Party Congress on February 25, 1956. Although the speech was considered confidential, it was soon leaked to outsiders. While safeguarding the moral authority of Lenin, Khrushchev attacked Stalin, revealing some of the crimes committed by him and his closest associates in the 1930s. The following passages from the speech draw on evidence collected by a special commission of inquiry.

We have to consider seriously and analyze correctly this matter [the crimes of the Stalin era] in order that we may preclude any possibility of a repetition in any form whatever of what took place during the life of Stalin, who absolutely did not tolerate collegiality in leadership and in work, and who practiced brutal violence, not only toward everything which opposed him, but also toward that which seemed to his capricious and despotic character, contrary to his concepts.

Stalin acted not through persuasion, explanation, and patient co-operation with people, but by imposing his concepts and demanding absolute submission to his opinion. Whoever opposed this concept or tried to prove his viewpoint, and the correctness of his position, was doomed to removal from the leading collective and to subsequent moral and physical annihilation. This was especially true during the period following the XVIIth Party Congress [1934], when many prominent Party leaders and rank-and-file Party workers, honest and dedicated to the cause of Communism, fell victim to Stalin's despotism. . . .

Stalin originated the concept "enemy of the people." This term automatically rendered it unnecessary that the ideological errors of a man or men engaged in a controversy be proven; this term made possible the usage of the most cruel repression, violating all norms of revolutionary legality, against anyone who in any way disa-

greed with Stalin, against those who were only suspected of hostile intent, against those who had bad reputations. This concept, "enemy of the people," actually eliminated the possibility of any kind of ideological fight or the making of one's views known on this or that issue, even those of a practical character. In the main, and in actuality, the only proof of guilt used, against all norms of current legal science, was the "confession" of the accused himself; and, as subsequent probing proved, "confessions" were acquired through physical pressures against the accused.

This led to glaring violations of revolutionary legality, and to the fact that many entirely innocent persons, who in the past had defended the Party line, became victims. . . .

The Commission [of Inquiry] has become acquainted with a large quantity of materials in the NKVD [secret police, forerunner to the KGB] archives and with other documents and has established many facts pertaining to the fabrication of cases against Communists, to false accusations, to glaring abuses of socialist legality — which resulted in the death of innocent people. It became apparent that many Party, Soviet and economic activists who were branded in 1937–1938 as "enemies" were actually never enemies, spies, wreckers, etc., but were always honest Communists; they were only so stigmatized, and often, no longer able to bear barbaric tortures, they charged themselves (at the order of the investigative judges — falsifiers) with all kinds of grave and unlikely crimes. . . .

Lenin used severe methods only in the most necessary cases, when the exploiting classes were still in existence and were vigorously opposing the revolution, when the struggle for survival was decidedly assuming the sharpest forms, even including a civil war.

Stalin, on the other hand, used extreme methods and mass repressions at a time when the revolution was already victorious, when the Soviet state was strengthened, when the exploiting classes were already liquidated and Socialist relations were rooted solidly in all phases of national economy, when our Party was politically consolidated and had strengthened itself both numerically and ideologically. It is clear that here Stalin showed in a whole series of cases his intolerance, his brutality and his abuse of power. Instead of proving his political correctness and mobilizing the masses, he often chose the path of repression and physical annihilation, not only against actual enemies, but also against individuals who had not committed any crimes against the Party and the Soviet government. . . .

An example of vile provocation, of odious falsification and of criminal violation of revolutionary legality is the case of the former candidate for the Central Committee Political Bureau, one of the most eminent workers of the Party and of the Soviet government, Comrade Eikhe, who was a Party member since 1905. (*Commotion in the hall.*)

Comrade Eikhe was arrested on April 29, 1938, on the basis of slanderous materials, without the sanction of the Prosecutor of the USSR, which was finally received 15 months after the arrest.

Investigation of Eikhe's case was made in a manner which most brutally violated Soviet legality and was accompanied by willfulness and falsification.

Eikhe was forced under torture to sign ahead of time a protocol of his confession prepared by the investigative judges, in which he and several other eminent Party workers were accused of anti-Soviet activity.

On October 1, 1939, Eikhe sent his declaration to Stalin in which he categorically denied his guilt and asked for an examination of his case. In the declaration he wrote: "There is no more bitter misery than to sit in the jail of a government for which I have always fought."

A second declaration of Eikhe has been preserved which he sent to Stalin on October 27, 1939; in it he cited facts very convincingly and countered the slanderous accusations made against him, arguing that his provocatory accusation was on the one hand the work of real Trotskyites whose arrests he had sanctioned as First Secretary of the West Siberian Krai Party Committee and who conspired in order to take revenge on him, and, on the other hand, the result of the base falsification of materials by the investigative judges. . . .

It would appear that such an important declaration was worth an examination by the Central Committee. This, however, was not done and the declaration was transmitted to Beria [head of the NKVD] while the terrible maltreatment of the Political Bureau candidate, Comrade Eikhe, continued.

On February 2, 1940, Eikhe was brought before the court. Here he did not confess any guilt and said as follows:

In all the so-called confessions of mine there is not one letter written by me with the exception of my signatures under the protocols which were forced from me. I have made my confession under pressure from the investigative judge who from the time of my arrest tormented me. After that I began to write all this nonsense. . . . The most important thing for me is to tell the court, the Party and Stalin that I am not guilty. I have never been guilty of any conspiracy. I will die believing in the truth of Party policy as I have believed in it during my whole life.

On February 4 Eikhe was shot. (*Indignation in the hall.*)

Aleksandr I. Solzhenitsyn
FORCED LABOR CAMPS

"Corrective labor" was part of Stalin's efforts to terrorize the peoples of the Soviet Union into compliance with his efforts to modernize the country's economy and society. All those accused of disloyalty to the party and not killed outright ended up in one of the *gulags*. *Gulag* is the Russian term for the Soviet forced-labor camps, scattered, like islands in an archipelago, over the entire Soviet Union. The inhabitants of that archipelago were the *zeks,* as the political prisoners were called. Their labor served a double purpose. It was designed as punishment for their alleged crimes and, more important, as a means of obtaining vital raw materials — including lumber and minerals — from areas too inhospitable for, or outright hostile to, regular labor. Forced labor also built the canal linking the Leningrad area with the White Sea in the far north.

The life of the zeks has been detailed by Aleksandr I. Solzhenitsyn (b. 1918), a heroic literary figure. He was a victim of Stalin's terror for nine years (1945–1953), spent mostly in the dreaded camps. He survived to tell the tale in a number of works, the most substantial of which are the three volumes of *The Gulag Archipelago* (published in the United States in 1975). In these volumes Solzhenitsyn draws not only on his own bitter experience, but also on those of countless others caught in Stalin's terror. He even expanded his investigations to cover life in the labor camps from the start of Soviet rule to the death of Stalin in 1953 — in all its human and inhuman detail.

During the "thaw" following Khrushchev's revelations about Stalin's terror, Solzhenitsyn published his novel *One Day in the Life of Ivan Denisovich,* which for the first time allowed the Soviet public a glimpse of gulag realities. Continuing his investigations, Solzhenitsyn was subsequently silenced again and barred from attending the ceremony awarding him the 1970 Nobel Prize for literature. Expelled in 1972 from his country, he eventually settled in the United States on a secluded Vermont farm. An embittered anticommunist, he yearns for the simplicity of rural life in traditional Russia. The following selection describes the life of the political prisoners, the zeks, who are the "natives" of *The Gulag Archipelago.*

. . . [T]he life of the natives consists of work, work, work; of starvation, cold, and cunning. This work, for those who are unable to push others out of the way and set themselves up in a soft spot, is that selfsame *general work* which raises socialism up out of the earth, and drives us down into the earth.

One cannot enumerate nor cover all the different aspects of this work, nor wrap your tongue about them. To push a wheelbar-row. . . . To carry hand barrows. To unload bricks barehanded (the skin quickly wears off the fingers). To haul bricks on one's own body by "goat" (in a shoulder barrow). To break up stone and coal in quarry and mine, to dig clay and sand. To hack out eight cubic yards of gold-bearing ore with a pick and haul them to the screening apparatus. Yes, and just to dig in the earth, just to "chew" up earth (flinty soil and in winter). To cut coal underground. And there are ores there too — lead and copper. Yes, and one can also . . . pulverize copper ore (a sweet taste in the mouth, and one waters at the nose). One can impregnate [railroad] ties with creosote (and one's whole body at the same time too). One can carve out tunnels for railroads. And build roadbeds. One can dig peat in the bog up to one's waist in the mud. One can smelt ores. One can cast metal. One can cut hay on hummocks in swampy meadows (sinking up to one's ankles in water). One can be a stableman or a drayman [cart driver] (yes, and steal oats from the horse's bag for one's own pot, but the horse is government-issue, the old grassbag, and she'll last it out, most likely, but you can drop dead). Yes, and generally at the *"selkhozy"* — the Agricultural Camps — you can do every kind of peasant work (and there is no work better than that: you'll grab something from the ground for yourself).

But the father of all is our Russian forest with its genuinely golden tree trunks. . . . And the oldest of all the kinds of work in the Archipelago is logging. It summons everyone to itself and has room for everyone, and it is not even out of bounds for cripples (they will send out a three-man gang of armless men to stamp down the foot-and-a-half snow). Snow comes up to your chest. You are a lumberjack. First you yourself stamp it down next to the tree trunk. You cut down the tree. Then, hardly able to make your way through the snow, you cut off all the branches (and you have to feel them out in the snow and get to them with your ax). Still dragging your way through the same loose snow, you have to carry off all the branches and make piles of them and burn them. (They smoke. They don't burn.) And now you have to saw up the wood to size and stack it. And the work norm for you and your brother for the day is six and a half cubic yards each, or thirteen cubic yards for two men working together. (In Burepolom the norm was nine cubic yards, but the thick pieces also had to be split into blocks.) By then your arms would not be capable of lifting an ax nor your feet of moving.

During the war years (on war rations), the camp inmates called three weeks at logging *"dry execution."* . . .

. . . [T]heir summer workday was sometimes sixteen hours long! I don't know how it was with sixteen, but for many it was thirteen hours long — on earth-moving work in Karlag and at the northern logging operations — and these were hours on the job itself, over and above the three miles' walk to the forest and three back. And anyway, why should we argue about the length of the day? After all, the *work norm* was senior in rank to the length of the workday, and when the brigade didn't fulfill the norm, the only thing that was changed at the end of the shift was the convoy, and the work sloggers were left in the woods by the light of searchlights until midnight — so that they got back to the camp just before morning in time to eat their dinner along with their breakfast and go out into the woods again.

There is no one to tell about it either. They all died.

And then here's another way they raised the norms and proved it was possible to fulfill them: In cold lower than 60 degrees below zero, workdays were written off; in other words, on such days the records showed that the workers had not gone out to work; but they chased them out anyway, and whatever they squeezed out of them on those days was added to the other days, thereby raising the percentages. . . .

———

And how did they feed them in return? They poured water into a pot, and the best one might expect was that they would drop unscrubbed small potatoes into it, but otherwise black cabbage, beet tops, all kinds of trash. Or else vetch or bran, they didn't begrudge these. (And wherever there was a water shortage, as there was at the Samarka Camp near Karaganda, only one bowl of gruel was cooked a day, and they also gave out a ration of two cups of turbid salty water.) Everything any good was always and without fail stolen for the chiefs, for the trusties, and for the thieves — the cooks were all terrorized, and it was only by submissiveness that they kept their jobs. Certain amounts of fat and meat "subproducts" (in other words, not real food) were signed out from the warehouses, as were fish, peas, and cereals. But not much of that ever found its way into the mouth of the pot. And in remote places the chiefs even took all the *salt* for themselves for their own pickling. (In 1940, on the Kotlas-Vorkuta Railroad, both the bread and the gruel were unsalted.) The worse the food, the more of it they gave the zeks. They used to give them horse meat from exhausted horses driven to death at work, and, even though it was quite impossible to chew it, it was a feast. . . .

It was impossible to try to keep nourished on Gulag norms anyone who worked out in the bitter cold for thirteen or even ten hours. And it was completely impossible once the basic ration had been plundered. . . .

———

. . . [N]o matter how many hours there are in the working day — sooner or later sloggers will return to the barracks.

Their barracks? Sometimes it is a dugout, dug into the ground. And in the North more often . . . *a tent* — true, with earth banked and reinforced hit or miss with boards. Often there are kerosene lamps in place of electricity, but sometimes there are the ancient Russian "splinter lamps" or else cotton-wool wicks. (In Ust-Vym for two years they saw no kerosene, and even in headquarters barracks they got light from oil from the food store.) It is by this pitiful light that we will survey this ruined world.

Sleeping shelves in two stories, sleeping shelves in three stories, or, as a sign of luxury, "vagonki" — multiple bunks — the boards most often bare and nothing at all on them; on some of the work parties they steal so thoroughly (and then sell the spoils through the free employees) that nothing government-issue is given out and no one keeps anything of his own in the barracks; they take both their mess tins and their mugs to work with them (and even tote the bags containing their belongings — and thus laden they dig in the earth); those who have them put their blankets around their necks . . . or else lug their things to trusty friends in a guarded barracks. During the day the barracks are as empty as if uninhabited. At night they might turn over their wet work clothes to be dried in the drier (if there is a drier!) — but undressed like that you are going to freeze on the bare boards! And so they dry their clothes on themselves. At night their caps may freeze to the wall of the tent — or, in a woman's case, her hair. They even hide their bast sandals under their heads so they won't be stolen off their feet. . . . In the middle of the barracks there is an oil drum with holes in it which has been converted into a stove, and it is good when it gets red-hot — then the steamy odor of drying footcloths permeates the entire barracks — but it sometimes happens that the wet firewood in it doesn't burn. Some of the barracks are so infested with insects that even four days' fumigation with burning sulphur doesn't help and when in the summer the zeks go out to sleep on the ground in the camp compound the bedbugs crawl after them and find them even there. And the zeks boil the lice off their underwear in their mess tins after dining from them. . . .

And later there was that constant, clinging (and, for an intellectual, torturing) *lack of privacy,* the condition of not being an individual but a member of a brigade instead, and the necessity of acting for whole days and whole years not as you yourself have decided but as the brigade requires. . . .

Now that is the way of life of my Archipelago.

REVIEW QUESTIONS

1. Why was Nikita Khrushchev careful to distinguish Stalin from Lenin?
2. What charges against Stalin did Khrushchev highlight in his speech?
3. What image of Stalin did Khrushchev draw?

4. How did Stalin use the concept of the "enemy of the people"?
5. What attitude did Comrade Eikhe express in court about the party policy just before he was shot? What did this reveal about his character and about the strength of communist ideology?
6. How would you explain the causes of the treatment meted out to the zeks as described by Aleksandr Solzhenitsyn?
7. Put yourself in the position of a zek. How would you try to survive under the conditions described by Solzhenitsyn?
8. How would you characterize the misery of the zek?

SOURCES OF THE WESTERN TRADITION

CHAPTER

▼▼▼

11

Fascism
and World War II

Following World War I, fascist movements arose in Italy, Germany, and many other European countries. Although these movements differed — each a product of separate national histories and the outlook of each movement's leader — they shared a hatred of liberalism, democracy, and communism; a commitment to aggressive nationalism; and a glorification of the party leader. Fascist leaders cleverly utilized myths, rituals, and pageantry to mobilize and manipulate the masses.

Several conditions fostered the rise of fascism. One factor was the fear of communism among the middle and upper classes. Inspired by the success of the Bolsheviks in Russia, communists in other lands were calling for the establishment of Soviet-style republics. Increasingly afraid of a communist takeover, industrialists, landowners, government officials, army leaders, professionals, and shopkeepers were attracted to fascist movements that promised to protect their nations from this threat. A second factor contributing to the growth of fascism was the disillusionment of World War I veterans and the mood of violence bred by the war. The thousands of veterans facing unemployment and poverty made ideal recruits for fascist parties that glorified combat and organized private armies. A third contributing factor was the inability of democratic parliamentary governments to cope with the problems that burdened postwar Europe. Having lost confidence in the procedures and values of democracy, many people joined fascist movements that promised strong leadership, an end to party conflicts, and a unified national will.

Fascism's appeal to nationalist feelings also drew people into the movement. In a sense, fascism expressed the aggressive racial nationalism that had emerged in the late nineteenth century. Fascists saw themselves as dedicated idealists engaged in a heroic struggle to rescue their nations from domestic and foreign enemies; they aspired to regain lands lost by their countries in World War I or to acquire lands denied them by the Paris Peace Conference.

Fascists glorified instinct, will, and blood as the true forces of life; they openly attacked the ideals of reason, liberty, and equality — the legacies of the Enlightenment

ADOLF HITLER AND BENITO MUSSOLINI stride through a crowd during Hitler's visit to Italy in 1935. They formed the Berlin-Rome Axis the next year. (*AP/ Wide World Photos*)

and the French Revolution. At the center of German fascism (National Socialism or Nazism) was a bizarre racial mythology that preached the superiority of the German race and the inferiority of others, particularly Jews and Slavs.

Benito Mussolini, founder of the Italian Fascist party, came to power in 1922. Although he established a one-party state, he was less successful than Adolf Hitler, the leader of the German National Socialists, in controlling the state and the minds of the people. After gaining power as chancellor of the German government in 1933, Hitler moved to establish a totalitarian state that controlled all phases of political, social, and cultural life. Utilizing modern methods of administration and communication, the Nazi state manipulated the lives and thoughts of its citizens to a much greater extent than had absolute and tyrannical governments of the past. Rejecting central liberal principles, it outlawed competing political parties, made terror a government policy, and drew no distinction between the individual's private life and the interests of the state. The Nazi regime aspired to shape a "new man," one who possessed a sense of mission and was willing to devote body and soul to the party, its ideology, and its leader, *Der Fuehrer,* who was endowed with attributes of infallibility.

Hitler's goal, which he pursued obsessively, was to forge a vast German empire in central and eastern Europe and to subjugate "inferior" races. Hitler explicitly laid out his philosophy of *Lebensraum* (living space) and racial nationalism, but Britain and France did not properly assess his intentions. Believing that the German dictator could be reasoned with and fearful of engulfing their nations in another disastrous world war, British and French statesmen gave in to Hitler's demands during the 1930s. This policy of appeasement only made Germany stronger and did not avert World War II.

Perhaps as many as fifty million people, both soldiers and civilians, died in World War II; of those, about twenty million were Russians, the Soviet Union suffering the most severe losses. Millions of people were murdered by the Nazis, including six million Jews, whom the Nazis aimed to exterminate. Nazi atrocities demonstrated anew the immense power of the irrational and the precariousness of Western civilization.

I ▼ Italian Fascism

Benito Mussolini (1883–1945) started his political life as a socialist and in 1912 was appointed editor of *Avanti,* the leading socialist newspaper. During World War I, Mussolini was expelled from the Socialist party for advocating Italy's entry into the conflict. Immediately after the war, he organized the Fascist party. Exploiting labor unrest, fear of communism, and thwarted nationalist hopes, Mussolini gained followers among veterans and the middle class. Powerful industrialists and landowners, viewing the Fascists as a bulwark against communism, helped to finance the young movement. An opportunist, Mussolini organized a march on Rome in 1922 to bring down the government. King Victor Emmanuel, fearful of civil war, appointed the Fascist leader prime minister. Had Italian liberals and the king taken a firm stand, the government could have crushed the 20,000 lightly armed marchers.

Benito Mussolini
FASCIST DOCTRINES

Ten years after he seized power, Mussolini, assisted by philosopher Giovanni Gentile (1875–1944), contributed an article to the *Italian Encyclopedia* in which he discussed fascist political and social doctrines. In this piece, Mussolini lauded violence as a positive experience; attacked Marxism for denying idealism by subjecting human beings to economic laws and for dividing the nation into warring classes; and denounced liberal democracy for promoting individual selfishness at the expense of the national community and for being unable to solve the nation's problems. The fascist state, he said, required unity and power, not individual freedom. The following excerpts are from Mussolini's article.

. . . Above all, Fascism, the more it considers and observes the future and the development of humanity quite apart from political considerations of the moment, believes neither in the possibility nor the utility of perpetual peace. It thus repudiates the doctrine of Pacifism — born of a renunciation of the struggle and an act of cowardice in the face of sacrifice. War alone brings up to its highest tension all human energy and puts the stamp of nobility upon the peoples who have the courage to meet it. All other trials are substitutes, which never really put men into the position where they have to make the great decision — the alternative of life or death. Thus a doctrine which is founded upon this harmful postulate of peace is hostile to Fascism. And thus hostile to the spirit of Fascism, though accepted for what use they can be in dealing with particular political situations, are all the international leagues and societies which, as history will show, can be scattered to the winds when once strong national feeling is aroused by any motive — sentimental, ideal, or practical. This anti-pacifist spirit is carried by Fascism even into the life of the individual; the proud motto of the *Squadrista,* "Me ne frego" [It doesn't matter], written on the bandage of the wound, is an act of philosophy not only stoic, the summary of a doctrine not only political — it is the education to combat, the acceptation of the risks which combat implies, and a new way of life for Italy. Thus the Fascist accepts life and loves it, knowing nothing of and despising suicide: he rather conceives of life as duty and struggle and conquest, life which should be high and full, lived for oneself, but above all for others — those who are at hand and those who are far distant, contemporaries, and those who will come after. . . .

. . . Fascism [is] the complete opposite of . . . Marxian Socialism, the materialist conception of history; according to which the history of human civilization can be explained simply through the conflict of interests among the various social groups and by the change and development in the means and instruments of production. That the changes in the economic field — new discoveries of raw materials, new methods of working them, and the inventions of science — have their importance no one can deny; but that these factors are sufficient to explain the history of humanity excluding all others is an absurd delusion. Fascism, now and always, believes in holiness and in heroism; that is to say, in actions influenced by no economic motive, direct or indirect. And if the economic conception of history be denied, according to which theory men are no more than puppets, carried to and fro by the waves of chance, while the real directing forces are quite out of their control, it follows that the existence of an unchangeable and unchanging class-war is also denied — the natural progeny of the economic conception of history. And above all Fascism denies that class-war can be the preponderant force in the transformation of society. . . .

After Socialism, Fascism combats the whole complex system of democratic ideology, and repudiates it, whether in its theoretical premises or in its practical application. Fascism denies that the majority, by the simple fact that it is a majority, can direct human society; it denies that numbers alone can govern by means of a periodical consultation, and it affirms the immutable, beneficial, and fruitful inequality of mankind, which can never be permanently leveled through the mere operation of a mechanical process such as universal suffrage. . . .

. . . Fascism denies, in democracy, the absur[d] conventional untruth of political equality dressed out in the garb of collective irresponsibility, and the myth of "happiness" and indefinite progress. . . .

. . . Given that the nineteenth century was the century of Socialism, of Liberalism, and of Democracy, it does not necessarily follow that the twentieth century must also be a century of Socialism, Liberalism, and Democracy: political doctrines pass, but humanity remains; and it may rather be expected that this will be a century of authority, . . . a century of Fascism. For if the nineteenth century was a century of individualism (Liberalism always signifying individualism) it may be expected that this will be the century of collectivism, and hence the century of the State. . . .

The foundation of Fascism is the conception of the State, its character, its duty, and its aim. Fascism conceives of the State as an absolute, in comparison with which all individuals or groups are relative, only to be conceived of in their relation to the State. The conception of the Liberal State is not that of a directing force, guiding the play and development, both material and spiritual, of a collective body, but merely a force limited to the function of recording results: on the other hand, the Fascist State is itself conscious and has itself a will and a personality — thus it may be called the "ethic" State. . . .

. . . The Fascist State organizes the nation, but leaves a sufficient margin of liberty to the individual; the latter is deprived of all useless and possibly harmful freedom, but retains what is essential; the deciding power in this question cannot be the individual, but the State alone. . . .

. . . For Fascism, the growth of empire, that is to say the expansion of the nation, is an essential manifestation of vitality, and its opposite a sign of decadence. Peoples which are rising, or rising again after a period of decadence, are always imperialist; any renunciation is a sign of decay and of death. Fascism is the doctrine best adapted to represent the tendencies and the aspirations of a people, like the people of Italy, who are rising again after many centuries of abasement and foreign servitude. But empire demands discipline, the coordination of all forces and a deeply felt sense of duty and sacrifice: this fact explains many aspects of the practical working of the régime, the character of many forces in the State, and the necessarily severe measures which must be taken against those who would oppose this spontaneous and inevitable movement of Italy in the twentieth century, and would oppose it by recalling the outworn ideology of the nineteenth century — repudiated wheresoever there has been the courage to undertake great experiments of social and political transformation; for never before has the nation stood more in need of authority, of direction, and of order. If every age has its own characteristic doctrine, there are a thousand signs which point to Fascism as the characteristic doctrine of our time. For if a doctrine must be a living thing, this is proved by the fact that Fascism has created a living faith; and that this faith is very powerful in the minds of men is demonstrated by those who have suffered and died for it.

REVIEW QUESTIONS

1. Why did Benito Mussolini consider pacifism to be the enemy of fascism?
2. Why did Mussolini attack Marxism?
3. How did Mussolini view majority rule and equality?
4. What relationship did Mussolini see between the individual and the state?

▼▼▼

2 ▼ Conservative Attack on the Weimar Republic

In November 1918 a revolution forced the German emperor, Kaiser William II, to flee, and a republic was proclaimed in Germany. Immediately afterward, the new government (soon to be called the Weimar Republic) signed an armistice agreement ending the war. The Weimar Republic, headed by democratic socialists, faced attacks from both the left and the right. In early 1919, radical Marxists, seeking to establish a proletarian state, took up arms against the republic. Although the communists were easily subdued, the middle and upper classes were deeply scarred by the uprising. Fear of communism led many of these people to support the right-wing parties that sought to bring down the republic.

The rightist attack on the republic was multifaceted. Traditional conservatives — aristocrats, army leaders, and industrialists — were contemptuous of democracy and sought a strong government that would protect the nation from communism and check the power of the working class. In a peculiar twist of logic, radical right-wing nationalists blamed Germany's defeat in World War I and the humiliation of the Versailles Treaty on the republic.

Friedrich Jünger
THE CULT OF BLOOD, SOIL, AND ACTION

The constitution of the Weimar Republic, premised intellectually and emotionally on the liberal-rational tradition, had strong opposition from German conservatives who valued the authoritarian state promoted by Bismarck and the
kaisers. In expressing their hostility to the Weimar Republic, conservatives attacked liberal democracy and reason and embraced an ultranationalist philosophy of blood, soil, and action. In the brittle disunity and disorientation of German society, conservative nationalists searched for community and certainty in
the special qualities of the German soul. Their antirationalism, hostility to democracy, and ultranationalism undermined the Weimar Republic and contributed to the triumph of Nazism.

The selection below is freely adapted from a small book, *The Rise of the
New Nationalism* (1926), written by Friedrich Georg Jünger, the brother of
Ernst Jünger, who is well known for his literary glorification of the war experi-
ence.

The new nationalism envisages a state elevated
by popular enthusiasm and gathering in itself
the fullness of power as the sole guarantor of
Germany's collective future. It is both armor
and sword, preserving indigenous culture and
destroying the alien elements that arrogantly
push against it.

The new nationalism in its formative state
throbs with revolutionary excitement. It lives
unrestrained in our gut feeling, seething in our
blood, although still full of confusion.

The November revolution was the result of a
moral collapse promoted by external pressures.
It happened at a time when the frightful struggle of the war should have demanded the concentration of all energies. Rightly it was called
a stab in the back, because it was led by Germans against Germans, provocatively and from
the rear. The revolution proved the shallowness
of its promoters. They could not radiate youth,
warmth, energy, or greatness. There were deputies, but no leaders. There was no man among
them who stood out by his exceptional qualities. We saw the feeble liberals and heard for
the hundredth time the promulgation of human
rights. One might say, a dusty storeroom was
thrown open from which emerged human rights,
freedom, toleration, parliament, suffrage, and

popular representation. Finally they wrote a
liberalist novel: the Weimar constitution.

But the Weimar regime was a body in which
there flowed no blood. You could talk about it
only in empty phrases. What an overabundance
of phrases and phrasemakers! They had plastered the last available fence, the last walls,
with their babble.

The new nationalism wants to awaken a sense
of the greatness of the German past. Life must
be evaluated according to the will to power,
which reveals the warlike character of all life.
The value of the individual is assessed according
to his military value for the state, and the state
is recognized as the most creative and toughest
source of power. . . .

It is necessary to look at the conditions that
have preceded and created the new nationalism.
The recent past has destroyed our inherited collective sense of tender intimacy by trying to
subvert and weaken all close bonds of community. It has denied all values that create cohe-
sion in the community. Everything conspired
to speed the disintegration of human ties in
state, church, marriage, family, and many
other institutions. A mad urge for throwing off
all restraints, for dissolution, for unbridled liberty, dissolved society into driftwood. This urge

shaped the flighty masses, depriving them of all convictions of meaningfulness. These excesses finally aroused disgust and a counter movement arose. A new consolidation of purpose began. From it arises the future success of the new nationalism, its resistance to the atomistic liberty and to the freedom of soulless decadence. Social life is never free. A mighty mysterious bond of blood links the lives of individuals and subsumes them in a fateful wholeness. Blood, as it were, sings the song of destiny.

Life is deeply bonded. And only as it remains true to these bonds and is rooted in them, can it fulfill itself. Life withers if these roots are cut or if it seeks nourishment from alien roots. It is tied to the blood; at its core it is part of a community of blood. The intellect enjoys freedom only to the degree to which it is loyal to the blood. The new nationalism is born of the new awareness of blood-bonded community; it wants to make the promptings of the blood prevail. Escaping from the boundlessness of contemporary life, it is driven forward by the yearning for the bonds of blood.

The new nationalism wants to strengthen the blood bonds and form them into a new state. Those who are part of an alien blood community, or those internationalists who feel joined to a transcendent community, are excluded. They have to be driven out, because they weaken the rich and fertile body of the nation that nourishes everything of significance.

The awareness of these blood bonds demands the fight against all movements weakening the spiritual bonds that affirm the community of blood. It judges all values according to that principle. It wants life to be whole, lived in a new intoxicating abundance, responsibly restricted, and not dissipated or fatigued by the intellect. In every nationalism there is something intoxicating, a wild and lusty pride, a mighty heroic vitality. It has no critical or analytic inclinations, which weaken life. It wants no tolerance, because life does not know tolerance. It is fanatical, because the promptings of the blood are fanatical and unjust. It does not care for scientific justification.

Nationalism must apply its force to the masses and try to set them afire by means peculiar to itself. These means are neither parliaments nor parties, but rather military units mobilized by a fierce loyalty to a leader. These units alone are called to carry out the will of the new nationalism. They will be the more powerful and successful the more they act in an organized and disciplined manner, the more unconditionally they subject themselves to the ideal of the nationalist state. The intensity of their discipline is the decisive factor. Next comes the urgent task to create a mighty organization covering all of Germany and to seize the reins of government. The community of blood is given the highest priority. It is defined racelike by the nationalist sentiment. It recognizes no European community, no common humanity. For us, mingling races and wiping out the difference between masters and slaves among the peoples of the world are an abomination. We want the sharpest separation of races.

The new state, obviously, will be authoritarian. The new nationalism is determined to make that authoritarianism absolute, all-surpassing, consolidating the state as the new steel-like instrument of power. It values the state as the highest historic fact and the most important vehicle for attaining the nationalist aims. That state shall be the mold for the nation's blood-bound will to power. For that reason the nationalist movement urges the annihilation of all political forms of liberalism. No more parties, parliaments, elections! No more hailshowers of prattle or the bustle of the senile parliamentary intrigues that burden the country! No more packs of petty politicians and literati poking fun at the state! Tremendous energies are wasted in the labyrinth of parliamentary procedure.

The madhouse of parliamentary activity in which every event is dragged out unconscionably without providing a sense of a great future, without consideration for the nation's dignity, reveals the foul sickness of liberalism. Masculine earnestness is dirtied by empty phrases; everything is befogged by the dense steam of corruption. There are no men of distinction in parliament. Universal suffrage is an ingenious sieve working in favor of bustling agitators and zealous blockheads. The assurance and righteousness with which it repels men of talent betray the hatred at the root of liberalistic thinking. These are the people who, after the November revolution, succeeded in driving wedges between people, inciting them against each other. They have paralyzed the nation's role in international relations and are responsible for the country's boundless misery.

While these people debate, vote, and slander each other in the battle of slogans, the new nationalism prepares for the crucial blow. The nationalist revolution proceeds on course; its thunderstorms loom over the horizon. And we can only wish that the explosion will be terrifying. May the elementary liberation of blood sweep away all the debris that burdens the times. The new nationalism is not given to compromise. Every institution needs to be examined whether it responsibly serves the nation or whether it is ripe to be smashed.

The nationalist state makes no claim to be the freest and most just state — that smacks of liberalism and negates its authoritarian character. The nationalist state aims at creating the most disciplined government devoid of any feeling of justice for its enemies. It wants a state permeated by a leader's personality. The personal element, inherent in all contemporary nationalist striving, belongs among the foundations of the new nationalism and of the state it wants to create. The will of the dictator is essential for the future. The craving for the blood-bond concentration of power raises the hope for an absolute leader even higher.

The adoption of the leader principle signifies the basic activation of the state — a state adapted to the tempo of the times; it shapes the nation's volcanic dynamism. The principle of the leader built into the structure of the state, almost resembling the military command structure, makes the will to resist external pressure more fanatical. The concentration of power in one man gives the state incredible strength and vitality. Decisions gain in strength and correctness; the choice of means becomes more effective; the frictions lessen; and the thrust of policy becomes more unified. The state must be prepared for something extraordinary, ready to jump. That this condition be achieved as soon as possible is the anxious yearning rising from our blood.

The great war has not ended. It has been the prelude to a brutal age of armed conflict. According to the deepest insight of the new nationalism, it is the beginning of a terrible, all-demanding struggle. Everything points to the fact that a new age of great violence is in the offing. Our blood is not deceived by the exhausted masses and the intellectual trends that passionately proclaim the dawn of freedom, human brotherhood, and sweet peace for all mankind. Nobody can prevent the war that arises from fateful depths and perhaps tomorrow will blanket the earth with corpses.

The savagery and corruption in the present world prepare mighty upheavals for the future. Then everything incapable and exhausted will be eliminated, and only he who carries within himself an unbounded fighting spirit and is armed to the teeth will be found worthy for the final decision. Under the surface of contemporary humanitarianism there looms a different attitude, vital, cruel, and merciless like steel. In the age of the machine, all means are legitimate. People and methods have been brutalized. Every restraint is like an opiate that diminishes the nation's will to power. At stake is the question: which people will finish the fight and administer the world and its resources in their own name? The convictions of the new nationalism are by necessity imperialist. The rule is: either domination or submission. Domination means being imperialist, having the will to exercise power and achieve superiority. Top priority, therefore, goes to mobilizing human wills. That is best done by the nationalist state. It guarantees total mobilization down to the last detail. The development of technology parallels the trends of political imperialism. It conveys a sense of the coming conflicts. The state, the economy, science — all are slowly geared to imperialist expansion, proving the fatefulness of the trend. Should we avoid it because it demands great sacrifices and the submission of the individual, or because the awesome aims make life cheap? "Never!" cries the nationalist, because he aims at domination and not submission. He does not want to reject fate. He will not retreat even before the prospect of getting wiped out. He looks forward to the great and mighty Germany of the future, the irresistible strength of a hundred million Germans at the core of Europe!

REVIEW QUESTIONS

1. What is the significance of the leader principle, military discipline, imperial conquest, war, peace, and the blood-bonded community for Friedrich Jünger?
2. Why did Jünger attack liberalism?
3. What political implications do you see in Jünger's statement that there is in nationalism "something intoxicating, a wild and lusty pride, a mighty heroic vitality"?
4. Why does Jünger regard fanaticism as a value? Do you agree or disagree? Explain.

▼▼▼

3 ▼ The World-View of Nazism

Many extreme racist-nationalist and paramilitary organizations sprang up in postwar Germany. Adolf Hitler, a veteran of World War I, joined one of these organizations, which became known as the National Socialist German Worker's party (commonly called the Nazi party). Hitler (1889–1945) had uncanny insight into the state of mind of postwar Germans and at mass meetings employed his power as an orator to play on their dissatisfactions with the Weimar Republic.

Adolf Hitler
≪ MEIN KAMPF ≫

In November 1923, Hitler attempted to overthrow the state government in Bavaria as the first step in bringing down the Weimar Republic. But the Nazis quickly scattered when the Bavarian police opened fire. Hitler was arrested and sentenced to five years' imprisonment — he served only nine months. While in prison, Hitler wrote *Mein Kampf (My Struggle)* in which he presented his views. The book came to be regarded as an authoritative expression of the Nazi world-view and served as a kind of sacred writing for the Nazi movement.

Hitler's thought — a patchwork of nineteenth-century anti-Semitic, Volkish, Social Darwinist, and anti-Marxist ideas — contrasted sharply with the core values of both the Judeo-Christian and the Enlightenment traditions. Central to Hitler's world-view was racial mythology: a heroic Germanic race that was descended from the ancient Aryans who once swept across Europe, and was battling for survival against racial inferiors. In the following passages excerpted from *Mein Kampf,* Hitler presents his views of race, of propaganda, and of the National Socialist territorial goals.

[THE PRIMACY OF RACE]

No more than Nature desires the mating of weaker with stronger individuals, even less does she desire the blending of a higher with a lower race, since, if she did, her whole work of higher breeding, over perhaps hundreds of thousands of years, might be ruined with one blow.

Historical experience offers countless proofs of this. It shows with terrifying clarity that in every mingling of Aryan blood with that of lower peoples the result was the end of the cultured people. North America, whose population consists in by far the largest part of Germanic elements who mixed but little with the lower colored peoples, shows a different humanity and culture from Central and South America, where the predominantly Latin immigrants often mixed with the aborigines on a large scale. By this one example, we can clearly and distinctly recognize the effect of racial mixture. The Germanic inhabitant of the American continent, who has remained racially pure and unmixed, rose to be master of the continent; he will remain the master as long as he does not fall a victim to defilement of the blood.

The result of all racial crossing is therefore in brief always the following:

(a) Lowering of the level of the higher race;

(b) Physical and intellectual regression and hence the beginning of a slowly but surely progressing sickness.

To bring about such a development is, then, nothing else but to sin against the will of the eternal creator. . . .

Everything we admire on this earth today — science and art, technology and inventions — is only the creative product of a few peoples and originally perhaps of *one* race. On them depends the existence of this whole culture. If they perish, the beauty of this earth will sink into the grave with them. . . .

All great cultures of the past perished only because the originally creative race died out from blood poisoning.

The ultimate cause of such a decline was their forgetting that all culture depends on men and not conversely; hence that to preserve a certain culture the man who creates it must be preserved. This preservation is bound up with the rigid law of necessity and the right to victory of the best and stronger in this world. . . .

If we were to divide mankind into three groups, the founders of culture, the bearers of culture, the destroyers of culture, only the Aryan could be considered as the representative of the first group. From him originate the foundations and walls of all human creation. . . .

Blood mixture and the resultant drop in the racial level is the sole cause of the dying out of old cultures; for men do not perish as a result of lost wars, but by the loss of that force of resistance which is contained only in pure blood.

All who are not of good race in this world are chaff. . . .

A state which in this age of racial poisoning dedicates itself to the care of its best racial elements must some day become lord of the earth.

▷ Modern anti-Semitism was a powerful legacy of the Middle Ages and the unsettling changes brought about by rapid industrialization; it was linked to racist doctrines that asserted the Jews were inherently wicked and bore dangerous racial qualities. Hitler grasped the political potential of anti-Semitism: by concentrating all evil in one enemy, he could provide non-Jews with an emotionally satisfying explanation for all their misfortunes and thus manipulate and unify the German people.

[ANTI-SEMITISM]

The mightiest counterpart to the Aryan is represented by the Jews. . . .

. . . The Jewish people, despite all apparent intellectual qualities, is without any true culture, and especially without any culture of its own. For what sham culture the Jew today possesses is the property of other peoples, and for the most part it is ruined in his hands.

In judging the Jewish people's attitude on the question of human culture, the most essential characteristic we must always bear in mind is that there has never been a Jewish art and accordingly there is none today either; that above all the two queens of all the arts, architecture and music, owe nothing original to the Jews. What they do accomplish in the field of art is either patchwork or intellectual theft. Thus, the Jew lacks those qualities which distinguish the races that are creative and hence culturally blessed. . . .

On this first and greatest lie, that the Jews are not a race but a religion, more and more lies are based in necessary consequence. Among them is the lie with regard to the language of the Jew. For him it is not a means for expressing his thoughts, but a means for concealing them. When he speaks French, he thinks Jewish, and while he turns out German verses, in his life he only expresses the nature of his nationality. As long as the Jew has not become the master of the other peoples, he must speak their languages whether he likes it or not, but as soon as they became his slaves, they would all have to learn a universal language. . . .

With satanic joy in his face, the black-haired Jewish youth lurks in wait for the unsuspecting girl whom he defiles with his blood, thus stealing her from her people. With every means he tries to destroy the racial foundations of the people he has set out to subjugate. . . .

For a racially pure people which is conscious of its blood can never be enslaved by the Jew. In this world he will forever be master over bastards and bastards alone.

And so he tries systematically to lower the racial level by a continuous poisoning of individuals.

And in politics he begins to replace the idea of democracy by the dictatorship of the proletariat.

In the organized mass of Marxism he has found the weapon which lets him dispense with democracy and in its stead allows him to subjugate and govern the peoples with a dictatorial and brutal fist.

He works systematically for revolutionization in a twofold sense: economic and political.

Around peoples who offer too violent a resistance to attack from within he weaves a net of enemies, thanks to his international influence, incites them to war, and finally, if necessary, plants the flag of revolution on the very battlefields.

In economics he undermines the states until the social enterprises which have become unprofitable are taken from the state and subjected to his financial control.

In the political field he refuses the state the means for its self-preservation, destroys the foundations of all national self-maintenance and defense, destroys faith in the leadership, scoffs at its history and past, and drags everything that is truly great into the gutter.

Culturally he contaminates art, literature, the theater, makes a mockery of natural feeling, overthrows all concepts of beauty and sublimity, of the noble and the good, and instead drags men down into the sphere of his own base nature.

Religion is ridiculed, ethics and morality represented as outmoded, until the last props of a nation in its struggle for existence in this world have fallen. . . .

And so the Jew today is the great agitator for the complete destruction of Germany. Wherever in the world we read of attacks against Germany, Jews are their fabricators, just as in peacetime and during the War the press of the Jewish stock exchange and Marxists systematically stirred up hatred against Germany until state after state abandoned neutrality and, renouncing the true interests of the peoples, entered the service of the World War coalition.

The Jewish train of thought in all this is clear. The Bolshevization of Germany — that is, . . . to make possible the sweating of the German working class under the yoke of Jewish world finance [which] is conceived only as a preliminary to the further extension of this

Jewish tendency of world conquest. As often in history, Germany is the great pivot in the mighty struggle. If our people and our state become the victim of these bloodthirsty and avaricious Jewish tyrants of nations, the whole earth will sink into the snares of this octopus; if Germany frees herself from this embrace, this greatest of dangers to nations may be regarded as broken for the whole world. . . .

▷ Hitler was a master propagandist and advanced his ideas on propaganda techniques in *Mein Kampf.* He mocked the learned and book-oriented German liberals and socialists whom he felt were entirely unsuited for modern mass politics. The successful leader, he said, must win over the masses through the use of simple ideas and images, constantly repeated, to control the mind by evoking primitive feelings. Hitler contended that mass meetings were the most effective means of winning over followers. What counted most at these demonstrations, he said, was will power, strength, and unflagging determination radiating from the speaker to every single individual in the crowd.

[PROPAGANDA AND MASS RALLIES]

The function of propaganda does not lie in the scientific training of the individual, but in calling the masses' attention to certain facts, processes, necessities, etc., whose significance is thus for the first time placed within their field of vision.

The whole art consists in doing this so skillfully that everyone will be convinced that the fact is real, the process necessary, the necessity correct, etc. . . . Its effect for the most part must be aimed at the emotions and only to a very limited degree at the so-called intellect.

All propaganda must be popular and its intellectual level must be adjusted to the most limited intelligence among those it is addressed to. Consequently, the greater the mass it is intended to reach, the lower its purely intellectual level will have to be. . . .

The art of propaganda lies in understanding the emotional ideas of the great masses and finding, through a psychologically correct form, the way to the attention and thence to the heart of the broad masses. . . .

The receptivity of the great masses is very limited, their intelligence is small, but their power of forgetting is enormous. In consequence of these facts, all effective propaganda must be limited to a very few points and must harp on these in slogans until the last member of the public understands what you want him to understand by your slogans. As soon as you sacrifice this slogan and try to be many-sided, the effect will piddle away, for the crowd can neither digest nor retain the material offered. In this way the result is weakened and in the end entirely cancelled out.

Thus we see that propaganda must follow a simple line and correspondingly the basic tactics must be psychologically sound. . . .

The function of propaganda is, for example, not to weigh and ponder the rights of different people, but exclusively to emphasize the one right which it has set out to argue for. Its task is not to make an objective study of the truth, in so far as it favors the enemy, and then set it before the masses with academic fairness; its task is to serve our own right, always and unflinchingly. . . .

But the most brilliant propagandist technique will yield no success unless one fundamental principle is borne in mind constantly and with unflagging attention. It must confine itself to a few points and repeat them over and over. Here, as so often in this world, persistence is the first and most important requirement for success. . . .

The purpose of propaganda is not to provide interesting distraction for blasé young gentlemen, but to convince, and what I mean is to convince the masses. But the masses are slow-moving, and they always require a certain time before they are ready even to notice a thing, and only after the simplest ideas are repeated thousands of times will the masses finally remember them.

When there is a change, it must not alter the

content of what the propaganda is driving at, but in the end must always say the same thing. For instance, a slogan must be presented from different angles, but the end of all remarks must always and immutably be the slogan itself. Only in this way can the propaganda have a unified and complete effect. . . .

All advertising, whether in the field of business or politics, achieves success through the continuity and sustained uniformity of its application. . . .

The mass meeting is . . . necessary for the reason that in it the individual, who at first, while becoming a supporter of a young movement, feels lonely and easily succumbs to the fear of being alone, for the first time gets the picture of a larger community, which in most people has a strengthening, encouraging effect. The same man, within a company or a battalion, surrounded by all his comrades, would set out on an attack with a lighter heart than if left entirely on his own. In the crowd he always feels somewhat sheltered, even if a thousand reasons actually argue against it.

But the community of the great demonstration not only strengthens the individual, it also unites and helps to create an *esprit de corps*. The man who is exposed to grave tribulations, as the first advocate of a new doctrine in his factory or workshop, absolutely needs that strengthening which lies in the conviction of being a member and fighter in a great comprehensive body. And he obtains an impression of this body for the first time in the mass demonstration. When from his little workshop or big factory, in which he feels very small, he steps for the first time into a mass meeting and has thousands and thousands of people of the same opinions around him, when, as a seeker, he is swept away by three or four thousand others into the mighty effect of suggestive intoxication and enthusiasm, when the visible success and agreement of thousands confirm to him the rightness of the new doctrine and for the first time arouse doubt in the truth of his previous conviction — then he himself has succumbed to the magic influence of what we designate as "mass suggestion." The will, the longing, and also

the power of thousands are accumulated in every individual. The man who enters such a meeting doubting and wavering leaves it inwardly reinforced: he has become a link in the community. . . .

▷ Hitler was an extreme nationalist who wanted a reawakened, racially united Germany to expand eastward at the expense of the Slavs, whom he viewed as racially inferior.

[LEBENSRAUM]

Only an adequately large space on this earth assures a nation of freedom of existence. . . .

If the National Socialist movement really wants to be consecrated by history with a great mission for our nation, it must be permeated by knowledge and filled with pain at our true situation in this world; boldly and conscious of its goal, it must take up the struggle against the aimlessness and incompetence which have hitherto guided our German nation in the line of foreign affairs. Then, without consideration of "traditions" and prejudices, it must find the courage to gather our people and their strength for an advance along the road that will lead this people from its present restricted living space to new land and soil, and hence also free it from the danger of vanishing from the earth or of serving others as a slave nation.

The National Socialist movement must strive to eliminate the disproportion between our population and our area — viewing this latter as a source of food as well as a basis for power politics — between our historical past and the hopelessness of our present impotence. . . .

. . . The demand for restoration of the frontiers of 1914 is a political absurdity of such proportions and consequences as to make it seem a crime. Quite aside from the fact that the Reich's frontiers in 1914 were anything but logical. For in reality they were neither complete in the sense of embracing the people of German nationality, nor sensible with regard to geo-military expediency. . . .

As opposed to this, we National Socialists must hold unflinchingly to our aim in foreign policy, namely, *to secure for the German people the land and soil to which they are entitled on this earth.* And this action is the only one which, before God and our German posterity, would make any sacrifice of blood seem justified. . . .

. . . Just as our ancestors did not receive the soil on which we live today as a gift from Heaven, but had to fight for it at the risk of their lives, in the future no folkish grace will win soil for us and hence life for our people, but only the might of a victorious sword.

Much as all of us today recognize the necessity of a reckoning with France, it would remain ineffectual in the long run if it represented the whole of our aim in foreign policy. It can and will achieve meaning only if it offers the rear cover for an enlargement of our people's living space in Europe. . . .

If we speak of soil in Europe today, we can primarily have in mind only *Russia* and her vassal border states. . . .

REVIEW QUESTIONS

1. How did Adolf Hitler account for cultural greatness? Cultural decline?
2. What comparisons did Hitler draw between Aryans and Jews?
3. What kind of evidence did Hitler offer for his anti-Semitic arguments?
4. Theodor Mommsen, a nineteenth-century German historian, said that anti-Semites do not listen to "logic and ethical arguments. . . . They listen only to their own envy and hatred, to the meanest instincts." Discuss this statement.
5. What insights did Hitler have about mass psychology and propaganda?
6. What foreign policy goals did Hitler have for Germany? How did he expect them to be achieved?

▼▼▼

4 ▼ The Great Depression and Hitler's Rise to Power

Had it not been for the Great Depression that began in late 1929, the National Socialists might have remained a relatively small and insignificant party, a minor irritant outside the mainstream of German politics. In 1928 the Nazis had 810,000 votes; in 1930, during the Depression, their share of votes soared to 6,400,000. To many Germans, the Depression was final evidence that the Weimar Republic had failed. The traumatic experience of unemployment and the sense of hopelessness led millions to embrace Hitler.

Heinrich Hauser
≪ WITH GERMANY'S UNEMPLOYED ≫

The following article excerpted from *Die Tat,* a National Socialist periodical, describes the loss of dignity suffered by the unemployed wandering Germany's roads and taking shelter in municipal lodging houses. Conditions in 1932 as described in the article radicalized millions of Germans, particularly young people.

An almost unbroken chain of homeless men extends the whole length of the great Hamburg-Berlin highway.

There are so many of them moving in both directions, impelled by the wind or making their way against it, that they could shout a message from Hamburg to Berlin by word of mouth.

It is the same scene for the entire two hundred miles, and the same scene repeats itself between Hamburg and Bremen, between Bremen and Kassel, between Kassel and Würzburg, between Würzburg and Munich. All the highways in Germany over which I traveled this year presented the same aspects. . . .

. . . Most of the hikers paid no attention to me. They walked separately or in small groups, with their eyes on the ground. And they had the queer, stumbling gait of barefooted people, for their shoes were slung over their shoulders. Some of them were guild members, — carpenters with embroidered wallets, knee breeches, and broad felt hats; milkmen with striped red shirts, and bricklayers with tall black hats, — but they were in a minority. Far more numerous were those whom one could assign to no special profession or craft — unskilled young people, for the most part, who had been unable to find a place for themselves in any city or town in Germany, and who had never had a job and never expected to have one. There was something else that had never been seen before — whole families that had piled all their goods into baby carriages and wheelbarrows that they were pushing along as they plodded forward in dumb despair. It was a whole nation on the march.

I saw them — and this was the strongest impression that the year 1932 left with me — I saw them, gathered into groups of fifty or a hundred men, attacking fields of potatoes. I saw them digging up the potatoes and throwing them into sacks while the farmer who owned the field watched them in despair and the local policeman looked on gloomily from the distance. I saw them staggering toward the lights of the city as night fell, with their sacks

on their backs. What did it remind me of? Of the War, of the worst periods of starvation in 1917 and 1918, but even then people paid for the potatoes. . . .

I saw that the individual can know what is happening only by personal experience. I know what it is to be a tramp. I know what cold and hunger are. I know what it is to spend the night outdoors or behind the thin walls of a shack through which the wind whistles. I have slept in holes such as hunters hide in, in hayricks, under bridges, against the warm walls of boiler houses, under cattle shelters in pastures, on a heap of fir-tree boughs in the forest. But there are two things that I have only recently experienced — begging and spending the night in a municipal lodging house.

I entered the huge Berlin municipal lodging house in a northern quarter of the city. . . .

. . . There was an entrance arched by a brick vaulting, and a watchman sat in a little wooden sentry box. His white coat made him look like a doctor. We stood waiting in the corridor. Heavy steam rose from the men's clothes. Some of them sat down on the floor, pulled off their shoes, and unwound the rags that were bound around their feet. More people were constantly pouring in the door, and we stood closely packed together. Then another door opened. The crowd pushed forward, and people began forcing their way almost eagerly through this door, for it was warm in there. Without knowing it I had already caught the rhythm of the municipal lodging house. It means waiting, waiting, standing around, and then suddenly jumping up.

We now stand in a long hall, down the length of which runs a bar dividing the hall into a narrow and a wide space. All the light is on the narrow side. There under yellow lamps that hang from the ceiling on long wires sit men in white smocks. We arrange ourselves in long lines, each leading up to one of these men, and the mill begins to grind. . . .

. . . As the line passes in single file the official does not look up at each new person to appear. He only looks at the paper that is handed to him. These papers are for the most part invalid cards or unemployment certificates. The very fact that the official does not look up robs the homeless applicant of self-respect, although he may look too beaten down to feel any. . . .

. . . Now it is my turn and the questions and answers flow as smoothly as if I were an old hand. But finally I am asked, "Have you ever been here before?"

"No."

"No?" The question reverberates through the whole room. The clerk refuses to believe me and looks through his card catalogue. But no, my name is not there. The clerk thinks this strange, for he cannot have made a mistake, and the terrible thing that one notices in all these clerks is that they expect you to lie. They do not believe what you say. They do not regard you as a human being but as an infection, something foul that one keeps at a distance. He goes on. "How did you come here from Hamburg?"

"By truck."

"Where have you spent the last three nights?"

I lie coolly.

"Have you begged?"

I feel a warm blush spreading over my face. It is welling up from the bourgeois world that I have come from. "No."

A coarse peal of laughter rises from the line, and a loud, piercing voice grips me as if someone had seized me by the throat: "Never mind. The day will come, comrade, when there's nothing else to do." And the line breaks into laughter again, the bitterest laughter I have ever heard, the laughter of damnation and despair. . . .

Again the crowd pushes back in the kind of rhythm that is so typical of a lodging house, and we are all herded into the undressing room. It is like all the other rooms except that it is divided by benches and shelves like a fourth-class railway carriage. I cling to the man who spoke to me. He is a Saxon with a friendly manner and he has noticed that I am a stranger here.

A certain sensitiveness, an almost perverse, spiritual alertness makes me like him very much.

Out of a big iron chest each of us takes a coat hanger that would serve admirably to hit somebody over the head with. As we undress the room becomes filled with the heavy breath of poverty. We are so close together that we brush against each other every time we move. Anyone who has been a soldier, anyone who has been to a public bath is perfectly accustomed to the look of naked bodies. But I have never seen anything quite so repulsive as all these hundreds of withered human frames. For in the homeless army the majority are men who have already been defeated in the struggle of life, the crippled, old, and sick. There is no repulsive disease of which traces are not to be seen here. There is no form of mutilation or degeneracy that is not represented, and the naked bodies of the old men are in a disgusting state of decline. . . .

It is superfluous to describe what follows. Towels are handed out by the same methods described above. Then nightgowns — long, sacklike affairs made of plain unbleached cotton but freshly washed. Then slippers. All at once a new sound goes up from the moving mass that has been walking silently on bare feet. The shuffling and rattling of the hard soles of the slippers ring through the corridor.

Distribution of spoons, distribution of enameledware bowls with the words "Property of the City of Berlin" written on their sides. Then the meal itself. A big kettle is carried in. Men with yellow smocks have brought it and men with yellow smocks ladle out the food. These men, too, are homeless and they have been expressly picked by the establishment and given free food and lodging and a little pocket money in exchange for their work about the house.

Where have I seen this kind of food distribution before? In a prison that I once helped to guard in the winter of 1919 during the German civil war. There was the same hunger then, the same trembling, anxious expectation of rations.

Now the men are standing in a long row, dressed in their plain nightshirts that reach to the ground, and the noise of their shuffling feet is like the noise of big wild animals walking up and down the stone floor of their cages before feeding time. The men lean far over the kettle so that the warm steam from the food envelops them and they hold out their bowls as if begging and whisper to the attendant, "Give me a real helping. Give me a little more." A piece of bread is handed out with every bowl.

My next recollection is sitting at table in another room on a crowded bench that is like a seat in a fourth-class railway carriage. Hundreds of hungry mouths make an enormous noise eating their food. The men sit bent over their food like animals who feel that someone is going to take it away from them. They hold their bowl with their left arm part way around it, so that nobody can take it away, and they also protect it with their other elbow and with their head and mouth, while they move the spoon as fast as they can between their mouth and the bowl. . . .

We shuffle into the sleeping room, where each bed has a number painted in big letters on the wall over it. You must find the number that you have around your neck, and there is your bed, your home for one night. It stands in a row with fifty others and across the room there are fifty more in a row. . . .

I curl up in a ball for a few minutes and then see that the Saxon is lying the same way, curled up in the next bed. We look at each other with eyes that understand everything. . . .

. . . Only a few people, very few, move around at all. The others lie awake and still, staring at their blankets, wrapped up in themselves but not sleeping. Only an almost soldierly sense of comradeship, an inner self-control engendered by the presence of so many people, prevents the despair that is written on all these faces from expressing itself. The few who are moving about do so with the tormenting consciousness of men who merely want to kill time. They do not believe in what they are doing.

Going to sleep means passing into the unconscious, eliminating the intelligence. And one can read deeply into a man's life by watching the way he goes to sleep. For we have not always slept in municipal lodgings. There are men among us who still move as if they were in a bourgeois bedchamber. . . .

. . . The air is poisoned with the breath of men who have stuffed too much food into empty stomachs. There is also a sickening smell of lysol. It seems completely terrible to me, and I am not merely pitying myself. It is painful just to look at the scene. Life is no longer human here. Today, when I am experiencing this for the first time, I think that I should prefer to do away with myself, to take gas, to jump into the river, or leap from some high place, if I were ever reduced to such straits that I had to live here in the lodging house. But I have had too much experience not to mistrust even myself. If I ever were reduced so low, would I really come to such a decision? I do not know. Animals die, plants wither, but men always go on living.

Lilo Linke
MASS SUGGESTION

The Nazis exploited the misery of the German people during the Depression. In mass rallies, Hitler provided simple explanations for Germany's misfortunes, attacked the Versailles Treaty, and denounced the Jews and the Weimar

Republic. In the following passage from *Restless Days: A German Girl's Autobiography* (1935), Lilo Linke described her experience at such a rally during the Depression.

At this moment the whole audience rose from their seats, most of them with wild cheers — from the back, behind an S.A. [Nazi storm-trooper] man who carried a large swastika flag, and a drumming and blowing and [deafening] band, a procession of S.A. men and Hitler Youth [Nazi youth movement] marched towards the platform. I enjoyed the right to remain seated as a member of the press. When they were half-way through the hall, the curtain draped behind the platform opened and Hitler, wearing a dark suit, stepped forward to the decorated desk. The audience howled with enthusiastic madness, lifting their right arms in the Fascist salute.

Hitler stood unmoved. At last, when the crowd was already hoarse with shouting, he made a commanding gesture to silence them, and slowly obeying, they grew calmer, as a dog, called to order by its master after wild play, lies down, exhaustedly snarling.

For an hour and a half Hitler spoke, every few minutes interrupted by fanatic acclamations which grew into a frenzy after such phrases as:

"Today the world treats us like outcasts. But they will respect us again when we show them our good old German sword, flashing high above our heads!"

Or: "Pacifism is the contemptible religion of the weak; a real man is not afraid of defending his rights by force."

Or: "Those foreign blood-suckers, those degenerate asphalt-democrats, those cunning Jews, those whining pacifists, those corrupted November criminals[1] — we'll knock them all down with our fists without pardoning a single one of them."

He thrust his chin forward. His voice, hammering the phrases with an obsessed energy, became husky and shrill and began to squeak more and more frequently. His whole face was covered with sweat: a greasy tress kept on falling on his forehead, however often he pushed it back.

Speaking with a stern face, he crossed his arms over his breast — the imposing attitude of one who stood under his own supreme control. But a moment later a force bursting out of him flung them into the air, where they implored, threatened, accused, condemned, assisted by his hands and fists. Later, exhausted, he crossed them on his back and began to march a few steps to and fro along the front of the platform, a lion behind the bars of his cage, waiting for the moment when the door will be opened to jump on the terror-stricken enemy.

The audience was breathlessly under his spell. This man expressed their thoughts, their feelings, their hopes; a new prophet had arisen — many saw in him already another Christ, who predicted the end of their sufferings and had the power to lead them into the promised land if they were only prepared to follow him.

Every word he said was true. They had won the war — yes. Been deprived of the reward for their heroism by a number of traitors — yes. Had suffered incessantly ever since — yes. Been enslaved, suppressed, exploited — yes, yes, yes. But the day had arrived when they would free and revenge themselves — *yes.*

A single question as to reason or proof or possibility would have shattered the whole argument, but nobody asked it — the majority because they had begun to think with their blood, which condemns all logic, and the others because they sat amazed, despairing, and hopeless in a small boat tossed about by the foaming waves of emotional uproar which surrounded it.

Under the sound of brass bands we pushed

---

[1]"November criminals" is a derogatory reference to the revolutionaries who overthrew the kaiser in November 1918 and established a republic.

out of the hall. Intimidated, I took hold of Rolf's arm:

"Oh, Rolf, this is terrible — so inhuman — so full of hatred against all we value — they don't understand what we want — you'll see, they'll demolish all we built up with our love and pains. The milkman, revenging his inferiority with a shining sword in his [swollen] hand and forcing his suppressors under his will — what a prospect for us, what a prospect for Germany!"

"Yet, my dear, something of what he said —"

"Good heavens, Rolf, what is the matter with you? Are you going Nazi, too?"

"You are absurd. But if you are just, you must admit that in many ways he is right."

"My dear Rolf, to 'admit that in many ways . . .' is always the beginning of the end. Of course, the Nazis are not mere villains, and they are striving for an ideal for which they are willing to suffer. On the other hand, much is rotten in the Republic and in the Republican parties. But that doesn't mean that Hitler is right and we are wrong, and you should know that well enough."

"Yes, but we are democrats, and we have to give them a chance —"

"To cut our throats. What a fool you are! You can't treat like a gentleman somebody who wants to murder you. The protection of the democratic rules can only be granted to those who follow them themselves. The others must be stamped out before they lift their heads too high."

"That is Bolshevism!"

"If you are right, I'll gladly be a Bolshevist, because I refuse to be made a Nazi."

REVIEW QUESTIONS

1. How did the Depression dehumanize people?
2. Judging from the description of the Nazi rally, what were the consequences of the Depression for German politics?
3. Account for Adolf Hitler's success at rallies.

▼▼▼

5 ▼ Nazism and Youth

Young people, in particular, were attracted to Nazism, in which they saw a cause worthy of their devotion. Victims of Nazi propaganda and led astray by their youthful idealism, they equated a total commitment to the Nazi movement with a selfless devotion to the nation.

Alice Hamilton
THE YOUTH WHO ARE HITLER'S STRENGTH

Dr. Alice Hamilton (1869–1970) wrote the following article in 1933 after her second post–World War I trip to Germany. An international authority on industrial diseases who was known for her social consciousness, she was the first woman on the faculty of the Medical School of Harvard University. Her familiarity with Germany had begun in the late nineteenth century when she pursued postgraduate studies there. Her article, which appeared in the *New York Times Magazine* eight months after Hitler gained power, shows how the Nazis exploited patriotism, idealism, and a deep-seated desire of youth for fellowship.

Hitler's movement is called a youth movement and during the first months of the Nazi rule, while I was in Germany, this certainly seemed to be true. The streets of every city swarmed with brown shirts [trademark Nazi uniform], echoed to the sound of marching men and Hitler songs; there were parades, monster mass meetings, celebrations of all kinds, day in and day out. The swastika flag flapped from every building. In Frankfurt-on-Main where I had spent, years ago, delightful student days, I went to the beautiful Römer Platz, only to find it unrecognizable, its lovely buildings hidden under fifty-three Nazi banners. Rathenau Square had been changed to Horst Wessel Square, for Wessel, the young organizer of storm detachments in the slums of Berlin, who died at the hands of Communists, is the new hero of Germany. . . .

To understand Hitler's enormous success with the young we must understand what life has meant to the post-war generation in Germany, not only the children of the poor but of the middle class as well. They were children during the years of the war when the food blockade kept them half starved, when fathers were away at the front and mothers distracted with the effort to keep their families fed. They came to manhood in a country which seemed to have no use for them. Even compulsory military training was no more and there was nothing to take its place. . . .

. . . A settlement worker told me that she knew families in which the children had come to manhood without ever realizing the connection between work and food. They had never had work, and food had come scantily and grudgingly from some governmental agency.

To these idle, hopeless youths two stirring calls to action came — one from the Communists, the other from Hitler; and to both of them German youth responded. Both appealed to hatred, both held out an ideal of a changed Germany, but Hitler's propaganda was cleverer than the Communists', because his program is narrower, more concrete. The Communist is internationally minded, his brothers are all over the world, his ideal State embraces all lands. Hitler repudiates internationalism; he is against all who are not German; his ideal State is a self-contained Germany, an object of fear to all her neighbors. The Communist is taught to hate a class, the capitalistic, the Hitlerite to hate each individual Jew. Many young Communists were brought under the banner of Hitler by appeals to national pride and race antagonism, but also by the ideal of a united Germany without class hatred.

Hitler made each insignificant, poverty-stricken, jobless youth of the slums feel himself one of the great of the earth, since the youth was a German, a Nordic, far superior to the successful Jew who was to be driven out of office and counting house to make place for the youth and his like. Hitler told the young men that the fate of Germany was in their hands, that if they joined his army they would battle with the Communists for the streets, they would see Jewish blood flow in streams, they would capture the government, deliver Germany from the Versailles treaty and then sweep triumphantly over the borders to reconquer Germany's lost land. He put them into uniforms, he taught them to march and sing together, he aroused that sense of comradeship and esprit de corps so precious to the young, and gave them what is even more precious — an object for hero worship. Life suddenly took on meaning and importance, with the call to danger, sacrifice, even death.

Among the hundreds of thousands who make up the audiences at Hitler's or Goebbels's [Joseph Goebbels, minister of propaganda] meetings, and who seem to an outsider to be carried away by a kind of mass hysteria, there are many who are actuated by real idealism, who long to give themselves unreservedly to the great vision of a resurgent Germany. Being young they are of course contemptuous of the slow and moderate methods of the republic; they are for action, quick, arrogant, ruthless.

But their program calls for a changed Germany, one purged of all selfishness and materialism. They repudiate liberalism, for that means to them capitalism, it means the profit-making system, it means class distinctions, inequalities. The Germany the young are planning will have no division between the classes and will substitute the common good for individual profit. They really believe that Hitler will bring about a genuine socialism without class warfare and this part of their program is highly idealistic and fine, but, as is to be expected, it is mixed with the intolerance of youth, it calls for the forcible repression of opposition within the country and a battling front to be presented to the outside world. This is the outpouring of a student writing in the official organ of the Nazi students' league:

A people organically united and filled with the spirit of sacrifice for the common good, strong and eager for battle. A people fused into an unconquerable fighting unit against a hostile world. This is what we must achieve in these incomparably important days. The millions who stand aside from our movement must be made to believe in it. He is a traitor who now holds back. Our revolution marches on, over saboteurs and counter-revolutionaries, whoever they be.

The students . . . dream of reform in the courts of justice which is to be brought about by requiring each candidate for the bar to serve for eight weeks in a labor camp, working shoulder to shoulder with men from all walks of life. In every way the barriers between workers and students must be abolished. "We must strive against intellec-

tualism and liberalism which are Jewish. We wish to be red-blooded men. Students, show the peasant and worker that you are not intellectuals." . . .

And here is one of the songs which the boys and girls sing as they march through the streets.

Seest thou the morning red in the East, a promise of sun and of freedom? We hold together for life or for death, no matter what may threaten. Many a year were we slaves to traitor Jews, but now has arisen a son of the people — he gives to Germany new hope and faith. Brothers, to arms! Young and old flock to the hooked cross banner, peasants and workers with sword and with hammer. For Hitler, for freedom, for work and for bread. Germany, awaken! Death to the Jew! Brothers, to arms! . . .

In spite of the strict censorship of the press, we heard many a bloody tale of the Storm Troopers, but we heard even more about their high-handed methods in business houses and in the universities. While we were in Berlin the struggle was going on between the Nazi students and the rector of the university. It was on the issue of academic freedom. The students had nailed up twelve theses in the entrance hall of the main building and refused to take them down at the command of the rector. These were the theses that called for the expulsion of all "non-German teachers," that demanded that Jews should write only in Hebrew and that repudiated "Jewish intellectualism." . . .

It was only too clear that whatever group had put up the theses ruled the university, and there were proofs aplenty that this was true. The rector threatened to resign if the proclamation was not removed. He did resign and his successor declared himself to be unreservedly behind the Nazi student movement. The new "Cultus-minister" soon afterward dissolved all student organizations and announced that there would be in the future one only, the Nazi students' league. He went on to praise the part played by the students in the revolution and to warn the faculties that they must no longer lag behind when youth led the way.

No wonder the students took things into their own hands, howled down the few Jewish professors who had received exceptional treatment because of war service, raided libraries, denounced suspected liberals right and left! The students of Kiel University demanded the discharge of twenty-eight professors. In Hamburg, when the university formally opened after the Spring holidays, a student arose and addressed the rector and faculty, telling them that any young Nazi was worth more to the Fatherland than the whole lot of them. His speech was received in silence. . . .

All this seemed simply stupid and ugly and primitive to an American, an incomprehensible swing-back to a day when physical force was the only thing respected and men of thought shut themselves in monasteries and were not always safe there. But this is an aspect which the students with whom I talked could not see. They were passionately behind the new movement, the revolt against intellectualism, against scientific objectivity, against all that the German universities had stood for. The burning of the books was their work and they were proud of it.

This revolt of youth against modern education is a part of Hitler's program, for Hitler has long preached the necessity for a new pedagogy, one that is directed first toward physical prowess, then character training, while purely intellectual subjects are to be left for specialists. Herr Frick, Minister of the Interior, said while I was there: "The mistake of the past was for the school to train the child as an individual.

This led, especially after the war, to the destruction of nation and State. We will supplant it by a training which will sink into the blood and flesh and cannot be uprooted for generations, a training which will fuse the German into his nation and bind him by the closest ties to his history and the destiny of his people."

The most important subject in the new curriculum is history, with the emphasis laid on German heroes, German inventors, German rulers, poets, artists. The German child must be taught that his nation is superior to every other in every field. Next to this comes politics and then everything that has to do with agriculture. Such subjects as mathematics and the physical sciences take a secondary place. Physical training and mental training find their culminating point in the last year, which is the year of compulsory service in labor camps. The training in these camps is military, for "defense warfare." For girls, education ends in a year of domestic service, with training for wifehood and motherhood. . . .

In his autobiography and in his voluminous speeches Hitler reveals himself as a man with the ambitions, the ideals, the crudities and the virtues of the adolescent. His physical courage and daring are those of the perfect soldier; he cares nothing for ease and comfort; he adores display, applause; he worships force and despises persuasion and mutual concession; he is intolerant of dissent, convinced of his own absolute rightness, and ready to commit any cruelty to carry out his own will.

It is this violent, fanatical, youthful despot, backed by some millions of like-minded youths, who now rules Germany. Truly it is a new thing in the world — a great modern country submitting itself to the will of its young men.

REVIEW QUESTIONS

1. How did Alice Hamilton interpret repression and coercion in the universities?
2. What educational theory did the Nazis espouse?
3. The idealism of youth has often been praised. What dangers did Hamilton see in this idealism?

▼▼▼

6 ▾ Nazification of Culture

The Nazis aspired to more than political power; they also wanted to have the German people view the world in accordance with National Socialist ideology. Toward this end the Nazis strictly regulated cultural life. Believing that the struggle of racial forces occupied the center of world history, Nazi ideologists tried to strengthen the racial consciousness of the German people. Numerous courses in "race science" introduced in schools and universities emphasized the superiority of the Nordic soul and the worthlessness of Jews, and their threat to the nation.

Hermann Gauch
≪ *NEW FOUNDATIONS OF RACIAL SCIENCE* ≫

The following excerpts from Hermann Gauch's *New Foundations of Racial Science* (1934) illustrate National Socialist racist thinking that was propagated by scholars, scientists, and school teachers.

The features of the Nordic [Aryan] race express noble and culture-carrying qualities . . . while non-Nordic features are more likely to express unmanliness and barbarous feelings. . . .

Even the Nordic woman is much more courageous, resolute and steadfast than the non-Nordic man.

Cowardliness and courage are therefore not differences typical of men and women, but they are like all other psychological qualities, purely differences of Nordic and non-Nordic races. . . .

The Nordic does not speak much. . . . The people of other races talk a lot, and what they say is superficial, devoid of judgment, and untrue. . . .

The Nordic chews his food with the mouth closed, by a grinding movement of the jaws, whereas other races tend to chew with a smacking noise like animals, owing to the pressing movement of the jaws and the repeated opening of the mouth.

The usual form of the Nordic mouth . . . is a friendly and happy smile.

The lips of Nordics are most expressive and look enticing and kissable. The trunks of all other races are more or less bent forward. . . .

Only the Nordic race walks and stands fully upright.

The crouching bodily bearing of the non-Nordic indicates lying-in-wait, perfidiousness and cunning attack.

The head of the Nordic "great man" expresses the "great mind." . . .

The swelled chest of the Nordic expresses his courageous and high-spirited love of freedom. . . .

The walk of the non-Nordic is cow-like. The non-Nordic waddles along and swings from one side to the other like a duck.

To "talk with hands and feet" is typical of the non-Nordic, whereas the Nordic stands quiet when speaking. He may even put his hands into his pockets. . . .

The physical forms of the Nordic women are special beauty, while with other races this is not the case. There the male is more beautiful, as in the animal world. . . .

The white of the eye is pure white in the

Nordic race only; that of the non-Nordic is blurred. . . .

The Nordic possesses a feeling for internal and external cleanliness, while the non-Nordic always lives in dirt when he is among his own people. Many of the animals even stand high above him so far as cleanliness is concerned. . . .

The mixture of races . . . causes and promotes diseases. It is a breach of the laws of order in the universe, a crime against the future generation, manslaughter and murder.

We come to the conclusion that all the better developed characteristics are typical of the Nordic body and the Nordic soul. . . . Non-Nordics are more or less equal to the animals or they form a . . . link to them. *The non-Nordic thus occupies an intermediate position between the Nordic and the animal and ranks next to the man-apes.* He is therefore not a hundred per cent human being. . . . He might be compared with the Neanderthal man, but better and more accurate is the description: "sub-man." . . .

The Nordic and the non-Nordic races have not a single characteristic in common. We are not justified, therefore, in speaking of a "human race." As a matter of fact there are actually some animals which have Nordic characteristics, such as the faithfulness of the dog, which is lacking in the non-Nordic.

The clear enunciation of sounds is found as a rule only with the Nordic race. The strongly non-Nordic peoples and individuals have a less clear pronunciation. The various sounds flow into each other and tend to resemble the sounds of animals, such as barking, snoring, sniffling, and squealing. . . .

Nordic man is therefore the creator of all culture and civilization. The salvation and preservation of the Nordic man alone will save and preserve culture and civilization. Lasting success can, of course, be achieved only through the unification of the whole Nordic humanity of the Germanic countries and a number of other strongly Nordic areas.

Johannes Stark
"JEWISH SCIENCE" VERSUS "GERMAN SCIENCE"

Several prominent German scientists endorsed the new regime and tried to make science conform to Nazi ideology. In 1934, Johannes Stark, who had won a Nobel Prize for his work in electromagnetism, requested fellow German Nobel Prize winners to sign a declaration supporting "Adolf Hitler . . . the savior and leader of the German people." In the following passage, Stark made the peculiar assertion that "German science" was based on an objective analysis of nature, whereas "Jewish science" (German Jews had distinguished themselves in science and medicine) sacrificed objectivity to self-interest and a subjective viewpoint.

But aside from this fundamental National Socialist demand, the slogan of the international character of science is based on an untruth, insofar as it asserts that the type and the success of scientific activity are independent of membership in a national group. Nobody can seriously assert that art is international. It is similar with science. Insofar as scientific work is not merely imitation but actual creation, like any other creative activity it is conditioned by the spiritual and characterological endowments of its practitioners. Since the individual members of a people have a common endowment, the creative activity of the scientists of a nation, as much as that of its artists and poets, thus assumes the stamp of a distinctive Volkish type. No, science is not international; it is just as national as art. This can be shown by the example of Germans and Jews in the natural sciences.

Science is the knowledge of the uniform interconnection of facts; the purpose of natural science in particular is the investigation of bodies and processes outside of the human mind, through observation and, insofar as possible, through the setting up of planned experiments. The spirit of the German enables him to observe things outside himself exactly as they are, without the interpolation of his own ideas and wishes, and his body does not shrink from the effort which the investigation of nature demands of him. The German's love of nature and his aptitude for natural science are based on this endowment. Thus it is understandable that natural science is overwhelmingly a creation of the Nordic-Germanic blood component of the Aryan peoples. Anyone who, in Lenard's classic work *Grosse Naturforscher (Great Investigators of Nature)*, compares the faces of the outstanding natural scientists will find this common Nordic-Germanic feature in almost all of them. The ability to observe and respect facts, in complete disregard of the "I," is the most characteristic feature of the scientific activity of Germanic types. In addition, there is the joy and satisfaction the German derives from the acquisition of scientific knowledge, since it is principally this with which he is concerned. It is only under pressure that he decides to make his findings public, and the propaganda for them and their commercial exploitation appear to him as degradations of his scientific work.

The Jewish spirit is wholly different in its orientation: above everything else it is focused upon its own ego, its own conception, and its self-interest — and behind its egocentric conception stands its strong will to win recognition for itself and its interests. In accordance with this natural orientation the Jewish spirit strives to heed facts only to the extent that they do not hamper its opinions and purposes, and to bring them in such a connection with each other as is expedient for effecting its opinions and purposes. The Jew, therefore, is the born advocate who, unencumbered by regard for truth, mixes facts and imputations topsy-turvy in the endeavor to secure the court decision he desires. On the other hand, because of these characteristics, the Jewish spirit has little aptitude for creative activity in the sciences because it takes the individual's thinking and will as the measure of things, whereas science demands observation and respect for the facts.

It is true, however, that the Jewish spirit, thanks to the flexibility of its intellect, is capable, through imitation of Germanic examples, of producing noteworthy accomplishments, but it is not able to rise to authentic creative work, to great discoveries in the natural sciences. In recent times the Jews have frequently invoked the name of Heinrich Hertz as a counter-argument to this thesis. True, Heinrich Hertz made the great discovery of electromagnetic waves, but he was not a full-blooded Jew. He had a German mother, from whose side his spiritual endowment may well have been conditioned. When the Jew in natural science abandons the Germanic example and engages in scientific work according to his own spiritual particularity, he turns to theory. His main object is not the observation of facts and their true-to-reality presentation, but the view which he forms about them and the formal exposition to which he subjects them. In the interest of his theory he will suppress facts that are not in keeping with it and likewise, still in the interest of his theory, he will engage in propaganda on its behalf.

Jakob Graf
HEREDITY AND RACIAL BIOLOGY FOR STUDENTS

The following assignments from a textbook entitled ***Hereditary and Racial Biology for Students*** (1935) show how young people were indoctrinated with racist teachings.

HOW WE CAN LEARN TO RECOGNIZE A PERSON'S RACE
Assignments

1. Summarize the spiritual characteristics of the individual races.

2. Collect from stories, essays, and poems examples of ethnological illustrations. Underline those terms which describe the type and mode of the expression of the soul.

3. What are the expressions, gestures, and movements which allow us to make conclusions as to the attitude of the racial soul?

4. Determine also the physical features which go hand in hand with the specific racial soul characteristics of the individual figures.

5. Try to discover the intrinsic nature of the racial soul through the characters in stories and poetical works in terms of their inner attitude. Apply this mode of observation to persons in your own environment.

6. Collect propaganda posters and caricatures for your race book and arrange them according to a racial scheme. What image of beauty is emphasized by the artist (a) in posters publicizing sports and travel? (b) in publicity for cosmetics? How are hunters, mountain climbers, and shepherds drawn?

7. Collect from illustrated magazines, newspapers, etc., pictures of great scholars, statesmen, artists, and others who distinguish themselves by their special accomplishments (for example, in economic life, politics, sports). Determine the preponderant race and admixture, according to physical characteristics. Repeat this exercise with the pictures of great men of all nations and times.

8. When viewing monuments, busts, etc., be sure to pay attention to the race of the person portrayed with respect to figure, bearing, and physical characteristics. Try to harmonize these determinations with the features of the racial soul.

9. Observe people whose special racial features have drawn your attention, also with respect to their bearing when moving or when speaking. Observe their expressions and gestures.

10. Observe the Jew: his way of walking, his bearing, gestures, and movements when talking.

11. What strikes you about the way a Jew talks and sings?

REVIEW QUESTIONS

1. In Hermann Gauch's view, what relationship did non-Nordic races have to the Nordic (Aryan) race and to animals? What qualities characterized Gauch's idea of the Nordic and non-Nordic races?

2. Why, in racial thinking, is the idea of the mixture of races regarded as the greatest evil?

3. Why would the idea of humanity be regarded as dangerous by Gauch?

4. What, in Johannes Stark's view, made the Nordic, Aryan people especially fitted for scientific creativity? What disqualified the non-Nordic, especially the Jewish, people from achievement in science? What is the fallacy in this line of thinking?

5. What does Stark's definition of scientific method share with the definitions of science given by such persons as Galileo (see page 42), Bacon (see page 45), and Isaac Newton (see pages 51–52)? How does it differ?

6. What was Jakob Graf's purpose in teaching students how to recognize a person's race? What would your reaction be if you were given such an assignment today?

▾▾▾

7 ▾ The Anguish of the Intellectuals

A somber mood gripped European intellectuals in the postwar period. The memory of World War I, the rise of totalitarianism, and the Great Depression caused intellectuals to have grave doubts about the nature and destiny of Western civilization. To many European liberals it seemed that the sun was setting on the Enlightenment tradition, that the ideals of reason and freedom, already gravely weakened by World War I, could not endure the threats posed by economic collapse and totalitarian ideologies.

José Ortega y Gasset
≪ THE REVOLT OF THE MASSES ≫

One of the thinkers who feared for the ideals of reason and freedom was the Spanish philosopher José Ortega y Gasset (1883–1955). In *The Revolt of the Masses* (1930), Ortega held that European civilization was degenerating into barbarism because of the growing power of the intellectually undisciplined and culturally unrefined masses. Ortega did not equate the masses with the working class and the elite with the nobility. For him, what distinguished the "mass-man" was an attitude that renounced rational dialogue in favor of violence and compulsion and demanded uniformity of thought. These threats to Western civilization, he said, were exemplified in both communism and fascism. Excerpts from *The Revolt of the Masses* follow.

There is one fact which, whether for good or ill, is of utmost importance in the public life of Europe at the present moment. This fact is the accession of the masses to complete social power. As the masses, by definition, neither should nor can direct their own personal existence, and still less rule society in general, this fact means that actually Europe is suffering from the greatest crisis that can afflict peoples, nations, and civilisation. . . .

Strictly speaking, the mass, as a psychological fact, can be defined without waiting for individuals to appear in mass formation. In the presence of one individual we can decide whether he is "mass" or not. The mass is all that which sets no value on itself — good or ill — based on specific grounds, but which feels itself "just like everybody," and nevertheless is not concerned about it; is, in fact, quite happy to feel itself as one with everybody else. . . .

. . . The mass believes that it has the right to impose and to give force of law to notions born in the café. I doubt whether there have been other periods of history in which the multitude has come to govern more directly than in our own. . . .

. . . *The characteristic of the hour is that the commonplace mind, knowing itself to be commonplace, has the assurance to proclaim the rights of the commonplace and to impose them wherever it will.* As they say in the United States: "to be different is to be indecent." The mass crushes beneath it everything that is different, everything that is excellent, individual, qualified and select. Anybody who is not like everybody, who does not think like everybody, runs the risk of being eliminated. . . .

. . . It is illusory to imagine that the mass-man of to-day . . . will be able to control, by himself, the process of civilisation. I say process, and not progress. The simple process of preserving our present civilisation is supremely complex, and demands incalculably subtle powers. Ill-fitted to direct it is this average man who has learned to use much of the machinery of civilisation, but who is characterised by root-ignorance of the very principles of that civilisation. . . .

The command over public life exercised today by the intellectually vulgar is perhaps the factor of the present situation which is most novel, least assimilable to anything in the past. At least in European history up to the present, the vulgar had never believed itself to have "ideas" on things. It had beliefs, traditions, experiences, proverbs, mental habits, but it never imagined itself in possession of theoretical opinions on what things are or ought to be. . . . To-day, on the other hand, the average man has the most mathematical "ideas" on all that happens or ought to happen in the universe. Hence he has lost the use of his hearing. Why should he listen if he has within him all that is necessary? There is no reason now for listening, but rather for judging, pronouncing, deciding. There is no question concerning public life, in which he does not intervene, blind and deaf as he is, imposing his "opinions."

But, is this not an advantage? Is it not a sign of immense progress that the masses should have "ideas," that is to say, should be cultured? By no means. The "ideas" of the average man are not genuine ideas, nor is their possession culture. . . . Whoever wishes to have ideas must first prepare himself to desire truth and to accept the rules of the game imposed by it. It is no use speaking of ideas when there is no acceptance of a higher authority to regulate them, a series of standards to which it is possible to appeal in a discussion. These standards are the principles on which culture rests. I am not concerned with the form they take. What I affirm is that there is no culture where there are no standards to which our fellow-men can have recourse. There is no culture where there are no principles of legality to which to appeal. There is no culture where there is no acceptance of

certain final intellectual positions to which a dispute may be referred. There is no culture where economic relations are not subject to a regulating principle to protect interests involved. There is no culture where aesthetic controversy does not recognise the necessity of justifying the work of art.

When all these things are lacking there is no culture; there is in the strictest sense of the word, barbarism. And let us not deceive ourselves, this is what is beginning to appear in Europe under the progressive rebellion of the masses. The traveller who arrives in a barbarous country knows that in that territory there are no ruling principles to which it is possible to appeal. Properly speaking, there are no barbarian standards. Barbarism is the absence of standards to which appeal can be made. . . .

. . . Under . . . Fascism there appears for the first time in Europe a type of man who does not want to give reasons or to be right, but simply shows himself resolved to impose his opinions. This is the new thing: the right not to be reasonable, the "reason of unreason." Here I see the most palpable manifestation of the new mentality of the masses, due to their having decided to rule society without the capacity for doing so. In their political conduct the structure of the new mentality is revealed in the rawest, most convincing manner. . . . The average man finds himself with "ideas" in his head, but he lacks the faculty of ideation. He has no conception even of the rare atmosphere in which ideas live. He wishes to have opinions, but is unwilling to accept the conditions and presuppositions that underlie all opinion. Hence his ideas are in effect nothing more than appetites in words. . . .

To have an idea means believing one is in possession of the reasons for having it, and consequently means believing that there is such a thing as reason, a world of intelligible truths. To have ideas, to form opinions, is identical with appealing to such an authority, submitting oneself to it, accepting its code and its decisions, and therefore believing that the highest form of intercommunion is the dialogue in which the reasons for our ideas are discussed. But the mass-man would feel himself lost if he accepted discussion, and instinctively repudiates the obligation of accepting that supreme authority lying outside himself. Hence the "new thing" in Europe is "to have done with discussions," and detestation is expressed for all forms of intercommunion which imply acceptance of objective standards, ranging from conversation to Parliament, and taking in science.

This means that there is a renunciation of the common life based on culture, which is subject to standards, and a return to the common life of barbarism. All the normal processes are suppressed in order to arrive directly at the imposition of what is desired. The hermetism [closing off] of the soul which, as we have seen before, urges the mass to intervene in the whole of public life. . . .

Thomas Mann
≪ AN APPEAL TO REASON ≫

Dismayed by the spread of fascism in Italy, Germany, and other lands, several thinkers attempted to reassert the ideals of reason and freedom. In 1931, two years before Hitler took power, the internationally prominent German author Thomas Mann (1875–1955) wrote an article entitled "An Appeal to Reason," in which he discussed the crisis in the European soul that gave rise to fascism. He saw National Socialism and the extreme nationalism it espoused as a rejection of the Western rational tradition and as a regression to primitive and barbaric modes of behavior. Some excerpts from Mann's article follow.

. . . The economic decline of the middle classes was accompanied — or even preceded — by a feeling which amounted to an intellectual prophecy and critique of the age: the sense that here was a crisis which heralded the end of the bourgeois epoch that came in with the French revolution and the notions appertaining to it. There was proclaimed a new mental attitude for all mankind, which should have nothing to do with bourgeois principles such as freedom, justice, culture, optimism, faith in progress. As art, it gave vent to expressionistic soul-shrieks; as philosophy it repudiated . . . reason, and the . . . ideological conceptions of bygone decades; it expressed itself as an irrationalistic throwback, placing the conception *life* at the centre of thought, and raised on its standard the powers of the unconscious, the dynamic, the darkly creative, which alone were life-giving. Mind, quite simply the intellectual, it put under a taboo as destructive of life, while it set up for homage as the true inwardness of life . . .

the darkness of the soul, the holy procreative underworld. Much of this nature-religion, by its very essence inclining to the orgiastic and to . . . [frenzied] excess, has gone into the nationalism of our day, making of it something quite different from the nationalism of the nineteenth century, with its bourgeois, strongly cosmopolitan and humanitarian cast. It is distinguished in its character as a nature-cult, precisely by its absolute unrestraint, its orgiastic, radically anti-humane, frenziedly dynamic character. . . .

. . . And there is even more: there are other intellectual elements come to strengthen this national-social political movement — a certain ideology, a Nordic creed, a Germanistic romanticism, from philological, academic, professorial spheres. It addresses the Germany of 1930 in a highflown wishy-washy jargon full of mystical good feeling, with hyphenated prefixes like race- and folk- and fellowship-, and lends to the movement a . . . fanatical cult-barbarism, . . . dangerous and estranging, with . . . power to clog and stultify the brain. . . .

Fed, then, by such intellectual and pseudo-intellectual currents as these, the movement which we sum up under the name of national-socialism and which has displayed such a power of enlisting recruits to its banner, mingles with the mighty wave — a wave of anomalous barbarism, of primitive popular vulgarity — that sweeps over the world to-day, assailing the nerves of mankind with wild, bewildering, stimulating, intoxicating sensations. . . . Humanity seems to have run like boys let out of school away from the humanitarian, idealistic nineteenth century, from whose morality — if we can speak at all of morality in this connection — our time represents a wide and wild reaction. Everything is possible, everything permitted as a weapon against human decency; if we have got rid of the idea of freedom as a relic of the bourgeois state of mind, as though an idea so bound up with all European feeling,

upon which Europe has been founded, for which she has made such sacrifices, could ever be utterly lost — it comes back again, this cast-off conception, in a guise suited to the time: as demoralization, as a mockery of all human authority, as a free rein to instincts, as the emancipation of brutality, the dictatorship of force. . . . In all this violence demonstrates itself, and demonstrates nothing but violence, and even that is unnecessary, for all other considerations are fallen away, man does not any longer believe in them, and so the road is free to vulgarity without restraint.

This fantastic state of mind, of a humanity that has outrun its ideas, is matched by a political scene in the grotesque style, with Salvation Army methods, hallelujahs and bell-ringing and dervishlike repetition of monotonous catchwords, until everybody foams at the mouth. Fanaticism turns into a means of salvation, enthusiasm into epileptic ecstasy, politics becomes an opiate for the masses, . . . and reason veils her face.

Arthur Koestler
THE APPEAL OF COMMUNISM

The 1930s have been called the Pink Decade, because many intellectuals, anguished by the Depression and fascism, found a new hope in communism and the Soviet Union. One such intellectual was Arthur Koestler (1905–1983), who joined the Communist party of Germany on December 31, 1931. However, disillusioned by Stalin's purges, he left the party in 1938. In the following passage, written in 1949, Koestler recalled the attraction communism had held for him.

A faith is not acquired by reasoning. One does not fall in love with a woman, or enter the womb of a church, as a result of logical persuasion. Reason may defend an act of faith — but only after the act has been committed, and the man committed to the act. Persuasion may play a part in a man's conversion; but only the part of bringing to its full and conscious climax a process which has been maturing in regions where no persuasion can penetrate. A faith is not acquired; it grows like a tree. Its crown

points to the sky; its roots grow downward into the past and are nourished by the dark sap of the ancestral humus. . . .

I became converted because I was ripe for it and lived in a disintegrating society thirsting for faith. But the day when I was given my Party card was merely the climax of a development which had started long before I had read about the drowned pigs or heard the names of Marx and Lenin. Its roots reach back into childhood; and though each of us, comrades of the

Pink Decade, had individual roots with different twists in them, we are products of, by and large, the same generation and cultural climate. It is this unity underlying diversity which makes me hope that my story is worth telling.

I was born in 1905 in Budapest; we lived there till 1919, when we moved to Vienna. Until the First World War we were comfortably off, a typical Continental middle-middle-class family: my father was the Hungarian representative of some old-established British and German textile manufacturers. In September, 1914, this form of existence, like so many others, came to an abrupt end; my father never found his feet again. He embarked on a number of ventures which became the more fantastic the more he lost self-confidence in a changed world. He opened a factory for radioactive soap; he backed several crank-inventions (everlasting electric bulbs, self-heating bed bricks and the like); and finally lost the remains of his capital in the Austrian inflation of the early 'twenties. I left home at twenty-one, and from that day became the only financial support of my parents.

At the age of nine, when our middle-class idyl collapsed, I had suddenly become conscious of the economic Facts of Life. As an only child, I continued to be pampered by my parents; but, well aware of the family crisis, and torn by pity for my father, who was of a generous and somewhat childlike disposition, I suffered a pang of guilt whenever they bought me books or toys. This continued later on, when every suit I bought for myself meant so much less to send home. Simultaneously, I developed a strong dislike of the obviously rich; not because they could afford to buy things (envy plays a much smaller part in social conflict than is generally assumed) but because they were able to do so without a guilty conscience. Thus I projected a personal predicament onto the structure of society at large.

It was certainly a tortuous way of acquiring a social conscience. But precisely because of the intimate nature of the conflict, the faith which grew out of it became an equally intimate part of my self. It did not, for some years, crystallize into a political creed; at first it took the form of a mawkishly sentimental attitude. Every contact with people poorer than myself was unbearable — the boy at school who had no gloves and red chilblains [inflamed swellings produced by exposure to cold] on his fingers, the former traveling salesman of my father's reduced to [begging] occasional meals — all of them were additions to the load of guilt on my back. The analyst would have no difficulty in showing that the roots of this guilt-complex go deeper than the crisis in our household budget; but if he were to dig even deeper, piercing through the individual layers of the case, he would strike the archetypal pattern which has produced millions of particular variations on the same theme — "Woe, for they chant to the sound of harps and anoint themselves, but are not grieved for the affliction of the people."

Thus sensitized by a personal conflict, I was ripe for the shock of learning that wheat was burned, fruit artificially spoiled and pigs were drowned in the depression years to keep prices up and enable fat capitalists to chant to the sound of harps, while Europe trembled under the torn boots of hunger-marchers and my father hid his frayed cuffs under the table. The frayed cuffs and drowned pigs blended into one emotional explosion, as the fuse of the archetype was touched off. We sang the "Internationale" [the communists' anthem], but the words might as well have been the older ones: "Woe to the shepherds who feed themselves, but feed not their flocks."

In other respects, too, the story is more typical than it seems. A considerable proportion of the middle classes in central Europe was, like ourselves, ruined by the inflation of the 'twenties. It was the beginning of Europe's decline. This disintegration of the middle strata of society started the fatal process of polarization which continues to this day. The pauperized bourgeois became rebels of the Right or Left; Schickelgrüber [Hitler] and Djugashwili [Stalin] shared about equally the benefits of the social migration. Those who refused to admit that they had become déclassé, who clung to the empty shell of gentility, joined the Nazis and found comfort in blaming their fate on Versailles and the Jews. Many did not even have that consolation; they lived on pointlessly, like a great black swarm of tired winterflies crawling over the dim windows of Europe, members of a class displaced by history.

The other half turned Left, thus confirming the prophecy of the "Communist Manifesto":

> Entire sections of the ruling classes are . . . precipitated into the proletariat, or are at least threatened in their conditions of existence. They . . . supply the proletariat with fresh elements of enlightenment and progress. . . .

I was ripe to be converted, as a result of my personal case-history; thousands of other members of the intelligentsia and the middle classes of my generation were ripe for it, by virtue of other personal case-histories; but, however much these differed from case to case, they had a common denominator: the rapid disintegration of moral values, of the pre-1914 pattern of life in postwar Europe, and the simultaneous lure of the new revelation which had come from the East.

I joined the Party (which to this day remains "the" Party for all of us who once belonged to it) in 1931. . . .

I lived at that time in Berlin. For the last five years, I had been working for the Ullstein chain of newspapers — first as a foreign correspondent in Palestine and the Middle East, then in Paris. Finally, in 1930, I joined the editorial staff in the Berlin "House.". . .

. . . With one-third of its wage-earners unemployed, Germany lived in a state of latent civil war, and if one wasn't prepared to be swept along as a passive victim by the approaching hurricane it became imperative to take sides. . . . The Communists, with the mighty Soviet Union behind them, seemed the only force capable of resisting the onrush of the primitive horde with its swastika totem. I began for the first time to read Marx, Engels and Lenin in earnest. By the time I had finished with *Feuerbach* and *State and Revolution,* something had clicked in my brain which shook me like a mental explosion. To say that one had "seen the light" is a poor description of the mental rapture which only the convert knows (regardless of what faith he has been converted to). The new light seems to pour from all directions across the skull; the whole universe falls into pattern like the stray pieces of a jigsaw puzzle assembled by magic at one stroke. There is now an answer to every question, doubts and conflicts are a matter of the tortured past — a past already remote, when one had lived in dismal ignorance in the tasteless, colorless world of those who *don't know.* Nothing henceforth can disturb the convert's inner peace and serenity — except the occasional fear of losing faith again, losing thereby what alone makes life worth living, and falling back into the outer darkness, where there is wailing and gnashing of teeth.

REVIEW QUESTIONS

1. How did José Ortega y Gasset define the "mass-man"?
2. According to Ortega, what were the attitudes of the mass-man toward liberal democracy, reason, and culture?
3. How did Ortega view fascism?
4. According to Thomas Mann, what new mental attitude emerged that heralded the end of the bourgeois age?
5. How did Mann view extreme nationalism and National Socialism?
6. What did Mann mean by "politics becomes an opiate of the masses"?
7. What factors led to Arthur Koestler's becoming a communist?

8 ▾ The Munich Agreement

Hitler sought power to build a great German empire in Europe, a goal that he revealed in *Mein Kampf.* In 1935, Hitler declared that Germany was no longer bound by the Versailles Treaty and would restore military conscription. In 1936, Germany remilitarized the Rhineland and in 1938 incorporated Austria into the Third Reich. Although these actions violated the Versailles Treaty, Britain and France offered no resistance.

In 1938, Hitler also threatened war if Czechoslovakia did not cede to Germany the Sudetenland with its large German population — of the 3.5 million people living in the Czech Sudetenland, some 2.8 million were Germans. In September 1938, Hitler met with other European leaders at Munich. Prime Minister Neville Chamberlain (1869–1940) of Great Britain and Prime Minister Édouard Daladier (1884–1970) of France agreed to Hitler's demands, despite France's mutual assistance pact with Czechoslovakia and the Czechs' expressed determination to resist the dismemberment of their country. Both Chamberlain and Daladier were praised by their compatriots for ensuring, as Chamberlain said, "peace in our time."

Neville Chamberlain
IN DEFENSE OF APPEASEMENT

Britain and France pursued a policy of appeasement — giving in to Germany in the hope that a satisfied Hitler would not drag Europe into another war. Appeasement expressed the widespread British desire to heal the wounds of World War I and to correct what many British officials regarded as the injustices of the Versailles Treaty. Some officials, lauding Hitler's anticommunism, regarded a powerful Germany as a bulwark against the Soviet Union. Britain's lack of military preparedness was another compelling reason for not resisting Hitler. On September 27, 1938, when negotiations between Hitler and Chamberlain reached a tense moment, the British prime minister addressed his nation. Excerpts of this speech and of another before the House of Commons, which appeared in his *In Search of Peace* (1939), follow.

First of all I must say something to those who have written to my wife or myself in these last weeks to tell us of their gratitude for my efforts and to assure us of their prayers for my success. Most of these letters have come from women — mothers or sisters of our own countrymen. But there are countless others besides — from France, from Belgium, from Italy, even from Germany, and it has been heartbreaking to read of the growing anxiety they reveal and their intense relief when they thought, too soon, that the danger of war was past.

If I felt my responsibility heavy before, to read such letters has made it seem almost overwhelming. How horrible, fantastic, incredible it is that we should be digging trenches and trying on gas masks here because of a quarrel in a far-away country between people of whom we know nothing. It seems still more impossible that a quarrel which has already been settled in principle should be the subject of war.

I can well understand the reasons why the Czech Government have felt unable to accept the terms which have been put before them in the German memorandum. Yet I believe after my talks with Herr Hitler that, if only time were allowed, it ought to be possible for the arrangements for transferring the territory that the Czech Government has agreed to give to Germany to be settled by agreement under conditions which would assure fair treatment to the population concerned. . . .

However much we may sympathise with a small nation confronted by a big and powerful neighbour, we cannot in all circumstances undertake to involve the whole British Empire in war simply on her account. If we have to fight it must be on larger issues than that. I am myself a man of peace to the depths of my soul. Armed conflict between nations is a nightmare to me; but if I were convinced that any nation had made up its mind to dominate the world by fear of its force, I should feel that it must be resisted. Under such a domination life for people who believe in liberty would not be worth living; but war is a fearful thing, and we must be very clear, before we embark on it, that it is really the great issues that are at stake, and that the call to risk everything in their defence, when all the consequences are weighed, is irresistible.

For the present I ask you to await as calmly as you can the events of the next few days. As long as war has not begun, there is always hope that it may be prevented, and you know that I am going to work for peace to the last moment. Good night. . . .

▷ On October 6, 1938, in a speech to Britain's House of Commons, Chamberlain defended the Munich agreement signed on September 30.

Since I first went to Berchtesgaden [to confer with Hitler in Germany] more than 20,000 letters and telegrams have come to No. 10, Downing Street [British prime minister's residence]. Of course, I have only been able to look at a tiny fraction of them, but I have seen enough to know that the people who wrote did not feel that they had such a cause for which to fight, if they were asked to go to war in order that the Sudeten Germans might not join the Reich. That is how they are feeling. That is my answer to those who say that we should have told Germany weeks ago that, if her army crossed the border of Czechoslovakia, we should be at war with her. We had no treaty obligations and no legal obligations to Czechoslovakia and if we had said that, we feel that we should have received no support from the people of this country. . . .

. . . When we were convinced, as we became convinced, that nothing any longer would keep the Sudetenland within the Czechoslovakian State, we urged the Czech Government as strongly as we could to agree to the cession of territory, and to agree promptly. The Czech Government, through the wisdom and courage of President Benes, accepted the advice of the French Government and ourselves. It was a hard decision for anyone who loved his country to take, but to accuse us of having by that advice betrayed the Czechoslovakian State is simply preposterous. What we did was to save her from annihilation and give her a chance of new life as a new State, which involves the loss of territory and fortifications, but may perhaps enable her to enjoy in the future and develop a national existence under a neutrality and security comparable to that which we see in Switzerland to-day. Therefore, I think the Government deserve the approval of this House for their conduct of affairs in this recent crisis which has saved Czechoslovakia from destruction and Europe from Armageddon.

Does the experience of the Great War and of the years that followed it give us reasonable hope that, if some new war started, that would end war any more than the last one did? . . .

One good thing, at any rate, has come out of this emergency through which we have passed. It has thrown a vivid light upon our preparations for defence, on their strength and on their weakness. I should not think we were doing our duty if we had not already ordered that a prompt and thorough inquiry should be made to cover the whole of our preparations, military and civil, in order to see, in the light of what has happened during these hectic days, what further steps may be necessary to make good our deficiencies in the shortest possible time.

Winston Churchill
A DISASTER OF THE FIRST MAGNITUDE

On October 5, 1938, Britain's elder statesman Winston Churchill (1874–1965) delivered a speech in the House of Commons attacking the Munich agreement and British policy toward Germany.

. . . I will begin by saying what everybody would like to ignore or forget but which must nevertheless be stated, namely, that we have sustained a total and unmitigated defeat, and that France has suffered even more than we have. . . .

. . . And I will say this, that I believe the Czechs, left to themselves and told they were going to get no help from the Western Powers, would have been able to make better terms than they have got — they could hardly have worse — after all this tremendous perturbation. . . .

. . . I have always held the view that the maintenance of peace depends upon the accumulation of deterrents against the aggressor, coupled with a sincere effort to redress grievances. . . . After [Hitler's] seizure of Austria in March . . . I ventured to appeal to the Government . . . to give a pledge that in conjunction with France and other Powers they would guarantee the security of Czechoslovakia while the Sudeten-Deutsch question was being examined either by a League of Nations Commission or some other impartial body, and I still believe that if that course had been followed events would not have fallen into this disastrous state. . . .

France and Great Britain together, especially if they had maintained a close contact with Russia, which certainly was not done, would have been able in those days in the summer, when they had the prestige, to influence many of the smaller States of Europe, and I believe they could have determined the attitude of Poland. Such a combination, prepared at a time when the German dictator was not deeply and irrevocably committed to his new adventure, would, I believe, have given strength to all those forces in Germany which resisted this departure, this new design. They were varying forces, those of a military character which declared that Germany was not ready to undertake a world war, and all that mass of moderate opinion and popular opinion which dreaded war, and some elements of which still have some influence upon the German Government. Such action would have given strength to all that intense desire for peace which the helpless German masses share with their British and French fellow men. . . .

. . . I do not think it is fair to charge those who wished to see this course followed, and followed consistently and resolutely, with having wished for an immediate war. Between submission and immediate war there was this third alternative, which gave a hope not only of peace but of justice. It is quite true that such a policy in order to succeed demanded that Britain should declare straight out and a long time beforehand that she would, with others, join to defend Czechoslovakia against an unprovoked aggression. His Majesty's Government refused to give that guarantee when it would have saved the situation. . . .

All is over. Silent, mournful, abandoned, broken, Czechoslovakia recedes into the darkness. She has suffered in every respect by her association with the Western democracies and with the League of Nations, of which she has always been an obedient servant. She has suffered in particular from her association with France, under whose guidance and policy she has been actuated for so long. . . .

We in this country, as in other Liberal and democratic countries, have a perfect right to exalt the principle of self-determination, but it comes ill out of the mouths of those in totalitarian States who deny even the smallest element of toleration to every section and creed within their bounds. . . .

What is the remaining position of Czechoslovakia? Not only are they politically mutilated, but, economically and financially, they are in complete confusion. Their banking, their railway arrangements, are severed and broken, their industries are curtailed, and the movement of their population is most cruel. The Sudeten miners, who are all Czechs and whose families have lived in that area for centuries, must now flee into an area where there are hardly any mines left for them to work. It is a tragedy which has occurred. . . .

I venture to think that in future the Czechoslovak State cannot be maintained as an independent entity. You will find that in a period of time which may be measured by years, but may be measured only by months, Czechoslovakia will be engulfed in the Nazi régime. Perhaps they may join it in despair or in revenge. At any rate, that story is over and told. But we cannot consider the abandonment and ruin of Czechoslovakia in the light only of what happened only last month. It is the most grievous consequence which we have yet experienced of what we have done and of what we have left undone in the last five years — five years of futile good intention, five years of eager search for the line of least resistance, five years of uninterrupted retreat of British power, five years

of neglect of our air defences. Those are the features which I stand here to declare and which marked an improvident stewardship for which Great Britain and France have dearly to pay. We have been reduced in those five years from a position of security so overwhelming and so unchallengeable that we never cared to think about it. We have been reduced from a position where the very word "war" was considered one which would be used only by persons qualifying for a lunatic asylum. We have been reduced from a position of safety and power — power to do good, power to be generous to a beaten foe, power to make terms with Germany, power to give her proper redress for her grievances, power to stop her arming if we chose, power to take any step in strength or mercy or justice which we thought right — reduced in five years from a position safe and unchallenged to where we stand now.

When I think of the fair hopes of a long peace which still lay before Europe at the beginning of 1933 when Herr Hitler first obtained power, and of all the opportunities of arresting the growth of the Nazi power which have been thrown away, when I think of the immense combinations and resources which have been neglected or squandered, I cannot believe that a parallel exists in the whole course of history. So far as this country is concerned the responsibility must rest with those who have the undisputed control of our political affairs. They neither prevented Germany from rearming, nor did they rearm ourselves in time. . . . They neglected to make alliances and combinations which might have repaired previous errors, and thus they left us in the hour of trial without adequate national defence or effective international security. . . .

We are in the presence of a disaster of the first magnitude which has befallen Great Britain and France. Do not let us blind ourselves to that. It must now be accepted that all the countries of Central and Eastern Europe will make the best terms they can with the triumphant Nazi Power. The system of alliances in Central Europe upon which France has relied for her safety has been swept away, and I can see no means by which it can be reconstituted. . . .

. . . If the Nazi dictator should choose to look westward, as he may, bitterly will France and England regret the loss of that fine army of ancient Bohemia [Czechoslovakia] which was estimated last week to require not fewer than 30 German divisions for its destruction. . . .

. . . Many people, no doubt, honestly believe that they are only giving away the interests of Czechoslovakia, whereas I fear we shall find that we have deeply compromised, and perhaps fatally endangered, the safety and even the independence of Great Britain and France. . . . [T]here can never be friendship between the British democracy and the Nazi Power, that Power which spurns Christian ethics, which cheers its onward course by a barbarous paganism, which vaunts the spirit of aggression and conquest, which derives strength and perverted pleasure from persecution, and uses, as we have seen, with pitiless brutality the threat of murderous force. That Power cannot ever be the trusted friend of the British democracy. . . .

. . . [O]ur loyal, brave people . . . should know the truth. They should know that there has been gross neglect and deficiency in our defences; they should know that we have sustained a defeat without a war, the consequences of which will travel far with us along our road; they should know that we have passed an awful milestone in our history, when the whole equilibrium of Europe has been deranged, and that the terrible words have for the time being been pronounced against the Western democracies:

Thou art weighed in the balance and found wanting.

And do not suppose that this is the end. This is only the beginning of the reckoning. This is only the first sip, the first foretaste of a bitter cup which will be proffered to us year by year unless by a supreme recovery of moral health and martial vigour, we arise again and take our stand for freedom as in the olden time.

REVIEW QUESTIONS

1. In Neville Chamberlain's view, how did the British people regard a war with Germany over the Sudetenland?
2. How did Chamberlain respond to the accusation that Britain and France had betrayed Czechoslovakia?
3. What did Chamberlain consider to be the "one good thing" to come out of the Sudetenland crisis?
4. Why did Winston Churchill believe that "there [could] never be friendship between the British democracy and the Nazi Power"?
5. Why did Churchill believe that the Munich agreement was "a disaster of the first magnitude" for Britain and France?
6. According to Chamberlain, how did Czechoslovakia benefit from the Munich agreement? What was Churchill's assessment of the impact of the Munich agreement on Czechoslovakia? What prediction did he make regarding post-Munich Czechoslovakia?
7. What policy toward Nazi Germany did Churchill advocate?

▼▼▼

9 ▼ Britain's Finest Hour

On September 1, 1939, German troops crossed into Poland, precipitating World War II. Poland fell in four weeks to the Nazi blitzkrieg, that is, lightning war marked by fast-moving mechanized columns. In the months that followed, land battles consisted only of a few skirmishes on the Franco-German border. Then in April 1940, Germany attacked Denmark and Norway. The swift conquest of these countries discredited the leadership of Britain's Neville Chamberlain, who was replaced as prime minister by Winston Churchill on May 10, the very day that Hitler struck against Holland, Belgium, Luxembourg, and France.

Winston Churchill
"BLOOD, TOIL, TEARS, AND SWEAT"

Churchill, at the age of sixty-six, proved to be an undaunted leader, sharing the perils faced by all and able by example and by speeches to rally British morale. When he first addressed Parliament as prime minister on May 13, 1940, he left no doubt about the grim realities that lay ahead. Excerpts from his speeches in 1940 follow.

May 13, 1940

I would say to the House, as I said to those who have joined this Government: "I have nothing to offer but blood, toil, tears, and sweat." We have before us an ordeal of the most grievous kind. We have before us many, many long months of struggle and suffering. You ask: "What is our policy?" I will say: "It is to wage war by sea, land, and air with all our might, and with all the strength that God can give us; to wage war against a monstrous tyranny, never surpassed in the dark lamentable catalogue of human crime." That is our policy.

You ask: "What is our aim?" I can answer in one word: "Victory!" Victory at all costs, victory in spite of all terror, victory however long and hard the road may be; for without victory there is no survival.

▷   When Churchill spoke next, on May 19, the Dutch had surrendered to the Germans, and the French and British armies were in retreat. Still, Churchill promised that "conquer we shall."

May 19, 1940

This is one of the most awe-striking periods in the long history of France and Britain. It is also beyond doubt the most sublime. Side

by side, unaided except by their kith and kin in the great Dominions and by the wide Empires which rest beneath their shield — side by side, the British and French peoples have advanced to rescue not only Europe but mankind from the foulest and most soul-destroying tyranny which has ever darkened and stained the pages of history. Behind them — behind us — behind the armies and fleets of Britain and France — gather a group of shattered states and bludgeoned races: the Czechs, the Poles, the Norwegians, the Danes, the Dutch, the Belgians — upon all of whom the long night of barbarism will descend unbroken even by a star of hope, unless we conquer, as conquer we must; as conquer we shall.

▷   By early June the Belgians had surrendered to the Germans, and the last units of the British Expeditionary Force in France had been evacuated from Dunkirk; the French armies were in full flight. Again Churchill spoke out in defiance of events across the Channel.

June 4, 1940

We shall not flag or fail. We shall go on to the end. We shall fight in France, we shall fight on the seas and oceans, we shall fight with growing confidence and growing strength in the air.

We shall defend our island, whatever the cost may be. We shall fight on the beaches, we shall fight on the landing-grounds, we shall fight in the fields and in the streets, we shall fight in the hills. We shall never surrender; and even if, which I do not for a moment believe, this island or a large part of it were subjugated and starving, then our Empire beyond the seas, armed and guarded by the British Fleet,' would carry on the struggle, until, in God's good time, the New World, with all its power and might, steps forth to the rescue and liberation of the Old.

▷ By June 18 the battle of France was lost; on June 22 France surrendered. Now Britain itself was under siege. Churchill again found the right words to sustain his people:

June 18, 1940

What General [Maxime] Weygand [commander of the French army] called the Battle of France is over. . . . The Battle of Britain is about to begin. Upon this battle depends the survival of Christian civilization. Upon it depends our own British life and the long continuity of our institutions and our Empire. The whole fury and might of the enemy must very soon be turned upon us. Hitler knows that he will have to break us in this island or lose the war.

If we can stand up to him, all Europe may be free and the life of the world may move forward into broad sunlit uplands. But if we fail, then the whole world, including the United States, including all that we have known and cared for, will sink into the abyss of a new Dark Age made more sinister and perhaps more prolonged by the lights of a perverted science.

Let us therefore brace ourselves to our duty and so bear ourselves that if the British Empire and Commonwealth last for a thousand years, men will still say, "This was their finest hour."

▷ The bombing of Britain began, in advance of the Germans' planned invasion, in July, reaching a climax in September with great raids on London and other cities. The Battle of Britain was fought in the air by British pilots defending their country. Early in the battle Churchill acknowledged the courage of British airmen and their contribution to Britain's survival.

August 20, 1940

The gratitude of every home in our island, in our Empire, and indeed throughout the world, except in the abodes of the guilty, goes out to the British airmen who, undaunted by odds, unwearied in their constant challenge and mortal danger, are turning the tide of world war by their prowess and by their devotion. Never in the field of human conflict was so much owed by so many to so few. All hearts go out to the fighter pilots whose brilliant actions we see with our own eyes day after day.

REVIEW QUESTIONS

1. According to Winston Churchill, what did a Nazi victory mean for Europe?
2. On whose help did Churchill ultimately count for the liberation of Europe?
3. Both Hitler and Churchill were gifted orators. Compare their styles.

▼▼▼

10 ▾ Stalingrad: A Turning Point

In July 1942, the Germans resumed their advance into the U.S.S.R. begun the previous summer, seeking to conquer Stalingrad, a vital transportation center located on the Volga River. Germans and Russians battled with dogged ferocity over every part of the city; 99 percent of Stalingrad was reduced to rubble. A Russian counteroffensive in November trapped the German Sixth Army. Realizing that the Sixth Army, exhausted and short of weapons, ammunition, food, and medical supplies, faced annihilation, German generals pleaded in vain with Hitler to permit withdrawal before the Russians closed the ring. On February 2, 1943, the remnants of the Sixth Army surrendered. More than a million people — Russian civilians and soldiers, Germans and their Italian, Hungarian, and Rumanian allies — perished in the epic struggle for Stalingrad. The Russian victory was a major turning point in the war.

Diary of a German Soldier

The following entries in the diary of a German soldier who perished at Stalingrad reveal the decline in German confidence as the battle progressed. While the German army was penetrating deeply into Russia, he believed that victory was not far away and dreamed of returning home with medals. Then the terrible struggles in Stalingrad made him curse the war.

Today, after we'd had a bath, the company commander told us that if our future operations are as successful, we'll soon reach the Volga, take Stalingrad and then the war will inevitably soon be over. Perhaps we'll be home by Christmas.

July 29 [1942]. . . . The company commander says the Russian troops are completely broken, and cannot hold out any longer. To reach the Volga and take Stalingrad is not so difficult for us. The Führer knows where the Russians' weak point is. Victory is not far away. . . .

August 2. . . . What great spaces the Soviets occupy, what rich fields there are to be had here after the war's over! Only let's get it over with quickly. I believe that the Führer will carry the thing through to a successful end.

August 10. . . . The Führer's orders were read out to us. He expects victory of us. We are all convinced that they can't stop us.

August 12. We are advancing towards Stalingrad along the railway line. Yesterday Russian "katyushi" [small rocket launchers] and then tanks halted our regiment. "The Russians are throwing in their last forces," Captain Werner explained to me. Large-scale help is coming up for us, and the Russians will be beaten.

This morning outstanding soldiers were presented with decorations. . . . Will I really go back to Elsa without a decoration? I believe that for Stalingrad the Führer will decorate even me. . . .

August 23. Splendid news — north of Stalingrad our troops have reached the Volga and captured part of the city. The Russians have two alternatives, either to flee across the Volga or give themselves up. Our company's interpreter has interrogated a captured Russian officer. He was wounded, but asserted that the Russians would fight for Stalingrad to the last round. Something incomprehensible is, in fact, going on. In the north our troops capture a part of Stalingrad and reach the Volga, but in the south the doomed divisions are continuing to resist bitterly. Fanaticism. . . .

August 27. A continuous cannonade on all sides. We are slowly advancing. Less than twenty miles to go to Stalingrad. In the daytime we can see the smoke of fires, at nighttime the bright glow. They say that the city is on fire; on the Führer's orders our Luftwaffe [air force] has sent it up in flames. That's what the Russians need, to stop them from resisting . . .

September 4. We are being sent northward along the front towards Stalingrad. We marched all night and by dawn had reached Voroponovo Station. We can already see the smoking town. It's a happy thought that the end of the war is getting nearer. That's what everyone is saying. If only the days and nights would pass more quickly . . .

September 5. Our regiment has been ordered to attack Sadovaya station — that's nearly in Stalingrad. Are the Russians really thinking of holding out in the city itself? We had no peace all night from the Russian artillery and aeroplanes. Lots of wounded are being brought by. God protect me . . .

September 8. Two days of non-stop fighting. The Russians are defending themselves with insane stubbornness. Our regiment has lost many men from the "katyushi," which belch out terrible fire. I have been sent to work at battalion H.Q. It must be mother's prayers that have taken me away from the company's trenches . . .

September 11. Our battalion is fighting in the suburbs of Stalingrad. We can already see the Volga; firing is going on all the time. Wherever you look is fire and flames. . . . Russian cannon and machine-guns are firing out of the burning city. Fanatics . . .

September 13. An unlucky number. This morning "katyushi" attacks caused the company heavy losses: twenty-seven dead and fifty wounded. The Russians are fighting desperately like wild beasts, don't give themselves up, but come up close and then throw grenades. Lieutenant Kraus was killed yesterday, and there is no company commander.

September 16. Our battalion, plus tanks, is attacking the [grain storage] elevator, from which smoke is pouring — the grain in it is burning, the Russians seem to have set light to it themselves. Barbarism. The battalion is suffering heavy losses. There are not more than sixty men left in each company. The elevator is occupied not by men but by devils that no flames or bullets can destroy.

September 18. Fighting is going on inside the elevator. The Russians inside are condemned men; the battalion commander says: "The commissars have ordered those men to die in the elevator."

If all the buildings of Stalingrad are defended like this then none of our soldiers will get back to Germany. I had a letter from Elsa today. She's expecting me home when victory's won.

September 20. The battle for the elevator is still going on. The Russians are firing on all sides. We stay in our cellar; you can't go out into the street. Sergeant-Major Nuschke was killed today running across a street. Poor fellow, he's got three children.

September 22. Russian resistance in the elevator has been broken. Our troops are advancing towards the Volga. . . .

. . . Our old soldiers have never experienced such bitter fighting before.

September 26. Our regiment is involved in constant heavy fighting. After the elevator was taken the Russians continued to defend themselves just as stubbornly. You don't see them at all, they have established themselves in houses and cellars and are firing on all sides, including from our rear — barbarians, they use gangster methods.

In the blocks captured two days ago Russian soldiers appeared from somewhere or other and fighting has flared up with fresh vigour. Our men are being killed not only in the firing line, but in the rear, in buildings we have already occupied.

The Russians have stopped surrendering at all. If we take any prisoners it's because they are hopelessly wounded, and can't move by themselves. Stalingrad is hell. Those who are merely wounded are lucky; they will doubtless be at home and celebrate victory with their families. . . .

September 28. Our regiment, and the whole division, are today celebrating victory. Together with our tank crews we have taken the southern part of the city and reached the Volga. We paid dearly for our victory. In three weeks we have occupied about five and a half square miles. The commander has congratulated us on our victory. . . .

October 3. After marching through the night we have established ourselves in a shrub-covered gully. We are apparently going to attack the factories, the chimneys of which we can see clearly. Behind them is the Volga. We have entered a new area. It was night but we saw many crosses with our helmets on top. Have we really lost so many men? Damn this Stalingrad!

October 4. Our regiment is attacking the Barrikady settlement. A lot of Russian tommy-gunners have appeared. Where are they bringing them from?

October 5. Our battalion has gone into the attack four times, and got stopped each time. Russian snipers hit anyone who shows himself carelessly from behind shelter.

October 10. The Russians are so close to us that our planes cannot bomb them. We are preparing for a decisive attack. The Führer has ordered the whole of Stalingrad to be taken as rapidly as possible.

October 14. It has been fantastic since morning: our aeroplanes and artillery have been hammering the Russian positions for hours on end; everything in sight is being blotted from the face of the earth. . . .

October 22. Our regiment has failed to break into the factory. We have lost many men; every time you move you have to jump over bodies. You can scarcely breathe in the daytime: there is nowhere and no one to remove the bodies, so they are left there to rot. Who would have thought three months ago that instead of the joy of victory we would have to endure such sacrifice and torture, the end of which is nowhere in sight? . . .

The soldiers are calling Stalingrad the mass grave of the Wehrmacht [German army]. There are very few men left in the companies. We have been told we are soon going to be withdrawn to be brought back up to strength.

October 27. Our troops have captured the whole of the Barrikady factory, but we cannot break through to the Volga. The Russians are not men, but some kind of cast-iron creatures; they never get tired and are not afraid of fire. We are absolutely exhausted; our regiment now has barely the strength of a company. The Russian artillery at the other side of the Volga won't let you lift your head. . . .

October 28. Every soldier sees himself as a condemned man. The only hope is to be wounded and taken back to the rear. . . .

November 3. In the last few days our battalion has several times tried to attack the Russian positions, . . . to no avail. On this sector also the Russians won't let you lift your head. There have been a number of cases of self-inflicted wounds and malingering among the men. Every day I write two or three reports about them.

November 10. A letter from Elsa today. Everyone expects us home for Christmas. In Germany everyone believes we already hold Stalingrad. How wrong they are. If they could only see what Stalingrad has done to our army.

November 18. Our attack with tanks yesterday had no success. After our attack the field was littered with dead.

November 21. The Russians have gone over to the offensive along the whole front. Fierce fighting is going on. So, there it is — the Volga, victory and soon home to our families! We shall obviously be seeing them next in the other world.

November 29. We are encircled. It was announced this morning that the Führer has said: "The army can trust me to do everything necessary to ensure supplies and rapidly break the encirclement."

December 3. We are on hunger rations and waiting for the rescue that the Führer promised.

I send letters home, but there is no reply.

December 7. Rations have been cut to such an extent that the soldiers are suffering terribly from hunger; they are issuing one loaf of stale bread for five men.

December 11. Three questions are obsessing every soldier and officer: When will the Russians stop firing and let us sleep in peace, if only for one night? How and with what are we going to fill our empty stomachs, which, apart from 3½-7 ozs of bread, receive virtually nothing at all? And when will Hitler take any decisive steps to free our armies from encirclement?

December 14. Everybody is racked with hunger. Frozen potatoes are the best meal, but to get them out of the ice-covered ground under fire from Russian bullets is not so easy.

December 18. The officers today told the soldiers to be prepared for action. General Manstein is approaching Stalingrad from the south with strong forces. This news brought hope to the soldiers' hearts. God, let it be!

December 21. We are waiting for the order, but for some reason or other it has been a long time coming. Can it be that it is not true about Manstein? This is worse than any torture.

December 23. Still no orders. It was all a bluff with Manstein. Or has he been defeated at the approaches to Stalingrad?

December 25. The Russian radio has announced the defeat of Manstein. Ahead of us is either death or captivity.

December 26. The horses have already been eaten. I would eat a cat; they say its meat is also tasty. The soldiers look like corpses or lunatics, looking for something to put in their mouths. They no longer take cover from Russian shells; they haven't the strength to walk, run away and hide. A curse on this war! . . .

REVIEW QUESTIONS

1. What were the expectations of the German soldier in July and August? How did he view Hitler and the war?
2. How did he view the Russians?
3. How did the hard fighting at Stalingrad alter his conception of the war and his attitude toward the Russians?

▼▼▼

11 ▼ The Holocaust

Over conquered Europe the Nazis imposed a "New Order" marked by exploitation, torture, and mass murder. The Germans took some 5.5 million Russian prisoners of war, of whom more than 3.5 million perished; many of these prisoners were deliberately starved to death. The Germans imprisoned and executed many Polish intellectuals and priests and slaughtered vast numbers of Gypsies. Using the modern state's organizational capacities and the instruments of modern technology, the Nazis murdered six million Jews, including one and a half million children — two-thirds of the Jewish population of Europe. Gripped by the mythical, perverted world-view of Nazism, the SS, Hitler's elite guard, carried out these murders with dedication and idealism; they believed that they were exterminating subhumans who threatened the German nation.

Hermann Graebe
SLAUGHTER OF JEWS IN THE UKRAINE

While the regular German army penetrated deeply into Russia, special SS units, the *Einsatzgruppen,* rounded up Jews for mass executions, killing about two million people. Hermann Graebe, a German construction engineer, saw such a mass slaughter in Dubno in the Ukraine. He gave a sworn affidavit before the Nuremberg tribunal, a court at which the Allies tried Nazi war criminals after the end of World War II.

Graebe had joined the Nazi party in 1931 but later renounced his membership, and during the war he rescued Jews from the SS. Graebe was the only German citizen to volunteer to testify at the Nuremberg trials, an act that earned him the enmity of his compatriots. Socially ostracized, Graebe emigrated to the United States, where he died in 1986 at the age of eighty-five.

On October 5, 1942, when I visited the building office at Dubno, my foreman told me that in the vicinity of the site, Jews from Dubno had been shot in three large pits, each about 30 metres long and 3 metres deep. About 1,500 persons had been killed daily. All the 5,000 Jews who had still been living in Dubno before the pogrom were to be liquidated. As the shooting had taken place in his presence, he was still much upset.

Thereupon, I drove to the site accompanied by my foreman and saw near it great mounds of earth, about 30 metres long and 2 metres high. Several trucks stood in front of the mounds. Armed Ukrainian militia drove the people off the trucks under the supervision of an S.S. man. The militiamen acted as guards on the trucks and drove them to and from the pit. All these people had the regulation yellow patches on the front and back of their clothes, and thus could be recognized as Jews.

My foreman and I went directly to the pits. Nobody bothered us. Now I heard rifle shots in quick succession from behind one of the earth mounds. The people who had got off the trucks — men, women and children of all ages — had to undress upon the orders of an S.S. man, who carried a riding or dog whip. They had to put down their clothes in fixed places, sorted according to shoes, top clothing and underclothing. I saw a heap of shoes of about 800 to 1,000 pairs, great piles of under-linen and clothing.

Without screaming or weeping, these people undressed, stood around in family groups, kissed each other, said farewells, and waited for a sign from another S.S. man, who stood near

the pit, also with a whip in his hand. During the fifteen minutes that I stood near I heard no complaint or plea for mercy. I watched a family of about eight persons, a man and a woman both about fifty with their children of about one, eight and ten, and two grown-up daughters of about twenty to twenty-nine. An old woman with snow-white hair was holding the one-year-old child in her arms and singing to it and tickling it. The child was cooing with delight. The couple were looking on with tears in their eyes. The father was holding the hand of a boy about ten years old and speaking to him softly; the boy was fighting his tears. The father pointed to the sky, stroked his head, and seemed to explain something to him.

At that moment the S.S. man at the pit shouted something to his comrade. The latter counted off about twenty persons and instructed them to go behind the earth mound. Among them was the family which I have mentioned. I well remember a girl, slim and with black hair, who, as she passed close to me, pointed to herself and said "23." I walked around the mound and found myself confronted by a tremendous grave. People were closely wedged together and lying on top of each other so that only their heads were visible. Nearly all had blood running over their shoulders from their heads. Some of the people shot were still moving. Some were lifting their arms and turning their heads to show that they were still alive. The pit was already two-thirds full. I estimated that it already contained about 1,000 people.

I looked for the man who did the shooting. He was an S.S. man, who sat at the edge of the narrow end of the pit, his feet dangling into the pit. He had a tommy-gun on his knees and was smoking a cigarette. The people, completely naked, went down some steps which were cut in the clay wall of the pit and clambered over the heads of the people lying there, to the place to which the S.S. man directed them. They lay down in front of the dead or injured people; some caressed those who were still alive and spoke to them in a low voice.

Then I heard a series of shots. I looked into the pit and saw that the bodies were twitching or the heads lying motionless on top of the bodies which lay before them. Blood was running from their necks. I was surprised that I was not ordered away, but I saw that there were two or three postmen in uniform nearby. The next batch was approaching already. They went down into the pit, lined themselves up against the previous victims and were shot.

When I walked back round the mound, I noticed another truckload of people which had just arrived. This time it included sick and infirm persons. An old, very thin woman with terribly thin legs was undressed by others who were already naked, while two people held her up. The woman appeared to be paralyzed. The naked people carried the woman around the mound. I left with my foreman and drove in my car back to Dubno.

On the morning of the next day, when I again visited the site, I saw about thirty naked people lying near the pit — about 30 to 50 metres away from it. Some of them were still alive; they looked straight in front of them with a fixed stare and seemed to notice neither the chilliness of the morning nor the workers of my firm who stood around. A girl of about twenty spoke to me and asked me to give her clothes and help her escape. At that moment we heard a fast car approach and I noticed that it was an S.S. detail. I moved away to my site. Ten minutes later we heard shots from the vicinity of the pit. The Jews alive had been ordered to throw the corpses into the pit, then they had themselves to lie down in it to be shot in the neck.

Rudolf Hoess
COMMANDANT OF AUSCHWITZ

To speed up the "final solution of the Jewish problem," the SS established death camps in Poland. Jews from all over Europe were crammed into cattle cars and shipped to these camps to be gassed or worked to death. At Auschwitz, the most notorious of the concentration camps, the SS used five gas chambers to kill 9,000 or more people a day. Special squads of prisoners, called *Sonderkommandos,* were forced to pick over the corpses for gold teeth, jewelry, and anything else of value for the German war effort. Some 1.3 million Jews perished at Auschwitz. In the following passage from *Commandant of Auschwitz,* Rudolf Hoess (1900–1947), who commanded the camp and was executed by Poland after the war, recalled the murder process when he was in a Polish prison.

In the spring of 1942 the first transports of Jews, all earmarked for extermination, arrived from Upper Silesia.

They were taken from the detraining platform to the "cottage" — to bunker I — across the meadows where later building site II was located. The transport was conducted by Aumeier and Palitzsch and some of the block leaders. They talked with the Jews about general topics, inquiring concerning their qualifications and trades, with a view to misleading them. On arrival at the "cottage," they were told to undress. At first they went calmly into the rooms where they were supposed to be disinfected. But some of them showed signs of alarm, and spoke of death by suffocation and of annihilation. A sort of panic set in at once. Immediately all the Jews still outside were pushed into the chambers, and the doors were screwed shut. With subsequent transports the difficult individuals were picked out early and most carefully supervised. At the first signs of unrest, those responsible were unobtrusively led behind the building and killed with a small-caliber gun, that was inaudible to the others. The presence and calm behavior of the Special Detachment [of *Sonderkommandos*] served to reassure those who were worried or who suspected what was about to happen. A further calming effect was obtained by members of the Special Detachment accompanying them into the rooms and remaining with them until the last moment, while an SS man also stood in the doorway until the end.

It was most important that the whole business of arriving and undressing should take place in an atmosphere of the greatest possible calm. People reluctant to take off their clothes had to be helped by those of their companions who had already undressed, or by men of the Special Detachment.

The refractory ones were calmed down and encouraged to undress. The prisoners of the Special Detachment also saw to it that the process of undressing was carried out quickly, so that the victims would have little time to wonder what was happening. . . .

Many of the women hid their babies among the piles of clothing. The men of the Special Detachment were particularly on the lookout for this, and would speak words of encouragement to the woman until they had persuaded her to take the child with her. The women believed that the disinfectant might be bad for their smaller children, hence their efforts to conceal them.

The smaller children usually cried because of the strangeness of being undressed in this fashion, but when their mothers or members of the Special Detachment comforted them, they became calm and entered the gas chambers, playing or joking with one another and carrying their toys.

I noticed that women who either guessed or knew what awaited them nevertheless found the courage to joke with the children to encourage them, despite the mortal terror visible in their own eyes.

One woman approached me as she walked past and, pointing to her four children who were manfully helping the smallest ones over the rough ground, whispered:

"How can you bring yourself to kill such beautiful, darling children? Have you no heart at all?"

One old man, as he passed by me, hissed:

"Germany will pay a heavy penance for this mass murder of the Jews."

His eyes glowed with hatred as he said this. Nevertheless he walked calmly into the gas chamber, without worrying about the others.

One young woman caught my attention particularly as she ran busily hither and thither, helping the smallest children and the old women to undress. During the selection she had had two small children with her, and her agitated behavior and appearance had brought her to my notice at once. She did not look in the least like a Jewess. Now her children were no longer with her. She waited until the end, helping the women who were not undressed and who had several children with them, encouraging them and calming the children. She went with the very last ones into the gas chamber. Standing in the doorway, she said:

"I knew all the time that we were being brought to Auschwitz to be gassed. When the selection took place I avoided being put with the able-bodied ones, as I wished to look after the children. I wanted to go through it all, fully conscious of what was happening. I hope that it will be quick. Goodbye!"

From time to time women would suddenly give the most terrible shrieks while undressing, or tear their hair, or scream like maniacs. These were immediately led away behind the building and shot in the back of the neck with a small-caliber weapon.

It sometimes happened that, as the men of the Special Detachment left the gas chamber, the women would suddenly realize what was happening, and would call down every imaginable curse upon our heads.

I remember, too, a woman who tried to throw her children out of the gas chamber, just as the door was closing. Weeping, she called out: "At least let my precious children live."

There were many such shattering scenes, which affected all who witnessed them.

During the spring of 1942 hundreds of vigorous men and women walked all unsuspecting to their death in the gas chambers, under the blossom-laden fruit trees of the "cottage" orchard. This picture of death in the midst of life remains with me to this day.

The process of selection, which took place on the unloading platforms, was in itself rich in incident.

The breaking up of families, and the separation of the men from the women and children, caused much agitation and spread anxiety throughout the whole transport. This was increased by the further separation from the others of those capable of work. Families wished at all costs to remain together. Those who had been selected ran back to rejoin their relations.

Mothers with children tried to join their husbands, or old people attempted to find those of their children who had been selected for work, and who had been led away.

Often the confusion was so great that the selections had to be begun all over again. The limited area of standing room did not permit better sorting arrangements. All attempts to pacify these agitated mobs were useless. It was often necessary to use force to restore order.

As I have already frequently said, the Jews have strongly developed family feelings. They stick together like limpets. . . .

Then the bodies had to be taken from the gas chambers, and after the gold teeth had been extracted, and the hair cut off, they had to be dragged to the pits or to the crematoria. Then the fires in the pits had to be stoked, the surplus fat drained off, and the mountain of burning corpses constantly turned over so that the draught might fan the flames. . . .

It happened repeatedly that Jews of the Special Detachment would come upon the bodies of close relatives among the corpses, and even among the living as they entered the gas chambers. They were obviously affected by this, but it never led to any incident.[1]

---

[1]On October 7, 1944, the *Sonderkommandos* attacked the SS. Some SS guards were killed, and one crematorium was burned. Most of the prisoners who escaped were caught and killed.

Y. Pfeffer
CONCENTRATION CAMP LIFE AND DEATH

Jews not immediately selected for extermination faced a living death in the concentration camp, which also included non-Jewish inmates, many of them opponents of the Nazi regime. The SS, who ran the camps, took sadistic pleasure in humiliating and brutalizing their helpless Jewish victims. In 1946, Y. Pfeffer, a Jewish survivor of Majdanek concentration camp in Poland, described the world created by the SS and Nazi ideology.

You get up at 3 a.m. You have to dress quickly, and make the "bed" so that it looks like a

matchbox. For the slightest irregularity in bed-making the punishment was 25 lashes, after which it was impossible to lie or sit for a whole month.

Everyone had to leave the barracks immediately. Outside it is still dark — or else the moon is shining. People are trembling because of lack of sleep and the cold. In order to warm up a bit, groups of ten to twenty people stand together, back to back so as to rub against each other.

There was what was called a wash-room, where everyone in the camp was supposed to wash — there were only a few faucets — and we were 4,500 people in that section (no. 3). Of course there was neither soap nor towel or even a handkerchief, so that washing was theoretical rather than practical. . . . In one day, a person there came a lowly person indeed.

At 5 a.m. we used to get half a litre of black, bitter coffee. That was all we got for what was called "breakfast." At 6 a.m. — a headcount (*Appell* in German). We all had to stand at attention, in fives, according to the barracks, of which there were 22 in each section. We stood there until the SS men had satisfied their game-playing instincts by "humorous" orders to take off and put on caps. Then they received their report, and counted us. After the headcount — work.

We went in groups — some to build railway tracks or a road, some to the quarries to carry stones or coal, some to take out manure, or for potato-digging, latrine-cleaning, barracks — or sewer — repairs. All this took place inside the camp enclosure. During work the SS men beat up the prisoners mercilessly, inhumanly and for no reason.

They were like wild beasts and, having found their victim, ordered him to present his backside, and beat him with a stick or a whip, usually until the stick broke.

The victim screamed only after the first blows, afterwards he fell unconscious and the SS man then kicked at the ribs, the face, at the most sensitive parts of a man's body, and then, finally convinced that the victim was at the end of his strength, he ordered another Jew to pour one pail of water after the other over the beaten person until he woke and got up.

A favorite sport of the SS men was to make a "boxing sack" out of a Jew. This was done in the following way: Two Jews were stood up, one being forced to hold the other by the collar, and an SS man trained giving him a knock-out. Of course, after the first blow, the poor victim was likely to fall, and this was prevented by the other Jew holding him up. After the fat, Hitlerite murderer had "trained" in this way for 15 minutes, and only after the poor victim was completely shattered, covered in blood, his teeth knocked out, his nose broken, his eyes hit, they released him and ordered a doctor to treat his wounds. That was their way of taking care and being generous.

Another customary SS habit was to kick a Jew with a heavy boot. The Jew was forced to stand to attention, and all the while the SS man kicked him until he broke some bones. People who stood near enough to such a victim, often heard the breaking of the bones. The pain was so terrible that people, having undergone that treatment, died in agony.

Apart from the SS men there were other expert hangmen. These were the so-called Capos. The name was an abbreviation for "barracks police." The Capos were German criminals who were also camp inmates. However, although they belonged to "us," they were privileged. They had a special, better barracks of their own, they had better food, better, almost normal clothes, they wore special red or green riding pants, high leather boots, and fulfilled the functions of camp guards. They were worse even than the SS men. One of them, older than the others and the worst murderer of them all, when he descended on a victim, would not revive him later with water but would choke him to death. Once, this murderer caught a boy of 13 (in the presence of his father) and hit his head so that the poor child died instantly. This "camp elder" later boasted in front of his peers, with a smile on his beast's face and with pride, that he managed to kill a Jew with one blow.

In each section stood a gallows. For being late for the headcount, or similar crimes, the "camp elder" hanged the offenders.

Work was actually unproductive, and its purpose was exhaustion and torture.

At 12 noon there was a break for a meal. Standing in line, we received half a litre of soup each. Usually it was cabbage soup, or some other watery liquid, without fats, tasteless. That was lunch. It was eaten — in all weather — under the open sky, never in the barracks. No spoons were allowed, though wooden spoons lay on each bunk — probably for show, for Red Cross committees. One had to drink the soup out of the bowl and lick it like a dog.

From 1 p.m. till 6 p.m. there was work again. I must emphasize that if we were lucky we got a 12 o'clock meal. There were "days of punishment" — when lunch was given together with the evening meal, and it was cold and sour, so that our stomach was empty for a whole day.

Afternoon work was the same: blows, and blows again. Until 6 p.m.

At 6 there was the evening headcount. Again we were forced to stand at attention. Counting, receiving the report. Usually we were left standing at attention for an hour or two, while some prisoners were called up for "punishment parade" — they were those who in the Germans' eyes had transgressed in some way during the day, or had not been punctilious in their performance. They were stripped naked publicly, laid out on specially constructed benches, and whipped with 25 or 50 lashes.

The brutal beating and the heart-rending cries — all this the prisoners had to watch and hear.

Richard von Weizsäcker
A GERMAN PERSPECTIVE ON THE HOLOCAUST

In a speech during a commemorative ceremony on May 8, 1985, Richard von Weizsäcker (b. 1920), president of the Federal Republic of Germany, reflected on the Holocaust and the need for remembrance.

May 8th is a day of remembrance. Remembering means recalling an occurrence honestly and undistortedly so that it becomes a part of our very beings. This places high demands on our truthfulness.

Today we mourn all the dead of the war and tyranny. In particular we commemorate the six million Jews who were murdered in German concentration camps. . . .

At the root of the tyranny was Hitler's immeasurable hatred of our Jewish compatriots. Hitler had never concealed this hatred from the public, and made the entire nation a tool of it. Only a day before his death, on April 30, 1945, he concluded his so-called "will" with the words: "Above all, I call upon the leaders of the nation and their followers to observe painstak-ingly the race laws and to oppose ruthlessly the poisoners of all nations: international Jewry." Hardly any country has in its history always remained free from blame for war or violence. The genocide of the Jews is, however, unparalleled in history.

The perpetration of this crime was in the hands of a few people. It was concealed from the eyes of the public, but every German was able to experience what his Jewish compatriots had to suffer, ranging from plain apathy and hidden intolerance to outright hatred. Who could remain unsuspecting after the burning of the synagogues, the plundering, the stigmatization with the Star of David, the deprivation of rights, the ceaseless violation of human dignity? Whoever opened his eyes and ears and sought information could not fail to notice that Jews were being deported. The nature and scope of the destruction may have exceeded human imagination, but in reality there was, apart from the crime itself, the attempt by too many people, including those of my generation, who were young and were not involved in planning the events and carrying them out, not to take note of what was happening. There were many ways of not burdening one's conscience, of shunning responsibility, looking away, keeping mum. When the unspeakable truth of the Holocaust then became known at the end of the war, all too many of us claimed that they had not known anything about it or even suspected anything.

There is no such thing as the guilt or innocence of an entire nation. Guilt is, like innocence, not collective, but personal. There is discovered or concealed individual guilt. There is guilt which people acknowledge or deny. Everyone who directly experienced that era should today quietly ask himself about his involvement then.

The vast majority of today's population were either children then or had not been born. They cannot profess a guilt of their own for crimes that they did not commit. No discerning person can expect them to wear a penitential robe simply because they are Germans. But their forefathers have left them a grave legacy. All of us, whether guilty or not, whether old or young, must accept the past. We are all affected by its consequences and liable for it. The young and old generations must and can help each other to understand why it is vital to keep alive the memories. It is not a case of coming to terms with the past. That is not possible. It cannot be subsequently modified or made undone. However, anyone who closes his eyes to the past is blind to the present. Whoever refuses to remember the inhumanity is prone to new risks of infection.

The Jewish nation remembers and will always remember. We seek reconciliation. Precisely for this reason we must understand that there can be no reconciliation without remembrance. The experience of millionfold death is part of the very being of every Jew in the world, not only because people cannot forget such atrocities, but also because remembrance is part of the Jewish faith.

"Seeking to forget makes exile all the longer; the secret of redemption lies in remembrance." This oft quoted Jewish adage surely expresses the idea that faith in God is faith in the work of God in history. Remembrance is experience of the work of God in history. It is the source of faith in redemption. This experience creates hope, creates faith in redemption, in reunification of the divided, in reconciliation. Whoever forgets this experience loses his faith.

If we for our part sought to forget what has occurred, instead of remembering it, this would not only be inhuman. We would also impinge upon the faith of the Jews who survived and destroy the basis of reconciliation. We must erect a memorial to thoughts and feelings in our own hearts.

Elie Wiesel
REFLECTIONS OF A SURVIVOR

Elie Wiesel (b. 1928), survivor of Auschwitz, author of numerous books and articles on the Holocaust and Jewish culture, human rights activist, and the 1986 Nobel Peace laureate, has also stressed the need for remembrance. In November 1987, Wiesel spoke at a conference center built inside the shell of the destroyed Reichstag, the German parliament during the Nazi era. The following is a journalistic report of his speech.

GHOSTS IN THE PARLIAMENT OF DEATH

. . . Elie Wiesel . . . delivered this speech from the rostrum of the Reichstag building in West Berlin. . . . The occasion was a planning conference for a museum to be built at Wannsee, the Berlin suburb where the formal decision to murder European Jewry was taken 45 years ago.

Elie Wiesel began his address in Yiddish. A literal translation follows:

"Hush, hush, let us be silent; tombs are growing here. Planted by the foe, they are green and turning to blue. . . . Hush, my child, don't cry, crying won't do us any good; the foe will never understand our plight. . . ."

This lullaby was written in the ghetto by Shmelke Katchegirsky. Grieving Jewish mothers would chant it, trying to put to sleep their hungry, weakened and agonizing children.

Tombs? These children — these innocent little children, perhaps the best our people ever had — were deprived of everything; their lives and even a burial place.

And so, hush, little children, one million of you, hush, come: we invite you. We invite you into our memory.

(The rest of Wiesel's speech was in English.)

Yiddish in the Reichstag? There is symbolism in using this warm, melancholy and compassionate language in a place where Jewish suffering and Jewish agony — some 50 years ago — aroused neither mercy nor compassion.

Yiddish was the tongue of many if not most of the Jewish victims who perished during the dark period when the Angel of Death seemed to have replaced God in too many hearts in this country.

There is symbolism, too — as there is irony and justice — in my speaking to you this afternoon from this very rostrum where my own death, and the death of my family, and the death of my friends, and the death of my teachers and the death of my entire people, was decreed and predicted by the legally elected leader of Germany.

I would betray the dead were I not to remind you that his poisonous words did *not* make him unpopular with his people. Most applauded with fervor; some, very few, remained silent. Fewer still objected.

How many Jews found shelter in how many German homes during the Kristallnacht? How many Germans tried to help extinguish the synagogues in flames? How many tried to save holy scrolls?

In those days and nights, humanity was distorted and twisted in this city, the capital of a nation proud of its distant history, but struggling with its recent memories.

Everything human and divine was perverted then. The law itself became immoral. Here, in this city, on this rostrum, it was made legal and commendable to humiliate Jews simply for being Jews — to hunt down children simply because they were Jewish children.

It became legal and praiseworthy to imprison, shame and oppress and, ultimately, to destroy human beings — sons and daughters of an ancient people — whose very existence was considered a crime.

The officials who participated in the Wannsee conference knew they acted on behalf of their government and in the name of the German people.

The atrocities committed under the law of the Third Reich *must* not and *will* not be forgotten; nor will they be forgiven.

I have no right to forgive the killers for having exterminated six million of my kinsmen. Only the dead can forgive, and no one has the right to speak on their behalf.

Still, not all Germans alive then were guilty. As a Jew, I have never believed in collective guilt. Only the guilty were guilty.

Children of killers are not killers but children. I have neither the desire nor the authority to judge today's generation for the unspeakable crimes committed by the generation of Hitler.

But we may — and we must — hold it responsible, not for the past, but for the way it remembers the past. And for what it does with the memory of the past.

Memory is the keyword. To remember is to

forge links between past and present, between past and present, between past and future.

It is in the name of memory that I address myself to Germany's youth. "Remember" is the commandment that dominates the lives of young Jews today; let it dominate your lives as well. Challenged by memory, we can move forward together. Opposed to memory, you will remain eternally opposed to us and to all we stand for.

I understand: of course, I understand: it is not easy to remember. It may be even more difficult for you than it is for us Jews. We try to remember the dead, you must remember those who killed them. Yes — there is pain involved in both our efforts. Not the same pain. Open yourselves to yours, as we have opened ourselves to ours.

You find it hard to believe that your elders did these deeds? So do I. Think of the tormentors as I think of their victims. I remember every minute of their agony. I see them constantly. I am afraid: if I stop seeing them, they will die. I keep on seeing them, and they died nevertheless.

I remember: 1942, in my childhood town, somewhere in the Carpathian Mountains. Jewish children were playing in the snow, others studied hard at school. They were already decreed dead here in Berlin, and they did not know it.

There is something in all this I do not understand — I never will. Why such obstinancy on the part of the killer to kill so many of my people? Why the old men and women? Why the children?

You, young men and women in Germany, must ask yourselves the same questions.

A people that has produced Goethe and Schiller, Bach and Beethoven, chose suddenly to put its national genius at the service of evil — to erect a monument to its dark power called Auschwitz.

A community that contributed to culture and education, as few nations have, called all of culture and education into question. After all: many of the killers had college degrees. And were products of the best universities in Germany. Many came from distinguished families.

Although I often wonder about the theological implications of Auschwitz, I must recognize that Auschwitz was not sent down from heaven. Auschwitz was conceived and built by human beings.

After Auschwitz, hope itself is filled with anguish.

But after Auschwitz, hope is necessary. Where can it be found? In remembrance alone.

How was remembrance handled after the war? Admit it, it took many Germans far too long to begin to confront their past.

Teachers did not teach, and pupils did not learn, the most tragic and important chapter in German and world history. Too painful, came the explanation.

It took the Eichmann trial in Jerusalem for German courts to indict 88 murderers who, after the war, had quietly returned to their homes and resumed their trades — as if nothing had happened.

True, the situation in East Germany is worse. Unlike the Federal Republic, which did make a serious effort, under Konrad Adenauer, to compensate the survivors and to help Israel, East Germany is hostile to Israel and refused to pay reparations. East Germany, like Austria, shows not the slightest trace of remorse.

The Federal Republic has chosen a more honest and enlightened course. In just a few decades, you have traveled from brutal totalitarianism to true democracy.

The freedom of the individual is respected here. Your commitment to the Western alliance is firm.

Among you are individuals and groups to whom we feel especially close. They have been seeking atonement, in word and in deed; some have gone to work in Israel; others are involved in religious dialogues.

Writers, artists, poets, novelists, statesmen: there are among them men and women who refuse to forget — and, make no mistake, the best books by German authors deal with the trauma of the past.

Now the museum. . . . What will it be?

Show pictures of Jews before they died.

Show the cold brutality of those who killed them.

Show the passivity, the cowardly indifference of the bystanders.

Remember the Jewishness of the Jewish victims, remember the uniqueness of their tragedy. True, not all victims were Jews, but all Jews were victims.

Be the conscience of your nation. And remember, a conscience that does not speak up when injustices are being committed is betraying itself. A mute conscience is a false conscience.

In remembering, you will help your own people vanquish the ghosts that hover over its history. Remember: a community that does not come to terms with the dead will continue to traumatize the living.

We remember Auschwitz and all that it symbolizes because we believe that, in spite of the past and its horrors, the world is worthy of salvation; and salvation, like redemption, can be found only in memory.

REVIEW QUESTIONS

1. What do the accounts of Hermann Graebe, Rudolf Hoess, and Y. Pfeffer reveal about the capacity of people to inflict oppression? How did the SS view its victims?
2. What do these accounts reveal about the ways in which people respond to overwhelmingly hopeless oppression?
3. Compare the views of the Holocaust of the German Richard von Weizsäcker and the Jew Elie Wiesel. What do they have to say about collective guilt, about the implications of forgetfulness and remembrance, and about the possibility of redemption, reconciliation, and salvation?
4. In your opinion what is the meaning of the Holocaust for Western civilization? For Jews? For Christians? For Germans?

Part Four

▾▾▾

The Contemporary World

The West in an Age of Globalism

CHAPTER
▼▼▼
12

SOURCES OF THE WESTERN TRADITION

END OF THE BERLIN WALL. Berliners sit on top of the soon-to-be-dismantled Berlin Wall and welcome East Germans flooding in to West Berlin on November 12, 1989. The 1990 reunification of East and West Germany occurred after over forty years of separation. (AP/ Wide World Photos)

Several major themes pervade the years since World War II: the Cold War, decolonization and independent statehood in the Third World, human rights, and humanity's prospects for survival amid the unprecedented changes in global conditions during the past half-century. The final selections in this volume reflect significant issues within these broad themes.

The Cold War between the United States and the Soviet Union has dominated world politics since 1945 and was the principal reason for global anxiety. The consequences of nuclear war threatened human life everywhere. The causes of the Cold War had deep roots. On one side the countries of Western liberal democracy, above all the United States, advanced their power and influence around the world. On the other side a large but historically backward country has labored — first under the tsars, and since 1917, under the Soviet dictatorship — to rise from humiliating defeats early in this century to global prestige and power, until Gorbachev revealed its continued weaknesses.

At the end of World War II the two political systems came into direct confrontation. At issue were not only the new U.S. pre-eminence in the world and Soviet penetration into central Europe and into Manchuria in the Far East, but also the competition between two systems of government and two approaches to fulfilling human aspirations for escape from backwardness and poverty. In this competition, each side dreaded the expansionism of the other, convinced of the worthlessness and immorality of the other's political system. All along, both sides have built up their military power to the utmost. But in recent years, tensions between the superpowers have eased. Burdened by severe economic and nationality problems and guided by younger and more enlightened leaders, the Soviet Union has repudiated the Stalinist past, permitted greater freedom of expression, and — aware of its profound domestic problems — demonstrated a conciliatory attitude in foreign affairs.

In the decades following World War II, Western imperial powers surrendered their empires. The human attitudes motivating the relations between the former colonial masters and their subjects, to whom they taught the ideals of freedom and self-determination, cover a wide spectrum.

The colonial peoples' attitudes range from plain envy to outright rejection.

These conflicting attitudes still swirl around the world, reflected in world politics as well as in the efforts of the developing countries to escape from poverty and instability. Decolonization, which began with high hopes, has produced turmoil in many lands; with political independence came civil strife, economic distress, and further economic dependence on the West. Western imperialism had bred high expectations in African and Asian lands. However, when former colonies with different and conflicting cultural traditions attempted to copy the trappings of Western civilization, the result was often cultural disorientation and political discord.

In the relations between the superpowers, as well as in global politics generally, the issue of human rights has played an important role. Having reasonably secured human rights in their own society, the Western democracies have promoted them as part of their responsibility in world affairs; Americans especially have pressed the issue. Unfortunately, the historically conditioned attitudes needed for orderly constitutional government and respect for individual liberty are often lacking in non-Western nations; consequently, these lands have often experienced revolutions and rule by force and terror.

In addition to international tensions and violations of human rights, humanity also faces serious social, economic, and environmental problems, including a population explosion that has tripled in less than one hundred years the number of people to be fed and employed. The immensity of human progress has raised expectations to a high level, but the earth's resources and the capacity of humankind to fulfill such expectations are burdened by a mushrooming population, cultural disorientation, political discord, and national antagonisms.

▼▼▼

I ▼ The Cold War

After World War II, the first Western statesman to express publicly his alarm over Soviet expansionism was Winston Churchill, the doughty and articulate wartime leader of Great Britain. Churchill surveyed the postwar world scene and noted that the United States stood "at the pinnacle of world power." But he also warned that "a shadow has fallen" on Europe and Asia, a shadow cast by Soviet hostility to the liberties that are a traditional part of Western democracy and had become embodied in the Charter of the United Nations as well. He still spoke of "our Russian friends," but the failure of appeasement and his war experiences prompted him to urge military strength and political unity for Western Europe and the United States in order to stop the communist advance.

Winston Churchill
THE IRON CURTAIN

In a famous speech at Fulton, Missouri, in early March 1946, when he was no longer in office, Churchill articulated his views on the duty of Western democracies in the face of Soviet expansion. Significant passages from that speech, in which the term *iron curtain* was first used, follow.

The United States stands at this time at the pinnacle of world power. It is a solemn moment for the American democracy. With primacy in power is also joined an awe-inspiring accountability to the future. As you look around you, you must feel not only the sense of duty done but also feel anxiety lest you fall below the level of achievement. Opportunity is here now, clear and shining, for both our countries. To reject it or ignore it or fritter it away will bring upon us all the long reproaches of the aftertime. . . .

. . . We cannot be blind to the fact that the liberties enjoyed by individual citizens throughout the British Empire are not valid in a considerable number of countries, some of which are very powerful. In these states, control is enforced upon the common people by various kinds of all-embracing police governments, to a degree which is overwhelming and contrary to every principle of democracy. The power of the state is exercised without restraint, either by dictators or by compact oligarchies operating through a privileged party and a political police. . . .

A shadow has fallen upon the scenes so lately lighted by the Allied victory. Nobody knows what Soviet Russia and its Communist international organization intends to do in the immediate future, or what are the limits, if any, to their expansive and proselytizing tendencies. I have a strong admiration and regard for the valiant Russian people and for my wartime comrade, Marshal Stalin. There is sympathy and good will in Britain — and I doubt not here also — toward the peoples of all the Russias and a resolve to persevere through many differences and rebuffs in establishing lasting friendships. We understand the Russians' need to be secure on her western frontiers from all renewal of German aggression. We welcome her to her rightful place among the leading nations of the world. Above all we welcome constant, frequent and growing contacts between the Russian people and our own people on both sides of the Atlantic. It is my duty, however, to place before you certain facts about the present position in Europe — I am sure I do not wish to, but it is my duty, I feel, to present them to you.

From Stettin in the Baltic to Triest in the Adriatic, an iron curtain has descended across the Continent. Behind that line lie all the capitals of the ancient states of central and eastern Europe. Warsaw, Berlin, Prague, Vienna, Budapest, Belgrade, Bucharest and Sofia, all these famous cities and the populations around them lie in the Soviet sphere and all are subject in one form or another, not only to Soviet influence but to a very high and increasing measure of control from Moscow. Athens alone, with its immortal glories, is free to decide its future at an election under British, American and French observation. The Russian-dominated Polish government has been encouraged to make enormous and wrongful inroads upon Germany, and mass expulsions of millions of Germans on a scale grievous and undreamed of are now taking place. The Communist parties, which were very small in all these eastern states of Europe, have been raised to pre-eminence and power far beyond their numbers and are seeking everywhere to obtain totalitarian control. Police governments are prevailing in nearly every case, and so far, except in Czechoslovakia, there is no true democracy. Turkey and Persia are both profoundly alarmed and disturbed at the claims which are made upon them and at the pressure being exerted by the Moscow government. An attempt is being made by the Russians in Berlin to build up a quasi-Communist party in their zone of occupied Germany by showing special favors to groups of Left-Wing German leaders. . . . Whatever conclusions may be drawn from these facts — and facts they are — this is certainly not the liberated Europe we fought to build up. Nor is it one which contains the essentials of permanent peace. . . . What we have to consider here today while time remains, is the permanent prevention of war and the establishment of conditions of freedom and democracy as rapidly as possible in all countries. Our difficulties and dangers will not be removed by closing our eyes to them. They will not be removed by mere waiting to see what happens; nor will they be relieved by a policy of appeasement. What is needed is a settlement and the longer this is delayed the more difficult it will be and the greater our dangers will become. From what I have seen of our Russian friends and allies during the war, I am convinced that there is nothing they admire so much as strength, and there is nothing for which they have less respect than for military weakness. . . . If the western democracies stand together in strict adherence to the principles of the United Nations Charter, their influence for furthering these principles will be immense and no one is likely to molest them. If, however, they become divided or falter in their duty, and if these all-important years are allowed to slip away, then indeed catastrophe may overwhelm us all.

Nikita S. Khrushchev
REPORT TO THE TWENTIETH PARTY CONGRESS

After World War II, the Korean War, and the escalation of the nuclear arms race into the deployment of hydrogen bombs, the Soviets perceived themselves to be in a worldwide struggle with the Western capitalists. In the Soviet view, the socialist system was advancing, whereas the capitalist system was in decline; the Cold War represented a desperate effort to preserve capitalism. Communists especially attacked the American desire to deal with the socialist countries from a position of superior strength.

Soviet international policy gave special attention to the aspirations of "the peoples of the East," the Asians and Africans emerging from colonial rule. Soviets described American aid to developing countries as a new form of imperialism, whereas Soviet aid was pictured as humanitarian assistance in the struggle against colonialism.

Nikita Khrushchev (1894–1971) summed up the Soviet perspective on world affairs for the benefit of a new generation of Soviet citizens. As first secretary of the Communist party, he delivered a report to the Twentieth Party Congress in February 1956, on the eve of his famous denunciation of the crimes of the Stalin era (see page 316). He sounded an optimistic but militant note. Alarmed by the progress of the arms race, Khrushchev gave vigorous support to an old

Soviet plea for the peaceful coexistence of the two competing sociopolitical systems — a coexistence in which victory would inevitably go to communism.

Soon after the Second World War ended, the influence of reactionary and militarist groups began to be increasingly evident in the policy of the United States of America, Britain and France. Their desire to enforce their will on other countries by economic and political pressure, threats and military provocation prevailed. This became known as the "positions of strength" policy. It reflects the aspiration of the most aggressive sections of present-day imperialism to win world supremacy, to suppress the working class and the democratic and national-liberation movements; it reflects their plans for military adventures against the socialist camp.

The international atmosphere was poisoned by war hysteria. The arms race began to assume more and more monstrous dimensions. Many big U.S. military bases designed for use against the U.S.S.R. and the People's Democracies [East European countries under Soviet control] were built in countries thousands of miles from the borders of the United States. "Cold war" was begun against the socialist camp. International distrust was artificially kindled, and nations set against one another. A bloody war was launched in Korea; the war in Indo-China dragged on for years.

The inspirers of the "cold war" began to establish military blocs, and many countries found themselves, against the will of their peoples, involved in restricted aggressive alignments — the North Atlantic bloc, Western European Union, SEATO (military bloc for South-East Asia) and the Baghdad pact.

The organizers of military blocs allege that they have united for defence, for protection against the "communist threat." But that is sheer hypocrisy. We know from history that when planning a redivision of the world, the imperialist powers have always lined up military blocs. Today the "anti-communism" slogan is again being used as a smokescreen to cover up the claims of one power for world domination. The new thing here is that the United States wants, by means of all kinds of blocs and pacts, to secure a dominant position in the capitalist world for itself, and to reduce all its partners in the blocs to the status of obedient executors of its will.

The inspirers of the "positions of strength" policy assert that this policy makes another war impossible, because it ensures a "balance of power" in the world arena. . . .

The winning of political freedom by the peoples of the former colonies and semi-colonies is the first and most important prerequisite of their full independence, that is, of the achievement of economic independence. The liberated Asian countries are pursuing a policy of building up their own industry, training their own technicians, raising the living standards of the people, and regenerating and developing their age-old national culture. History-making prospects for a better future are opening up before the countries which have embarked upon the path of independent development. . . .

To preserve, and in some places also to re-establish their former domination, the colonial powers are resorting to the suppression of the colonial peoples by the force of arms, a method which has been condemned by history. They also have recourse to new forms of colonial enslavement under the guise of so-called "aid" to underdeveloped countries, which brings colossal profits to the colonialists. Let us take the United States as an example. The United States renders such "aid" above all in the form of deliveries of American weapons to the underdeveloped countries. This enables the American monopolies to load up their industry with arms orders. Then the products of the arms industry, worth billions of dollars and paid for through the budget by the American taxpayers, are sent to the underdeveloped countries. States receiving such "aid" in the form of weapons, inevitably fall into dependence; they increase their armies, which leads to higher taxes and a decline in living standards. . . .

Naturally, "aid" to underdeveloped countries is granted on definite political terms, terms providing for their integration into aggressive military blocs, the conclusion of joint military pacts, and support for American foreign policy aimed at world domination, or "world leadership," as the American imperialists themselves call it. . . .

[In contrast,] the exceptionally warm and friendly welcome accorded the representatives of the great Soviet people has strikingly demonstrated the deep-rooted confidence and love the broad masses in the Eastern countries have for the Soviet Union. Analyzing the sources of this confidence, the Egyptian *Al Akhbar* justly wrote: "Russia does not try to buy the conscience of the peoples, their rights and liberty. Russia has extended a hand to the peoples and said that they themselves should decide their destiny, that she recognizes their rights and aspirations and does not demand their adherence to military pacts or blocs." Millions of men and women ardently acclaim our country for its uncompromising struggle against colonialism, for its policy of equality and friendship among all nations and for its consistent peaceful foreign policy. *(Stormy, prolonged applause.)*

. . . The Leninist principle of peaceful co-existence of states with different social systems has always been and remains the general line of our country's foreign policy. . . . To this day the enemies of peace allege that the Soviet Union is out to overthrow capitalism in other countries by "exporting" revolution. It goes without saying that among us Communists there are no supporters of capitalism. But this does not mean that we have interfered or plan to interfere in the internal affairs of countries where capitalism still exists. . . . It is ridiculous to think that revolutions are made to order. We often hear representatives of bourgeois countries reasoning thus: "The Soviet leaders claim that they are for peaceful co-existence between the two systems. At the same time they declare that they are fighting for communism, and say that communism is bound to win in all countries. Now if the Soviet Union is fighting for communism, how can there be any peaceful co-existence with it?" This view is the result of bourgeois propaganda. The ideologists of the bourgeoisie distort the facts and deliberately confuse questions of ideological struggle with questions of relations between states in order to make the Communists of the Soviet Union look like advocates of aggression.

When we say that the socialist system will win in the competition between the two systems — the capitalist and the socialist — this by no means signifies that its victory will be achieved through armed interference by the socialist countries in the internal affairs of the capitalist countries. Our certainty of the victory of communism is based on the fact that the socialist mode of production possesses decisive advantages over the capitalist mode of production. Precisely because of this, the ideas of Marxism-Leninism are more and more capturing the minds of the broad masses of the working people in the capitalist countries, just as they have captured the minds of millions of men and women in our country and the People's Democracies. *(Prolonged applause)*. We believe that all working men in the world, once they have become convinced of the advantages communism brings, will sooner or later take the road of struggle for the construction of socialist society.

REVIEW QUESTIONS

1. Where did Winston Churchill observe evidence of Soviet expansionism? Find on a map of Europe and Asia the areas he mentioned.
2. What were Churchill's recommendations for countering Soviet expansionism?
3. What, according to Nikita Khrushchev, were the "imperialist powers" (the

United States, England, and France) trying to accomplish in their pursuit of a
"position of strength"?

4. How did Khrushchev describe the aims of American policy in regard to the Soviet Union?

5. What were Khrushchev's hopes for the future? What were his reasons for viewing socialism as superior to capitalism?

2 ▼ Imperialism: Its Decline and Legacy

African and Asian nationalists often denounced imperialism as a crime against humanity and blamed many of their nation's ills on the imperialist past. In this attack, they were joined by some Western intellectuals who saw little benefit in the spread of Western values and techniques to other parts of the globe.

Frantz Fanon
≪ *THE WRETCHED OF THE EARTH* ≫
THE EVILS OF COLONIALISM

One of the keenest modern critics of colonialism was Frantz Fanon (1925–1961). A black from the French West Indies, Fanon was familiar with racial discrimination, and he was influenced by Marxism. He was trained in France as a psychiatrist and decorated for valor in World War II. In the 1950s he sided with the Algerian rebels in their fight for independence from France and became an embattled advocate of African decolonization. In his book *The Wretched of the Earth,* published in 1961 when colonial rule in Africa had virtually ended, he analyzed the relations between the colonial masters and their subject peoples with the keen eye of a psychoanalyst. Reflecting the tensions built up under colonialism and the fury of the Algerian war, Fanon focused on the oppressive and dehumanizing aspects of imperialism. He did not even spare the Christian churches from criticism, although they had often trained those who eventually led the anticolonial struggles.

Fanon also anticipated the ambitions of the emerging African leaders. As he observed, "The colonised man is an envious man," who wanted what the masters possessed — wealth and power in an independent state. Rejection of colonial domination did not rule out imitation of the colonial masters' way of life — an attitude that sometimes brought a new dependence, branded as neocolonialism. Yet the memory of colonial exploitation that Fanon so vividly described persists, kept alive by the poverty and powerlessness of the new African states. In the following passage from *The Wretched of the Earth,* Fanon starkly compares the two realms of the colonial world: ruler and ruled.

The colonial world is a world cut in two. The dividing line, the frontiers are shown by barracks and police stations. In the colonies it is the policeman and the soldier who are the official, instituted go-betweens, and spokesmen of the settler and his rule of oppression. In capitalist societies the educational system, whether lay or clerical, the structure of moral reflexes handed down from father to son, the exemplary honesty of workers who are given a medal after fifty years of good and loyal service, and the affection which springs from harmonious relations and good behaviour — all these esthetic expressions of respect for the established order serve to create around the exploited person an atmosphere of submission and of inhibition which lightens the task of policing considerably. In the capitalist countries a multitude of moral teachers, counsellors and "bewilderers" separate the exploited from those in power. In the colonial countries, on the contrary, the policeman and the soldier, by their immediate presence and their frequent and direct action, maintain contact with the native and advise him by means of rifle-butts and napalm not to budge. It is obvious here that the agents of government speak the language of pure force. The intermediary does not lighten the oppression, nor seek to hide the domination; he shows them up and puts them into practice with the clear conscience of an upholder of the peace; yet he is the bringer of violence into the home and into the mind of the native.

The zone where the natives live is not complementary to the zone inhabited by the settlers. The two zones are opposed, but not in the service of a higher unity. . . .

. . . No conciliation is possible, for of the two terms, one is superfluous. The settlers' town is a strongly-built town, all made of stone and steel. It is a brightly-lit town; the streets are covered with asphalt, and the garbage-cans swallow all the leavings, unseen, unknown and hardly thought about. The settler's feet are never visible, except perhaps in the sea; but there you're never close enough to see them. His feet are protected by strong shoes although the streets of his town are clean and even, with no holes or stones. The settler's town is a well-fed town, an easy-going town; its belly is always full of good things. The settler's

town is a town of white people, of foreigners.

The town belonging to the colonised people, or at least the native town, the negro village, the medina,[1] the reservation, is a place of ill fame, peopled by men of evil repute. They are born there, it matters little where or how; they die there, it matters not where, nor how. It is a world without spaciousness; men live there on top of each other, and their huts are built one on top of the other. The native town is a hungry town, starved of bread, of meat, of shoes, of coal, of light. The native town is a crouching village, a town on its knees, a town wallowing in the mire. It is a town of niggers and dirty arabs. . . . The look that the native turns on the settler's town is a look of lust, a look of envy; it expresses his dreams of possession — all manner of possession: to sit at the settler's table, to sleep in the settler's bed, with his wife if possible. The colonised man is an envious man. And this the settler knows very well; when their glances meet he ascertains bitterly, always on the defensive "They want to take our place." It is true, for there is no native who does not dream at least once a day of setting himself up in the settler's place.

This world divided into compartments, this world cut in two is inhabited by two different species. The originality of the colonial context is that economic reality, inequality and the immense difference of ways of life never come to mask the human realities. When you examine at close quarters the colonial context, it is evident that what parcels out the world is to begin with the fact of belonging to or not belonging to a given race, a given species. In the colonies the economic substructure is also a superstructure. The cause is the consequence; you are rich because you are white, you are white because you are rich. . . .

. . . As if to show the totalitarian character of colonial exploitation the settler paints the na-

---

[1]The term *medina* here connotes a quarter of a North African city inhabited by indigenous people; the Saudi Arabian city of Medina is the sacred center of the Islamic faith.

tive as a sort of quintessence of evil. . . . Native society is not simply described as a society lacking in values. It is not enough for the colonist to affirm that those values have disappeared from, or still better never existed in, the colonial world. The native is declared insensible to ethics; he represents not only the absence of values, but also the negation of values. He is, let us dare to admit, the enemy of values, and in this sense he is the absolute evil. . . .

. . . I speak of the Christian religion, and no one need be astonished. The Church in the colonies is the white people's Church, the foreigner's Church. She does not call the native to God's ways but to the ways of the white man, of the master, of the oppressor. And as we know, in this matter many are called but few chosen.

At times this Manicheism [conflict between light and dark] goes to its logical conclusion and dehumanises the native, or to speak plainly it turns him into an animal. In fact, the terms the settler uses when he mentions the native are zoological terms. He speaks of the yellow man's reptilian motions, of the stink of the native quarter, of breeding swarms, of foulness, of spawn, of gesticulations. When the settler seeks to describe the native fully in exact terms he constantly refers to the bestiary. The European rarely hits on a picturesque style; but the native, who knows what is in the mind of the settler, guesses at once what he is thinking of. Those hordes of vital statistics, those hysterical masses, those faces bereft of all humanity, those distended bodies which are like nothing on earth, that mob without beginning or end, those children who seem to belong to nobody, that laziness stretched out in the sun, that vegetative rhythm of life — all this forms part of the colonial vocabulary.

Jacques Ellul
≪ THE BETRAYAL OF THE WEST ≫
A REAFFIRMATION OF WESTERN VALUES

In recent years a number of Western intellectuals have attacked the values and deeds of the West. At the same time, they exalt the other civilizations of the world. That many Westerners have lost confidence in their own tradition constitutes a profound spiritual crisis. Jacques Ellul (b. 1912), a French sociologist with a pronounced moralist bent, is known for his study of the impact of technology and bureaucracy on the modern world. In the following passages from *The Betrayal of the West* (1978), he assessed the historical uniqueness and greatness of Western civilization.

. . . I am not criticizing or rejecting other civilizations and societies; I have deep admiration for the institutions of the Bantu and other peoples (the Chinese among them) and for the inventions and poetry and architecture of the Arabs. I do not claim at all that the West is superior. In fact, I think it absurd to lay claim to superiority of any kind in these matters. What criterion would you apply? What scale of values would you use? I would add that the greatest fault of the West since the seventeenth century has been precisely its belief in its own unqualified superiority in all areas.

The thing, then, that I am protesting against is the silly attitude of western intellectuals in hating their own world and then illogically exalting all other civilizations. Ask yourself this question: If the Chinese have done away with binding the feet of women, and if the Moroccans, Turks, and Algerians have begun to liberate their women, whence did the impulse to these moves come from? From the West, and nowhere else! Who invented the "rights of man"? The same holds for the elimination of exploitation. Where did the move to socialism originate? In Europe, and in Europe alone. The Chinese, like the Algerians, are inspired by western thinking as they move toward socialism. Marx was not Chinese, nor was Robespierre an Arab. How easily the intellectuals forget this! The whole of the modern world, for better or for worse, is following a western model; no one imposed it on others, they have adopted it themselves, and enthusiastically.

I shall not wax lyrical about the greatness and benefactions of the West. Above all, I shall not offer a defense of the material goods Europe brought to the colonies. We've heard that kind of defense too often: "We built roads, hospitals, schools, and dams; we dug the oil wells. . . ." And the reason I shall say nothing of this invasion by the technological society is that I think it to be the West's greatest crime, as I have said at length elsewhere. The worst thing of all is that we exported our rationalist approach to things, our "science," our conception of the state, our bureaucracy, our nationalist ideology. It is this, far more surely than anything else, that has destroyed the other cultures of the world and shunted the history of the entire world onto a single track.

But is that all we can say of the West? No, the essential, central, undeniable fact is that the West was the first civilization in history to focus attention on the individual and on freedom. Nothing can rob us of the praise due us for that. We have been guilty of denials and betrayals (of these we shall be saying something more), we have committed crimes, but we have also caused the whole of mankind to take a gigantic step forward and to leave its childhood behind.

This is a point we must be quite clear on. If the world is everywhere rising up and accusing the West, if movements of liberation are everywhere under way, what accounts for this? Its sole source is the proclamation of freedom that the West has broadcast to the world. The West, and the West alone, is responsible for the movement that has led to the desire for freedom and to the accusations now turned back upon the West.

Today men point the finger of outrage at slavery and torture. Where did that kind of indignation originate? What civilization or culture cried out that slavery was unacceptable and torture scandalous? Not Islam, or Buddhism, or Confucius, or Zen, or the religions and moral codes of Africa and India! The West alone has defended the inalienable rights of the human person, the dignity of the individual, the man who is alone with everyone against him. But the West did not practice what it preached? The extent of the West's fidelity is indeed debatable: the whole European world has certainly not lived up to its own ideal all the time, but to say that it has never lived up to it would be completely false.

In any case, that is not the point. The point is that the West originated values and goals that spread throughout the world (partly through conquest) and inspired man to demand his freedom, to take his stand in the face of society and affirm his value as an individual. I shall not be presumptuous enough to try to "define" the freedom of the individual. . . .

. . . The West gave expression to what man — every man — was seeking. The West turned the whole human project into a conscious, deliberate business. It set the goal and called it freedom, or, at later date, individual freedom. It gave direction to all the forces that were working in obscure ways, and brought to light the value that gave history its meaning. Thereby, man became man.

The West attempted to apply in a conscious, methodical way the implications of freedom. The Jews were the first to make freedom the key to history and to the whole created order. From the very beginning their God was the God who liberates; his great deeds flowed from a will to give freedom to his people and thereby to all mankind. This God himself, moreover, was understood to be sovereignly free (freedom here was often confused with arbitrariness or with omnipotence). This was something radically new, a discovery with explosive possibilities. The God who was utterly free had nothing in common with the gods of eastern and western religions; he was different precisely because of his autonomy.

The next step in the same movement saw the Greeks affirming both intellectual and political liberty. They consciously formulated the rules for a genuinely free kind of thinking, the conditions for human freedom, and the forms a free society could take. Other peoples were already living in cities, but none of them had fought so zealously for the freedom of the city in relation to other cities, and for the freedom of the citizen within the city.

The Romans took the third step by inventing civil and institutional liberty and making political freedom the key to their entire politics. Even the conquests of the Romans were truly an unhypocritical expression of their intention of freeing peoples who were subject to dictatorships and tyrannies the Romans judged degrading. It is in the light of that basic thrust that we must continue to read Roman history. Economic motives undoubtedly also played a role, but a secondary one; to make economic causes the sole norm for interpreting history is in the proper sense superficial and inadequate. You cannot write history on the basis of your suspicions! If you do, you only project your own fantasies.

I am well aware, of course, that in each concrete case there was darkness as well as light, that liberty led to wars and conquests, that it rested on a base of slavery. I am not concerned here, however, with the excellence or defects of the concrete forms freedom took; I am simply trying to say (as others have before me) that at the beginning of western history we find the awareness, the explanation, the proclamation of freedom as the meaning and goal of history.

No one has ever set his sights as intensely on freedom as did the Jews and Greeks and Romans, the peoples who represented the entire West and furthered its progress. In so doing, they gave expression to what the whole of mankind was confusedly seeking. In the process we can see a progressive approach to the ever more concrete: from the Jews to the Greeks, and from the Greeks to the Romans there is no growth in consciousness, but there is the ongoing search for more concrete answers to the question of how freedom can be brought from the realm of ideas and incarnated in institutions, behavior, thinking, and so on.

Today the whole world has become the heir of the West, and we Westerners now have a twofold heritage: we are heirs to the evil the West has done to the rest of the world, but at the same time we are heirs to our forefathers' consciousness of freedom and to the goals of freedom they set for themselves. Other peoples, too, are heirs to the evil that has been inflicted on them, but now they have also inherited the consciousness of and desire for freedom. Everything they do today and everything they seek is an expression of what the western world has taught them. . . .

. . . Everything used to be so organized that wealth and poverty were stable states, determined (for example) by the traditional, accepted hierarchy, and that this arrangement was regarded as due to destiny or an unchangeable divine will. The West did two things: it destroyed the hierarchic structures and it did away with the idea of destiny. It thus showed the poor that their state was not something inevitable. This is something Marx is often credited with having done, but only because people are ignorant [of history]. It was Christianity that did away with the idea of destiny and fate. . . .

Once Christianity had destroyed the idea of destiny or fate, the poor realized that they were poor, and they realized that their condition was not inevitable. Then the social organisms that had made it possible to gloss over this fact were challenged and undermined from within.

Against all this background we can see why the whole idea of revolution is a western idea. Before the development of western thought, and apart from it, no revolution ever took place. Without the individual and freedom and the contradictory extremes to which freedom leads, a society cannot engender a revolution. Nowhere in the world — and I speak as one with a knowledge of history — has there ever been a revolution, not even in China, until the western message penetrated that part of the world. Present-day revolutions, whether in China or among the American Indians, are the direct, immediate, unmistakable fruit of the western genius. The entire world has been pupil to the West that it now rejects. . . .

. . . I wish only to remind the reader that the West has given the world a certain number of values, movements, and orientations that no one else has provided. No one else has done quite what the West has done. I wish also to remind the reader that the whole world is living, and living almost exclusively, by these values, ideas, and stimuli. There is nothing original about the "new" thing that is coming into existence in China or Latin America or Africa: it is all the fruit and direct consequence of what the West has given the world.

In the fifties it was fashionable to say that "the third world is now entering upon the stage of history." The point was not, of course, to deny that Africa or Japan had a history. What the cliché was saying, and rightly saying, was that these peoples were now participating in the creative freedom of history and the dialectic of the historical process. Another way of putting it is that the West had now set the whole world in motion. It had released a tidal wave that would perhaps eventually drown it. There had been great changes in the past and vast migrations of peoples; there had been planless quests for power and the building of gigantic empires that collapsed overnight. The West represented something entirely new because it set the world in movement in every area and at every level; it represented, that is, a coherent approach to reality. Everything — ideas, armies, the state, philosophy, rational methods, and social organization — conspired in the global change the West had initiated.

It is not for me to judge whether all this was a good thing or bad. I simply observe that the entire initiative came from the West, that everything began there. I simply observe that the peoples of the world had abided in relative ignorance and [religious] repose until the encounter with the West set them on their journey.

Please, then, don't deafen us with talk about the greatness of Chinese or Japanese civilization. These civilizations existed indeed, but in a larval or embryonic state; they were approximations, essays. They always related to only one sector of the human or social totality and tended to be static and immobile. Because the West was motivated by the ideal of freedom and had discovered the individual, it alone launched society in its entirety on its present course.

Again, don't misunderstand me. I am not saying that European science was superior to Chinese science, nor European armies to Japanese armies; I am not saying that the Christian religion was superior to Buddhism or Confucianism; I am not saying that the French or English political system was superior to that of the Han dynasty. I am saying only that the West discovered what no one else had discovered; freedom and the individual, and that this discovery later set everything else in motion. Even the most solidly established religions could not help changing under the influence. . . .

It was not economic power or sudden technological advances that made the West what it is. These played a role, no doubt, but a negligible one in comparison with the great change — the discovery of freedom and the individual — that represents the goal and desire implicit in the history of all civilizations. That is why, in speaking of the West, I unhesitatingly single out freedom from the whole range of values. After all, we find justice, equality, and peace everywhere. Every civilization that has attained a certain level has claimed to be a civilization of justice or peace. But which of them has ever spoken of the individual? Which of them has been reflectively conscious of freedom as a value?

The decisive role of the West's discovery of freedom and the individual is beyond question, but the discovery has brought with it . . . tragic consequences. First, the very works of the West now pass judgment on it. For, having proclaimed freedom and the individual, the West played false in dealing with other peoples. It subjected, conquered, and exploited them, even while it went on talking about freedom. It made the other peoples conscious of their enslavement by intensifying that enslavement and calling it freedom. It destroyed the social structures of tribes and clans, turned men into isolated atoms, and shaped them into a worldwide proletariat, and all the time kept on talking of the great dignity of the individual: his autonomy, his power to decide for himself, his capacity for choice, his complex and many-sided reality. . . .

. . . Reason makes it possible for the individual to master impulse, to choose the ways in which he will exercise his freedom, to calculate the chances for success and the manner in which a particular action will impinge upon the group, to understand human relations, and to communicate. Communication is the highest expression of freedom, but it has little meaning unless there is a content which, in the last analysis, is supplied by reason. . . . Here precisely we have the magnificent discovery made by the West: that the individual's whole life can be,

and even is, the subtle, infinitely delicate interplay of reason and freedom.

This interplay achieved its highest form in both the Renaissance and classical literature since the Enlightenment. No other culture made this discovery. We of the West have the most rounded and self-conscious type of man. For, the development of reason necessarily implied reason's critique of its own being and action as well as a critique of both liberty and reason, through a return of reason upon itself and a continuous reflection which gave rise to new possibilities for the use of freedom as controlled by new developments of reason. . . .

Let me return to my main argument. It was the West that established the splendid interplay of freedom, reason, self-control, and coherent behavior. It thus produced a type of human being that is unique in history: true western man. (I repeat: the type belongs neither to nature nor to the animal world; it is a deliberate construct achieved through effort.) I am bound to say that I regard this type as superior to anything I have seen or known elsewhere. A value judgment, a personal and subjective preference? Of course. But I am not ready on that account to turn my back on the construction and on the victory and affirmation it represents. Why? Because the issue is freedom itself, and because I see no other satisfactory model that can replace what the West has produced.

REVIEW QUESTIONS

1. Why did Frantz Fanon think that no conciliation is possible between the colonial masters and their subjects?
2. How did Fanon define the "totalitarian character" of colonial exploitation?
3. In saying that colonized people are envious, does Fanon reject what colonial exploitation stands for?
4. What contribution, according to Jacques Ellul, did the West make to human life everywhere?
5. According to Ellul, what was the West's "greatest crime"?
6. Ellul asserts on one hand that he does "not claim at all that the West is superior," and on the other he characterizes Chinese or Japanese civilization as existing only "in a larval or embryonic state." Compare these statements in the context of the entire passage. Are they contradictory?

▼▼▼

3 ▼ Feminism

In the advanced Western countries, the feminist movement, also called the women's liberation movement, has sought for two centuries to obtain legal and social rights for women, giving them equal status with men. Mary Wollstone-craft in *A Vindication of the Rights of Woman* (see page 181) proposed in 1792 that women receive the same education, work opportunities, and political rights as men.

Since the 1960s, women's organizations have proliferated worldwide. Goals range from legal and cultural changes in developed countries, such as bans on sex-based discrimination and freedom of choice in matters related to childbearing, to elemental improvements in the Third World, such as the abolition of the bride price in some African countries. On some issues the movement does have opponents among women as well as men. Because of cultural differences, the extent to which women's rights are recognized varies from country to country, and there are still countries where women have few "rights," notably among the developing nations.

Simone de Beauvoir
≪ THE SECOND SEX ≫

Simone de Beauvoir (1908–1986), the French philosopher and feminist, published *The Second Sex* in 1949. It described the role of women in a traditional society, in which the majority of women were married, depended on men for their role in society, and were tied to their home and their children; only a minority of women (including the author) led independent lives. De Beauvoir traced the role of women through history and through their contemporary life cycle as evidence for her thesis: because the forces of social tradition are controlled by men, women have been relegated to a secondary place in the world.

In the excerpts that follow, de Beauvoir argues that despite considerable change in their social status, women are still prevented from becoming autonomous individuals and taking their places as men's equals. Marriage is still expected to be women's common destiny, with their identity defined in relation to their husbands. In discussing the status of newly independent women, de Beauvoir implies that because of their failure to escape the psychological trap of secondary status, they lack confidence and creativity in their work.

. . . Woman has always been man's dependant, if not his slave; the two sexes have never shared the world in equality. And even today woman is heavily handicapped, though her situation is beginning to change. Almost nowhere is her legal status the same as man's, and frequently it is much to her disadvantage. Even when her rights are legally recognized in the abstract, long-standing custom prevents their full expression in the mores. In the economic sphere men and women can almost be said to make up two castes; other things being equal, the former hold the better jobs, get higher wages, and have more opportunity for success than their new competitors. In industry and politics men have a great many more positions and they monopolize the most important posts. In addition to all this, they enjoy a traditional prestige that the education of children tends in every way to support, for the present enshrines the past — and in the past all history has been made by men. At the present time, when women are beginning to take part in the affairs of the world, it is still a world that belongs to men — they have no doubt of it at all and women have scarcely any. To decline to be the Other, to refuse to be a party to the deal — this would be for women to renounce all the advantages conferred upon them by their alliance with the superior caste. Man-the-sovereign will provide woman-the-liege with material protection and will undertake the moral justification of her existence; thus she can evade at once both economic risk and the metaphysical risk of a liberty in which ends and aims must be contrived without assistance. Indeed, along with the ethical urge of each individual to affirm his subjective existence, there is also the temptation to forgo liberty and become a thing. This is an inauspicious road, for he who takes it — passive, lost, ruined — becomes henceforth the creature of another's will, frustrated in his transcendence and deprived of every value. But it is an easy road; on it one avoids the strain involved in undertaking an authentic existence. When man makes of woman the *Other,* he may, then, expect to manifest deep-seated tendencies towards complicity. Thus, woman may fail to lay claim to the status of subject because she lacks definite resources, because she feels the necessary bond that ties her to man regardless of reciprocity, and because she is often very well pleased with her role as the *Other.* . . .

Marriage is the destiny traditionally offered to women by society. It is still true that most women are married, or have been, or plan to be, or suffer from not being. The celibate woman is to be explained and defined with reference to marriage, whether she is frustrated, rebellious, or even indifferent in regard to that institution. We must therefore continue this study by analysing marriage.

Economic evolution in woman's situation is in process of upsetting the institution of marriage: it is becoming a union freely entered upon by the consent of two independent persons; the obligations of the two contracting parties are personal and reciprocal; adultery is for both a breach of contract; divorce is obtainable by the one or the other on the same conditions. Woman is no longer limited to the reproductive function, which has lost in large part its character as natural servitude and has come to be regarded as a function to be voluntarily assumed; and it is compatible with productive labour, since, in many cases, the time off required by a pregnancy is taken by the mother at the expense of the State or the employer. In the Soviet Union marriage was for some years a contract between individuals based upon the complete liberty of the husband and wife; but it would seem that it is now a duty that the State imposes upon them both. Which of these tendencies will prevail in the world of tomorrow will depend upon the general structure of society, but in any case male guardianship of woman is disappearing. Nevertheless, the epoch in which we are living is still, from the feminist point of view, a period of transition. Only a part of the female population is engaged in production, and even those who are belong to a society in which ancient forms and antique values survive. Modern marriage can be understood only in the light of a past that tends to perpetuate itself.

Marriage has always been a very different thing for man and for woman. The two sexes are necessary to each other, but this necessity has never brought about a condition of reciprocity between them; women, as we have seen, have never constituted a caste making exchanges and contracts with the male caste upon a footing of equality. A man is socially an independent and complete individual; he is regarded first of all as a producer whose existence is justified by the work he does for the group: we have seen why it is that the reproductive and domestic role to which woman is confined has not guaranteed her an equal dignity. Certainly the male needs her; in some primitive groups it may happen that the bachelor, unable to manage his existence by himself, becomes a kind of outcast; in agricultural societies a woman co-worker is essential to the peasant; and for most men it is of advantage to unload certain drudgery upon a mate; the individual wants a regular sexual life and posterity, and the State requires him to contribute to its perpetuation. But man does not make his appeal directly to woman herself; it is the men's group that allows each of its members to find self-fulfilment as husband and father; woman, as slave or vassal, is integrated within families dominated by fathers and brothers, and she has always been given in marriage by certain males to other males. In primitive societies the paternal clan, the gens, disposed of woman almost like a thing: she was included in deals agreed upon by two groups. The situation is not much modified when marriage assumes a contractual form in the course of its evolution; when dowered or having her share in inheritance, woman would seem to have civil standing as a person, but dowry and inheritance still enslave her to her family. During a long period the contracts were made between father-in-law and son-in-law, not between wife and husband; only widows then enjoyed economic independence. The young girl's freedom of choice has always been much restricted; and celibacy — apart from the rare cases in which it bears a sacred character — reduced her to the rank of parasite and pariah; marriage is her only means of support and the sole justification of her existence. It is enjoined upon her for two reasons.

The first reason is that she must provide the society with children; only rarely — as in Sparta and to some extent under the Nazi régime — does the State take woman under direct guardianship and ask only that she be a mother. But even the primitive societies that are not aware of the paternal generative role demand that woman have a husband, for the second reason why marriage is enjoined is that woman's function is also to satisfy a male's sexual needs and to take care of his household. These duties placed upon woman by society are regarded as a *service* rendered to her spouse: in return he is supposed to give her presents, or a marriage settlement, and to support her. Through him as intermediary, society discharges its debt to the woman it turns over to him. The rights obtained by the wife in fulfilling her duties are represented in obligations that the male must assume. He cannot break the conjugal bond at his pleasure; he can repudiate or divorce his wife only when the public authorities so decide, and even then the husband sometimes owes her compensation in money; the practice even becomes an abuse in Egypt under Bocchoris [Egyptian King] or, as the demand for alimony, in the United States today. Polygamy has always been more or less openly tolerated: man may bed with slaves, concubines, mistresses, prostitutes, but he is required to respect certain privileges of his legitimate wife. If she is maltreated or wronged, she has the right — more or less definitely guaranteed — of going back to her family and herself obtaining a separation or divorce.

Thus for both parties marriage is at the same time a burden and a benefit; but there is no symmetry in the situations of the two sexes; for girls marriage is the only means of integration in the community, and if they remain unwanted, they are, socially viewed, so much wastage. . . .

It must be said that the independent woman is justifiably disturbed by the idea that people do not have confidence in her. As a general rule, the superior caste is hostile to newcomers from the inferior caste: white people will not consult a Negro physician, nor males a woman doctor; but individuals of the inferior caste, imbued with a sense of their specific inferiority and often full of resentment towards one of their kind who has risen above their usual lot, will also prefer to turn to the masters. Most women, in particular, steeped in adoration for man, eagerly seek him out in the person of the doctor, the lawyer, the office manager, and so on. Neither men nor women like to be under a woman's orders. Her superiors, even if they esteem her highly, will always be somewhat condescending; to be a woman, if not a defect, is at least a peculiarity. Woman must constantly win the confidence that is not at first accorded her: at the start she is suspect, she has to prove herself. If she has worth she will pass the tests, so they say. But worth is not a given essence; it is the outcome of a successful development. To feel the weight of an unfavourable prejudice against one is only on very rare occasions a help in overcoming it. The initial inferiority complex ordinarily leads to a defence reaction in the form of an exaggerated affectation of authority.

Most women doctors, for example, have too much or too little of the air of authority. If they act naturally, they fail to take control, for their life as a whole disposes them rather to seduce than to command; the patient who likes to be dominated will be disappointed by plain advice simply given. Aware of this fact, the woman doctor assumes a grave accent, a peremptory tone; but then she lacks the bluff good nature that is the charm of the medical man who is sure of himself.

Man is accustomed to asserting himself; his clients believe in his competence; he can act naturally: he infallibly makes an impression. Woman does not inspire the same feeling of security; she affects a lofty air, she drops it, she makes too much of it. In business, in administrative work, she is precise, fussy, quick to show aggressiveness. As in her studies, she lacks ease, dash, audacity. In the effort to achieve she gets tense. Her activity is a succession of challenges and self-affirmations. This is the great defect that lack of assurance engenders: the subject cannot forget himself. He does not aim gallantly towards some goal: he seeks rather to make good in prescribed ways. In

boldly setting out towards ends, one risks disappointments; but one also obtains unhoped-for results; caution condemns to mediocrity.

We rarely encounter in the independent woman a taste for adventure and for experience for its own sake, or a disinterested curiosity; she seeks "to have a career" as other women build a nest of happiness; she remains dominated, surrounded, by the male universe, she lacks the audacity to break through its ceiling, she does not passionately lose herself in her projects. She still regards her life as an immanent enterprise: her aim is not at an objective but, through the objective, at her subjective success. This is a very conspicuous attitude, for example, among American women; they like having a job and proving to themselves that they are capable of handling it properly; but they are not passionately concerned with the *content* of their tasks. Woman similarly has a tendency to attach too much importance to minor setbacks and modest successes; she is turn by turn discouraged or puffed up with vanity. When a success has been anticipated, one takes it calmly; but it becomes an intoxicating triumph when one has been doubtful of obtaining it. This is the excuse when women become addled with importance and plume themselves ostentatiously over their least accomplishments. They are for ever looking back to see how far they have come, and that interrupts their progress. By this procedure they can have honourable careers, but not accomplish great things. It must be added that many men are also unable to build any but mediocre careers. It is only in comparison with the best of them that woman — save for very rare exceptions — seems to us to be trailing behind. The reasons I have given are sufficient explanation, and in no way mortgage the future. What woman essentially lacks today for doing great things is forgetfulness of herself; but to forget oneself it is first of all necessary to be firmly assured that now and for the future one has found oneself. Newly come into the world of men, poorly seconded by them, woman is still too busily occupied to search for herself.

Sue Ellen M. Charlton
≪ WOMEN IN THIRD WORLD DEVELOPMENT ≫

How have women in the Third World countries been affected by the processes of development? Professor Sue Ellen M. Charlton, who teaches political science at Colorado State University, examines the impact of development planning on women's lives in the following passages from *Women in Third World Development* (1984).

In the 1950s, scholars and policymakers had just begun to discuss the meaning of development for most of the world, and the role of the individual in the process of economic and social development was barely addressed and even less frequently understood. Only since the 1970s have development discussions focused on the majority of the human race, women. Now the phrase "women and development" is used so widely that it seems almost faddish. . . .

Since 1970, there has been a proliferation of policy pronouncements, research projects, and publicity brochures designed to promote an awareness of, and a concern for, the impact of development planning on women's lives. National and international agencies have begun to argue that women should have some control over the direction that development takes, at least on the local level.

This relatively new interest in women reflects the far-reaching changes that are taking place throughout the world in the late twentieth century. These changes are sometimes spectacular, sometimes subtle. The world is being revolutionized by women. Feminist movements in industrialized states, the 1975 International Women's Year, and sporadic headline events all mark this revolution. But it is also marked by nutritional changes for a woman and her child, by a change in educational opportunity for girls, or by a woman's decision to seek paid employment in a town or city. The headline events contribute to the debate about women and development for they serve as a constant reminder that women care about themselves, each other, their families, and their

communities and that they are both demanding and receiving more control over their own lives. However, the reality of the revolution must be sought also at the local level.

In addition to the attention generated by women themselves, another factor contributes to the discussions of women and development: our growing awareness of the complexity of the developmental process itself. Explanations for low productivity or poverty that seemed straightforward in the 1950s or 1960s are now widely viewed as inadequate and misguided or, worse, patronizing and imperialistic. Anyone who attempts to rethink what happens in development and why, or to understand simply what the word "development" means, can ill afford to ignore the majority of the human race. . . .

CONCEPTUALIZING DEVELOPMENT . . .
Defining Development

History.   The very use of the term "development" implies a notion of historical change derived from Western European secular and scientific thought. We assume that change is more linear than cyclical. Development is, by definition, a historical process, so one presumes direction in this process. Thus, the study of history is an essential source of information on the changes countries have gone through as they have developed. . . .

Science, Human Needs, and Human Wishes.   The notion of development assumes the human ability to influence and control the natural and social environment. . . . What is distinctive about our modern times is the rationality that is associated with scientific knowledge in societies' efforts to influence and control.

. . . One of the political realities of development in the late twentieth century, however, is that policymakers typically define the developmental process in terms of Western rationality and scientific knowledge. . . .

If specialization is a characteristic of development, as historical experience suggests it has been in Western Europe and North America, this fact has significant implications for those women who are not in a position to acquire the education or skills that are necessary if they are to have specialized roles in their societies. Thus the question of what is meant by development has major practical consequences for women.

There are four clusters of issues surrounding the definitions of development that are especially important for women. . . .

1. The role of ethical and moral choice in development
2. The structure of the international system in the late twentieth century
3. The influence and, in some instances, domination of Western norms and institutions in development concepts and policies
4. The political control of development.

ETHICAL CHOICE . . .

Since the political and social status of women is secondary to that of men in most societies, proposing an improvement in their status may be viewed as a threat by those people who have more status (or wealth, or power). The seemingly straightforward goal of "integrating women into development projects" at once challenges social and political structures, the distribution of wealth, and cultural mores. It is, in short, revolutionary in its implications. . . .

All people concerned with development must recognize that there are different value systems throughout the world, and it is precisely this diversity that makes the concern for moral and ethical questions so pressing. For most people, the ideal development process harmonizes with the traditional values of a particular society, but in reality, value systems in the late twentieth century are seldom static. Changes originate both inside and outside a society. . . .

THE INTERNATIONAL SYSTEM

The growing preoccupation with the fate of women in the development process has occurred in the midst of a rapidly changing international system. In fact, it is as a result of these changes that concern about women is even articulated. . . .

Third World

Beginning with the 1950s, the bipolar nature [predominant role of the United States and the Soviet Union] of international relations has been progressively muted by the policies of those nation-states that have refused to identify solely with capitalist or socialist causes. Originally, the term "Third World" characterized those countries that eschewed alignment with either the First World of the West or the Second World of the East. Although the term now has an economic meaning as well, the idea of the Third World is still most accurately described as a political concept. . . .

. . . [T]he [Third World] countries . . . are the focus of development projects and [their] populations are usually described by planners as the "targets" of development efforts. . . . [H]owever weak the government of a Third World state may be in some spheres, that government is still most often the key factor in determining whether development occurs, how it occurs, and who benefits from it. Hence, all discussions of development projects for women must recognize the role of the national governments in the countries in question and acknowledge that politically, development is what a national government says it is.

WESTERN INFLUENCE

The pervasiveness of the West in the conceptualization and implementation of development projects is only one part of Western influence. This influence ranges from the most common definitions of development, which rely heavily on Western scientific thought and reflect Western cultural and religious norms (such as equality), to the effects of the historical experience of industrialization in Western Europe and North America. The Western heritage of colonialism throughout most of the Third World is important both directly and indirectly. The direct importance lies in the history of colonial control over the structures of government in the colonies or territories and colonial influence in determining the boundaries of governmental jurisdiction. Indirectly, formal education . . . reflected British, French, Spanish, Portuguese, Dutch, or U.S. ideas about the proper subjects to teach and the students to be taught.

The socioeconomic impact of colonialism was also both direct and indirect. Slaves were taken, plantations were organized, and markets and trade routes were created. Although colonial regimes generally assumed that the people directly affected by these and other such policies would be men, the indirect effects on women included the opportunities and disadvantages presented by urbanization, the shift in female labor caused by the introduction of cash crops, the introduction of Western diseases as well as of Western cures, along with innumerable other changes in the traditional ways of life. . . .

. . . Even in the 1980s, however, Western influence continues to be extensive, and it is important to stress that this influence is predominantly male. . . .

THE POLITICAL DEPENDENCY OF WOMEN

One way to conceptualize the relative powerlessness of women in development decision making is to view them as being caught in a triad of dependency. In this context, the dependency triad describes the situation that exists in virtually every country in the world, one in which women are dependent upon men in formal politics at the local, national, and international levels. Equally important in this conceptualization is the recognition that these three levels are increasingly interrelated. Events at the local level, whether in the private (family/kin group) sphere or public sphere are more and more influenced by the institutions of the nation-state. Moreover, the expansion of multinational organizations means that virtually no country can be considered impermeable to influences that originate outside its border. This phenomenon of interdependence and nation-state permeability can be illustrated by the complex issue of child nutrition and multinational corporations, which has been discussed widely in the past few years. The choice by a village woman to breast-feed her infant is conditioned in part by forces over which she has no control: the availability of manufactured formulas, advertising and other sources of information (such as health workers), prices and cash income, and government policies regulating the operations of multinational corporations. This example is a reminder that the conditions of a woman's life — even in remote villages — are influenced by institutions and events that are physically far removed from her.

Recent research on women in Third World countries points to a number of factors that determine the quantity and quality of the changes the women experience in the course of development. Four of these factors are especially significant: traditional cultural norms, the productive roles of women, political values and structures, and the position of the country (nation-state) in the international system. . . . The factors that are of primary importance are those that initially define the status women hold in a particular society and the roles they play. Anthropologists and historians have provided reasonably detailed descriptions of the culturally defined roles women have played in many societies, and we know that these roles have varied widely: female life has been circumscribed by such practices as foot-binding or suttee (sāti) in some cultures, and relative autonomy and power have been given to women in other cultures.

Whatever their traditional condition, women in general have little or no formal, institutionalized power at the local, national, and international levels in comparison to men. Even when they do acquire public influence locally or nationally, that influence is often undermined by the limited autonomy of their nation-state. . . .

From Personal to Political Dependency, the Private and the Public Spheres

Marxist-feminist scholarship has been instrumental in suggesting the way in which patriarchal control within the family or kin group is linked to the division of labor by gender. . . . As men become more involved in production for exchange (rather than for immediate consumption), the work the women do is increasingly restricted to the domestic sphere. . . .

A number of scholars have argued that the greater the involvement of women in the nondomestic, or public, sphere, the greater their status in their culture and the greater their influence in community matters. This linkage between the nondomestic functions performed by women, cultural norms, and ultimately, status and influence has often been characterized as a private/public dichotomy or paradigm. The linkage relies on two arguments: One, women's lives have always been defined by dual activities — reproductive and productive — but male activity is productive only, and two, there is a direct relationship between the ability of women to define themselves by nonreproductive labor and their broader social status and influence. . . .

Social, cultural, and religious institutions may reflect or reinforce female dependency, even as they guarantee women love, honor, protection, or worship. The political-economic relationship analyzed in private/public paradigms does not imply the absence of reciprocal obligations between men and women in social and economic activities or mutual psychological bonds. However, reciprocal obligations are as much a quality of hierarchical relationships as egalitarian ones, and they do not erase the dominance found in male-female political intercourse, even at the most fundamental level of social organization.

Even when women traditionally have had informal political power, research now suggests that female status has tended to decline historically as differentiation between the private and public spheres increases and as political institutions become more complex and the nation-state becomes more modern. This declining status is generally accompanied by a loss of female power in the new institutions of the state. The political history of the second half of the twentieth century in most of the Third World shows state after state attempting to expand government influence and control to enhance the state's capacity for extracting resources and regulating activities and behavior. The tools of state expansion may be political parties or armies — with increasing frequency, they are extension workers, tax collectors, and development planners. Part of the decline in women's status may be measured by the creation of male-dominated state bureaucracies at the local, regional, and national levels. As public agencies influence or absorb activities that formerly were handled privately, women may lose ground in their ability to control their lives. . . .

The historical trend of declining female power is not irreversible, as the experiences of societies in Western Europe and North America make clear. The expansion of political participation offers women the same opportunities it formerly offered propertyless or uneducated men, ex-slaves, and ethnic minorities, but there is nothing easy or automatic about the expansion of political participation to women. . . .

. . . [But there] is the grim reality of the . . . increasing militarization of politics throughout the world. [I]t is clear that the military will be dominant in national politics around the world for years to come. It is equally obvious that female suffrage and other tangible political gains for women in Western and socialist states have not produced greater female control over, or penetration of, the military establishments, nor have these gains resulted in a decreased emphasis on military priorities, expenditures, or methods.

Over and over, women have pointed out their underrepresentation in all government institutions, including development agencies, and in public international agencies, the picture is hardly better for the future of women's concerns. Although it is recognized that some women in powerful positions identify with men and not women, the absence of women in these positions is still not healthy. Two different lines of argument lead to the same conclusion on this issue.

The late Margaret Mead argued for a greater internationalization of the female role to counteract the increasing dehumanization of the world.

> When there are no women's voices heard in the international councils related to food or population control, the debate is one-sided, limited to the traditionally or recently preempted activities of men. . . . Whether there are any inherent differences between men and women's capacities to hear and consider the needs of others is of long term significance in social planning for the future division of labor. At present, however, it is enough to know that because such matters have been women's concern throughout the ages, if women are excluded from decision making at the present time, there will be no one to take these matters into account. . . .

> . . . It is while the majority of the world's women are still concerned with the care and feeding of children, with the preservation, processing and distribution of food, with the care of the sick. . . . that we have some chance of promoting these concerns in a world that is becoming increasingly dehumanized, hurtling towards slow, possibly complete, deterioration and destruction.

In her book [*Domestication of Women*] on discrimination against women in the Third World, Barbara Rogers focuses on the dominance of male planners and a male bias in planning, and she notes that women planners do not automatically reverse preexisting discrimination against women in development projects. . . . However, at least "women working as professionals in planning organizations, regardless of their degree of identification with the women's movement, can be observed to be disinclined to describe the world in terms of 'men' as a synonym for people. They are also less likely . . . to express boredom and hostility with the question of women in development."

In summary, the movement of women to organize themselves from the village to the transnational level; the integration of women into political and administrative bodies, both public and private; the equalization of political power at every stage and level of organization; and the formal, legal recognition of women's rights are all "women-and-development issues" as much as the questions of maternal and child nutrition or credit for farm women are.

REVIEW QUESTIONS

1. What, in Simone de Beauvoir's view, is the position of women in regard to men and in regard to marriage?
2. Why, from de Beauvoir's feminist perspective, is the epoch in which we are living a period of transition?
3. What are the obstacles, according to de Beauvoir, that face "the independent woman" with "a taste for adventure and for experience for its own sake"?

4. What does Sue Ellen M. Charlton see as a reality in how policymakers today define developmental process, and what are its implications for women?
5. In what ways has the West influenced development programs, according to Charlton?
6. What does Charlton's examination of the political power of Third World women reveal?

▼▼▼

4 ▾ Tensions in Eastern Europe

When at the end of World War II the Soviet armies pursued the retreating Germans deep into central Europe, they subjected all of Eastern Europe to Soviet domination. By 1948 all countries except Yugoslavia had fallen under Stalin's iron grip. Soviet domination was buttressed by the Warsaw Pact, the military alliance of all countries within the Soviet bloc formed in 1955 to counter the North Atlantic Treaty Organization (NATO). It was further strengthened by the Council for Mutual Economic Assistance (COMECON), created in 1958 in response to the emerging European Economic Community; it tried to weld the disparate economies of Eastern Europe into a viable unit for the benefit of the Soviet boss.

Yet Soviet rule did not take firm root. The peoples under Soviet domination traditionally had looked westward, benefiting from economic, religious, and cultural ties with Western Europe. They also carried over from their past a strong nationalist ambition for independence. As Western Europe recovered from World War II, the discrepancy between the poverty of the Soviet bloc and the prosperity of its Western neighbors, especially the Federal Republic of Germany, added a further source of anti-Soviet agitation.

Inevitably the craving for independence and freedom caused mounting tensions in Soviet-controlled Eastern Europe. Within each country Soviet lackeys struggled against the reformers who were asserting, however cautiously, the yearnings of their peoples. Tensions occasionally erupted in dramatic protests, as evidenced in Hungary (1956), Czechoslovakia (1968), and Poland (1980). Then during 1989–1990 in country after country, people showed their distaste for communist leadership and demanded democratic reforms. Faced with a mounting tide of popular discontent, communist leaders resigned or agreed to reforms. The hard-line communist leadership in East Germany, shamed and contrite, was driven from power and the Berlin Wall came down. A coalition of parties allied with the West German Christian Democrats won; this was also a crucial step in the reunification of Germany. Repudiated by the people, the Polish Communist party occupied a subordinate position in a new government headed by democratic-minded reformers. Hungary legalized opposition parties and permitted free elections, in which the communists lost. Noncommunists also dominated the newly established government in Czechoslovakia. In Rumania, after a brief but bloody uprising, the hard-line dictator Nicolae Ceausescu was executed.

Milovan Djilas
≪ THE NEW CLASS ≫

Milovan Djilas, a Yugoslav author and political commentator (b. 1911), became a communist after finishing his studies in 1933. In World War II, he was a leader of the partisans fighting the German occupation. Starting as a close friend of Marshal Tito, the all-powerful communist leader of Yugoslavia, in 1953 he turned critic, not only of his friend's personal creed, but also of communist practice and ideology in general. Jailed in 1956 for his heresies, he wrote several books, the best known of which is *The New Class: An Analysis of the Communist System* (1957). In this work he traced the source of the communist system of power to the unprecedented new class of political bureaucrats dominating state and society. Under communism, he argued, the state did not wither away, as early theorists had expected. On the contrary, it grew more powerful, thanks to that highly privileged "exploiting and governing class." Aware of the dynamics of nationalism at work in the special conditions of each communist regime (fresh in his mind were the events of 1956 in Hungary), Djilas also pointed to the growing desire for national self-assertion among the leaders of the Soviet satellite states. The following selections from his book provide helpful insights into the explosions of discontent in Hungary, Czechoslovakia, and Poland related in the subsequent pages.

Earlier revolutions, particularly the so-called bourgeois ones, attached considerable significance to the establishment of individual freedoms immediately following cessation of the revolutionary terror. Even the revolutionaries considered it important to assure the legal status of the citizenry. Independent administration of justice was an inevitable final result of all these revolutions. The Communist regime in the U.S.S.R. is still remote from independent administration of justice after forty years of tenure. The final results of earlier revolutions were often greater legal security and greater civil rights. This cannot be said of the Communist revolution. . . .

In contrast to earlier revolutions, the Communist revolution, conducted in the name of doing away with classes, has resulted in the most complete authority of any single new class. Everything else is sham and an illusion. . . .

This new class, the bureaucracy, or more accurately the political bureaucracy, has all the characteristics of earlier ones as well as some new characteristics of its own. Its origin had its special characteristics also, even though in essence it was similar to the beginnings of other classes. . . . The new class may be said to be made up of those who have special privileges and economic preference because of the administrative monopoly they hold. . . .

The mechanism of Communist power is perhaps the simplest which can be conceived, although it leads to the most refined tyranny and the most brutal exploitation. The simplicity of this mechanism originates from the fact that one party alone, the Communist Party, is the backbone of the entire political, economic, and ideological activity. The entire public life is at a standstill or moves ahead, falls behind or turns around according to what happens in the party forums. . . .

. . . Communist control of the social machine . . . restricts certain government posts to party members. These jobs, which are essential in any government but especially in a Communist one, include assignments with police, especially the secret police; and the diplomatic and officers corps, especially positions in the information and political services. In the judiciary only top positions have until now been in the hands of Communists. . . .

Only in a Communist state are a number of both specified and unspecified positions reserved for members of the party. The Communist government, although a class structure, is a party government; the Communist army is a party army; and the state is a party state. More precisely, Communists tend to treat the army and the state as their exclusive weapons.

The exclusive, if unwritten, law that only party members can become policemen, officers, diplomats, and hold similar positions, or that only they can exercise actual authority, creates a special privileged group of bureaucrats. . . .

The entire governmental structure is organized in this manner. Political positions are reserved exclusively for party members. Even in non-political governmental bodies Communists hold the strategic positions or oversee administration. Calling a meeting at the party center or publishing an article is sufficient to cause the entire state and social mechanism to begin functioning. If difficulties occur anywhere, the party and the police very quickly correct the "error.". . .

The classes and masses do not exercise authority, but the party does so in their name. In every party, including the most democratic, leaders play an important role to the extent that the party's authority becomes the authority of the leaders. The so-called "dictatorship of the proletariat," which is the beginning of and under the best circumstances becomes the authority of the party, inevitably evolves into the dictatorship of the leaders. In a totalitarian government of this type, the dictatorship of the proletariat is a theoretical justification, or ideological mask at best, for the authority of some oligarchs. . . .

Freedoms are formally recognized in Communist regimes, but one decisive condition is a prerequisite for exercising them: freedoms must be utilized only in the interest of the system of "socialism," which the Communist leaders rep-

resent, or to buttress their rule. This practice, contrary as it is to legal regulations, inevitably had to result in the use of exceptionally severe and unscrupulous methods by police and party bodies. . . .

. . . It has been impossible in practice to separate police authority from judicial authority. Those who arrest also judge and enforce punishments. The circle is closed: the executive, the legislative, the investigating, the court, and the punishing bodies are one and the same. . . .

Communist parliaments are not in a position to make decisions on anything important. Selected in advance as they are, flattered that they have been thus selected, representatives do not have the power or the courage to debate even if they wanted to do so. Besides, since their mandate does not depend on the voters, representatives do not feel that they are answerable to them. Communist parliaments are justifiably called "mausoleums" for the representatives who compose them. Their right and role consist of unanimously approving from time to time that which has already been decided for them from the wings. . . .

Though history has no record of any other system so successful in *checking* its opposition as the Communist dictatorship, none ever has *provoked* such profound and far-reaching discontent. It seems that the more the conscience is crushed and the less the opportunities for establishing an organization exist, the greater the discontent. . . .

In addition to being motivated by the historical need for rapid industrialization, the Communist bureaucracy has been compelled to establish a type of economic system designed to insure the perpetuation of its own power. Allegedly for the sake of a classless society and for the abolition of exploitation, it has created a closed economic system, with forms of property which facilitate the party's domination and its monopoly. At first, the Communists had to turn to this "collectivistic" form for objective reasons. Now they continue to strengthen this form — without considering whether or not it is in the interest of the national economy and of further industrialization — for their own sake, for an exclusive Communist class aim. They first administered and controlled the entire economy for so-called ideal goals; later they did it for the purpose of maintaining their absolute control and domination. That is the real reason for such far-reaching and inflexible political measures in the Communist economy. . . .

A citizen in the Communist system lives oppressed by the constant pangs of his conscience, and the fear that he has transgressed. He is always fearful that he will have to demonstrate that he is not an enemy of socialism, just as in the Middle Ages a man constantly had to show his devotion to the Church. . . .

. . . Tyranny over the mind is the most complete and most brutal type of tyranny; every other tyranny begins and ends with it. . . .

History will pardon Communists for much, establishing that they were forced into many brutal acts because of circumstances and the need to defend their existence. But the stifling of every divergent thought, the exclusive monopoly over thinking for the purpose of defending their personal interests, will nail the Communists to a cross of shame in history. . . .

In essence, Communism is only one thing, but it is realized in different degrees and manners in every country. Therefore it is possible to speak of various Communist systems, i.e., of various forms of the same manifestation.

The differences which exist between Communist states — differences that Stalin attempted futilely to remove by force — are the result, above all, of diverse historical backgrounds. . . . When ascending to power, the Communists face in the various countries different cultural and technical levels and varying social relationships, and are faced with different national intellectual characters. . . . Of the former international proletariat, only words and empty dogmas remained. Behind them stood the naked national and international interests, aspirations, and plans of the various Communist oligarchies, comfortably entrenched.

The nature of authority and property, a sim-ilar international outlook, and an identical ideology inevitably identify Communist states with one another. Nevertheless, it is wrong to ignore and underestimate the significance of the inevitable differences in degree and manner between Communist states. The degree, manner, and form in which Communism will be realized, or its purpose, is just as much of a given condition for each of them as is the essence of Communism itself. No single form of Communism, no matter how similar it is to other forms, exists in any way other than as national Communism. In order to maintain itself, it must become national.

The form of government and property as well as of ideas differs little or not at all in Communist states. It cannot differ markedly since it has an identical nature — total authority. However, if they wish to win and continue to exist, the Communists must adapt the degree and manner of their authority to national conditions. . . .

. . . The Communist East European countries did not become satellites of the U.S.S.R. because they benefited from it, but because they were too weak to prevent it. As soon as they become stronger, or as soon as favorable conditions are created, a yearning for independence and for protection of "their own people" from Soviet hegemony will rise among them.

The subordinate Communist governments in East Europe can, in fact must, declare their independence from the Soviet government. No one can say how far this aspiration for independence will go and what disagreements will result. The result depends on numerous unforeseen internal and external circumstances. However, there is no doubt that a national Communist bureaucracy aspires to more complete authority for itself. This is demonstrated . . . by the current unconcealed emphasis on "one's own path to socialism," which has recently come to light sharply in Poland and Hungary. The central Soviet government has found itself in difficulty because of the nationalism existing even in those governments which it installed in the Soviet republics (Ukraine,

Caucasia), and still more so with regard to those governments installed in the East European countries. Playing an important role in all of this is the fact that the Soviet Union was unable, and will not be able in the future, to assimilate the economies of the East European countries.

The aspirations toward national independence must of course have greater impetus. These aspirations can be retarded and even made dormant by external pressure or by fear on the part of the Communists of "imperialism" and the "bourgeoisie," but they cannot be removed. On the contrary, their strength will grow.

Andor Heller
THE HUNGARIAN REVOLUTION, 1956

After Stalin's death in 1953, the rigid political controls in Hungary were relaxed, leading to an unstable balance between Soviet-oriented hard-liners and patriotic reformers willing to grant greater freedom to the spirit of nationalism and individual enterprise stirring among the people. In 1956, the year of Khrushchev's attack on Stalin, the Hungarian yearning for escape from Soviet domination exploded. On October 23 a student demonstration in Budapest, the capital, provided the spark. Throughout the country, communist officials were ousted and the Soviet troops forced to withdraw. A coalition government under Imre Nagy was formed to restore Hungary's independence; it even appeared that the country would withdraw from the newly formed Warsaw Pact controlled by Moscow. In Budapest especially, the popular excitement over the country's liberation from the Soviet yoke knew no bounds, as described in the following eye-witness account.

Deep dejection followed the anger caused by the Soviet counterattack that killed thousands of people and drove 200,000 into exile. A new "peasant-worker government" under János Kádár boasted of having saved the country from "fascist counter-revolution." Subsequently, however, Kádár transformed his country's economy. Dubbed "goulash communism" for its mixture of state and private enterprise, it became the freest in the Soviet bloc and a model for Gorbachev's *perestroika*.

I saw freedom rise from the ashes of Communism in Hungary: a freedom that flickered and then blazed before it was beaten down — but not extinguished — by masses of Russian tanks and troops.

I saw young students, who had known nothing but a life under Communist and Russian control, die for a freedom about which they had only heard from others or from their own hearts.

I saw workers, who had been pushed to the limit of endurance by their hopeless existence under Communism, lay down their tools and take up arms in a desperate bid to win back freedom for our country.

I saw a girl of fourteen blow up a Russian tank, and grandmothers walk up to Russian cannons.

I watched a whole nation — old and young, men and women, artists and engineers and doctors, clerks and peasants and factory workers — become heroes overnight as they rose up in history's first successful revolt against Communism.

Tuesday, October 23, 1956

No Hungarian will forget this day. . . .

. . . In spite of the cold and fog, students are on the streets early in the morning, marching and singing. No one shows up for classes at the universities. After a decade of Communist control over our country, we are going to show our feelings spontaneously, in our own way — something never allowed under Communist rules.

The students carry signs with slogans that until now we have never dared express except to members of our own family — and not in every family. The slogans read:

RUSSIANS GO HOME!

LET HUNGARY BE INDEPENDENT!

BRING RAKOSI TO JUSTICE!

WE WANT A NEW LEADERSHIP!

SOLIDARITY WITH THE POLISH PEOPLE!

WE TRUST IMRE NAGY — BRING IMRE

NAGY INTO THE GOVERNMENT!

The walls of Budapest are plastered with leaflets put up by the students during the night. They list the fourteen demands adopted at the stormy meetings held at the universities:

1. Withdrawal of all Soviet troops from Hungary.
2. Complete economic and political equality with the Soviet Union, with no interference in Hungary's internal affairs.
3. Publication of Hungary's trade agreements, and a public report on Hungary's reparations payments to the U.S.S.R.
4. Information on Hungary's uranium resources, their exploitation, and the concessions given to the U.S.S.R.
5. The calling of a Hungarian Communist Party congress to elect a new leadership.
6. Reorganization of the government, with Imre Nagy as Premier.
7. A public trial of Mihaly Farkas and Matyas Rakosi [notorious Stalinists].
8. A secret general multi-party election.
9. The reorganization of Hungary's economy on the basis of her actual resources.
10. Revision of the workers' output quotas, and recognition of the right to strike.
11. Revision of the system of compulsory agricultural quotas.
12. Equal rights for individual farmers and cooperative members.
13. Restoration of Hungary's traditional national emblem and the traditional Hungarian army uniforms.
14. Destruction of the giant statue of Stalin.

During the morning a radio announcement from the Ministry of Interior bans all public meetings and demonstrations "until further notice," and word is sent to the universities that the student demonstrations cannot be held. At that moment the students decide that the will to freedom is greater than the fear of the A.V.H. — the Russian-controlled Hungarian secret police. The meeting will be held! . . .

At 3 P.M. there are 25,000 of us at the Petofi Monument. We weep as Imre Sinkovits, a young actor, declaims the *Nemzeti Dal* ("National Song"), Sandor Petofi's [a great Hungarian poet and revolutionary hero in the anti-Austrian rebellion of 1848–1849] ode to Hungary and our 1848 "freedom revolution." With tears in our eyes, we repeat the refrain with Sinkovits: . . .

"We swear, we swear, we will no longer remain slaves."

The student voices are tense with feeling. No policeman or Communist official is in sight. The young people are keeping order on their own.

. . . [W]e have swelled to some 60,000. Someone grabs a Hungarian flag and cuts out the hated hammer and sickle that the Communists had placed at its center.

One after another of the purified Hungarian flags appear. Suddenly someone remembers to put the old Kossuth [Lajos Kossuth was the leader of the Hungarian uprising of 1848–1849] coat-of-arms on the flag, in place of the Communist emblem.

We have created a new flag of freedom!

Meantime we all sing the . . . *Appeal to the Nation,* and the *Hungarian National Hymn* that begins "God Bless the Magyar" — both of which had been banned under the Communist rule.

We cannot get enough. The actor Ferenc Bessenyei recites the *National Song* again, and follows once more with *Appeal to the Nation.* Peter Veres, the head of the Hungarian Writers' Federation, leaps to the top of a car equipped with a loudspeaker. He reads the Hungarian writers' demands for more freedom — many of them the same as those in the fourteen points of the students.

The day is ending. We begin to march toward the Parliament Building. The crowds are peaceful, marching in orderly lines. We carry the new Hungarian flag.

As we march we are joined by workers leaving their jobs. By the time we arrive in Kossuth Lajos Square there are at least 150,000 of us, in front of the Parliament Building. On the square, all traffic stops. . . .

Suddenly everyone makes torches of newspapers, and lights them. It is a marvelous spectacle — ten thousand torches burning in the Square before the Parliament Building. . . .

But finally, Imre Nagy appears on the balcony. "Comrades!" he begins, but the crowd interrupts him with a roar: "There are no more comrades! We are all Hungarians!" . . .

The crowd grows still bigger, and we head for the Stalin statue. Now the demonstration has spread so large that it is going on simultaneously in three places: at the Parliament Building: in Stalin Square, where the crowd is trying to pull down the huge Stalin statue with tractors and ropes; and at the building of Radio Budapest, where part of the crowd has gone to demand the right of patriots to be heard over the air. . . .

I go with the group that heads for Stalin Square. Some of the workers have got hold of acetylene torches. They and the students are trying to cut down the dictator's twenty-five-foot metal figure. At the edge of the crowd the first Russian tanks appear, but at the moment they are only onlookers. The crowd pulls hard at the cables that have been attached to the Stalin statue. It leans forward, but is still held by its boots — a symbol, we feel. The cables are now being pulled by tractors, and the men with the torches work feverishly. The statue, though still in one piece, begins to bend at the knees. The crowds burst into cheers. . . .

. . . [W]e watch the Stalin statue, cut off at the knees, fall to the ground with a thunderous crash. . . .

Suddenly shooting breaks out from all sides. The security police — the A.V.H. — are firing into the crowds. In minutes the streets are strewn with the dying and wounded. News of the A.V.H. attack spreads. All over Budapest the workers and students are battling the hated A.V.H.

The peaceful demonstrations of the youth and the workers have been turned by Communist guns into a revolution for national freedom.

For four days — from October 31 to November 3, 1956 — Hungary was free. Although the Russian forces were still in our country, they had withdrawn from the cities and the fighting had stopped. The whole nation recognized the Imre Nagy government, which, knowing it had no other alternative, was ready to carry out the will of the people. . . .

On November 3, Radio Free Kossuth summed up: "The over-whelming weight of Hungarian public opinion sees the result of the revolution as the establishment of a neutral, independent and democratic country, and just as it was ready to sweep out Stalinst tyranny, so it will protect with the same determination and firmness its regained democratic achievement.". . .

In those four days of freedom, political liberty came quickly to life. . . .

Before October 23 there had been only five newspapers in Budapest, all under complete Communist control. On November 4 there were twenty-five. Neither news nor opinions could be suppressed any longer.

Plans for a free general election were speeded.

Religious freedom, like political freedom, came back to strong life in those four days. . . .

In the countryside, the peasants and their spokesmen were mapping the changes of the farm laws and regulations. All were agreed on the goal of a free farm economy based on the individual working farmers and peasants. Peasants would be free to join or leave the farm collectives. If the collectives were dissolved, the land, tools and stock were to be distributed to the individual peasants. Compulsory deliveries at government fixed prices were abolished.

The factory committees and workers' groups were putting forward the needs and demands of the workers, not the government. The right to strike — a criminal act under the Communists — was upheld. Wages, prices, pension rights, working conditions were eagerly discussed and debated.

The economy was slowly getting on its feet. Everyone wanted to be on the streets together. . . .

Return of the Russians

At dawn on November 4, 1956, Soviet Russia attacked Hungary with 6,000 tanks, thousands of guns and armored cars, squadrons of light bombers, 200,000 soldiers — and a tidal wave of lies.

Vaclav Havel
THE FAILURE OF COMMUNISM

Established as a sovereign state at the end of World War I, Czechoslovakia enjoyed two decades of independence until it fell under Hitler's rule in 1938–1939; in World War II it was brutally occupied by the German army. Liberated by Soviet soldiers in 1945, it regained a measure of independence before Stalin installed a ruthless communist regime in 1948.

In 1968, enlightened party members, with the support of the Czech people, sought to loosen the oppressive restraints of the Soviet-imposed socialist order and to establish ties with Western Europe. Alexander Dubček replaced Antonin Novotny, the rigid and unimaginative head of the Communist party, and an air of freedom intoxicated the country. Seeking a humane version of Marxism, the reformers rehabilitated the victims of the Stalinist past and stopped censorship.

On August 21, 1968, Soviet troops invaded the country, joined by Polish, East German, Hungarian, and Bulgarian military units. The Soviet leaders took no chances, fearing a repetition of the events in Hungary, where they had lost control for a time in 1956. And worse: liberalization in Czechoslovakia might endanger their own political system and end their domination of Eastern Europe. Thereafter, the Soviet government moved slowly but relentlessly to regain political control. Dubček was replaced by Gustav Husak, a pro-Soviet hard-liner, in April 1969; exiled from his country as ambassador to Turkey, Dubček was dropped from the party in 1970. It seemed that Czechoslovakia's hope for "socialism with a human face," as Dubček's program was sometimes called, had come to an end. In this manner the Soviet government enforced the Brezhnev Doctrine, which allowed it to intervene in any Soviet satellite state if "the socialist order" (that is, Soviet domination) was threatened. Under Husak, Czechoslovakia became a stronghold of Soviet communism in Eastern Europe.

In 1989, Vaclav Havel, a frequently imprisoned dissident playwright, was elected president. In his 1990 New Year's Day address, excerpted below, Havel told the Czech people how the previous communist regime had abused its power.

THE TRUTH, UNVARNISHED

For 40 years you have heard on this day from the mouths of my predecessors, in a number of variations, the same thing: how our country is flourishing, how many more millions of tons of steel we have produced, how we are all happy, how we believe in our Government and what beautiful prospects are opening ahead of us. I assume you have not named me to this office so that I, too, should lie to you.

Our country is not flourishing. The great creative and spiritual potential of our nations is not being applied meaningfully. Entire branches of industry are producing things for which there is no demand while we are short of things we need.

The state, which calls itself a state of workers, is humiliating and exploiting them instead. Our outmoded economy wastes energy, which we have in short supply. The country, which could once be proud of the education of its people, is spending so little on education that today, in that respect, we rank 72d in the world. We have spoiled our land, rivers and forests, inherited from our ancestors, and we have, today, the worst environment in the whole of Europe. Adults die here earlier than in the majority of European countries. . . .

LEARNING TO BELIEVE AGAIN

The worst of it is that we live in a spoiled moral environment. We have become morally ill because we are used to saying one thing and thinking another. We have learned not to believe in anything, not to care about each other, to worry only about ourselves. The concepts of love, friendship, mercy, humility or forgiveness have lost their depths and dimension, and for many of us they represent only some sort of psychological curiosity or they appear as long-lost wanderers from faraway times, somewhat ludicrous in the era of computers and space ships. . . .

COGS NO LONGER

The previous regime, armed with a proud and intolerant ideology, reduced people into the means of production, and nature into its tools. So it attacked their very essence, and their mutual relations. . . . Out of talented and responsible people, ingeniously husbanding their land, it made cogs of some sort of great, monstrous, thudding, smelly machine, with an unclear purpose. All it can do is slowly but irresistibly, wear itself out, with all its cogs.

If I speak about a spoiled moral atmosphere I don't refer only to our masters. . . . I'm speaking about all of us. For all of us have grown used to the totalitarian system and accepted it as an immutable fact, and thereby actually helped keep it going. None of us are only its victims; we are all also responsible for it.

It would be very unwise to think of the sad heritage of the last 40 years only as something foreign; something inherited from a distant relative. On the contrary, we must accept this heritage as something we have inflicted on ourselves. If we accept it in such a way, we shall come to understand it is up to all of us to do something about it.

Let us make no mistake: even the best Government, the best Parliament and the best President cannot do much by themselves. Freedom and democracy, after all, mean joint participation and shared responsibility. If we realize this, then all the horrors that the new Czechoslovak democracy inherited cease to be so horrific. If we realize this, then hope will return to our hearts.

———

Everywhere in the world, people were surprised how these malleable, humiliated, cynical citizens of Czechoslovakia, who seemingly believed in nothing, found the tremendous strength within a few weeks to cast off the totalitarian system, in an entirely peaceful and dignified manner. We ourselves are surprised at it.

And we ask: Where did young people who had never known another system get their longing for truth, their love of freedom, their political imagination, their civic courage and civic responsibility? How did their parents, precisely the generation thought to have been lost, join them? How is it possible that so many people immediately understood what to do and that none of them needed any advice or instructions?. . .

RECALLING RUINED LIVES

Naturally we too had to pay for our present-day freedom. Many of our citizens died in prison in the 1950's. Many were executed. Thousands of human lives were destroyed. Hundreds of thousands of talented people were driven abroad. . . . Those who fought against totalitarianism during the war were also persecuted. . . . Nobody who paid in one way or another for our freedom could be forgotten.

Independent courts should justly evaluate the possible guilt of those responsible, so that the full truth about our recent past should be exposed.

But we should also not forget that other nations paid an even harsher price for their present

freedom, and paid indirectly for ours as well. All human suffering concerns each human being. . . . Without changes in the Soviet Union, Poland, Hungary, and the German Democratic Republic, what happened here could hardly have taken place, and certainly not in such a calm and peaceful way.

Now it depends only on us whether this hope will be fulfilled, whether our civic, national and political self-respect will be revived. Only a man or nation with self-respect, in the best sense of the word, is capable of listening to the voices of others, while accepting them as equals, of forgiving enemies and of expiating sins. . . .

[A HUMANE REPUBLIC]

Perhaps you are asking what kind of republic I am dreaming about. I will answer you: a republic that is independent, free, democratic, a republic with economic prosperity and also social justice, a humane republic that serves man and that for that reason also has the hope that man will serve it. . . .

THE PEOPLE HOLD SWAY

My most important predecessor started his first speech by quoting from Comenius. Permit me to end my own first speech by my own paraphrase. Your Government, my people, has returned to you.

POLAND: THE EMERGENCE OF SOLIDARITY

Soviet-occupied in 1945 and fully Stalinized in 1948, Poland was officially a Marxist-socialist workers' state led by the Polish United Workers party. It was therefore not surprising that major political changes there since World War II have resulted from workers' protests against poor living conditions and lack of freedom, most often expressed in strikes. In 1956, after Khrushchev's anti-Stalin speech, striking workers in the city of Poznan forced a relaxation of Soviet-style totalitarianism, returning to power Wladyslaw Gomulka (who had previously led the country from 1945 to 1948). In 1970, major strikes broke out along the Baltic coast, provoked by price hikes; they were violently suppressed, with several hundred workers killed — ironically, within a "workers' state." In the turmoil, Gomulka, who had turned authoritarian and rigid, was ousted and replaced by Edward Gierek, who promised improvements in the material welfare of the country. Yet the workers' unrest continued, supported by intellectuals in Warsaw, the capital. The Roman Catholic church was an even more significant ally, with added prestige after Cardinal Wojtyla became Pope John Paul II in 1978.

As the Polish economy continued in crisis, Gierek was forced to announce new price hikes in July 1980. The workers immediately protested, striking for higher wages and greater influence at their places of work; by August 8, 150 strikes had been reported. A few days later, the strike wave hit the city of Gdansk on the Baltic coast, the location of the Lenin shipyard (employing 16,000 workers), and the nearby city of Gdynia with its Paris Commune shipyard (employing 12,000 workers). Though these workers were the best paid in Poland, they too were dissatisfied with their harsh living conditions and their inability to make their grievances heard; they wanted more freedom for themselves and their fellow citizens as well.

One employee at the Lenin shipyard was an electrician named Lech Walesa. Of peasant background and a devout Catholic, he had worked there since 1967 and emerged as a leader in the strikes of 1970. Dismissed and banned from the shipyard in 1976, he continued his agitation, watching events locally and nationally while gaining the respect of his fellow workers. In August 1980, agitation for higher wages and anger against the dismissal of Anna Walentynowicz, a fifty-one-year-old widow, crane operator, and political activist, escalated into a resounding political protest. The Solidarity movement took off, culminating in a political program called the Twenty-One Demands, which outlined the major reforms requested by Solidarity in the years to come. On August 31, the Gierek government and the leaders of Solidarity reached an agreement at last, granting most of the strikers' demands. Gierek lost face; he soon thereafter resigned.

Amidst public unrest, tension heightened between Solidarity and the government during the next twelve months. How much freedom could the party grant the workers without upsetting the political order in Eastern Europe imposed by the Soviet Union? Gierek's eventual successor, General Wojciech Jaruzelski, was determined to restore order with the help of the army. In late December 1981, he declared martial law. Solidarity was outlawed, Walesa detained. Yet Solidarity survived underground, gaining political recognition with Jaruzelski's help in 1989. "The Twenty-One Demands" are reproduced below.

THE TWENTY-ONE DEMANDS

of the striking workforces represented on the Inter-Factory Strike Committee of Gdansk Shipyard

The following are the Committee Demands:

1. Acceptance of free trade unions independent of the Communist Party and of enterprises, in accordance with convention No. 87 of the International Labour Organisation concerning the right to form free trade unions, which was ratified by the Communist Government of Poland.

2. A guarantee of the right to strike and of the security of strikers and those aiding them.

3. Compliance with the constitutional guarantee of freedom of speech, the press and publication, including freedom for independent publishers, and the availability of the mass media to representatives of all faiths.

4. (a) A return of former rights to:
— People dismissed from work after the 1970 and 1976 strikes.
— Students expelled from school because of their views.
(b) The release of all political prisoners, among them Edmund Zadrozynski, Jan Kozlowski and Marek Kozlowski.
(c) A halt in repression of the individual because of personal conviction.

5. Availability to the mass media of information about the formation of the Inter-factory Strike Committee and publications of its demands.

6. The undertaking of actions aimed at bringing the country out of its crisis situation by the following means:
(a) Making public complete information about the social-economic situation.
(b) Enabling all sectors and social classes to take part in discussion of the reform programme.

7. Compensation of all workers taking part in the strike for the period of the strike, with vacation pay from the Central Council of Trade Unions.

8. An increase in the base pay of each worker by 2,000 zlotys [$50.00] a month as compensation for the recent rise in prices.

9. Guaranteed automatic increases in pay on the basis of increases in prices and the decline in real income.

10. A full supply of food products for the domestic market, with exports limited to surpluses.

11. The abolition of "commercial" prices and of other sales for hard currency in special shops.

12. The selection of management personnel on the basis of qualifications, not party membership. Privileges of the secret police, regular police and party apparatus are to be eliminated by equalizing family subsidies, abolishing special stores, etc.

13. The introduction of food coupons for meat and meat products (during the period in which control of the market situation is regained).

14. Reduction in the age for retirement for women to 50 and for men to 55, or after 30 years' employment in Poland for women and 35 years for men, regardless of age.

15. Conformity of old-age pensions and annuities with what has actually been paid in.

16. Improvements in the working conditions of the health service to insure full medical care for workers.

17. Assurances of a reasonable number of places in day-care centres and kindergartens for the children of working mothers.

18. Paid maternity leave for three years.

19. A decrease in the waiting period for apartments.

20. An increase in the commuter's allowance to 100 zlotys from 40, with a supplemental benefit on separation.

21. A day of rest on Saturday. Workers in the brigade system or round-the-clock jobs are to be compensated for the loss of free Saturdays with increased leave or other paid time off.

REVIEW QUESTIONS

1. How did Milovan Djilas characterize the "new class"? What were its qualities?
2. How, according to Djilas, did the new class wield its immense power?
3. Why, according to Djilas, would the communist governments in Eastern Europe sooner or later declare their independence from the Soviet government?
4. What would you say was the climax of the Budapest demonstration on October 23?
5. What was at stake for the workers and farmers of Hungary in the anti-Soviet uprising?
6. How did the Hungarians in those crucial October days assert their freedom?
7. What evidence of nationalism did you observe in the anti-Soviet demonstrations?
8. What did Vaclav Havel mean when he said that the Czechs had lived in a "morally spoiled environment for the past forty years"?

9. What kind of affliction did he accuse the previous regime of having imposed on the Czech people? Whom did he hold responsible for it?
10. According to Havel, what made it possible for the Czechs to cast off the totalitarian system? Who was responsible for it?
11. What kind of future did Havel envisage?
12. What were the essential demands in the Polish workers' twenty-one points?

▼▼▼

5 ▼ The Soviet Union: Restructuring and Openness

Mikhail Sergeyevich Gorbachev, Soviet leader since 1985 and president of the USSR after 1988, has started a new era in Soviet life and government. There was need for drastic change. The Soviet system of centralized control over all aspects of life had failed alarmingly. The planned economy had fallen behind free enterprise economies; productivity had declined. The official ideology of Marxism-Leninism had been discredited, and the Soviet claim of setting a model for developing countries had collapsed. Under the slogans of *perestroika* (restructuring) and *glasnost* (openness), Gorbachev has begun reforming the Soviet system. He has loosened the strict state controls in order to stimulate the creative energies of the people; he has emphasized the need for official truthfulness and open discussion of vital issues.

He has also called for "new political thinking," setting new perspectives for his country's role in global politics. The need for concentrating on domestic Soviet reform requires a relaxation of tensions around the world. For that reason the Soviet Union has pulled out of Afghanistan and has reduced its control over its Eastern European satellites. As a result, Gorbachev has established friendly relations with Western leaders. His foreign policy has been remarkably successful.

Yet his domestic measures have created baffling problems for him. In trying to liberate private initiative and to open discussion, he has also stirred up the hidden tensions in Soviet society. Revelations of Stalin's terror, of the corruption under Brezhnev, and of the misrule of party officials have divided public opinion. In addition, people accustomed to rigid order and strict authority are uneasy about the command for self-reliance; workers dread the prospect of unemployment in a competitive economy. Even worse, the national minorities agitate for self-determination and liberation; the unity of the multinational Soviet state is threatened. As Gorbachev himself admitted: "The Soviet Union is entering a long period of uncertainty."

Mikhail S. Gorbachev
≪ PERESTROIKA ≫

A man of seemingly inexhaustible energy with a sure way of building public confidence, Mikhail Gorbachev (b. 1931) has talked freely to all sorts of people in his own country ever since he assumed the leadership of the Communist party. He has also taken his case to audiences in Western Europe and the United States, capturing the attention of the world as a statesman eager to reduce the threat of nuclear war and to promote awareness of the responsibilities of global interdependence. In 1987 he spelled out his political views in a book appropriately called *Perestroika.* The following selections present key passages, the first from his opening address "To the Reader" and the second consisting of scattered excerpts from the substance of his book. .

TO THE READER

Perestroika is the focus of the intellectual life of our society now. That is natural, because it concerns the future of this country. The changes it is bringing affect all Soviet people and deal with the most vital issues. Everyone is anxious to know the kind of society we ourselves, and our children and grandchildren, will live in.

Other socialist countries are showing a natural and lively interest in the Soviet restructuring. They, too, are living through a difficult but highly important period of quest in their development, devising and trying out ways of accelerating economic and social growth. Success here is largely linked with our interaction, with our joint undertakings and concerns. . . .

. . . The Soviet Union is truly living through a dramatic period. The Communist Party made a critical analysis of the situation that had developed by the mid-1980s and formulated this policy of perestroika, or restructuring, a policy of accelerating the country's social and economic progress and renewing all spheres of life. Soviet people have both understood and accepted this policy. Perestroika has animated the whole of society. True, our country is huge. Many problems have accumulated and it won't be easy to solve them. But change has begun and society cannot now turn back. . . .

. . . [P]erestroika has been largely stimulated by our dissatisfaction with the way things have been going in our country in recent years. But it has to a far greater extent been prompted by an awareness that the potential of socialism had been underutilized. We realize this particularly clearly now in the days of the seventieth anniversary of our Revolution. We have a sound material foundation, a wealth of experience and a broad world outlook with which to perfect our society purposefully and continuously, seeking to gain ever greater returns — in terms of quantity and quality — from all our activities.

I would say from the start that perestroika has proved more difficult than we at first imagined. We have had to reassess many things. Yet, with every step forward we are more and more convinced that we have taken the right track and are doing things properly.

Some people say that the ambitious goals set forth by the policy of perestroika in our country have prompted the peace proposals we have lately made in the international arena. This is an oversimplification.

True, we need normal international conditions for our internal progress. But we want a world free of war, without arms races, nuclear-weapons and violence; not only because this is an optimal condition for our internal development. It is an objective global requirement that stems from the realities of the present day.

But our new thinking goes further. The world is living in an atmosphere not only of nuclear threat, but also of unresolved major social problems, of new stresses created by scientific and technological advancement and by the exacerbation of global problems. Mankind today faces unprecedented problems and the future will hang in the balance, if joint solutions are not found. All countries are now more interdependent than ever before, and the stockpiling of weapons, especially nuclear missiles, makes the outbreak of a world war, even if unsanctioned or accidental, increasingly more probable, due simply to a technical failure or human fallibility. Yet all living things on Earth would suffer.

Everyone seems to agree that there would be neither winners nor losers in such a war. There would be no survivors. It is a mortal threat for all. . . .

In short, we in the Soviet leadership have come to the conclusion — and are reiterating it — that there is a need for new political thinking. Furthermore, Soviet leaders are vigorously seeking to translate this new thinking into action, primarily in the field of disarmament. This is what prompted the foreign policy initiatives we have honestly offered the world. . . .

Politics should be based on realities. And the most formidable reality of the world today is the vast military arsenals, both conventional and nuclear of the United States and the Soviet Union. This places on our two countries a special responsibility to the whole world. Con[s]cious of this fact, we genuinely seek to improve Soviet-American relations and attain at least that minimum of mutual understanding needed to resolve issues crucial to the world's future.

We openly say that we reject the hegemony-seeking aspirations and global claims of the United States. We do not like certain aspects of American politics and way of life. But we respect the right of the people of the United States, as well as that of any other people, to live according to their own rules and laws, customs and tastes. We know and take into account the great role played by the United States in the modern world, value the Americans' contribution to world civilization, reckon with the legitimate interests of the United States, and realize that, without that country, it is impossible to remove the threat of nuclear catastrophe and secure a lasting peace. We have no ill intent toward the American people. We are willing and ready to cooperate in all areas.

But we want to cooperate on the basis of equality, mutual understanding and reciprocity. Sometimes we are not only disappointed but have serious misgivings when in the United States our country is treated as an aggressor, an

"empire of evil." All manner of tall stories and falsehoods are spread about us, distrust and hostility are shown toward our people, all kinds of limitations imposed and, simply, uncivilized attitudes are assumed toward us. This is impermissible shortsightedness.

Time slips past and must not be wasted. We have to act. The situation does not allow us to wait for the ideal moment: constructive and wide-ranging dialogue is needed today. That is what we intend when we arrange television links between Soviet and American cities, between Soviet and American politicians and public figures, between ordinary Americans and Soviet citizens. We have our media present the full spectrum of Western positions, including the most conservative of them. We encourage contacts with exponents of different outlooks and political convictions. In this way we express our understanding that this practice helps us to move toward a mutually acceptable world.

We are far from regarding our approach as the only correct one. We have no universal solutions, but we are prepared to cooperate sincerely and honestly with the United States and other countries in seeking answers to all problems, even the most difficult ones.

NEW THINKING

The new atmosphere is, perhaps, most vividly manifest in glasnost. We want more openness about public affairs in every sphere of life. People should know what is good, and what is bad, too, in order to multiply the good and to combat the bad. That is how things should be under socialism. . . .

Truth is the main thing. Lenin said: More light! Let the Party know everything! As never before, we need no dark corners where mold can reappear and where everything against which we have started a resolute struggle could start accumulating. That's why there must be more light.

Today, glasnost is a vivid example of a normal and favorable spiritual and moral atmosphere in society, which makes it possible for people to understand better what happened to us in the past, what is taking place now, what we are striving for and what our plans are, and, on the basis of this understanding, to participate in the restructuring effort consciously.

. . . The people should know life with all its contradictions and complexities. Working people must have complete and truthful information on achievements and impediments, on what stands in the way of progress and thwarts it. . . .

. . . [T]he concept of economic reform . . . is of an all-embracing, comprehensive character. It provides for fundamental changes in every area, including the transfer of enterprises to complete cost accounting, a radical transformation of the centralized management of the economy, fundamental changes in planning, a reform of the price formation system and of the financial and crediting mechanism, and the restructuring of foreign economic ties. It also provides for the creation of new organizational structures of management, for the all-round development of the democratic foundations of management, and for the broad introduction of the self-management principles. . . .

The essence of what we plan to do throughout the country is to replace predominantly administrative methods by predominantly economic methods. That we must have full cost accounting is quite clear to the Soviet leadership. . . .

Now, after a nationwide discussion, we have adopted programs for a radical transformation of higher and secondary schools. The main direction of efforts is training young people for future work with a view to meeting the requirements of scientific and technological progress and getting rid of everything of secondary importance which gives people little except unnecessary burdens. The humanistic education of the young, the aim of which is a proper upbringing and the acquisition of adequate cultural standards, is being improved. Colleges and secondary schools lay emphasis on stimulating creative methods of instruction and education and fostering initiative and independence in secondary and higher school collectives. The new tasks call for restructuring the material base and, most importantly, for teachers to attain a new level in their work. Those who upgrade their skills will be encouraged materially. The programs have the necessary financial backing, and their realization is proceeding. . . .

We will firmly continue the struggle against drinking and alcoholism. This social evil has been deeply rooted in our society for centuries and has become a bad habit. Hence it is not easy to combat. But society is ripe for a radical turn around. Alcohol abuse, especially in the past decades, has increased at an alarming rate and threatens the very future of the nation. . . . The per capita consumption of alcohol has dropped by half over the past two years. However, moonshining has gone up. It is impossible to resolve this issue by administrative measures alone. The most reliable way to get rid of such an evil as alcoholism is to develop the sphere of recreation, physical fitness, sport and mass cultural activities, and to further democratize the life of society as a whole. . . .

In my talks with people in the street or at the workplace I constantly hear: "Everybody supports perestroika here." I am convinced of the sincerity and fairness of these words, yet I reply every time that the most important thing right now is to talk less about perestroika and do more for it. What is needed is greater order, greater conscientiousness, greater respect for one another and greater honesty. We should follow the dictates of conscience. . . .

Observance of law is a matter of principle for us and we have taken a broad and principled view of the issue. There can be no observance of law without democracy. At the same time, democracy cannot exist and develop without the rule of law, because law is designed to protect society from abuses of power and guarantee citizens and their organizations and work collectives their rights and freedoms. This is the reason why we have taken a firm stand on the issue. . . .

The January 1987 Plenary Meeting of the

Central Committee called upon Party leaders to pay greater attention to the labor, ideological and moral steeling of young people. A didactic tone and regimentation are intolerable in work with young people. Whatever the reasons — distrust of the maturity of young people's aspirations and actions, elementary overcautiousness, a desire to make things easy for one's children — we cannot agree with such a stand. There are two prime areas in the life and work of the young. First, they have to master the entire arsenal of the ways to democracy and autonomy and breathe their youthful energy into democratization at all levels, and to be active in social endeavors. . . . Intellectual renewal and enrichment of society are what we expect of the young. . . .

Today it is imperative for the country to more actively involve women in the management of the economy, in cultural development and public life. For this purpose women's councils have been set up throughout the country. . . . We have discovered that many of our problems — in children's and young people's behavior, in our morals, culture and in production — are partially caused by the weakening of family ties and slack attitude to family responsibilities. This is a paradoxical result of our sincere and politically justified desire to make women equal with men in everything. Now, in the course of perestroika, we have begun to overcome this shortcoming. That is why we are now holding heated debates in the press, in public organizations, at work and at home, about the question of what we should do to make it possible for women to return to their purely womanly mission. . . .

Universal security in our time rests on the recognition of the right of every nation to choose its own path of social development, on the renunciation of interference in the domestic affairs of other states, on respect for others in combination with an objective self-critical view of one's own society. A nation may choose either capitalism or socialism. This is its sovereign right. Nations cannot and should not pattern their life either after the United States or the Soviet Union. Hence, political positions should be devoid of ideological intolerance. . . .

. . . We do not claim to be able to teach others. Having heard endless instructions from others, we have come to the conclusion that this is a useless pastime. Primarily, life itself teaches people to think in a new way.

William M. Mandel
GLASNOST IN ACTION

In 1987, William M. Mandel, a peace activist and expert on Soviet affairs, participated in a peace march from Leningrad to Moscow, stopping in Novgorod on the way. In that ancient city famous in Russian history, he attended a peace vigil *(vakhta mira),* which allows a glimpse of Gorbachev's glasnost in action. Mandel begins his article "Street-Corner Democracy" by describing the setting.

The Novgorod outdoor meeting of *Vakhta mira* was in the form of a circle next to their nine-foot-high placard-symbol with the sign *"Vakhta mira"* planted in the ground. Attendance during the time I was present fluctuated between 20 and 60, more or less in proportion to the strength of the rain that was falling. Uniformed police ("militia") came by twice, listened from the outside of the crowd with more or less interest, and wandered off. There was no chair or order of business, and no platform or "soapbox" was used.

My transcript is verbatim. The only omissions are when two or more spoke at once and I was unable to decipher either. People interrupted each other exactly as in a conversation around a kitchen table. The general tone was intense, but without hostility toward anyone present or authorities or personalities not present but referred to.

I said nothing, but simply taped, until very late in the meeting. No one seemed bothered or even curious about my presence, perhaps because I arrived in the company of individuals they knew. The meeting was already under way. A very tall young man, blond, in his middle or late 20s, whom I call "First Organizer" was speaking.

FIRST ORGANIZER We organized this to give people a place and time to foregather, not as a brigade (*organized group*), but independent of anything, to have a discussion among concerned people, a plain conversation among human beings, so as for the first time in our lives to feel ourselves free, freedom of association and communication (obshchenie), when no one brings pressure upon you, when you are not subject to anything, when you are not asked to state who you are. We do not set any conditions for people (*to speak*). . . .

The times today demand of us that we act. For the moment, the following form has been suggested to me — that we simply learn how to speak out, to re-establish the contact among human beings that has been lost, to restore that contact.

I see that when people are asked to, they name problems. But until now we were disunited. Today, however, we can speak out, you understand? Simply talk things over. That's the kind of times we are living in. The time in which we will keep our mouths shut and again await instructions from above will not return, will not. Our conscience as citizens will not permit this anymore. Tomorrow we will act. This is the essence of the *Vakhta mira* for which we have assembled.

SECOND ORGANIZER The point is they have given us permission to open our mouths.

FIRST ORGANIZER Permitted us to open our mouths. We *are* speaking. But we have come up against that wall, the same one we faced be-

fore the proclamation of glasnost. And now our voices are bouncing back off that wall. We feel that resistance. It's still here.

WOMAN'S VOICE It isn't opposition that we are up against, but that we aren't capable yet of doing anything. We have only just emerged from an inert state. We are placid and even lazy. We are lazy.

FIRST ORGANIZER We were trained to be that way.

THE WOMAN Yes! It was inculcated, and now they are demanding things of us.

SECOND ORGANIZER What do you mean, demanding?

FIRST ORGANIZER They're not demanding. Our conscience is demanding. Conscience demands. It is now we who want this. No one is demanding. They have given us the opportunity.

SECOND ORGANIZER Opportunity.

WOMAN I don't want to take that upon myself. I don't want to think. I don't want to take the responsibility.

SECOND ORGANIZER That's *your* position. *Your* position.

(*Her statement has caused laughter in the crowd.*) SHE GOES ON: At school they told me: "Here, learn this, learn it." My mother told me: "Learn it." At college the instructor told me: "Learn this."

THE FIRST ORGANIZER *tries to put the discussion back on track* You understand, today they're showing confidence in us. Our government is expressing its faith in us. Seek! Seek out how to do things right.

SECOND ORGANIZER Go and think!

MAN Think for yourselves!

FIRST ORGANIZER And responsibility! They're showing trust in us.

SECOND ORGANIZER But no one ever took off our shoulders the responsibility for what tomorrow will bring. That's what underlies the watchword of the day: responsibility and trust, interwoven together. And if I'm not ready for that yet today, you are now in a position to see that. . . .

A CALM WOMAN *whose voice has been heard*

previously Is a bridge going to be built across the Volkhov downstream? It will make the place look ugly.

A MAN You think so?

ANOTHER WOMAN A footbridge?

A footbridge. There used to be a bridge there.

THE WOMAN *who opened this subject* But not that kind.

ONE OF THE ORGANIZERS Not that kind, because the rivers and barges that now ply the river are bigger than those back then.

WOMAN You know, when they built the previous bridges, it blocked off the streams flowing into the river. Now people have gotten used to that. Isn't that going to happen again? You know, something else that will offend the eye. How can one tolerate that?

ORGANIZER No. The point is that, when they build it — you know, they had a competition for the design, within the organization, privately; they examined it from all angles before they approved it. It *may* turn out to be a very good bridge. There may be aspects that won't please one person or another, but that bridge is needed.

SHE Is it necessary?

ANOTHER MAN It has to be built.

FIRST ORGANIZER It had to be. The bridge is needed as a link. In the first place, the district will be brought together. Secondly, when people go to see the historical things. . . .

SHE Yes, I know all that.

FIRST ORGANIZER And think of it structurally. The previous one was old, wooden. That was bad.

SEVERAL PEOPLE JOINED IN, *and the discussion briefly became a babble, in which the woman was clearly for keeping or restoring everything as it was in olden times. There was some debate over the use and/or preservation of poplar trees.*

THE WOMAN People grew up accustomed to that view. And it is being destroyed. . . .

Again, the FIRST ORGANIZER *who had opened the meeting tried to get people to keep their eyes on the ball, saying* You don't understand the nub of the problem. Excuse me, excuse me for interrupting. You are putting the issue correctly. In one respect, you are right; on the other, they are. But that is not the issue. The issue is that *no one consulted us on these matters.* Neither with you nor with him. The question is to find out which is better, to learn the opinion of the people of the city. Maybe those trees don't have to be cut down. Maybe that bridge does have to be built. But if all this had been explained to you; if they had said this was the location of the old bridge, here is the present situation as far as transport is concerned, here are the proposed design plans: maybe you might then have voted in favor of that bridge before anyone else.

ANOTHER MAN It's a problem of glasnost.

THE WOMAN *who earlier had said "I don't want to think"* now says But we are not from that district. They don't notice us.

FIRST ORGANIZER What do you mean, you are not noticed. Sure, if you stay home and lie on your couch, no one will notice you.

She joins in the laughter.

HE GOES ON People came here to talk about this.

ANOTHER MAN They've been coming here for a month and a half, two months. That's how long our Peace Vigil has been going. And many pass by without stopping. Understand, the problem is that we haven't been brought up (*to take part*).

WOMAN *who had pressed about bridge and trees* Will this amount to anything more than a lot of chatter?

SECOND ORGANIZER, *confidently* No. But we have to deal with real problems. For example, to restore the Peredoskov House, we need only to *want* that, we also need construction materials. Can *you* find the materials? Can *you* send out a general call for people to come out to do the work? It is the authorities who have to handle such problems.

MALE VOICE What about the factories?

SECOND ORGANIZER The factories?

FIRST ORGANIZER There are organizations that handle such matters. The assistant general manager of a factory deals with such things. Things have to be decided in proper order. We have Soviet government, you understand? It is its *duty* to carry out its functions.

ANOTHER MAN, *calmly* You say you need materials. Come over to my place. I'll steal them for you.

FIRST ORGANIZER Not by stealing. We can't just go to some factory and take things. We can go to the manager and say, give us some. He will. He'll find appropriate stored supplies. . . .

FIRST ORGANIZER But you have problems that bother you. I cited that as an example. You have your problems. Go out and find people who think as you do about them. This is a time for creativity. The whole things rests in one's own soul. We have got to be active citizens. That's what we are talking about. We are very different kinds of people here. The solution of problems has to begin with the people, whether one is a plain worker or is a member of the City Committee of the Party. Any way you slice it, everything starts with human beings.

ANOTHER They may be people, it's true, but they're too high up for us. They do what they have instructions to do. And you are trying to bust into those instructions. And a year won't do, nor two, nor three, nor ten, to break that pattern.

FIRST ORGANIZER Today we just don't want to wait any more. Today we simply can't wait any longer.

OTHER You'll have to wait, whether you like it or not.

SECOND ORGANIZER That depends upon us.

YET ANOTHER We have been trying for two years, and nothing has changed. (*Gorbachev had then been in office two years.*)

SOMEONE *addresses the last speaker* And what have you done about it? What have you tried?

FIRST ORGANIZER What do you mean, we haven't moved off the dime? Look about you. There *have* been changes. Let's look at them. They've begun to give free rein to radio, TV, the press, the movies.

VOICE *in the background* New kinds of things are being written.

SKEPTIC That's just talk. I'm speaking of reality, not chatter. Action.

He is challenged What do you call action? They've begun to show confidence in us.

FIRST ORGANIZER. . . The evening news didn't show the things it is showing today.

OTHER Everything depends upon industry. If industry doesn't produce, we'll remain right where we are. Or we'll go backward, into the past. For industry to run right, we need laws in the sphere of the economy. We need incentives. And so far they don't exist.

FIRST ORGANIZER We have already built our economic base, but we are not using it adequately, not putting it to full use. The economic potential of our country, of our social system — I don't know how to put it strongly enough: we are underutilizing it to a criminal degree. It is precisely because of this that socialism has lost its prestige in recent years. That's why we can't even offer to the other socialist countries goods that can compete with those offered by the West. We can't compete. . . .

ANOTHER We have to ask that we be given rooms in which we can meet. Today we came together without leaders, without anything. We just came together and talked.

ANOTHER There are community centers we could arrange to use, to bring people to, so we can meet under a roof.

ANOTHER It's okay to have a specific group of initiators, but we don't need any leaders.

SECOND ORGANIZER Okay, here's a question that's to the point. Will *you* show up here next Saturday?

(*General laughter: they've been put on the spot, and know it.*)

SOMEONE And bring someone else with us.

ANOTHER Understand, the idea is to move on to action. Here so far we're just running off at the mouth.

FIRST ORGANIZER The fact that you have offered a concrete idea is already action. But no one can take a long stride without first learning how to walk. And now we are in a time in which we are learning to walk. And those who are taking this first step feel in their souls that they are doing something for their country.

REVIEW QUESTIONS

1. What were the essential ideas in Mikhail Gorbachev's plea for "new political thinking"?
2. What, according to Gorbachev, does *glasnost* mean?
3. What are the major targets of *perestroika?*
4. How did the meeting in Novgorod illustrate the working of glasnost?
5. What were the issues raised by the participants in the peace vigil?
6. To what extent did the discussion reflect Gorbachev's "new thinking"?

▼▼▼

6 ▼ Human Rights

The West has attempted to apply its liberal-democratic principles in condemning oppression, persecution, and terror. Through the United Nations and other bodies, the Western democracies have attempted to uphold standards of human rights for the entire world. However, in many cases, efforts to police human rights violations have met with only limited success.

Amnesty International
POLITICAL MURDER

Amnesty International was founded in England in 1961 by Peter Benenson, a lawyer long interested in upholding human rights. The organization now has chapters in forty-one countries around the world. Preferring a low-key approach to its work, Amnesty International tracks down evidence about the fate of political prisoners and tries to help them by sending supportive letters to unjustly imprisoned individuals and by writing to their governments and asking for their release. Amnesty International also issues occasional reports on the most flagrant violations of elemental human rights. The following reading from *Amnesty International Report 1989* surveys human rights violations throughout the world in 1988.

Tens of thousands of people were deliberately killed in 1988 by government agents acting beyond the limits of the law. They were victims of executions that evaded the judicial process.

Killing grounds were many and varied. Some alleged opponents of governments, or people targeted because of their religion, ethnic group, language or political beliefs were killed in full public view; others in secret cells and remote camps. Some victims were shot down near battlefields, others in mosques and churches, hospital beds, public squares and busy city streets. Prison cells and courtyards, police stations, military barracks and government offices were all sites of political killing by agents of the state. Many people were killed in their own homes, some in front of their families.

Victims were assassinated by snipers, blown up by explosive devices or gunned down in groups by assailants using automatic weapons. Others were stabbed, strangled, drowned, hacked to death or poisoned. Many were tortured to death. In Colombia, Guatemala, El Salvador, Syria and the Philippines victims were often severely mutilated before they were killed. Their bodies were burned or slashed, ears and noses were severed and limbs amputated.

A state of armed conflict was frequently the pretext, as well as the context, for government campaigns of extrajudicial execution against those they considered undesirable. Warfare makes it easier to evade accountability: not only is access by independent observers limited but the dead can be characterized as combatants killed in encounters or as the unavoidable civilian casualties of war. In Afghanistan forces of the Afghan Government and the USSR summarily killed civilians and captive guerrillas. In one incident a mosque was demolished, killing nine of the 12 captured guerrillas held within. In Ethiopia troops combating guerrilla movements in Eritrea and Tigray carried out mass executions of civilians accused of supporting the guerrillas. On one occasion hundreds of people were reportedly forced into a shallow ditch and then crushed by army tanks. In Burma measures to control the people in areas of insurgency included instant, illegal executions of those found outside their communities or in possession of quantities of food or other goods. In Peru massacres and summary executions largely replaced imprisonment and trial by the courts in counter-insurgency zones under the control of the military.

Many people became victims simply because they lived in an area where the population as a whole was seen as the enemy. In Iraq the Kurdish population was attacked with chemical weapons; survivors were arrested and summarily executed — in one town over 1,000 executions were reported. In Somalia government forces bombarded and strafed fleeing refugees in the north, killing thousands, and executed hundreds of other members of the Issaq clan, which was associated with a guerrilla opposition movement.

In Sri Lanka, both Sri Lankan and Indian troops used deliberate killings of non-combatants in their efforts to suppress armed opposition groups. They were also responsible for "disappearances" — secret, unacknowledged arrests which often resulted in execution.

Mass killings were also carried out outside the immediate context of armed conflict. In Burundi tensions between the dominant Tutsi minority and the Hutu community — which makes up over 80 per cent of the population — led to the reported massacre by Tutsi-dominated troops of thousands of unarmed Hutu. In Guatemala people were killed each month for their political beliefs. During the 1980s tens of thousands of Guatemalan civilians have been killed by agents of the government's security services. Among those executed, apparently because they were deemed subversive, have been teachers, community leaders, trade unionists, human rights workers and peasant farmers active in community life.

In many countries prisoners died as a consequence of torture. . . .

Some prisoners died as a result of deliberate neglect — by being denied medical attention, by exposure, or from starvation. . . .

Not all victims of extrajudicial execution were formally in custody when they were killed, although all were under the state's control.

The violence of non-governmental entities often provided the background to extrajudicial executions by government forces. Violent opposition groups and sectarian movements in many countries were responsible for the random killing and maiming of civilians on a large scale and tortured and killed their captives. The torture and murder of captives by non-governmental groups in Afghanistan, Sri Lanka, Peru, Colombia and elsewhere were a grim part of the context of gross human rights abuse.

As an organization concerned particularly

with prisoner-related human rights and dedicated to the abolition of torture and the death penalty, Amnesty International condemns the torture or killing of prisoners by non-governmental groups. It does not, however, treat such groups as though they had the status of governments in the sense of international human rights law. Nor does it address them unless they have the essential attributes of a government, including the exercise of effective power over substantial territory and population. Amnesty International works within the framework of international human rights law and with the governments bound by it.

Extrajudicial execution on a large scale often arises in the context of internal armed conflict, inter-communal violence, economic crisis, or even rampant drug-related criminality — and of course international armed conflict. The context is important. But it cannot excuse gross human rights abuse, or justify setting aside the norms of international law concerning governmental obligations to respect human rights. Acknowledgement of the context within which governments resort to torture and extrajudicial execution should never be mistaken or misused to suggest that the particular problems of states may in any way justify gross and persistent abuses of the rights that can *never* be set aside in time of peace or war. International law does not recognize the argument of necessity to justify the violation of the rights to life and personal integrity through torture and extrajudicial execution. . . .

Although governments often explained deliberate killings by saying they were a result of law enforcement or armed conflict, they often made enormous efforts to conceal or destroy evidence of killings and their own responsibility for them. Sometimes they denied that killings had taken place and destroyed all traces of the victims. Corpses were burned, placed in quicklime, buried in secret graveyards or dumped in the sea or in dense jungle. Arrest records were destroyed. In Peru a press exposé of an army massacre of 28 people in the hamlet of Cayara was followed by a campaign to eliminate all evidence of the killings. Graves were dug up and the bodies removed, witnesses were killed and access to the region by independent investigators was severely restricted.

Governments sometimes targeted domestic human rights defenders for liquidation — setting out to kill the people who most effectively monitor, report on and combat human rights abuse. The victims have included leaders of local and national human rights commissions, human rights lawyers and members of religious orders who have worked actively for human rights and have helped dismantle the walls of silence, fear and lies concealing gross human rights abuse. Some have been killed outright — in El Salvador, Guatemala, Colombia, and the Philippines. Others have been the object of persistent death threats or have survived assassination attempts in public places.

Government denials and measures to muzzle or eliminate local witnesses were often combined with efforts to exclude outsiders. In Burundi the authorities denied reports of a pogrom of the Hutu majority and refused to allow an international commission of inquiry to investigate how thousands of civilians had died. The Government of Iraq refused a request by the United Nations Secretary-General to permit on-site investigation of the reported killings of members of the Kurdish population.

Suppression of evidence can extend to silencing a government's institutions established to investigate disputed killings. In India a government-established committee investigating the "disappearance" of several dozen Muslims in 1987 was not allowed to make public its findings, which reportedly implicated the provincial police. . . .

Some of those killed are among the "disappeared," although efforts at concealment may break down. In Colombia, El Salvador, Guatemala, Peru, the Philippines and elsewhere the bodies of "disappeared" prisoners were periodically found in remote mass graves and dumping grounds — in sandpits, overgrown ravines, caves and abandoned wells — or washed up on beaches.

One way for governments to deflect criticism is to attribute responsibility for killings to private citizens "taking the law into their own hands." . . . In Colombia since 1981 the authorities have attributed killings by the security forces to mysterious civilian "death squads" — groups they say cannot be apprehended. Military courts which claim jurisdiction over such cases have refused to take action even when civilian legal authorities have identified police and military personnel as responsible. . . .

In many parts of the world conventional security services operate jointly with part-time civilian auxiliary services organized in paramilitary formations. Paramilitary forces responsible for extrajudicial executions sometimes have both official status and an identity of their own. Some are built around religious sects — as in the Philippines; some are connected to political organizations — as in the case of Haiti's *tonton macoutes;* some are part of ethnic groupings — as with the forces raised by officials of South Africa's "homelands." Governments often deny that paramilitary forces enjoy official status, and may set out their legal basis and regulations in secret decrees. They claim such forces are acting spontaneously in self-defence or against law-breakers.

Civilian militias often provide the framework for part-time irregular forces to be incorporated into government service. In the Philippines, Guatemala, El Salvador and Peru, official civil defence or civil self-defence militias participate in joint operations with conventional forces. The governments in question evade accountability for routine extrajudicial executions by blurring the official status of the forces involved.

Blaming phantom "death squads," outraged private citizens or intercommunal violence for killings often goes hand in hand with policies to publicize such executions deliberately as a medium of terror. Whole sectors of the population are intimidated by "death lists" naming candidates for imminent elimination and by manifestos pledging annihilation of political critics.

Bodies of victims may be publicly displayed as grotesque tokens of power and symbols of terror. The dead themselves are used to sow terror. They may be placed in public places and hung with posters threatening others; often corpses are grossly mutilated to further intimidate the target population. . . .

The refusal of governments to acknowledge secret executions may also extend to executions carried out after secret, summary and arbitrary trials. The killing of more than 1,200 prisoners in Iran in late 1988 was summary and arbitrary — but government secrecy has made it impossible to determine whether some form of trial preceded them or if they were carried out without any recourse to the judicial process.

Assessing whether killings carried out in the context of crowd control and against violent opposition groups are lawful may depend on whether official policies on the use of lethal force comply with international legal standards. Orders issued to security personnel were in question in many countries in which unarmed civilians were shot dead during demonstrations in 1988. They included Israel and the Occupied Territories, where over 300 Palestinian civilians were killed; Algeria, where at least 176 demonstrators died; Tibet, where armed Chinese police killed dozens of pro-independence demonstrators; Burma, where troops normally assigned to counter-insurgency operations killed hundreds of demonstrators calling for an end to military rule. . . .

International awareness of extrajudicial executions as a major human rights issue has grown dramatically in the 1980s. The strengthening of human rights monitoring at a local level in many countries and concerted efforts by international human rights organizations — both governmental and nongovernmental — have helped turn this awareness into action.

The United Nations Commission on Human Rights has developed important mechanisms to counter extrajudicial executions. Its Special Rapporteur's brief on summary and arbitrary executions covers the full range of extrajudicial executions and those killings at the fringe of legality — executions that follow sham trials and trials in which inadequate safeguards for fairness make a mockery of justice. The Commission's Special Rapporteurs and Representatives appointed to deal with particular countries have confronted the crisis of deliberate political killings head-on, notably in Afghanistan, El Salvador and Iran. Its Working Group on Enforced or Involuntary Disappearances has investigated thousands of cases of "disappeared" prisoners, showing that many of the "disappeared" have been secretly executed. However, the Commission has balked at subjecting to the scrutiny of a Rapporteur the extreme situations in Colombia, Iraq and Peru, despite the copious testimony it has received from Amnesty International and others about these situations. Moreover, too many countries simply ignore the approaches of the Special Rapporteur on Summary and Arbitrary Executions and the Working Group or fail to act on their recommendations.

The 1980s have been marked by an extraordinary level of mass killings and individual assassinations by government forces and by a significant change in the way they are viewed by international public opinion. The international community receives more and better information and is readier to cut through the fog of secrecy and deceit that cloaks illicit government actions.

It is common practice for governments to attribute state-sponsored killings to independent "death squads," vigilantes or uncontrollable intercommunal violence but it is increasingly obvious that this may merely be a device to deflect public criticism from those in authority.

Killings continue but the fact that reports of extrajudicial executions now rapidly become known around the world is a new element in international relations. In the 1990s the impact of public opinion and the remedial action of the international community should make it more difficult for governments that aim to carry out killings which are murder by any other name.

REVIEW QUESTIONS

1. What role does Amnesty International play in influencing international public opinion in condemning extrajudicial executions?
2. Describe some of the circumstances in which executions take place and the ways in which governments evade responsibility.
3. What mechanisms has the United Nations Commission on Human Rights developed to counter extrajudicial executions?

▼▼▼

7 ▼ Global Problems

The *global village,* meaning the world, is a term in common use today. This phrase succinctly states a truth that has become self-evident in the past decades: the interdependence of all nations in the vital areas of food, energy, economics, and the environment. Given this interdependence, the problems that affect one part of the world affect the rest of it. For example, the burgeoning population, especially in Third World countries, puts pressure on increasing the food supply, but such increase has limits, with finite land, water, and other resources. Larger populations also mean dwindling forests and subsequent soil erosion as people clear trees for fuel and farmland. More people need more energy, using up non-renewable energy sources as well as renewable sources; more people seek more jobs for their livelihood. Another problem that adds to the economic distress of many Third World countries is the immense debt that they have accumulated. A more volatile and immediate problem is the arms race of the superpowers and other countries. Not only does it drain their nations' gross national product, but the stockpiling of nuclear weaponry carries the threat of the annihilation of humanity. All these threats and pressures on the global village and its inhabitants present the greatest challenge humankind has ever faced.

World Commission on Environment and Development
≪ OUR COMMON FUTURE ≫

A widespread feeling of inadequacy and frustration has permeated the international community concerning the ability of human beings to deal with the global issues that threaten life on this planet. This concern resulted in the General Assembly of the United Nations calling for "a global agenda for change," and late in 1984 the World Commission on Environment and Development started meeting to formulate this agenda. The twenty-one Commissioners from as many countries published their report in *Our Common Future* (1987). The following excerpts are taken from the overview, titled "From One Earth to One World."

In the middle of the 20th century, we saw our planet from space for the first time. Historians may eventually find that this vision had a greater impact on thought than did the Copernican revolution of the 16th century, which upset the human self-image by revealing that the Earth is not the centre of the universe. From space, we see a small and fragile ball dominated not by human activity and edifice but by a pattern of clouds, oceans, greenery, and soils. Humanity's inability to fit its doings into that pattern is changing planetary systems, fundamentally. Many such changes are accompanied by life-threatening hazards. This new reality, from which there is no escape, must be recognized — and managed.

Fortunately, this new reality coincides with more positive developments new to this century. We can move information and goods faster around the globe than ever before; we can produce more food and more goods with less investment of resources; our technology and science gives us at least the potential to look deeper into and better understand natural systems. From space, we can see and study the Earth as an organism whose health depends on the health of all its parts. We have the power to reconcile human affairs with natural laws and to thrive in the process. In this our cultural and spiritual heritages can reinforce our economic interests and survival imperatives.

This Commission believes that people can build a future that is more prosperous, more just, and more secure. . . . We see . . . the possibility for a new era of economic growth, one that must be based on policies that sustain and expand the environmental resource base. And we believe such growth to be absolutely essential to relieve the great poverty that is deepening in much of the developing world.

But the Commission's hope for the future is conditional on decisive political action now to begin managing environmental resources to ensure both sustainable human progress and human survival. We are not forecasting a future; we are serving a notice — an urgent notice based on the latest and best scientific evidence — that the time has come to take the decisions needed to secure the resources to sustain this and coming generations. . . .

I. THE GLOBAL CHALLENGE
Successes and Failures

Those looking for success and signs of hope can find many: Infant mortality is falling; human life expectancy is increasing; the proportion of the world's adults who can read and write is climbing; the proportion of children starting school is rising; and global food production increases faster than the population grows.

But the same processes that have produced these gains have given rise to trends that the planet and its people cannot long bear. These have traditionally been divided into failures of "development" and failures in the management of our human environment. On the development side, in terms of absolute numbers there are more hungry people in the world than ever before, and their numbers are increasing. So are the numbers who cannot read or write, the numbers without safe water or safe and sound homes, and the numbers short of woodfuel with which to cook and warm themselves. The gap between rich and poor nations is widening — not shrinking — and there is little prospect, given present trends and institutional arrangements, that this process will be reversed.

There are also environmental trends that threaten to radically alter the planet, that threaten the lives of many species upon it, including the human species. Each year another 6 million hectares of productive dryland turns into worthless desert. Over three decades, this would amount to an area roughly as large as Saudi Arabia. More than 11 million hectares of forests are destroyed yearly, and this, over three decades, would equal an area about the size of India. Much of this forest is converted to low-grade farmland unable to support the farmers who settle it. In Europe, acid precipitation kills forests and lakes and damages the artistic and architectural heritage of nations; it may have acidified vast tracts of soil beyond reasonable hope of repair. The burning of fossil fuels puts into the atmosphere carbon dioxide, which is causing gradual global warming. This "greenhouse effect" may by early next century have increased average global temperatures enough to shift agricultural production areas, raise sea levels to flood coastal cities, and disrupt national economies. Other industrial gases threaten to deplete the planet's protective ozone shield to such an extent that the number of human and animal cancers would rise sharply and the oceans' food chain would be disrupted. Industry and agriculture put toxic substances into the human food chain and into underground water tables beyond reach of cleansing.

There has been a growing realization in national governments and multilateral institutions that it is impossible to separate economic development issues from environment issues; many forms of development erode the environmental resources upon which they must be based, and environmental degradation can undermine economic development. Poverty is a major cause and effect of global environmental problems. It is therefore futile to attempt to deal with environmental problems without a broader perspective that encompasses the factors underlying world poverty and international inequality. . . .

Through our deliberations and the testimony of people at the public hearings we held on five continents, all the commissioners came to focus on one central theme: many present development trends leave increasing numbers of people poor and vulnerable, while at the same time degrading the environment. How can such development serve next century's world of twice as many people relying on the same environment? This realization broadened our view of development. We came to see it not in its restricted context of economic growth in developing countries. We came to see that a new development path was required, one that sustained human progress not just in a few places for a few years, but for the entire planet into the distant future. Thus "sustainable development" becomes a goal not just for the "developing" nations, but for industrial ones as well.

The Interlocking Crises

. . . These are not separate crises: an environmental crisis, a development crisis, an energy crisis. They are all one.

The planet is passing through a period of dramatic growth and fundamental change. Our human world of 5 billion must make room in a finite environment for another human world. The population could stabilize at between 8 billion and 14 billion sometime next century, according to UN projections. More than 90 per cent of the increase will occur in the poorest countries, and 90 per cent of that growth in already bursting cities.

Economic activity has multiplied to create a $13 trillion world economy, and this could grow five- or tenfold in the coming half-century. Industrial production has grown more than fiftyfold over the past century, four-fifths of this growth since 1950. Such figures reflect and presage profound impacts upon the biosphere, as the world invests in houses, transport, farms, and industries. Much of the economic growth pulls raw material from forests, soils, seas, and waterways.

A mainspring of economic growth is new technology, and while this technology offers the potential for slowing the dangerously rapid consumption of finite resources, it also entails high risks, including new forms of pollution and the introduction to the planet of new variations of life forms that could change evolutionary pathways. Meanwhile, the industries most heavily reliant on environmental resources and most heavily polluting are growing most rapidly in the developing world, where there is both more urgency for growth and less capacity to minimize damaging side effects.

These related changes have locked the global economy and global ecology together in new ways. We have in the past been concerned about the impacts of economic growth upon the environment. We are now forced to concern ourselves with the impacts of ecological stress — degradation of soils, water regimes, atmosphere, and forests — upon our economic prospects. We have in the more recent past been forced to face up to a sharp increase in economic interdependence among nations. We are now forced to accustom ourselves to an accelerating ecological interdependence among nations. Ecology and economy are becoming ever more interwoven — locally, regionally, nationally, and globally — into a seamless net of causes and effects. . . .

The recent crisis in Africa best and most tragically illustrates the ways in which economics and ecology can interact destructively and trip into disaster. Triggered by drought, its real causes lie deeper. They are to be found in part in national policies that gave too little attention, too late, to the needs of smallholder agriculture and to the threats posed by rapidly rising populations. Their roots extend also to a global economic system that takes more out of a poor continent than it puts in. Debts that they cannot pay force African nations relying on commodity sales to overuse their fragile soils, thus turning good land to desert. Trade barriers in the wealthy nations — and in many developing ones — make it hard for Africans to sell their goods for reasonable returns, putting yet more pressure on ecological systems. Aid from donor nations has not only been inadequate in scale, but too often has reflected the priorities of the nations giving the aid, rather than the needs of the recipients. The production base of other developing world areas suffers similarly both from local failures and from the workings of international economic systems. As a consequence of the "debt crisis" of Latin America, that region's natural resources are now being used not for development but to meet financial obligations to creditors abroad. This approach to the debt problem is short-sighted from several standpoints: economic, political, and environmental. It requires relatively poor countries simultaneously to accept growing poverty while exporting growing amounts of scarce resources. . . .

The deepening and widening environmental crisis presents a threat to national security — and even survival — that may be greater than well-armed, ill-disposed neighbours and unfriendly alliances. Already in parts of Latin America, Asia, the Middle East, and Africa, environmental decline is becoming a source of political unrest and international tension. The recent destruction of much of Africa's dryland agricultural production was more severe than if an invading army had pursued a scorched-earth policy. Yet most of the affected governments still spend far more to protect their people from invading armies than from the invading desert.

Globally, military expenditures total about $1 trillion a year and continue to grow. In many countries, military spending consumes such a high proportion of gross national product that it itself does great damage to these societies' development efforts. . . .

The arms race — in all parts of the world — pre-empts resources that might be used more productively to diminish the security threats created by environmental conflict and the resentments that are fuelled by widespread poverty. . . .

Sustainable Development

Humanity has the ability to make development sustainable — to ensure that it meets the needs of the present without compromising the ability of future generations to meet their own needs. . . . The Commission believes that widespread poverty is no longer inevitable. Poverty is not only an evil in itself, but sustainable development requires meeting the basic needs of all and extending to all the opportunity to fulfil their aspirations for a better life. A world in which poverty is endemic will always be prone to ecological and other catastrophes. . . .

Sustainable global development requires that those who are more affluent adopt life-styles within the planet's ecological means — in their use of energy, for example. Further, rapidly growing populations can increase the pressure on resources and slow any rise in living standards; thus sustainable development can only be pursued if population size and growth are in harmony with the changing productive potential of the ecosystem.

Yet in the end, sustainable development is not a fixed state of harmony, but rather a process of change in which the exploitation of resources, the direction of investments, the orientation of technological development, and institutional change are made consistent with future as well as present needs. We do not pretend that the process is easy or straightforward. Painful choices have to be made. Thus, in the final analysis, sustainable development must rest on political will.

The Institutional Gaps

The objective of sustainable development and the integrated nature of the global environment/development challenges pose problems for institutions, national and international, that were established on the basis of narrow preoccupations and compartmentalized concerns. Governments' general response to the speed and scale of global changes has been a reluctance to recognize sufficiently the need to change themselves. The challenges are both interdependent and integrated, requiring comprehensive approaches and popular participation. . . .

There is a growing need for effective international co-operation to manage ecological and economic interdependence. Yet at the same time, confidence in international organizations is diminishing and support for them dwindling. . . .

The ability to anticipate and prevent environmental damage requires that the ecological dimensions of policy be considered at the same times as the economic, trade, energy, agricultural, and other dimensions. They should be considered on the same agendas and in the same national and international institutions.

This reorientation is one of the chief institutional challenges of the 1990s and beyond. Meeting it will require major institutional development and reform. Many countries that are too poor or small or that have limited managerial capacity will find it difficult to do this unaided. They will need financial and technical assistance and training. But the changes required involve all countries, large and small, rich and poor.

II. THE POLICY DIRECTIONS

The Commission has focused its attention in the areas of population, food security, the loss of species and genetic resources, energy, industry, and human settlements — realizing that all of these are connected and cannot be treated in isolation one from another. This section contains only a few of the Commission's many recommendations.

Population and Human Resources

In many parts of the world, the population is growing at rates that cannot be sustained by available environmental resources, at rates that are outstripping any reasonable expectations of improvements in housing, health care, food security, or energy supplies.

The issue is not just numbers of people, but how those numbers relate to available resources. Thus the "population problem" must be dealt with in part by efforts to eliminate mass poverty, in order to assure more equitable access to resources, and by education to improve human potential to manage those resources.

Urgent steps are needed to limit extreme rates of population growth. Choices made now will influence the level at which the population stabilizes next century within a range of 6 billion people. But this is not just a demographic issue; providing people with facilities and education that allow them to choose the size of their families is a way of assuring — especially for women — the basic human right of self-determination.

Governments that need to do so should develop long-term, multifaceted population policies and a campaign to pursue broad demographic goals: to strengthen social, cultural, and economic motivations for family planning, and to provide to all who want them the education, contraceptives, and services required.

Human resource development is a crucial requirement not only to build up technical knowledge and capabilities, but also to create new values to help individuals and nations cope with rapidly changing social, environmental, and development realities. Knowledge shared globally would assure greater mutual understanding and create greater willingness to share global resources equitably. . . .

Food Security: Sustaining the Potential

Growth in world cereal production has steadily outstripped world population growth. Yet each year there are more people in the world who do not get enough food. Global agriculture has the potential to grow enough food for all, but food is often not available where it is needed.

Production in industrialized countries has usually been highly subsidized and protected from international competition. These subsidies have encouraged the overuse of soil and chemicals, the pollution of both water resources and foods with these chemicals, and the degradation of the countryside. Much of this effort has produced surpluses and their associated financial burdens. And some of this surplus has been sent at concessional rates to the developing world, where it has undermined the farming policies of recipient nations. . . .

Most developing nations need more effective incentive systems to encourage production, especially of food crops. In short, the "terms of trade" need to be turned in favour of the small farmer. Most industrialized nations, on the other hand, must alter present systems in order to cut surpluses, to reduce unfair competition with nations that may have real comparative advantages, and to promote ecologically sound farming practices.

Food security requires attention to questions of distribution, since hunger often arises from lack of purchasing power rather than lack of available food. It can be furthered by land reforms, and by policies to protect vulnerable subsistence farmers, pastoralists, and the landless — groups who by the year 2000 will include 220 million households. Their greater prosperity will depend on integrated rural development that increases work opportunities both inside and outside agriculture. . . .

Species and Ecosystems: Resources for Development

The planet's species are under stress. There is a growing scientific consensus that species are disappearing at rates never before witnessed on the planet, although there is also controversy over those rates and the risks they entail. Yet there is still time to halt this process.

The diversity of species is necessary for the normal functioning of ecosystems and the biosphere as a whole. The genetic material in wild species contributes billions of dollars yearly to the world economy in the form of improved crop species, new drugs and medicines, and raw materials for industry. But utility aside, there are also moral, ethical, cultural, aesthetic, and purely scientific reasons for conserving wild beings.

A first priority is to establish the problem of disappearing species and threatened ecosystems on political agendas as a major economic and resource issue.

Governments can stem the destruction of tropical forests and other reservoirs of biological diversity while developing them economically. . . .

Energy: Choices for Environment and Development

A safe and sustainable energy pathway is crucial to sustainable development; we have not yet found it. Rates of increase in energy use have been declining. However, the industrialization, agriculture development, and rapidly growing populations of developing nations will need much more energy. Today, the average person in an industrial market economy uses more than 80 times as much energy as someone in sub-Saharan Africa. Thus any realistic global energy scenario must provide for substantially increased primary energy use by developing countries. . . .

Any new era of economic growth must therefore be less energy-intensive than growth in the past. Energy efficiency policies must be the cutting edge of national energy strategies for sustainable development, and there is much scope for improvement in this direction. Modern appliances can be redesigned to deliver the same amounts of energy-services with only two-thirds or even one-half of the primary energy inputs needed to run traditional equipment. And energy efficiency solutions are often cost-effective.

After almost four decades of immense technological effort, nuclear energy has become widely used. During this period, however, the nature of its costs, risks, and benefits have become more evident and the subject of sharp controversy. . . . The highest priority should be accorded to research and development on environmentally sound and ecologically viable alternatives, as well as on means of increasing the safety of nuclear energy.

Energy efficiency can only buy time for the world to develop "low-energy paths" based on renewable sources, which should form the foundation of the global energy structure during the 21st century. Most of these sources are currently problematic, but given innovative development, they could supply the same amount of primary energy the planet now consumes. However, achieving these use levels will require a programme of coordinated research, development, and demonstration projects commanding funding necessary to ensure the rapid development of renewable energy. Developing countries will require assistance to change their energy use patterns in this direction.

Millions of people in the developing world are short of fuelwood, the main domestic energy of half of humanity, and their numbers are growing. The wood-poor nations must organize their agricultural sectors to produce large amounts of wood and other plant fuels. . . .

A safe, environmentally sound, and economically viable energy pathway that will sustain human progress into the distant future is clearly imperative. It is also possible. But it will require new dimensions of political will and institutional co-operation to achieve it. . . .

Industry: Producing More with Less

The world manufactures seven times more goods today than it did as recently as 1950. Given population growth rates, a five- to ten-fold increase in manufacturing output will be needed just to raise developing-world consumption of manufactured goods to industrialized world levels by the time population growth rates level off next century.

Experience in the industrialized nations has proved that anti-pollution technology has been cost-effective in terms of health, property, and environmental damage avoided, and that it has made many industries more profitable by making them more resource-efficient. . . .

Emerging technologies offer the promise of higher productivity, increased efficiency, and decreased pollution, but many bring risks of new toxic chemicals and wastes and of major accidents of a type and scale beyond present coping mechanisms. There is an urgent need for tighter controls over the export of hazardous industrial and agricultural chemicals. Present controls over the dumping of hazardous wastes should be tightened.

Many essential human needs can be met only through goods and services provided by industry, and the shift to sustainable development must be powered by a continuing flow of wealth from industry. . . .

The Urban Challenge

By the turn of the century, almost half of humanity will live in urban centres; the world of the 21st century will be a largely urban world.

Over only 65 years, the developing world's urban population has increased tenfold, from around 100 million in 1920 to 1 billion today. In 1940, one person in 100 lived in a city of 1 million or more inhabitants; by 1980, one in 10 lived in such a city. Between 1985 and the year 2000, Third World cities could grow by another three-quarters of a billion people. This suggests that the developing world must, over the next few years, increase by 65 per cent its capacity to produce and manage its urban infrastructure, services, and shelter merely to maintain today's often extremely inadequate conditions.

Few city governments in the developing world have the power, resources, and trained personnel to provide their rapidly growing populations with the land, services, and facilities needed for an adequate human life: clean water, sanitation, schools, and transport. The result is mushrooming illegal settlements with primitive facilities, increased overcrowding, and rampant disease linked to an unhealthy environment. . . .

Governments will need to develop explicit settlements strategies to guide the process of urbanization, taking the pressure off the largest urban centres and building up smaller towns and cities, more closely integrating them with their rural hinterlands. This will mean examining and changing other policies — taxation, food pricing, transportation, health, industrialization — that work against the goals of settlements strategies.

Good city management requires decentralization — of funds, political power, and personnel — to local authorities, which are best placed to appreciate and manage local needs. But the sustainable development of cities will depend on closer work with the majorities of urban poor who are the true city builders, tapping the skills, energies, and resources of neighbourhood groups and those in the "informal sector." Much can be achieved by "site and service" schemes that provide households with basic services and help them to get on with building sounder houses around these. . . .

III. INTERNATIONAL CO-OPERATION AND INSTITUTIONAL REFORM

The Role of the International Economy

Two conditions must be satisfied before international economic exchanges can become beneficial for all involved. The sustainability of ecosystems on which the global economy depends must be guaranteed. And the economic partners must be satisfied that the basis of exchange is equitable. For many developing countries, neither condition is met.

Growth in many developing countries is being stifled by depressed commodity prices, protectionism, intolerable debt burdens, and declining flows of development finance. If living standards are to grow so as to alleviate poverty, these trends must be reversed.

A particular responsibility falls to the World Bank and the International Development Association as the main conduit for multilateral finance to developing countries. In the context of consistently increased financial flows, the World Bank can support environmentally sound projects and policies. In financing structural adjustment, the International Monetary Fund should support wider and longer term development objectives than at present: growth, social goals, and environmental impacts.

The present level of debt service of many countries, especially in Africa and Latin America, is not consistent with sustainable development. Debtors are being required to use trade surpluses to service debts, and are drawing heavily on non-renewable resources to do so. Urgent action is necessary to alleviate debt burdens in ways that represent a fairer sharing between both debtors and lenders of the responsibilities and burdens. . . .

Multinational companies can play an important role in sustainable development, especially as developing countries come to rely more on foreign equity capital. But if these companies are to have a positive influence on development, the negotiating capacity of developing countries vis à vis transnationals must be strengthened so they can secure terms that respect their environmental concerns. . . .

IV. A CALL FOR ACTION. . . .

. . . As the century closes, not only do vastly increased human numbers and their activities have [the power radically to alter planetary systems], but major, unintended changes are occurring in the atmosphere, in soils, in waters, among plants and animals, and in the relationships among all of these. The rate of change is outstripping the ability of scientific disciplines and our current capabilities to assess and advise. . . .

The onus lies with no one group of nations. Developing countries face the obvious life-threatening challenges of desertification, deforestation, and pollution, and endure most of the poverty associated with environmental degradation. The entire human family of nations would suffer from the disappearance of rain forests in the tropics, the loss of plant and animal species, and changes in rainfall patterns. Industrial nations face the life-threatening challenges of toxic chemicals, toxic wastes, and acidification. All nations may suffer from the releases by industrialized countries of carbon dioxide and of gases that react with the ozone layer, and from any future war fought with the nuclear arsenals controlled by those nations. All nations will have a role to play in changing trends, and in righting an international economic system that increases rather than decreases inequality, that increases rather than decreases numbers of poor and hungry.

The next few decades are crucial. The time has come to break out of past patterns. Attempts to maintain social and ecological stability through old approaches to development and environmental protection will increase instability. Security must be sought through change. . . .

First and foremost, this Commission has been concerned with people — of all countries and all walks of life. And it is to people that we address our report. The changes in human attitudes that we call for depend on a vast campaign of education, debate, and public participation. This campaign must start now if sustainable human progress is to be achieved. . . .

We are unanimous in our conviction that the security, well-being, and very survival of the planet depend on such changes, now.

Arnold Toynbee
≪ FOR THE FIRST TIME IN 30,000 YEARS ≫

Appropriately, this volume ends with the observations of Arnold Toynbee (1889–1975). Toynbee authored the monumental work *The Study of History,* which traces the rise and fall of civilizations; as Director of the Royal Institute of International Affairs in London, he was for years a perceptive analyst of events around the world. In the following passages from an essay written in 1972, Toynbee sets his assessment of the contemporary age and its problems into the historical context of the past thirty millennia, combining in his person the roles of historian, observer of his own times, and prophet of human destiny.

As a prophet, Toynbee hardly offers a reassuring message: humankind's future is once again in doubt. He points to the threat of nuclear weapons, the despoliation of the human habitat, and the effects of the population explosion. Assessing the causes of political hostility in the world, he stresses the dangers of nationalism, pleading for a voluntary union of all humankind on a global scale as the main hope for survival.

Till now, mankind has either taken it as a matter of course that it is going to survive, or, alternatively, assumed that its destiny will be decided by forces beyond human control: the gods or God or Nature. We have now woken up to the truth that, today, we are in greater danger of extinction than we have been at any time since the date — perhaps 30,000 years ago — at which our ancestors gained the upper hand over all other forms of life on this planet except microbes and viruses. In the present age we have discovered and conquered the microbes, and we have hopes of getting the better of the viruses. But our recent victories over nonhuman menaces to human life are far outweighed by new threats to us from ourselves. These threats have no precedents; for man, armed with the power of science applied to technology, is a vastly more formidable enemy for man than any non-human enemy that man has yet encountered.

The present human threats to mankind's survival are notorious. The three principal current man-made menaces are nuclear weapons, the pollution of mankind's habitat on this planet, together with the using up of the planet's irreplaceable natural resources, and the population explosion produced by a reduction in the death-rate without a simultaneous corresponding reduction in the birth-rate.

Taken together, these man-made menaces threaten mankind with extinction, because they threaten to make the surface of our planet uninhabitable, and this limited area is the only habitat we have or are likely ever to have. At least this seems to be the lesson of the progressive increase in the range of astronomical observation and of the recent feat of breaking out into the nearest reaches of outer space. . . .

. . . It is surely clear that the first business on mankind's agenda ought now to be securing its own survival by making sure that its habitat on Earth, which is mankind's sole patrimony, should continue to be habitable by human beings. It is also surely clear that, since the whole habitable and traversable and exploitable and pollutable part of the Earth's crust and air-envelope has been knit together, for technological purposes, into a global unity, the necessary effort to conserve it for human use must be a united and concerted effort by the whole human race. The menaces of nuclear armaments, pollution, prodigality, and overcrowding threaten us on a global scale. They cannot be dealt with effectively by a cooperative human effort of less than global comprehensiveness.

The technological unification of our habitat is now an accomplished fact. Its economic unification is hardly less complete, and even its social and cultural unification has been accomplished at some levels. This is the result of the global radiation during the last five centuries of West European technology, trade, investment, government, population, institutions, ideas, and ideals. For the non-Western majority of mankind, these West-European exports were originally alien imports, intrusions, and impositions, but gradually they have begun to become common possessions of all mankind. From being something specifically Western, they are turning into something generically modern, to which the living non-Western civilizations are making increasingly important contributions. On the cultural and professional planes, there are now people who are already citizens of the world — for instance, the members of the medical profession, and of university faculties and student bodies. The global bond of feeling that unites people in these walks of life is stronger than their juridical segregation from each other as citizens, in the political sense, of the planet's present 140 local sovereign states.

The present situation and, still more, the current tendency on the political plane presents a disturbing contrast to the situation and tendency on other planes of human activity. On these other planes, the history of human affairs during the last five hundred years has resulted in at least a beginning of the process of unification which is the outcome that we should expect. On the political plane, on the other hand, there has so far been little discernible progress toward unification.

Indeed, there has been a quite marked accentuation of political disunity, both in fact and in feeling. This increasing disharmony between politics and other human activities has now reached a degree at which it is manifestly threatening mankind with catastrophe. Why are we exposing ourselves to this fearful risk? Why, in our political life, are we so allergic to the unifying tendency which has prevailed in other fields? It is important to try to identify and understand the causes of this political misfit. To lay bare the causes is the most promising first step toward finding a cure.

The most obvious cause is the persistent disunity of the Western civilization, since it is the Western peoples who, within the last five hundred years, have initiated the global unification of mankind on a number of non-political planes. Since the collapse of the Roman Empire in its western provinces in the fifth century, the new Western civilization that has sprung up out of the Roman Empire's ruins has been disunited politically, though united culturally, technologically and to some extent also economically.

This initial combination of political disunity with unity on other planes is not peculiar to the West. Other civilizations — for instance, the Sumerian, the "classical" Greek, the Chinese — have started life with the same cultural and political configuration. The peculiarity of the Western civilization's political disunity has been its persistence. Its predecessor, the "classical" Greek civilization, was eventually unified politically in the Roman Empire, and similarly the Sumerian civilization in the Akkadian Empire and the Chinese civilization in the Chinese Empire — a political union that survives today, in the form of the People's Republic, nearly 2,200 years after its original establishment in 221 B.C. Moreover, when the Roman Empire disintegrated in its western provinces, it survived in its Levantine heartland; and when, in the seventh century, it broke down here too, it was quickly re-established, first as the Byzantine Greek Empire and then as the Ottoman Turkish Empire. The Ottoman Empire maintained itself till within living memory; it was not till after the First World War that it was extinguished by the youngest of its national successor-states, the present Turkish Republic.

These examples indicate that normally a cultural unity becomes a political unity as well — in course of time. But, if this is the normal rule, the political history of the Western civilization has been a conspicuous exception to it so far. In the West, the Roman Empire was replaced first by a number of local successor-states carved out by invading barbarian war-bands; and here, in contrast to the Levant, the attempt to re-establish the Roman Empire was a failure. The so-called "Holy Roman Empire" of Charlemagne and his successors never embraced the whole of the contemporary domain of the Western civilization, and its authority became more and more ineffective. The "Holy Roman Empire" was defeated by the medieval Papacy, but the Papacy's apparently promising attempt to unify the West under ecclesiastical auspices failed in its turn. In the Western Middle Ages, the most effective forms of political organization were the local city-states in Italy, Flanders, and Germany. In the modern age of Western history, the nation-state has supplanted the city-state as the standard form of Western polity. The global unification of mankind on the non-political planes within the last five hundred years has been accomplished through a competition between half-a-dozen rival West European nation-states — each of them expanding its trade, planting its settlers, and annexing territory all around the globe in chronic warfare with each of the others.

This political division of the modern Westerners into a number of mutually hostile nation-states has now been imitated by the non-Western majority of mankind. During the two

centuries and a half that ended in the two world wars, the West was manifestly dominant in the world. Consequently, Western institutions acquired prestige. Non-Western peoples who revolted against Western domination adopted the Western political ideology of nationalism because they believed this had been the source of the West's strength. The dissolution of the West European national states' colonial empires during and since the Second World War has resulted in a doubling of the number of the world's local sovereign independent states. Each formerly subject territory that has recovered its political independence has set itself up as a national state in imitation of the Western national state whose rule it has shaken off.

The tendency to increase the number and to reduce the average size of local sovereign states has been stimulated, both in the West and elsewhere, by the nineteenth-century Western political doctrine of self-determination. . . .

Nationalism is the most potent of the causes of the political disunity of the present-day world. Another cause is a revulsion from the impersonalness of modern life. Today, human beings feel that they are being dehumanized; they are being reduced to ciphers, to serial numbers, or to clusters of holes punched in cards made for "processing" through a computer. People recognize that this dehumanization is a consequence of the increase in the number of persons and things, e.g., in the size of the populations of states. They know by experience that personal relations between human beings are more satisfactory than impersonal relations. They infer that life would become more human in a state in which it was possible for all the citizens to be acquainted with each other personally, and they argue from this premise that the breakup of states into smaller and smaller pieces is to be welcomed.

The premise is correct, but the conclusion drawn from it is fallacious because the objective is unattainable. A sovereign independent state small enough to become a family affair would not be viable. No state — not even a non-sovereign component of a federation — has ever been as small as that. In the smallest of the historical city-states, the political relations between the citizens have always been impersonal. They are inevitably impersonal in a population of, say, as many as 10,000 men, women, and children all told; when once this figure is reached, it makes no difference if it is increased to one million or to ten million or to five hundred million. Present-day Scottish and Welsh nationalists dream that they would find life more cosy in a separate Scottish or Welsh sovereign national state. In truth, they would find themselves no less depersonalized in a state of this smaller scale than they find themselves today as citizens of the United Kingdom. . . .

In most previous cases, political unity has been imposed eventually by military conquest. The cost, psychological as well as physical, of this barbarous method of unification has proved, again and again, to be prohibitively high. Unification by conquest has sometimes postponed the dissolution of a civilization, but it has seldom averted it and, insofar as the dissolution of a forcibly unified civilization has been postponed, the civilization has been preserved in most cases only in a state of petrification. However, in the age of atomic weapons by which mankind has now been overtaken, the traditional violent method of unification is no longer practicable anyway. A world war fought with atomic weapons could not unify mankind; it would only annihilate it. In the atomic age, the only possible method of unification is some form of voluntary association.

It has been noted already that since 1945 — the year in which the Second World War culminated and ended in the invention and use of atomic weaponry — some of the sovereign national states of Western Europe have taken the radically new departure of entering into a voluntary association in the E.E.C. This is a good augury, considering how deeply ingrained is nationalism in the tradition of Western European peoples and how often one or other of them has tried to subjugate the rest by force. If the Western European peoples can unite with each other voluntarily, as they are now demonstrating they can, a voluntary union of all mankind, on a global scale, is not a utopian objective.

The objective is not utopian, but will it be achieved? That is to say, will it be achieved in time to avert the catastrophe which is the alternative to it? This question will be answered by the three present superpowers [United States, Soviet Union, and China]; their answer is still unknown — probably even to themselves. Will the superpowers' governments and peoples recognize in time that the winning of successes in their competition with each other is not the paramount interest of any one of them? Will they recognize that their paramount interest is the preservation of the human race; that this interest is common to them all and also to the rest of mankind; and that the pursuit of this objective is not only their interest but their duty, both to themselves and to their fellow men? If and when the views and intentions of the superpowers become clear, we shall be better able than we are today to forecast the future of mankind. Today we know only that mankind's future is once again in doubt for the first time, perhaps, within the last 30,000 years.

REVIEW QUESTIONS

1. What does the World Commission on Environment and Development see as the major threats to life on this planet?
2. How does the Commission interpret "sustainable development"?
3. What are some of the Commission's policy recommendations in the areas of population and human resources, food, species, and ecosystems, energy, industry, and the urban explosion?

4. What does the Commission view as the two conditions needed before international economic exchanges can benefit all nations? Explain why for many developing nations these conditions are not being met.
5. What, according to Arnold Toynbee, is "the present human threat to mankind's survival"?
6. What obstacles to political unity in the world did Toynbee observe?
7. What did Toynbee identify as the causes of modern nationalism?
8. What hopes for the future did Toynbee hold out?

Taylor, *Thought and Expression in the Sixteenth Century,* 2d rev. ed. (New York: Frederick Ungar, 1930; repub. 1959), I, 36–37. P. 10: "On Learning and Literature" from *Vittorino de Feltre and Other Humanist Educators,* ed. W. H. Woodward (Cambridge University Press, 1897), pp. 124, 127–129, 132–133. *Section 2* P. 12: From Giovanni Pico della Mirandola, "Oration on the Dignity of Man," trans. Elizabeth L. Forbes in *The Renaissance Philosophy of Man,* ed. Ernst Cassirer, Paul Oskar Kristeller, and John H. Randall Jr., pp. 223–225. Reprinted by permission of The University of Chicago Press, © 1948 The University of Chicago Press. *Section 3* P. 14: From *The Prince* by Niccolò Machiavelli, translated by Luigi Ricci, revised by E. R. P. Vincent (1935), pp. 92–93, 97–99, 101–103, by permission of Oxford University Press. *Section 4* P. 19: "On Papal Power" from Martin Luther, *Luther's Works,* Vol. 44, ed. James Atkinson and Helmut Lehmann, pp. 126–127, 136–137, copyright © 1966 Fortress Press. Used by permission of Augsburg Fortress. P. 19: "Justification by Faith" from Martin Luther, *Luther's Works,* Vol. 31, ed. H. J. Grimm and Helmut Lehmann, pp. 346–347, 372–373, copyright © 1957 by Fortress Press. Used by permission of Augsburg Fortress. P. 20: "The Interpretation of the Bible" from Martin Luther, *What Luther Says: An Anthology,* ed. Ewald Plass, 1959, Vol. 1, p. 943; Vol. 2, pp. 1062–1063; Vol. 3, pp. 1139–1140. Reprinted by permission of Concordia Publishing House. *Section 5* P. 22: From *Select Statutes and Other Constitutional Documents Illustrative of the Reigns of Elizabeth and James I,* 3rd ed., ed. G. W. Prothero (Oxford: Clarendon Press, 1906), pp. 400–401, 293–294. *Section 6* P. 24: From *The English Works of Thomas Hobbes of Malmesbury: Leviathan, or the Matter Form and Power of a Commonwealth Ecclesiastical and Civil,* collected and ed. Sir William Molesworth (London: John Bohn, 1839), III, 110–113, 116, 117, 154, 157–158, 160–161. *Section 7* P. 28: From *Select Documents of English Constitutional History,* ed. George Burton Adams and M. Morse Stephens (New York: Macmillan Company, 1902), pp. 464–465.

Chapter 2

Section 1 P. 34: From Copernicus, *On the Revolutions,* trans. Edward Rosen, ed. Jerry Dobrzycki. Reprinted by permission of Macmillan, London and Basingstoke. P. 36: From *Galileo Affair: A Documentary History,* ed. Maurice A. Finocchiaro, pp. 67–68. Copyright © 1989 The Regents of the University of California. Reprinted by permission of The University of California Press. *Section 2* P. 37: Excerpts from *Discoveries and Opinions of Galileo* by Galileo Galilei, translated by Stillman Drake, pp. 28–31, 51–53, 57. Translation copyright © 1957 by Stillman Drake. Used by permission of Doubleday, a division of Bantam, Doubleday, Dell Publishing Group, Inc. *Section 3* P. 40: From Galileo Galilei, *Dialogue Concerning The Two Chief World Systems,* trans. Stillman Drake, pp. 107–108, 112–113, 175–177, 179–184, 190. Copyright © 1962 The Regents of the University of California. Reprinted by permission of The University of California Press. *Section 4* P. 44: From *The Philosophy of Francis Bacon,* ed. and trans. Benjamin Farrington (Liverpool: Liverpool University Press, 1970), pp. 114–115. P. 45: From *The Works of Francis Bacon,* ed. Spedding, Ellis, and Heath (Boston: Taggard and Thompson, 1863), VIII, 67–69, 71–72, 74, 76–79, 142. *Section 5* P. 47: Extracts reprinted with permission of Macmillan Publishing Company from René Descartes, *Discourse on Method,* trans. Laurence J. Lafleur. Copyright 1956 by Macmillan Publishing Company. *Section 6* P. 50: From Sir Isaac Newton, *The Mathematical Principles of Natural Philosophy, Book III,* trans. Andrew Motte (London: H. D. Symonds, 1803), II, 160–162, 313–314. P. 51: From Sir Isaac Newton, *The Mathematical Principles of Natural Philosophy, Book III,* trans. Andrew Motte (London: H. D. Symonds, 1803), II, 310–313.

Chapter 3

Section 1 P. 57: From Immanuel Kant, *The Philosophy of Kant,* translated and edited by Carl J. Friedrich, pp. 132–134, 138–139. Copyright 1949 by Random House, Inc. Reprinted by permission of the publisher. *Section 2* P. 59: From John Locke, *Two Treatises on Civil Government* (London: 1688, 7th reprinting by J. Whiston et al., 1772), pp. 292, 315–316, 354–355, 358–359, 361–362. P. 62: First printing of the Declaration of Independence, July 4, 1776, Papers of the Continental Congress No. 1, Rough Journal of Congress, III. *Section 3* P. 63: From *Candide and Other Writings* by Voltaire, edited by Haskell M. Block, pp. 114, 368, 374, 375, 441, 443–444, 525. Copyright © 1956 & renewed 1984 by Random House, Inc. Reprinted by permission of the publisher. *Section 4* P. 67: From Thomas Paine, *Age of Reason being an investigation of True and Fabulous Theology* (New York: Peter Eckler, 1892), pp. 5–11. P. 69: From Paul Heinrich Dietrich Baron d'Holbach, *Good Sense or Natural Ideas opposed to Ideas that are Supernatural* (New York: G. Vale, 1856), pp. vii–xi. *Section 5* P. 71: From Denis Diderot, *The Encyclopedia: Selections,* ed. and trans. Stephen J. Gendzier, pp. 92–93, 104, 124–125, 134, 136, 153, 183–187, 199, 229–230. Reprinted by permission of Stephen J. Gendzier. *Section 6* P. 74: Extracts reprinted with permission of Macmillan Publishing Company from Denis Diderot, *Rameau's Nephew and Other Works,* trans. Jacques Barzun and Ralph H. Bowen, pp. 188–190, 194–195, 197–199, 213. Copyright © 1956 by Jacques Barzun and Ralph H. Bowen; copyright renewed 1984. *Section 7* P. 78: From Jean Jacques Rousseau, *The Social Contract* in *The Social Contract and Discourse,* trans. G. D. H. Cole (New York: E. P. Dutton, 1950), pp. 8–9, 13–15, 18–19, 23, 26–28. Reprinted by permission of J. M. Dent & Everyman's Library as Publishers. P. 81: From Jean Jacques Rousseau, *Émile,* trans. Barbara Foxley, pp. 80–84. Everyman's Library Series, reprinted by permission of J. M. Dent & Everyman's Library as Publishers. *Section 8* P. 83: From Antoine-Nicolas de Condorcet, *Sketch for a Historical Picture of the Progress of the Human*

Mind, trans. June Barraclough, pp. 4–5, 9–10, 128, 136, 140–142, 173–175, 179. Reprinted by permission of George Weidenfeld & Nicolson Ltd.

Chapter 4

Section 1 P. 92: From Arthur Young, *Travels During the Years 1787, 1788, and 1789* (London: Printed for W. Richardson, 1792), pp. 533–540. P. 93: Selections reprinted with permission of Macmillan Publishing Company from John Hall Stewart, *A Documentary Survey of the French Revolution,* pp. 76–82. Copyright 1951 by Macmillan Publishing Company, renewed 1979 by John Hall Stewart. P. 95: From Emmanuel Joseph Sieyès, *What Is the Third Estate?* trans. M. Blondel (1964). Reprinted by permission of Praeger and Phaidon Press Limited. *Section 2* P. 97: From Thomas Paine, *Rights of Man* (New York: Peter Eckler, 1892), pp. 94–96. *Section 3* P. 99: From Edmund Burke, *Reflections on the Revolution in France* (London: Printed for J. Dodsley, 1791), pp. 51–55, 90–91, 116–117, 127–129. P. 101: From Thomas Paine, *Rights of Man* (New York: Peter Eckler, 1892), pp. 9, 127, 162–164, 167. *Section 4* P. 103: Excerpts from *The French Revolution* edited by Paul Beik. Copyright © 1971 by Paul Beik. Reprinted by permission of Harper & Row, Publishers, Inc. P. 104: From *The French Revolution as Told by Contemporaries,* ed. E. L. Higgins (Boston: Houghton Mifflin, 1938), p. 301. *Section 5* P. 105: Selections reprinted with permission of Macmillan Publishing Company from John Hall Stewart, *A Documentary Survey of the French Revolution,* pp. 672–673. Copyright 1951 by Macmillan Publishing Company, renewed 1979 by John Hall Stewart. P. 106: Diary passages from *The Corsican: A Diary of Napoleon's Life in His Own Words,* ed. R. M. Johnston (Boston & New York: Houghton Mifflin, The Riverside Press, Cambridge, 1910), pp. 140, 143–145, 166, 189, 322. P. 108: Lesson VII from *The Constitutions and other Select Documents Illustrative of the History of France, 1789–1907,* ed. Frank Malloy Anderson (Minneapolis: H. W. Wilson, 1908), pp. 312–313. P. 108: Letter to Fouché from *Napoleon: Was He the Heir of the Revolution?* ed. David L. Dowd (New York: Holt, Rinehart and Winston, 1966), p. 41. P. 109: From *Letters of Napoleon,* trans. and ed. J. M. Thompson, pp. 207–208. Reprinted by permission of Basil Blackwell.

Chapter 5

Section 1 P. 113: From Wordsworth and Coleridge, *The Lyrical Ballads 1798–1805,* introduction and notes by George Sampson (London: Methuen, 1940), pp. 20–26. P. 114: William Wordsworth, "Tables Turned," *The Poetical Works of William Wordsworth* (London: Edward Moxon, Son and Co., 1869), p. 361. P. 114: From William Blake, *Milton: A Poem in Two Books* (London: Printed by William Blake, 1804), pp. 42, 44. P. 115: Excerpts reprinted with permission of Macmillan Publishing Company from Johann Wolfgang von Goethe, *Faust,* Part II, trans. Bayard Quincy Morgan, pp. 13–15. Copyright © 1964 by The Bobbs-Merrill Co. Translation copyright © 1954 by Macmillan Publishing Com-

pany, renewed 1982. *Section 2* P. 117: From Klemens von Metternich, *Memoirs,* trans. Mrs. Alexander Napier (London: Richard Bentley & Son, 1881), III, 458–459, 461–463, 465–475. P. 120: From Joseph de Maistre, *On God and Society: Essay on the Generative Principle of Political Constitutions,* ed. Elisha Greifer and trans. with the assistance of Laurence M. Porter, pp. 3, 12–14, 29–30, 33, 40, 45, 51, 54, 86. Reprinted by permission of Regnery-Gateway. *Section 3* P. 122: From John Stuart Mill, *On Liberty* (Boston: Ticknor and Fields, 1863), pp. 22–23, 27–29, 35–36. *Section 4* P. 124: From *The Dynamics of Nationalism: Readings in Its Meaning and Development,* ed. Louis L. Snyder, pp. 146–147, © 1964 by D. Van Nostrand Co., Inc. Reprinted by permission of Wadsworth, Inc. P. 125: From *Metternich's Europe,* ed. Mack Walker, pp. 45–47. Reprinted by permission of Mack Walker. P. 126: From Great Britain, *Annual Register,* 1819, pp. 159–160. *Section 5* P. 127: From *Joseph Mazzini: His Life, Writings, and Political Principles* (New York: Hurd and Houghton, 1872), pp. 62, 69, 71–74. *Section 6* P. 129: From *The Recollections of Alexis de Tocqueville,* trans. A. T. De Mattos (New York: Macmillan, 1896), pp. 14, 187–189, 197–200. P. 131: From *The Reminiscences of Carl Schurz,* (New York: The McClure Co., 1907), I, 112–117.

Chapter 6

Section 1 P. 137: From Edward Baines, *The History of the Cotton Manufacture in Great Britain* (London: Fisher, Fisher and Jackson, 1835), pp. 84–89. P. 139: From Adam Smith, *An Inquiry into the Nature and Causes of the Wealth of Nations;* reprint of the edition of 1812, ed. J. R. McCulloch (London: Ward Lock, n.d.), pp. 19, 20, 22. *Section 2* P. 141: From Edward Baines, *The History of the Cotton Manufacture in Great Britain* (London: Fisher, Fisher and Jackson, 1835), pp. 148, 183, 195–196. *Section 3* P. 142: From A. Schroter and Walter Becker, *Die deutsche Maschinenbau industrie in der industriellen Revolution* in S. Pollard and C. Holmes, *Documents of European Economic History,* pp. 534–536. Reprinted by permission of S. Pollard and Colin Holmes. *Section 4* P. 145: From Report from the Committee on the Bill to Regulate the Labour of Children in the Mills and Factories of the United Kingdom, *British Sessional Papers, 1831–1832,* House of Commons, XV, 5–6, 95–96, 99–100. P. 148: From Frederick Engels, *The Condition of the Working Class in England,* ed. and trans. W. O. Henderson and W. H. Chaloner, pp. 30–31, 33. Reprinted by permission of Basil Blackwell Ltd. *Section 5* P. 150: From Andrew Ure, *The Philosophy of Manufactures* (London: Charles Knight, 1835), pp. 309–311, 347, 353–354. *Section 6* P. 153: From Adam Smith, *An Inquiry into the Nature and Causes of the Wealth of Nations;* reprint of the edition of 1813, ed. J. R. McCulloch (London: Ward Lock, n.d.), pp. 352, 354, 544–545. P. 154: From Thomas Robert Malthus, *First Essay on Population, 1798,* reprinted for the Royal Economic Society (London: Macmillan & Co. Ltd., 1926), pp. 7, 11–14, 16–17. P. 155: "Population and Poverty" from Thomas Robert Malthus, *An Essay on the Principle of Population, or, a View of Its Past and Present Effects on Human Happi-*

ness, 7th ed. (London: Reeves and Turner, 1872), pp. 6–8, 404–405. *Section 7*   P. 157: From Karl Marx and Frederick Engels, *Manifesto of the Communist Party,* Authorized English Translation, ed. and annotated by Frederick Engels, pp. 8–11, 16–20, 21–25, 28–29, 31–34, 48. Reprinted by permission of the Charles B. Kerr Publishing Company, Chicago.

Chapter 7
Section 1   P. 168: From Samuel Smiles, *Self-Help; with Illustrations of Conduct and Perserverance* (London: John Murray, 1897), pp. 1–3. P. 168: From Samuel Smiles, *Thrift* (New York: A. L. Burt n.d.), pp. 6, 14, 18–21. *Section 2*   P. 170: From *The German Worker, Working-Class Autobiographies from the Age of Industrialization,* ed. Alfred Kelly, pp. 164–165, 168–172, 175. Copyright © 1987 by The Regents of the University of California. Reprinted by permission of The University of California Press. P. 173: From William Booth, *In Darkest England, and The Way Out* (London: International Headquarters of the Salvation Army, 1890), pp. 9, 11–16, 18–20. *Section 3*   P. 177: From Thomas Hill Green, *Liberal Legislation and Freedom of Contract, A Lecture* (Oxford: Slattery & Rose and London: Simpkin, Marshall & Co., 1861), pp. 9–15. P. 179: From Herbert Spencer, *The Man versus the State* (London: William & Norgate, 1884), pp. 28, 33, 34, 38–39, 41, 107. *Section 4*   P. 181: From Mary Wollstonecraft, *Vindication of the Rights of Woman,* together with excerpts from John Stuart Mill, *Subjection of Women* (London: J. M. Dent & Sons, 1929), pp. 3–6, 10–12, 15, 60–61, 64, 73, 82, 161–164, 214–215. P. 185: From John Stuart Mill, *The Subjection of Women* (London: Longmans, Green, 1869), pp. 1, 8, 24–28, 91–92, 95–97, 185–186. P. 187: From Emmeline Pankhurst, October 21, 1913, Speech, *Suffrage and the Pankhursts,* ed. Jane Marcus, pp. 153–157, 159–161. Reprinted by permission of Routledge & Kegan Paul Ltd. P. 190: From Hubertine Auclert, *La Citoyenne,* from *Victorian Women: A Documentary History of Women's Lives in Nineteenth-Century England, France and the United States,* trans. Karen M. Offen, ed. Erna Olafson Hellerstein, Leslie Parker Hume, and Karen M. Offen, pp. 445–446. © 1981 by the Board of Trustees of the Leland Stanford Junior University and Harvester Press. Reprinted with the permission of the publishers, Stanford University Press and Harvester Press. *Section 5*   P. 192: From *Bismarck,* ed. Frederic B. M. Hollyday, pp. 60, 63, 65–66. © 1970. Used by permission of the publisher, Prentice-Hall, Inc., Englewood Cliffs, N. J. *Section 6*   P. 195: From Sergei Witte, *The Journal of Modern History,* XXVI (March 1954), pp. 66, 68–69, 73. Reprinted by permission of the publisher, The University of Chicago Press. P. 197: Abridged excerpt from Basil Dmytryshyn, *Imperial Russia: A Sourcebook, 1700–1917,* 2/e, copyright © 1974 by the Dryden Press, a division of Holt, Rinehart and Winston, Inc. reprinted by permission of the publisher. P. 199: From M. I. Pokzovskaya, "The Woman Factory Worker in Russia — II," trans. Sonia Lethes, *Jus Suffragii,* 8, February 1, 1914, pp. 68–69. *Section 7*   P. 202: Excerpt from *Rehearsal for Destruction: A Study of Political Anti-Semitism*

in Imperial Germany by Paul W. Massing. Copyright © 1949 by the American Jewish Committee. Reprinted by permission of Harper & Row, Publishers, Inc. P. 204: From Édouard Drumont, *La France Juive. Essai d'Histoire Contemporaine,* Vol. 1, 50th ed., orig. pub. in 1886, trans. Theodore H. Von Laue (Paris: C. Marpon & E. Flammarion, n.d.), from the Intro. & Ch. 1. P. 206: Die zur Erforschung der Pogrom Eingesetzten Kommission, *Die Judenpogrome in Russland: Herausgegeben im Auftrage des Zionistischen Hilfsfonds in London, Vol. 2, Einzeldarstellungen,* trans. Theodore H. Von Laue (Koln: Judischer Verlag GmbH, 1910), pp. 11–24 passim. P. 208: From Theodor Herzel, *The Jewish State: An Attempt at a Modern Solution of the Jewish Question* (New York: American Zionist Emergency Council, 1946), pp. 76–77, 85–86, 91–93, 96. Reprinted by permission of the American Zionist Federation. *Section 8*   P. 211: From Cecil Rhodes, "Confession of Faith," in John E. Flint, *Cecil Rhodes.* Copyright © pp. 248–252. Reprinted by permission of Little, Brown and Company. P. 213: From Joseph Chamberlain, *Foreign and Colonial Speeches* (London: G. Routledge and Sons, 1897), pp. 102, 131–133, 202, 244–246. P. 215: From Karl Pearson, *National Life from the Standpoint of Science* (London: Adam and Charles Black, 1905), pp. 21, 23–27, 36–37, 44, 46–47, 60–61, 64. *Section 9*   P. 218: From J. A. Hobson, *Imperialism* (London: James Nisbet & Co. Ltd., 1902), pp. 132–134, 139, 234–235, 295–297.

Chapter 8
Section 1   P. 223: From Émile Zola, *The Experimental Novel and Other Essays,* trans. Belle M. Sherman (New York: The Lassell Publishing Co., 1893), pp. 20–21, 23, 54. *Section 2*   P. 225: From Charles Darwin, *His Life Told in an Autobiographical Chapter and in a Selected Series of his Published Letters,* edited by his son Francis Darwin (New York: D. Appleton, 1893), pp. 41–43, 45, 49. P. 226: From Charles Darwin, *The Origin of the Species* (New York: D. Appleton, 1872), I, 77, 79, 98, 133–134. P. 227: From Charles Darwin, *The Descent of Man* (New York: D. Appleton, 1876), pp. 606–607, 619. *Section 3*   P. 229: From Andrew D. White, *A History of the Warfare of Science with Theology in Christendom* (New York: Appleton, 1896), Vol. 1, pp. 70–74, 78–81, 86. *Section 4*   P. 232: From Fyodor Dostoevsky, *Notes from the Underground and the Grand Inquisitor,* trans. Ralph E. Matlaw, pp. 18–20, 23, 25–29, 31. Copyright © 1960 by E. P. Dutton, renewed © 1988 by E. P. Dutton. Reprinted by permission of the publisher, Dutton, an imprint of New American Library, a division of Penguin Books, Inc. USA. *Section 5*   P. 237: From Friedrich Nietzsche, *The Birth of Tragedy and the Genealogy of Morals,* trans. Francis Golffing, pp. 93–95, 109–111. Translation copyright © 1956 by Doubleday, a division of Bantam, Doubleday, Dell Publishing Group, Inc. Reprinted by permission of the publisher. P. 239: From *The Will to Power* by Friedrich Nietzsche, translated by Walter Kaufman and R. J. Hollingdale, pp. 383–384, 386, 397, 399, 401, 457–459, 465–468, 518–519, 550. Copyright © 1967 by Walter Kaufmann. Reprinted by permission of Random House, Inc.

Chapter 12

Section 1 P. 381: From Winston Churchill, *Vital Speeches of the Day,* March 15, 1946, pp. 329, 332. Reprinted by permission of City News Publishing Co. P. 383: From Nikita S. Khrushchev, *Report on the Twentieth Party Congress,* from *Current Soviet Policies II. The Documentary Record of the Twentieth Party Congress and Its Aftermath,* 1957, pp. 32–34, 36–37. Published and reprinted by permission of The Current Digest of the Soviet Press, Columbus, Ohio. *Section 2* P. 385: From Frantz Fanon, *The Wretched of the Earth,* pp. 31–35. Reprinted by permission of Grove Weidenfeld and Grafton Books, a division of Harper Collins Publishers Ltd. Copyright © 1963 by Presence Africaine. P. 387: From Jacques Ellul, *The Betrayal of the West,* trans. Matthew J. O'Connell (New York: Continuum Publishing Company, 1978), pp. 16–21, 23–24, 28–30, 44–45. Reprinted by permission of the publisher. *Section 3* P. 392: From *The Second Sex* by Simone de Beauvoir, translated and edited by H. M. Parshley. Copyright 1952 by Alfred A. Knopf, Inc. Reprinted by permission of Alfred A. Knopf, Inc. and Jonathan Cape on behalf of the Estate of Simone de Beauvoir. P. 396: From Sue Ellen M. Charlton, *Women in Third World Development,* pp. 7–9, 11, 13, 15–16, 23–28. Copyright © 1984 by Westview Press, Inc. Reprinted by permission of Westview Press. *Section 4* P. 402: Excerpts from Milovan Djilas, *The New Class: An Analysis of the Communist System,* Copyright © 1957 by Harcourt Brace Jovanovich, Inc. and renewed 1985 by Milovan Djilas and Harcourt Brace Jovanovich, Inc. reprinted by permission of the publisher. P. 405: From Andor Heller, *No More Comrades,* 1957, pp. 9–10, 12, 13, 15, 18, 21, 23, 25, 156–158, 160–163. Reprinted by permission of Regnery-Gateway. P. 409: From "Havel's Vision — Excerpts from Speech by the Czech President," January 2, 1990. Copyright © 1990 by The New York Times Company. Reprinted by permission. P. 411: Reprint by permission of Greenwood Publishing Group, Inc., Westport, CT, from *The Promise of Solidarity: Inside the Polish Worker's Struggle, 1980–82,* by Jean-Yves Potel. Copyright © 1982 by Praeger. *Section 5* P. 414: Excerpts from *Perestroika* by Mikhail Gorbachev. Copyright © 1987 by Mikhail Gorbachev. Reprinted by permission of Harper & Row, Publishers, Inc. P. 417: From William M. Mandel, "Street-Corner Democracy," in *The Station Relay: Facts and Views on Daily Life in the Soviet Union,* 3 (March, May 1988, Nos. 4–5), pp. 3–4, 6–8, 20. Reprinted by permission of Highgate Road Social Science Research Station Inc. *Section 6* P. 421: From *Amnesty International Report, 1989,* pp. 9–15. (AI Index: POL 10/02/89). Reprinted by permission of Amnesty International. International Secretariat. *Section 7* P. 426: From World Commission on Environment and Development, *Our Common Future* (Oxford/New York: Oxford University Press, 1987), pp. 1–18, 22–23. © World Commission on Environment and Development 1987, Palais Wilson, 52 rue des Paquis, 1201 Geneva, Switzerland. Reprinted by permission of Oxford University Press. P. 434: From Arnold Toynbee, "For the First Time in 30,000 Years," *Worldview,* 15, March 1972, pp. 5–9. Reprinted by permission of the Carnegie Council on Ethics and International Affairs.